DICTIONARY OF
LEGAL
TERMS

Definitions and explanations for non-lawyers!

Fifth Edition

DICTIONARY OF
LEGAL
TERMS

Definitions and explanations for non-lawyers!

Fifth Edition

STEVEN H. GIFIS
Former Associate Professor of Law
Rutgers University School of Law/Newark

Barron's books are available at special quantity discounts to use as premiums and sales promotions, or for use in corporate training programs. For
more information, please write to the Special Sales Manager, Barron's
Educational Series, Inc. at the mailing address indicated below.

All inquiries should be addressed to:
Barron's Educational Series, Inc.
250 Wireless Boulevard
Hauppauge, New York 11788
www.barronseduc.com

Library of Congress Control Number: 2015009342

ISBN: 978-1-4380-0512-6

Gifis, Steven H. author.
   Dictionary of legal terms : definitions and explanations for non-lawyers /
      Steven H. Gifis. — Fifth edition.
      pages cm
   Summary: "This book provides basic definitions of thousands of the
      most common legal terms. It is meant for both laymen and legal
      specialists"— Provided by publisher.
   ISBN 978-1-4380-0512-6 (paperback)
   1. Law—United States—Dictionaries. I. Title.
   KF156.G53 2015
   349.7303—dc23

                                        2015009342

PRINTED IN CHINA
9 8 7 6 5 4 3 2 1

CONTENTS

PREFACE

Professions tend to insulate themselves from lay understanding by the development of specialized jargon. The legal profession has achieved this insulation so successfully that the uninitiated is overwhelmed by the incomprehensibility of his or her lawyer's prose. Despite the increasing pervasiveness of law into every facet of modern life, the special language of the law remains a barrier to nonlawyers. In recent years "plain language" statutes have been passed by several states, requiring that consumer contracts, such as residential leases, be written in plain, everyday language. Yet, even with these reforms, the language of the lawyer often remains a mystery to the client.

The lawyer's language is replete with words having particular meanings. Thus, a lawyer "moves" to "evict a holdover tenant" when his or her client wants to kick the tenant out. The lawyer seeks to "partition a co-tenancy" gone sour and to "compel an accounting" to the "aggrieved party." A client's home is destroyed by earthquake and the insurance company refuses to pay. An attorney asks if the "risk" of earthquake is included in the insured's policy and, if not, whether "representations" were made to the homeowner that would support an action to "reform" the policy or that might create an "estoppel" against the company's denial of "liability." A merchant finds an umbrella in a coat rack; the attorney asks whether it has been "abandoned" or "mislaid" and explains to the merchant the "duty" that the law imposes upon a "finder" of "lost property."

In 1975 I authored a paperback law dictionary primarily for law students who were trying to comprehend what I and their other law professors were saying. That book has been used by hundreds of thousands of law students. It is hoped they have found it of assistance in understanding the baffling new world of law. Paralegals, legal secretaries and other professionals who regularly interact with lawyers have also purchased the law dictionary. It occurred to me, however, that the greatest need for communication existed between the lawyer and the client. And, even for the general citizens, it seemed to me that comprehending the ordinary newspaper article had to be growing more and more difficult as the news of the day became more and more entangled with legal jargon. The available law dictionaries were either too sophisticated for the average lay person or too simplistic and incomplete to be helpful. The purpose of this book is to provide a ready, accessible and useful source of understanding of the language of law and law-related processes and concepts.

The text of the book has been drawn in large part from my companion publication *Law Dictionary.* The definitions have been re-drafted in lay terms and the citations to authority have been deleted. Users of this book who need a more detailed explanation of a term may find resort to the *Law Dictionary* appropriate. And, in addition to the greater readability of the text, many new terms were added that law students might not encounter in their studies and that might not be thought of as technically "legal terms" but that have special meaning and arise in legal contexts. Hundreds of definitions have been added from the fields of securities, finance and taxation, which will assist the average person in understanding the business section of a newspaper. Abbreviations such as "N.O.V." have been defined so that the user will not have to fumble through many other sources until he or she discovers that the phrase refers to non obstante verdicto.

Although the book is titled a *Dictionary of Legal Terms* and may be used as one would use any other dictionary, it is contemplated that the user may want to skim through the book from time to time, stopping to read definitions touching upon jargon that he or she has noticed but not comprehended. In this fashion the book will be a primer for the lay person and hopefully will bridge the communication gap between the reader and the law.

STEVEN H. GIFIS

Lawrenceville, New Jersey

ACKNOWLEDGMENTS

A number of persons contributed to the first edition of this book. The financial and securities terms were drafted by Michael B. Perkins, C.F.A.; the taxation terms, by David Mills, Esq. The task of editing the Law Dictionary into a layman's version was handled very ably by Keith Roberts, Esq., and significant editorial assistance was rendered by Alan Dexter Bowman, Esq., and Joseph C. Mahon, Esq. The examples were drafted by Andrew Levine, Rutgers School of Law-Newark, Class of 1984. The overall editing of the entire manuscript was performed with great skill and precision by my wife, Susan Pollard Gifis, Esq. Finally, the entire manuscript was typed and retyped with great care and cheerfulness by my secretary, Angela Di Pierro.

I was most fortunate to persuade my wife once again to lend her considerable talents to the editing of the second edition. The cross-references were improved, new terms were added, the text was made more gender-neutral, and the examples and definitions sharpened and made more readable. This fifth edition incorporates much of the improvements in the sixth edition of the companion volume, *Law Dictionary*. The manuscript for this edition was reviewed by Amira Rahman Scurato and her husband Michael and daughter Katie. Without their efforts, this new edition would not have been possible. I am deeply indebted to them for their excellent input.

PRONUNCIATION GUIDE

The decision as to which Latin words, maxims and expressions should be included in this dictionary, in view of the thousands that the user might encounter, was necessarily a somewhat arbitrary one; but an earnest effort has been made to translate and, where appropriate, to illuminate those terms and phrases considered likely to be crucial to a full understanding of important legal concepts. Hopefully, there are no significant omissions and we have erred only on the side of overinclusiveness.

Each of the Latin and French words and phrases—at least those that continue to be recognized as such and have not become, functionally, a part of the English language—includes a phonetic spelling designed to assist the user in the pronunciation of terms that are probably unfamiliar to her or him. The purpose in providing this pronunciation guide, however, has not been to indicate the "correct" mode of pronouncing the terms; rather, the goal has been to afford the user a guide to an acceptable pronunciation of them. In the case of Latin words, therefore, neither the classic nor the ecclesiastical pronunciation has been strictly followed; instead, the phonetic spellings provided herein reflect the often considerable extent to which pronunciation has been "Anglicized" and/or "Americanized," partly through widespread legal usage.

Of course, such a system is anything but uniform, and adoption of it is clearly hazardous from the standpoint of general acceptance as well as that of scholarship. Many, if not most, of these terms have alternative pronunciations in common usage throughout the English-speaking legal world, and there has been some deference to classical or ecclesiastical pronunciation and, hopefully, to consistency. Thus, the choices made here, while in most cases meant to reflect the most commonly accepted pronunciation, inevitably have been the product of the author's personal preferences.

The phonetic symbols employed herein were drawn from what the author perceives as a commonly recognized and understood "system." The following guide should be of some assistance in interpreting them.

Vowels		*Consonants*
ă as in ăt	ĭ as in ĭll	g as in gas
ä as in ärmy	ī as in īce	
à as in àrrive		j as in jump or as
ā as in āpe	ŏ as in ŏx	the g in rouge
aủ as in out	ô as in ôrgy	or bourgeois
	ō as in ōpen	
ĕ as in ĕgg		
ē as in ēvil	ŭ as in ŭp	
ė as in ėarn	û as in ûrge	
	ū as in rūde	

KEY TO EFFECTIVE USE OF THIS DICTIONARY

Alphabetization: The reader should note carefully that all entries have been alphabetized letter by letter rather than word by word. Thus *ab initio,* for example, is located between *abeyance* and *abortion,* rather than at the beginning of the listings. In the same manner, *actionable* appears before, not after *action ex delicto.*

Brackets: Material in brackets [thus] represents an alternate expression for the preceding phrase. For example, "Federal Bureau of Investigation [FBI]" indicates that FBI is another way of expressing the entry for Federal Bureau of Investigation. It is also used as an alternative. **ABANDONED CHILD [SPOUSE]** would be the entry for an abandoned child or an abandoned spouse. When the reader is referred to a different main entry for the definition of a particular word, brackets are also used to indicate that the word to be defined appears as a subentry of the main word to which the reader is referred. Thus, **"COMPENSATORY DAMAGES** see **damages [ACTUAL DAMAGES]"** indicates that the definition of compensatory damages appears under the subentry **ACTUAL DAMAGES,** which in turn is found under the heading **DAMAGES.**

Cross-References: **Boldface type** has been used within the text of the definitions and at the end of them, to call attention to terms that are defined in the dictionary as separate entries and that should be understood and, if necessary, referred to specifically, in order to assure the fullest possible comprehension of the word whose definition has been sought in the first instance.

Terms emphasized in this manner include many that appear in the dictionary only in a different form or as a different part of speech. For example, although the term "alienate" may appear in boldface in the text of a definition, it will not be found as a separate entry, since it is expected that the reader can readily draw the meaning of that term from the definition given for the word "alienation"; likewise, the reader coming across the word "estop" printed in boldface should not despair upon discovering that it is not in fact an entry here, but should instead refer to the term "estoppel."

Also, the reader must not assume that the appearance of a word in regular type precludes the possibility of its having been included as a separate entry, for by no means has every such word been printed in boldface in every definition. Terms emphasized in this manner include primarily those an understanding of which was thought to be essential or very helpful in the reader's quest for adequate comprehension. Many terms that represent very basic and frequently used concepts, such as "property," "possession" and "crime," are often printed in regular type. Furthermore, boldface is used to emphasize a word only the first time that that word appears in a particular definition.

Examples: Examples have been included to clarify many terms. Where these appear, they are clearly marked *"EXAMPLE:"*

Gender: Where masculine nouns and pronouns have been used, they are intended to refer to both men and women and should be so read.

Subentries: Words printed in boldface SMALL CAPITALS include:

(1) those whose significance as legal concepts was not deemed sufficiently substantial to warrant their inclusion in the dictionary as separate entries, though some explanation or illumination was thought desirable, and

(2) those which, though important, are most logically and coherently defined in the context of related or broader terms.

Words emphasized in this manner either have been separately and individually defined in the manner of "subcategories" or have been defined or illustrated, implicitly or explicitly, within the text of the definition of that main entry.

A

ABA see **American Bar Association.**

ABANDONED CHILD [SPOUSE] person who has not been in contact with or received support from the parent or spouse. A court finding of child abandonment terminates parental rights and allows the child to be adopted without permission of the parents. An abandoned spouse is one whose spouse has deserted them without consent. It may be grounds for divorce. For tax filing purposes, an abandoned spouse may qualify as unmarried. See **desertion.**

ABANDONMENT the intentional giving up of rights or property with no future intention to regain title or possession.

EXAMPLE: Paul finishes reading his newspaper while waiting for a doctor to see him. Upon leaving the doctor's office, Paul intentionally decides not to take the paper with him. Paul *abandons* the newspaper. Had he merely forgotten the paper and returned to the office to retrieve it, he would not be considered to have abandoned the property.

ABATABLE NUISANCE see **nuisance [ABATABLE NUISANCE].**

ABATEMENT generally, a lessening or reduction: also, either a termination or a temporary suspension of a lawsuit. An **ABATEMENT OF A LEGACY** means that the **legacy** to a **beneficiary** is either reduced or completely eliminated because of debts that must first be paid out of the decedent's estate. An **ABATEMENT OF TAXES** is a tax rebate or decrease. See **nuisance [ABATEMENT OF A NUISANCE].**

ABDUCTION the criminal or wrongful act of forcibly taking away another person through **fraud,** persuasion or violence. (Compare **kidnapping.**)

ABET see **aid and abet.**

ABEYANCE an undetermined or incomplete state of affairs; in property law, the condition of a **freehold** or estate in **fee** when there is no existing person in whom the estate **vests.**

ABILITY TO STAND TRIAL see **competent.**

AB INITIO *(ăb ĭn-ĭ'-shē-ō)* Lat.: from the beginning. Commonly used in referring to the time when an action or instrument or interest in property becomes legally valid.

ABJURE retract, recant, or repudiate.

ABNORMALLY DANGEROUS ACTIVITY see **ultrahazardous activity.**

ABOLISH to repeal, recall, or revoke; to cancel and eliminate entirely. This term refers especially to things of a permanent nature such as institutions, customs, and usages, as in the abolition of slavery by the **Thirteenth Amendment** to the United States **Constitution.**

ABORIGINAL TITLE see **Indian law [INDIAN TITLE].**

ABORTION the premature termination of a pregnancy; may be either spontaneous (miscarriage) or induced. A woman enjoys a constitutional right to have an abortion during the first trimester of her pregnancy. During the second trimester, however, the state may regulate the abortion procedure, and during the third trimester the state may even proscribe abortion except where medically necessary to preserve the health of the mother.

ABRIDGE to shorten, condense; diminish.

ABROGATE to annul, repeal, put an end to; to make a law void by legislative repeal.

ABSCOND to travel secretly out of the **jurisdiction** of the courts, or to hide in order to avoid a legal **process** such as a lawsuit or arrest. See **jump bail.**

ABSENTIA see **in absentia.**

ABSENT WITHOUT LEAVE see **desertion [ABSENT WITHOUT LEAVE].**

ABSOLUTE LIABILITY see **strict liability.**

ABSOLUTE SALE see **sale [ABSOLUTE SALE].**

ABSQUE HOC *(äb'-skwā hŏc)* Lat.: without this. If it had not been for this; a phrase used to introduce a denial in a pleading.

ABSTENTION (DOCTRINE) the policy that a federal district court may decline to exercise its **jurisdiction** and may allow a state court to decide a federal constitutional question or questions of state law. Abstention is based on **comity** and is intended to restrict federal court interference in state proceedings. See **federalism.**

EXAMPLE: A prisoner in a state prison brings a lawsuit in federal district court claiming that under federal law he is entitled to have access to a law library. The state in which the prisoner is jailed may require by law that each state prison maintain an adequate law library. The federal court applies the *abstention doctrine* in refusing to hear the case, instructing the prisoner to raise the issue in a state court.

ABSTRACT OF RECORD a condensed history of a case, taken from the trial court records and prepared for use by the **appellate court.**

ABSTRACT OF TITLE a short history of **title** to land, noting all **conveyances,** transfers, **grants, wills** and judicial proceedings, and all **encumbrances** and **liens,** together with evidence of **satisfaction** and any other facts affecting title.

EXAMPLE: Rishi wants to sell a parcel of land to Bill. In order to protect himself from claims by any other persons concerning that parcel, Bill insists that Rishi provide an *abstract of title* before Bill purchases the land. Only with that abstract can Bill be satisfied that Rishi is the rightful owner of the property. Bill can also purchase a policy of title insurance to protect himself from any problems that develop arising from claims of ownership in the land. The insurance will be based on the abstract of title.

ABUSE harm; injury; damage; neglect; mental, physical, and/or emotional mistreatment. See **child abuse; cruelty; domestic violence; endangering; rape.** Also, improper use or exercise. See **abuse of discretion; abuse of process.**

ABUSE DEFENSE [EXCUSE] claim which attempts to justify a person's improper action based upon that person's history of victimization. May be used to negate the **mens rea** of a crime and/or to **mitigate** punishment. See **battered person's syndrome.**

ABUSE OF DISCRETION on appeal, the characterization by a reviewing court of a lower court or administrative agency decision or ruling as arbitrary and unreasonable, leading the reviewing court to overturn the decision. See **discretion.**

ABUSE OF PROCESS improper use of a legal **process;** for example, serving a **summons** to frighten the recipient or to prompt a response from him or her, where no **suit** has been filed, or filing a lawsuit for an improper purpose.

EXAMPLE: Nick desperately needs information from Sam to aid Nick in preparing for a lucrative business deal. Sam refuses to provide that information because of its confidential nature. Nick files a lawsuit against Sam so he can acquire the information by claiming that he needs it in connection with the lawsuit. Nick has thus participated in an *abuse of process* because he used service of summons, which is a legal process, to institute a lawsuit, for the sole purpose of acquiring information not otherwise lawfully available to him.

ABUSE, SEXUAL   see **rape [SEXUAL ABUSE].**

ABUT   to adjoin, touch boundaries, border on.

ACA   see **Affordable Care Act.**

ACCELERATED COST RECOVERY SYSTEM   see **depreciation [ACCELERATED COST RECOVERY SYSTEM].**

ACCELERATION   1. the hastening of the time for **enjoyment** of a **remainder** interest due to the premature termination of a **preceding estate;** 2. the process by which, under the terms of a **mortgage** or similar obligation, an entire debt is to be regarded as due upon the borrower's failure to pay a single installment or to fulfill some other duty. See **acceleration clause.**

ACCELERATION CLAUSE   a provision in a **contract** or document that, upon the happening of a certain event, a person's expected interest in the property will become **vested** sooner than expected. Often found in **installment contracts,** this clause, if invoked, causes the entire debt to become due upon a party's failure to make payment on time.

EXAMPLE: Dave signs a loan agreement with the bank, promising to repay the bank in monthly payments over a three-year period. The agreement includes an *acceleration clause* which provides that if Dave fails to pay the required amount for any month or months, the bank can demand that Dave repay the remaining amount of the loan in one payment.

Although acceleration clauses are frequently found in loan or mortgage agreements, they are not generally resorted to until other methods of repayment are attempted.

ACCEPTABLE USE POLICY   regulations establishing who may use a network, website, or service's resources; the purposes allowed; and the privacy and security rules involved.

ACCEPTANCE   the voluntary act of receiving something or of agreeing to certain terms. 1. In contract law, acceptance is consent to the terms of an **offer,** creating a binding **contract.**

EXAMPLE: A homeowner contracts with an aluminum siding company to cover the house with new siding. The homeowner is not happy with two of the clauses in the contract, but the company is unwilling to change the clauses. When the homeowner signs the contract with the clauses unchanged, his signature acts as an *acceptance* of those clauses as they are printed. The fact that he has questioned those clauses has no effect as they are a valid part of the contract.

2. In real property law, acceptance is essential to completion of a gift **inter vivos.** 3. "Acceptance" by a bank of a check or other **negotiable instrument** is a formal procedure whereby the bank on which the check is drawn promises to honor the **draft** by paying the payee named on the check.

ACCEPTOR individual or institution that assumes an obligation to pay by signing for or consenting to a check or draft. Also spelled "accepter." See **drawee.**

ACCESS the opportunity to approach, communicate, or pass to and from without obstruction as with an **easement.** Also refers to the opportunity for sexual intercourse. A husband's nonaccess to his wife may be a defense to a **paternity** suit, as may "multiple access" be the defense of several lovers in a paternity suit. The absence of opportunity for copying may provide a nonaccess defense to a **plagiarism** action. The right of access to **public records** includes such laws as the **Freedom of Information Act.**

ACCESSION something added; a right, derived from the **civil law,** to all that one's property produces, and to that which is united to it either naturally or artificially. The civil law required the thing to be changed completely, as grapes into wine, before the original owner could lose title. By **common law** the article in its altered form is still the property of the owner of the original material if the owner can prove the identity of the original material.

EXAMPLE: Cobbler Conroy kills some of Farmer Bob's cows and turns the leather into shoes. Bob can take the shoes by *accession* if he can establish the leather came from his cows.

ACCESSORY a person who aids or contributes to a crime as a subordinate. An accessory performs acts that aid others in committing a crime or in avoiding apprehension. In some jurisdictions an accessory is called an **aider and abettor.** See also **accomplice; conspirator.** Compare **principal.**

ACCESSORY AFTER THE FACT a person who harbors or assists a criminal knowing that the criminal has committed a **felony** or is sought in connection with a crime.

ACCESSORY BEFORE THE FACT a person who incites, counsels or orders another to commit a crime, but who is not present when it is committed.

ACCIDENT an unforeseen, unexpected event; an occurrence by chance and not by design. In the context of an automobile insurance policy, the term includes any event that occurs unintentionally, even if due to **negligence** rather than to forces beyond anyone's control. An **UNAVOIDABLE ACCIDENT** is one that is not the product or fault of another, such as one caused by an **act of God.**

ACCOMMODATION INDORSEMENT see **indorsement** [ACCOMMODATION INDORSEMENT].

ACCOMMODATION MAKER [PARTY] one who, as a favor to another, signs a **note** as acceptor, **maker** or **indorser**, without receiving compensation or other benefit, and who thus guarantees the debt of the other person.

ACCOMPLICE one who voluntarily joins another in committing a crime. An accomplice has the same degree of liability as the one who commits the crime. See also **accessory; aid and abet; conspirator.** Compare **principal.**

ACCORD an agreement whereby one party takes, in settlement of a **claim,** something other than what he or she considers himself or herself entitled to receive. **Satisfaction** takes place when the accord is **executed,** after which there has been an **accord and satisfaction.** See **novation; settlement.**

ACCORD AND SATISFACTION the payment of money or other valuable consideration (usually less than the amount owed) in exchange for **extinguishment** of a debt. There must be an express or implied agreement that accepting the smaller sum discharges the obligation to pay the larger sum.

ACCOUNT a detailed statement of the mutual demand in the nature of debt and credit between parties, arising out of contracts or some fiduciary relation. In general business terminology, a particular client or customer. See **capital account; discretionary account; joint account; open account.**

ACCOUNT DEBTOR person who is obligated on an account.

ACCOUNTS PAYABLE the amount owed by a business to its suppliers and other regular trading partners.

ACCOUNTS RECEIVABLE amounts owing on open account. Running accounts that are usually disclosed in the **creditor**'s account books, representing unsettled **claims** and transactions not reduced to writing. In neither commercial nor legal contexts does an account receivable embrace an isolated transaction wholly outside of the account creditor's normal business dealings. The **Uniform Commercial Code** has rejected "exact and detailed" descriptions in favor of those that reasonably identify what is described. All that is required under the code to describe an accounts receivable is that the financing statement be sufficiently descriptive so as reasonably to generate further inquiry.

CAPITAL ACCOUNT see **capital [CAPITAL ACCOUNTS].**

DISCRETIONARY ACCOUNT see **discretion [DISCRETIONARY ACCOUNT].**

JOINT ACCOUNT see **joint account.**

OPEN ACCOUNT see **open account.**

ACCOUNTING, ACTION FOR refers to an action, usually brought in **equity,** to secure a formal statement of account from one partner to others in order to obtain a judicial determination of the rights of the parties in a shared asset. If one or more partners feel another has been diverting funds or otherwise cheating them, they may bring an action for an accounting and ask for the appointment of a temporary **receiver.** Sometimes an equity judge will appoint a **master** to perform the accounting.

ACCOUNTING METHOD the method used by a business (**corporation, partnership,** or **sole proprietorship**) in keeping its books and records for purposes of computing income and **deductions** and determining taxable **income.**

ACCRUAL METHOD an accounting method under which income is subject to tax when the right to receive such income becomes fixed, and deductions are allowed when the obligation to pay becomes fixed, regardless of when the income is actually received or when the obligation is actually paid. The accrual method must be utilized by any business taxpayer that has inventory.

CASH METHOD an accounting method under which income is subject to tax when received and deductions are allowed when paid.

INSTALLMENT METHOD a method of accounting which may be elected by a **taxpayer** who is either on the cash or the accrual method of accounting which allows the taxpayer to postpone the **recognition** of gain from the **sale or exchange** of assets if at least one payment is to be received after the close of the year of sale. If this method is utilized, a pro-rata portion of the payment received each year reduces the taxpayer's **basis** and the remainder is taxed as gain from the sale or exchange of the asset.

ACCOUNTS PAYABLE the list of moneys currently owed by the debtor to the creditor, such as a business to its suppliers. This list is kept in the **ordinary course** of the debtor's business. Compare **accounts receivable.**

ACCOUNTS RECEIVABLE the list of moneys owed on current accounts to a **creditor** kept in the normal course of the creditor's business and representing unsettled claims and transactions. Compare **accounts payable.**

ACCREDITED INVESTOR knowledgeable and sophisticated persons or institutions who qualify to purchase securities in transactions exempt from registration under the **Securities Act of 1933.** See **private offering [placement].**

ACCRETION 1. the act of adding something to property, as when a co-**heir** or co-**legatee** dies or rejects his or her inheritance or legacy, thereby increasing the shares of the other heirs or legatees.

EXAMPLE: A father's will leaves equal amounts of a bank account to his son and daughter. If the son takes his share, the added tax burden on him will virtually eliminate all of his gains. He therefore decides to reject the legacy. The daughter benefits by the *accretion* in the amount of the bank account the father left her if the son's share goes to her.

2. the gradual, imperceptible addition of soil to the shore by the natural action of waters. Compare **avulsion.** 3. in situations involving a **trust,** any addition to principal or income that results from an extraordinary occurrence, that is, an event that, while foreseeable, rarely occurs.

ACCRUAL METHOD see **accounting method [ACCRUAL METHOD].**

ACCRUE 1. to accumulate, become due, as **interest** added to **principal.** ACCRUED INTEREST is the interest that has become due, whether or not it has been paid. 2. in a **cause of action,** to come into existence as an enforceable claim. For example, the pedestrian's cause of action against the driver accrues when the driver hits and injures the pedestrian.

ACCUMULATED DEPRECIATION the total **depreciation** charged against all productive **assets** as stated on the **balance sheet.** The charge is made to allow realistic reduction in the value of productive assets and to allow tax-free recovery of the original investment in assets.

ACCUMULATED EARNINGS AND PROFITS see **earnings and profits [ACCUMULATED EARNINGS AND PROFITS].**

ACCUSATION a **charge** of wrongdoing against a person or corporation, in the form of an **indictment, presentment,** or **information.**

ACCUSATORY INSTRUMENT refers to the initial **pleading** or other paper that forms the procedural basis for a criminal charge.

It may take the form of an **indictment, information, presentment,** or **accusation.** If the accusatory instrument is defective, the entire proceeding will be rendered **null and void.**

ACCUSE   to institute legal proceedings charging someone with a crime.

ACCUSED   the person charged with a crime; the **defendant.**

ACKNOWLEDGMENT   affirmation, admission or declaration recognizing ownership, indicating authenticity, accepting responsibility, or undertaking an obligation to do something, such as pay a debt.

ACLU   see **American Civil Liberties Union.**

A COELO USQUE AD CENTRUM   (*ä kō-ā'-lō ūs'-kwā äd sĕn'-trŭm*)—Lat.: from the sky [heavens] all the way to the center of the earth; a very old **property** maxim which marked the boundaries within which an owner owned his property. This maxim no longer strictly applies because the owner of property in modern times owns subject to the rights of airplanes and oil and gas exploration.

ACQUIESCENCE   conduct that may imply consent; a tacit acceptance, often through silence when some objection ought to be forthcoming. Thus, if one makes a statement and another does not respond negatively, acquiescence may be inferred. An **estoppel** may be created in appropriate circumstances in this manner. Compare **laches,** which implies a neglect to do that which one would be expected to do for his or her own benefit.

ACQUIRE   to gain by any means; to obtain by any endeavor such as practice, purchase, or investment; in the law of contracts, to become the owner of property; to make something one's own. This implies some positive action as opposed to a more passive obtaining such as by an accrual. See **accrue.**

ACQUIRED CORPORATION   see **corporation** [ACQUIRED CORPORATION].

ACQUIRING CORPORATION   see **corporation** [ACQUIRING CORPORATION].

ACQUIT   1. to set free from an **accusation** of guilt by a verdict of not guilty; 2. in older **contract** terminology, to release from a debt or other obligation.

ACQUITTAL   a legal finding that an individual charged with a crime is not guilty and is therefore set free.

ACRS see **depreciation** [ACCELERATED COST RECOVERY SYSTEM].

ACT see **overt act; wrongful act.**

ACTIO *(äk'-tē-ō)* Lat.: action. Used to refer to a legal **proceeding, lawsuit, process, action,** or permission for a suit.

ACTIONABLE forming the legal basis for a **civil action,** such as wrongful conduct.

ACTIONABLE PER QUOD see **per quod** [ACTIONABLE PER QUOD].

ACTIONABLE PER SE see **per se** [ACTIONABLE PER SE].

ACTIONABLE TORT the existence of facts sufficient for legal **filing** requirements for a legitimate **lawsuit** by one injured. See **cause of action.**

ACTION (AT LAW) a **judicial** proceeding whereby one party **prosecutes** another for a wrong done, or for protection of a right or prevention of a wrong; at common law, to be distinguished from an action in equity which could not be brought before the law courts but only before a court of **equity**. See **collusive action; derivative action; penal action.**

ACTION EX CONTRACTU see **ex contractu.**

ACTION EX DELICTO a **cause of action** based on a **tort.**

ACTION FOR ACCOUNTING see **accounting, action for.**

ACTION FOR POSSESSION see **possessory action.**

ACTION IN CASE see **trespass** [TRESPASS ON THE CASE].

ACTIO NON *(äk'-tē-ō nŏn)* Lat.: no action. In **pleading,** a Latin term referring to a nonperformance, **nonfeasance;** also, a **nonsuit.**

ACTIONS IN PERSONAM see **in personam**; **jurisdiction.**

ACTIONS IN REM see **in rem; jurisdiction.**

ACTIONS QUASI IN REM see **jurisdiction; quasi** [QUASI IN REM].

ACTIVE CONCEALMENT see **concealment** [ACTIVE CONCEALMENT].

ACTIVE EUTHANASIA see **euthanasia** [ACTIVE EUTHANASIA].

ACTIVE INCOME see **income** [ACTIVE INCOME].

ACTIVISM see **judicial activism.**

ACT OF GOD [NATURE; PROVIDENCE] a violent and cat-astrophic event caused by forces of nature, which could not have been prevented or avoided by foresight or prudence. Examples include high tides, storms, lightning, earthquakes, sharp frosts, or sudden death. Proof that an injury was caused by an act of God demonstrates that **negligence** was not the cause. An act of God that makes performance of a contractual **duty** impossible may excuse performance of that duty. See **impossibility.**

EXAMPLE: During heavy rain, a tree fell on Bayshawn's car. He claimed it was an act of nature and therefore covered under his par-ticular insurance policy. The insurance company denied coverage, pointing first to the fact that no other trees fell during the storm and also to the fact that the tree in question was diseased and had not been properly pruned.

ACTUAL AUTHORITY see **agency.**

ACTUAL BAILMENT see **bailment [ACTUAL BAILMENT].**

ACTUAL CASH VALUE see **market value.**

ACTUAL DAMAGES see **damages [ACTUAL DAMAGES].**

ACTUAL EVICTION see **eviction [ACTUAL EVICTION].**

ACTUAL NOTICE see **notice [ACTUAL NOTICE].**

ACTUAL POSSESSION see **possession [ACTUAL POSSESSION].**

ACTUAL VALUE see **market value.**

ACTUARY one who calculates insurance and property costs, espe-cially, the cost of life insurance risks and insurance premiums.

ACTUS REUS *(äkt'-ŭs rā'-ŭs)* Lat.: the criminal act. More prop-erly, the physical act that had been declared a crime. In murder, the actus reus is **homicide;** in burglary, it is breaking into another's home; in check **forgery,** it is presenting the forged check for payment.

ADA see **Americans with Disabilities Act [ADA].**

AD DAMNUM *(äd däm'-nŭm)* Lat.: to the damage. The amount of **damages** demanded in a civil suit.

ADDENDUM something added; a supplemental section of a docu-ment containing material added after the document was prepared. It may be executed simultaneously or at a later time.

ADDITUR *(ăd'-dĭ-tûr)* Lat.: it is increased. An increase by the court in the amount of **damages** awarded by the jury, which is done with the defendant's consent in return for the plaintiff's agreeing not to seek a new trial.

ADEEM see **ademption.**

ADEMPTION the extinction or withdrawal of a **devise** or **bequest** by some act of the decedent clearly indicating an intent to revoke it, e.g., by giving away during one's life the property to be devised or bequeathed.

AD FEMINAM see **ad hominem [AD FEMINAM].**

ADHESION CONTRACT a contract so heavily restrictive of one party, while so nonrestrictive of another, that doubts arise as to whether it is a voluntary agreement. The term signifies a grave inequality of bargaining power that may lead the contract to be declared invalid. The concept often arises in standard-form printed contracts submitted by one party to the other on a take-it-or-leave-it basis. See also **overreaching; unconscionable.**

AD HOC *(ăd hŏk)* Lat.: for this, for this particular purpose. An ad hoc committee is one commissioned for a special purpose; an ad hoc attorney is one designated for a particular client in a special situation.

AD HOMINEM attacking an opponent's character rather than the opponent's argument. Appealing to irrelevant personal considerations, especially prejudice, instead of intellect or reason. If the target is a woman, the adjective "**AD FEMINAM**" is used.

ADJECTIVE LAW the rules of legal **practice** and **procedure** that make **substantive law** effective. Adjective law determines the methods of enforcing the legal rights created and defined by substantive law. For instance, **service of process** is a matter of adjective law.

ADJOURN to postpone; to delay briefly a court proceeding through **recess.** An adjournment for a longer duration is termed a **continuance.** A session postponed indefinitely is termed an **ADJOURNMENT SINE DIE.** See **sine die.**

The term has a special meaning in the rules of legislatures which adjourn between legislative sessions, but recess for periods, of whatever duration, within a single session.

ADJUDICATION the determination of a **controversy** and pronouncement of **judgment.**

ADJUSTABLE RATE MORTGAGE see **mortgage [ADJUSTABLE RATE MORTGAGE].**

ADJUSTED BASIS   see **basis [ADJUSTED BASIS].**

ADJUSTED GROSS INCOME   see **income [ADJUSTED GROSS INCOME].**

ADJUSTER   one who determines the amount of an insurance claim and then makes an agreement with the insured as to a settlement.

AD LITEM   *(ăd lī'-těm)*   Lat.: for the suit. For the purposes of the lawsuit being prosecuted. See **guardian [GUARDIAN AD LITEM].**

ADMINISTRATION FOR NATIVE AMERICANS   see **Indian law [ADMINISTRATION FOR NATIVE AMERICANS].**

ADMINISTRATION OF JUSTICE   see **justice [ADMINISTRATION OF JUSTICE].**

ADMINISTRATIVE AGENCY   see **regulatory agency.**

ADMINISTRATIVE HEARING   see **hearing [ADMINISTRATIVE HEARING].**

ADMINISTRATIVE LAW   law created by administrative agencies by way of rules, regulations, orders, and decisions.

ADMINISTRATIVE LAW JUDGE   the presiding officer at an administrative **hearing,** whose power is essentially one of recommendation. In the federal system, he or she can administer **oaths,** issue **subpoenas,** rule on **evidence,** take **depositions** and make or recommend decisions, which can be appealed first to the federal agency for which he or she hears cases and then to a court of law.

ADMINISTRATIVE PROCEDURE ACT [APA]   an act designed to create uniformity and provide guidelines regarding the rule-making and adjudicative proceedings of administrative agencies including intra-agency and judicial review, public access to agency rules and decisions, and personal information collected by an agency.

ADMINISTRATIVE SERVICES ONLY [ASO]   arrangement in an employee **benefit** plan whereby an employer engages an insurance company to handle the administrative tasks of the plan (such as billing and claims processing) in order to lower costs. The employer continues to pay the claims.

ADMINISTRATOR [ADMINISTRATRIX]   someone appointed to handle the affairs of a person who has died **intestate,** that is, without leaving a **will.** If the decedent left a will, an **executor** performs the same function. A male is an *administrator*, while a female is an *administratrix*. See **letters of administration [SUCCESSOR ADMINISTRATOR].**

ADMIRALTY AND MARITIME JURISDICTION jurisdiction over all actions related to events occurring at sea, including transactions relating to commerce and navigation, to damages and injuries upon the sea, and to all maritime **contracts**, and **torts.** In most cases, admiralty and maritime jurisdiction in the United States is given to the federal courts.

ADMIRALTY COURTS tribunals that hear cases involving **maritime law,** the law governing disputes arising on or in relation to business transacted at sea or involving commerce or navigation.

ADMIRALTY LAW see **maritime law**.

ADMISSIBLE EVIDENCE evidence that may be introduced in court to aid the trier of fact—i.e. , the judge or jury—in deciding the **merits** of a case. Each jurisdiction has established rules of evidence to determine what evidence is admissible. A judge may exclude otherwise admissible evidence when he or she determines that its probative value is outweighed by such factors as undue consumption of time, prejudice, confusion of issues or a danger that the jury will be misled. A lurid, gory photograph, for example, depicting the scene of the crime, the weapon used or the injury to the victim may have very high probative value as to several issues in a criminal trial, but since it may cause undue prejudice in the minds of the jurors, it will be excluded if there is any other way to prove the necessary facts.

ADMISSION the voluntary acknowledgment that certain facts are true; a statement by the **accused** or by an **adverse party** that tends to support the charge or claim against him or her but is not necessarily sufficient to establish guilt or liability.

EXAMPLE: Vijay's admission that he was in the bar and spoke to the victim was insufficient to prove that they left the bar together.

In civil procedure, an admission is a pretrial **discovery** device by which one party asks another for a positive affirmation or denial of a **material** fact or **allegation** at issue.

ADMISSIONS BY A PARTY-OPPONENT see **declaration against interest** [ADMISSIONS BY A PARTY-OPPONENT].

ADMIT 1. to permit into **evidence.** A judicial determination to admit some evidence and to exclude other evidence is a function of the perceived usefulness such evidence will have on the outcome of the case. See **relevancy.**

2. Admit can also mean *acknowledged*, as in the accused admitted being present at the scene of the crime. See **admission.**

ADMIT TO BAIL to permit an accused person to be released from custody until trial upon posting of sufficient **surety (bail).**

ADMIT TO PRACTICE to certify by a court that a lawyer possesses the required qualifications to practice law within that jurisdiction. An admission **pro hac vice** is for a limited purpose.

ADMIT TO THE BAR see **ADMIT TO PRACTICE** above.

ADOPT 1. to agree to, appropriate, borrow, derive from, make use of. 2. the formal process terminating legal rights between a child and his or her natural parents and creating new rights between the child and the adopting parents. See **adoption.**

ADOPTION the legal process by which the parent/child relationship is created between persons not so related by blood. The adopted child becomes an heir and is entitled to all other privileges belonging to a natural child of the adoptive parent.

ADR see **alternative dispute resolution [ADR]; American Depository Receipt [ADR].**

ADS. abbreviation for ad sectum meaning "at the suit of."

AD TESTIFICANDUM *(äd tĕs-tĭ-fĭ-căn'-dūm)* Lat.: for testifying. A person sought ad testificandum is sought to appear as a witness. See **subpoena [AD TESTIFICANDUM].**

ADULT a person who has reached the **age of majority.**

ADULTERY voluntary sexual intercourse between a married person (or, under common law, a married woman) and someone other than his or her spouse. Adultery is grounds for divorce, in which case the person who committed the act with the estranged spouse is called a **CORESPONDENT.** Adultery is not criminalized in close to half of the states, is a misdemeanor in nearly half of the states and is a felony in just a handful of states. See **cuckold.**

AD VALOREM *(ăd và-lô'-rĕm)* Lat.: according to value. Commonly used to designate an assessment of taxes against property at a certain rate upon its value.

AD VALOREM TAX see **tax [VALUE ADDED TAX].**

ADVANCE moneys paid before payment is legally due, such as to an author for a novel yet to be written.

ADVANCEMENT a gift given by a parent to his or her child that is intended to represent all or part of the child's share of the estate in the event the parent dies **intestate.**

EXAMPLE: Eva desires that her son receive $20,000 upon her death. During her life, the son requires money to start up his new business. Eva gives him $10,000 without requiring repayment but informs the son that the money reduces the amount to which he will be entitled upon her death. The $10,000 constitutes an *advancement.*

ADVANCE SHEETS   printed judicial opinions published in paperback or loose-leaf form prior to being incorporated into a bound volume with other reported cases in a **reporter** series. The volume and page number of the advance sheet is usually the same as its future bound counterpart for ease in citation. Compare **SLIP OPINION,** which is an individual judicial decision published after its issuance by the court and prior to its incorporation into advance sheets.

ADVERSARY   opponent or **litigant** in a legal controversy or **litigation**. See **adverse party.**

ADVERSARY PROCEEDING   a hearing involving a **controversy** between two opposing parties, the outcome of which is expected to be favorable to only one of the parties.

ADVERSE INFERENCE   unfavorable deduction that may be drawn by the fact-finder from the failure of a party to produce a normally expected witness or other evidence. It may be presumed that the failure to produce was because the testimony or other evidence would have been harmful to that party.

ADVERSE INTEREST   an interest contrary to and inconsistent with that of some other person.

ADVERSE PARTY   the opposing party in a lawsuit. See **adversary.**

ADVERSE POSSESSION   a method of acquiring legal **title** to land through actual, continuous, open occupancy of the property, for a prescribed period of time, under claim of right, and in opposition to the rights of the true owner. See **hostile possession; notorious possession.**

EXAMPLE: Jim owned an empty piece of land next to his house. Dmitri, a neighbor, built an extension on his home which overlapped a considerable amount of Jim's land. For over 15 years, Jim never said anything to Dmitri about building on his property, but after a dispute arose, Jim told Dmitri to remove any part of the extension that was on Jim's land. A court would find that Dmitri's continuous use of the property, which Jim always knew about, meant that Dmitri had legal title to the land by *adverse possession.*

ADVERSE WITNESS   see **witness [ADVERSE [HOSTILE] WITNESS].**

ADVICE AND CONSENT term relating to the provision of the **Constitution** requiring the President to have approval (advice and consent) of two-thirds of the Senate before entering into **treaties** or before appointing federal **judges** or Supreme Court **justices.** See **Treaty Clause.**

ADVISORY OPINION a formal opinion by a judge, court or law officer upon a question of law submitted by a legislative body or government official but not presented in an actual court case or **adversarial proceeding.** Such an opinion has no binding force as law.

ADVOCACY the active taking up of a legal cause; the art of persuasion. A legal advocate is a lawyer.

ADVOCATE a legal advocate is an **attorney.** An INMATE ADVOCATE is a person who advances issues common to prisoners such as being provided with proper health care, educational programs or job training skills. It may also be a person who is not admitted to practice law but provides general legal assistance to a prisoner in such circumstances as an internal prison disciplinary hearing. In such a role they may be known as "COUNSEL SUBSTITUTE."

AFDC see **social security** [AID TO FAMILIES WITH DEPENDENT CHILDREN].

AFF'D abbreviation for "affirmed."

AFFECTED WITH A PUBLIC INTEREST see **public interest** [AFFECTED WITH A PUBLIC INTEREST].

AFF'G abbreviation for "affirming."

AFFIANT a person who makes and signs a written statement under oath [**affidavit**].

AFFIDAVIT a written statement made under **oath** before an officer of the court, a **notary public** or other person legally authorized to certify the statement.

EXAMPLE: As part of the defendant's sentence, the judge intends to include a large dollar amount for restitution to the victim. Rather than conduct a trial to determine the defendant's ability to pay the fine, the judge permits the defendant to file an *affidavit* outlining his financial situation. The affidavit also includes the defendant's name, address, age and other technicalities required by law, and an acknowledgment of the truthfulness of the statements made. A legally authorized person is required to administer an oath to the signer (called the **affiant**) and witness his signature.

AFFINITY attraction existing between persons; penchant. Also, a term used to describe a relationship created by marriage. Examples follow.

COLLATERAL AFFINITY   would exist between a wife and her husband's collateral relatives such as uncles or cousins.

DIRECT AFFINITY   would exist between a wife and her husband's brother.

SECONDARY AFFINITY   would exist between a wife and her husband's brother's wife.

AFFIRM   to approve or confirm; refers to an **appellate court** decision that a lower court judgment is correct and should stand.

AFFIRMATION   a person's indication that one affirms the truth of one's statement. An *affirmation* serves the same purpose as an **oath,** in which a person swears to God the truth of the statement made. When persons object to making an oath on religious or ethical grounds, an affirmation is commonly accepted in the place of an oath. A person who makes an affirmation is subject to the same penalties for **perjury** as a person who makes an oath.

AFFIRMATIVE ACTION   a positive step taken to correct conditions resulting from past discrimination or from violations of a law.

AFFIRMATIVE ACTION PROGRAMS   hiring practices and other employment programs adopted to eliminate discrimination in the employment of minority persons. Such programs are required by federal law.

AFFIRMATIVE DEFENSE   see   **defense**   [**AFFIRMATIVE DEFENSE**].

AFFIRMATIVE EASEMENT   see   **easement**   [**AFFIRMATIVE EASEMENT**].

AFFIRMATIVE PLEADINGS   see   **pleadings**   [**AFFIRMATIVE PLEADINGS**].

AFFIRMATIVE RELIEF   that **relief** granted a **defendant** (D) in a situation in which the defendant might maintain an **action** entirely independent of **plaintiff's** (P's) **claim,** and which claim D might proceed to establish and recover even if P abandoned his or her **cause of action,** or failed to establish it. In other words, D's answer must be in the nature of a cross-claim, thereby rendering the action the defendant's as well as the plaintiff's.

AFFIX   1. to attach to. In real estate, to attach something permanently to the land (e.g., a tree or an addition to a building). 2. to inscribe (e.g., a signature is affixed to a document).

AFFORDABLE CARE ACT common name for the "Patient Protection and Affordable Care Act of 2010." Federal health care mandate providing an open health insurance marketplace of health care options with the requirement that individuals select and pay for a plan (in some cases with federal tax credits) or pay a "fee" on their federal income tax return to opt out of coverage. The comprehensive health insurance reforms severely curtail areas such as bans on preexisting conditions and lifetime maximum limits on most benefits as well as cancellation of coverage. Coverage includes preventive care, choice of doctors and prescription drug benefits. It provides small businesses with tax credits for providing coverage for employees. Passage in 2010 provides the most significant overhaul of health care since **MEDICARE** (below) and **MEDICAID** (below) were established in 1965.

COBRA [**CONSOLIDATED OMNIBUS BUDGET RECONCILIATION ACT OF 1985**] federal law, passed in 1986, providing continuation of health insurance coverage to certain employees for a period of time after leaving employment. Employers that have 20 or more full-time-equivalent employees that do not offer such coverage must pay an excise tax. Qualifying events include employee retirement, termination, layoff, divorce, medical leave, or where a dependent child beneficiary reaches an age where coverage would not apply. Coverage generally lasts 18 months and the employee must pay the full cost of the premium although the cost is generally lower than in the Healthcare Marketplace under the ACA.

HEALTH INSURANCE PORTABILITY AND ACCOUNTABILITY ACT [**HIPPA**] 1996 federal law providing safeguards to protect confidential medical information. It also protects health insurance coverage for workers and their families when they change or lose their jobs. It also helps the healthcare industry control administrative costs. Most importantly, the HIPAA privacy rule or PHI (Protected Health Information) protects patient record confidentiality including any information held by a covered entity which concerns health status, provision of health care, or payment for health care that can be linked to an individual (other than for facilitating treatment or payment). Any other disclosure of PHI (Protected Health Information) requires the covered entity to obtain written authorization from the individual for the disclosure. HIPAA remains largely intact although the ACA expanded support for administrative technology.

MEDICAID state-run programs (partially paid for with federal funds) that provides hospital and medical coverage for people with low income. Each state has its own rules about who is eligible and what is covered under their state Medicaid program. The affordable care act left in place the state-run programs while attempting to adjust the amount of federal contributions.

MEDICARE federal health insurance program for citizens age 65 or older (although individuals under age 65 with certain disabilities may also qualify). The program helps with the cost of health care, but it does not cover all medical expenses or the cost of most long-term care. Individuals may buy a Medicare supplement policy (called **MEDIGAP**) from a private insurance company to cover some of the costs that Medicare does not. Medicare is financed by a portion of the payroll taxes paid by workers and their employers. It also is financed in part by monthly premiums, usually deducted from Social Security checks. There are four main parts: hospital insurance (Part A); medical insurance (Part B); medicare advantage plans (Part C); and prescription drug coverage (Part D). Medicare recipients are not required to obtain coverage in the health insurance marketplace as Medicare coverage remains in full effect under the Affordable Care Act.

MEDICARE ADVANTAGE PLAN method of obtaining Medicare benefits offered by private companies which are approved by and paid by Medicare to administer care, similar to an HMO (health maintenance organization) or PPO (preferred provider organization). This is different than a **MEDIGAP** (Medicare Supplement Insurance) policy (above), which just pays for costs that Medicare does not cover.

AFFREIGHTMENT shipping **contract.**

AFIS see **fingerprint [AFIS].**

AFORETHOUGHT see **malice aforethought.**

A FORTIORI *(ä fôr-shē-ô'-rē)* Lat.: with stronger reason. An inference that because a certain conclusion or fact is true, then the same reasoning makes it even more certain that a second conclusion is true.

EXAMPLE: Dan is accused of aiding in a bank robbery in which all of the participants were over six feet tall. One suspect has already been cleared by police because he is only five feet six inches. Since Dan is only five feet two inches, *a fortiori* he could not have participated in the robbery and will also be cleared.

AFTER-ACQUIRED PROPERTY 1. in commercial law, property acquired by a debtor after he has entered into an agreement in which other property is put up as **security** for a loan. Commonly used in security agreements, such a clause subjects any additional property to the creditor's mortgage or other interest and makes it clear that improvements, repairs, and additions made after the agreement are included as part of the security. 2. in **bankruptcy** law, property acquired by the bankrupt after he or she has filed to be declared a bankrupt. This property is generally free of all claims of the bankrupt's creditors.

AFTER-ACQUIRED TITLE a property law doctrine that says that if a person without good **title** to land sells it and then subsequently gets good title to it, the title will automatically go to the one who had bought the land.

AFTER-THE-FACT see **accessory** [ACCESSORY AFTER-THE-FACT].

AGAINST PUBLIC POLICY see **public interest** [AGAINST PUBLIC POLICY].

AGAINST THE [MANIFEST] [WEIGHT OF THE] EVIDENCE a determination by the trial judge that the jury's **verdict** is against the clear weight of the evidence presented, is based upon false evidence, or will result in a **miscarriage of justice,** or that the jury has acted mistakenly or improperly, in which case it is his or her duty, upon motion, to set aside the verdict and grant a new trial. See **n.o.v.** Compare **directed verdict.**

AGE DISCRIMINATION the denial of privileges as well as other unfair treatment of employees on the basis of age, which is prohibited by federal law under the Age Discrimination Unemployment Act of 1967. This act was amended in 1978 to protect employees up to 70 years of age.

AGENCY a relationship in which one person **(agent)** acts on behalf of another **(principal)** with the authority of the latter. Compare **partnership.**

AGENT one who is authorized by another person to act in that person's behalf. The acts of an agent are binding on his **principal.**

EXAMPLE: Kim, an artist, instructs Lorenzo to sell her paintings to various art galleries and to private parties. Lorenzo is considered Kim's *agent,* regardless of whom he sells to, since he will have **apparent authority** to act on her behalf.

AGE OF CONSENT age set by statute at which persons may marry without parental consent. Also refers to age at which an actor may consent to sexual intercourse, and below which age another commits an offense such as **statutory rape** or **sexual assualt,** even if the sexual conduct is engaged in voluntarily by both parties. An erroneous belief that another is at or above the age of consent is generally not a defense.

> *EXAMPLE:* Ashley, 19, meets Lee, 14, and thinks Lee looks 18. They have consentual intercourse. Ashley is nonetheless guilty of statutory rape.

AGE OF MAJORITY see **majority, age of.**

AGGRAVATED ASSAULT see **assault.**

AGGRAVATED FELONY a **felony** is a serious crime, usually punishable by more than one year in prison, as compared to a **misdemeanor**, which is a lesser offense. For **immigration** purposes, the term *aggravated felony* includes but is not limited to crimes of violence, treason, drug and weapon offenses, theft and fraud, prostitution and child pornography, racketeering, bribery and perjury, and bail jumping. It is a ground for deportability (see **deportation**). An offense not considered "aggravated" under state law may still be considered "aggravated" under federal law.

AGGRAVATED SEXUAL ABUSE [ASSAULT] see **rape.**

AGGRAVATING CIRCUMSTANCES special circumstances tending to increase the severity of the crime charged (comparing sexual assault with aggravated sexual assault on a minor) or the severity of punishment. Enhanced punishment may be applied for offenses involving murder for hire or other crimes for profit such as arson; extreme cruelty or depravity; substantial prior criminal record; failure of rehabilitative efforts; particular vulnerability of the victim due to advanced age, extreme youth, or disability; and many other factors that may be considered by the court. Compare **mitigating circumstances.**

AGGREGATE a total of all the parts; the whole, the complete amount; also, to combine, as to aggregate several **causes of action** in a single **suit;** similarly, to aggregate many persons whose causes of action are closely related to a **class action.** See **joinder.**

AGGRIEVED PARTY one who has been injured or has suffered a loss. A person is aggrieved by a **judgment, order** or **decree** whenever it operates prejudicially and directly upon his or her property, monetary or personal rights.

AGREEMENT mutual assent between two or more legally **competent** persons, ordinarily leading to a **contract.** In common usage, it is a broader term than contract, **bargain** or **promise,** since it includes executed **sales, gifts** and other transfers of **property,** as well as promises without legal obligation. While agreement is often used as a synonym for contract, some authorities narrow it to mean only mutual assent.

AID AND ABET   to knowingly encourage or assist another in the commission or attempted commission of a crime. See also **accessory; accomplice; conspirator.** Compare **principal.**

AID TO FAMILIES WITH DEPENDENT CHILDREN   see **social security [AID TO FAMILIES WITH DEPENDENT CHILDREN].**

AIR PIRACY   see **hijacking.**

AIR RIGHTS   the legal ownership of land includes the ownership of the airspace above the land. A tree that has branches extending over a neighbor's property may therefore interfere with the neighbor's air rights. The rights are not limitless since, for example, airplanes are allowed to fly at certain altitudes. Conversely, the rights do not allow an owner to pollute the air.

AIRSPACE   see **air rights.**

A.J.   abbreviation for Associate Judge or Justice.

AKA   abbreviation for "also known as." See **alias.**

ALCOMETER see **breathalyzer.**

ALEATORY   uncertain; risky. An **ALEATORY CONTRACT** is an agreement in which performance by one party depends upon an uncertain or contingent event—for example, a fire insurance contract is aleatory because it is uncertain when or if benefits will be paid.

ALFORD PLEA see **plea [ALFORD PLEA].**

ALI   see **restatement.**

ALIAS   "otherwise known as"; an indication that a person is known by more than one name. "AKA" and "a/k/a" mean "also known as" and are used in **indictments** to introduce the listing of an alias.

ALIBI   an excuse that proves the physical impossibility that a suspected person could have committed the crime.

ALIEN   one who is not a citizen of the country in which he lives. A **RESIDENT ALIEN** is a person who has been admitted to permanent resident status but has not been granted citizenship. An **ILLEGAL ALIEN** is a noncitizen who has not been given permission by immigration authorities to reside in the country in which he is living.

ALIENATION   in real property law, the voluntary transfer of **title** and **possession** of **real property** to another person. The law recognizes the power to alienate (or transfer) property as an essential ingredient of **fee simple** ownership of property and generally prohibits unreasonable restraints on alienation.

ALIENATION OF AFFECTIONS   a **tort** based upon willful and malicious interference with the marriage relationship by a third party, causing mental anguish, loss of social position, disgrace, embarrassment or actual monetary loss. (Most states no longer recognize this as the basis for a lawsuit.) If the interference is in the nature of adultery, the tort is called CRIMINAL CONVERSATION. However, it may result from lesser acts which deprive the other spouse of affection from his marital partner. See **consortium.**

ALIENATION, ORDER OF   see **marshaling [marshalling].**

ALIEN REGISTRATION   see **green card.**

ALIEN TORT CLAIMS ACT adopted in 1789, provides that federal district courts shall have original jurisdiction of any **civil** cause of action by a foreign national alien for a **tort** committed in violation of the law of nations or a treaty of the United States. The act thus permits federal courts to hear **human rights** cases brought by foreign nationals for conduct committed outside the United States. A more recent codification, passed in 1992, is the TORTURE VICTIM PROTECTION ACT which allows both aliens and citizens to bring civil actions against individuals (in an official capacity for a foreign country that is on a specified list) who torture, kill, or commit other human rights abuses.

ALIMONY   court-ordered payment for the support of one's estranged spouse in the case of **divorce** or separation. For federal income tax purposes, alimony payments are **deductions** to the paying spouse and **income** to the receiving spouse if they are payable over an indefinite period, or over a definite period lasting more than ten years.
  CHILD SUPPORT, the amount of money the court requires one spouse to pay to the other who has **custody** of the children born of the marriage, may be imposed by the court with or without an award of alimony. See **deadbeat dad [mom].**

ALIQUOT   *(ä'-lē-kwō)* Lat.: an even, fractional part of the whole. In a **trust,** it is a particular fraction of the whole property involved, as distinguished from a general interest.

ALI TEST   see **insanity [ALI TEST].**

ALIUNDE   *(äl-ē-ŭn'-dā)* Lat.: from another source; from elsewhere; from outside. ALIUNDE RULE refers to the doctrine that a **verdict** may not be **impeached** by evidence offered by a juror unless the foundation for introducing the evidence is laid first by competent, **admissible evidence** from another source.

ALLEGATION   in a **pleading,** an assertion of fact; a statement of the issue that the contributing party expects to prove. See **averment.**

ALLEN CHARGE   an instruction by the court to a jury that is having difficulty reaching a **verdict** in a criminal case, to encourage the jury to make a renewed effort to arrive at a decision. Because it may have a coercive effect upon the jury, some jurisdictions no longer permit the instruction to be given after the jury reports a deadlock.

ALLOCUTION   the requirement in **common law** that, following the **verdict** of conviction, the judge ask the **defendant** to show legal cause why sentence should not be pronounced. It continues to be part of the **sentencing** procedure in a majority of states and is a mandatory part of a valid sentencing in the federal system. The modern allocution does not ask the defendant why sentence should not be imposed but rather asks if he or she has anything to say in his or her own behalf in mitigation of punishment. See **mitigating circumstances.**

ALLODIAL   owned freely; not subject to the restriction on **alienation** that existed in feudal law.

ALLOWANCE   see depletion [DEPLETION ALLOWANCE].

ALLUVION   a deposit of sedimentary material (earth, sand, gravel, etc.) that has accumulated gradually and imperceptibly along the bank of a river or the sea. Alluvion is the result of **accretion** and is considered part of the property to which it has become attached. See also **avulsion.**

ALSO KNOWN AS [AKA]   see **alias.**

ALTERATION   see **material alteration.**

ALTER EGO   *(äl'-tèr ē-gō)*   Lat: the other self. Under the doctrine of alter ego, the law will disregard the limited personal liability one enjoys when he or she acts in a corporate capacity and will regard the act as his or her personal responsibility. To invoke the doctrine, it must be shown that the corporation was a mere conduit for the transaction of private business and that no separate identity of the individual and the corporation really existed.

ALTERNATIVE DISPUTE RESOLUTION [ADR]   alternatives to the slow and costly process of litigation. Includes **arbitration**, **conciliation**, **mediation**, and **summary** proceedings. Some of these processes, such as mediation and arbitration, are being used by court systems to attempt to resolve disputes before trial.

ALTERNATIVE MINIMUM TAX [AMT]   the AMT attempts to ensure that individuals who benefit from tax advantages such as deductions, credits, and exemptions pay at least a minimum amount of tax. It effectively creates a tax liability for individuals who would pay little or no tax. In practice, the AMT is controversial, as it applied to more and more taxpayers each year, beyond the intended targets of the tax. Congress is attempting to correct or repeal the AMT.

ALTERNATIVE PLEADING in **common law,** a pleading that alleged facts so inconsistent that it was difficult to determine upon which set of facts the person pleading intended to rely. Alternative pleading is generally permitted under modern procedure.

EXAMPLE: Corey is accused of murder. At his trial, he *alternatively pleads* the insanity defense and self-defense. The two are alternatives: the insanity plea means that Corey admits the murder but claims that his mental state prevents him from being criminally responsible, while the plea of self-defense means that he was justified in using deadly force in the particular circumstance.

ALTERNATIVE WRIT OF MANDAMUS see **preemptory writ.**

AMBULANCE CHASING see **barratry.**

AMELIORATING WASTE see **waste [AMELIORATING WASTE].**

AMEND to alter. One amends a statute by changing (but not abolishing) an established law. One amends a **pleading** by adding to or subtracting from an already existing pleading.

EXAMPLE: Lily sues a manufacturing company for injuries resulting from a defect in one of their products. After she files her papers with the court, she discovers new facts which indicate that the company was negligent in developing the product. Lily seeks to *amend* her pleading to include these new facts, and, as is generally the case, she is permitted to amend.

AMENDED PLEADINGS see **pleadings [AMENDED PLEADINGS].**

AMENDED RETURN see **return [AMENDED RETURN].**

AMENDMENTS see **respective entries** (e.g., **First Amendment**).

A MENSA ET THORO see **divorce [SEPARATION].**

AMERCEMENT a monetary penalty or fine or a chastisement, especially of a public official.

AMERICAN BAR ASSOCIATION [ABA] a national organization of lawyers and law students that promotes improvements in the delivery of legal services and the administration of justice. Membership is open to any lawyer who is in good standing in any state or to any student attending an accredited law school. The **AMERICAN BAR FOUNDATION** is a subsidiary of the ABA that sponsors and funds projects in legal research, education, and social studies.

AMERICAN BAR FOUNDATION see **American Bar Association [AMERICAN BAR FOUNDATION].**

AMERICAN CIVIL LIBERTIES UNION [ACLU] a national organization, founded in 1920, that seeks to enforce and preserve the rights and civil liberties guaranteed by the federal and state constitutions. Its activities include handling cases, opposing allegedly repressive legislation and publishing reports and informational pamphlets.

AMERICAN DEPOSITORY RECEIPT [ADR] a receipt issued by American banks to domestic buyers as a convenient substitute for direct ownership of stock in foreign companies. ADR's are traded on **stock exchanges** and in **over-the-counter markets** like stocks of domestic companies. **Rights, offers,** stock **dividends** and similar adjustments to the underlying shares are paid in cash or ADR dividends by the bank.

AMERICAN INDIAN LAW see **Indian law.**

AMERICAN LAW INSTITUTE see **restatement.**

AMERICAN LAW INSTITUTE TEST see **insanity [ALI TEST].**

AMERICAN STOCK EXCHANGE **Stock exchange** which merged with the **New York Stock Exchange.** It was formerly known as the **NEW YORK CURB EXCHANGE** or "Curb" and is abbreviated today as either **AMEX** or **ASE.**

AMERICANS WITH DISABILITIES ACT [ADA] wide-ranging federal legislation intended to make American society more accessible to people with disabilities. Disability is defined as a physical or mental impairment that substantially limits one or more major life activities. The ADA has several key components including the following: businesses of fifteen or more employees must provide reasonable accommodations for disabled employees; all public services, including state and local governments, cannot deny services or participation in programs or activities which are available to people without disabilities; public transportation systems must be accessible; public accommodations including facilities such as restaurants, hotels, and stores must be barrier free and accessible in new construction and in existing facilities, barriers to services must be removed if readily achievable; telecommunications companies must make provisions for use by hard-of-hearing persons; and discrimination against persons with disabilities or persons who assert rights under the ADA is not permitted.

AMEX see **American Stock Exchange.**

AMICUS CURIAE *(à-mē'-kŭs kyū'-rē-ī)* Lat.: friend of the

27

court. A qualified person who is not a party to the **action** but gives information to the court on a question of law. The function of an amicus curiae is to call attention to some information that might escape the court's attention. An AMICUS CURIAE BRIEF (or AMICUS BRIEF) is one submitted by someone not a party to the lawsuit, to give the court information needed to make a proper decision, or to urge a particular result on behalf of the public interest or of a private interest of third parties who will be indirectly affected by the resolution of the dispute. Thus, a court might permit a group of retarded citizens to participate in a proceeding brought by a prisoner rights group to challenge a statute authorizing the expenditure of funds for the construction of prisons and mental health facilities, since invalidation of the statute would adversely affect the interests of retarded citizens.

AM. JUR. (2D)   American Jurisprudence (second edition). An encyclopedia of United States law.

AMNESTY   a **pardon** extended to a group of persons excusing them for offenses against the government. See **executive clemency.**

EXAMPLE: In an attempt to end the dissension caused by the Vietnam War, President Carter granted *amnesty* to all draft evaders on certain conditions. Those individuals entitled to amnesty were absolved of liability for selective service violations.

AMORTIZATION   the reduction of a **debt** by periodic charges to assets or liabilities, such as payments on mortgages.

EXAMPLE: A landlord paves the parking lot for an apartment building. In charging each tenant rental for a parking space, the landlord *amortizes* the cost of the pavement so that, over a period of time, the tenant actually pays for the work. If the landlord had borrowed the money to fund the improvement, the landlord would amortize the loan by paying it back over a fixed period of time.

In accounting statements, the term usually refers to charges against investments in intangibles such as patents, copyrights, goodwill, organization, expenses, etc. Compare **depreciation.**

AMOUNT REALIZED   see **realization [GAIN OR LOSS REALIZED].**

AMT   see **alternative minimum tax [AMT].**

AMW   average monthly wage.

ANACONDA CLAUSE   see **mother hubbard clause [ANDACONDA CLAUSE].**

ANCIENT DEMESNE manors that were in the actual possession of the Crown during the reign of William the Conqueror and that were recorded as such in the **Domesday Book.** This type of tenure was abolished in England by the Law of Property Act (1922). See **demesne.**

ANCILLARY JURISDICTION the jurisdiction under which a federal court is permitted to decide an entire controversy (including matters which it would not have authority to consider were they raised independently) if the controversy contains other issues that the law specifically authorizes federal courts to decide. Thus, when the court has jurisdiction of the principal action, it may also hear any ancillary proceeding, regardless of any other factor that would normally determine jurisdiction. Compare **pendent jurisdiction.**

AND HIS HEIRS see **heirs.**

ANIMO *(än'-ĭ-mō)* Lat.: intentionally.

   AMINO REVERTENDI *(rĕ-vĕr-tĕn'-dē)* with the intention to return.

   AMINO REVOCANDI *(rĕ-vō-kän'-dē)* with the intention to revoke.

   AMINO TESTANDI *(tĕs-tän'-dē)* with the intention to make a **will.**

ANIMUS see **animo.**

ANNOTATION a comment upon or collection of cases citing a particular case or statute. An annotated statute is one that has the relevant cases interpreting the statute appended to it. Thus, United States Code Annotated (U.S.C.A.) or New Jersey Statutes Annotated (N.J.S.A.) are annotated versions of the official statutes of those jurisdictions. American Law Reports (A.L.R.) is an annotated set of recent cases from the various state and federal courts. The current versions are A.L.R. 5th and A.L.R. Fed.

ANNUAL PERCENTAGE RATE standardized method for expressing a rate of interest on borrowed money (on a yearly basis) so that the borrower will know the true cost of borrowing.

ANNUAL REPORT a formal financial statement issued yearly. The annual report of publicly owned corporations must comply with **SEC** reporting requirements, which include **balance sheet, income statement,** and cash flow reports audited by an independent certified public accountant.

ANNUITANT one who receives the benefits of an **annuity.**

ANNUITY a fixed sum payable periodically, subject to the limitations imposed by the grantor—generally, either for life or for a number of years.

ANNUL to make void; to dissolve that which once existed, as to annul a marriage. Annulment wipes out or invalidates the entire marriage, whereas **divorce** only ends the marriage from that point on and does not affect the former validity of the marriage.

ANSWER the **defendant's** principal **pleading** in response to the **plaintiff's complaint.** It must contain a **denial** of all the **allegations** the defendant wishes to dispute, as well as any affirmative **defenses** by the defendant and any **counterclaim** against the plaintiff.

ANTENUPTIAL AGREEMENT see **prenuptial agreement.**

ANTICIPATORY BREACH (OF CONTRACT) breaking a contract before the actual time of required performance. It occurs when one person repudiates his contractual obligation before it is due, by indicating that he will not or cannot perform his contractual duties.

EXAMPLE: Steven contracted with a fuel oil company to supply heating oil to it. The contract called for twelve monthly deliveries over a year period. After three months, Steven realized the contract would be too costly for him to continue supplying the oil. He informed the company that he would not deliver the oil at the next delivery date. His action constitutes an *anticipatory breach* of his contract with the fuel oil company.

Where anticipatory repudiation is by conduct rather than by declaration, it may be called VOLUNTARY DISABLEMENT.

ANTICYBERSQUATTING CONSUMER PROTECTION ACT see **cybersquatting [cyberpiracy]** [ANTICYBERSQUATTING CONSUMER PROTECTION ACT].

ANTI-DISCRIMINATION ACT see **Robinson-Patman Act.**

ANTI-DUMPING LAW see **dumping.**

ANTILAPSE STATUTES statutes that allow the **heirs** of a devisee or **legatee** who predeceases the **testator** to inherit what the testator had **bequeathed** to the deceased devisee or legatee. Under common law, a bequest lapsed upon the death of the specified recipient, so that, in particular, when a parent died before the testator/grandparent, the grandchildren were disinherited.

ANTITRUST LAWS statutes that promote free competition by outlawing such things as **monopolies,** price discrimination, and collaboration, for the purpose of **restraint of trade,** between two or more business enterprises in the same market. The two major U.S. antitrust laws are the **SHERMAN ACT** and the **CLAYTON ACT.**

APA   see **Administrative Procedure Act [APA].**

A POSTERIORI   *(ä pŏs-tĕr-ē-ô'-rē)*   Lat.: from the most recent point of view. Relates to knowledge gained through actual experience or observation, rather than through logical conclusions. Compare **a priori.**

APOSTILLE (SEAL)   a certificate authenticating the signature of officials on official documentation such as birth or death certificates, diplomas, contracts or court orders from countries that are party to the **Hague Convention.** Provides an international notarization accepted by signatory countries. See also **notary public.**

APPARENT AUTHORITY   a reference to the doctrine that a **principal** is responsible for the acts of his or her **agent** where the principal by words or conduct suggests to a third person that the agent may act in the principal's behalf, and where the third person believes in the authority of the agent.

EXAMPLE: A business organization that sells athletic equipment used Tim, a local sports star, to advertise and promote their products. His actions made it seem that he was part of the business, and the business did nothing to qualify that image. A manufacturer contracted with Tim to supply the business with various types of equipment under their belief that Tim was a part of that business. Although the business may not want that equipment, they are forced to purchase it. Tim's *apparent authority* as agent of the business organization was due to the organization's acquiescence, and this false impression obliges them to act in accordance with the contract.

APP. DIV.   abbreviation for Appellate Division.

APPEAL   a request to a higher court to review and reverse the decision of a lower court. On appeal, no new evidence is introduced; the higher court is limited to considering whether the lower court erred on a question of law or gave a decision plainly contrary to the evidence presented during trial. Unless special permission is granted by the higher court to hear an **interlocutory** appeal, an appeal cannot be made until the lower court renders a final **judgment.**

NOTICE OF APPEAL   document **filed** with the **appellate court** giving notice of an intention to appeal. It must be **served** on the opposing party and must comply with specified deadlines for filing.

TRIAL DE NOVO   historically, the appeal as it existed in **equity** allowed a trial de novo on law and facts, while proceedings **at law**

allowed only a review on the **record** produced in the lower court for errors of law. Today this distinction largely has merged into one system. Equitable proceedings still, however, require a trial de novo more often than legal proceedings, unless it has been specifically proscribed by **statute.** For example, appeals from **probate** court **decrees** often are by trial de novo.

APPEARANCE the required coming into court of a plaintiff or defendant in an **action** either by himself or herself (**PRO SE**) or through an attorney. An appearance involves a voluntary submission to the **jurisdiction** of the court.

EXAMPLE: Suze is arrested for possessing more than 25 grams of marijuana. Once she employs an attorney, the attorney files a notice of *appearance* with the court stating that he or she is Suze's attorney and will represent her in the forthcoming trial.

COMPULSORY APPEARANCE an appearance compelled by **service of process.**

GENERAL APPEARANCE a party's appearance at a **proceeding** for any reason other than for questioning the court's jurisdiction.

SPECIAL APPEARANCE an appearance for the sole purpose of questioning the **jurisdiction** of the court over the defendant and the authority of the court to compel his appearance for any other purpose.

EXAMPLE: A seller agrees to provide a buyer with certain goods. One clause in the contract states that, if the goods are defective, the buyer can only sue in the seller's home state. The goods turn out to be defective, but the buyer files suit in a court in the buyer's home state. The seller makes a *special appearance* in the court only for the purpose of challenging that court's jurisdiction based on the clause in the contract. By such an appearance, the seller does not acknowledge the court's right to entertain the buyer's suit against him.

VOLUNTARY APPEARANCE an appearance by one who has not been required to appear by **service of process.**

APPEARANCE DE BENE ESSE see **de bene esse.**

APPELLANT the party to a lawsuit who appeals the decision to a higher court. See **plaintiff [PLAINTIFF IN ERROR].** Compare **appellee.**

APPELLATE [APPEALS] COURT a court having authority to review the law applied by a lower court in the same case. In most instances, the trial court first decides a lawsuit, with review of its decision then available in an appellate court.

APPELLATE JURISDICTION see **jurisdiction.**

APPELLATION OF ORIGIN   a term that refers to the specific characteristics of wines, cheeses, butters, and other agricultural products which are unique to a region. For example, the **INDICATION OF SOURCE** would be "blue cheese from France" while the *appellation of origin* might be "Roquefort" which is only applied to those cheeses aged in the natural Cambalou caves of Roquefort-sur-Soulzon.

APPELLEE   the party prevailing in the lower court who argues, on **appeal,** against setting aside the lower court's **judgment.** In some state courts this party is referred to as the **respondent.** See **defendant [DEFENDANT IN ERROR].** Compare **appellant.**

APPOINTED COUNSEL   see **public defender; right to counsel.**

APPOINTMENT OF RECEIVER   the placing, by court order, of contested property in the hands of a **receiver** in order to protect someone's ownership or **trust** interests in said property or funds. For instance, the **creditor** of a **bankrupt** can have the bankrupt's assets placed in the **custody** of a receiver to stop the bankrupt from selling the assets for cash or to prevent other creditors from seizing the assets.

APPOINTMENT, POWER OF   see **power of appointment.**

APPORTION   to divide fairly or proportionately, according to the parties' respective interests.

APPRAISAL RIGHTS   a **statutory** remedy available in many states to minority stockholders [**SHAREHOLDERS**] who object to an extraordinary action taken by the **corporation** (such as a **merger**). This remedy requires the corporation to repurchase the stock of dissenting stockholders at a price equivalent to its value immediately prior to the extraordinary corporate action.

APPRAISE   to estimate the value of property. Compare **assess.**

APPRECIATE   1. increase in value; 2. to understand the significance of something; in criminal law, used in some statutes as part of the insanity test, to signify that the defendant understands the wrongfulness of his or her conduct.

APPRECIATION   the excess of the fair market value of property over the taxpayer's **basis** in such property.

    UNREALIZED APPRECIATION   the amount of appreciation in property that has not yet been subject to tax. See **realization.**

APPROPRIATE   1. to set apart for, or assign to, a particular purpose or use; 2. to wrongfully use or take the property of another.

APPROPRIATION 1. the designation of funds for a specific government expenditure. 2. the **tort** arising from the use of a person's name, picture, or likeness as a symbol of his or her identity without compensation.

APPURTENANT attached to something else. In property law, the term refers especially to the attachment of a restriction (e.g., an **easement** or **covenant**) to a piece of land, which benefits or restricts the owner of such land in his use and enjoyment. To illustrate: if A allows B the right-of-way over A's land so that B has access to the highway, this is an easement appurtenant to B's land. See **easement** [EASEMENT APPURTENANT].

APR see **annual percentage rate.**

A PRIORI *(ä prē-ô'-rē)* Lat.: from the former, from the first. Modern usage has deviated significantly from the Latin. An a priori conclusion or judgment is one that is necessarily true, that is neither proved by nor capable of being disproved by experience, and that is known to be true by a process of reasoning independent of all factual evidence.

The term is commonly used to indicate a judgment that is widely believed to be certain, or that is introduced presumptively, without analysis or investigation. Thus to accuse someone of having assumed a fact or conclusion a priori is often to disparage him or her for having failed to support a judgment through evidence or analysis. Compare **a posteriori.**

ARBITER *(är'-bĭt-ėr)* Lat.: referee. A person (other than a judicial officer) appointed by the court to decide a controversy according to the law. Unlike an **arbitrator,** the arbiter needs the court's confirmation of his decision for it to be final.

ARBITRAGE a kind of hedged investment wherein the arbitrageur simultaneously buys and sells the same assets (such as securities or commodities) in different markets or exchanges in order to profit from slight differences in price. True arbitrage positions are completely HEDGED—that is, the performance of both sides of the transaction is guaranteed at the time the position is assumed—and are thus without risk of loss.

KIND ARBITRAGE purchase of a security that is without restriction, other than the purchase of money, exchangeable or convertible within a reasonable time into a second security together with a simultaneous offsetting sale of the second security.

SPACE ARBITRAGE purchase in one market against sale in another market.

TIME ARBITRAGE   most common form — the purchase of a commodity against a present sale of the identical commodity for future delivery.

ARBITRARY AND CAPRICIOUS   see **abuse of discretion.**

ARBITRATION   submitting a controversy to an impartial person, the **arbitrator,** chosen by the two parties in the dispute to determine an equitable settlement. Where the parties agree to be bound by the determination of the arbitrator, the process is called **BINDING ARBITRATION.**

In labor law, arbitration has become an important means of settling disputes, and the majority of labor contracts provide for arbitration of disputes over the meaning of contract clauses.

COMPULSORY ARBITRATION, in which the parties are forced to agree, is generally not provided for in federal law. The states, however, have increasingly provided for compulsory arbitration in areas beyond the control of federal law, such as police and firefighters' contracts.

NONBINDING ARBITRATION   process where the parties are free to follow the arbitrator's findings or disregard them and proceed to court. The arbitrator's decision is not final.

ARBITRATION CLAUSE   a clause in a **contract** providing for **arbitration** of disputes arising under the contract. Arbitration clauses are treated as separable parts of the contract so that the illegality of another part of the contract does not nullify such agreement and a **breach** or repudiation of the contract does not preclude the right to arbitrate.

ARBITRATOR   an impartial person chosen by the parties to solve a dispute between them, who is empowered to make a final determination concerning the issue(s) in controversy, who is bound only by his or her own **discretion,** and from whose decision there is no appeal. The decision of the arbitrator (the counterpart of a court's **order** or **judgment**) is called the **AWARD.** A court order enforcing an arbitrator's award is called **CONFIRMATION.** Compare **arbiter; conciliator; mediator.**

ARGUENDO   *(är-gyū-ĕn'-dō)*   Lat.: for the sake of argument.

EXAMPLE: Ace Chemical Company is accused of dumping toxic wastes in a canal outside the city. Although the company does not want to admit that it polluted the canal, for public relations reasons it is willing to pay the cleanup costs. In approaching the city to determine the dollar figure for those costs, the company will state, "Assuming, *arguendo,* that we did pollute the canal, how much will the cleanup cost?" By "assuming arguendo," the company avoids admitting guilt and moves on to the more important questions of cleanup.

ARGUMENT   a course of reasoning intended to establish a position and to induce belief.

ARM'S LENGTH   a relatively equal bargaining position between contracting parties, in which the agreement reached is seen as free of one-sidedness, **duress, unconscionability,** or **overreaching** by either party.

ARRAIGN   to bring a defendant to court to answer the charge under which an **indictment** has been handed down.

ARRAIGNMENT   an initial step in the criminal process in which the defendant is formally charged with an offense, given a copy of the **complaint, indictment, information,** or other accusatory instrument, and informed of his or her constitutional rights, including the **pleas** he or she may enter. Where the appearance is shortly after the arrest, it may properly be called a **presentment** since often no plea is taken. Compare **preliminary hearing.**

ARRANGEMENTS   see **bankruptcy [CHAPTER 11 REORGANIZATION].**

ARRAY   see **challenge [CHALLENGE TO JURY ARRAY].**

ARREARS   that which is unpaid although due to be paid. A person in arrears is behind in payment.

ARREST   to deprive a person of liberty by legal authority; in the technical criminal law sense, to seize an alleged or suspected offender to answer for a crime.

ARREST OF JUDGMENT   the court's withholding of **judgment** because of some error in the **record.**

ARREST RECORD   see **criminal record.**

ARSON   the willful and malicious burning of another's house; sometimes expanded by statute to include acts similar to burning (such as exploding) or the destruction of property other than dwellings.

ARTICLES OF IMPEACHMENT   a formal statement of the grounds upon which the removal of a public official is sought, similar to an **indictment** in an ordinary criminal proceeding. In the federal system, articles of **impeachment** are voted by the House of Representatives, with the trial occurring before the Senate.

ARTICLES OF INCORPORATION the document that creates a private corporation, according to the general corporation laws of the state.

ARTIFICE a **fraud** or a cunning device used to accomplish some wrong; usually implies craftiness or deceitfulness.

ARTIFICIAL PERSON see **corporation.**

ART, WORDS OF see **words of art.**

ASA assistant state's attorney. See **prosecutor.**

AS A MATTER OF LAW see **operation of law.**

ASE see **American Stock Exchange.**

AS IS a commercial term denoting agreement that buyer shall accept delivery of goods in the condition in which they are found on inspection prior to purchase, even if they are damaged or defective.

ASO see **administrative services only.** Also may mean "as **subrogee** of."

ASPORTATION see **caption; trespass [TRESPASS DE BONIS ASPORTATIS].**

ASSAULT an attempt or apparent attempt to inflict bodily injury upon another by using unlawful force, accompanied by the apparent ability to injure that person if not prevented. An assault need not result in a touching so as to constitute a **battery.** Thus, no physical injury need be proved to establish an assault. An assault may be either a civil or criminal offense. Some jurisdictions have defined criminal assault to include battery—the actual physical injuring.

AGGRAVATED ASSAULT an assault where serious bodily injury is inflicted on the person assaulted; an assault with a dangerous or **deadly weapon.**

ASSAULT, SEXUAL see **rape [SEXUAL ASSAULT].**

ASSEMBLY, UNLAWFUL see **unlawful assembly.**

ASSESS 1. to determine the value of something; 2. to fix the value of property on the basis of which property taxes will be calculated. Compare **appraise.**

ASSESSMENT OF DEFICIENCY in general, the amount of tax determined to be due after an appellate review within the **Internal Revenue Service** and a **Tax Court** adjudication (if requested).

JEOPARDY ASSESSMENT an immediate assessment of the deficiency by the Internal Revenue Service without appellate review and Tax Court hearing, which is permitted if, in the opinion of the Internal Revenue Service, the assessment and collection of a deficiency would be jeopardized by delay.

ASSET   anything owned that has monetary value; any interest in **real property** or **personal property** that can be used for payment of *debts*.

EXAMPLE: Luciana wants to borrow a sizeable amount of money to build a summer house in the mountains. Although banks are generally unwilling to lend money for such projects, they will lend to Luciana because she has substantial *assets*, including ownership of several buildings and a large number of stocks. Such assets are generally pledged as **collateral.** With respect to real property, Luciana might give the bank a mortgage as a form of collateral.

Assets appear as one of three major **balance sheet** categories and are counterbalanced by **liabilities** and **net assets.** In corporations, net assets are usually referred to as shareholder's equity or **book value.**

CURRENT ASSETS   for accounting purposes, property that can be easily converted into cash, such as marketable **securities, accounts receivable** (goods or services sold but not paid for) and inventories (raw materials, work in process and finished goods intended for future sale).

FIXED ASSETS   in accounting, property used for production of goods and services, such as plant and machinery, buildings, land, mineral resources.

Other categories of assets include intangibles, such as **goodwill,** patent rights and acquisition costs in excess of fair market value, and tangibles, such as long-term investments in other companies, long-term receivables, insurance owned.

ASSET VALUE   see **net asset value.**

ASSEVECATION   oath or declaration.

ASSIGN   to transfer one's interest in property, contract or other rights to another.

ASSIGNED COUNSEL   see **public defender; right to counsel.**

ASSIGNED RISK   in automobile insurance, a class of persons to whom insurance companies will not issue policies voluntarily, usually because their record of prior accidents has made them a high risk, and who therefore are assigned by state law to insurance companies and must pay higher rates. Many states have **FINANCIAL RESPONSIBILITY LAWS** that prohibit such persons from driving unless adequate insurance has been obtained.

ASSIGNEE   see **assigns [assignees].**

ASSIGNMENT   the transfer to another of one's **interest** in a right or property.

   ASSIGNMENT FOR BENEFIT OF CREDITORS   a **debtor's** transfer of his property to another party to be held in **trust** and applied to the debts of the assignor (debtor).

   ASSIGNMENT OF A LEASE   the transfer of the **lessee's** entire interest in the **lease,** by which the assignee of the lease becomes primarily liable for any rent required to be paid under the lease, and the **assignor** (original lessee) remains secondarily liable for the rent if the assignee does not pay it.

ASSIGNMENT OF ERROR   the **appellant's** declaration or complaint against the trial judge that he committed an **error** in the lower court proceedings. Assignments of error establish the issues to be argued on **appeal.**

ASSIGNMENT OF INCOME   a taxpayer's direction that income earned by him or her be paid to another person, so that it will be considered the other person's income for federal tax purposes. An effective assignment of income would be to transfer a share of dividend-paying stock *before* the dividend declaration date—in such a case the dividend would be taxed to the transferee; an ineffective assignment of income would be to transfer the share *after* the dividend declaration date—here the dividend would be taxed to the transferor.

ASSIGNMENT OF MORTGAGE   see **mortgage [ASSIGNMENT OF MORTGAGE].**

ASSIGNOR   one who transfers property to another. Synonymous with **GRANTOR**. The grantor of a trust is the creator of the trust.

ASSIGNS [ASSIGNEES]   all those who take from another by deed upon the transfer of real property, or under a will, or, in the absence of a valid will, those who inherit the property of the **intestate** by operation of law. See **descent.**

ASSISTED SUICIDE   see **euthanasia [ACTIVE EUTHANASIA].**

ASSIZE   ancient writ issued from a **court of assize** to the sheriff for the recovery of property; actions of the special court that issues the writ. See **Court of Assize and Nisi Prius.**

ASSOCIATE JUSTICE   a member of the United States Supreme Court, other than the **Chief Justice;** the title held by a judge, other than the presiding judge, on the highest court of some states.

ASSOCIATION   a group of persons joined together for a certain object.

ASSUMPSIT   *(à-sŭmp'-sĭt)*   Lat.: he promised; he undertook. In contract law, the term signifies an express or implied promise or undertaking, made either orally or in writing not under **seal.** The term refers especially to one of the old **forms of action** in **common law** comprising an action in **equity** and applicable to almost every case in which money had been received that in equity and good conscience ought to have been refunded.

ASSUMPTION OF MORTGAGE   see **mortgage.**

ASSUMPTION OF RISK   1. in torts, an affirmative **defense** used by the defendant in a **negligence** suit, claiming that plaintiff had knowledge of an obviously dangerous condition or situation and yet voluntarily exposed himself to the hazard, thereby relieving the defendant of legal responsibility for any resulting injury; 2. in contract law, the agreement by an employee to assume the risks of ordinary hazards arising out of his occupation.

Contributory negligence arises when plaintiff fails to exercise due care, while assumption of risk arises regardless of the care used and is based fundamentally on consent.

ASSURANCE   see **covenant** [COVENANT OF FURTHER ASSURANCE].

ASSURED   see **insured.**

ASYLUM   a shelter for the unfortunate or afflicted—the insane, the crippled, the poor. A POLITICAL ASYLUM is a state that accepts a citizen of another state to shelter him from prosecution by that other state.

AT BAR   see **bar.**

AT EQUITY   see **equity.**

AT ISSUE   see **issue.**

AT LAW   that which pertains to or is governed by the rules of law, as distinguished from the rules of equity; according to the rules of the **common law.** In England, and later in the United States, courts of law developed strict rules establishing the kinds of **causes of action** that could be maintained and the kinds of remedies that were available. Courts of equity established different rules and remedies, partly to mitigate the rigors of the law courts. "At law" and "in equity" thus refer to two different bodies of **jurisprudence.**

The term also may be used to mean by **operation of law.**

ATM abbreviation for automated [automatic] teller machine.

AT-RISK see **tax shelter [AT-RISK RULES].**

ATROCIOUS outrageously wicked and vile. An atrocious act demonstrates depraved and insensitive brutality and exhibits a senselessly immoderate use of extreme violence for a criminal purpose.

ATTACHMENT a legal **proceeding** by which a defendant's property is taken into custody and held for payment of a **judgment** in the event plaintiff's demand is later established and judgment is rendered in his favor.

ATTAINDER in common law, the elimination of all civil rights and liberties, and the forfeiture of property, caused by one's conviction for a **felony** or **capital offense.** See **bill of attainder.**

ATTAINDER, BILL OF see **bill of attainder.**

ATTAINT to pass sentence of attainder or to be under such a sentence; more generally to be stained or degraded by a conviction. In early common law practice this referred to a writ used to challenge a jury verdict.

ATTEMPT an **overt act,** beyond mere preparation, moving directly toward the actual commission of a criminal offense. The attempt to accomplish a criminal act is often made a crime itself, separate and distinct from the crime that is attempted. See **inchoate.** Compare **conspiracy.**

ATTENDANT CIRCUMSTANCES loose facts surrounding an event. In criminal law the definitions of crimes often require the presence or absence of attendant circumstances. For example, **statutory rape** requires that the minor be under the **age of consent,** the age of the minor being the attendant circumstance.

ATTEST to affirm as true; to sign one's name as a witness to the execution of a document; to bear witness to.

EXAMPLE: Where a person writes a will, that person must understand the nature of what he or she is doing when the will is signed and what the various provisions of the will mean. The laws of most states require that at least two persons *attest* to, or formally confirm, the writer's ability to meet these requirements. These persons are witnesses to the will.

ATTESTATION the act of **authentication** by **witnessing** an **instrument** of writing, at the request of the party making the instrument, and subscribing it as a witness. Attestation entails witnessing and certification that the instrument exists.

ATTORNEY synonymous with lawyer. May refer to an attorney in fact or an attorney at law. An **ATTORNEY IN FACT** is one who is an agent or representative of another given authority to act in that person's place and name. The document giving the attorney authority is called a **power of attorney.**

The general reference to an attorney is usually intended to designate an **ATTORNEY AT LAW.** This is one of a class of persons admitted by the state's highest court or by a federal court to practice law in that jurisdiction. The attorney is regarded as an officer of the court and is always subject to the admitting court's jurisdiction as to his or her ethical and professional conduct. Violations of those standards of conduct may result in discipline of the attorney in the form of censure, suspension, or **disbarment**. See **counsel [COUNSELLOR]; district attorney; public defender.**

ATTORNEY-CLIENT PRIVILEGE privilege that confidential communications between an attorney and a client in the course of the professional relationship cannot be disclosed without the consent of the client. It is the oldest of the privileges for confidential communications known to the common law. Its purpose is to encourage full and frank communication between attorneys and their clients and thereby promote broader public interests in the observance of law and administration of justice. Such communications may take the form of oral or written statements or may be actions and gestures. Communications made to an attorney while seeking to obtain representation, even though the attorney did not ultimately represent the client, are nonetheless privileged. The privilege protects discussions of past crimes but does not extend to the client's proposed commission of future crimes. If third parties (generally including relatives and friends but excluding law clerks, stenographers, or interpreters) are present, the privilege may be destroyed. The privilege extends indefinitely, and does not terminate when the attorney/client relationship ends or when either party dies. Communications between a corporate general counsel and corporate employees have been found to be protected. Finally, the privilege to prohibit disclosure belongs to the client, and as such may be waived by the client.

ACCOUNTANT-CLIENT PRIVILEGE available in about one-third of the states rendering confidential all communications to an accountant. Such communications are not otherwise privileged. If the accountant is also an attorney, the attorney-client privilege may not apply if the accountant-attorney was acting in the capacity of an accountant. If, however, a client communicates to an accountant designated by the client's attorney in confidence for the purpose of obtaining legal advice from the lawyer, it is then privileged. See **privileged communications**.

ATTORNEY GENERAL   the chief law enforcement officer of the federal government or of a state government.

ATTORNEY OF RECORD   see **of record** [ATTORNEY OF RECORD].

ATTORNEY, POWER OF   see **power of attorney.**

ATTORNEY'S FEE   the attorney's charge for services in representing a client; also, the additional award made by the court to the successful party in a lawsuit to compensate for the reasonable value of the services of the attorney.

ATTRACTIVE NUISANCE   the doctrine in **tort** law which holds that one who maintains something dangerous on his premises that is likely to attract children is required to reasonably protect the children against the dangers of that attraction. Thus, one has a duty to fence swimming pools, to remove doors from discarded refrigerators, to enclose partially constructed buildings and to be sensitive to other potentially dangerous conditions that attract curious children.

AUCTION   see **sale** [AUCTION SALE].

AUDIT   an inspection of the accounting records and procedures of a business, government unit or other reporting entity by a trained accountant, for the purpose of verifying the accuracy and completeness of the records. It may be conducted by a member of the organization (internal audit) or by an outsider (independent audit).

EXAMPLE: Since its inception, a welfare agency has been criticized for mismanagement of federal money by the agency directors and for allowing people to file double and sometimes triple claims. The General Accounting Office, an agency of the federal government, agrees to conduct an *audit* to determine if these allegations are true and to trace where the money had been spent.

See **audit of return.**

AUDIT OF RETURN   a review by an agent of the **Internal Revenue Service** of the tax return filed by the taxpayer and of the books and records supporting the information contained on the tax return. See **return, income tax.**

AUDITOR   1. a public officer charged by law with the duty of examining and verifying the expenditure of public funds; 2. an accountant who performs a similar function for private parties.

AUTHENTICATE   certify; corroborate; to prove genuine. Authentication may be established by witness testimony or by an expert.

AUTHORITY   the permission or power delegated to another. This may be express or implied. See **de facto [DE FACTO AUTHORITY].** If express, it is usually embraced in a document called a **power of attorney. IMPLIED AUTHORITY** stems from a relationship such as that of **principal** and **agent.** If the agent does not have **EXPRESS AUTHORITY** by some writing, he or she nonetheless will have **apparent authority.** If the authority is given to the agent for a **consideration,** it is said to be an **AUTHORITY COUPLED WITH AN INTEREST.** Where not to infer an authority would result in an injustice, the law will imply an authority so as not to mislead another. In this circumstance the law speaks of an **AUTHORITY BY ESTOPPEL.** Where the principal intended the agent to have the right to act on the principal's behalf, the authority is called an **ACTUAL AUTHORITY.**

The term may also refer to the jurisdiction of a court such as "within the court's authority." It is also used to denote judicial or legislative **precedent.**

AUTHORIZED ISSUE   the total number of shares of capital stock that a corporation may issue under its charter.

AUTOMATED CRIME see **computer crime.**

AUTOMATIC [ELECTRONIC] DATA CAPTURE   technologies such as magnetic stripes, radio frequency identification tags, bar codes and speech, iris, or facial recognition systems, which provide identifying information by way of stored digital files without the need to manually re-enter the data.

AUTOMOBILE, DEATH BY   see **homicide; manslaughter [DEATH BY AUTOMOBILE].**

AUTOMOBILE GUEST STATUTE   see **guest statute.**

AUTOPSY   the dissection of a cadaver to determine the cause of death. It may involve the inspection of important organs in order to determine the nature of a disease or abnormality.

AVERMENT   a positive statement or **allegation** of facts in a **pleading,** as distinguished from one based on reasoning or on inference.

AVOID   to cancel or make void; to prevent a certain result.

AVOIDANCE see **confession and avoidance.**

AVOIDANCE OF TAX   the method by which a taxpayer reduces his tax liability without committing **fraud**—e.g., by investing in a **tax shelter.** Compare **evasion of tax.**

AVULSION   an abrupt change in the course or channel of a stream that forms the boundary between two parcels of land, resulting in an apparent loss of part of the land of one **riparian** landowner and an apparent increase in the land of the other. The sudden and perceptible nature of this change distinguishes avulsion from **accretion:** when the change is abrupt, as in avulsion, the boundary between the two properties remains unaltered. When the changes are brought about by accretion—i.e., gradually, as a result of natural causes—the changed boundaries are recognized, and ownership interests are affected.

AWARD   see **arbitrator [AWARD].**

AWOL   see **desertion [ABSENT WITHOUT LEAVE].**

B

BAD CHECK   a check that is dishonored on presentation because of **nonsufficient funds [NSF],** unavailable funds, or a closed bank account. Issuing a bad check is a form of **larceny** [theft] and is generally punished as a **misdemeanor** although in some jurisdictions it is a more serious offense if the amount of the check is substantial. An affirmative defense is usually provided if the maker of the check, upon notice of dishonor, promptly satisfies the **payee.** See **check kiting.**

BAD DEBT   a **debt** that is not collectible and is therefore worthless to the **creditor;** a debt that becomes uncollectible because the debtor is insolvent. A nonbusiness bad debt is deductible from gross income as a short-term capital loss whereas a business bad debt is allowable as a **deduction** against ordinary income. See **income [GROSS INCOME; ORDINARY INCOME]; capital gains or losses [SHORT-TERM CAPITAL GAINS OR LOSSES].**

BAD FAITH   **breach** of faith; a willful failure to respond to plain, well-understood statutory or contractual obligations; dishonesty in fact in the conduct or transaction concerned.

BADGES OF FRAUD   facts or circumstances surrounding a transaction that indicate it may be fraudulent, especially in **fraud** of **creditors.** These badges include fictitious **consideration,** false statements as to consideration, transactions different from the usual method of doing business, transfer of all of a debtor's property, **insolvency,** confidential relationship of the parties, and transfers in anticipation of a lawsuit or an **execution** of judgment.

BAD TITLE   a purported title that is legally insufficient to **convey** property to the purchaser. A title that is not a **marketable title** is not necessarily a bad title, but a title that is bad is not marketable and is one that a purchaser ordinarily may not be compelled to accept.

BAIL   a monetary or other **security** given to secure the release of a **defendant** until time of trial and to assure his or her **appearance** at every stage of the **proceedings.** Very often today an accused will be released "ROR" **(release on recognizance)** without bail so long as he promises to appear as required.

BAIL BOND the document executed in order to secure the release of an individual in legal **custody.** The BAIL BONDSMAN, who acts as **surety,** generally forfeits his or her security in the event the **defendant** jumps bail—that is, fails to appear as required for court dates.

BAILEE a party who holds the **personal property** of another for a specific purpose agreed to between the parties. See **bailment.**

EXAMPLE: Clark owns a considerable amount of bonds that are payable on a certain date to whoever holds the documents. As a security precaution, Clark delivers the bonds to his bank to hold for him in a custodial capacity. The bank acts as a *bailee* of the bonds; Clark is the **bailor.** If Clark had placed the bonds in a rented safety deposit box, no bailment would have been created.

BAILIFF 1. a court attendant; 2. a person to whom some care, **guardianship** or **jurisdiction** is entrusted: e.g., a steward who has charge of lands, goods and **chattels** to get the best benefit for the owner; a person appointed by private persons to collect rents and manage their estate; or a court-appointed guardian of an **incompetent.**

BAIL JUMPING see **jump bail.**

BAILMENT a delivery of **personal property** to be held in **trust;** the relationship that arises where one person, the **bailor,** delivers property to another, the **bailee,** to hold, with control and **possession** of the property passing to the bailee.

ACTUAL BAILMENT one established by an actual or constructive delivery of the property to the bailee or the bailee's agents.

BAILMENT FOR HIRE one that arises from contract in which the bailor agrees to compensate the bailee as, for example, in the case of delivering one's car to a garage attendant. If the bailment is intended to result in some additional benefit for the bailor, such as a repair of his or her vehicle during the bailment, it may be referred to as a BAILMENT FOR MUTUAL BENEFIT.

BAILMENT FOR MUTUAL BENEFIT one in which the parties contemplate some compensation for benefits flowing from the bailment resulting from an express or implied undertaking to that effect. Compare BAILMENT FOR HIRE.

CONSTRUCTIVE BAILMENT one that arises when the person having possession holds it under such circumstances that the law imposes an obligation to deliver to another, even where such person did not come into possession voluntarily, and where therefore no bailment was voluntarily established.

GRATUITOUS BAILMENT one that results when care and custody of the **bailor's** property is accepted by the **bailee** without charge and without any **consideration** or expectation of benefit. In a gratuitous bailment, the bailee is liable to the bailor for the loss of bailed property only if the loss is caused by bailee's gross **negligence.**

INVOLUNTARY BAILMENT one that arises when the owner accidentally and without negligence leaves **personal property** in the **possession** of any person. An involuntary bailment arises if an umbrella is left with the coat check at a restaurant. Compare **abandonment.**

BAILOR a person who delivers **personal property** to another to be held in **bailment.** The bailor need not be the owner of the property involved.

EXAMPLE: A hotel maid finds a necklace in a hallway. She leaves it with the clerk responsible for locking up the guests' jewelry, who will hold it until the rightful owner claims the necklace. The maid is the *bailor* of the necklace. In this instance, the bailment is involuntary and gratuitous. In instances where one pays a fee for another to hold his property (as in a parking lot situation), the bailment is one "for hire."

BAIT AND SWITCH a method of consumer deception practiced by retailers that involves advertising in such an attractive way as to bring the customer in, followed by disparagement of the advertised product (that the seller in truth does not desire to sell) to cause the customer to switch to a more expensive product. This device is also frequently termed **DISPARAGEMENT.** Statutes in many states prohibit this sort of advertising.

BALANCE SHEET a financial statement that gives an accounting picture of property owned by a company and of claims against the property on a specific date. See **assets, liabilities.**

BALANCING (TEST) principle basic to the **justice** system of weighing both sides of an issue; examining the pros and cons. The ultimate goal is to seek **equality** or evenhandedness (a perfect balance). Constitutionally, it involves individual **rights** guaranteed by the **Constitution** weighed against states rights in such areas as **equal protection** and **freedom of speech** and **press.**

BALANCING OF EQUITIES weighing of conveniences, hardships, and policies as would be done in a **Court of Equity.**

BALANCING OF INTERESTS involves constitutional principles; the individual versus the State. Often involved in issues of **interstate commerce.**

BALLOON MORTGAGE [NOTE] see **mortgage [BALLON MORTGAGE [NOTE]]**.

BANC bench. See **en banc.**

BANK a corporation formed to maintain savings and checking accounts, issue loans and credit, and deal in negotiable **securities** issued by government agencies and by corporations. Banks are strictly regulated and fall into the following three categories according to the limitations upon their activities:

COMMERCIAL BANK the most common and most unrestricted type of bank, allowed the most latitude in its services and investments. Its major limitation: it must keep on reserve a larger percentage of its deposits than the other two types of banks.

SAVINGS AND LOAN ASSOCIATION (or BUILDING AND LOAN ASSOCIATION) similar to a savings bank in history and operation, except that the savings and loan association's primary purpose has been to provide loans for purchasing and building homes. In 1981 these institutions were authorized to offer a variant on checking accounts called a negotiable order of withdrawal **("NOW" account),** which allows depositors to write checks against their interest-bearing savings account.

SAVINGS BANK the least common type of bank, prevalent only on the East Coast and in the Midwest. Its major service traditionally has been the time-savings account, from which money could be withdrawn only after a set period or upon thirty days' notice. Its services, however, have been expanded in some instances. By law a savings bank's investments are usually limited to certain corporate and government bonds and securities. Its advantages: it can pay higher interest rates than commercial banks, has certain tax benefits and can keep on reserve a smaller percentage of deposits. Usually, the bank is owned by its depositors as **creditors** whose dividends are paid as interest on their accounts. See **member bank; nonmember bank**. See also **thrift institutions.**

BANKER'S LIEN the authority enjoyed by a banker to appropriate a depositor's funds or securities that are in the banker's possession and are not dedicated to a special purpose (as a trust) in order to satisfy a debt owed by the depositor to the bank.

BANKRUPTCY popularly defined as **insolvency,** the inability of a **debtor** to pay his or her **debts** as they become due. Technically, however, it is the legal process under the Federal Bankruptcy Act by which assets of the debtor are **liquidated** as quickly as possible to pay off creditors and to **discharge** the bankrupt, or free the debtor of his or her debts, so that he or she may start anew. In **reorganization,** on the other hand, liquidation may be avoided and the debtor may continue to function, pay **creditors** and carry on business. At the state level, INSOLVENCY PROCEEDINGS may be brought to obtain more limited relief. BANKRUPTCY TRUSTEE refers to the person who takes legal title to the property of the debtor and holds it "in trust" for equitable distribution among the creditors. In most districts, the trustee is appointed by the bankruptcy judge or selected by the creditors and approved by the judge. In a limited number of "pilot districts," a UNITED STATES TRUSTEE, appointed by the Attorney General, served as or supervised the trustee.

DEBTOR REHABILITATION refers to those provisions of the Code that enable the rehabilitation and reorganization of the debtor. Creditors are paid out of future earnings of the debtor rather than the liquidation of the debtor's property. This includes business reorganizations (see **chapter 11** reorganization). See **trustee [TRUSTEE IN BANKRUPTCY].** Compare **receivership.**

CHAPTER 11 REORGANIZATION in addition to voluntary and involuntary proceedings in which a debtor is adjudged bankrupt, under Chapter 11 a debtor is permitted to postpone all payments on debts so that he or she can reorganize his or her business. While other **bankruptcy** proceedings seek to have the debtor's assets sold and to have all the creditors paid to the extent possible, Chapter 11 seeks to give the debtor a breathing spell with the hope that the business will recover and all the creditors will be fully repaid. The goal is a plan that specifies how much the creditors will be paid, in what form they will be paid, and other details. See **debt; insolvency.**

INVOLUNTARY PROCEEDING a **proceeding** to seize all the insolvent debtor's nonexempt property, to distribute it equally among creditors and to release the debtor from liability. Additional qualified creditors have an absolute right to join in the original lawsuit at any time before **judgment** is entered.

VOLUNTARY PROCEEDING a proceeding under the Federal Bankruptcy Act whereby an insolvent **debtor** may file a **petition** to be declared a voluntary bankrupt.

BANKRUPTCY COURT a United States district court created specifically to carry out the Federal Bankruptcy Act.

BANKRUPTCY PETITION see **petition in bankruptcy.**

BAR 1. in procedure, a barrier to the relitigating of an **issue.** A bar operates to deny a party the right or privilege of rechallenging issues in subsequent litigation. The prevailing party in a lawsuit can use his or her favorable decision to bar retrial of the action. See **collateral [COLLATERAL ESTOPPEL]; res judicata.**

2. a particular position in the courtroom; hence, the defendant standing before the judge is sometimes called the prisoner **AT BAR.** The complete body of attorneys is called the bar because they are the persons privileged to enter beyond the bar that separates the general courtroom audience from the judge's bench. The **CASE AT BAR** refers to the particular action before the court.

BARGAIN a mutual voluntary **agreement** between two parties for the **exchange** or purchase of some specified goods. The term also implies negotiation over the terms of an agreement.

EXAMPLE: As a favor to his neighbor, Craig agrees not to erect a swing set in his yard. Two years later, Craig's grandson moves in with him. Craig decides to build the swing set to keep the grandson happy. He is not prevented from building the set even though he had previously told his neighbor he would not erect one. The earlier agreement is not binding on Craig because it was not a bargained-for exchange. The neighbor provided nothing in the agreement as **consideration** for Craig's promise; the promise was a gratuitous one.

BARGAIN AND SALE a **contract,** or **deed** in the form of a contract, that conveys **property** and transfers title to the buyer but lacks any **guarantee** from the seller as to the validity of the title. It is commonly used to convey title to real estate today and in effect transfers to the new owner whatever interest the **grantor** had. It is often combined with a **COVENANT AGAINST GRANTOR'S ACTS,** an assurance that the grantor has not impaired the title by, for example, conveying the property, or part of it, to someone else. Compare **quitclaim deed; warranty deed.**

BARGAINING UNIT the labor union or other group that represents employees in **collective bargaining.**

BARRATRY in **common law,** the crime of stirring up suits and quarrels, either at law or otherwise. Generally, the statutory crime of barratry is restricted to the practice of instigating groundless lawsuit, to the lawyer's profit.

BARRISTER in England, a legal practitioner whose function is similar to that of an American trial lawyer, although the barrister does not prepare the case from the start. His **SOLICITOR** assembles the materials necessary for presentation to the court and settles cases out of court.

BAR SINISTER the fact or condition of being born out of wedlock.

EXAMPLE: Fearing that he would be labeled a **bastard,** Seth kept his background a secret until he realized that the bar sinister made no difference to his friends.

BARTER   the exchange of goods or services without using money. See **exchange.**

BASIS   an amount usually representing the **taxpayer's** cost in acquiring an **asset.** It is used for a variety of tax purposes including computation of gain or loss on the **sale or exchange** of the asset and **depreciation** with respect to the asset.

ADJUSTED BASIS   during the time that a taxpayer holds an asset, certain events require that the taxpayer adjust (either up or down) his or her original basis to reflect the event, thus resulting in an adjusted basis. In general, depreciation deductions allowable in a taxable year with respect to an asset reduce the taxpayer's basis in the asset. On the other hand, if the taxpayer made a CAPITAL EXPENDITURE (see **capital**) for the asset, the amount of the expenditure would increase the taxpayer's basis.

CARRYOVER or SUBSTITUTED BASIS   in certain cases a taxpayer's basis is computed by reference to the basis of the property when held by the previous owner or to the basis of the property exchanged for the assets. In both these situations, the taxpayer's basis is said to be a **carryover** basis. For example, if a taxpayer received a **gift** of property, his basis in the property is the transferor's basis in the property. In other words, the transferor's basis carries over to the taxpayer.

RECOVERY OF BASIS   the process by which a taxpayer recovers the basis through **distributions** or payments with respect to the property.

STEP-UP BASIS   the process by which a taxpayer's basis is increased to a certain level (usually fair **market value**) as of a certain date. Such a basis is generally available for property received by an **heir** from a decedent.

BASTARD   an illegitimate child, one who is not born either in lawful wedlock or within a competent time after its termination; also, a child of a married person conceived with one other than the spouse. See **bar sinister.**

BASTARDY PROCEEDING   see **paternity suit [bastardy proceeding].**

BATTERY   the unlawful touching of or use of force on another person **willfully** or in anger. Battery may be considered either a tort, giving rise to **civil liability** for damages to the victim, or a crime. Compare **assault.**

BATTERY, SEXUAL   see **rape.**

BEARER   the person in possession of an **instrument, document of title,** or **security** payable to bearer or endorsed in blank. A note payable to "bearer" is payable to any person who successively holds the note **bona fide,** not by virtue of any assignment of promise, but by an original and direct promise moving from the maker to the "bearer."

BEARER BOND   see **bond [BEARER BOND].**

BEARER PAPER   commercial paper that is negotiable upon delivery by any party or that does not designate a specific party by whom it is negotiable. Such commercial paper is said to be **PAYABLE TO BEARER.** The most popular domestic bearer instruments are government securities, such as **treasury bills** and **municipal bonds.** Foreign stocks and bonds are normally in bearer form. A major disadvantage of bearer instruments is that they offer little protection in the event of theft or loss.

EXAMPLE: A thief steals several notes that are payable to bearer and sells them to Willie, who does not know they are stolen. Because the notes are *bearer paper,* Willie can demand payment according to the terms of the notes. The fact that they are stolen has no effect on his ability to collect. Willie is the bearer. The notes are payable to whoever has possession and is therefore the bearer.

See **negotiable instrument.** Compare **order paper.**

BEAR HUG   a hostile takeover strategy wherein the suitor seeks to acquire a company by making an offer at a premium price. This strategy is designed to overcome resistance from the target's board of directors who are bound to act in the best interest of their shareholders.

BED AND BOARD   see **divorce.**

BEFORE-THE-FACT   see **accessory [ACCESSORY BEFORE-THE-FACT].**

BELIEF   see **information and belief.** See also **reasonable belief.**

BENCH   1. the court; the judges composing the court collectively; 2. the place where the trial judge sits. Compare **bar**.

BENCH TRIAL   see **trial [BENCH TRIAL].**

BENCH WARRANT   a court order for the arrest of a person; commonly issued to compel a person's attendance before the court to **answer** a **charge** of **contempt** or if a **witness** or a **defendant** fails to attend after a **subpoena** has been duly served.

EXAMPLE: Wendy was arrested for a traffic violation and ordered to appear in court in two weeks. The order to appear notwithstanding, Wendy continued with her vacation plans and found herself in another state on the required date. As a result of her failure to appear, the court ordered a *bench warrant* for Wendy. On the basis of that order she will be arrested and brought before the court. The issuance of the warrant also subjects Wendy to a penalty for contempt of court.

BEND SINISTER   see **bar sinister.**

BENEFICIAL INTEREST   the **equitable** interest in a **trust** held by the **beneficiary** of the trust, as distinguished from the interest of the **trustee** who holds legal **title.** Any person who under the terms of a trust instrument has the right to the income or **principal** of the trust fund has a beneficial interest in the trust.

BENEFICIAL USE   a right to the use and enjoyment of property that exists where legal title to that property is held by another, in **trust**.

BENEFICIARY   1. a person for whose benefit property is held in **trust**.

EXAMPLE: Curtis wants to insure that his two granddaughters, Lisa and June, will have sufficient money to pursue a college education. In the trust that Curtis establishes, the bank is named as trustee and Lisa and June are named as *beneficiaries*. As trustee, the bank holds the money until Lisa and June attend college, at which point the bank pays their education costs. The bank holds the money for the benefit of Lisa and June.

2. a person to whom another is in a **fiduciary** relation, whether the relation is one of **agency,** trust, **guardianship, partnership** or otherwise; 3. a person named to receive the proceeds or benefits of an **insurance** policy; 4. a person named in a **will** to receive certain property.

INCIDENTAL BENEFICIARY   a person who may incidentally benefit from the creation of a trust. Such a person has no actual interest in the trust and cannot enforce any right to such incidental benefit.

BENEFIT   for tax purposes, a benefit is received by a **taxpayer** whenever anything occurs that results in an economic benefit to the taxpayer. However, not all benefits are included in gross **income** since many benefits are not **realized** in the **taxable year** or are not subject to **tax** under the **Internal Revenue Code** or judicially or administratively developed principles.

FRINGE BENEFITS benefits other than direct salary or compensation (such as parking, health insurance, tuition reimbursement, etc.) received by employees from employers as a result of their employment. Generally, fringe benefits are not subject to tax.

BENEFIT OF CLERGY under Old English law, the right of clergymen to avoid nonchurch trials. Also means solemnized by the church.

BENEFIT OF COUNSEL with an attorney's advice. See **right to counsel.**

BENEFIT OF THE BARGAIN (RULE) method of measuring **damages** in **breach** of **contract** or **warranty** cases or cases involving **fraud** or **misrepresentation.** Calculated as the difference between the real **value** and the represented or warranted value. Also known as **LOSS OF BARGAIN.** See **bargain.** Compare **out-of-pocket (rule).**

BEQUEATH in a will, a **gift** of **personal property,** distinguishing it from a **devise,** a gift of **real property.** The term **disposition** encompasses both a **bequest** of personalty and a devise of realty.

BEQUEST a **gift** of **personal property** by **will.** A **devise** ordinarily passes **real estate,** and a bequest passes personal property. See **legacy.**

CONDITIONAL BEQUEST a bequest that depends upon the occurrence or nonoccurrence of a particular event.

EXECUTORY BEQUEST a bequest of **personalty** or money that does not take effect until the happening of some future event, upon which it is contingent.

RESIDUARY BEQUEST a bequest consisting of the remainder of an **estate** after the payment of **debts** and of general legacies and other specific gifts.

SPECIFIC BEQUEST A bequest of particular items, or of a part of a **testator's** estate that can be distinguished from all others of the same kind, which may be satisfied only by delivery of the particular thing (given by the will) and not merely by a corresponding amount in value or similar property.

BERNE CONVENTION see **copyright [BERNE CONVENTION].**

BEST EVIDENCE RULE a rule of **evidence** requiring that the most reliable evidence available be used. Thus, where the original of a document is available, a copy will not be accepted as evidence.

BESTIALITY sexual intercourse with an animal. Bestiality constitutes a **crime against nature.**

BEYOND A REASONABLE DOUBT   see **reasonable doubt.**

B.F. bona fide or "approved."

BFOQ   see **bona fide occupational qualification [BFOQ].**

BFP   see **bona fide purchaser.**

BIAS   preconception; prejudice; taint; partiality. Since most persons have various biases, the issue is whether the bias is such that impartiality cannot be achieved and a fair outcome cannot occur. Any predisposition that a judge or arbitrator may have may be grounds for **recusal;** any predisposition that a witness may have may be grounds for **impeachment** through cross-examination; any predisposition that a juror may have may be grounds for **excusal** determined through a process known as **voir dire.** Biases may exist for or against certain religious, racial, ethnic, or minority groups and they may exist for or against police officers, the very rich or the very poor, athletes, attorneys, immigrants, and virtually any recognizable group of persons.

EXAMPLE: Nicholas, an avid Red Sox fan, is called as a juror in a medical malpractice case. He agrees to set aside the fact that Dr. Kylie is an avid Yankees fan and judge her strictly on her treatment of the patient.

BIAS CRIME   commission of an offense where the person acted, at least in part, with ill will, hatred, or **bias** toward, and with a purpose to intimidate, an individual or group because of race, color, religion, sexual orientation, or ethnicity. Offenses such as **assult, harassment, intimidation,** or **criminal mischief** may have enhanced sentences imposed upon the perpetrator if it is proved that the act was a bias crime. Examples of hate or bias crimes include defacing a Jewish cemetery with symbols of anti-Semitism; throwing rocks through the windows of Chinese restaurants; or attacking persons believed to be gay. The **FBI** collects statistics relating to such crimes.

BID   an offer by an intending purchaser to buy goods or services at a stated price, or an offer by an intending seller to sell his or her goods or services for a stated price. Building **contractors** usually solicit bids based on building specifications from several subcontractors in order to complete a project. Government units are often required by law to construct highways and buildings, and to buy goods and services, through competitive bidding solicited by public advertisement, with the lowest competent bid winning the contract. See also **responsibility [RESPONSIBLE BIDDERS].**

BID SHOPPING   the practice of a general **contractor** who, before the award of the prime contract, discloses to interested **subcontractors** the current low subbids on certain subcontracts in an effort to obtain lower subbids.

BIGAMY   the criminal offense of having two or more wives or husbands at the same time. A bigamous marriage is **void.**

BILATERAL CONTRACT   see **contract** [BILATERAL CONTRACT].

BILATERAL MISTAKE   see **mistake** [MUTUAL [BILATERAL] MISTAKE].

BILL   l. an order drawn by one person on another to pay a certain sum of money; 2. in commercial law, an account for goods sold, services rendered and work done; 3. in the law of **negotiable instruments,** any form of paper money; 4. in legislation, a draft of a proposed statute submitted to the legislature for enactment; 5. in **equity pleadings,** the name of the pleading by which the complainant sets out his cause of action.

BILL FOR A NEW TRIAL   a bill submitted to a **court of equity** stating **equitable** grounds for suspending **execution** of a **judgment** rendered in a **court of law** and proposing a new suit in **equity.**

BILL OF ATTAINDER   see **bill of attainder.**

BILL OF CERTIORARI   a **petition** for **writ** of **certiorari.**

BILL OF DISCOVERY   see **discovery.**

BILL OF EXCEPTIONS   a writing submitted to a trial court stating for the **record** objections to rulings made and instructions given by the trial judge. See **exceptions**.

BILL OF EXCHANGE   a written order directing another party to pay a certain sum to a third party. See **draft.**

BILL OF INTERPLEADER   see **interpleader.**

BILL OF LADING   see **bill of lading.**

BILL OF PARTICULARS   see **bill of particulars.**

BILL OF REVIEW   a form of equitable proceeding brought to secure an explanation, alteration or reversal of a final **decree** by the court that rendered it, because of errors on the face of the record, or new evidence or new matters that have appeared after entry of that decree.

BILL OF RIGHTS   the first eight amendments to the United States Constitution creating individual rights. Because they were adopted at the same time, Amendments 9 and 10 are generally considered part of the Bill of Rights. See **Bill of Rights.**

BILL OF SALE a written agreement under which **title** to personal **chattels** is transferred.

CROSS BILL a pleading in a court of equity by the defendant against the plaintiff or against another defendant in the suit; similar to **counterclaim** and **cross-claim** at law.

TREASURY BILL a promissory note, having maturity of no longer than one year, issued by the Treasury Department of the U.S. government. See **treasury bill.**

BILL OF ATTAINDER a legislative act that applied either to individuals or to members of a group in such a way as to pronounce sentence on them without a trial. Such acts are prohibited by the Constitution because they are, in effect, a legislative judgment of conviction without a hearing. See **attainder.**

BILL OF EXCHANGE see **bill; draft; exchange.**

BILL OF LADING in commercial law, the receipt a **carrier** gives to a shipper for goods given to the carrier for transportation. The bill evidences the contract between the shipper and the carrier, and can also serve as a document of *title* creating in the person possessing the bill ownership of the goods shipped.

EXAMPLE: Jordan Ski Company agrees to ship goods to Peyton Sporting World. When Jordan leaves the goods with Sydney Transport, the transportation company, Sydney issues Jordan a bill of lading, acknowledging receipt of the goods. The bill of lading specifies the exact terms of the freight, its value, and delivery specifications, such as the mode of transportation and any terms regarding damage.

ORDER BILL OF LADING a negotiable bill of lading that can be negotiated like any other **negotiable instrument,** so that the shipper can sell it to anyone, not just the intended recipient of the goods. The bill not only states that the carrier is to deliver the goods to a specified person at a specified place, but also requires the carrier to release the goods only when the bill of lading is given him by the recipient. An order bill operates as a document of title and must be presented by the recipient before possession of goods will be delivered. Under this arrangement, the shipper can withhold the bill of lading, and thus the goods themselves, until the intended recipient pays for them.

STRAIGHT BILL OF LADING a nonnegotiable bill of lading, which merely states that the carrier is to deliver the goods to a specified person at a specified place.

BILL OF PARTICULARS a detailed statement provided in a criminal case, as an amplification of the **pleading** to which it relates, in order to advise the court, and, more particularly, the defendant, of the specific facts or allegations he will be required to respond to.

BILL OF REVIEW form of **equitable proceedings** brought to secure an explanation, alteration, or **reversal** of a final **decree** by the court that rendered it. Most commonly, only errors of law appearing on the face of the **record,** new evidence not susceptible to use at the trial and coming to light after the decree is issued, and **new matter** arising after entry of the decree, could have been the basis for a successful bill of review. It is also appropriate where there is evidence of **fraud** impeaching the original transaction.

BILL OF RIGHTS the first ten amendments to the United States Constitution; that part of any constitution that sets forth the fundamental rights of citizenship. It is a declaration of rights that are substantially immune from government interference. See **Fourteenth Amendment.**

BIND something that obligates or constrains the bound individual. To **guaranty,** to promise, to secure, to warrant, and to defend. A bind places one under legal duties and obligations. One can "bind" oneself as in a **contract** or one can be "bound" by a **judgment.**

BINDER 1. a written memorandum of the most important items of a preliminary **contract;** 2. an insurer's acknowledgment of its contract to protect the insured against accidents of a specified kind until a formal policy can be issued or until insurer gives notice of its election to terminate.

BINDER RECEIPT a memorandum that serves as evidence of an approved application for **insurance** and is intended to take the place of an ordinary policy until the policy can be issued.

BINDING obligatory.

BINDING AGREEMENT a conclusive agreement.

BINDING ARBITRATION see **arbitration [BINDING ARBITRATION].**

BINDING INSTRUCTION an instruction that directs the jury how to determine an issue in the case if certain conditions stated in that instruction are shown to exist.

BIND OVER to order that a defendant be placed in **custody** pending the outcome of a **proceeding** (usually criminal) against him or her. He or she may thereafter be released on **bail** or on other conditions of release.

BITCOIN anonymous digital currency that is not tied to any government and, unlike bank accounts, bitcoins are not insured by the **FDIC.**

Bitcoins are stored in a digital wallet, which exists either in the cloud or on a user's computer. The wallet is similar to a virtual bank account that allows users to send or receive bitcoins peer to peer, without an intermediary, to pay for goods or to save.

BLACKACRE   a hypothetical piece of **real estate** used in teaching **real property** or **future interests** courses in law school.

BLACK LETTER LAW   see **hornbook law.**

BLACKMAIL   the demanding of money either for performing an existing duty, or for preventing an injury or for exercising an influence; the **extortion** of things of value from a person by threats of personal injury, or by threatening to accuse that person of crime or immoral conduct, which, if true, would tend to disgrace him or her.

EXAMPLE: As a child, Evan had once been caught shoplifting. Now, Evan occupies a position of high standing in the community and enjoys an untarnished reputation. Tom wants Evan to lend him a considerable amount of money. To persuade Evan to advance the loan, Tom *blackmails* Evan by threatening to reveal the childhood incident, which would discredit Evan. The criminal nature of Tom's attempt to blackmail is not affected by the truthfulness underlying the threat.

BLACKMAIL SUITS   see **strike suits.**

BLANKET MORTGAGE [NOTE]   see **mortgage [BLANKET MORTGAGE [NOTE].**

BLANK INDORSEMENT   see **indorsement.**

BLASPHEMY   at common law, the **misdemeanor** of reviling or ridiculing the established religion (Christianity) and the existence of God. See **establishment clause.**

BLIND CERTIFICATE   see **digital certificate [BLIND CERTIFICATE].**

BLIND TRUST   see **trust [BLIND TRUST].**

BLOOD, CORRUPTION OF THE   see **corruption of blood.**

BLUEBOOK   see **Uniform System of Citation [BLUE BOOK].**

BLUE CHIP STOCK   the common stock of a company known nationally for the quality and wide acceptance of its products or services, and for its ability to generate consistent profits and pay increased dividends. The term probably evolved from its use in gambling casinos, where blue chips are valued at $100, since common stocks of leading companies were offered at $100 per share around the turn of the last century.

BLUE LAWS   strict statutes or local ordinances most frequently enacted to preserve observance of the Sabbath by prohibiting commercial activity on Sundays.

EXAMPLE: In Ewing Township, local *blue laws* prevent a merchant from selling automobile tires on Sunday but permit him to sell toothpaste and soap. The difference is rationalized by the belief that selling tires promotes working on a car instead of attending church. Toothpaste sales will have no such effect.

With increasing frequency, blue laws are being abolished so that people may freely choose activities without regard to societal notions as to appropriate Sunday conduct.

BLUE RIBBON JURY   see **jury [BLUE RIBBON JURY]**.

BLUE SKY LAWS   state laws regulating the sale of corporate **securities** through investment companies, enacted to prevent the sale of securities of fraudulent enterprises. See also **Securities and Exchange Commission [SEC]**.

BOARD OF DIRECTORS   a group elected by **shareholders** to set company policy and appoint the chief executives and operating officers.

BOARD ROOM   a stockbroker's office where **registered representatives** (that is, securities salespersons registered with the SEC) work and where the public is allowed to visit and obtain stock price quotations throughout the market day. Offices are equipped with electronic machines that provide information on trading in **listed stocks,** and **over-the-counter markets** and also provide business news.

BOILERPLATE   1. any standardized or preprinted form for agreements.

EXAMPLE: Scott is a rental agent and rents apartments for many landlords throughout the city. Although both the apartments and the landlords' requirements differ greatly, each rental agreement includes, in addition to clauses related to each particular group of apartments, nineteen *boilerplate* provisions covering liability of the various parties, damage deposits, security arrangements and other matters common to such agreement.

2. also, standardized language, as on a printed form containing the terms of a lease or sales contract, often phrased to the advantage of the party furnishing the form, with the expectation that the contract will be signed without being carefully examined. See **adhesion contract; unconscionable.**

BOILER ROOM [SHOP]   a place devoted to high-pressure

61

promotion by telephone of stocks, bonds, diamonds, commodities, contracts, etc., which are of very questionable value. Extensive **fraud** is usually involved, but successful prosecution may be difficult since operations often disband before detection and since little tangible evidence is obtainable.

BONA *(bō'-nà)* Lat.: good, virtuous; also, goods, property.

BONA FIDE *(bō'-nà fīd)* Lat.: in *good faith*. Without fraud or deceit; genuine.

BONA FIDE OCCUPATIONAL QUALIFICATION [BFOQ] statutory provision that permits discriminatory practices in employment if a person's religion, sex, or national origin is a bona fide occupational qualification reasonably necessary to the normal operation of that particular business or enterprise. It is also permissible for an educational institution with a particular religious orientation to hire only employees of that religion. Courts have placed the burden of proof of establishing a BFOQ on the defendant and the exception provided by the BFOQ has been narrowly interpreted. In this manner it is more difficult to justify a BFOQ than to defend against a constitutionally based claim of sex discrimination under the Equal Protection Clause of the **Fourteenth Amendment**. The BFOQ exception would only be permitted if, in the example of a woman working at a job requiring the frequent lifting of substantial amounts of weights, the defendant proved by a preponderance of the evidence that all or substantially all females would be unable to perform safely and efficiently the duties involved in the job. Sex has been found to be a BFOQ in terms of community standards of morality where, for example, a man works as an attendant in a men's washroom and a woman works as a fitter in a lingerie establishment.

BONA FIDE PURCHASER [BFP] one who pays a valuable **consideration,** has no notice of outstanding rights of others and acts in **good faith** concerning the purchase. In commercial law, the phrase **holder in due course** signifies the same thing. See **buyer in ordinary course of business.**

EXAMPLE: George owns a textile mill and stores his products in a warehouse. The owner of the warehouse sells several boxes of shirts to Jerry without George's permission. Jerry suspects no wrongdoing because he has frequently dealt with the warehouse in a similar manner without any trouble. Since George left the goods with the warehouse, the subsequent sale to Jerry for value makes Jerry a *bona fide purchaser* who is legally entitled to own the goods. Jerry even has superior claim to the goods over George, so that in order to be compensated for his loss, George must pursue his claim against the warehouse owner.

BOND evidence of a long-term debt that is legally guaranteed as to the principal and interest specified on the face of the bond certificate. The rights of the holder are specified in the bond **indenture,** which contains the legal terms and conditions under which the bond was issued. Bond debt is secured or guaranteed primarily by the ability of the issuer (borrower) to pay the interest when due and to repay the principal at maturity.

Bonds are available in two forms. **REGISTERED BONDS** are recorded on the books of the issuer by the trustee, and interest is paid by mail to the **holder** of record. **BEARER BONDS** are **negotiable instruments** that must be safeguarded by the owner to prevent loss. Interest is paid by **coupon** redemptions.

BOND DISCOUNT a reduction from the face amount of a bond that occurs where bonds are sold on the market for cash at a price less than the face amount. Since bonds **mature** (become due) years after issue, they are discounted to reflect present value.

BONDED DEBT that part of the entire indebtedness of a **corporation** or state that is represented by bonds it has issued; a debt contracted under the obligation of a bond.

BOND FOR DEED [TITLE] a document given by the owner of **real estate** to **convey** the property upon being paid money; an agreement to convey **title** in the future that, so long as it remains **executory** (not yet performed), allows title to remain **vested** in the original owner.

BOND FOR GENERAL PURPOSES government bonds that are a charge against the taxpayers generally, as distinguished from bonds for improvements, the cost of which is charged to the property specially benefited.

BOND ISSUE the offering of bonds for sale to investors.

BOND PREMIUM the amount that the purchaser pays in buying a bond that exceeds the face or call value of the bond.

BOND YIELD see **yield.**

PERFORMANCE BOND a contractor's bond, guaranteeing that the contractor will perform the contract and providing that, in the event of a default, the surety may complete the contract or pay damages up to the bond limit.

SERIAL [SERIES] BONDS bonds issued in a series by a public entity that are payable at different times.

SURETY BOND a bond issued by one party, the **surety,** guaranteeing that he or she will perform certain acts promised by another or pay a stipulated sum, up to the bond limit, in lieu of performance, should the principal fail to perform. In a criminal case, the surety bond assures the appearance of the **defendant** or the repayment of bail forfeited upon the defendant's failure to appear in court.

BONDSMAN a **surety;** one who serves as security for another; a person who obtains surety bonds for others for a fee; also, the individual who arranges for the defendant in a criminal case to be released from jail by posting a **bail bond.** Compare **underwriter.**

BONUS STOCK **common stock** offered as an additional incentive to **underwriters** or buyers of a **bond** or **preferred stock issue.**

BOOK VALUE the value of individual **assets,** calculated as actual cost less allowances for any **amortization** such as **depreciation.** It may be quite different from **market value,** giving rise to hidden assets. Book value on an overall **balance sheet** basis is **net asset value;** that is, total assets less all **liabilities.** In reports to shareholders of publicly held corporations, common shareholders' per-share **equity** or book value is obtained by dividing book value less any **liquidation** price for preferred issues by the outstanding issue of **common stock.**

EXAMPLE: A corporation decides to close ten of its branch offices located throughout the country. As part of the closing, it makes a deal with another company to sell the buildings in which the offices were located. The original cost of the buildings was $6 million, and their *book value* has been reduced to $4 million through depreciation. The actual market value is $8 million since in fact the buildings have appreciated in value.

Companies that invest in stock of other companies usually carry the investment at its original cost as book value. The true market value may be many times the cost if the stock has been held a long time.

BOOLEAN SEARCH basic method of locating information in a data system such as LEXIS or WESTLAW by use of key words whose relationships are expressed by the logical operators AND, OR, and NOT. See **search engine.**

BOOT term referring to the **taxable** portion of a nontaxable exchange. The general rule for nonrecognition tax treatment in a **like-kind** exchange applies only to qualifying property exchanged solely for other qualifying property. However, if an exchange that otherwise qualifies for nonrecognition treatment includes the transfer of cash or non-like-kind property (called "boot"), the transaction still qualifies for like-kind exhange treatment, but is also partially nontaxable.

BORDELLO see **prostitution [BORDELLO].**

BOROUGH ENGLISH   see **primogeniture.**

BOYCOTT   to refrain from commercial dealing with someone by concerted effort; to persuade someone to refrain from doing business with another.

SECONDARY BOYCOTT economic pressure by a union upon an employer with whom the union has no dispute. By engaging in such activity, the union hopes to compel that employer from ceasing to doing business with the employer with which the union has its dispute. Secondary boycotts are a violation of the **Taft-Hartley Act**.

EXAMPLE: An ironworker's union has a dispute with Grayson Bridging. The union puts pressure on Quinn Steel, the major supplier of steel to Grayson, by stating it will call upon the public to boycott all of Quinn Steel's products in order to pressure Grayson into accepting the union's demands.

BRADY LAW   the Brady Handgun Violence Prevention Act of 1993 is an act of Congress that instituted background checks on the purchaser before firearms may be purchased from a licensed dealer or manufacturer. Intended to prevent persons with certain mental illnesses, drug addictions, felony criminal records, misdemeanor domestic violence convictions or restraining orders, dishonorable service discharges, and noncitizens from purchasing firearms.

BRADY MATERIAL   discovery which must be provided to the defense in a criminal prosecution which is in the possession of the prosecution and is favorable to the defendant and material to the question of guilt or to punishment. The prosecution cannot withhold such information.

EXAMPLE: Davi has been charged in a series of home burglaries occurring on the same residential street. Prior to Davi's arrest, the police obtained fingerprints from the broken window in one of homes that was burglarized and determined that the prints belong to Jude, a person who was never authorized to be in that home. Davi is entitled to the police reports and fingerprint evidence in order to defend himself on the charge of burglary of that particular home. Such exculpatory evidence may also provide Davi with a defense to the remaining burglaries as well.

BRAIN DEATH   the irreversible cessation of brain function; statutory or case law definitions of death are being expanded in many jurisdictions to include this. Among the factors considered are the failure to respond to external stimuli, the absence of breathing or spontaneous movement, the absence of reflex movement, and a flat electroencephalograph reading following a 24-hour observation period.

BREACH   failure to perform some contracted-for or agreed-upon act, or to comply with a legal duty owed to another or to society.

ANTICIPATORY BREACH   see **anticipatory breach.**

BREACH OF CONTRACT   a wrongful nonperformance of any contractual duty of immediate performance; failing to perform acts promised, by hindering or preventing such performance or by repudiating the duty to perform.

BREACH OF PROMISE   failure to fulfill a promise; often used as a short form for breach of the promise of marriage.

BREACH OF THE PEACE   conduct that destroys or menaces public order and tranquillity, including violent acts or acts and words likely to produce violence in others. In its broadest sense the term refers to any criminal offense.

BREACH OF TRUST   a **trustee's** violation, whether willful and **fraudulent,** or because of **negligence,** oversight or forgetfulness, of a **duty** that **equity** places upon him or her.

BREACH OF WARRANTY   infraction of an express or implied agreement as to the **title,** quality, content or condition of a thing sold.

MATERIAL BREACH   see **material.**

PARTIAL BREACH   see **partial breach.**

BREAKING A CLOSE   the **common law trespass** of unlawful entering upon the land of another.

BREAKING AND ENTERING   two of the elements necessary to constitute a **burglary,** consisting of the use of physical force, however slight, to remove an obstruction to an entrance. For example, pushing open a door that is ajar, followed by unauthorized entry into a building, is sufficient to constitute the breaking and entering elements of burglary.

BREAKING BULK   refers to a doctrine whereby a **bailee** could be charged with **larceny** by trespass if the person opened a chest, parcel, or case containing goods entrusted to his or her care and converted some to his or her own use; the trespass necessary for larceny was complete even if the goods were not in a container but were themselves delivered in bulk provided that the bailee separated only a portion of the goods entrusted to him or her. If he or she converted all of the goods, there was, however, no breaking bulk and hence no trespass and no larceny.

BREATHALYZER   a chemical test of a person's breath to determine whether he or she is intoxicated, usually when the person is suspected of drunken driving. The test is normally administered by a police officer trained in the use of the equipment, and the equipment must be calibrated on a regular basis. A person operating a motor vehicle is usually presumed to have consented to taking the test, and refusal to take the test may result in the automatic loss of one's driver's license. The results of the test are admissible as evidence in court.

BRETHREN   plural of brother, although its usage in **wills** can include sisters. Reference used among **Justices** of the **United States Supreme Court** to refer to fellow Justices. Since the appointment of female Justices the term has fallen from usage or has been replaced with the awkward "brethren/sistern."

BRIBERY   the voluntary giving of something of value to influence the performance of an official duty.

EXAMPLE: Franco wants to build a shopping center in town, but for years his requests for building permits have been turned down. Another company is then granted the permits after one request. When Franco inquires why that company is treated differently, he is informed that they "make sure" their requests are granted. Franco understands that to mean he needs to pay money to town council members. If Franco pays the money, he is guilty of *bribery* even though payment is the only means to secure permits.

COMMERCIAL BRIBERY   includes the breach of duty by an employee in accepting secret compensation from another in exchange for the exercise of some **discretion** conferred upon the employee by his employer, as in the approval of a contract.

BRICK AND MORTAR   traditional business with a physical building location for customers to interact on a face-to-face basis and having rental and utility costs, in contrast to a business with Internet customers, no physical presence, and thus lower operating costs.

BRIEF   a written argument concentrating upon legal points and authorities (i.e., **precedents**) used by the lawyer to convey to the court (trial or **appellate**) the essential facts of his or her client's case, a statement of the questions of law involved, the law that should be applied and the application that he or she desires made of that law by the court. The brief is submitted in connection with an application, **motion, trial** or **appeal**. Compare **memorandum [MEMORANDUM OF LAW].**

BROKER   one who for a commission or fee brings parties together and assists in negotiating **contracts** between them, a person whose business it is to bring buyer and seller together.

BROTHEL   see **prostitution.**

BROTHER-SISTER CORPORATION   see **corporation [BROTH-ER-SISTER CORPORATION].**

BRUTUM FULMEN   *(brū'-tŭm fŭl'-mĕn)*   Lat.: inert thunder. An empty threat or charge, or a void **judgment** that is in legal effect no judgment at all. A brutum fulmen is any potentially powerful and effective **order,** document, **decree** or judgment that is powerless due to some imperfection causing it to be unenforceable.

BUGGERY   see **sodomy.**

BUGGING   see **wiretap.**

BUILDING AND LOAN ASSOCIATION   see **bank [SAVINGS AND LOAN ASSOCIATION].**

BUILDING PERMIT   see **certificate of occupancy.**

BULK SALES ACTS   statutes designed to prevent the defrauding of **creditors** by the secret sale in bulk of substantially all of a merchant's goods. These laws generally require that notice be given to creditors before any sale of **debtor's** goods. See **bulk transfer.**

BULK TRANSFER   a type of commercial **fraud** in which a merchant (or the owner of a business) transfers the business or a major part of it for **consideration** and then fails to pay his **creditors** with the proceeds. Any transfer in bulk of a major part of the materials, supplies, merchandise or other inventory, not in the ordinary course of the retailer's business, is subject to the provisions of the **Uniform Commercial Code [UCC].**

BUNCHING   the concentration of gross **income** in one or more **taxable years.** This results in adverse tax consequences because, under the progressive **tax rate** structure, in the years that have the larger amount of income there is a higher effective rate of tax. These adverse effects are minimized by **income averaging** and by the preferential tax treatment afforded to **capital gains.**

BURDEN   anything that is grievous, wearisome or oppressive; in property law, any restriction on the use of land, such as a **zoning ordinance** or **covenants running with the land.**

BURDEN OF PROOF   1. the duty of a party to substantiate an **allegation** or **issue,** either to avoid **dismissal** of that issue early in the trial or to convince the court of the truth of that claim and hence to prevail in a civil or criminal **suit.**

EXAMPLE: Jean files a lawsuit claiming that Don fraudulently induced her to buy a vacuum cleaner. Don replies that he has never met Jean and that he has never sold vacuum cleaners in Jean's section of town. Jean has a *burden of proof* to show facts that Don sold her a vacuum cleaner and did so by fraudulent means.

2. the duty of a **plaintiff,** at the beginning of a trial, to make a **prima facie** showing of each fact necessary to establish the existence of a **cause of action;** referred to as the DUTY OF PRODUCING EVIDENCE (also BURDEN OF EVIDENCE or PRODUCTION BURDEN). 3. the obligation to plead each element of a cause of action or AFFIRMATIVE DEFENSE (see **defense**) or suffer a dismissal; referred to as the PLEADING BURDEN.

BUREAU OF INDIAN AFFAIRS   see **Indian law** [BUREAU OF INDIAN AFFAIRS].

BURGLARY   in common law, an actual breaking into a dwelling, at night, with intent to commit a **felony.** Some statutes have expanded burglary to include any unlawful entry into or remaining in a building or vehicle with intent to commit a crime.

BUSINESS, COURSE OF   see **ordinary course of business.**

BUSINESS CYCLE   the periodic expansion and contraction of economic activity. Economic researchers have identified three overlapping cycles of approximately 4 years', 10 to 20 years', and 45 to 60 years' duration. Causes of the short-term cycles (average duration: 52 months, as measured by the U.S. National Bureau of Economic Research) are believed to be a combination of money expansion and contraction (monetary theory), alternate savings and spending patterns of consumers (consumer confidence theory), and alternate expansion and contraction patterns of business inventory and business capital investment. It has also been suggested that the attitudes and perceptions of consumers and business managers guide their spending decisions and thus determine the business cycle (psychological theory). The longer-term economic cycles are dependent on more fundamental forces such as growth in labor force and productivity, capital investments, technological innovation, and long-term weather cycles.

BUSINESS EXPENSE   see **expense** [TRADE OR BUSINESS EXPENSE].

BUSINESS GUEST   see **invitee.**

BUSINESS INVITEE   see **invitee.**

BUSINESS JUDGMENT RULE   deference given by **courts** to the **good faith** operations and transactions of a **corporation** by its executives. Reasonable decisions, even if not the most profitable, will not be disturbed by a court upon application by a disgruntled **party** such as a **stockholder.** The rationale behind the rule is that stockholders accept the risk that an informed business decision, honestly made and rationally thought to be in the corporation's best interests, may not be second-guessed. Therefore, courts afford business judgments special protection in order to limit litigation and avoid judicial intrusiveness in private sector business decision making.

BUSINESS RECORDS EXCEPTION see **hearsay rule [BUSINESS RECORDS EXCEPTION].**

BUSINESS TRUST see **Massachusetts trust.**

BUT FOR in **tort** and in criminal law, a test of whether an individual's action caused a particular event. The test is applied by asking whether an accident or injury would have occurred "but for" (or in the absence of) the individual's act. See **cause [PROXIMATE CAUSE].** See also **causa [CAUSA SINE QUA NON].**

BUY AMERICAN ACT [PROVISION] federal legislation establishing preference for the purchase of American-made supplies over foreign-made supplies. The Buy American provision in the American Recovery and Reinvestment Act of 2009 provides that, unless one of three listed exceptions applies (nonavailability, unreasonable cost, and inconsistent with the public interest), and a waiver is granted, none of the funds appropriated or otherwise made available by the act may be used for a project for the construction, alteration, maintenance, or repair of a public building or public work unless all the iron, steel, and manufactured goods used are produced in the United States.

BUYDOWN advances made to a buyer by a home builder to reduce the monthly mortgage payments ·as an inducement to purchase. May be for a specified number of years or for the entire term of the loan.

BUYER IN ORDINARY COURSE OF BUSINESS a person who, in **good faith** and without knowledge that the sale to him or her violates a third party's ownership rights or **security interest** in the **goods,** buys in the usual manner from a person in the business of selling goods of that kind. The buyer acquires the goods free of any security interest created by the seller. See **bona fide purchaser; holder in due course.**

EXAMPLE: Rich, a truck driver, fraudulently obtains a truckload of computer parts from a manufacturing company and sells them to a parts supplier. Unless the supplier frequently buys large amounts of new parts from truck drivers, the supplier cannot be a *buyer in the ordinary course of business* and therefore cannot claim ownership of the parts over the manufacturing company. If the supplier had bought the parts from a normal dealer in computer parts, the supplier would have ownership rights superior to the manufacturing company. The buyer should have suspected that the truck driver was not in legitimate possession of the goods. In purchasing goods from him, the buyer assumed the risk that the truck driver might later be exposed as a thief.

BUY-SELL AGREEMENT   an arrangement entered into between owners of a business providing for the disposition of the respective interest of each in the event one or more owners withdraws from the business at some future time. Under such an agreement, the withdrawing owner agrees to sell, and the remaining owner(s) agree to buy, his or her proportionate share of the business upon his or her departure for a predetermined price, fixed, either as to the amount or the method of computing that amount, at the time the agreement is entered into.

BYLAWS   rules adopted for the regulation of an **association's** or **corporation's** own actions. In corporation's law, bylaws are self-imposed rules that constitute an agreement or contract between a corporation and its members to conduct the corporate business in a particular way. In the absence of law to the contrary, under **common law** the power to make bylaws resides in the members or **shareholders** of the corporation. When used by corporations, the term bylaws deals with matters of corporate structure and machinery as distinguished from regulations, which are imposed by a board of directors to deal with problems relating to the day-to-day management.

BY OPERATION OF LAW   see **operation of law.**

BY THE ENTIRETY   see **tenancy [TENANCY BY THE ENTIRETY].**

C

C Lat.: abbreviation for the Latin "cum" meaning "with."

CAB see **Civil Aeronautics Board [CAB].**

CADAVER the body of a deceased person.

CALENDAR (CALL) a hearing in court in a pending cause to ascertain the status of the matter and to establish a date for trial.

CALENDAR YEAR see **fiscal year** [CALENDAR YEAR].

CALL 1. a demand by a **corporation** on a **shareholder** to pay an additional sum to the corporation proportionate to his or her share of **stock;** also, an obligation of a corporation to issue stock at a certain price on demand, in which case the privilege of calling for the stock belongs to the buyer; 2. in property law, an identifiable natural object designated in a **deed** or other **instrument** of **conveyance** as a landmark, to mark the boundary of the land conveyed.

CALLABLE BOND a bond that the issuer may retire at any time before its maturity. Usually the issuer must pay a premium (an amount more than the face value of the bond) to call the bond.

CALL OPTION see **stock option** [CALL OPTION].

CALUMNY **slander, defamation;** false prosecution or accusation.

CAMERA see **in camera.**

CANNABIS see **controlled substances** [CANNABIS].

CANON 1. a rule of **ecclesiastical law,** primarily concerning the clergy, but also at times embracing lay members of a congregation. 2. a rule of **construction.** One of a body of rules to guide the interpretation of statutes, ordinances, etc. A **PROFESSIONAL CANON** is a rule or standard of conduct adopted by a professional group to guide the professional conduct of its members.

CAPACITY mental ability to make a rational decision, which includes the ability to perceive and appreciate all relevant facts. Capacity is not necessarily synonymous with sanity. No one can be guilty of a **crime** who lacks the legal capacity to commit it. To render a **contract** binding, the parties involved must have the capacity to contract. **Testamentary** capacity with respect to personalty is governed by the law of the **testator's domicile,** and, with respect to **realty,** by the law of the place where the realty is situated. The **objection** of "lack of capacity to sue" refers to a general legal **disability** to maintain the **action.**

CAPACITY TO SUE   see **legal capacity to sue.**

CAPIAS   *(kā'-pē-ăs)*   Lat.: that you take. In common law, a **writ** executed by seizing either the property or the person of the **defendant** to compel his answering a particular **charge** in court. The term describes several types of judicial writs or **process,** by which **actions** in a court of law were commenced. The writs have been largely replaced by service of process.

CAPIAS AD AUDIENDUM JUDICIUM   *(ăd ô-dē-ĕn'-dŭm jū-dŭ'-shē-ŭm)*   Lat.: that you take to hear judgment. A writ to bring to court a defendant who has **appeared** and been found **guilty** of a **misdemeanor,** to receive the court's judgment.

CAPIAS AD RESPONDENDUM   *(ăd rĕs-pŏn-dĕn'-dŭm)*   Lat.: that you take to answer. A writ directing the arrest and production of a defendant before **judgment.** It not only notifies a defendant to defend **suit,** like a **summons,** but also enables his or her **arrest** as security for the **plaintiff's** claim.

CAPIAS AD SATISFACIENDUM   *(ăd sä-tĭs-fä-shē-ĕn'-dŭm)*   Lat.: that you take to satisfy. A writ for the arrest of a judgment **debtor** until the **debt claim** is satisfied. See **service of process.**

CAPITA   see **per capita.**

CAPITAL   the money and other property of a corporation or other enterprise used in transacting its business. Compare **capitalization.**

CAPITAL ACCOUNTS   that part of a business's accounting records where capital assets and expenditures, and the liabilities incurred to acquire such assets and make such expenditures, are taken into account. The capital account usually consists of **CAPITAL ASSETS** [below] and capital liabilities, such as long-term debt, and stock and other **equity** ownership.

CAPITAL ASSETS   property with a relatively long life, or the fixed **assets** in a trade or business. In U.S. tax law, the term refers to property held for investment by the taxpayer that when sold is subject to special tax treatment (as **capital gains** and **losses**). Property that is part of one's stock in trade does not qualify as a capital asset.

CAPITAL EXPENDITURE   expenditure made for the acquisition, repair or improvement of a capital asset. Compare **expenses.**

EXAMPLE: Aerospace Corporation, a thriving industry, wants to expand its production capabilities to meet the increase in demand for its products. Its minimum needs are two new plants and four new office buildings in various parts of the country. Regardless of where Aerospace obtains the money for the new construction, whether from a bank or from profits the corporation has retained, the money spent to acquire these buildings represents a *capital expenditure*.

CAPITAL GAINS OR LOSSES gains or losses **realized** from the **sale or exchange** of CAPITAL ASSETS, calculated as the difference between the **amount realized** on the sale or exchange and the taxpayer's **basis** in the assets.

CAPITAL INTENSIVE an industry or economic sector that requires a large amount of machinery, equipment, and so on, relative to the quantity of labor or land required. The energy industries—oil production and refining, coal mining, and electric power generation—require large amounts of capital equipment per unit of output. Historically, coal mining was a labor intensive industry requiring a large labor force to dig the product using hand tools. This is no longer the case, however, as modern strip-mining machinery can dig more coal per hour than 50 miners using hand tools could dig in a shift.

CAPITAL INVESTMENT money paid out to acquire something for permanent use or value in a business or home; also, moneys paid out for an interest in a business, as in a **stock** purchase.

CAPITAL MARKET the organized buying and selling of long-term fixed-income securities such as **bonds** or **mortgages,** proceeds from the sale of which are used to finance **CAPITAL EXPENDITURES**. In contrast to the capital market, the money market is used to raise short-term funds and the **EQUITY MARKET** (see **equity**) is used to obtain permanent capital through the sale of stock.

CAPITAL STOCK the amount of money or property contributed by **shareholders** to be used as the financial foundation for the **corporation.** The total of a corporation's capital stock is divided into **shares.**

CAPITAL SURPLUS see **surplus [CAPITAL SURPLUS].**

LONG-TERM CAPITAL GAINS OR LOSSES are capital gains or losses from the sale or exchange of capital assets held for the required **holding period.** The net long-term capital gain or loss for the year is combined with the net short-term capital gain or loss for the year to arrive at an overall (net) capital gain or loss. If capital gains exceed capital losses, the overall gain is included with the taxpayer's other income but is subject to a maximum tax rate of 28% for individuals and 35% for corporations. If capital losses exceed capital gains, the overall losses are subject to deduction limitations, generally $3,000 per year for noncorporate taxpayers.

In order to encourage the flow of capital to small businesses, the 1993 Revenue Act permits noncorporate taxpayers to exclude 50% of any gain realized on the sale or exchange of "qualified small business stock" ("QSBS") held for more than 5 years, subject to certain limitations and special rules. **SHORT-TERM CAPITAL GAINS OR LOSSES** are gains or losses from the sale or exchange of capital assets held for a period shorter than the required **holding period.**

§1231 PROPERTY depreciable business property, business real property, and certain other types of property are §1231 property. These assets produce long-term capital gain and ordinary loss.

CAPITAL ACCOUNT the group of accounting records that involves transactions in the **equity** or ownership of the business.

CAPITAL ASSETS see **capital [CAPITAL ASSETS].**

CAPITAL EXPENDITURE see **capital [CAPITAL EXPENDI- TURE].**

CAPITAL GAINS OR LOSSES gains or losses **realized** from the **sale or exchange** of **CAPITAL ASSETS** (see **capital**) and calculated as the difference between the amount realized on the sale or exchange and the taxpayer's **basis** in the assets.

LONG-TERM CAPITAL GAIN OR LOSS a capital gain or loss from the sale or exchange of capital assets held for the required holding period (generally, one year for the **taxable years** beginning after 1977).

SHORT-TERM CAPITAL GAIN OR LOSS a gain or loss from the sale or exchange of capital assets held for a period shorter than the required holding period.

CAPITAL INTENSIVE an industry or economic sector that requires a large amount of machinery, equipment, etc., relative to the quantity of labor or land required. The energy industries—oil production and refining, coal mining and electric power generation—require large amounts of capital equipment per unit of output. Historically, coal mining was a labor intensive industry requiring a large labor force to dig the product using hand tools. Today, however, this is no longer the case, as modern strip-mining machinery can dig more coal per hour than fifty miners using hand tools could dig in a shift.

CAPITAL INVESTMENT see **capital [CAPITAL INVESTMENT].**

CAPITALIZATION 1. for accounting purposes, the process of converting expected earnings or an expense item into an **asset;** 2. the total of long-term **capital,** such as long-term loans and notes, bonds, mortgages, and stock, used by a business to purchase assets.

CAPITALIZED VALUE the current worth of money expected to be earned or received in the future, calculated by using an appropriate discount rate to accurately express current value.

CAPITAL MARKET the organized buying and selling of long-term fixed-income securities such as **bonds** or **mortgages,** proceeds from the sale of which are used to finance **capital expenditures.** In contrast to the capital market, the money market is used to raise short-term funds and the **EQUITY MARKET** (see **equity**) is used to obtain permanent **capital** through the sale of stock.

CAPITAL OFFENSE a criminal offense punishable by death, for which **bail** is generally unavailable to the **defendant.**

CAPITAL PUNISHMENT imposition of the **death penalty**.

CAPITAL STOCK see **capital [CAPITAL STOCK].**

CAPITAL SURPLUS see **surplus [CAPITAL SURPLUS].**

CAPITE see **in capite.**

CAPTION 1. the heading of a legal document containing the names of the **parties,** the court, the index or **docket** number of the case, etc.; 2. the act of seizing, which, together with **ASPORTATION** (the act of carrying away), was a necessary element of common law **larceny.**

CAPTURE acquiring ownership where no prior ownership existed, as with wild animals, **mining,** and water. Also refers to taking by a military group.

CARBON FOOTPRINT calculation of the negative impact on the environment by the fuel consumption choices of a person or business, measured in terms of carbon dioxide emissions or greenhouse gases.

CARE attention, charge, or management implying responsibility for safety; also **custody,** temporary charge. In the law of **negligence,** the care owned by a **defendant** to those who may be injured by his or her actions is measured by the risks that those actions create. Occasionally, statutes fix the duty of care owed and an unexplained violation of that statutory standard renders the defendant negligent as a matter of law. Generally, degrees of care set a relative standard by which conduct is tested to determine whether it constitutes negligence. See **due care; duty [DUTY OF CARE]; utmost care.**

GREAT CARE   degree of care usually exercised in similar circumstances by the most competent, prudent, and careful class of persons engaged in similar conduct. Care greater than that usually bestowed by persons of ordinary prudence in similar circumstances. For example, the great care expected of an airplane pilot is the care that would be exercised by the most competent, conscientious, prudent, and careful pilot in similar circumstances.

ORDINARY CARE   reasonable diligence and exercise of good judgment; care a reasonably careful person would use under similar circumstances.

REASONABLE CARE   degree of care that, under the circumstances, would usually be exercised by or might be reasonably expected from an ordinary, prudent person. Often viewed as the only true measure of care. Reasonable care is synonymous with ordinary and due care.

SLIGHT CARE   such as persons of ordinary prudence usually exercise about their own affairs of slight importance. Includes such care as careless or inattentive persons usually exercise.

CAREGIVER STRESS   the strain of long-term care for another person with physical or mental needs. The caregiver may suffer a toll on his or her physical, emotional, or financial health from providing care such as cooking, bathing, and feeding the person in need.

CA. RESP.   see **capias [CAPIAS AD RESPONDENDUM].**

CARJACKING   see **hijacking [CARJACKING].**

CARNAL KNOWLEDGE   sexual intercourse; the slightest penetration of the female sexual organ by the male sexual organ; does not require rupture of the hymen. Known as "statutory rape" when conducted with a child under the age of consent. See **rape.**

CARRIER [COMMON CARRIER]   one who is in the business of transporting goods or persons for hire, as a public utility. A private carrier, in contrast, is not in the business of transporting as public employment, but hires out to deliver goods in particular cases.

CARRYBACK   a process by which the **deductions** or **credits** of one **taxable year** that cannot be used to reduce tax liability in that year are applied against tax liability in an earlier year or years. Carrybacks are available, for example, with respect to operating losses of businesses, **charitable deductions** and investment tax credits. Compare **carryover.**

CARRYOVER   a process by which the **deductions** and **credits** of one **taxable year** that cannot be used to reduce tax liability in that year are applied against tax liability in subsequent years. Compare **carryback.**

CARRYOVER BASIS see **basis [CARRYOVER OR SUBSTITUTED BASIS].**

CARTEL a group of independent industrial **corporations,** usually operating internationally, which agree to restrict trade to their mutual benefit.

CARVE OUT the process by which a **taxpayer** separates the present **income** stream of property from the property itself. For example, if an owner of mineral property sells for a certain number of years a portion of the future mineral production from such property, the sale of such future production is a "carved out" interest in the mineral property.

CA. SA. see **capias [CAPIAS AD SATISFACIENDUM].**

CASE an **action,** cause, **suit,** or **controversy, at law** or in **equity.** ACTION IN CASE see **trespass [TRESPASS ON THE CASE].**

   PRIMA FACIE CASE see **prima facie case.**

CASE AT BAR see **bar [CASE AT BAR].**

CASE LAW see **common law.** Compare **statutory law.**

CASE OF FIRST IMPRESSION see **first impression.**

CASE, ON THE see **trespass [TRESPASS ON THE CASE].**

CASE OR CONTROVERSY see **controversy [CASE OR CONTROVERSY].**

CASE REPORTS see **advance sheets; reports.**

CASH EQUIVALENT DOCTRINE see **income [CASH EQUIVALENT DOCTRINE].**

CASHIER'S CHECK see **check [CASHIER'S CHECK].**

CASH METHOD see **accounting method [CASH METHOD].**

CASH SALE if a contract for the sale of **goods** does not specify the manner of payment, the law requires that the purchase price be paid in cash. Under the CASH SALE DOCTRINE a seller who sells to a middleman under "cash sale" terms has priority over other secured creditors to that middleman's assets if he or she goes bankrupt.

CASH SURRENDER VALUE the amount the insurance company will pay on a given life insurance policy if the policy is canceled prior to the death of the insured.

CASH VALUE   see **market value.** Compare **book value.**

CASUALTY LOSS   a loss of property due to fire, storm, shipwreck or other casualty, which is allowable as a **deduction** in computing **TAXABLE INCOME** (see **income**). For a loss to qualify as a casualty loss it must be due to a sudden, unexpected or unusual event. Thus, while property damage due to a storm would normally qualify as a casualty loss, gradual erosion by wind or water would not.

CAUSA   *(käw'-zà)*   Lat.: **cause,** motive, reason. A lawsuit or case.

CAUSA MORTIS   *(môr'-tǐs)*   Lat.: in anticipation of approaching death.

CAUSA PROXIMA   *(prŏk'-sǐ-mà)*   Lat.: proximate cause; most closely related cause. A cause sufficiently related to the result to justify imposing legal liability on the actor who produces the cause. See **cause [PROXIMATE CAUSE];** see also **cause [DIRECT CAUSE].**

CAUSA SINE QUA NON   *(se'-nà kwä nŏn)*   Lat.: a cause without which it would not have occurred. Used most often in connection with the **"but for"** test of causation. See **cause.**

CAUSE   that which effects a result.

DIRECT CAUSE   the active cause that sets in motion a chain of events that brings about a result without the intervention of any other source; often used interchangeably with **PROXIMATE CAUSE.**

IMMEDIATE CAUSE   the nearest cause in time and space.

INTERVENING [SUPERVENING] CAUSE   the cause that actively produces the result *after* the **negligence** or **breach** or **culpable** act of the defendant.

PROXIMATE CAUSE   that which in natural and continuous sequence, unbroken by any new independent cause, produces an event, and without which the injury would not have occurred.

REMOTE CAUSE   that which does not necessarily produce an event without which injury would not occur. Thus, a cause which is not considered to be "proximate" will be regarded as "remote."

SUPERSEDING CAUSE   an intervening cause so substantially responsible for the ultimate injury that it cuts off the liability of preceding actors regardless of whether their prior negligence was a substantial factor in bringing about the injury.

EXAMPLE: Danita pulls into a gasoline station and asks the attendant to fill up her car. In the process, the attendant accidentally squeezes the handle, and gas spills on the pavement, something that is not uncommon. Sal, who is near the car and is unaware of what happened, lights a cigarette and tosses the match in the puddle of gas. Danita's car is destroyed. Courts would find that, although the attendant may have been negligent in spilling gasoline, Sal's action is the superseding cause of the fire. The gas on the pavement would not have created a problem had Sal never lighted a cigarette near the pumps.

SUPERVENING CAUSE see **INTERVENING CAUSE.**

CAUSE OF ACTION a claim in law and fact sufficient to form the basis of a valid lawsuit, as a **BREACH OF CONTRACT.** A **RIGHT OF ACTION** is the legal right to sue; a cause of action is the composite of facts that gives rise to a right of action.

CAUTIONARY INSTRUCTION that part of a judge's **charge** (instruction) to a **jury** telling them not to allow any extraneous or outside matter to influence their **verdict,** not to consider certain rulings of the court as an intimation of opinion, and not to discuss their deliberation process with anyone. The giving of cautionary instructions is within the discretion of the court and is not improper if it does not prejudice either party, but there is authority holding that such instructions should not be given if unnecessary.

CAVEAT *(kä'-vē-ât)* Lat.: let him beware. 1. A warning or caution; a suggestion to a judicial officer that he or she ought to take care how he or she acts in a particular matter and should suspend the proceeding until the merits of the issue thus raised (the caveat) are determined; 2. an **in rem** proceeding attacking the validity of an **instrument** purporting to be a **will,** or a remedy given to prevent a **patent** from being issued in cases where the directions of the law have been violated.

CAVEAT EMPTOR *(kä'-vē-ät ĕmp'-tŏr)* Lat.: let the buyer beware. This phrase expresses the rule of law that the purchaser buys at his or her own risk.

CBP see **Customs and Border Protection [CBP].**

CD see **certificate of deposit.**

CEASE AND DESIST ORDER an order of a court or other body having judicial authority prohibiting the person or entity to which it is directed from undertaking or continuing a particular activity or course of conduct. Such an order may be issued upon a showing, to a degree of certainty or probability, that the conduct is unlawful or likely to be found unlawful.

EXAMPLE: Timber Company had received permission from the Interior Department to cut wood in a section of one of California's giant redwood forests. Several environmental groups brought a court action to stop Timber, claiming that any lumbering activities in the forests would violate the express purpose of Congress in establishing the forests and would result in irreparable harm. The court agreed and issued a *cease and desist order* requiring Timber to stop cutting wood.

CELL PARDE   see **sentence** [CELL PAROLE].

CENSURE   1. a reproach or reprimand, especially when delivered by a judicial or other official body; 2. the act of pronouncing such a reproach or reprimand.

CENTER OF GRAVITY   see **conflict of laws.**

CERT.   see **certiorari.**

CERTIFICATE OF DEPOSIT [CD]   an acknowledgment by a bank of receipt of money with an agreement to repay within a specified time.

CERTIFICATE OF INCORPORATION   similar to **articles of incorporation.** In some states the certificate is issued by a state agency after the articles of incorporation have been properly filed; the corporation's existence begins upon the issuance of the certificate.

CERTIFICATE OF OCCUPANCY [CO]   a document by a local government agency signifying that a building or dwelling conforms to local building code regulations. Generally, entry or transfer of title requires a valid certificate of occupancy.

CERTIFICATE OF TITLE   a document indicating ownership, similar to a **BILL OF SALE** (see **bill**) and usually associated with the sale of new motor vehicles.

CERTIFICATION   see **certiorari.**

CERTIFIED CHECK   see **check.**

CERTIFIED LEGAL ASSISTANT   see **National Association of Legal Assistants** [CLA].

CERTIORARI   *(sèr-shē-ô-rä'-rē)*   Lat.: to be informed of. A means of gaining **appellate** review; a **common law writ,** issued by a superior court to a lower court, commanding the latter to certify and return to the former a particular case record so that the higher court may inspect the proceedings for irregularities or errors.

CESTUI QUE   *(sĕs'-tĭ kā* or *sĕs'-twē kā;* pl.: **CESTUIS QUE**)   Old Fr.: the one who; the person who. Used only in the following phrases:

  CESTUI QUE TRUST *(trŭst)*   Old Fr.: the one who trusts. The beneficiary. See *trust.*

CESTUI QUE USE (*ūz*)   Old Fr.: the one who has the use. The person for whose use the property is held by another. *Cestui que use* enjoys the equitable and beneficial rights to the profits and income of the estate, while the legal title and obligations remain in the **trustee.**

CESTUI QUE VIE (*vē*)   Old Fr.: the one who lives. The person by whose life the duration of an estate is measured.

CF.   abbreviation for the Latin word confer meaning "compare."

CFI   see **CIF**

C.F.R.   Code of Federal Regulations.

CFTC   see **Commodity Futures Trading Commission [CFTC].**

CHAIN OF TITLE   the succession of **conveyances** of **title** to property, commencing with the **patent** from the government (or other original source) down to and including the conveyance to the pres-ent holder. The **recorded** chain of title consists only of the documents affecting title that have been recorded in a manner that makes their existence readily discoverable by a **bona fide purchaser.** Of the two systems for recording such documents, the **TRACT INDEX** records in the same place all **instruments** relating to a particular property, while the **GRANTOR-GRANTEE INDEX** indexes all such instruments under the names of the various grantors or grantees of the property. See **recording acts; title search.**

CHALLENGE   in general, to call one out to answer for something; an objection or exception calling into question the existence of a right, the validity or sufficiency of an instrument, or the capability of a person for a specific function. Also, an objection by a party (or lawyer) to the inclusion of a particular prospective juror as a member of the jury that is to hear that party's cause or trial, with the result that the prospective juror is disqualified from the case. See **voir dire**.

CHALLENGE FOR CAUSE   a challenge based upon a particular reason (such as bias) specified by law or procedure as a reason that a party (or his lawyer) may use to disqualify a prospective juror.

CHALLENGE TO JURY ARRAY   a formal objection to the entire panel of grand or petit jurors. The basis of such a challenge is that something has been done or omitted to the prejudice of the substantial rights of the challenging party.

GENERAL CHALLENGE   a type of challenge for cause based on grounds from which, if shown to exist, the disqualification of the juror follows as a legal conclusion. Known as a **CHALLENGE FOR PRINCIPAL CAUSE** at common law.

PEREMPTORY CHALLENGE   a right given to attorneys at trial to dismiss a prospective juror for no particular reason; the number of times an attorney can invoke this right is usually limited. If a specific reason exists why a particular juror may not fairly decide a matter, the juror may be **CHALLENGED FOR CAUSE.** This conserves the peremptory challenges. Even the government can use these challenges.

CHAMBERS   see **in camera.**

CHAMPERTY   in common law, an unlawful agreement between an attorney and his or her client that the attorney will sue and pay the costs of the client's suit in return for a portion of the damages rewarded. Today the prohibition against champerty survives only in a few jurisdictions and only in modified form. See also **criminal maintenance.** Compare **barratry.**

CHANCELLOR   1. in early English law, the King's minister who would dispense justice in the King's name by extraordinary **equitable relief** where the remedy **at law** was inadequate; later, the name of the chief judge of the court of **chancery;** 2. in American law, a judge in a court of chancery.

CHANCERY   the jurisprudence that is exercised in a **court of equity;** synonymous with **equity** or equitable jurisdiction.

CHAPTER 11   see **bankruptcy [CHAPTER 11 REORGANIZATION].**

CHARACTER WITNESS   see **witness.**

CHARGE   1. in criminal law, a description of the underlying offense in an **accusation** or **indictment;** 2. in trial practice, an address delivered by the court to the **jury** at the close of the **case,** telling them the principles of law they are to apply in reaching a decision.

EXAMPLE: At the end of the trial for assault and robbery, the judge *charged* the jury with (i.e., explained to them) the necessary elements of law that must be proved in order to convict the defendant. As in all criminal trials, the judge also charged the jury that they are the sole deciders (triers) of fact and should not be influenced by impressions from the judge or any attorney. Finally, the jurors were instructed to apply the law only as charged by the judge and not to base their decision on their own conception of the law.

The charge may also include instructions given during the trial for the jury's guidance.

See also *complaint.*

CHARITABLE CONTRIBUTION a contribution for the use of a state, the United States, or a **corporation** organized and operated exclusively for religious, charitable, scientific, literary, educational, or like purposes. Charitable contributions are deductible under the federal income tax laws.

POLITICAL CONTRIBUTION donations to political candidates, parties, and newsletter funds.

CHARITABLE DEDUCTION   see **charitable contribution.**

CHARITY   a nonprofit institution organized and operated exclusively for charitable, religious, scientific, literary, educational or like purposes, whose income is exempt from federal income tax. Contributions to such organizations are allowable, with limitations, as a **deduction** in computing one's **TAXABLE INCOME** (see income).

PRIVATE FOUNDATIONS   organizations that, although charities, are deemed to receive a substantial portion of their support from nonpublic sources, usually from small groups of individuals. A private foundation is subject to additional restrictions on its activities and its financial dealings, including accumulation of income.

PUBLIC CHARITY   a charity that, under certain tests, is deemed to receive the major portion of its support from the public rather than from a small group of individuals.

CHARTER   a document issued by the government establishing a corporate entity. See **articles of incorporation; certificate of incorporation.**

CHATTEL   any tangible, movable thing; **personal property** as opposed to **real property; goods.**

CHATTEL MORTGAGE   a mortgage on personal property created to secure the payment of moneys owed or the performance of some other obligation. This security device has for the most part been replaced by the security agreements available under the **Uniform Commercial Code.**

CHATTEL PAPER   a document that shows both a debt and a **security interest** in or a **lease** of specific goods.

CHECK   a **draft** upon a bank, payable on **demand,** and by the **maker** or **drawer,** containing a promise to pay an amount of money to the **payee.** Compare **bad check; NSF [nonsufficient funds] check; raised check.**

CASHIER'S CHECK   a check issued by an officer of a bank to another person, authorizing the **payee** to receive upon demand the amount of the check. It is drawn on the bank's own account, not that of a private person, and is therefore accepted for many transactions where a personal check would not be.

CERTIFIED CHECK a check containing a certification that the drawer of the check has sufficient funds in the bank to cover payment.

MEMORANDUM CHECK a bank check with the word "memorandum" written across its face, which is not intended for immediate presentation, but simply as evidence of an indebtedness by the **drawer** to the **holder.**

CHECK KITING an illegal scheme that establishes a false line of credit by the exchange of worthless checks between two banks. For instance, a check kiter might have empty checking accounts at two different banks, *A* and *B*. The kiter writes a check for $50,000 on the Bank *A* account and deposits it in the Bank *B* account. If the kiter has good credit at Bank *B*, he will be able to draw funds against the deposited check before it clears (i.e., is forwarded to Bank *A* for payment and paid by Bank *A*.) Since the clearing process usually takes a few days, the kiter can use the $50,000 for a few days, and then deposit it in the Bank *A* account before the $50,000 check drawn on that account clears.

CHECKS AND BALANCES see **separation of power.**

CHIEF JUSTICE the presiding member of certain courts with more than one judge; especially, the presiding member of the U.S. Supreme Court, who is the principal administrative officer of the federal judiciary.

CHILD AND DEPENDENT CARE CREDIT a **tax credit** allowed for 20 percent of the expenses incurred for household services or for care of a child or other dependent where a **taxpayer** maintains a household that includes one or more **dependents** who are under 15 years of age or mentally or physically incapacitated.

CHILD CITIZENSHIP ACT see **citizen [CHILD CITIZENSHIP ACT].**

CHILD CUSTODY see **custody of children.**

CHILD PORNOGRAPHY see **obscene material; sexual exploitation.**

CHILD SEXUAL ABUSE ACCOMMODATION SYNDROME [CSAAS] a pattern of behavior that is found to occur in children who are victims of sexual abuse. The behavior is often contrary to basic adult assumptions and thus courts may allow expert testimony on CSAAS to establish that a victim's symptoms are consistent with sexual abuse and to explain a delay in reporting abuse or recanting allegations of abuse. CSAAS consists mainly of five parts. The first is secrecy. Most people would expect that a child would tell if they had been sexually assaulted but statistically they rarely tell. Usually the child will keep it a secret. The other parts are helplessness; entrapment or accommodation; delayed, conflicted or unconvincing disclosure; and retraction or recantation. See **rape.**

CHILD SUPPORT   see **alimony [CHILD SUPPORT].**

CHILL [CHILLING EFFECT]   limitations on the exercise of **First Amendment** rights imposed not by law but by individuals who, fearful of the possible application of laws and sanctions, choose not to exercise their legitimate rights rather than risk prosecution.

EXAMPLE: A protest group schedules a weekend march to show support for that group's position. Even though the group has a permit, word is spread that the police plan to use tear gas and arrest marchers. The rumor has a *chilling effect* and keeps some people home who would otherwise have joined the protest.

CHOATE   *(kō'-āt)* completed or perfected; a right in regard to which no additional events need occur for it to be operative. Compare **inchoate.**

CHOICE OF LAW   see **conflict of law [CHOICE OF LAW].**

CHOSE   *(shōz)*   Fr.: a thing.

CHOSE IN ACTION   a **claim** or **debt** upon which recovery may be made in a lawsuit; not a present possession, but merely a right to sue, becoming a possessary thing only upon successful completion of a lawsuit.

CHOSE IN POSSESSION   a thing actually possessed or possessable.

CHURNING   excessive trading in a stock investment account. If the pattern of activity is inappropriate for the customer and if the prime result is excessive brokerage commissions for the **registered representative,** then the practice is unethical and recovery of damages by the customer is possible.

CIF   cost, insurance and freight; also written CFI In a **contract** of sale it means that the cost of the goods, the insurance and the freight to the destination is included in the contract price, and unless there is something in a CFI contract to indicate to the contrary, the seller completes the contract when he or she delivers the merchandise to the shipper, pays the freight to point of destination and forwards to the buyer the **bill of lading,** invoice, insurance policy and receipt showing payment of freight.

CIMT abbreviation for "crime involving **moral turpitude."**

CIR. CT. abbreviation for Circuit Court.

CIRCUIT judicial divisions of a state or the United States; originally so called because judges traveled from place to place within the circuit, holding court in various locations. There are now thirteen federal judicial circuits wherein the United States Courts of Appeal are allocated the appellate jurisdiction of the United States.

CIRCUIT COURT one of several courts in a given jurisdiction; a part of a system of federal courts extending over one or more counties or districts; formerly applied to the U. S. courts of appeals. Compare **district court.**

CIRCUMSTANTIAL EVIDENCE indirect evidence; secondary facts by which a principal fact may be reasonably inferred.

EXAMPLE: There are no eyewitnesses to place Julio at the site of the car accident, but there is a variety of *circumstantial evidence* to suggest that Julio was involved. The prints at the scene of the accident match the tires on his car, the color of several scratches on the other person's car is the same as the color of Julio's car, and his car is dented precisely where the other driver said it would be. That evidence could be used to implicate Julio in the collision. Compare **direct evidence.**

CITATION 1. a reference to a legal authority—for example, a citation to a statute or case; 2. a writ similar to a **summons,** in that it commands the appearance of a party in a **proceeding.** The object of a citation is to give the court proper **jurisdiction** and to notify the **defendant** that a **suit** has been filed.

CITE 1. to summon; to order to appear, as before a tribunal; 2. to make reference to a text, statute, case or other legal authority in support of a proposition or argument; also the reference thus made.

CITE CHECKING see **spading.**

CITIZEN a member of a nation or political community; one who owes allegiance to, and may claim protection from, its government. Under the **Fourteenth Amendment** to the **Constitution**, all persons born or naturalized in the United States, and subject to the jurisdiction thereof, are citizens of the United States and of the state wherein they reside. Citizenship is the status of being a citizen. In the United States, there is usually a double citizenship, that is, citizenship in the nation and citizenship in the state in which one resides.

Generally, in the United States, one may acquire citizenship by birth in the United States or by naturalization therein. See **naturalized citizen**. However, a person who becomes a United States citizen through naturalization is not considered a NATURAL BORN CITIZEN (a person born within the jurisdiction of the United States) and consequently, is not eligible to become President or Vice-President of the United States. Compare **legal permanent resident [LPR]**. A child born in the United States of **alien** parents is a citizen of the United States. A foreign-born child of citizens of the United States, subject to certain qualifications and limitations, is a citizen of the United States. A child born in the United States of a diplomatic representative, such as an ambassador or minister, takes the nationality of such representative. When a foreign child from a **Hague Convention** country is adopted by a citizen of the United States, the child receives an immigrant visa and automatically acquires citizenship if the child enters prior to his or her eighteenth birthday. For orphan, non-Hague country adoptions, and where the child was not seen prior to adoption, the child becomes a permanent resident upon entry and will acquire citizenship upon the child's finalized adoption in the United States. When the child is between 18 and 21, the rules vary. The **Child Citizenship Act** of 2000 controls. American **Indians** [Native Americans] are citizens of the United States and of the states in which they reside. They are also citizens of their Tribes according to the criteria established by each Tribe. For purposes of **diversity jurisdiction**: a municipality may be considered a citizen; a corporation is deemed a citizen of the state in which it maintains its principal place of business; counties are citizens; the United States is not a citizen; and states are not citizens. See also **Immigration and Customs Enforcement [ICE]**.

CITIZEN, NATURAL BORN see **citizen [NATURAL BORN CITIZEN]**.

CITIZEN, NATURALIZED see **naturalized citizen.**

CITIZENSHIP AND IMMIGRATION SERVICES [USCIS] part of the **Department of Homeland Security** that oversees lawful **immigration** to the United States. This agency processes citizenship and naturalization eligibility, immigration of family members, and international adoption documents. It also manages the process that allows individuals from other countries to work in the United States and administers humanitarian programs that provide protection to individuals inside and outside the United States who are displaced by war, famine, and civil and political unrest, and those who are forced to flee their countries to escape the risk of death and torture at the hands of persecutors. See *www.uscis.gov*. See also **alien; citizen; deportability; green card; Immigration and Customs Enforcement [ICE]; legal permanent resident [LPR]; naturalized citizen.**

CIVIL   1. the branch of law that pertains to suits other than criminal practice and is concerned with the rights and duties of persons in **contract, tort,** etc.; 2. civil law as opposed to **common law.**

CIVIL ACTION   an action to protect a private right or to compel a civil remedy in a dispute between private parties, as distinguished from a criminal **prosecution.**

CIVIL AERONAUTICS BOARD [CAB]   an independent federal agency established by Congress in 1938 to regulate commercial aviation and provide public air safety and navigation facilities. In 1958, Congress transferred all the functions except economic regulation of air carriers, aircraft registration, pilot licensing, and accident investigation to the **Federal Aviation Administration [FAA].**

CIVIL CONTEMPT   see **contempt of court.**

CIVIL COURTS see **court.**

CIVIL DAMAGE ACTS   see **dram shop act.**

CIVIL DEATH   at common law, civil death was the status given to a person who, though alive, had been convicted of a **felony** and sentenced to life imprisonment. It referred to the fact that the convicted person had lost all **civil rights** and was thus thought to be dead as regards his or her participation in society. The convict could not, for example, sue or inherit since in contemplation of law he or she did not exist; in fact, a **next friend** was often designated to represent the interests of a civilly dead person. Some states still apply civil death to persons serving life sentences; however, there is no general agreement as to the scope of the civil rights lost. Most states deny specific rights to convicted felons such as the right to vote or to hold public office.

CIVIL DISOBEDIENCE   the refusal to obey a law for the purpose of demonstrating its unfairness or social undesirability; generally does not apply to violent efforts to oppose laws.

EXAMPLE: Katie leads a group of protestors who sit down in a roadway to prevent vehicles from entering a nuclear weapons site and thus disrupt the activities at that site. The group may be forceably removed by the police and/or charged with various offenses such as trespassing or obstructing a passageway, yet they feel they have achieved their goal of calling attention to their concern.

CIVIL DISORDER any public disturbance involving acts of violence by a group of three or more persons causing immediate danger, damage, or injury to the property or person of another individual.

CIVIL LAW 1. Roman law embodied in the Justinian Code and presently prevailing in most Western European states; it is also the foundation of the law of Louisiana; 2. the law concerned with noncriminal matters; 3. the body of laws established by a state or nation, as distinguished from **natural law.**

CIVIL LIABILITY amenability to **civil action** as distinguished from criminal action; a liability to actions seeking private remedies or the enforcement of personal rights, based on **contract, tort,** etc.

CIVIL LIBERTIES see **civil rights.**

CIVIL PARTNERSHIP see **civil union; marriage.**

CIVIL PENALTIES fines or money damages imposed by a regulatory scheme. Civil penalties are imposed as punishment for a certain activity and act as a criminal sanction, while civil remedies redress wrongs between private parties.

CIVIL PROCEDURE the body of rules of **practice** to be adhered to in adjudicating a controversy before a court of **civil,** as opposed to criminal, **jurisdiction.** The term refers to matters of form rather than to the principles of **substantive law** that must be applied to determine the rights of the parties.

CIVIL RIGHTS the nonpolitical rights of all citizens, especially those rights relating to personal liberty. Civil rights differ from CIVIL LIBERTIES in that civil rights are positive in nature, and civil liberties, negative; that is, civil liberties are immunities from governmental interference or limitations on governmental action (as in the **First Amendment**) that have the effect of reserving rights to individuals.

EXAMPLE: Neal is harassed as he enters a building designated as a polling place. The purpose is to prevent Neal from voting. The harassment violates Neal's *civil rights,* since he is guaranteed his right to vote.

CIVIL RIGHTS ACT OF 1964 federal act passed to amend statutes passed after the Civil War to provide stronger protection for individual rights guaranteed by the Constitution.

CIVIL SERVICE COMMISSIONS see **patronage [CIVIL SERVICE COMMISSIONS].**

CIVIL UNION ceremony between same-sex persons which conveys to them certain aspects of marriage for purposes of that state's laws (but not those of other states or the federal government). States which recognize civil unions provide that those persons receive the same rights as married persons with respect to mutual financial support, child custody and support, property division and maintenance, adoption, survivorship, insurance and health care coverage, causes of action for wrongful death or other tort laws, tax laws of that state, prohibitions against discrimination, and other rights. Parties to civil unions are included in the definitions for spouse, family, immediate family, dependent, and next of kin. At time of press, civil unions are largely replaced by state **marriage** laws allowing marriage between same-sex persons.

EXAMPLES: Ebony and Gretchen enter into a civil union and adopt a child, Deb. Ebony is critically injured in an automobile accident and Gretchen makes the decision to terminate life support and to donate Ebony's organs. Gretchen also inherits Ebony's share of their **tenancy by the entirety** and retains full custody of Deb.

Carter and Sanjay dissolve their union and since Carter's job pays substantially more than Sanjay's, Sanjay is entitled to receive spousal support from Carter. See **alimony.**

CIVITAS *(sĭ'-vĭ-täs)* Lat: in the Roman Law, any body of people living under the same laws; citizenship, state, commonwealth, community.

C.J. abbreviation for **Chief Justice** or Chief Judge.

C.J.S. Corpus Juris Secundum.

CLA see **National Association of Legal Assistants [CLA].**

CLAIM 1. the assertion of a right to money or **property;** 2. in pleading, the facts giving rise to a right enforceable in the courts, which must show the existence of a right, an injury and **damages.** One who makes a claim is the claimant.

CLAIMANT the **party** who asserts a right to money or property. See **claim.**

CLAIM FOR REFUND a claim by a **taxpayer** to the **Internal Revenue Service** that he or she is entitled to a refund of all or part of the **taxes** paid by him or her in earlier years; such a claim must be made in writing within a specified time from the filing date of the **return** to which it relates and is a necessary prerequisite to any allowance of a refund by the IRS or to any suit by the taxpayer against the IRS for disallowance of a claimed refund.

CLAIM OF RIGHT a doctrine that requires **taxpayers** to include in their gross **income** all amounts received by them under claim that they are entitled to the amounts, whether or not they are legally entitled to keep them and whether they are required to repay them in a subsequent year. When repayment occurs, a **deduction** is allowed under a special section of the **Internal Revenue Code** designed to minimize the tax distortion caused by the inclusion of such amounts in the wrong tax years.

CLASS ACTION a **suit** brought by one or more members of a large group of persons on behalf of all members of the group. If the court permits the class action, all members must receive notice of the action and must be given an opportunity to exclude themselves. Members who do not exclude themselves are bound by the **judgment,** whether favorable or not.

EXAMPLE: In accordance with securities law, a corporation files a registration statement with the Securities and Exchange Commission concerning a stock sale. After investors buy several million shares of stock and a few years pass, the corporation files for bankruptcy. At that point, a few of the investors realize the statement was false and misleading. Those investors, on behalf of all investors of the corporation, file a *class action* lawsuit seeking to recover the money they originally paid for the stock.

CLASS GIFT a gift of an aggregate sum to a body of persons uncertain in number at the time of the gift, to be ascertained at a future time, who are all to take in equal, or other definite proportions, the share of each being dependent for its amount upon the ultimate number.

CLASSIFIED STOCK common stock divided into two or more classes. A typical approach is for a company to issue Class A **stock** to raise the bulk of **equity** capital while vesting voting rights in Class B stock, which is retained by management and/or founders. The practice is usually confined to promotional ventures, and very few publicly held companies have classified stock as part of their **capitalization.**

CLAUSE see respective entries, e.g., **escalator clause.**

CLAYTON ACT a federal statute amending the **Sherman Antitrust Act.** The Act prohibits certain types of price and other discriminations, now covered by the **Robinson-Patman Act;** tying, exclusive dealing, and total requirements agreements; mergers or acquisitions tending substantially to lessen competition in any line of commerce, and interlocking directorates. See **antitrust laws.**

CLEAN ELECTIONS   the public financing of political campaigns. To qualify for public funding, a candidate would have to raise a threshold amount of small contributions (for example, $10 per person), depending on the size of the district's population, and reach a threshold amount (for example, $15,000). Once that amount is raised, the candidate gets grants (for the primary election and then for the general election) in exchange for an agreement to raise no more money. The candidate would be eligible for additional matching funds to keep pace in an election where the opponent is a privately funded candidate. Such elections are thought to encourage politicians to be accountable to constituents rather than campaign contributors, level the playing field by giving all citizens a fair possibility of being elected, and save taxpayers money.

CLEAN HANDS (DOCTRINE)   the concept in **equity** that a **claimant** who seeks **equitable relief** must not himself or herself have acted unfairly or unjustly in the transaction in which relief is sought.

CLEAN MONEY   see **clean elections.**

CLEAR   see **free and clear.**

CLEAR AND CONVINCING   as a standard of proof, the amount of evidence that is beyond mere **preponderance** but is not "beyond **reasonable doubt,**" which will convince the trier of fact (**fact finder**) as to the facts sought to be established.

CLEAR AND PRESENT DANGER   in constitutional law, a standard used to determine if one's **First Amendment** right to speak may be curtailed or punished. If the words are spoken in such circumstances and are of such a nature as to create a clear and present danger that they will bring about certain evils that government has a right to prevent, the government may prohibit or punish the use of those words.

CLEARINGHOUSE   1. an association, usually formed voluntarily by banks, to exchange checks, drafts or other forms of indebtedness held by one member and owed to another. Its object is to effect at one time and place the daily settlement of balances between the banks of a city or region with a minimum of inconvenience and labor. 2. in a stock or commodities exchange, an organization to facilitate settlement of the debits and credits of its members with each other. In essence, it operates on the same principles of centrality and convenience as does the clearinghouse association for banks. For example, if broker *A* is obligated to deliver 5,000 shares of *XYZ* stock and is entitled to receive 4,500 such shares from brokers *B*, *C*, and *D*, at the end of the day he would deliver to the clearinghouse only 500 shares.

CLEAR TITLE **title** free from any **encumbrance,** obstruction, **burden** or limitation that presents a doubtful or even a reasonable question of law or fact as to its validity. See **good title; marketable title.**

CLEMENCY the act of forgiving a person the criminal liability of his or her acts. The term is generic and embraces **pardon, amnesty,** and **commutation**. The power of clemency is usually vested in the chief executive. See **executive clemency.**

CLERGYMEN'S PRIVILEGE see **priest-penitent privilege.**

CLERICAL ERROR a mistake made while copying or transmitting legal documents as distinguished from a JUDICIAL ERROR, which is an error made in the exercise of judgment or discretion.

CLERIC'S PRIVILEGE see **priest-penitent privilege.**

CLERK an assistant or a subordinate. A COURT CLERK is an officer whose duties include keeping records, issuing process and entering judgment. A LAW CLERK is an assistant to a lawyer or a judge, whose primary job is to aid in the research and writing of briefs or opinions and the handling of cases.

CLICKWRAP [CLICKTHROUGH] LICENSE **terms of service** providing access to software or a web site. The user agrees to the terms by clicking yes or indicating agreement in the installation or sign-in process. A SHRINKWRAP LICENSE is one where the user agrees to terms by opening the shrinkwrap which encloses the boxed software. Rejection of the terms means the software or web site cannot be accessed. Most provisions of such a unilateral contract are upheld in legal challenges but not necessarily every term of the contract. See **adhesion contract.**

CLOSE see **breaking a close; enclosure.**

CLOSE CORPORATION see **corporation.**

CLOSED END FUNDS see **investment company [TRUST].**

CLOSED-END MANAGEMENT COMPANY a management **investment company** that issues a fixed number of **shares.** The shares are redeemable through secondary market transactions rather than directly from the investment management company as in an open-end management investment company [MUTUAL FUND]. The shares of a closed-end management company are generally listed for trading on a **stock exchange.**

CLOSED-END MORTGAGE see **mortgage [CLOSED-END MORTGAGE].**

CLOSED SHOP an enterprise in which, because it is required by the terms of a collective bargaining agreement between a labor union and the owners/managers of the enterprise, all workers must be union members, as a condition of their employment.

CLOSELY HELD CORPORATION see **corporation** [CLOSE CORPORATIONS].

CLOSING the consummation of a transaction involving the sale of real estate or of an interest in real estate, usually by payment of the purchase price (or some agreed portion), delivery of the **deed** or other **instrument** of **title,** and finalizing of collateral matters.

CLOSING AGREEMENT a written agreement between a **taxpayer** and the **Internal Revenue Service** that conclusively settles his or her tax liability for the **taxable year** ending prior to the agreement date or settles one or more issues affecting his or her tax liability. The agreement is binding on both the taxpayer and the IRS unless **fraud** or misrepresentation of a **material** fact is demonstrated.

CLOSING LAWS see **blue laws; Sunday closing laws.**

CLOSING STATEMENT see **statement** [CLOSING STATEMENT]; **summation** [summing up].

CLOTURE in legislative assemblies that permit unlimited debate **(FILIBUSTER),** a procedure or rule by which debate is ended so that a vote may be taken on the matter. In the U.S. Senate, a two-thirds majority vote of the body is required to invoke cloture and terminate debate.

CLOUD ON TITLE any matter appearing in the record of a **title** to real estate that on its face appears to reflect the existence of an outstanding **claim** or **encumbrance** that, if valid, would defeat or impair title, but that might be proven invalid by evidence outside the title record.

EXAMPLE: Sadie locates a house she wants to buy but demands an abstract of title to be sure that no one else may have a claim to the land or house. The abstract shows a *cloud on the title* from about 60 years ago concerning a transfer of the land wherein a joint owner did not sign the deed transferring title. Sadie may not want to purchase the house, or she may want title insurance to cover a problem if one arises.

Where a cloud on a title exists, the seller ordinarily gives the purchaser a **quitclaim deed,** which transfers all of the interest the seller owns and no more. Title companies usually will not insure a clouded title or will insure it subject to that cloud which is listed in the policy as an exception.

CO Prefix meaning equal, with. Abbreviation for commanding officer, company, county, central office or contractual obligation. Also, **certificate of occupancy.**

COAST GUARD see **Department of Homeland Security [DHS] [UNITED STATES COAST GUARD].**

COBRA see **affordable care act [COBRA].**

COCONSPIRATOR EXCEPTION see **hearsay rule.**

CODE a systematic compilation of laws, for example, the Criminal Code (referring to penal laws) and the Motor Vehicle Code (referring to laws relating to motor vehicles).

CO-DEFENDANT a **defendant** who is joined together with one or more other defendants in a single **action.** See **joinder.**

CODE OF MILITARY JUSTICE see **military law [UNIFORM CODE OF MILITARY JUSTICE].**

CODE OF PROFESSIONAL RESPONSIBILITY a set of rules based on ethical considerations that govern the conduct of lawyers; passed by the American Bar Association and **adopted** by most states; enforced by state disciplinary boards. Some states require lawyers to prove their knowledge of the Code by passage of a course or test before being allowed to practice in that state.

CODE PLEADING the term applied to the system of **pleading,** now abandoned, which was developed in this country through practice codes enacted in a majority of the states, to consolidate and improve the **common law** and **equity** systems of pleading previously used.

CODICIL a supplement to a **will,** whose purpose is to add to, subtract from, or qualify, modify or revoke the provisions of a prior will.

EXAMPLE: Constantine executed his will at a time when his relationship with his brother was at a low point. As the relationship improves, Constantine writes a *codicil* to his will providing that a certain amount of money pass to the brother. The codicil also revokes any prior statement in the will that specifically denies the brother anything.

CODIS Combined DNA Index System. A **Federal Bureau of Investigation** laboratory that blends forensic science and computer technology into an effective tool for solving violent crimes. CODIS enables federal, state, and local crime labs to exchange and compare **DNA testing** profiles (taken from blood, saliva, or semen samples) electronically, thereby linking crimes to each other and to convicted offenders.

COERCION any form of compulsion or constraint that compels or induces a person to act otherwise than freely. It may be physical force but is more often used to describe any pressure that is brought to bear on another's free will. In testamentary law, if undue influence is exerted upon the **testator,** the coercion will vitiate the effect of the instrument. In criminal law, improper conduct that coerces the defendant into making an incriminatory statement will void the **confession.** See **criminal coercion; duress.**

COGENT appealing forcibly to the mind or reason; compelling; convincing. The word is frequently used to describe the quality of a particular legal argument. It is derived from the Latin cogo, cogere, which means "to bind, drive, or compress into a mass."

COGNIZABLE within the **jurisdiction** of the court. An interest is cognizable in a court of law when that court has the power to decide the controversy.

COGNOVIT JUDGMENT see **confession of judgment.**

COGNOVIT NOTE a **promissory note** in which the debtor authorizes an attorney to enter a confession of judgment against him or her in the event of nonpayment.

COHABITATION literally, the act of living together; often statutorily expanded to include living together publicly, as a couple. Cohabitation among unmarried persons was once proscribed by local laws, as it produced an **inference** of criminal **fornication.** Where **common law** marriages are recognized, cohabitation for a period of time is required.

CO-HEIR one who inherits a property with another.

COHORT(S) associate or companion. Also can be plural, as in a group with members that have shared characteristics.

COIF headdress formerly worn by English sergeants at law. "Order of the Coif" is an honorary legal fraternity in the United States.

COINSURANCE an **insurance** plan in which the insurer provides **indemnity** for only a certain percentage of the insured's loss, reflecting the relative division of risk between insurer and **insured.**

COLA see **cost of living adjustment.**

COLLATERAL 1. secondary; on the side; 2. in commercial transactions, the property offered as **security,** usually as an inducement to another party to lend money or extend credit.

IMPAIRMENT OF COLLATERAL lessening of the effect of the collateral; an act whose effect is to reduce the value of the collateral as security for the obligation it is intended to assure.

COLLATERAL AFFINITY see **affinity** [COLLATERAL AFFINITY].

COLLATERAL ATTACK a challenge to the integrity of a prior **judgment,** brought in a special **proceeding** intended for that express purpose. A **direct attack,** on the other hand, is an attempt to impeach a judgment within the same **action** in which the judgment was rendered, through an appeal, request for new trial, etc. Lack of proper jurisdiction and constitutional infirmities in the original judgment are often grounds for collateral attack. **Habeas corpus** is a "collateral attack" remedy.

COLLATERAL CONSANGUINITY [LINE] see **consanguinity** [COLLATERAL CONSANGUINITY]; **lineal** [COLLATERAL LINE].

COLLATERAL ESTOPPEL the doctrine recognizing that the determination of facts **litigated** between two **parties** in a **proceeding** is binding on those parties in all future proceedings against each other; also known as issue preclusion. In a subsequent **action** between the parties on a different **claim,** the judgment is conclusive as to the **issues** raised in the subsequent action, if these issues were actually litigated and determined in the prior action. The constitutional prohibition against **double jeopardy** includes within it the right of the **defendant** (but not the state) to plead "collateral estoppel" and thereby preclude proof of some essential element of the state's case found in the defendant's favor at an earlier trial. See **estoppel.** See also **bar; merger; res judicata.**

EXAMPLE: Damien is charged with robbing six persons at a poker game and his defense in the first trial involving the alleged robbery of only one of the victims is that he wasn't there [ALIBI], and if he is **acquitted** at that trial due to the jury's specific acceptance of his alibi, the state will be **estopped** to relitigate the alibi question with respect to the other related robberies.

COLLATERAL FRAUD see **fraud** [EXTRINSIC [COLLATERAL] FRAUD].

COLLATERAL HEIRS see **heirs** [COLLATERAL HEIRS].

COLLATERAL SOURCE RULE **benefits** or **compensation** received by an injured person from a separate source such as insurance do not serve to reduce the damages owed by a **tortfeasor.**

COLLATION the preparation of an estimate of the value of **advancements** made by an **intestate** [person who dies without a

will] to his or her children, in order that the whole of the **estate** may be divided in accordance with law.

COLLECTIVE BARGAINING the process of settling labor disputes by negotiation between the employer and representatives of employees. Compare **arbitration.**

COLLOQUIUM allegation in a **declaration** or **complaint** of **libel** under **common law pleadings,** which purport to connect the libelous words with the **plaintiff** by setting forth extrinsic facts showing that they applied to the plaintiff and were so intended by the defendant.

COLLUSION 1. the making of a secret agreement with another to commit **fraud** or engage in other illegal activity, or in legal activity with an illegal end in mind; 2. an agreement between husband and wife to suppress facts or to make up **evidence** important to the existence of lawful grounds for divorce.

COLLUSIVE ACTION an **action** brought by **parties** not actually **adversaries** to determine a hypothetical point of law or to produce a desired legal **precedent.** Because such a suit does not involve a genuine **controversy,** it will not be entertained by a court.

COLOR deceptive appearance or disguise; designates hiding a set of facts behind a false, but technically proper, legal theory. See **color of law; color of title.**

COLORABLE that which presents an appearance that does not correspond with the reality, or an appearance intended to conceal or to deceive.

COLOR OF LAW the semblance of legal right. An action under color of law has the apparent authority of law but is actually contrary to law.

COLOR OF TITLE an **instrument** that appears to pass title, and on which one relies as passing title, but that is not valid, either because title is lacking in the person conveying or because the **conveyance** itself is defective.

COMAKERS two (or more) persons who sign a **note.** Upon such signature, each assumes full liability in the event of **default** by the other person(s). Generally used to assist a borrower with questionable creditworthiness to obtain financing (such as a parent signing on a child's car loan). Considered synonymous with **surety.** Often considered synonymous with COSIGNER although the specific terms of the contract may vary depending upon the signature location, whether any loan proceeds were received by the cosigner, and the parties' intent. A cosigner might recover full value in a suit brought against a borrower (after default) while a comaker's recovery against the borrower might be limited. Compare **accommodation maker.**

EXAMPLE: Aida graduates with a teaching degree and decides to open her own preschool. Unfortunately she has not established a sufficient credit history to qualify for low-rate loans so her father Abdul signs as a comaker and the bank issues the loan at the rate sought by Aida.

COMITY [COMITAS] a rule of courtesy by which one court defers to the concomitant **jurisdiction** of another; most often used in reference to the long-standing public policy against federal court interference with state criminal proceedings.

EXAMPLE: Jack kidnaps a young girl and takes her across state lines, a crime that violates both federal and state laws. Although Jack could be prosecuted by both jurisdictions or either of them, under principles of *comity* the federal prosecutor allows the state to proceed first, because of the anger of the community and their desire to try Jack in a local setting.

COMMENT statements made by a judge or counsel concerning a defendant, where such statements are not based on fact, but rather on alleged facts.

COMMERCE CLAUSE Art. I, Sec. 8, Cl. 3 of the **Constitution** providing ". . . Congress shall have Power . . . to regulate Commerce with foreign Nations, and among the several States, and with the Indian Tribes. . . ." Federal regulations regarding business such as the **Occupational Safety and Health Act** have their roots in the commerce clause. See **interstate commerce.**

COMMERCE POWER see **power, constitutional [COMMERCE POWER].**

COMMERCIAL BANK see **bank [COMMERCIAL BANK].**

COMMERCIAL BRIBERY see **bribery [COMMERCIAL BRIBERY].**

COMMERCIAL FRUSTRATION see **frustration (of purpose).**

COMMERCIAL LAW the body of law that concerns the rights and obligations of persons in their commercial dealings with one another (such as the **Uniform Commercial Code,** laws prohibiting unfair trade practices, etc.). See **law merchant; mercantile law; Uniform Commercial Code.**

COMMERCIAL NAME see **trade name.**

COMMERCIAL PAPER a **negotiable instrument,** that is, a writing **indorsed** by the **maker** or **drawer,** containing an unconditional promise or order to pay a certain sum on demand or at a specified time, and payable to order or to bearer. See also **order paper.**

COMMERCIAL PREFERENCE   see **preference.**

COMMERCIAL UNIT   a unit considered by trade or usage to be a whole that cannot be divided without materially impairing its value, character or use; for example, a machine or a suite of furniture. Since acceptance of any part of a commercial unit constitutes acceptance of the whole, the term becomes significant when a buyer attempts to reject part of a **contract** for nonconformance. If the item rejected is part of a commercial unit, the rejection will not be allowed.

COMMINGLING OF FUNDS   the act of a **fiduciary** or **trustee,** including a lawyer, in mixing his or her own funds with those belonging to a client or customer; generally prohibited unless the fiduciary maintains an exact accounting of the client's funds and how they have been used.

EXAMPLE: The bank trustee felt he had an excellent tip on a stock, so he *commingled the funds* of one of the bank trusts with his own funds. The investment is successful, but the trustee is still disciplined because he never made an exact accounting of the stock purchased with trust money.

COMMISSION   a fee paid to an employee or agent for services performed—especially, a percentage of a total amount received in a transaction—as distinguished from salary, which is a fixed amount payable periodically.

COMMISSION, MILITARY   see **military law [MILITARY COMMISSION].**

COMMITMENT   1. a judge's order directing that a person be taken to prison or jail, either to await trial or following an imposition of sentence; 2. an order mandating a person to confinement in a medical institution.

COMMITTEE   1. in legislative practice, a group appointed to investigate some special matter or area of interest and report its findings and recommendations to the legislative body; 2. a person appointed by the court to manage the affairs of a legally **incompetent** person. See **guardian; ward.**

COMMODITY [COMMODITIES]   any tangible **good;** a product that is the subject of **sale** or barter. See also **futures.**

COMMODITY   FUTURES   TRADING   COMMISSION [CFTC]   the federal agency that regulates commodity futures and option markets in the United States. The CFTC's mission is to

101

protect market users and the public from fraud, manipulation, and abusive practices related to the sale of commodity and financial futures and options, and to foster open, competitive, and financially sound futures and options markets. The **Securities and Exchange Commission** fulfills a similar function in the securities markets.

COMMON AREA   in landlord-tenant law, portions of premises used in common by all tenants. A large number of cases have imposed **liability** on the **landlord** on the basis of "retained control" with injuries sustained when the landlord has failed to maintain common areas in reasonably safe condition. Implicit in these decisions is the notion that since no individual **tenant** controls the common area, control remains with the landlord. Common areas to which the landlord's obligation has been extended include stairways, porches, hallways and entrance areas, elevators, yards, and basements.

COMMON CARRIER   see **carrier [COMMON CARRIER]**.

COMMON LAW   the system of **jurisprudence,** which originated in England and was later applied in the United States, that is based on judicial **precedent** (court decisions or case law) rather than legislative enactment (statutes) and is therefore derived from principles rather than rules.

In the absence of **statutory law** regarding a particular subject, the judge-made rules of **common law** are the law on that subject. Thus the traditional phrase "at common law" refers to the state of the law in a particular field prior to the enactment of legislation in that field.

COMMON LAW COPYRIGHT   see **copyright [COMMON LAW COPYRIGHT]**.

COMMON LAW MARRIAGE   one based not upon ceremony and compliance with legal formalities, but upon the agreement of two persons, legally competent to marry, to **cohabit** with the intention of being husband and wife, usually for a minimum period of seven years.

COMMON LAW TRUST   see **Massachusetts trust.**

COMMON NUISANCE   see **nuisance [PUBLIC [COMMON] NUISANCE]**.

COMMON PROPERTY   see **community property; property.**

COMMONS   1. land set aside for public use, for example, public parks; 2. the untitled class of Great Britain, represented in Parliament by the House of Commons.

COMMON STOCK   a security representing an ownership interest in a corporation. Ownership may also be shared with **preferred stock,** which has prior claim on any **dividends** to be paid and, in the event of liquidation, prior claim to the distribution of the corporation's **assets.** As owners of the corporation, common stockholders (**shareholders**) assume the primary risk if business is poor, realize the greater return in the event of success and elect the **board of directors** that controls the company.

COMMONWEALTH   the public; the people; a government which concerns itself with the rights of the people rather than the rulers. From "common weal," a term for the public good. Four of the 50 states (Kentucky, Massachusetts, Pennsylvania, and Virginia) use "Commonwealth of" rather than "State of."

COMMUNITY NOTIFICATION   see **registration of offenders** [COMMUNITY NOTIFICATION].

COMMUNITY PROPERTY   all property that a husband and wife acquire by joint effort during marriage. Property owned prior to marriage or acquired by gift or inheritance is considered SEPARATE PROPERTY.

EXAMPLE: As a result of hard work and prudent investing, Anji has acquired a great deal of property during her marriage. If the marriage fails, her spouse is entitled to one-half of whatever property she has acquired in her work if the couple reside in a state that follows *community property* law. That law applies regardless of the fact that Anji's efforts alone resulted in accumulation of the property.

Currently, nine states have adopted the community property doctrine. Other states have instead adopted EQUITABLE DISTRIBUTION statutes to achieve a similar distribution of the marital estate upon dissolution of a marriage.

Community property is similar to, but should be distinguished from, TENANCY BY THE ENTIRETY and JOINT TENANCY (see **tenancy**).

COMMUTATION   change; in criminal law, substituting a lesser punishment for a greater one, such as life imprisonment for a death sentence, a shorter term for a longer one. Commutation is the prerogative of the chief executive (president or governor), who possess the power of **executive clemency.** A commutation can be granted only after a conviction, whereas other forms of clemency, such as a **pardon,** can be granted at any time. Also, a commutation merely lessens punishment, while a pardon removes all legal disabilities of a conviction. Compare **reprieve.**

EXAMPLE: Several years ago, eight persons were sentenced to fifteen years' imprisonment for possession of a small quantity of marijuana. In light of the new attitude towards personal use of the drug and the recent decriminalization of many marijuana laws, the governor *commuted* (reduced) the prisoners' sentences to time already served, allowing the prisoners to be released immediately.

COMPACT CLAUSE Art. I, Sec. 10, Cl. 3 of the **Constitution** providing "No State shall, without the Consent of Congress . . . enter into any Agreement or Compact with another State, or with a foreign Power. . . ." **INTERSTATE COMPACTS** that have been congressionally approved include those relating to boundaries and ports, conservation and flood control, and educational and correctional interests.

COMPANY a group of people organized to perform an activity, business or industrial enterprise.

HOLDING COMPANY see **holding company.**

JOINT STOCK COMPANY a company or association, usually unincorporated, that has the capital of its members pooled in a common fund; the **CAPITAL STOCK** (see **capital**) is divided into **shares** and distributed to represent ownership **interest** in the company. A form of partnership, it is distinguished from a partnership in that the membership of a joint stock company is changeable, its shares are transferable, its members can be many and not necessarily known to each other, and its members cannot act or speak for the company.

COMPARATIVE NEGLIGENCE see **negligence.**

COMPELLING INTEREST see **equal protection of the laws.**

COMPENSATION payment for work done or for an injury.

COMPENSATORY DAMAGES see **damages [ACTUAL DAMAGES].**

COMPETENT properly or legally qualified; able; capable of understanding or of acting reasonably. **COMPETENT EVIDENCE** is both relevant and proper to the issue being **litigated.** A **COMPETENT COURT** has proper jurisdiction over the person or property at issue. A criminal defendant is competent to stand trial if he or she is able to consult with his or her lawyer with a reasonable degree of rational understanding and has a rational as well as a factual understanding of the **proceedings** against him or her. An individual is competent to make a **will** if he or she understands the extent of his or her **property,** the identity of the natural objects of his or her bounty, and the consequences of making a will.

EXAMPLE: Upon their father's death, his children learned that his will left all his property to his mistress. The children brought a lawsuit to invalidate the will, claiming the father was not *competent* to understand what he was signing or to whom he was leaving his property. The children's evidence included examples of frequent outbursts of rage and depression by the father, as well as occasional stays at a nearby mental health facility.

COMPLAINANT the party who initiates the **complaint** in an **action** or **proceeding;** practically synonymous with **petitioner** and **plaintiff.** The appropriate term to use is determined by the nature of the proceeding and the court in which it is instituted. Compare **accused; defendant; respondent.**

COMPLAINT 1. in a civil action, the first **pleading** of the **plaintiff** setting out the facts on which the claim is based; the purpose is to give notice to the adversary of the nature and basis of the claim asserted; 2. in criminal law, the preliminary **charge** or accusation made by one person against another to the appropriate court or officer, usually a magistrate. However, court proceedings, such as a trial, cannot be instituted until an **indictment** or **information** has been handed down against the defendant.

COMPOS MENTIS *(kŏm'-pōs měn'-tĭs)* Lat.: mentally competent. Compare **non compos mentis.**

COMPOUND CONCLUSION see **question of law [COMPOUND CONCLUSION].**

COMPOUNDING A FELONY the refusal by one injured by a **felony** to **prosecute** the felon, in exchange for which the injured party receives a bribe or reparation.

COMPOUND INTEREST see **interest [COMPOUND INTEREST].**

COMPROMISE VERDICT see **verdict [COMPROMISE VERDICT].**

COMPULSORY APPEARANCE see **appearance [COMPULSORY APPEARANCE].**

COMPULSORY ARBITRATION see **arbitration [COMPULSORY ARBITRATION].**

COMPULSORY COUNTERCLAIM see **counterclaim [COMPULSORY COUNTERCLAIM].**

COMPULSORY JOINDER see **joinder [COMPULSORY JOINDER].**

COMPULSORY LABOR see **involuntary servitude.**

COMPULSORY PROCESS the right of a **defendant** to have the **subpoena** power of the court used on his or her behalf to compel the **appearance** of **witnesses.** In civil actions, the right to compulsory process is often secured through state constitutional or statutory provisions. In a criminal proceeding, this right is guaranteed to the defendant by the **Sixth Amendment** to the United States Constitution. The right extends only to competent, **material** witnesses who are subject to the court's process and whose expected testimony will be **admissible.**

COMPURAGATOR in early English law, one of a group of neighbors called by a person accused of a crime to swear that the accused was testifying truthfully. See **wager of law.**

COMPUTER CRIME illegal activity that either uses a computer to commit the offense (such as **cyberstalking, identity theft, theft, fraud,** or child **sexual exploitation)** or attacks another computer system by way of **hacking** or the unleashing of a program **virus.**

CONCEALMENT an act making more difficult the discovery of that which one is legally obligated to reveal or not to withhold, such as the failure of a **bankrupt** to schedule all his or her **assets,** or the failure of an applicant for an insurance policy to disclose information relevant to the insurer's decision to insure the risk.

ACTIVE CONCEALMENT concealing by words or deeds that which one has a duty to reveal.

PASSIVE CONCEALMENT maintaining silence when a duty to speak exists.

CONCERTED ACTION [CONCERT OF ACTION] 1. action that has been arranged and agreed upon between parties, in pursuit of some common design or in accordance with some scheme. In criminal law, concerted action is found only where there has been a conspiracy to commit an illegal act—that is, all share the criminal intent of the actual perpetrator. 2. The term also applies to joint tortfeasors where there is tort liability for conspiracy.

CONCILIATION amicable agreement between parties that resolves a dispute. Usually arrived at with the assistance of a CON-CILIATOR (similar to a **mediator)** but it is the parties themselves who resolve the dispute. Compare **arbitration** where an **arbitrator** renders a decision that binds the parties.

CONCILIATOR see **conciliation [**CONCILIATOR**].**

CONCLUSION OF FACT a conclusion as to a factual matter,

reached solely through the use of facts and natural reasoning, rather than rules of law. See **finding [FINDING OF FACT].**

EXAMPLE: The legal issue before the judge is simple; if the manufacturer does not provide necessary safeguards, the manufacturer is liable for the workman's injury. The only issue is a question of fact: Did the manufacturer provide the safeguards which the workman subsequently disregarded or were the safeguards never provided? After hearing the evidence, the judge ruled as a *conclusion of fact* that the safeguards were in place but had been disregarded by the workman.

CONCLUSION OF LAW a conclusion as to a legal issue, reached by applying the rules of law. See **finding [FINDING OF LAW].**

EXAMPLE: In a particular case, the facts were not in question; but the defense counsel never called a witness who might have been crucial to the defendant's case. A few years later, when the defendant attempts to have the conviction reversed, the legal issue concerns the standard to be used when a lawyer's incompetency results in a conviction. As a *conclusion of law,* the judge finds that, in his particular state, the law requires a stronger showing of incompetence than the one made in this case and therefore refuses to reverse the conviction.

CONCLUSIVE EVIDENCE evidence that is incontrovertible; not open or not able to be questioned. Where a thing is conclusively proved, it means that such result follows from the facts shown as the only possibility. The term contemplates the degree of **proof,** and its meaning in a particular statute depends largely on its context and the intention of the legislature.

CONCLUSIVE PRESUMPTION see **presumption.**

CONCUR to agree. A concurring opinion agrees with the conclusion of the majority but may state different reasons why such a conclusion is reached.

CONCURRENT existing together; in conjunction with. In criminal law, **CONCURRENT SENTENCE** describes multiple sentences that a convicted defendant is to serve at the same time.

CONCURRENT CONDITION see **condition [CONCURRENT CONDITION].**

CONCURRENT COVENANTS see **covenant [CONCURRENT COVENANTS].**

CONCURRENT JURISDICTION see **jurisdiction [CONCURRENT JURISDICTION].**

CONCURRENT NEGLIGENCE   see **negligence** [CONCURRENT NEGLIGENCE].

CONCURRENT SENTENCES   see **sentence** [CONCURRENT SENTENCES].

CONCURRING OPINION   see **opinion** [CONCURRING OPINION].

CONDEMN   1. to take private property for public use, such as the building of a highway, with or without consent but for **just compensation;** to declare legally useless or unfit for habitation, as an unsafe building. 2. to sentence to death a person convicted of a **capital offense.**

CONDITION   1. a prerequisite or requirement; 2. a possible future event, which will trigger the duty to perform a legal obligation or will cause a **real property** interest to arise, vest or be extinguished.

CONCURRENT CONDITION   a condition precedent that exists only when parties to a contract are obligated to perform at the same time.

CONDITION PRECEDENT   an act or event that must occur before a duty of immediate performance of a promise arises, or before a real property interest will arise or vest.

CONDITION SUBSEQUENT   a fact that will extinguish a duty to make compensation for BREACH OF CONTRACT after the breach has occurred, or whose occurrence will result in the extinguishment of an interest in real property.

CONDITIONAL   dependent upon the happening or non-happening of the **condition;** implies a type of **incumbrance.**

CONDITIONAL BEQUEST   see **bequest** [CONDITIONAL BEQUEST].

CONDITIONAL CONTRACT   see **contract** [CONDITIONAL CONTRACT].

CONDITIONAL DISCHARGE   see **sentence** [SUSPENDED SENTENCE].

CONDITIONAL FEE [ESTATE]   a limited **fee simple** that must eventually pass from the **donee** to certain **heirs** or to the **issue** (children) of the donee (**heirs of the body**). Should the designated heir fail to be alive at the time of the **donee's** death, the property **reverts** to the **donor** or the donor's **estate.** However, the entire estate remains with the donee until his or her death, the donor having the mere **possibility of a reverter.**

EXAMPLE: The mother gave Kim, her daughter, title to a home and instructed Kim to pass the home to Kim's daughter or, if she did not have a daughter, to Kim's son, upon Kim's death. This gift to Kim was a *conditional fee,* since if Kim died without a daughter or son, title to the home returned to the mother. If the mother predeceased Kim, the home would return to the mother's estate and pass under the mother's will.

CONDITIONAL SALE see **sale [CONDITIONAL SALE].**

CONDITION PRECEDENT see **condition [CONDITION PRECEDENT].**

CONDITION SUBSEQUENT see **condition [CONDITION SUBSEQUENT].**

CONDOMINIUM a type of ownership associated with multi-unit projects, which consists of individual ownership (in **fee**) of a single unit and shared ownership (**tenancy** in common) of the common areas (such as elevators, grounds, etc.). A condominium is distinguished from a **COOPERATIVE,** in which a corporate or business **trust** entity holds **title** to the **premises** and grants rights of occupancy to apartments through proprietary **leases** or similar arrangements.

CONFERENCE, PRETRIAL see **pretrial conference.**

CONFESSION an admission of guilt or other incriminating statement by the **accused;** not admissible at trial unless voluntarily made. See **Miranda Rule.** See **involuntary [INVOLUNTARY CONFESSION]; oral [ORAL CONFESSION].**

CONFESSION AND AVOIDANCE a **pleading** by which a **party** admits the **allegations** against him or her, either expressly or by implication, but presents **new matter** that **avoids** or annuls the effect of his or her admitting those allegations. See **defense [AFFIRMATIVE DEFENSE].**

CONFESSION OF JUDGMENT the entry of a **judgment** upon the written **admission** or **confession** of a **debtor,** without a legal **proceeding.** It is accomplished through an advance, voluntary submission to the **jurisdiction** of the court, as when a buyer of goods on **credit** agrees in the purchase **contract** that if he or she fails to pay on time the amounts due he or she will consent to the entry of a judgment against him or her for the amount outstanding (and, often, reasonable **attorney's fees** not exceeding a fixed percentage).

CONFIDENCE GAME a scheme by which a swindler wins the confidence of his or her victim and then cheats the victim of his or her money by taking advantage of the confidence reposed in him or her.

CONFIDENTIAL COMMUNICATION   see **privileged communication.**

CONFIRMATION   see **arbitrator [CONFIRMATION].**

CONFISCATE   1. with regard to acts by a government entity, to take private property without **just compensation;** 2. to seize goods or property and divest the owner of his proprietary rights, usually as a result of some violation of the law involving the goods or property seized. Compare **condemn.**

CONFLICT[S] OF INTEREST[S]   a situation in which regard for one duty results in disregard for another, as when one attorney seeks to represent two persons whose interests are adverse potentially or in fact; an inconsistency between the public interest and the personal interest of a public official which arises in connection with the performance of official duties.

CONFLICT OF LAW [CHOICE OF LAW]   the body of law that contains the rules by which the court in which an **action** is brought chooses between the applicable law of the court's state (the "forum state") and the differing applicable law of another **jurisdiction** connected with the controversy.

EXAMPLE: Mary died intestate (i.e., without a will). At her death, she lived and owned property in Florida but had set up a trust in Delaware for her children and grandchildren. Florida claims that, because Mary was a resident of Florida, that state's intestate laws should apply to all of Mary's property. Delaware feels that its intestate laws should apply to the trust accounts since she purposefully set up the account in Delaware. A court will consider the rules concerning *conflict of laws* to determine which state's law applies to the trust.

CONFORMED COPY   an exact copy of a document, often certified to be so by a **clerk** of a **court,** with handwritten notations duplicating those on the original document. Thus, an order may have the date, precise terms, and signature of the judge (s/Judge) written by hand on another copy of a proposed order that had not been signed. This then becomes a conformed copy of the order that was completed and signed by the court.

EXAMPLE: Court Clerk Bailey conforms a copy of Judge Davis' order by writing "s/Judge Davis" on the copy.

CONFORMING   **goods** or conduct including any part of a performance are "conforming" or conform to the **contract** when they are in accordance with the obligations under the contract.

CONFORMING USE   see **nonconforming use.**

CONFRONTATION CLAUSE   under the **Sixth Amendment** of the Constitution, the accused in a criminal prosecution is entitled "to be confronted with the witnesses against him." This right entitles the accused to be present at the trial, and to hear and cross-examine all witnesses against him or her. Evidence that is not subject to confrontation, such as the confession of a codefendant who is not subject to cross-examination, may not be used against the accused.

CONFUSION OF GOODS   a mixing together of **personal property** belonging to two or more owners so the property of any of them no longer can be identified except as part of a mass of like goods.

CONGLOMERATE   a group of **corporations** engaged in unrelated businesses and controlled by a single corporate entity. See **merger** [CONGLOMERATE MERGER].

CONGRESS   1. a formal body of delegates or representatives; 2. in the United States, the national legislative body consisting of the Senate and the House of Representatives. The lawmaking power of the United States vests in this body.

CONGRESSIONAL REFERENCE CASES   see **Federal Claims Court.**

CONJECTURE   a tenuous inference based upon facts within a person's knowledge. A witness may only testify as to facts within his or her knowledge and may not present conjecture to the jury. A jury cannot render a verdict on the basis of conjecture, but must find its verdict based upon the evidence admitted in the trial of the matter.

CONJUGAL RIGHTS   the rights of married persons, which include companionship, domestic happiness, the comforts of dwelling together, joint property rights, and the intimacies of domestic relations. In prison, a CONJUGAL VISITATION permits an opportunity for sexual intimacy between the inmate and his or her spouse.

CONJUNCTIVE DENIAL   see **denial** [CONJUNCTIVE DENIAL]; **negative pregnant** [CONJUNCTIVE DENIAL].

CONNECTED PACS   see **political action committee** [CONNECTED PACS].

CONSANGUINITY   the familial relationship of persons united by one or more common ancestors. LINEAL CONSANGUINITY refers to persons who are descended in a direct line from a common ancestor such as grandparents, parents, children, grandchildren. COLLATERAL CONSANGUINITY refers to persons who are descended from a common ancestor but not in a direct line such as aunts and nephews, uncles and grandnieces. Degrees of collateral consanguinity are determined by counting generations up to the common ancestor, and then down to the related party. Degrees of consanguinity sometimes control **inheritance.** See **descent and distribution; heirs; lineal.**

CONSCIENCE OF THE COURT   refers to the power of the **court of equity** to resolve a controversy by applying common standards of decency and fairness. The term does not refer to the private opinion of a particular judge but to uniformly held judgment of the community. The proper application of the doctrine rests upon general principles of equitable law and to established precedent. Conduct that shocks the conscience of the court will lead to the invalidation in part or in whole of an **unconscionable contract,** or to the **suppression** of evidence as violative of **due process of law.**

CONSCIENTIOUS OBJECTOR   a status recognized by U.S. Selective Service ("draft") laws and accorded to one who, in good conscience, because of religious belief, is opposed to war. Such a person may be excused from participation in military service otherwise required by law and may be permitted to substitute community service.

CONSCIOUS PARALLELISM   in **antitrust law,** an independent decision by one party, aware that a particular course of conduct has been followed by a competitor, to follow the same course; distinguished from **conspiracy,** which requires an agreement, either implied or express, between the parties engaged in the parallel conduct.

EXAMPLE: Shopper Supermarkets decides to end its three-month promotion of offering double coupons. Because of Shopper's action, other area supermarkets end similar promotions. When complaints arise against the supermarkets for acting together to raise prices by ending the discounts, in violation of antitrust laws, the supermarkets reply that their action was not unlawful but represented *conscious parallelism*—when Shopper ended the discounts, the other supermarkets felt they could do the same without losing business but they did not act together in an anticompetitive and illegal way.

CONSECUTIVE SENTENCE see **sentence** [CONSECUTIVE [CUMULATIVE] SENTENCE].

CONSENT   voluntary agreement; an act of reason, not based on fraud, duress or mistake. Consent is implied in every agreement.

CONSENT DECREE see **consent judgment** [CONSENT DECREE]; **decree.**

CONSENT, INFORMED   see **informed consent.**

CONSENT JUDGMENT   recorded agreement of parties to a lawsuit concerning the form the **judgment** should take. Such a contract cannot be nullified without consent of the parties, except for **fraud** or **mistake.** Consent judgments have the same force as any other judgment. Because the agreement of the parties waives exception to irregularities before agreement, **appeal** from a consent judgment is limited to attack for mistake, fraud or lack of **jurisdiction.**

CONSENT DECREE   the counterpart of a consent judgment issued in a **court of equity;** only as binding as any other **equitable** remedy. For instance, in antitrust cases, the court can modify a consent decree according to changed circumstances.

CONSENT ORDER   any court **order** to which the opposing party agrees; in **antitrust law,** an agreement between the **Federal Trade Commission** and a party being investigated; the party consents to cease activities that could be subject of antitrust action and the FTC refrains from initiating suit.

CONSENT ORDER   see **consent judgment [CONSENT ORDER].**

CONSENT SEARCH   a search made by an authorized person after the subject of the search has voluntarily consented. The constitutional immunity from unreasonable searches and seizures may be waived by consent to a search or seizure. Once an individual has consented to a search he or she cannot later **challenge** the **search.** In order to constitute a lawful waiver the consent must be given intelligently and voluntarily.

CONSEQUENTIAL DAMAGES   see **damages [CONSEQUENTIAL [SPECIAL] DAMAGES].**

CONSERVATOR   temporary court-appointed **guardian** or custodian of **property.**

CONSIDERATION   something of value given in return for performance or promise of performance for the purpose of forming a **contract;** generally required to make a promise binding and to make agreement of the parties enforceable as a contract. Consideration distinguishes a contract from a **gift.**

FAILURE OF CONSIDERATION or WANT OF CONSIDERATION refers to the circumstance in which consideration was bargained for but either has become worthless, has ceased to exist or has not been provided as promised.

EXAMPLE: Although Paula ran a prosperous business on the West Coast and was enjoying life as a "single," she agreed to return East to care for her aging mother. As a demonstration of her gratitude, the mother promised Paula the money located in a bank account. Nothing was ever signed, and upon the mother's death, the other children contested Paula's claim to the whole account. They felt that there was no contract between the mother and Paula because Paula gave no *consideration* in return for the money in the account. A court would probably find that Paula's care for the mother at the mother's request, as well as the giving up of a prosperous business, constituted consideration and hence the promise is enforceable.

CONSIDERED DICTUM   see **dictum [CONSIDERED DICTUM].**

CONSIGNMENT   **bailment** for care or sale. A delivery of goods, without **sale,** to a dealer, who must sell the goods and remit the price to the person making delivery; or if the goods are not sold, the dealer must return them to the owner.

CONSIGNEE   1. a person to whom goods are shipped for sale under a consignment contract; 2. the person named in a **bill of lading** to whom the bill promises delivery; 3. one to whom a carrier may lawfully make delivery in accordance with his or her contract of carriage. See **carrier [COMMON CARRIER].**

CONSIGNOR   one who sends a consignment; a shipper of goods; the person calling upon a common carrier for transportation service, who is not necessarily the person in whose name a bill of lading is made.

CONSOLIDATE   combine; unite; bring together, as with two or more loans.

CONSOLIDATED APPEAL   if two or more persons are entitled to **appeal** from a **judgment** or order of a district court, and their interests are such as to make **joinder** practicable, they may file a joint notice of appeal, or may join in appeal after filing separate notices of appeal, and they may thereafter proceed on appeal as a single appellant. Appeals may be consolidated by order of the court of appeals upon its own motion or upon motion of a party, or by stipulation of the parties of the several appeals.

CONSOLIDATED OMNIBUS BUDGET RECONCILIATION ACT   see **affordable care act [COBRA].**

CONSOLIDATION   see **merger.**

CONSORTIUM   the conjugal fellowship of husband and wife, and the right of each to the aid of the other in every conjugal relation. A person willfully interfering with this relation, depriving one spouse of the consortium of the other, is liable in **damages** and may give rise to action for **alienation of affection.** Loss of consortium can figure in action for injury or **wrongful death** of a spouse. See **conjugal rights.**

CONSPIRACY   a combination of two or more persons to commit an unlawful act, or to commit a lawful act by unlawful means. A conspiracy to injure another is an actionable **tort;** it may also be a criminal offense. Compare **accomplice.**

CONSPIRATOR [COCONSPIRATOR]   one involved in a **conspiracy;** one who acts with another, or others, in furtherance of an unlawful transaction. See **accessory.** Compare **principal.**

CONSTITUTION   the fundamental principles of **law** by which a government is created and a country is administered. In Western democratic theory, a **mandate** from the people in their **sovereign** capacity, concerning how they shall be governed. Distinguished from a **statute,** which is a rule decided by legislative representatives and is subject to limitations of the Constitution.

CONSTITUTIONAL RIGHT[S]   individual liberties granted by the State or Federal **Constitutions** and protected from governmental interference.

CONSTRUCTION   an interpretation of something not totally clear. To determine construction of a **statute** or **constitution** is to decide the meaning of an ambiguous part of it.

LIBERAL [EQUITABLE] CONSTRUCTION   a liberal construction expands the meaning of a statute or provision to give broad effect to its purposes so as to encompass circumstances clearly within the spirit if not the letter of the statute. Statutes which are intended to be remedial in purpose are generally accorded a liberal construction so as to meet the evils which the statute was intended to remedy.

STRICT [LITERAL] CONSTRUCTION   a conservative or literal interpretation of statutes, stressing rigid adherence to terms specified.

CONSTRUCTIVE   not actual, but accepted in law as a substitute for whatever is otherwise required. Thus, anything the law finds to exist constructively will be treated by the law as though it were actually so.

CONSTRUCTIVE BAILMENT   see **bailment [**CONSTRUCTIVE BAILMENT**].**

CONSTRUCTIVE BREACH   see **breach [**CONSTRUCTIVE BREACH**].**

CONSTRUCTIVE CONTEMPT   see **contempt of court [**CONSTRUCTIVE CONTEMPT**].**

CONSTRUCTIVE DELIVERY   see **delivery** [CONSTRUCTIVE DELIVERY].

CONSTRUCTIVE EVICTION   see **eviction** [CONSTRUCTIVE EVICTION].

CONSTRUCTIVE FRAUD   see **fraud** [CONSTRUCTIVE [LEGAL] FRAUD].

CONSTRUCTIVE NOTICE   see **notice** [CONSTRUCTIVE NOTICE].

CONSTRUCTIVE POSSESSION   see **possession** [CONSTRUCTIVE POSSESSION].

CONSTRUCTIVE RECEIPT OF INCOME   see **income** [CONSTRUCTIVE RECEIPT OF INCOME].

CONSTRUCTIVE SERVICE   see **service (of process)** [SERVICE BY PUBLICATION].

CONSTRUCTIVE TRUST   see **trust** [CONSTRUCTIVE [INVOLUNTARY] TRUST].

CONSTRUE   to interpret a statute, case, regulation, treaty, or other legal authority.

CONSUMER   in economics, an individual who buys goods and services for personal use rather than for manufacture. It has been said that the consumer is the last person to whom property passes in the course of ownership and that this is the test of a retail transaction.

CONSUMER GOODS   goods that are used or bought for use primarily for personal, family, or household purposes. "Consumer goods" is one of four categories of goods distinguished by the Uniform Commercial Code. The classifications are important for such purposes as determining the rights of persons who buy goods subject to a security interest, rights after a default, and rights among those with conflicting security interests in the same collateral. Thus, consumer goods are to be distinguished from EQUIPMENT, which are goods used or bought for use primarily in business; from FARM PRODUCTS, which are goods in the possession of one engaged in a farming operation if they are crops or livestock or supplies used or produced in farming operations or if they are products of crops or livestock in their unmanufactured states and from INVENTORY, which are goods held for sale. The classification of goods is determined by its primary use.

CONSUMER PROTECTION   refers to laws designed to aid retail consumers of goods and services that have been improperly manufactured, delivered, performed, handled, or described. Such laws provide the retail consumer with additional protections and remedies not generally provided to merchants and others who engage in business transactions, on the premise that consumers do not enjoy an **"arm's-length"** bargaining position with respect to the businesspeople with whom they deal and therefore should not be strictly limited by the legal rules that govern **recovery** for **damages** among businesspeople.

EXAMPLE: Harry contracted with a company to put aluminum siding on his house. The company transfers the contract to a finance agency and receives the amount Harry had agreed to pay the company, less a small discount so that the finance agency can make a profit on the transfer. Under basic commercial law, if the company does not perform the work satisfactorily, Harry will still have to pay the finance agency, because that area of law protects the agency [as a **holder in due course**] from claims against the company once the agency assumes the contract. But under some states' *consumer protection* laws, the finance agency must take responsibility for the company's work.

CONTACTS APPROACH   see **conflict of laws.**

CONTACT, SEXUAL   see **rape [SEXUAL CONTACT].**

CONTEMPLATION OF DEATH   see **causa [CAUSA MORTIS].**

CONTEMPT OF COURT   an act or omission tending to interfere with orderly administration of justice, or to impair the dignity of the court or respect for its authority. **DIRECT CONTEMPT** takes place openly and in the presence of the court. **CONSTRUCTIVE CONTEMPT** occurs outside the court; an example is failure to comply with court orders.

CIVIL CONTEMPT consists of failure to do something ordered by the court for the benefit of another party to the proceedings (sometimes called **RELIEF TO LITIGANTS**); **CRIMINAL CONTEMPT** includes acts disrespectful of the court or its processes that obstruct administration of justice.

EXAMPLE: A judge orders a litigant to disclose several important documents to his adversary. The litigant refuses because he feels that the documents will give away trade secrets. The court has certain formulas and designs deleted, and orders that the documents be relinquished. If the litigant still refuses, he can be held in *contempt of court,* resulting in a jail sentence and/or a fine. The nature of the sanction is within the trial judge's discretion. As a general legal proposition, an order of a court must be obeyed or appealed. It may not be disregarded.

CONTIGUOUS adjacent, connected.

CONTINGENT BENEFICIARY one who will receive the benefit or proceeds of an **estate, trust,** life insurance policy or the like but only if some particular event or circumstance, whose happening or outcome is not presently known or assured, does in fact occur.

EXAMPLE: A husband establishes a trust to take effect at his death and names his wife as beneficiary. The trust instrument also provides that if the wife should remarry, the husband's son and daughter become the beneficiaries and the wife is no longer eligible to take under the trust. Since there is no assurance that the wife will ever remarry, the son and daughter are considered *contingent beneficiaries*.

CONTINGENT ESTATE [INTEREST] an **interest** or **estate** in land that might or might not begin in the future, depending upon occurrence of a specific but uncertain event or depending on the determination or existence of the person[s] to whom the estate is limited. Compare **conditional fee; future interest.**

EXAMPLE: The brother grants land to Janet until she dies and then provides that the land go to Xavier's children. Xavier has no children at this time, so the grant of the land to them following Janet's death is a *contingent estate*. If Xavier has no children when Janet dies, the title to the land reverts back to the brother (who first granted it).

CONTINGENT FEE a charge made by an attorney for services rendered to his or her client, recovery of which depends upon a successful outcome of the case. The amount is often agreed to be a percentage of the client's recovery. Such fee arrangements are often used in **negligence** cases, but it is unethical for an attorney to charge a criminal defendant a fee contingent upon the result. See **attorney's fee.**

CONTINGENT LIABILITY a liability that will not accrue unless facts or circumstances that are not certain to occur do in fact occur at some future time. For instance, in a contract to sell a business, the seller will incur a contingent liability if he or she agrees to refund some or all of the purchase price in the event that the purchaser is sued for the seller's negligent acts in operating the business.

CONTINUANCE the adjournment or postponement, to a specified subsequent date, of an **action** pending in a court.

CONTRA *(kôn'-tră)* Lat.: against. In opposition to; in violation of; the reverse of.

CONTRABAND any property, the possession or transportation of which is illegal. For instance, narcotic drugs, firearms, counterfeit money, or untaxed cigarettes that an individual intends to illegally distribute or use are contraband.

CONTRA BONOS MORES *(kôn'-trà bō'-nōs mô'-rāz)* Lat.: against good morals. Refers to conduct that offends the average conscience and commonly accepted standards.

CONTRACT a promise, for the **breach** of which the law provides a **remedy,** or the **performance** of which the law recognizes as a **duty;** a transaction involving two or more individuals whereby each has reciprocal rights to demand performance of what is promised.

ADHESION CONTRACT see **adhesion contract.**

ALEATORY CONTRACT see **aleatory [ALEATORY CONTRACT].**

BILATERAL CONTRACT one in which there are mutual promises between two parties, each being both a promisor and a promisee.

CONDITIONAL CONTRACT a contract whose performance depends upon a future event; e.g., a contract to purchase a car if it passes a motor vehicle inspection.

EXAMPLE: Glen wants to purchase a large tract of land from seller to build a manufacturing plant but is unsure whether he can get a loan from the bank to finance the construction costs. Therefore, he signs a *conditional contract* with the seller that he will purchase the land only if he obtains a construction loan from the bank.

CONTRACT OF ADHESION see **adhesion contract.**

CONTRACT OF HAZARD see **sale [SALE IN GROSS].**

CONTRACT UNDER SEAL see SPECIAL CONTRACT (below). See also **sealed instrument; specialty.**

COST-PLUS CONTRACT one providing that the contractor receives payment of his or her total costs, plus a stated percentage or profit.

FORMAL CONTRACT see **sealed instrument.**

FREEDOM OF CONTRACT see **freedom of contract.**

IMPLIED CONTRACT see QUASI [IMPLIED] CONTRACT (below).

INSTALLMENT CONTRACT see **installment contract.**

OPTION CONTRACT see **option contract.**

ORAL CONTRACT one that is not in writing or that is not signed by the parties.

OUTPUT CONTRACT one whereby a party promises to deliver his

or her entire output to another and the other promises to accept the entire output supplied.

QUASI CONTRACT see **quasi [QUASI CONTRACT].**

REQUIREMENTS CONTRACT one whereby a party agrees to purchase all his or her requirements of a particular product from another, and the other agrees to supply the need.

SEVERABLE CONTRACT see **severable contract.**

SIMPLE CONTRACT see **sealed instrument [SIMPLE CONTRACT].**

SPECIAL CONTRACT a contract under seal; a **specialty.** See **sealed instrument.** See also **adhesion contract; breach (of contract); privity [PRIVITY OF CONTRACT]; retail installment contract; tender; usurious contract; yellow dog contract.**

UNILATERAL CONTRACT agreement whereby one makes a promise to do, or refrain from doing, something in return for an actual performance by the other, rather than a mere promise of performance.

CONTRACT OF ADHESION see **adhesion contract.**

CONTRACT OF HAZARD see **sale [SALE IN GROSS].**

CONTRACTOR 1. a party to a **contract;** 2. one who contracts to do work for another. An **INDEPENDENT CONTRACTOR** makes an agreement to do a specific piece of work, retaining control of the means and method of doing the job; neither party has the right to terminate the contract at will. A **GENERAL BUILDING CONTRACTOR** contracts directly with the owner of the property upon which the construction occurs, as distinguished from a **SUBCONTRACTOR,** who would deal only with one of the general contractors.

CONTRACTUAL BREACH see **breach (of contract).**

CONTRACT UNDER SEAL see **sealed instrument.**

CONTRA PACEM *(kŏn'-trà pä'-kĕm)* Lat.: against the peace. Used in Latin forms of **indictments,** and also in **actions** for **trespass,** to signify that the alleged offense was committed against the public peace.

CONTRIBUTION 1. sharing, by another person jointly responsible for injury to a third person, of the amount required to compensate the victim. One who is partly responsible for an injury is often entitled to demand contribution from another who is also responsible. The duty generally involves equal sharing of the penalty, but in some **jurisdictions** it may be apportioned among the **joint tortfeasors** according to degree of fault. Compare **indemnity;** 2. In tax law, a tax deductible contribution is a **DONATION.**

CHARITABLE CONTRIBUTION a contribution for the use of a state, the United States, or a **NOT-FOR-PROFIT CORPORATION** (see **corporation**) organized exclusively for religious, charitable, scientific, literary, or educational purposes.

CONTRIBUTORY NEGLIGENCE see **negligence** [**CONTRIBUTORY NEGLIGENCE**].

CONTROLLED CORPORATION see **corporation** [**CONTROLLED CORPORATION**].

CONTROLLED SUBSTANCE a drug whose general availability is restricted; any substance that is strictly regulated or outlawed because of its potential for abuse or addiction. Controlled substances include narcotics, stimulants, depressants, hallucinogens, and cannabis.

CONTROVERSY a dispute. In constitutional law, in order to constitute a "case or controversy" sufficient to permit an **adjudication** by the court, a controversy must be real, not one inquiring what the law would be in a hypothetical situation. See **standing.** Compare **advisory opinion.** See also **justiciable; separable controversy.**

CONTUMACY willful disobedience to the **summons** or orders of a court; overt defiance of authority. Contumacious conduct may result in a finding of **contempt of court.**

CONVERSATION, CRIMINAL see **alienation of affections.**

CONVERSION a **tort** consisting of deprivation of another's property without authorization and without **justification.**

EXAMPLE: Ralph steals a check made payable to Overland Corporation and cashes it at his bank. Ralph is guilty of theft, which by definition includes *conversion*. But, in most instances, the bank is also guilty of conversion. It has contributed to the unauthorized taking of the check by giving Ralph cash even though the check was not made out to him. Absent complicity in the theft, the bank is not criminally liable, unlike Ralph. The bank is, however, monetarily liable to Overland Corporation.

CONVERTIBLE SECURITIES **bonds** and **preferred stock** that can be exchanged for **common stock** or other lesser security usually of the same **corporation.** Terms of the exchange specify the exchange ratio and expiration of the right to exchange.

CONVEY in **real property** law, to transfer property from one to another, by means of a written **instrument** and other formalities. Compare **alienation.** See also **grant.**

CONVEYANCE see **convey.**

CONVICT 1. one who has been determined by the court to be guilty of the crime charged; 2. to determine such guilt.

CONVICTION the result of a legal **proceeding** in which the guilt of a **party** is ascertained and upon which **sentence** or **judgment** is founded. The **confession** of an **accused** in open court or a **verdict** that ascertains and publishes the fact of guilt are both sufficient to constitute a conviction. See **guilty.**

COOPERATIVE [CO-OP] see **condominium [COOPERATIVE].**

COOPERATIVE ASSOCIATION a union of individuals, commonly laborers, farmers, or small capitalists, formed for the pursuit in common of a productive enterprise, the profits being shared in proportion to the capital or labor contributed by each.

COORDINATE JURISDICTION see **jurisdiction [CONCURRENT JURISDICTION].**

COPARCENARY at common law, the estate of two or more females inherited from a common ancestor in default of male heirs. The rights of coparceners were in the nature of a **joint tenancy** in that they could sue and be sued jointly in regards to the property, but were in the nature of a **tenancy in common** in that no right of survivorship existed.

COPARCENERS persons who, by virtue of **descent,** have become concurrent owners. See **parcener.**

EXAMPLE: Beth and Nathan were left a summer home by their father. As a result of that devise, the two are **coparceners.**

COPARTNER see **partner.**

COPY, CONFORMED see **conformed copy.**

COPYHOLD a medieval form of land tenure in England. A copyhold was a parcel of land granted to a peasant by a lord in return for agricultural services. The transaction was recorded on the rolls of the manor by the steward, who gave the tenant an authenticated copy of the recordation. Transfer of lands held by copyhold was achieved by surrender and admittance; that is, the copyholder surrendered his land to the baronial court and the steward admitted the person designated by the previous holder to the land by recording the transfer on the rolls and issuing a copy to the new tenant. Tenure was at the will of the lord, but in time the custom of the manor arising over many years gave the tenant a degree of security against arbitrary action by the lord. Thus, copyhold, though not originally entitling the holder to the absolute ownership character-istic of a freehold estate, came to represent a form of permanent tenure with rights of descent and alienability, while money rents or symbolic consideration were substituted for agricultural services. Copyhold was abolished in England in 1926.

Also used to refer generally to any form of land tenure other than a **freehold.**

COPYRIGHT   protection by **statute** or by the **common law,** giving authors and artists exclusive right to publish their works or to deter-mine who may so publish. When by statute, copyright is exclusively a matter of federal law.

COMMON-LAW COPYRIGHT   a protection that exists before a work is published or otherwise placed in the public domain; protects against unauthorized publication of the unpublished work; also called **RIGHT OF FIRST PUBLICATION.**

COPYRIGHT INFRINGEMENT   the offense of unauthorized use of a work protected by copyright. See **plagiarism.**

CORAM NOBIS, WRIT OF   see **writ of coram nobis.**

CORESPONDENT   see **adultery.** Another meaning is a co-respon-dent (a co-party who responds to an appeal or a petition.) Finally, compare the spelling and meanings of correspondent.

CORONER   a public official who investigates the causes and circum-stances of suspicious deaths that occur within his or her jurisdiction and makes a finding in a coroner's **inquest.** See also **post mortem.**

CORPORAL PUNISHMENT   punishment inflicted upon the body. The term may or may not include imprisonment; often serves simply to distinguish physical punishment from nonphysical pun-ishment, such as a fine.

CORPORATE OPPORTUNITY   the legal doctrine that **direc-tors** or others invested with a **fiduciary duty** toward a corporation may not appropriate for their own benefit a business opportunity properly belonging to the corporation. Persons found guilty of this practice are deemed to hold the property or profits thus obtained in **CONSTRUCTIVE TRUST** (see **trust**) for the benefit of the corporation, and **injunctive** relief as well as money damages may be available to the victimized shareholders. See **conflict of inter-ests; insider.**

CORPORATE POWER   see **power, corporate.**

CORPORATION   an association of **shareholders** (or a single shareholder) created under law as an **ARTIFICAL PERSON,** having a legal entity separate from the individuals who compose it, with the capacity of continuous existence or **succession,** and the capacity of taking, holding, and conveying **property,** suing and being sued, and exercising, like a **natural person,** other powers that are conferred on it by law. A corporation's **liability** is normally limited to its **assets;** the shareholders are thus protected against personal liability for the corporation. The corporation is taxed at special tax rates, and the stockholders must pay an additional tax upon **dividends** or other profits from the corporation. Corporations are subject to regulation by the state of incorporation and by the **jurisdictions** in which they carry on their business.

Special statutes have been enacted in many jurisdictions to permit single individuals or closely knit small groups of individuals to form **CLOSE CORPORATIONS** to limit their personal liability but to carry on business without the formality of annual meetings and action by boards of directors.

EXAMPLE: Yancey runs several clothing shops as a sole proprietor. After speaking with other businesspeople, he decides to form a *close corporation.* Under that arrangement, Yancey still controls the company, although there may be others, such as a wife and siblings, who hold a number of shares of stock in the corporation. He also enjoys the limited liability aspect of a corporation in that, if the corporation owes money, a creditor will be limited to the assets of the corporation.

A small corporation with limited earnings may elect to be taxed as an ordinary **partnership;** its stockholders thus enjoy limited personal liability and only individual (not also corporate) taxation. A corporation electing this federal income tax option is a **SUBCHAPTER S CORPORATION.**

ACQUIRED CORPORATION a corporation which has been the target of a successful acquisition attempt.

ACQUIRING CORPORATION the corporation seeking to acquire the target corporation.

AFFILIATED CORPORATION generally applied to any member of an affiliated group of corporations related through common ownership.

BROTHER-SISTER CORPORATION two or more corporations having a common parent corporation.

CONTROLLED CORPORATION a corporation which is deemed to be controlled by another entity or individual who satisfies certain control requirements relating to stock ownership. Control is usually established by voting rights; for some purposes, however, it can be defined by the relative fair market value of a shareholder's stock.

DE FACTO CORPORATION one existing in fact, but without actual authority of law.

EXAMPLE: Flange Brothers, a partnership, decides to incorporate. After filing what they believe are the necessary papers, the partnership changes it name to Flange Corporation and continues to carry on its business. Several years later, a creditor sues both the corporation and the partners who run it claiming that the partners are not protected from personal liability because they failed to file certain papers for incorporation and a corporation, therefore, was never legally formed. Unless the omission was intentional or under other rare circumstances, a court will generally find that the error was inadvertent, a *de facto corporation* was formed, and the persons running the corporation are protected from liability.

MEMBER CORPORATION see **member corporation.**

MUNICIPAL CORPORATION see **municipal corporation.**

NONSTOCK CORPORATION see **nonstock corporation.**

NOT-FOR-PROFIT CORPORATION one organized for some charitable, civil, social or other purpose that does not entail the generating of profit or the distribution of its income to members, principals, shareholders, officers or others affiliated with it. Such corporations are accorded special treatment under the law for some purposes, including federal income taxation.

PROFESSIONAL CORPORATION see **professional corporation.**

PRIVATE CORPORATION the common corporation, created by and for private individuals for nongovernmental purposes.

PUBLIC [POLITICAL] CORPORATIONS those created by the state to fulfill certain purposes, such as to form lesser governmental bodies (towns, cities), organize school districts, operate water districts.

QUASI CORPORATION a body that exercises certain functions of a corporate character, but that has not been established as a corporation by any statute.

S CORPORATION a small corporation which elects to be taxed as a partnership for federal income taxation purposes. Prior to 1982 these entities were called **SUBCHAPTER S CORPORATIONS**. The number of shareholders is limited; individual shareholders enjoy the benefits under state law of limited corporate liability but avoid corporate federal taxation.

SHELL CORPORATION a company that is **incorporated** but has few or no assets and no real business. Such corporations are formed for the purpose of going public and later acquiring existing businesses or obtaining financing. Also a term for a truly nonexistent corporation used for **tax evasion** purposes.

TARGET CORPORATION a corporation which is the subject of an acquisition attempt.

CORPOREAL having material reality; opposite of **INCORPOREAL**, intangible.

CORPOREAL HEREDITAMENT see **hereditaments.**

CORPUS *(kôr'-pŭs)* Lat.: body. The main substance of a thing.
1. The principal or **res** of an **estate, trust, devise** or **bequest** from which income is derived; can consist of funds, real estate or other tangible or intangible property.

EXAMPLE: Sean creates a trust naming his children as beneficiaries. An office building is stated to be the trust *corpus* in the trust instrument. The rents collected from the building's tenants constitute the income that is distributed to the children.

2. In **civil law,** corpus refers to a positive fact as distinguished from a possibility. See **corpus delicti.**

CORPUS DELICTI *(kôr'-pŭs dĕ-lĭk'-tī)* Lat.: body of the crime. The objective proof that a crime has been committed; sometimes refers to the body of the victim of a **homicide,** but the term has a broader meaning. For the state to introduce a **confession** or convict the **accused** it must prove a corpus delicti; i.e., the occurrence of specific injury or loss and a criminal act as the source of the loss. See **moral certainty.**

EXAMPLE: At his trial for murder, Qiang asks the court to dismiss his prosecution because no body was ever found. He does not prevail on that theory alone. Although there is no body, the state can still prove a *corpus delicti.* It is possible to prove a murder by showing that the person has not been seen for several years, that items of particular importance which had belonged to the person were found in Qiang's house, and that a knife with bloodstains matching the blood type of the person was found in Qiang's car. It should be observed that corpus delicti is not related exclusively to homicide. The corpus delicti of a robbery is the stolen money.

CORPUS JURIS *(kôr'-pŭs jūr'-is)* Lat.: body of law. A series of texts containing much of the **civil** and **canon [ecclesiastical]** law.

CORRECTIONAL INSTITUTION a general term used to describe a jail, prison, reformatory or other government-maintained detention facility.

CORRESPONDENT   1. a financial or other institution that has regular business relations with another distant but similar institution; 2. a person who engages in written communication with another; 3. consistent; similar; equivalent; fitting. Compare the spelling and meaning of **corespondent.**

CORROBORATING EVIDENCE   evidence complementary to evidence already given and tending to strengthen or confirm it; additional evidence of a different character on the same point.

CORRUPTION OF THE BLOOD   incapacity to **inherit** or pass **property,** usually because of **attainder,** such as for treason. A doctrine of feudal origin stated that the blood of the attained person was deemed to be corrupt, so that neither could he or she transmit his or her **estate** to **heirs,** nor could the heirs take by **descent** from their ancestors. This doctrine has been constitutionally abolished in the United States.

COSIGN   the act of affixing one's signature in addition to the principal signature of another in order to verify the authenticity of the principal signature.

COSIGNER   see **comakers [COSIGNER].**

COST DEPLETION   see **depletion [COST DEPLETION].**

COST, INSURANCE, AND FREIGHT   see **CIF**

COST OF COMPLETION   in a **breach of contract** situation, a measure of damages representing the total amount of additional expense, over and above the **contract** price, that the injured party would have to incur in order to obtain a substituted **performance** that would place that party in the same position he or she would have been in if the contract had not been breached. Often used as a measure of damages for breaches of construction contracts. Compare **diminution in value; expectation damages; specific performance.**

COST OF GOODS SOLD   see **income statement [COST OF GOODS SOLD]; inventory [COST OF GOODS SOLD].**

COST OF LIVING ADJUSTMENT   automatic adjustments to Social Security and Supplemental Security Income (SSI) benefits, as well as some pension plans, to maintain purchasing power that is not eroded by inflation. Adjustments are based on a complicated formula derived from the Consumer Price Index.

COST OF LIVING CLAUSE   in a long-term contract, a clause that adjusts the price paid for the goods or services received in an amount equal to the change in the cost of living. For instance, in a lease of commercial property, the contract often provides that the rent will be increased once a year in an amount equal to the rise in the consumer price index for the area, published by the Bureau of Labor Statistics.

COST-PLUS CONTRACT see **contract** [COST-PLUS CONTRACT].

COSTS   court expenses of the victorious **party** in a lawsuit and that may be reimbursed by the losing party as part of recovery. Such an allowance is therefore incidental to judgment and compensates for the expense of asserting one's rights in court. Costs may be allowed to the **plaintiff** if the **default** of a **defendant** made it necessary to sue, and to a defendant if the plaintiff sued without cause. Generally, costs of litigation are recoverable as of right if provided by **statute.** If there is no applicable statute, court rules may provide for allowance of costs to be at the discretion of the trial court. However, pursuant to the **American rule,** the prevailing practice in most jurisdictions is that each party bears his or her own costs.

COSTS TO ABIDE THE EVENT   court order requiring the losing party to pay legal expenses of the prevailing party up to and including the decision of the court of appeals (see **appellate court**) and sometimes on retrial.

COTENANCY   possession of and the holding of rights in a unit of property by two or more persons simultaneously. The term does not describe the **estate,** but the relationship between persons who share the property. It encompasses TENANCY IN COMMON, JOINT TENANCY, and TENANCY BY THE ENTIRETY (see **tenancy**).

COUNSEL [COUNSELOR]   1. **attorney**, lawyer, legal adviser; 2. the advice or aid given with respect to a legal matter; 3. In criminal law, the term may refer to the advising or encouraging of another to commit a crime.

COUNSEL SUBSTITUTE   see **advocate** [COUNSEL SUBSTITUTE].

COUNT   a distinct statement of **plaintiff's cause of action.** In **indictments,** a count, like a **charge,** is an **allegation** of a distinct offense. A **complaint** or indictment may contain one or more counts.

COUNTERCLAIM   a counterdemand by **defendant** against the **plaintiff;** it is not a mere **answer** or **denial** of plaintiff's allegation, but asserts an independent **cause of action** in favor of defendant.

EXAMPLE: A retail store owner sues a manufacturer for a shipment of defective clocks. Regardless of the validity of that suit, the manufacturer could *counterclaim* against the store owner if, for example, the owner owed the manufacturer money for past shipments. Both the storeowner's and the manufacturer's claims would then be decided by the courts.

In federal practice, a **COMPULSORY COUNTERCLAIM** arises out of the subject matter of the opposing party's claims, and unless the defendant makes such a counterclaim in the suit that has been brought against him or her, he or she may be barred from ever raising that claim again. A **PERMISSIVE COUNTERCLAIM** is any other counterclaim and may be made by the defendant in the action that has been brought against him or her or in a subsequent suit. See **setoff.** Compare **cross-claim.**

COUNTERFEIT   forged; fabricated without right; made in imitation of something else to defraud by passing the false copy for genuine.

COUPLED WITH AN INTEREST   see **authority** [**AUTHORITY COUPLED WITH AN INTEREST**].

COUPONS   certificates, usually attached to an **instrument** evidencing a loan, which may be presented separately for payment of a specific sum representing interest on the main instrument. See **bond** [**BEARER BOND**].

COURSE OF BUSINESS   see **ordinary course of business.**

COURSE OF DEALING   see **trade usage** [**COURSE OF DEALING**].

COURT   the branch of government responsible for the resolution of disputes arising under the laws of government. A court system is usually divided into various parts that specialize in hearing different types of cases. **Trial courts** receive evidence and make initial determinations of fact and law that may then be reviewed by **appellate courts.** Trial courts are usually divided into **CIVIL COURTS,** which hear disputes arising under the common law and civil statutes, **CRIMINAL COURTS,** which hear prosecutions under the criminal laws, **MATRIMONIAL COURTS,** which hear divorce proceedings, and **SURROGATE'S COURTS,** which hear proceedings regarding the estates of deceased and incompetent persons. **Federal courts** hear cases arising under federal laws. All states have a separate court system to decide cases arising under state laws. See **court of claims; court of equity; court of law; de facto** [**DE FACTO COURT**]; **district court; drug court; federal courts; inferior court; international court of justice; juvenile courts; kanga-**

roo court; moot court; open court; probate [PROBATE COURT]; small claims court; supreme court; tax court; term of court; territorial court; trial court.

COURT CALENDAR a schedule of cases awaiting disposition in a given court, also referred to as the TRIAL LIST or the COURT DOCKET.

COURT EN BANC see **en banc.**

COURT-MARTIAL l. a military or naval tribunal with jurisdiction over offenses against the law of the service in which the offender is engaged; 2. a proceeding in such a court. (plural: courts-martial).

GENERAL COURT-MARTIAL one presided over by a law officer and not fewer than five members, having jurisdiction over all members of the armed services of which it is a part, and authorized to try defendants for all military offenses and to prescribe any permitted sanctions.

SPECIAL COURT-MARTIAL one presided over by three members, that may try all noncapital offenses and that is limited in its authority to prescribe sanctions such as dismissal, hard labor and extended confinement, but may not authorize execution.

SUMMARY COURT-MARTIAL one presided over by a single commissioned officer, and limited in respect to the military personnel over whom it has jurisdiction and the sanctions it may prescribe. The accused may refuse trial by a summary court-martial, but the charges may then be referred to a higher level court-martial.

COURT OF APPEALS see **appellate [appeals] court.** Also the name of Maryland's and New York's highest state court.

COURT OF ASSIZE AND NISI PRIUS an English law court composed of two or more commissioners, who were sent twice in every year by the king's special commission all around the kingdom to try by jury cases under their jurisdiction.

COURT OF CLAIMS the court of the United States, created to determine all presented claims founded upon any law of Congress, upon any regulation of an executive department, or upon any **contract,** express or implied, with the government of the United States, and also all claims that may be referred to the court by either house of Congress. It has no power over matters in **equity.** See **Federal Claims Court.**

COURT OF CUSTOMS AND PATENT APPEALS see **federal courts.**

COURT OF EQUITY a court having **jurisdiction** in cases where an adequate and complete remedy cannot be had at law. Courts of equity in **common law** developed their own principles and unique remedies (e.g., **injunction, specific performance**). Actions were brought either equitably in **chancery** or legally **at law.** Today, courts that are guided primarily by equitable doctrine are still said to be courts of equity. Thus, a **bankruptcy court** is a court of equity. Courts of equity, which arose independent of courts of law in England, have merged with the latter in most jurisdictions of the United States. See **equity.**

COURT OF EXCHEQUER *(ĕks'-chĕk-èr)* an ancient English court of **record.** It was established by William the Conqueror to recover the king's **debts** and **duties.** It was inferior to both the court of the **King's Bench** and the court of common pleas, but served as both a **court of law** and **equity.** It took its name from the chequered cloth that covered its table and was marked and scored when the king's accounts were prepared. It consisted of two divisions, one that handled the royal revenue and the court, which was subdivided into courts of **equity** and **common law.**

THE COURT OF EXCHEQUER CHAMBER a court of **appeal** established to determine causes upon **writs** of error from the **common law** side of the **court of exchequer.**

COURT OF INQUIRY see **military law** [MILITARY COURT OF INQUIRY].

COURT OF KING'S [QUEEN'S] BENCH see **King's [Queen's] Bench.**

COURT OF LAW a **tribunal** with **jurisdiction** over cases at **law.** The term applies to courts that administer justice according to federal or state law or **common law,** as distinguished from courts that follow the principles of **equity** and are called **chancery** courts. Law courts and equity courts, however, are generally no longer distinguished, and a court of law is any tribunal administering the law.

COURT OF MILITARY APPEAL see **military law** [COURT OF MILITARY APPEAL].

COURT OF MILITARY REVIEW see **military law** [COURT OF MILITARY REVIEW].

COURT OF RECORD a court that, like most modern courts, is required by law to keep a record of its proceedings, including the orders and judgments it enters, and that has the authority to imprison and to levy fines.

COURT OF STAR CHAMBER   see **star chamber.**

COURT REPORTERS   persons certified to operate tape-recording devices or to use shorthand or stenographic means to record that which is said in court or at a **deposition.** The recording is later turned into a **transcript** and forms the official **record** of the proceeding. Contemporaneous transcripts made by computer systems and that are viewable by persons in the courtroom are known as REAL TIME or LIVE VIEW transcripts.

COURT REPORTS   see **advance sheets; reports.**

COVENANT   1. to enter a formal agreement; to bind oneself in **contract;** to make a stipulation; 2. an agreement to do or not to do a particular thing; 3. a promise incidental to a **deed** or contract, either express or implied.

EXAMPLE: Rita wants to sell a large tract of land adjacent to her home. As an inducement to Salman, the buyer, Rita is willing to *covenant* with (i.e., promise) him that he has access to and use of her driveway so that he will not have to build one.

CONCURRENT COVENANTS   those that require the performance by one party of his or her obligation, when the other party is ready and offers performance.

COVENANT NOT TO COMPETE   see **covenant not to compete.**

DEPENDENT COVENANTS   those in which the obligation to perform one covenant arises only upon the prior **performance** of another; therefore, until the prior **condition** of performance has been met, the other party is not liable in an **action** on his covenant.

INDEPENDENT [MUTUAL] COVENANTS   those that must be performed by one party without reference to the obligations of the other party.

In deeds, the usual **COVENANTS OF TITLE,** which may be deemed by law to be a part of certain kinds of real property conveyances, include:

COVENANT AGAINST ACTS OF THE GRANTOR   one often inserted into a **bargain and sale** deed to assure that the grantor has not done, nor caused to be done, any act by means of which the premises or any part thereof may be encumbered in any way.

COVENANT AGAINST ENCUMBRANCES   a guarantee given to the grantee of an estate that the estate is without **encumbrances.** Compare **run with the land.**

COVENANT OF FURTHER ASSURANCE   one that obligates the covenantor to perform whatever acts are reasonably demanded by the covenantee for the purpose of perfecting or assuring the **title** that is conveyed. This type of covenant is no longer in general use.

COVENANT OF HABITABILITY see **warranty [WARRANTY OF HABITABILITY]**.

COVENANT OF QUIET ENJOYMENT see **quiet enjoyment.**

COVENANT OF SEISIN AND RIGHT TO CONVEY covenant that the grantor has an **estate,** or the right to **convey** an estate, of the quality and quantity that he or she purports to convey (which, in the case of a covenant of **seisin,** is a **fee simple**).

COVENANT OF WARRANTY AND QUIET ENJOYMENT one that obligates the covenantor to protect the estate against the existence of lawful claims of ownership by third parties. A cause of action arises only when there is **eviction,** actual or constructive.

RESTRICTIVE COVENANT see **restrictive covenant.**

COVENANTEE one who receives the **covenant,** or for whom it is made.

COVENANT NOT TO COMPETE a contractual promise to refrain from conducting business or professional activities similar to those of another party. These covenants are encountered principally in contracts of employment, partnership, or sale of a business.

EXAMPLE: A chain of discount appliance stores is bought by a large corporation. The corporation offers to hire Trent, the owner of the chain, and to allow him to organize a separate business if he wants. The only condition on the offer is that Trent sign a *covenant not to compete,* which would prohibit Trent from organizing another chain of discount appliance stores or selling any other merchandise this corporation distributes. Ordinarily, such covenants have geographic and duration limits, i.e., that for a period of three years Trent may not open a competitive store within 50 miles of the chain he sold.

The protection of **trade secrets,** customer lists, business methods specific to a particular employer, and the unique qualifications of the employee have been held to constitute legitimate interests for protection by covenants not to compete.

COVENANTOR one who makes a **covenant.**

COVER in commercial law, refers to a buyer's purchase on the open market of **goods** similar or identical to the goods contracted for after a seller has **breached** a contract of sale by failure to deliver the goods contracted for. Under the **Uniform Commercial Code,** after a seller breaches and the buyer covers, the buyer is entitled to the difference between the cost of the substitute goods and the original contract price, provided the buyer has acted in good faith and without unreasonable delay in effecting such cover.

EXAMPLE: Phil contracts with the Prime Leather Company to supply him with raw leather hides at a certain price. By the delivery date, the cost of hides has risen so sharply that Prime would lose a considerable amount of money if it ships the hides to Phil. Prime decides to breach the contract. If Phil *covers* on this contract by purchasing the hides from another company, he can sue Prime for the difference between his purchase price with the new company and the price agreed to in the contract with Prime.

COVERTURE in **common law,** the state of a married woman whereby the existence of the wife was for many civil purposes merged with that of her husband, particularly with regard to ownership of property.

CREDIBILITY whether or not a witness is being truthful. The primary measure of credibility is whether the testimony is probable or improbable when judged by common experience.

CREDIT 1. a privilege of delayed payment extended to a buyer or borrower on the seller's or lender's belief that what is given will be repaid; 2. in accounting, a credit represents money due.

CREDIT LINE a promised maximum amount of money made available to a borrower by a bank or store merchant to allow for ongoing transactions. Compare **home equity line of credit [heloc]**.

CREDIT CARD an indication to sellers of commodities that the person who received the card from the issuer has a satisfactory credit rating and that if **credit** is extended, the issuer of the card will pay (or see to it that seller receives payment) for the merchandise delivered.

CREDITOR one to whom money is owed by the **debtor;** one to whom an obligation exists. In its strict legal sense, a creditor is one who voluntarily gives credit to another for money or other property; in its more general sense it is one who has a right by law to demand and recover of another a sum of money on any account. See **judgment creditor**.

CREDITOR BENEFICIARY see **third party beneficiary [CREDITOR BENEFICIARY]**.

CREDITOR'S BILL [SUIT] a **proceeding** in **equity** in which a **judgment creditor** (a **creditor** who has secured **judgment** against a **debtor** and whose **claim** has not been satisfied) attempts to gain a **discovery,** accounting and delivery of **property** owed to him or her by the **judgment debtor,** which property cannot be reached by execution (seizure and forced sale) at law.

CREDIT UNION see **bank [CREDIT UNION].**

CRIME a wrong that the government has determined is injurious to the public and that may therefore be prosecuted in a **criminal proceeding.** Crimes include **felonies** and **misdemeanors.** A common law crime was one declared to be an offense by the developed case law of the **common law** courts. Today all criminal offenses are exclusively statutory in nearly every American jurisdiction. See **infamous crime.**

CRIME AGAINST NATURE sexual deviation, including **sodomy** and **bestiality,** considered a crime in common law and carried over into statutory law.

CRIME INVOLVING MORAL TURPITUDE [CIMT] see **moral turpitude.**

CRIMEN FALSI *(krǐ'-měn fǎl'-sē)* Lat.: a **crime** of **deceit.** In **common law** a crime involving falsehood and **fraud.** Having committed such a crime generally disqualified a person as a **witness** in a judicial **proceeding.** Examples of *crimen falsi* include **forgery, perjury, subornation of perjury,** suppression of **testimony, conspiracy** in the absence of a **witness** and fraudulent making or alteration of a document.

CRIME OF PASSION a crime committed under the influence of sudden or extreme passion. That an act was committed in the heat of passion may provide a defense to a charge of murder, since it negates the element of **premeditation,** a necessary element of murder. See **manslaughter.**

EXAMPLE: Nancy comes home and finds her husband in bed with another lover. In a fit of rage she shoots both of them. Although Nancy is charged with murder, she claims that the shootings were a *crime of passion.* As part of her proof, she states that her act resulted from seeing her husband in bed with someone else and not from a rational or premeditated plan to kill, which would be required to support a first degree murder conviction. If the jury accepts her claim she would be convicted of the lesser-degree offense of manslaughter.

CRIME, ORGANIZED see **organized crime; racketeering.**

CRIMINAL 1. done with **malicious intent,** with a disposition to injure persons or property; 2. one who has been convicted of a violation of the criminal laws. A **HABITUAL OFFENDER** has been repeatedly convicted of crimes and therefore is subject to extended imprisonment under the habitual offender laws of many **jurisdictions.**

CRIMINAL CODE see **penal law [code].**

CRIMINAL COERCION the common law offense of **extortion** has been broadened by modern statutes to encompass any person who, acting with purpose to restrict unlawfully another's freedom of action to his or her detriment, threatens to commit any criminal offense, accuse anyone of a criminal offense, expose any secret tending to subject any person to hatred, contempt, or ridicule, impair his or her credit or business repute, or threatens to take or withhold action as an official, or cause an official to take or withhold action. Common law extortion was limited to the corrupt collection of an unlawful fee by an officer acting under **color** of office with no proof of threat, force, or **duress** required. If property is obtained as the result of criminal coercion, the conduct then constitutes **theft** by extortion since that form of theft encompasses today any conduct that is now proscribed by the criminal coercion statute. See **coercion.**

CRIMINAL CONTEMPT see **contempt of court.**

CRIMINAL CONVERSATION see **alienation of affections.**

CRIMINAL COURTS see **court [CRIMINAL COURTS].**

CRIMINALISTICS the science of crime detection, including **DNA** and **fingerprint** technology and other laboratory analyses. See **forensic.**

CRIMINAL MAINTENANCE unauthorized interference in a lawsuit by helping one party, with money or otherwise, to prosecute or defend a **cause of action** so as to obstruct justice, promote unnecessary litigation or unsettle community peace. Unlike **champerty,** criminal maintenance does not necessarily involve personal profit. See **also barratry.**

CRIMINAL MISCHIEF a crime against property; the willful damaging of the property of another. Punishable in a criminal court but may also be dealt with as a civil **tort.** Such offenses may include throwing rocks through windows, spray painting graffiti, slashing car tires, or other acts of vandalism. Adding the element of personal ill will or hatred such as defacing a Jewish cemetery with symbols of anti-Semitism raises the act to a **hate** or **bias crime,** which has significantly higher levels of punishment.

CRIMINAL NEGLIGENCE see **negligence [CRIMINAL [CULPABLE] NEGLIGENCE].**

CRIMINAL POSSESSION see **possession** [CRIMINAL POSSESSION].

CRIMINAL PROCEDURE see **procedure** [CRIMINAL PROCEDURE].

CRIMINAL RECORD a summary of an individual's contacts with law enforcement generally computerized in the **NCIC.** All **arrests** are noted with an explanation of the result including **convictions** (and **sentences** received), dismissals, not guilty verdicts, or **bench warrant** status. Parole or probation violations and escapes are noted as well as alias names, different dates of birth or social security numbers used, fingerprint classification, race, and state and federal identification numbers, Height, weight, eye and hair color, and identifying marks such as scars or tattoos are included, but some of these factors are subject to change. Also known as a **RAP SHEET,** the information is used by courts in determining the appropriate punishment or bail, and by prison authorities in determining minimum custody or job status.

CRIMINAL THREAT see **threat** [TERRORISTIC THREAT].

CROSS-BILL see **bill** [CROSS-BILL].

CROSS-CLAIM a claim **litigated** by co**defendants** or co**plaintiffs** against each other, and not against a party on the opposite side of the litigation. Compare **counterclaim.**

CROSS-EXAMINATION the questioning of a witness, by a party or lawyer other than the one who called the witness, concerning matters about which the witness has testified during **DIRECT EXAMINATION.** The purpose is to discredit or clarify testimony already given so as to neutralize damaging testimony or present facts in a light more favorable to the party against whom the direct testimony was offered.

DIRECT EXAMINATION the initial questioning of a witness by the party who called the witness. The purpose is to present testimony containing the factual argument the party is making.

REDIRECT EXAMINATION the questioning of a witness by a party who called the witness, which occurs after that witness has been subjected to cross-examination. The purpose of redirect examination is to rebut or to clarify any damaging testimony elicited on cross-examination.

CRUEL AND UNUSUAL PUNISHMENT a penalty tantamount to torture, or excessive in proportion to the offense for which it is imposed, or inherently unfair, or by contemporary standards shocking to people of reasonable sensitivity. A punishment not inherently cruel and unusual may become so by the manner in which it is inflicted. Such punishment is prohibited by the **Eighth Amendment** to the U.S. Constitution.

CSAAS see **child sexual abuse accommodation syndrome [CSAAS].**

CTA see **letters of administration [CTA].**

CUCKOLD a man whose wife is unfaithful; the husband of an adulteress. It is explained that the word alludes to the habit of the female cuckold, which lays her eggs in the nests of other birds to be hatched by them. To make a cuckold of a man is to seduce his wife.

CULPA *(kŭl'-pă)* Lat: a term from the civil law meaning fault, neglect, or negligence. Compare **DOLUS,** also from the civil law meaning fraud, guile, or deceit.

CULPABLE deserving of moral blame or punishment; at fault; having acted with indifference to consequences and to the rights of others.

CULPABLE MENTAL STATE the state of mind necessary to commit a crime. In common law, both intent to commit a crime, called **mens rea,** and the acts that constitute the crime were required to establish guilt.

EXAMPLE: After a long night drinking, Rod stumbles into what he believes is his car and attempts to start the car with his own set of keys. As it turns out, the car is not his, and the rightful owner, who comes out seconds later, sees Rod and has him arrested for attempting to steal a car. Rod argues that he did not have the *culpable mental state* required for theft since he had no intention to steal the car.

See also **negligence [CRIMINAL [CULPABLE] NEGLIGENCE].**

CUM TESTAMENTO ANNEXO see **letters of administration [CUM TESTAMENTO ANNEXO].**

CUMULATIVE DIVIDEND see **dividend [CUMULATIVE DIVIDEND].**

CUMULATIVE SENTENCE see **sentence [CONSECUTIVE [CUMULATIVE] SENTENCE].**

CUMULATIVE VOTING a system of **shareholder** voting for a board of **directors,** that allows all the votes an individual is eligible to cast to be cast for a single candidate. The system is designed to give minority shareholders representation on the board. For example, the owner of a single share of stock voting in an election for five directors would be able to cast one vote for each position under a straight voting system, but would be able to cast all five votes for a single position or distribute them in any manner desired under a cumulative voting system.

CUPOS census term meaning cohabiting unmarried person of the opposite sex. The term **POSSLQ** "person of opposite sex sharing living quarters" encompasses married and unmarried persons.

CURATIVE correcting a legal error or defect. A judge will give a curative **instruction** to the jury to negate the effect of an erroneous instruction or of tainted evidence. A curative statute is enacted to remedy a defect in previously enacted legislation.

CURIA REGIS *(kū'-rē-à rā'-gĭs)* Lat.: the king's court. See **King's Bench.**

CURRENT ASSETS see **asset; balance sheet.**

CURRENT LIABILITIES debts incurred by the reporting entity as part of normal operations and that are expected to be repaid during the following twelve months. Examples are **accounts payable,** short-term loans and that portion of long-term loans due in one year. See **balance sheet.**

CURTESY the husband's right in **common law,** upon the death of his wife, to a **life estate** in all lands of which his wife was **seised** in **fee simple** or in **fee tail** at any time during the marriage, provided that there was **issue** born of the marriage capable of inheriting the estate. Compare **dower.**

CURTILAGE in **common law** the land around the **dwelling house.**

CUSTODY 1. as applied to property, the condition of holding a thing within one's personal care and control; 2. as applied to persons, such control over a person as will insure his or her presence at a **hearing,** or the actual imprisonment of a person resulting from a criminal **conviction;** 3. **Custody of children** is legal **guardianship.**

CUSTODY OF CHILDREN the care and control of minor children awarded by the court to one parent in a divorce proceeding. Where parents both make application for **JOINT CUSTODY,** and circumstances render the arrangement feasible, some courts have awarded custody to both parents so that responsibility for the children is shared. Under a joint custody order, each parent would assume custody of the children for a fixed period, such as for six months or for the school year or for the summer vacation.

CUSTOM DUTIES **taxes** imposed on the importation of foreign goods into the United States. Custom duties and other restrictions are imposed in order to regulate trade between the United States and other countries.

CUSTOMS AND BORDER PROTECTION [CBP] a federal law enforcement agency under the **Department of Homeland Security** with a priority mission of keeping **terrorists** and their weapons out of the United States. Missions also include preventing the illegal entry of people and goods while facilitating legitimate travel and trade. Specifically, the CBP prevents persons, illicit drugs, and contraband from entering the country illegally. It also protects American businesses from **intellectual property** theft and provides agricultural inspection to curtail harmful pests and diseases. See *www.cbp.gov*.

CUSTOMS COURT   see **federal courts.**

CYBERLAW   an evolving area of the law that deals with communications technology involving e-commerce, copyright, **First Amendment** issues (such as privacy and speech) and governmental regulations.

CYBERSQUATTING [CYBERPIRACY]   the illegal practice of registering a **domain** site (such as a company name) with the intention of profiting by selling that domain name to the company to which it rightfully belongs. Federal law prohibits such practices under the ANTICYBERSQUATTING CONSUMER PROTECTION ACT. See also **Digital Millennium Copyright Act.**

CYBERSTALKING   actions by a user of a computer that harass, monitor, or threaten another person and cause that person to be annoyed or alarmed by the user's conduct. See **stalking.**

CYPRÈS   *(sī'-prĕ)*   Fr.: so near, as near. In the law of **trusts** and **wills,** the principle that a court of **equity** will, when a charity bequest is illegal or becomes impossible or impracticable, substitute another charitable object that is believed to approach closely the original purpose of the **testator** or **settlor.**

EXAMPLE: In her will, Ruth provided that $10,000 go to the Animal Humanitarian Society for their work in placing lost or abandoned pets and for running an animal hospital. At her death, the society no longer existed. Under the doctrine of *cyprès,* the court awarded the $10,000 to the American Society for the Prevention of Cruelty to Animals.

D

D.A.   abbreviation for **District Attorney.**

DAILY   see **per diem.**

DAMAGE   see **injury; irreparable injury [damage; harm].**

DAMAGES   monetary compensation that the law awards to one who has been injured by the action of another; monetary recompense for a legal wrong such as a **breach of contract** or a **tortious** act. There are various measures used for calculating damages, including **diminution of value** and **cost of completion.** Compare **specific performance.**

ACTUAL [COMPENSATORY; GENERAL] DAMAGES   losses directly referrable to the breach or tortious act; losses that can readily be proven to have been sustained, and for which the injured party should be compensated as a matter of right.

COMPENSATORY DAMAGES   see **ACTUAL DAMAGES** above.

CONSEQUENTIAL [SPECIAL] DAMAGES   indirect loss or injury. In contract law, consequential damages are recoverable if it was reasonably foreseeable at the time of contract that the injury would probably result if the contract were broken. The availability of award of such damages depends upon the defaulting party's actual or **constructive** knowledge of conditions that make likely some special injury upon default. Special damages should be distinguished from **ACTUAL [GENERAL] DAMAGES,** which are presumed directly caused by the injury. Because special damages do not necessarily flow from the injury, they must be specially pleaded and proven. The distinction between special and general damages is not absolute but, rather, is relative and depends upon the circumstances of each case. For instance, in an action for failure to provide widgets as agreed in a contract, the general damages would be the price paid under the contract. Any claim for damages to business reputation for reliability would be special damages. In an action for the tort of interference with a business relationship, however, damage to the business reputation would be the general damage. Under the UCC, in order for a buyer to recover consequential damages resulting from a seller's breach, the damages must not have been avoidable by **cover.**

141

EXAMPLE: Crystal Lighting contracts with a construction company to install unique light fixtures throughout a new building. On the basis of that contract, Crystal also contracts with one of its suppliers to have several hundred fixtures delivered to Crystal. Since this is not a normal order for Crystal, Crystal explains what all the fixtures are for. The supplier then breaches his contract. Ordinary light fixtures do not fit in the building design. Any damages in the contract between Crystal and the construction company that result from the breach are the direct foreseeable result of the supplier's breach. As such, those damages are called *consequential damages.*

DOUBLE [TREBLE] DAMAGES twice [or three times] the amount of damages that a court or jury would normally award, recoverable for certain kinds of injuries pursuant to a statute authorizing the double [or treble] recovery. These damages are intended in certain instances as punishment for improper behavior. Treble damages is a statutory remedy most often awarded in antitrust violations.

EXEMPLARY [PUNITIVE] DAMAGES compensation in excess of actual damages that is a form of punishment to the wrongdoer and reparation to the injured. Exemplary damages are awarded only in rare instances of **malicious** and **willful** misconduct.

EXAMPLE: Several corporations are found guilty of fixing the price of milk over a nine-year period. In addition to assessing a fine on the corporations, a judge awards an additional amount as *punitive damages.* Since all purchases of milk were affected by the price-fixing, the judge might order that the amount of the punitive damages be repaid to consumers by a coupon offering.

EXPECTATION DAMAGES a measure of the money damages available to **plaintiff** in an action for breach of contract, based on the value of the benefit he would have received from the contract if the **defendant** had not breached, but had completed **performance** as agreed. The amount is generally the monetary value of full performance of the contract to the plaintiff minus costs plaintiff avoided by not performing his own part of the contract.

GENERAL DAMAGES see **ACTUAL DAMAGES** above.

INCIDENTAL DAMAGES losses reasonably incident to conduct giving rise to a claim for actual damages. A buyer's incidental damages would include expenses reasonably incurred in inspection, receipt, transportation, and care and custody of goods rightfully rejected while the seller's incidental damages would include any commercially reasonable charges, expenses or commissions incurred in stopping delivery, in the transportation, care and custody of goods after the buyer's breach, in connection with return or resale of the goods.

LIQUIDATED DAMAGES   see **liquidated damages.**

NOMINAL DAMAGES   a trivial sum awarded as recognition that a legal injury was sustained, though slight. Nominal damages will be awarded for a breach of contract or for an intentional tort to vindicate the plaintiffs claim where no recoverable loss can be established.

PUNITIVE DAMAGES   see **EXEMPLARY [PUNITIVE] DAMAGES** above.

SPECIAL DAMAGES   see **CONSEQUENTIAL [SPECIAL] DAMAGES** above.

TREBLE DAMAGES   see **DOUBLE [TREBLE] DAMAGES** above.

DAMNUM ABSQUE INJURIA   *(däm'nūm äb'-skwā ĭn-jū'-rē-ä)*   Lat.: harm without **injury.** Refers to damage without violation of law, or to damage caused by nature, where the law provides no **cause of action** to recover for the loss. Compare **compensation.**

DANGEROUS WEAPON [INSTRUMENTALITY]   almost any device that has the potential to cause serious bodily injury or endanger life.

DATA CAPTURE   see **automatic [electronic] data capture.**

DATA PROTECTION   requirements for ensuring the effectiveness of information security controls over information resources that support business or governmental operations. Also, prevention of the dissemination of personal information without consent of the individual.

DATE RAPE   see **rape [DATE RAPE].**

DAY IN COURT   refers broadly to the opportunity afforded a party to a lawsuit to be heard by the court. See **appearance; due process of law.**

DAY ORDER   see **order [DAY ORDER].**

DBA [D/B/A]   abbreviation for "doing business as." **Trade name.**

   EXAMPLE: William and Lorna Scott are doing business under the name of Scott's Hockey Supplies and a **lawsuit** is brought. Its caption might read *Britton Michael* v. *William and Lorna Scott DBA Scott's Hockey Supplies.*

DB(k)   a hybrid **retirement plan** that would combine the features of a defined benefit plan with a defined contribution (401(k)) plan. The DB(k) features an employer-funded monthly retirement payment that can be augmented with tax-deferred employee contributions. The **Pension Protection Act** will provide businesses with less than 500 employees the opportunity to offer this plan starting in 2010.

DBN see **letters of administration [DBN].**

DEADBEAT DAD [MOM] a person who fails to pay court-ordered **child support** and may, as a result, be subjected to any of the following penalties: garnishment of wages; refusal to allow the parent to obtain a legal passport; interception of unemployment compensation and/or offsetting federal and/or state income tax refunds, or even incarceration for contempt of court.

DEAD HAND see **mortmain.**

DEADLY FORCE see **force [DEADLY FORCE].**

DEADLY WEAPON any device capable of causing death or serious bodily injury. An instrument may be intrinsically deadly, as a knife or pistol, or deadly because of the way it is used, as a wrench or hammer.

DEALER one who produces or acquires something in order to sell it. One is a dealer if he or she has structured his or her business so that he or she can, upon reasonable **notice, deliver** his or her commodity once a sale has been made.

DEATH the point at which life ceases; permanent and irreversible termination of vital signs. Several states have adopted **statutes** defining death to include brain criteria. See **brain death.**

DEATH BY AUTOMOBILE see **homicide; manslaughter [DEATH BY AUTOMOBILE].**

DEATH PENALTY the ultimate punishment imposed for murder or other capital offenses. The U.S. Supreme Court has determined that the death penalty is not in every instance to be considered unconstitutional, as **cruel and unusual punishment**.

DEATH TAX see **tax [ESTATE TAX; INHERITANCE TAX].**

DEBAUCHERY overindulgences in sensual pleasures; sexual immorality; as used in the Mann Act [prohibiting travel across state lines for immoral purposes]. It is a broad term and includes all sexual immoralities, whether for hire or not for hire, or for **cohabitation.**

DE BENE ESSE *(dĕ bĕ'-nĕ ĕs'-sĕ)* Lat.: conditionally; provisionally.

   APPEARANCE DE BENE ESSE a conditional **appearance,** by which one appearing in the jurisdiction intends not to thereby subject himself or herself to the authority of the court for all purposes.

DEPOSITIONS DE BENE ESSE conditional **depositions** that cannot be introduced in evidence if the **witness** is available at the trial.

EVIDENCE DE BENE ESSE **evidence** whose **admissibility** is conditioned upon a subsequent showing of facts necessary to support its admission.

DEBENTURE written acknowledgment of a **debt** secured only by the general **credit** or promise to pay of the issuer. Debentures are the common type of **bond** issued by large, well-established corporations with adequate credit ratings. The written agreement under which the debentures are sold, the **indenture,** is specific as to maturity date, interest rate, **call** features and **convertibility.** Holders of debentures representing corporate indebtedness are creditors of the corporation and entitled to payment before **shareholders** upon **dissolution** of the corporation.

DEBIT a sum charged as due or owing. In bookkeeping, a term used to denote an entry on the left, or **asset** side of a ledger or account indicating the creation of or addition to an asset or an expense, or the reduction or elimination of a **liability.** Also, the balance of an account where it is shown that something remains due to the person keeping the account. Compare **credit.**

DE BONIS NON see **letters of administration [DE BONIS NON].**

DEBT any obligation of one person to pay or compensate another. See **bad debt; bankruptcy; bond [BONDED DEBT]; creditor; floating debt; insolvency.** See also **satisfaction (of a debt).**

DEBT CAPITAL see **security [DEBT CAPITAL].**

DEBTOR one who owes another anything, or is under obligation, arising from express agreement, implication of law, or principles of natural justice, to pay money or to fulfill some other obligation; in **bankruptcy** or similar proceedings, the person who is the subject of the proceeding.

DECEASED one who has died. In property law, the alternate term **DECEDENT** is generally used. In criminal law, "the deceased" refers to the victim of a **homicide.**

DECEDENT see **deceased.**

DECEIT the **tort** or **fraudulent** representation of a **material** fact made with knowledge of its falsity, or recklessly, or without reasonable grounds for believing its truth and with intent to induce **reliance** on it; the **plaintiff** justifiably relies on the deception, to his **injury.**

DECISION act of determining; forming a definite opinion; or coming to a conclusion. A resort to a choice of possibilities is "guess-work," not a "decision." A final determination arrived at after consideration, an opinion formed, or a course of action decided upon. A decision necessarily involves a dispute, actual or potential. See **judgment; opinion.**

DECISION ON THE MERITS   see **judgment [JUDGMENT ON THE MERITS].**

DECLARANT   person making a statement. See **deponent; witness.** See also **declaration.**

DECLARATION   in common law, the formal document specifying plaintiff's **cause of action,** including the facts necessary to sustain a proper cause of action and to advise **defendant** of the grounds upon which he or she is being sued. See **complaint.**

DECLARATION AGAINST INTEREST   a statement that *at the time of its making* was so contrary to the declarant's pecuniary, proprietary, or penal interest that a reasonable person would not have made the statement unless he or she believed it to be true. Further, the declarant must have personal knowledge and, in some jurisdictions, must be unavailable at the time of trial. Because of its special trustworthiness, a declaration against interest is an exception to the **hearsay** rule.

EXAMPLE: A statement by a juvenile that he had thrown a bicycle frame out an eighth floor stairwell window of the defendant's building is admissible hearsay in an action against the defendant housing authority for failure to repair the stairwell window.

ADMISSIONS BY A PARTY-OPPONENT   distinguishable from declarations against interest in that admissions of a party-opponent are **per se** admissible and thus do not have to satisfy the above requirements for a declaration against interest and they do not have to, although they may, be against interest when made. Further, the party making the admission need not be unavailable and need not have personal knowledge.

EXAMPLE: A statement by a defendant, questioned in Nebraska about a homicide committed in New Jersey, that he had never been to New Jersey is admissible as an admission by a party (along with proof of his ten-year residency in New Jersey) to show that the defendant lied to throw off the investigation.

DECLARATION OF ESTIMATED TAX   see **return [DECLARATION OF ESTIMATED TAX].**

DECLARATION OF TRUST   see **trust [DECLARATION OF TRUST].**

DECLARATORY JUDGMENT   a **judgment** of the court to

establish the rights of the parties or express the opinion of the court on a question of law, without ordering anything to be done or granting any remedy.

EXAMPLE: A state legislature passes a taxing measure that will have a widespread effect on corporations doing interstate business within that state. A payment of the tax with a subsequent refund if the tax is found invalid would result in administrative difficulties. Therefore, one of the affected corporations asks a court for a *declaratory judgment* on the validity of the tax.

Compare **advisory opinion; injunction.** See **controversy; justiciability.**

DECLARATORY STATUTE a statute that merely declares the existing law without proposing changes, for the purpose of resolving conflicts concerning the meaning of a previous statute or portion of the **common law.**

DECREE 1. the judicial decision in a **litigated** cause rendered by a **court of equity;** 2. the determination of a cause in courts of **admiralty** and **probate.** It is accurate to use the word **judgment** for a decision of a **court of law,** and decree from a court of equity, although the former term now includes both.

CONSENT DECREE an agreement of the parties made under sanction of the court, not the result of a judicial determination, but merely agreement to be bound by certain stipulated facts.

DECREE NISI in English law, a provisional decree of divorce, which becomes absolute only after a specified interval, usually six months, during which parties have the opportunity to show cause why the decree should not become absolute.

FINAL DECREE one that ultimately disposes of every matter of contention between the parties and constitutes a bar to another action on the same subject matter between the same parties.

INTERLOCUTORY DECREE one made upon some point arising during the progress of the suit that does not determine finally the **merits** of the entire suit.

DECREE NISI see **decree [DECREE NISI]; nisi [DECREE NISI].**

DECRIMINALIZATION the adoption or repeal of legislation, the effect of which is that acts or omissions formerly considered criminal are no longer so characterized, and penal sanctions for such acts or omissions are removed.

DEDICATION a **conveyance** of land as a **grant** to the public by a private owner and an acceptance of that land on behalf of the public.

EXAMPLE: Pollard Company buys a large area of land, on which it plans to locate its national headquarters. To promote goodwill between the company and the surrounding communities, the company *dedicates* a portion of land to the county parks committee that accepts permanent ownership of the land.

DEDUCTIONS amounts allowed to taxpayers under the **Internal Revenue Code** as offsets against GROSS INCOME or ADJUSTED GROSS INCOME (see **income**).

ITEMIZED DEDUCTIONS specific individualized deductions, allowed under provisions of the Code for specific expenses incurred by the **taxpayer** during the **taxable year.** These deductions are allowed in computing TAXABLE INCOME (see **income**) to the extent they exceed the ZERO BRACKET AMOUNT.

MARITAL DEDUCTION a deductible amount under the unified estate and gift tax for certain interests in property transferred to a spouse.

PERSONAL EXPENSES DEDUCTION personal expenses as opposed to expenses for income-producing or business expenses. Personal expenses are not allowed as deductions except as specifically enumerated in the Internal Revenue Code.

STANDARD DEDUCTION a provision allowing a taxpayer to deduct, in lieu of itemized deductions, a percentage of gross income up to certain specified amounts, repealed and replaced by the ZERO BRACKET AMOUNT.

ZERO BRACKET AMOUNT DEDUCTION an amount of income below the amounts at which, according to the tax tables, income taxes must be paid.

DEED an **instrument** in writing that **conveys** an **interest** in land (**realty**) from the grantor to the grantee. Its main function is to pass **title** to land. See **bargain and sale; quitclaim deed; warranty.**

DEED OF TRUST a transfer of legal **title** to property from owner to a **trustee,** so that the trustee may hold the title as security for the **performance** of certain obligations, monetary or otherwise, by the owner of a third party. Compare **mortgage.**

DEED POLL a **deed** made by and obligatory upon one **party** alone.

DEEP ROCK DOCTRINE a doctrine that makes available a **remedy** for improper conduct in connection with a loan to a corporation by a controlling **shareholder.** Though generally loans to a corporation by a shareholder are entitled to equal priority with loans made by outside **creditors,** the doctrine allows, when there are **bankruptcy** proceedings involving the corporation, subordination of the shareholder loans to the claims of other creditors where it would be manifestly unfair to permit a controlling shareholder to participate equally with these other creditors.

The unfairness occurs most commonly where the corporation is undercapitalized and frequently involves a parent corporation as the controlling shareholder of a **subsidiary.**

DE FACTO *(dĕ fäk'-tō)* Lat.: in fact. By virtue of the deed or accomplishment; actually. Used to refer to a situation in which a condition or institution is operating as though it were official or pursuant to law, but that is not legally authorized. Such situations may arise where, for example, an authorizing law is declared invalid, or because required legal formalities have not been satisfied.

EXAMPLE: Nursing homes were established throughout a particular state under the authority of a newly enacted state law. Now, two years later, portions of the law are found to be unconstitutional. Instead of closing all the homes that were set up, the state permits them to continue to operate under its *de facto* authority until the law is amended and legal.

The de facto acts of a person or entity may for some purposes be regarded as legally binding. Compare **de jure.**

DE FACTO AUTHORITY authority exercised in fact.

DE FACTO BOARD OF DIRECTORS the board which in fact is in charge of the affairs of a company and is recognized as such and is performing the legitimate functions and duties of a board.

DE FACTO CORPORATION one which has inadvertently failed to comply with the provisions of the laws relating to the creation of a **corporation** but has made a good faith effort to do so and has in **good faith** exercised the **franchise** of a corporation. See also **corporation [DE FACTO CORPORATION].**

DE FACTO COURT one established and exercising judicial functions under the authority of an apparently valid statute. If the statute is subsequently declared invalid, the court exists in fact though not in law. See **de jure.**

DE FACTO INCUMBENT one who was elected in an election which is later declared void.

DE FACTO JUDGE one acting under color of right, and who exercises the judicial functions he assumed while the appointment is contested.

DE FACTO JURY a jury selected in pursuance of a **void** law.

DE FACTO OFFICER one whose title is not good in law, but who in fact possesses an office and discharges his duties.

DE FACTO SEGREGATION segregation which results without purposeful action by government officials; real or actual segregation which results from social, psychological, or economic conditions.

DE FACTO TRUSTEE one who assumes an office or position under **color** of right or title and who exercises the duties of the office.

DEFALCATION failure of one entrusted with money to pay over the money when it is due to another. The term is like misappropriation and **embezzlement,** but is wider in scope because it does not imply criminal **fraud.**

DEFAMATION the publication of anything injurious to the reputation of another. Defamation designed to be read is **libel;** oral defamation is **slander.**

EXAMPLE: A reporter publishes an article that Ryan is being investigated for misapplication of public funds. The article has no basis in fact, but, as a result of it, Ryan is forced to temporarily leave his position as director. Ryan has been **libeled** and probably has a *defamation* action against the reporter.

DEFAULT failure to discharge a duty. The term is often used in the context of **mortgages** to describe failure of the mortgagor to pay **installments** when due, and in the context of judicial **proceedings** to describe failure of one of the parties to take **procedural** steps to prevent entry of a **judgment** against him (called a **default judgment**). See **delict.**

DEFAULT JUDGMENT 1. a **judgment** against **defendant** who has failed to respond to **plaintiff's action** or to appear at the **trial** or hearing.

EXAMPLE: A carpenter files a suit against a homeowner, claiming that the homeowner failed to pay the carpenter for work performed six months ago. Under the state's court rules, the homeowner has twenty days to file an answer to the carpenter's claim. If the homeowner fails to do so within twenty days, the court will enter a *default judgment* against him declaring that the homeowner must pay the carpenter what is claimed.

2. judgment given without the defendant being heard in his own defense. Compare **confession of judgment; ex parte.**

DEFEASANCE an **instrument** that negates the effectiveness of a **deed** or of a **will;** a **collateral** deed that defeats the force of another deed upon the performance of certain conditions.

DEFEASIBLE subject to revocation if certain **conditions** are not met; capable of being avoided or annulled, or liable to such avoidance or annulment.

DEFEASIBLE FEE see **determinable fee.**

DEFECT see **inherent defect; latent defect; patent defect.**

DEFECTIVE 1. incomplete, faulty; 2. not reasonably safe for a use that can be reasonably anticipated. See **products liability; strict liability; warranty.**

DEFECTIVE PLEADING any **pleading** [complaint, answer, cross-claim, etc.] which fails to conform in form or substance to minimum standards of accuracy or sufficiency. Under strict common law pleading rules, a defective pleading was often fatal to the **lawsuit.** Under modern relaxed standards, such occurrences are rare and are curable by amendment.

DEFECTIVE TITLE unmarketable right of ownership. 1. With reference to land, it means that the **title** held by the person making the **conveyance,** claiming to own **good title,** is or might be subject to partial or complete **ownership** by someone else.

EXAMPLE: Allie wants to sell her house to a friend who is moving into the state. Prior to purchasing the house, the friend has a title search done to determine if anyone else has claimed ownership of the house besides Allie. That search discloses a bank note that has never been paid but that the bank has never acted upon. Still, the outstanding bank note gives rise to a *defective title,* which now makes the friend reluctant to buy the house.

2. As to **negotiable instruments,** the term denotes title obtained through **fraud** or other illegal means.

DEFENDANT 1. in **civil proceedings,** the **party** responding to the **complaint;** one who is sued and called upon to make satisfaction for a wrong complained of by another; 2. in criminal proceedings, the **accused.** See also **respondent.**

CO-DEFENDANT see **co-defendant.**

DEFENDANT IN ERROR the prevailing party in the lower court who is the adverse party in the appellate proceeding where review has been sought on a writ of error. The person who brings the **action** at the **appellate** level is called the PLAINTIFF IN ERROR. See **appellee.**

DEFENSE a denial, answer or plea disputing the validity of plaintiff's case, or making some further contention that renders the defendant not liable upon the facts alleged by the plaintiff.

AFFIRMATIVE DEFENSE one that serves as a basis for proving some new fact, whereby defendant does not simply **deny** a **charge** but offers new **evidence** to avoid **judgment** against him or her.

EQUITABLE DEFENSE a defense that is recognized by **courts of equity** acting solely upon rules of **equity.** Such defenses can now be asserted in **courts of law** as well.

DEFENSE ATTORNEY lawyer representing a **defendant.** Includes both civil and criminal defense. A criminal defendant who cannot afford counsel is entitled to one appointed at the state's expense. See **public defender.**

DEFENSE OF MARRIAGE ACT [DOMA] 1996 federal law allowing a state to refuse to recognize a same-sex marriage granted under the laws of another state. As of press time, the act is undergoing multiple challenges. Portions of the act have been ruled unconstitutional and, as a result, same-sex married couples qualify as "spouses" for purposes of federal laws. Social security survivor benefits, bankruptcy action status, immigration issues, and insurance for federal employees are some of the areas affecting spousal recognition.

DEFERMENT postponing or putting off to a future time. May apply to the vesting or enjoyment of an estate, or to the calling of a person to serve in the armed forces. To defer does not mean to abolish or omit.

DEFERRED COMPENSATION see **retirement plans** [DEFERRED COMPENSATION].

DEFERRED PAYMENTS payments extended over a period of time or put off to a future date.

DEFICIENCY the excess of a **taxpayer's** correct tax liability for the **taxable year** over the amount of **taxes** previously paid for such year. The **Internal Revenue Service** is authorized to assess deficiencies during an **audit** of the taxpayer's return, and a deficiency may be used to assess penalties for the underpayment of tax, such as for **negligence** or **fraud** in filing the return.

DEFICIT insufficiency in an account or number, whether as the result of **defaults** and misappropriations or of mistake or shrinkage in value.

DEFINITE FAILURE OF ISSUE see **failure of issue.**

DEFLORATION the act of taking a person's virginity.

DEFRAUD to deprive a person of **property** or **interest, estate** or right by **fraud** or **deceit.**

DEGREE a measure. Also, the certificate of achievement that a school, college, or university gives to a student who completes a specified course of study or curriculum.

DEGREE OF CONSANGUINITY [KINSHIP] see **consanguinity.**

DEGREE OF CRIME the measure of the seriousness of a criminal act that determines the range of criminal sanctions that may be imposed for the crime. For instance, under the Model Penal Code, assault can be classified into any of four degrees depending upon the victim or the manner of commission. A simple assault could be a petty misdemeanor carrying a sentence of not more than 30 days, or a misdemeanor carrying a sentence of not more than one year; an aggravated assault could be a crime of the third degree exposing the defendant to five years, or a crime of the second degree carrying a maximum sentence of ten years.

DEGREE OF NEGLIGENCE the measure of **negligence** necessary for liability to result. Parties under an obligation to exercise great **care,** such as common **carriers,** may be liable for **slight negligence,** whereas parties only required to exercise slight **care,** such as the driver of an automobile in a state that has a **guest statute,** will be liable to a passenger only for **gross negligence.**

DEGREE OF PROOF the measure of probability necessary in order for a **court** or other fact finder to render a decision or a **verdict** with regard to the evidence **presented** to it. See **preponderance of the evidence; clear and convincing; reasonable doubt.**

DE JURE *(dĕ ju'-rā)* Lat.: by right; lawful; legitimate.

EXAMPLE: a new corporation is set up exactly according to both state and federal incorporation laws. The corporation is therefore a *de jure* (i.e., legal) corporation.

Generally used in contrast to **de facto;** de jure connotes "as a matter of law," whereas de facto connotes "as a matter of practice not founded upon law."

DEL CREDERE an **agent,** employed to make transactions, who guarantees (to the **principal**) the solvency of the purchaser and the performance of the contract in exchange for a higher **commission.**

DELEGABLE DUTY a **duty** that an obligor is able to transfer to another. The term does not imply a giving up of authority but, rather, the conferring of authority to another to do things that otherwise must be done by the obligor. When delegation occurs, it does not free the obligor from his or her duty to see to it that performance is properly complied with. Only by **novation** may the original obligor totally discharge his or her responsibilities and liabilities.

Where performance by the delegate would vary materially from the performance of the obligor, the duty is **NONDELEGABLE.** Thus, under a contract to paint a portrait or where a contract is premised on the unique abilities of the obligor, the duties are nondelegable. Construction contracts, however, are generally held to be delegable because it is contemplated by the parties that the work will be performed by persons other than the obligor.

DELEGATE 1. to appoint, authorize or commission; the **transfer** of authority by one person to another; 2. a person commissioned to act instead of another.

DELEGATED POWER power conferred by one person on another who will act for his or her benefit.

DELIBERATE to consider all of the evidence and arguments presented in regard to a particular matter. For instance, after the evidence has been presented, the parties to a lawsuit have made their closing arguments, and the judge has given the jury its instructions, the jury will retire to deliberate and render its verdict.

DELIBERATE SPEED forthwith, immediate. In certain instances, such as the desegregation of public facilities, the term implies that desegregation should occur as quickly as the maintenance of law and order and the welfare of all citizens will allow.

DELIBERATION the process by which the reasons for and against a **verdict** are weighed by **jurors.** While such verdict should be the consensus of the judgments of each juror, the purpose of deliberation is to allow opinions to be changed by conference in the **jury** room.

DELICT a **tort;** a wrong or injury; any statutory violation; sometimes used in the sense of a **default** on a monetary obligation.

DELICTUM Latin for tort. An action **EX DELICTO** is an action in tort as distinguished from one **EX CONTRACTU,** in **contract.**

DELICTUM Latin for **tort.** An **ACTION EX DELICTO** is an action in tort as opposed to one **EX CONTRACTU,** in contract. This distinction was significant when the early forms of **code pleading** were very strict. If, for example, one alleged a cause of action ex delicto for fraud but the proof established a breach of warranty (an action ex contractu) the case would be dismissed for **variance.**

DELINQUENT in a monetary context, payable but overdue and unpaid. See **default.** See also **juvenile delinquent.**

DELISTING removal of an issue from trading on an organized exchange such as the **New York Stock Exchange.** Organized exchanges have minimum listing requirements that must be met before listed trading is allowed. If the issuer fails to maintain the minimum requirements, trading in its listed securities can be suspended or eliminated.

DELIVERY a voluntary transfer of **title** or **possession** from one **party** to another; a legally recognized handing over to another one's possessory rights. Where actual delivery is cumbersome or impossible, the courts may find **constructive** delivery sufficient if the intention is clearly to transfer title. Thus, one may deliver the contents of a safety deposit box by handing over the key together with any necessary authorization. Such action is also called **SYMBOLIC DELIVERY.** Compare **bailment.**

DELUSION a false belief that is produced by a mental disorder and that people of the same age, class, and education would find incredible. A delusion can be the basis for the **insanity defense** to a **crime.**

DEMAND see **on demand.**

DEMAND NOTE 1. an **instrument** that by its express terms is payable immediately on an agreed-upon date of **maturity** without further demand for payment; 2. an instrument payable at sight, or upon presentation, or one in which no time for payment is stated.

DEMESNE *(de-mēn')* Fr: domain. Something owned; held in one's own right, and not of a superior; not allotted to tenants. In the language of pleading, own, proper, or original. See **ancient demesne.**

DE MINIMIS *(dĕ mĭ'-nĭ-mĭs)* Lat.: trifling. Of insufficient significance to warrant judicial attention.

DE MINIMIS NON CURAT LEX *(nŏn kū'-rät lĕx)* Lat.: the law does not care for small things; the law does not bother with trifles.

EXAMPLE: Cy is arrested for possession of one marijuana cigarette. Although marijuana possession has not been decriminalized in the state where Cy is arrested, the prosecutor decides not to prosecute Cy for the possession since it is only a *de minimis* infraction.

DEMISE term used to describe a **conveyance** of an **estate** in **real property;** to let, especially pursuant to a **lease** for a term of years.

DEMONSTRATIVE EVIDENCE evidence consisting of an object or thing, such as a weapon used in a crime, a stolen item, or a photograph or X-ray, that may aid the jury in understanding the crime before it but has no effect on the question of guilt; evidence other than a person's oral testimony but that may help to explain that testimony.

DEMUR to present a **demurrer.** More broadly, to take an exception to a point of law or an allegation of facts on the basis that even if it is so it does not advance the interests of the party making the statement.

DEMURRER formal **allegation** that facts as stated in the **pleadings,** even if true, are not legally sufficient for the case to proceed further. It does not admit anything but tests whether the **complaint** is sufficient to state a **cause of action.** In modern **procedure,** a **motion** to **dismiss** for failure to state a **claim** upon which relief may be granted replaces the demurrer. Compare **summary judgment.**

DENIAL a contradiction or **traverse;** in practice, a refutation of affirmative **allegations** contained in the **pleading** of an adversary. A defendant's **answer** must admit, deny, or state there is insufficient information upon which to admit or deny the plaintiff's allegations. Any allegation in a complaint to which a responsive pleading is required, other than for amount of damages, is admitted when not denied in the responsive pleading. **Averments** in a pleading to which no responsive pleading is required or permitted shall be taken as denied or avoided. See **confession and avoidance; negative pregnant.**

CONJUNCTIVE DENIAL a denial that denies all of the allegations as wholly untrue.

DISJUNCTIVE DENIAL a denial that denies the allegations as untrue in the alternative.

GENERAL DENIAL a denial of all of the plaintiff's allegations.

SPECIFIC DENIAL a denial of one or several, but not all, of the plaintiff's allegations.

DE NOVO *(dĕ nō'-vō)* Lat.: anew. A second time, as though the first had never taken place. See **plenary.**

DE NOVO HEARING a new hearing, in which the **judgment** of the first hearing is suspended and the case proceeds as if it had originated in the reviewing **tribunal.**

EXAMPLE: A state statute gives a defendant convicted in a municipal court the right to appeal that conviction *de novo* in a higher court. That right means that the defendant will have a new trial in which the facts and issues will be reviewed anew.

DEODAND see **forfeiture.**

DEPARTMENT OF HOMELAND SECURITY [DHS] leverages resources within federal, state, and local governments, coordinating the transition of multiple agencies and programs into a single, integrated agency focused on protecting the American people and their homeland. It has four essential missions: (1) information analysis and infrastructure protection (reviews intelligence and law enforcement information from all agencies of government and produces a single daily picture of threats against the homeland); (2) chemical, biological, radiological, and nuclear countermeasures (brings together the country's best scientists to develop technologies that detect biological, chemical, and nuclear weapons to best protect citizens); (3) emergency preparedness and response (works with state and local authorities to respond quickly and effectively to emergencies); and (4) border and transportation security (controls the borders and prevents terrorists and explosives from entering the country). Some of the specific agencies falling under the DHS include: the **TRANSPORTATION SECURITY ADMINISTRATION [TSA]** (protects the nation's transportation systems to ensure freedom of movement for people and commerce); the United States **Customs and Border Protection [CBP]** (responsible for protecting our nation's borders in order to prevent terrorists and terrorist weapons from entering the United States, while facilitating the flow of legitimate trade and travel); United States **Citizenship and Immigration Services [USCIS]** (responsible for the administration of immigration and naturalization adjudication functions and establishing immigration services policies and priorities); United States **Immigration and Customs Enforcement [ICE]** (responsible for identifying and shutting down vulnerabilities in the nation's border, economic, transportation, and infrastructure security); the **UNITED STATES COAST GUARD** (protects the public, the environment, and U.S. economic interests in the nation's ports, waterways, coastline, and on international waters as required to support national security); the **FEDERAL EMERGENCY MANAGEMENT AGENCY [FEMA]** (prepares the nation for hazards, manages federal response and recovery efforts following any national incident, and administers the National Flood Insurance Program); the **UNITED STATES SECRET SERVICE** (protects the President and other high-level officials and investigates counterfeiting and other financial crimes, including financial institution fraud, identity theft, computer fraud, and computer-based attacks on our nation's financial, banking, and telecommunications infrastructure); and the Office of Health Affairs (coordinates all medical activities to ensure appropriate preparation for and response to incidents having medical significance). See *www.dhs.gov*.

DEPENDENCY   a territory or possession not within the boundaries of the country that has jurisdiction to govern it. Dependencies of the United States include Puerto Rico, the Virgin Islands, Guam, and various other islands located in the Pacific Ocean.

DEPENDENT   any person with respect to whom a **taxpayer** can claim a dependency **exemption;** defined by the **Internal Revenue Code** as any individual supported by the taxpayer who is related to the taxpayer in specified ways or who makes his principal abode in the taxpayer's household.

DEPENDENT CARE   see **child and dependent care credit.**

DEPENDENT COVENANTS   see **covenant [DEPENDENT COVE-NANTS].**

DEPENDENT RELATIVE REVOCATION   the doctrine that provides that when a **will** revokes an earlier will executed by the same person, the earlier will is only revoked if the latter will is effective; otherwise, the earlier will remains in full effect and force.

DEPLETION   the exhaustion of a natural resource, the amount of the original deposit being hidden and thus necessarily unknown. Depletion is most often referred to in federal income **tax deduction** provisions that deal with exhaustion of natural resources.

The **DEPLETION ALLOWANCE** is a formula for computing and excluding from the proceeds of natural resource operations that part of the operations' proceeds that is in effect a return of **capital.**

EXAMPLE: Petro Corporation purchases several leases of land on which it plans to drill oil. If oil is extracted from any of those leased lands, the value of the lease is reduced. The *depletion allowance* determines a figure based on that reduction in value. Petro then uses that figure to reduce its tax obligation.

Depletion allowance should be contrasted with **depreciation** deduction provisions that deal with deterioration of tangible physical **property** incident to its use that shortens its period of service.

DEPONENT   a **witness;** especially one who gives information under oath, in a **deposition** concerning facts known to him or her.

DEPORTATION   the transfer of an **alien** to a foreign country because the deporting government refuses to harbor a person whose presence is deemed inconsistent with the public welfare. Compare **extradition.**

DEPOSE   1. to give **evidence** or **testimony,** especially in response to interrogation during a **deposition;** 2. the act of interrogating and eliciting testimony during a deposition, typically conducted by a lawyer.

DEPOSIT [EARNEST] MONEY see **earnest.**

DEPOSITION a method of pretrial **discovery** that consists of a stenographically transcribed statement of a **witness** under oath, in response to an attorney's questions, with opportunity for the opposing party or his or her attorney to be present and to cross-examine. Such a statement is the most common form of discovery and may be taken of any witness (whether or not a **party** to the **action**). When taken in the form described, it is called an oral deposition. Depositions may also be taken upon written **interrogatories,** where the questions are read to the witness by the officer who is taking the deposition.

DEPOSITION DE BENE ESSE see **de bene esse.**

DEPRECIATION a **deduction** allowed to a **taxpayer** representing a reasonable allowance for the exhaustion of property used in a trade or business, or property held for the production of income. The purpose of charging depreciation against equipment is to generate a tax-free stream of income equal to the portion of the **asset** that has been "used up" and to distinguish the portion of income that is a return of **capital.** Compare **depletion.**

ACCELERATED DEPRECIATION any one of a number of allowed methods of calculating depreciation that permit greater amounts of deductions in earlier years than are permitted under the straight line method, which assumes equal depreciation during each year of the asset's useful life.

SALVAGE VALUE the estimated value of the property when the taxpayer completes his or her use of the property. In determining the amount of depreciation allowable, salvage value must be subtracted from **basis.**

STRAIGHT LINE DEPRECIATION a method that calculates the depreciation deduction available by subtracting the asset's SALVAGE VALUE from its total value and dividing the difference by the number of years of the asset's useful life.

USEFUL LIFE the reasonable estimate of the term of an asset's usefulness to the taxpayer in his or her business.

DEPRECIATION RESERVE the total **depreciation** charged against all productive **assets** as stated on the **balance sheet.** The charge is made to allow realistic reduction in the value of productive assets and to allow tax-free recovery of the original investment in assets. See **accumulated depreciation.**

DEPREDATION see **piracy.**

DEPRESSANTS see **controlled substances.**

DERELICTION a recession of waters of the sea, a navigable river or other stream, by which land that had been covered with water is left dry. If the alteration is sudden and noticeable, ownership remains according to former bounds; but if recession is gradual and imperceptible, the derelict or dry land belongs to the **riparian** owner from whose shore the water has so receded. The term may also refer to the land that is thus left uncovered. For **contiguous** landowners to gain ownership of the newly uncovered land, the withdrawal of the water must appear permanent, not merely seasonal. Compare **accretion; avulsion.**

DERIVATIVE ACTION 1. an **action** based upon a primary right of a **corporation,** but asserted on its behalf by the **shareholder** because of the corporation's failure, deliberate or otherwise, to assert the right; 2. a **cause of action** founded upon an injury to another, as when a husband sues for loss of **consortium** or services of his wife on account of injury to her by the **defendant,** or when a father sues for loss of services of children. See **stockholders' derivative action.**

DERIVATIVE TORT an action in **tort** based on the **criminal** conduct of **defendant** that resulted in **injury** to **plaintiff** for which he seeks **compensation.** The action is distinct from any criminal prosecution that may result from the same conduct by defendant.

DEROGATION partial taking away of the effectiveness of a law; partially repealing or abolishing a law.

DESCENT a method of acquiring **property,** usually **real property,** through the laws of **descent and distribution** from a decedent without the use of a **will;** generally applied to **inheritance** only by **intestate succession.** Compare **devise.** See **worthier title, doctrine of.**

DESCENT AND DISTRIBUTION the transmission of an **intestate's property** to his **heirs.**

DESEGREGATION see **segregation.**

DESERTION act of abandonment of a relation or service in which one owes duties. In matrimonial law, an unjustified cessation from cohabitation, with intent not to resume it and without the consent of the other spouse, is desertion and is grounds for divorce. In military law, **ABSENT WITHOUT LEAVE [AWOL]** signifies an intention by a member of the armed forces not to return to service. It is punishable under the Code of Military Justice.

DESIGNEE one who is designated or delegated, usually to perform a specific role or duty.

DESIST see **cease and desist order.**

DESTINATION CONTRACT see **tender** [TENDER OF DELIVERY].

DESTRUCTIBILITY refers to a **common-law** rule that when a **contingent remainder** does not **vest** at or before the termination of the preceding freehold estate, the remainder **interest** is destroyed. Thus, the termination of the preceding estate, because of its inherent limitation, or as a result of forfeiture or **merger,** destroys the nonvested contingent remainder.

DESTRUCTIVE DEVICE a firearm or explosive or incendiary device. Includes poison gas, bombs, grenades, rockets, missiles, mines, or similar devices.

DESUETUDE a term applied to obsolete laws and practices that may therefore be regarded as no longer in effect.

DETAINER 1. keeping a person from goods or land to which he or she has a legal right; 2. a **writ** or **instrument,** issued by a competent officer, authorizing a prison warden to keep in his or her **custody** a person therein named. See also **detention.**

FORCIBLE DETAINER see **forcible detainer; forcible entry** [FORCIBLE ENTRY AND DETAINER].

UNLAWFUL DETAINER refusal to deliver on demand, as where the **tenant,** after termination of the lease, refuses to deliver possession to the **landlord.** Compare **tenancy** [TENANCY AT SUFFERANCE]; **trespass.**

DETENTION holding of a person charged with crime following the person's arrest on that charge; restraining a person for some official purpose, by establishing control over the person. See also **preventive detention**.

DETENTION CENTER see **jail** [DETENTION CENTER].

INVESTIGATIVE DETENTION refers to the holding of a suspect without formal arrest during the investigation of his possible participation in a crime. Such investigative detention is unconstitutional if **probable cause** does not exist to charge him with the crime.

DETERMINABLE FEE [FEE SIMPLE DETERMINABLE] an **interest** in **property** that may last forever, but that will automatically terminate upon the happening or nonhappening of a specified event. Also called a **DEFEASIBLE FEE** or a **FEE SIMPLE DEFEASIBLE.**

EXAMPLE: A brother conveys a large office building to his

sister provided she remains unmarried. If she is unmarried at her death, she can dispose of it as she pleases in her will. But once she marries, the ownership of the building reverts to the brother. The sister's interest in the building after the brother's conveyance is a *determinable fee.*

DETERMINATION a decision by a court or other adjudicative body. See **holding; judgment; verdict.**

DETINUE in **common law,** an **action** for the wrongful detention of **personal property;** a legal claim provided for the recovery of a specific thing, and for obtaining **damages** for its detention. Compare **detainer [UNLAWFUL DETAINER].**

DEVISE a gift of **real property** made by **will.** In modern usage, the term may also embrace **testamentary** gifts of **personal property.** Compare **bequest; legacy.**

DEVOLVE to pass property from one person to another by **operation of law,** without any voluntary act of the previous owner.

DICTA plural form of **dictum.**

DICTUM a statement in a judicial **opinion** not necessary for the decision of the case. Dictum differs from the **holding** in that it does not establish a rule binding on the courts in subsequent cases.

EXAMPLE: Sandor claims that the issue of his liability for damage on his sidewalk resulting in injury to another was settled in a previous case. The judge reminds Sandor that the previous case concerned the city's obligation to keep the sidewalks in good repair and the city's liability for injury to a person. The part of the case addressed to a private citizen's liability was not necessary to the decision and hence was only *dictum* and is not binding on this judge.

CONSIDERED DICTUM refers to a discussion of a point of law that, although it is dictum, is nevertheless so well developed that it is later incorporated into an opinion of a court as though it were authority.

DIE WITHOUT ISSUE see **failure of issue.**

DIGITAL CERTIFICATE encoded data of identifying information certifying that the sender or receiver is who it claims to be, by way of third-party verification. A method of tracking visitors to a web site. A **BLIND CERTIFICATE** verifies limited information without revealing the party's identity.

DIGITAL MILLENNIUM COPYRIGHT ACT primarily implements treaties of the WORLD INTELLECTUAL PROPERTY ORGANIZA-

TION (WIPO). Enacted in 1996, it criminalizes the circumvention of anti-piracy features of software and calls for payments of fees to record companies for webcasts of music.

DILATORY PLEA [PLEA IN ABATEMENT] in **common law,** a **plea** not responsive to the **merits** of a controversy, but a **defense** that simply delays or defeats the present **action,** leaving the **cause of action** unsettled. If a defendant, by establishing the facts, can defeat the plaintiff's cause of action in whole or in part, or can obtain substantial relief against the plaintiff, the plea is not dilatory, but **on the merits.** This kind of plea has largely disappeared under modern practice. Instead these defenses are now raised by **motion** or in an **answer.**

DILIGENCE attention to the matter at hand. **DUE DILIGENCE** or **REASONABLE DILIGENCE** is that level of attention required by the circumstances in order to avoid liability in **negligence.**

DILUTING THE SHARES see **watered stock.**

DIMINISHED CAPACITY in criminal law, the inability to have the state of mind, or **mens rea,** required for the commission of a particular crime. A successful defense of diminished capacity will usually result in conviction of a lesser offense, not an **acquittal.** Compare **insanity.**

DIMINISHED RESPONSIBILITY see **diminished capacity.**

DIMINUTION IN VALUE a measure of **damages** for **breach of contract** that reflects a decrease, occasioned by the breach, in the value of property with which the contract was concerned. In a building contract, for example, it is the difference between the value of the building as constructed and its value had it been constructed in conformance with the contract. Compare **cost of completion; damages [EXPECTATION DAMAGES]; specific performance.**

DIRECT AFFINITY see **affinity [DIRECT AFFINITY].**

DIRECT ATTACK a proceeding instituted to amend, **vacate** or enjoin **execution** of a judgment; an attempt by **appellants** to **avoid** or correct a **judgment** in a manner provided by law, as by an **appeal.** Compare **collateral [COLLATERAL ATTACK].**

DIRECT CAUSE see **cause [DIRECT CAUSE].**

DIRECT CONTEMPT see **contempt of court [DIRECT CONTEMPT].**

DIRECTED VERDICT a verdict returned by the **jury** at the direction of the trial judge, by whose direction the jury is bound. In **civil**

proceedings either party may receive a directed verdict in its favor if the opposing party fails to present a **prima facie case** or a necessary **defense.** In criminal proceedings, there may be a directed verdict of **acquittal,** but not a directed verdict of conviction, which would violate the defendant's constitutional right to a jury determination of his guilt or innocence.

DIRECT ESTOPPEL   see **estoppel [DIRECT ESTOPPEL].**

DIRECT EVIDENCE   proof based upon the witness's own observations that do not require any additional **inferences** to be drawn. Compare **circumstantial evidence.**

EXAMPLE: Direct Evidence: Susan testified that she looked out into her hallway at 4 A.M. and observed her neighbor Mae hitting her husband with a hammer. Circumstantial Evidence: Susan testified that at 4 A.M. she was awakened by screams and banging noises from the adjoining apartment and the next morning found the injured body of Mae's husband in the hallway. Additional inferences need to be drawn to link Mae to the crime of assaulting her husband.

DIRECT EXAMINATION   see **cross-examination [DIRECT EXAMINATION].**

DIRECTOR   a member of a board of directors of a **company** or **corporation,** who shares with others directors the legal responsibility of control over the officers and affairs of the company or corporation. A director has a **fiduciary** duty to the corporation and to its **shareholders** to manage the corporation in a manner consistent with their interests.

DIRECT ORDER OF ALIENATION   see **marshaling [marshalling] [DIRECT ORDER OF ALIENATION].**

DIRECT REDUCTION MORTGAGE   see **mortgage [DIRECT REDUCTION MORTGAGE].**

DISABILITY   state of being not fully capable of performing all functions, whether mental or physical; want of legal capacity such as **infancy, insanity** or past criminal conviction that renders a person legally **incompetent;** one person's inability to alter a given legal relation with another person. Compare **Durham Rule.**

DISBAR   to rescind an attorney's license to practice law because of illegal or unethical conduct.

DISCHARGE   1. to satisfy or dismiss the obligations of **contract** or **debt;** 2. the method by which a legal **duty** is extinguished. Compare **performance; rescission.**

DISCHARGE IN BANKRUPTCY the release of the **bankrupt** from all his or her provable debts, whether then payable or not, and debts founded on a contract, express or implied; but not a release from debts specifically excepted from discharge by the bankruptcy statute.

3. to release from **custody, acquit.** See **sentence** [SUSPENDED SENTENCE]. Compare **reprieve.**

DISCLAIMER 1. denial of a person's **claim** to a thing, though previously that person insisted on such a claim or right; 2. renunciation of the right to **possess** and of claim of **title;** 3. denial of a right of another, e.g., where an **insurer** disclaims an allegation of **liability** against its **insured** and thereby refuses to **indemnify** or defend the insured in a **lawsuit** [DISCLAIMER OF LIABILITY].

DISCONTINUANCE cessation of **proceedings** in an **action** where the **plaintiff** voluntarily puts an end to it, with or without judicial approval. Judicial approval may be required, depending upon each jurisdiction's rules of practice. Compare **dismissal; nonsuit.**

DISCOUNT a deduction from a specified sum; often used with transactions in negotiable **commercial paper** in which the instrument is bought at a price below its face amount to reflect the fact that the debt it represents is not due until a future date.

EXAMPLE: Sidney regularly enters into contracts where he is not to be paid until the work is completed. But Sidney needs the money before he starts the work to purchase work materials and pay other debts. Because the contracts represent obligations to pay by other parties, a bank is willing to give Sidney the money that the contracts call for less a *discount.* That discount mainly covers the difference in the value of the money given to Sidney now versus what the money will be worth when the bank is paid by the other parties, as well as a small profit margin for the bank. The discount will also factor in that percentage of the contracts which are not likely to be collected.

DISCOUNT BOND see **bond** [BOND DISCOUNT].

DISCOUNTED CASH FLOW measure of the present value of a future income stream generated by a **capital** investment.

DISCOVERY modern pretrial procedure by which one **party** gains information held by the adverse party, concerning the case; the disclosure by the adverse party of facts, deeds and documents that are exclusively within his or her possession or knowledge and that are necessary to support the other party's position. Common types of discovery are **depositions, interrogatories,** production of documents and requests for admissions.

EXAMPLE: Alina gets into an accident when her rear wheels stop for no reason, causing the car to skid into a highway divider. In her lawsuit against the car manufacturer, Alina uses the *discovery* procedure to obtain memos and test-run results that the manufacturer used in designing the car. Without discovery, Alina may not be able to acquire that information.

DISCRETION the freedom of a public officer to make choices, within the limits of his or her authority, among possible courses of action.

    ABUSE OF DISCRETION see **abuse of discretion.**

    DISCRETIONARY ACCOUNT in the **securities** trade, one in which the customer gives the **broker** or a third party complete or partial discretion to buy and sell securities. Such discretion typically extends to selection, price, timing, and amount purchased.

    JUDICIAL DISCRETION the reasonable use of judicial power, i.e., the court's freedom to decide within the bounds of law and fact.

    EXAMPLE: Jason, a juvenile, is charged with an assault upon another teenager. In Jason's state, the law provides the juvenile judge with the judicial discretion to have the case heard in the juvenile court or to transfer the case to an adult court. Previous cases and the law itself establish certain standards to use in determining whether a transfer is appropriate, but the judge has the discretion to decide which court shall hear the matter. The decision, though, may be appealed to a higher court.

    LEGAL DISCRETION the use of one of several equally satisfactory provisions of law.

    PROSECUTORIAL DISCRETION the wide range of alternatives for a **prosecutor** in criminal cases, including decision to prosecute, particular charges to be brought, bargaining, mode of trial conduct, recommendations for sentencing, **parole,** etc.

DISCRIMINATION the unequal treatment of parties who are similarly situated. Federal law prohibits discrimination on the basis of race, sex, nationality, religion, and age in matters of employment, housing, education, voting rights, and access to public facilities.

DISHONOR to refuse, rightly or wrongly, to make payment on a **negotiable instrument** when such an instrument is duly presented for payment.

DISINHERITANCE the act by the **donor** that dissolves the right of a person to **inherit** that **property** to which he or she previously had such right.

DISINTERMEDIATION movement of savings from banks and savings and loan associations into money market instruments, such as **treasury bills** and **notes.**

DISJUNCTIVE ALLEGATIONS [DENIAL] those that **charge** the **defendant** with either one act or another. The word "or" may not leave the **averment** uncertain as to which of two or more things is meant. An **allegation** that charges the commission of a **crime** by one act "or" another is **defective** if it does not clearly inform the defendant of the charge so that a **defense** can be prepared to meet it. The same standard is applied to **pleadings** in **civil** cases, where both disjunctive allegations and disjunctive denials generally constitute defective pleadings and are therefore inadmissible.

DISMISS to terminate a case or some part of it. Before or during the trial of a **civil action,** the suit may be dismissed voluntarily by the **plaintiff,** or involuntarily by the court upon **defendant's motion** to dismiss the **complaint** or any **count** thereof. See **demurrer.**

DISMISSAL a cancellation. Dismissal of a **motion** is a denial of the motion. Dismissal of a **complaint** or a related **count** terminates proceedings on the **claim** asserted in the complaint. Dismissal of an **appeal** places the parties in the condition as if there had been no appeal, confirming the **judgment** of the lower court.

DISMISSAL WITH PREJUDICE usually an adjudication upon the **merits** that operates as a **bar** to future action by preventing plaintiff from making further attempts at a claim based upon the same facts.

EXAMPLE: Jorge brings a lawsuit against a company, claiming that it never refunded his money for an item he returned. The company shows the judge a check made payable to Jorge and cashed by him, with a large notation on the check that it was payment for the return of the item. Jorge then tries to make an additional claim that the company owes him more money for other reasons. The judge will usually **dismiss with prejudice** Jorge's claim for the refund price alone and instruct him to file a separate claim if he is seeking more money. The "with prejudice" aspect of the court's decision means that Jorge can never again sue on the same claim unless he successfully appeals the decision.

DISMISSAL WITHOUT PREJUDICE such a dismissal is not **on the merits** and does not bar a subsequent **suit** on the same **cause of action,** nor affect any right or **remedy** of the parties.

DISORDERLY CONDUCT generic term embracing minor offenses that are generally below the grade of **misdemeanor,** but that nevertheless are somewhat criminal; broadly signifies conduct that tends to **breach** the peace or endanger the morals, safety or health of the community.

DISORDERLY HOUSE see **prostitution.**

DISPARAGEMENT the **tort** of discrediting a person's business (such as the quality of the merchandise) to third persons resulting in economic injury. Also applies to calling into question a person's **title** to property. An **injurious falsehood** applying to things is *disparagement* and applying to persons is **defamation.** See **bait and switch.**

DISPOSITION 1. the giving up of anything; often used in reference to a testamentary **proceeding,** as in "the disposition of the estate"; 2. courts "dispose of" **cases,** i.e., determine the rights of the parties or otherwise terminate the proceedings; 3. In criminal law, the **sentence** of the **defendant** is the disposition.

DISPOSSESS to oust, eject or exclude another from the possession of lands or premises, whether by legal process (as where a landlord lawfully evicts a tenant) or wrongfully. Compare **disseisin.**

DISPUTABLE PRESUMPTION see **presumption [REBUTTABLE PRESUMPTION].**

DISQUALIFICATION the inability to perform some act due to the existence of factors rendering the performance improper or inappropriate. For instance, a judge may be disqualified from hearing a particular case because of having previously represented one of the parties involved.

DISSEISIN 1. the act of wrongfully depriving a person of **seisin** of land; the taking of **possession** of land under claim or **color of title;** 2. any act, with or without the owner's consent, the necessary effect of which is to **divest** him of the **estate.**

DISSENT 1. to disagree; 2. a reasoned **opinion** that differs from that of the majority of the court.

DISSENTING OPINION see **opinion [DISSENTING OPINION].**

DISSOLUTION in **corporation** law, the end of the legal existence of a corporation, whether by expiration of **charter, decree** of court, act of legislature, vote of **shareholders,** or other means.

DISTINGUISH to demonstrate that an apparently similar case is so sufficiently different from the case at hand that it is of limited value as **precedent.**

DISTRAINER see **distress [DISTRAINER].** Also spelled distrainor.

DISTRAINT see **distress.**

DISTRESS the act or process of **DISTRAINT,** by which a person (the **DISTRAINER**), without prior court approval, seizes the **per-**

sonal property of another in **satisfaction** of a claim, as a pledge for **performance** of a duty or in reparation of an injury. Where goods are seized in satisfaction of a claim, the distrainer may hold the goods until the claim is paid and, failing payment, may sell them in satisfaction. The person whose goods are distrained has recourse against the wrongful distrainer in **replevin.**

EXAMPLE: A warehouseman stores goods for a farmer. When the farmer fails to pay the storage costs for over a year, the warehouse-man seizes in *distress* whatever goods the farmer presently has in the warehouse. If the farmer does not then pay for the storage charges that are past due, the warehouseman can sell the goods, take out what he is owed and refund the amount remaining to the farmer.

Originally, distress was a landlord's remedy; see **lien [LAND-LORD'S LIEN],** distinguishable from **attachment,** which is a court-ordered seizure of property. See **impounding; garnishment.**

DISTRESS, EMOTIONAL see **emotional distress.**

DISTRIBUTION a payment of yield in cash or in property to one entitled to such payment.

EXAMPLE: At the end of every three months, a corporation distrib-utes dividends to all of its shareholders. A *distribution* takes place whether the dividends represent checks, an increase in the number of shares each shareholder has, or any other method of payment.

DISTRICT ATTORNEY an officer of the governmental body under which he or she is operating, such as a state, county, or municipality, with the duty to prosecute all those accused of crimes. A district attorney will frequently have assistants who are similarly empowered. In the federal government, district attorneys are called **UNITED STATES ATTORNEYS.**

DISTRICT COURT 1. a court, established by the U.S. Constitution, having territorial **jurisdiction** over a district that may include a whole state or part of it. A district court has **original jurisdiction,** exclusive of courts of the individual states, over all offenses against laws of the United States, and is a court of general jurisdiction for **suits** between **litigants** of different states. See **diversity of citizen-ship; federal question jurisdiction.** 2. an inferior court in several states having limited jurisdiction to try certain minor cases.

DISTURBANCE OF THE PEACE any public act that molests inhabitants or that excites fear among normal persons.

DIVERS many, several, sundry; a grouping of unspecified persons, things, acts, etc.

DIVERSIONARY PROGRAMS   see **pretrial intervention [PTI]** [DIVERSIONARY PROGRAMS].

DIVERSITY JURISDICTION   see **diversity of citizenship.**

DIVERSITY OF CITIZENSHIP   the circumstance that grants to federal courts **original jurisdiction** over **cases** and **controversies** between citizens of different states or between a citizen of a state and an alien, subject to a minimum **jurisdictional amount** (the value in controversy) of $75,000.

DIVESTITURE   1. loss or surrender of a right or title or interest; 2. a **remedy** by which the court orders the offending party to rid itself of assets before the party would normally have done so. Divestiture, like **restitution,** has the purpose of depriving a defendant of the gains of wrongful conduct. It is a remedy sometimes used in the enforcement of the **antitrust laws.**

EXAMPLE: One of the top three oil companies purchases the sixth largest oil company. After a long investigation, the government determines that the purchase will remove gasoline price competition in many states. If a court agrees with the government's position, it will order the larger company to *divest* itself of the smaller company.

DIVIDEND   a **corporation's** profits or earnings appropriated for **distribution** among **shareholders.**

CUMULATIVE DIVIDEND   a dividend whose unpaid residue is added to the following distribution.

DIVIDEND ADDITION   life insurance in addition to the face value of the policy, purchased with dividends of the policy.

EX-DIVIDEND see **ex-dividend.**

EXTRAORDINARY DIVIDENDS   dividends of unusual form and amount, paid at unscheduled times from accumulated surplus.

LIQUIDATION DIVIDEND   dividend resulting from *winding up* affairs of a business, settling with its **debtors** and **creditors,** and appropriating and distributing to its shareholders a residue proportionate to the profit and loss.

PREFERRED DIVIDEND   fund paid to owners of **preferred stock** in priority over that to be paid to another class of shareholders.

SCRIP DIVIDEND   a dividend payable not in cash, but in certificates of indebtedness that give the holder certain rights against the corporation.

STOCK DIVIDEND   a dividend paid not in cash, but in **stock.**

DIVISIBLE CONTRACT   see **severable contract.**

DIVORCE   dissolution of the bonds of **marriage**. Compare **annul.**

NO-FAULT DIVORCE   a divorce granted without the necessity of a spouse guilty of marital misconduct. The most common no-fault ground is voluntary separation for a period of time, which creates a statutory presumption of incompatibility or irreconcilable differences. See **community property; equitable distribution.**

SEPARATION [DIVORCE A MENSA ET THORO] *(à měn'-sà ět thô'-rō)*   Lat.: from table and bed. A partial divorce decree, usually entered in the course of divorce proceedings, which directs the parties to live separately—indeed, forbids them to **cohabit**—but does not dissolve the marriage.

DNA TESTING   scientific evidence used in **criminal** cases and in **paternity** suits. DNA (deoxyribonucleic acid) molecules contain hereditary (genetic) information. The theory on which DNA testing is based consists of the following: all cells in the human body (except red blood cells) contain DNA; the structure of the DNA of a person is identical throughout a person's body; the DNA structure is constant from a person's infancy through their death; and, finally, that no two people (except identical twins) have the same DNA. DNA can be extracted from blood (white blood cells and plasma), skin, tissue, sperm, saliva, vaginal swabs, mouth scrapings, bones, and hair. The technique is widely accepted as scientifically reliable. While also known as "DNA FINGERPRINTING," the process has nothing to do with **fingerprints** themselves but rather with the concept of uniqueness and the ability to link an individual to a crime (or establish paternity). It is a test of exclusion (proving that this could not have been the person) as well as a test that can include a person as one of a percentage of a population that could be the source. In the first case of a person convicted of a crime by DNA evidence (through semen recovered from a rape victim), bands from the defendant's blood and the semen "matched" and the probability of such a match occurring at random was 0.0000002 (or the chance that it did not belong to the defendant was 1 in 833,333,333). It is this last area—the probability calculation—that has received the most criticism. Some courts exclude such calculations.

At the risk of oversimplification, the following terms frequently are used when discussing DNA testing. Methods of DNA analysis are noted below:

HLA DQ ALPHA [DQ ALPHA]   refers to the PCR method. HLA stands for human leukocyte antigen and DQ Alpha refers to the locus of the antigens.

MITOCHONDRIAL DNA [mtDNA]   a newer type of analysis used

to identify war remains, samples subjected to extreme conditions, or even unsolved crimes. Older biological samples that lack nucleated cellular material, such as hair, bones, and teeth, cannot be analyzed with older methods, but they can be analyzed with mtDNA. Nuclear DNA must be extracted for use in RFLP, PCR, and STR methods; however, mtDNA analysis uses DNA extracted from mitochondrion. Also used in cases of disputed maternity since mtDNA is inherited solely from the mother.

POLYMERASE CHAIN REACTION [PCR]   this method can analyze as little as one-tenth of the biological material that is needed for RFLP. PCR is also able to give quicker results; however, the results are less discriminating. The PCR technique consists of extraction of the biological material, amplification (replication), and then typing. It is an in vitro process through which repeated cycling of the reaction reproduces a specific region of DNA, yielding millions of copies from the original.

RECOMBINANT DNA TECHNOLOGY   procedure used to join together DNA sequences since a recombinant DNA molecule can enter a cell and replicate there.

RESTRICTION FRAGMENT LENGTH POLYMORPHISM [RFLP]   is a process that breaks DNA into small fragments at specific points on the DNA chain that are then measured. A disadvantage of the RFLP method is that it requires a large amount of non-degraded DNA.

SHORT TANDEM REPEATS [STR]   copies of an identical DNA sequence arranged in direct succession in a particular region of a chromosome. Short tandem repeats, or **VARIABLE NUMBER OF TANDEM REPEATS [VNTR],** is a method which uses markers for short, repeating segments combined with computer system analysis although visual detection is possible.

Y CHROMOSOME ANALYSIS   genetic markers on the Y chromosomes are especially useful for analyzing biological evidence, including relationships among males or where there are multiple male contributors, since the Y chromosome is passed directly from father to son.

States are increasingly requiring mandatory submission of blood samples from certain convicted persons for DNA identification and placement in an information bank that can then be used in the event that future crimes are committed. See **CODIS.**

DOB   date of birth.

DOCK   historically, criminal court enclosure wherein the prisoner was held during trial.

DOCKET 1. a list of cases on a court's calendar; 2. in **procedure,** a formal **record** of the proceedings in the court whose decision is being appealed.

DOCTOR-PATIENT PRIVILEGE see **physician-patient privilege.**

DOCTRINE OF WORTHIER TITLE see **worthier title, doctrine of.**

DOCUMENT any writing, recording, computer tape, blueprint, X-ray, photograph, or other physical object upon which information is set forth by means of letters, numbers, or other symbols.

DOCUMENTARY EVIDENCE a **document** having legal effect that is offered as **evidence.** Prior to being admitted as evidence, the authenticity of the document must be established by testimony as to how the writing was produced or the circumstances under which it has been kept.

DOCUMENT OF TITLE a **bill of lading,** dock warrant, warehouse receipt, or order for the delivery of **goods,** or any other document that in the regular course of business or financing is treated as adequate evidence that the person in possession of it is entitled to receive, hold, and dispose of the document and the goods it covers.

DOCUMENT, ORIGINAL see **best evidence rule.**

DOLUS see **culpa.**

DOMA see **defense of marriage act [doma].**

DOMAIN 1. land of which one is absolute owner. See **eminent domain; public domain; public easement;** 2. DOMAIN [NAME] denotes an Internet address representing a specific web page. URL stands for "uniform resource locator" and represents the entire address. An example of a URL is *http://www.barronseduc.com/.* The domain name is barronseduc.com. See **hyperlink.**

DOMESDAY BOOK a record made in the time of William the Conqueror (1066–87) consisting of accurate and detailed surveys of the lands in England and the means by which the alleged owners obtained title.

DOMESTIC PARTNERSHIP see **civil union.** Compare **marriage.**

DOMESTIC VIOLENCE physical abuse, including sexual abuse, emotional abuse, or victim isolation by one person upon another whether dating, married, or formerly in such a relationship. Most states include family members or cohabitants of a residence under the concept for purposes of legal remedies.

DOMICILE an individual's permanent home or principal establishment. Residence is not the same as domicile, since a person can have many transient residences but only one legal domicile, which is the home address to which he or she always intends to return for prolonged periods.

EXAMPLE: As the result of a long and prosperous business career, Ricardo has bought houses in Florida, New Jersey, Colorado and California. But Ricardo spends most of his time at his house in New Jersey because that is only fifteen minutes from his corporation's headquarters. Ricardo's *domicile* is New Jersey and would remain so even if in one particular year he spent more time at one of his other homes. Should he sell his business and leave New Jersey to permanently live in California, his domicile would then change.

The domicile of a business is the address where the establishment is maintained or where the governing power of the enterprise is exercised. For purposes of taxation, it is often a principal place of business.

DOMICILIARY an individual who is domiciled in a particular state or country is a domiciliary of that state or country. See **domicile.**

DOMINANT ESTATE [TENEMENT] **property** retained by an original grantor when a particular tract is subdivided and a portion is **conveyed,** and to which there attaches a right to some beneficial use of the conveyed or **servient estate** or a portion of it. The owner of the retained land (dominant estate) is said to have a right of **easement** in the servient estate.

DOMINION having both **title** to and possession of **property;** having control of both ownership and use.

DONATED SURPLUS see **unearned surplus [DONATED SURPLUS].**

DONATIO *(dō-nä'-shē-ō)* Lat.: a **gift;** donation.

DONATION see **contribution.**

DONATIVE INTENT voluntary intent on the part of a **donor** to make a **gift.**

DONEE the recipient of a **gift** or **trust;** one who takes without first giving **consideration;** one who is given a power, right or interest. Compare **bailee; trustee.**

DONEE BENEFICIARY see **third party beneficiary [DONEE BENEFICIARY].**

DONOR one who gives a **gift;** creator of a **trust;** the party conferring a power, right, or interest.

DOUBLE DAMAGES see **damages [DOUBLE [TREBLE] DAMAGES].**

DOUBLE JEOPARDY prosecution or punishment twice for the same offense, which is prohibited by the U.S. Constitution and by many state constitutions.

EXAMPLE: Ray is charged with destroying government property. After a long trial, a jury finds Ray not guilty. Immediately after the trial, new evidence is discovered that unquestionably links Ray to the destruction. Under principles of *double jeopardy,* the prosecutor cannot retry Ray for the crime even with the new evidence.

See **collateral [COLLATERAL ESTOPPEL].**

DOUBT see **reasonable doubt.**

DOWAGER generally, a widow supported by the property of her deceased husband. In real property, a widow who has a life estate in the real property of her husband by her right of **dower.**

DOWER a **life estate** to which a wife is entitled upon the death of her husband. At **common law,** the widow was entitled to one-third of all the property in which her husband was **seized** in **fee** at any time during the marriage [coverture]. Her dower is a **freehold** estate, and cannot derive from an **estate for years.** Compare **homestead rights.** See **curtesy; inchoate dower.**

Dower rights have been abrogated in many jurisdictions or limited to interests that the husband holds at his death. Where they still exist, a wife can join in a **conveyance** and thereby give up her dower rights. See **widow's election.**

DOWNZONING see **zoning [DOWNZONING].**

DOWRY the money and personal property that a wife brings to her husband in marriage.

DQ ALPHA see **DNA testing [HLA DQ ALPHA].**

DRAFT 1. an order in writing directing a person other than the **maker** to pay a specified sum to a named person. Drafts may or may not be **negotiable instruments,** depending upon whether the elements of negotiability are satisfied. Draft is synonymous with **BILL OF EXCHANGE.** 2. the preliminary form of a legal document (e.g., the draft of a contract—often called "rough draft"); 3. the process of preparing or **DRAWING** a legal document (e.g., drafting a will) or piece of proposed legislation; 4. in a military context, conscription of citizens into the military service.

SIGHT DRAFT one that is payable on demand; a **bill** of exchange for immediate collection.

TIME DRAFT a draft which is not payable until a specified future time. For instance, a post-dated check is a time draft.

DRAGNET CLAUSE see **mother hubbard clause [DRAGNET CLAUSE]**.

DRAM SHOP ACT a legislative enactment imposing **strict liability** upon the seller of intoxicating beverages when the sale results in the harm of a third party's person, **property** or means of support.

EXAMPLE: Jake left a tavern after consuming an excessive amount of alcohol. His drinking caused an accident. The victim of the accident sues the tavern owner under that state's *Dram Shop Act.* Since the act imposes strict liability on the owner, he is liable even if he did not realize or had no way of realizing that Jake was drunk.

DRAW 1. to withdraw money from an account in a bank or other depository; 2. to execute a check or **draft** for the withdrawal of money; 3. to prepare a draft of a legal document, such as a **complaint,** a **deed** or a **will.**

DRAWEE one whom a **BILL OF EXCHANGE** (see **bill; draft**) or a **check** directs to pay to another a specified sum of money. In the typical checking account situation, the bank is the drawee, the person writing the check is the **maker** or **drawer,** and the person to whom the check is written is the **payee.**

DRAWER person by whom a **check** or **BILL OF EXCHANGE** (see **bill**) is drawn; person directing payment by another by way of a **draft.**

DRAWING see **draft [DRAWING].**

DRIVING WHILE INTOXICATED [DWI] the criminal offense of operating a motor vehicle while under the influence of alcohol or drugs. State law controls both the definition of "operating," such as whether it includes the actual driving of the car or merely sitting in the car, and the level of intoxication needed in order to be found in violation of the law.

DROIT *(drwäh)* Fr.: a right; law; the whole body of the law.

DRUG ABUSE the repeated or uncontrolled use of **controlled substances.** While possession or use of controlled substances may be a crime, addiction to drugs is a disease that cannot be made a crime under the **due process** clause of the Constitution. Drug abuse or addition is a ground for **divorce** in some states.

DRUG COURT   the coordination of treatment for substance abuse with judicial oversight. In recognition of the link between substance abuse and criminal activity, some progressive courts have embraced the concept of stopping the illicit use and abuse of all addictive substances and thereby curtailing related criminal activity. In a comprehensive plan, the prosecutor's office screens candidates who are judicially approved for participation in treatment-based programs, coordinated with job training, and pretrial, probation, and parole agencies. In exchange for successful completion of the treatment program, the court may dismiss the original criminal charge, reduce or set aside a sentence, offer some lesser penalty, or offer a combination of these. Other programs named "drug courts" may refer to focusing on expediting case processing under expanding court dockets, clogged with drug-related offenses. They may look similar, but they may not provide the orientation toward treatment and judicial supervision.

DRUG LAW   see **generic** [GENERIC DRUG LAW].

DRUGS   see **controlled substances; driving while intoxicated.**

DUAL CITIZENSHIP   concept whereby two different sovereigns within their respective territorial confines may lawfully claim citizenship of the same person and the person may claim citizenship to each of the sovereignties. For an American **citizen** to be deprived of United States citizenship the government must show the commission of an expatriating act as defined by statute done voluntarily and with intent to relinquish citizenship. Also refers to the fact that an American citizen is a citizen of the United States and of the state in which the citizen resides.

DUCES TECUM   *(dū'-chĕs tā'-kŭm)*   Lat.: bring with you. See **subpoena** [SUBPOENA DUCES TECUM].

DUE CARE   the degree of care that a person of ordinary prudence and reason (a **reasonable man**) would exercise under given circumstances. The concept is used in **tort** law to indicate the standard of care or the legal **duty** one normally owes to others. **Negligence** is the failure to use due care.

EXAMPLE: Basic construction trade usage mandates that a certain size beam be used to support a certain amount of weight. In its hurry, a construction company uses a smaller beam because it is all that is available. The floor supported by that beam collapses, and three workers are injured. The use of the smaller beam represents a failure on the part of the company to use *due care.*

DUE COURSE   see **payment in due course.**

DUE DATE   time fixed for payment of **debt, tax, interest,** etc.

DUE DILIGENCE see **diligence [DUE DILIGENCE].**

DUE PROCESS OF LAW   a phrase introduced into American jurisprudence in the **Fifth** and **Fourteenth Amendments** to the U.S. Constitution; the principle that the government may not deprive an individual of life, liberty or property unless certain rules and procedures required by law are followed. The phrase does not have a fixed meaning, but embodies society's fundamental notions of legal fairness. Specifically, the constitutional safeguard of **SUBSTANTIVE DUE PROCESS** requires that all legislation, state or federal, must be reasonably related to a legitimate government objective. The concept of **PROCEDURAL DUE PROCESS** guarantees procedural fairness where the government attempts to deprive one of his or her property or liberty; this requires notice and a fair hearing prior to a deprivation of life, liberty or property.

EXAMPLE: Police in a municipality devise a scheme to produce a confession from Randy, who was accused of murder. The trial judge permits the prosecution to use the confession, and Randy is convicted. On appeal, a judge could find that the scheme violates *procedural due process of law,* based on the nature of the police scheme and the general nature of the American judicial system, which looks to produce convictions based on evidence acquired from sources other than the accused. In essence, due process is that level of process which is deemed fair based on a balancing of all interests.

DUI   driving under the influence of alcohol or drugs. See **driving while intoxicated [DWI].**

DUMMY   a strawman, a sham.

DUMMY CORPORATION   a **corporation** that has no business purpose other than to provide protection from liability or the disclosure of the principal behind its activities.

DUMMY DIRECTOR   a **director** who serves in name only and has no real control over the corporation's activities.

DUMMY SHAREHOLDER   a **shareholder** who owns **stock** in name only and has no financial interest in the corporation.

DUMPING   the sale of manufactured goods for a price lower than its fair value; sale of commodities in foreign market at a price that is lower than the price or value of comparable commodities in the country of their origins. Under the **ANTIDUMPING LAW,** the United States may impose special **custom duties** on foreign manufacturers that attempt to import goods into this country for less than their fair value if an industry in the United States is or may be materially injured. Also, discharge of waste material into the environment.

DUPLICITOUS refers to a **pleading** that joins in the same **count** two or more distinct grounds of **action** to enforce a single right. To allege more than one distinct claim in the same **indictment** is *duplicitous.*

DUPLICITY the technical invalidity resulting from uniting two or more **causes of action** in one **count** of a **pleading,** or multiple defenses in one plea, or multiple **crimes** in one count of an **indictment,** or two or more incongruous subjects in one legislative act, all contrary to proper **procedural** or constitutional requirements. See also **joinder; misjoinder.**

DURESS refers to conduct that has the effect of compelling another person to do what he need not otherwise do. It is a recognized **defense** to any act, such as a **crime,** contractual **breach** or **tort,** all of which must be voluntary to create **liability.** See **involuntary.**

EXAMPLE: Ximao is held at gunpoint until she agrees to help some people rob a bank. At her trial for the robbery, Ximao pleads *duress* and explains what happened. If her version of the facts is accepted, her defense of duress prevents a finding of guilty against her.

DURHAM RULE a test of criminal responsibility that states that an accused is not criminally responsible if his unlawful act was the product of mental defect. The Durham Rule was the first major modification of the **common law M'Naghten Rule** but is no longer in force in the District of Columbia (where it was adopted), having been superseded by the American Law Institute's Model Penal Code test. This new test asks whether the defendant lacks substantial capacity to conform his conduct to the requirements of law, and is now used by a number of jurisdictions. See **insanity.**

DUTY 1. obligation of one person to another. 2. In **tort** law, duty is a legally sanctioned obligation the **breach** of which results in the **liability** of the actor. Thus, an individual owes a **DUTY OF CARE** to conduct himself to avoid **negligent** injury to others. See **due care.** 3. In tax law, a duty is a levy [tax] on **imports** and exports.

DELEGABLE DUTY a duty that the person under legal obligation is able to transfer to another.

DUTY, LEGAL see **legal duty.**

DUTY OF PRODUCING EVIDENCE see **burden of proof.**

DUTY TO MITIGATE DAMAGES see **mitigation of damages.**

DWELLING HOUSE one's residence; a structure or apartment used as a home for a family unit; a house in which the occupier and his family usually reside. In the law of real property, it includes everything attached to or considered an accessory to the main building, such as a garage or barn, and may consist of a cluster of buildings.

DWI   see **driving while intoxicated [DWI].**

DYING DECLARATIONS   see **hearsay rule [DYING DECLARATIONS].**

E

EARMARK Congressional provision setting aside a portion of revenue for a specified project, program, or grant.

EARNEST in **civil law,** something of value given by one party to another to bind a **contract,** usually a sales agreement; serves both as part payment or **performance** and as a method of predetermining **liquidated damages** for **breach** of the contract. On breach by buyer, seller retains the earnest, while in seller's breach, buyer is entitled to twice the value of the earnest.

In **common law,** earnest often denotes a down payment, but unlike a down payment, earnest is by definition forfeited on breach of contract.

EARNINGS AND PROFITS a tax term referring to the income of the **corporation** that, if distributed to its **shareholders,** would constitute a **dividend** to each shareholder.

ACCUMULATED EARNINGS AND PROFITS the amount of earnings and profits from prior years earned by a corporation but not yet distributed to its shareholders.

CURRENT EARNINGS AND PROFITS the earnings and profits of a corporation earned during the current taxable year. For dividend purposes, **distributions** to shareholders are deemed paid first out of current earnings and profits.

EARNINGS REPORT see **income statement.**

EASEMENT a right, created by an express or implied agreement, to make lawful and **beneficial use** of the land of another. Such use must not be inconsistent with any other uses already being made of the land. An easement is a privilege connected with the land and is therefore not a **possessory interest** or **fee.**

AFFIRMATIVE EASEMENT an easement that allows its owner to do affirmative acts on the subservient property, such as to use the subservient property as a right of way.

DEDICATION see **dedication.**

EASEMENT APPURTENANT a pure easement, or easement proper, that is, one that belongs to whomever owns the **dominant estate** to which the benefit of the easement attaches. In contrast to an

EASEMENT IN GROSS (definition follows), an easement appurtenant passes with the dominant estate to all subsequent **grantees** and is **inheritable.** See **appurtenant.**

EASEMENT BY IMPLICATION see **IMPLIED EASEMENT** (below).

EASEMENT BY PRESCRIPTION see **PRESCRIPTIVE EASEMENT** (below).

EASEMENT IN GROSS   a personal privilege to make use of another's land. It is not appurtenant to a dominant estate and is therefore not **assignable** or **inheritable.** See **license.**

EASEMENT OF NECESSITY   one necessary for the continued use of the land when a larger tract of land has been subdivided. If without the easement either the grantee or grantor cannot make use of his or her property, the existence of an easement of necessity is implied by **operation of law.**

EQUITABLE EASEMENT an equitable servitude, and therefore only enforceable in equity. To be enforceable at law, there must be **privity** between the grantor and grantee. As an equitable servitude, however, privity is not necessary to enforce the easement so long as the subsequent grantee has either actual or constructive notice of the easement. Violation of this easement is remedied by an injunction rather than money damages.

IMPLIED EASEMENT   one created by operation of law from the particular circumstances involved rather than by a written instrument. A **QUASI EASEMENT** will be implied where at the time of the grant there existed an apparent, permanent, continuous and necessary use of the land from which it can be inferred that an easement permitting its continuation was intended, as, for example, where a lot containing a driveway is severed from the lot containing the house.

NEGATIVE EASEMENT   an easement that restricts a landowner from doing certain acts he or she would normally be permitted to do in connection with his or her own land. See **restrictive covenant.**

PRESCRIPTIVE EASEMENT [EASEMENT BY PRESCRIPTION]   an easement that is acquired through the uninterrupted use of another's land for a period of time that would be sufficient to acquire title to the land by **adverse possession.**

PUBLIC EASEMENT   see **public easement.**

RECIPROCAL NEGATIVE EASEMENTS   an implied restriction upon the use of property that can arise where a common grantor of several adjoining parcels (especially a subdivision) has failed to insert the restrictions from prior deeds into deeds to parcels conveyed later. See **license.** Compare **run with the land.**

EXAMPLE: When Sunbelt Housing Cooperative sold the first half of a housing complex, they included a provision that no commercial establishments would be allowed on any property owned by Sunbelt. The contracts for sale on the second half of the complex included no such provision. Still, a purchaser of a lot on the second half cannot set up a psychologist's clinic in his home. A court will usually imply a *reciprocal negative easement* based on the sales contracts of the first half of the complex, thereby limiting all structures throughout Sunbelt to residential use.

EAVESDROPPING the monitoring of communications by a third party without the knowledge of the communicating parties. See **invasion of privacy; wiretapping.**

ECCLESIASTICAL LAW English **law** pertaining to matters concerning the church. This law was administered by ecclesiastical courts and is considered a branch of English **common law.** It was intended to vindicate the dignity and peace of the church by reforming the ecclesiastical state and persons, and all manner of errors, heresies, schisms, abuses, offenses, **contempts** and enormities. Today, in **equity** and **divorce** cases, courts still rely on the principles and doctrines established by ecclesiastical law insofar as these principles are consistent with relevant constitutional and statutory law. American law specifically adopted the practice of granting **alimony,** as incident to **divorce,** from English ecclesiastical law.

Historically, the ecclesiastical courts had undisturbed jurisdiction over rights of marriage, actions for divorce, restitution of **conjugal rights,** and testamentary and intestacy cases. There is, however, a conflict of opinion as to whether ecclesiastical law has been adopted as part of the common law of this country. Some courts hold that this code of laws cannot be considered part of the common law since it is based on a union of church and state that has no place in our legal system. Other courts consider some of this law part of the common law, especially if these laws afford a good rule of **construction** for a particular American law. See **canon, corpus juris.**

ECONOMIC STIMULUS federal funds provided to generate economic recovery in a recession by saving or creating jobs, providing energy savings and infrastructure improvements, and generally restoring confidence in the economy. See **TARP.**

ECU see **Eurodollar.**

EEOC see **equal opportunity** [EQUAL EMPLOYMENT OPPORTUNITY COMMISSION].

EFFECTS, PERSONAL see **personal effects.**

E.G. abbreviation for exemplia gratia; for example.

EGRESS see **ingress and egress.**

EIGHTH AMENDMENT one of the **Bill of Rights** passed in 1791 prohibiting **cruel and unusual punishment** and excessive **bail** and fines. The ban against cruel and unusual punishment has been applied against a state's imposition of a penalty for the status of being addicted to the use of narcotics, but the **Supreme Court** has given the state courts great deference in determining what constitutes cruel and unusual punishment in terms of sentencing for various crimes. However, the amendment does limit the kinds of punishment that can be imposed, proscribes punishment grossly disproportionate to the severity of the crime, and imposes substantive limits on what can be made criminal and punished as such.

EIS [EIR] see **environmental impact statement [report].**

EJECTMENT a legal action brought by one claiming a right to possess **real property** against another who has **adverse possession** of the premises or who is a **holdover** (**tenant** who remains beyond the termination of a **lease**). In **common law** the action was originally commenced by a **lessee** against an intruder. Later it became a possessory action brought by the holder of legal **title** to recover possession from one holding under an invalid title. Compare **eviction.**

EJUSDEM GENERIS *(ĕ-yūs'-dĕm jĕn'-ĕr-ĭs)* Lat.: of the same class. A rule of statutory **construction,** generally accepted by both state and federal courts, providing that where general words follow enumerations of particular classes of persons or things, the general words shall be construed as applicable only to persons or things of the same general kind as those enumerated.

EXAMPLE: A state law forbids concealing on one's person "pistols, revolvers, derringers, or other dangerous weapons." Jed is arrested under that law for concealing a long-blade knife. Under the rule of *ejusdem generis,* the law will probably not apply to Jed since "other dangerous weapons" as used here implies firearms or, perhaps even more narrowly, handguns.

Compare **sui generis.**

ELECTION the selection of a public official by the citizens of a country, state, or other political body; the choice between two or more legal rights, whether they arise under a statute, by contract, or otherwise.

ELECTION OF REMEDIES a choice of possible **remedies**

permitted by law for an injury suffered; a rule of **procedure** that requires the party to make a choice among alternative and inconsistent remedies all of which are allowed by law on the same facts. Once a choice is made, the alternatives not chosen are **waived.** Thus, while the plaintiff may seek the alternative remedies of **specific performance** or **damages** for a **breach** of **contract,** he or she may not ask for alternative inconsistent remedies such as **rescission** and damages, since rescission elects to treat the contract as **void** and the request for damages seeks to enforce a valid contract. Many jurisdictions do not require election of remedies until late in the proceedings.

ELECTION UNDER THE WILL the principle that to take under a **will** is to submit to all its provisions. Specifically, it consists of the choice of accepting the benefit given under the will and relinquishing a claim, such as **dower,** that one may have to a portion of the **estate** of another, or retaining that claim and rejecting the request provided by the will.

ELECTION, WIDOW'S see **widow's election.**

ELECTIVE FRANCHISE see **franchise** [ELECTIVE FRANCHISE].

ELECTIVE SHARE see **right of election.**

ELEGIT see **fieri facias** [ELEGIT].

ELEMENT an ingredient or factor, as the elements of an offense.

ELEMENTS the forces of nature: fire, air, earth, and water. References to "caused by the elements" is used synonomously with "caused by an **Act of God.**"

ELEVENTH AMENDMENT an amendment to the U.S. Constitution effectively prohibiting the federal courts from hearing cases against a state by citizens of that state or of another state unless the state consents to be sued. The amendment is rooted in the doctrine of **sovereign immunity.**

ELIGIBLE COMBINED PLAN see **DB(k).**

EMANCIPATION 1. freeing of someone from control of another; 2. express or implied relinquishing by a parent of rights in, or authority and control over, a **minor** child.

EMBARGO prohibition on the transportation of goods into or out of a country, usually done to control trade or in wartime.

EMBEZZLEMENT **fraudulent** appropriation for one's own use of property lawfully in his **possession,** a type of **larceny** that did not exist in **common law** because it does not involve a **trespassory** taking; thus it is a crime created by statute. Embezzlement is often associated with bank employees, public officials or officers of organizations, who may in the course of their lawful activities come into possession of property, such as money, actually owned by others.

EXAMPLE: A bank teller is short of cash one month and takes some money out of the deposits received with the full intention of returning it in a few weeks. The intent to return the money, though, has no relevance to the fact that the money was embezzled. The only defense in this instance would be that the teller thought the money belonged to him or that he had the owner's consent to borrow the money.

Compare **defalcation; misapplication [misappropriation] of property; theft.**

EMBLEMENTS 1. the right of a **tenant** of agricultural land to remove crops that he or she has planted, even if the tenancy has expired before harvest; 2. vegetable **chattels** such as corn, produced annually as the result of one's labor and deemed **personal property** in the event of the death of the farmer before the harvest.

EMBRACERY the common-law **misdemeanor** of attempting to bribe or corruptly influence a **juror;** also called JURY TAMPERING. See **obstruction of justice.**

EMERGENCY ECONOMIC STABILIZATION ACT see **TARP** [EMERGENCY ECONOMIC STABILIZATION ACT].

EMINENT DOMAIN the inherent right of the state to take private property for **public use,** without the individual property owner's consent; but just compensation must be paid to the property owner. See **expropriation.** Compare **public domain; public easement.**

EMOLUMENT profit derived from office, rank, employment, or labor, including salary, fees and other **compensation.**

EMOTIONAL DISTRESS extreme personal suffering caused by the **intentional** or **negligent** actions of another. Physical injury (or even physical contact) is no longer a required element for the recovery of **damages.** Monetary awards have been issued in cases of **harassment, sexual harassment, libel,** and **slander.** INTENTIONAL INFLICTION OF EMOTIONAL DISTRESS and NEGLIGENT INFLICTION OF EMOTIONAL DISTRESS involve those two respective **states of mind.** Examples might include a lab technician calling and deliberately falsely stating, "Your lab results show that you have HIV" (intentional) versus the loss of a coffin and its contents by an airline (negligent).

EMOTIONAL INSANITY see **insanity [EMOTIONAL INSANITY].**

EMPLOYEE SHARE OWNERSHIP PLAN [ESOP] a plan designed to provide a retirement benefit and a stake in the corporation for the employee. Such plans are also used by employees to purchase plants that are being closed.

EMPLOYEE STOCK OPTION see **stock option [EMPLOYEE STOCK OPTION].**

EMPLOYERS LIABILITY ACTS statutes specifying the extent to which employers shall be **liable** to make **compensation** for **injuries** sustained by their employees in the course of employment. Unlike in **workers' compensation** laws, which have replaced these acts in many states, the employer is made liable only for injuries resulting from his **breach** of a **duty** owed the employee, i.e., his **negligence.** See **assumption of risk; Federal Employers Liability Act; fellow servants.**

EMPLOYMENT RETIREMENT INCOME SECURITY ACT OF 1974 see **ERISA [Employment Retirement Income Security Act of 1974].**

ENABLING CLAUSE a provision in most new laws or statutes that gives appropriate officials the power to implement and enforce the law.

EXAMPLE: A statute that provides extra money for public housing is passed. The statute will include an *enabling clause* permitting the Department of Housing and Urban Development to spend the money accordingly.

ENACTING CLAUSE generally, the **preamble** of a **statute,** or the part that identifies the statute as a legislative act and authorizes it as law. Thus, "Be it enacted by the Senate and House of Representatives of the United States in Congress assembled," etc., is the enacting clause used in Congressional legislation.

EN BANC *(än bänk)* Fr.: by the full court. Many **appellate courts** sit in divisions of three or more judges from among a larger number on the full court. Sometimes either on the court's **motion** or at the request of a **litigant** the court will consider a case by the full court rather than by only a part of it. A matter reconsidered by the whole court after a part of it has rendered its decision is called a **REHEARING EN BANC,** sometimes spelled "en bank."

ENCLOSURE land enclosed by something other than an imaginary boundary line, i.e., a wall, hedge, fence, ditch or other actual obstruction; also called a **CLOSE.**

ENCROACH to intrude gradually upon the rights or property of another. An encroachment is any infringement on the property or authority of another.

ENCUMBRANCE any right to, interest in or legal **liability** upon **real property** that does not prohibit passing **title** to the land but that diminishes its value. Encumbrances include **easements, licenses, leases,** timber privileges, **homestead** privileges, **mortgages,** judgment **liens,** etc.

EXAMPLE: A piece of land Raj wants is *encumbered* by a mortgage that is greater than the stated value of the land. He purchases the property anyway, believing that the value is understated and that one day he will be able to sell the land at a great profit.

ENDORSEMENT see **indorsement.**

ENDOWMENT a permanent fund of **property** or money bestowed upon an institution or a person, the income from which is used to serve the specific purpose for which the gift was intended.

ENEMY COMBATANT designation under which a detainee is not provided rights otherwise entitled to under the laws of the country detained in. An *enemy combatant* is either (1) a person who has engaged in or supported hostilities against the United States or its co-belligerents who is not a "lawful enemy combatant." A "lawful enemy combatant" is defined generally as a member of the regular forces of a state party engaged in hostilities against the United States; or (2) an *enemy combatant* is a person who has been determined to be so by a competent tribunal established under the authority of the President or the Secretary of Defense. They are not considered to qualify under the **Geneva Conventions** as prisoners of war.

ENFEOFF to create a **feoffment.** The term refers to an early common law means of conveying **freehold** estates and has been used in some modern **deeds** to signify a conveyance of **title.**

EN GROS *(än grō)* Fr.: in gross (large) amount; total; by wholesale.

ENJOIN to command or instruct with authority; to suspend or restrain. One may be enjoined or commanded by a court either to do a specific act or to refrain from doing a certain act. See **injunction.**

EXAMPLE: Plastics Company has been disposing of its waste products in an adjacent river for over a decade. Environmentalists finally determine that some of the liquid waste contains a deadly carcinogen. A court *enjoins* (i.e., forbids) Plastics from using the river for disposal based on the environmentalists' proofs.

ENJOYMENT   substantial present economic benefit; **beneficial use** and purpose to which **real** or **personal property** may be put; implies right to use and to profits and income from use, rather than mere technical ownership. In common usage, synonymous with use and occupancy; usually infers **possession.**

ADVERSE ENJOYMENT   see **adverse possession**.

COVENANT OF QUIET ENJOYMENT   see **quiet enjoyment.**

ENJOYMENT, QUIET   see **quiet enjoyment.**

ENLARGEMENT   a rule of civil procedure permitting a court to extend the expiration period for any act required or allowed to be done at or within a specified time. Once cause is shown, the court may act in its discretion with or without motion or notice if the period has not expired. If the period has expired, the court can only act upon motion where the failure to act was the result of excusable neglect. Certain of the time periods found in specific rules may not be enlarged by this general rule, but can only be enlarged by conditions within those rules themselves.

EN MASSE   all together, as a group.

ENRICHMENT   see **unjust enrichment.**

ENTAIL   to create a **fee tail;** to create a fee tail from a **fee simple.**

ENTERPRISE   any individual, partnership, corporation, or any union or group of individuals associated in fact though not a legal entity. Some states have expanded the meaning to include sole proprietorships, business or charitable trusts, governmental entities, and illicit as well as licit entities.

ENTIRETY   see **tenancy [TENANCY BY THE ENTIRETY].**

ENTITY   a being that exists for tax, accounting or other particular purpose, such as a corporation, governmental body or an estate. A **legal entity** is one that, while not a person, can sue, be sued and make decisions as an individual could, e.g., a corporation.

ENTRAPMENT   in criminal law, an AFFIRMATIVE DEFENSE (see **defense**) created either by statute or by court decision in the given jurisdiction that excuses a **defendant** from criminal liability for **crimes** induced by trickery on the part of law enforcement officers or other agents of the government. To sustain the defense, the defendant must demonstrate that but for the objectionable police conduct, he or she would not have committed the crime, or that an ordinary, law-abiding citizen would have been persuaded, under the same circumstances, to commit the crime.

  EXAMPLE: Kurt does not touch or go near anything related to drugs since his conviction for drug dealing six years ago. One day, an undercover police officer asks Kurt to buy some drugs. He refuses, but the officer continues his request over several days and even offers to provide the narcotics to Kurt on credit. Low on cash, Kurt accepts, acquires the drugs and is then arrested. The officer's conduct in continually pressing Kurt after he refused on several occasions may constitute *entrapment.*

ENTRY, FORCIBLE see **forcible entry.**

ENTRY, UNLAWFUL see **unlawful entry.**

ENUMERATED POWERS express powers specifically granted by the **Constitution** such as the **taxing power** and the **spending power** granted to Congress. See **inherent powers.** Compare **implied powers.**

ENURE see **inure.**

EN VENTRE SA MERE in gestation; in the womb of one's mother. In the law of property, a person who is en ventre sa mere has the same rights as, and is entitled to the same protections as, a person who has been born.

ENVIRONMENTAL IMPACT STATEMENT [REPORT] requirement under federal and state laws for developers to file documents and receive approval where projects may affect the environment. Such documents must detail efforts to minimize adverse polution, disruption to wildlife or traffic, or use of protected areas such as wetlands.

ENVIRONMENTAL PROTECTION AGENCY [EPA] an agency of the federal government charged with a variety of responsibilities relating to protection of the quality of the natural environment, including research and monitoring, promulgation of standards for air and water quality, control of the introduction of pesticides and other hazardous materials into the environment, and the like. See **police power.**

E. O. executive officer; also, **executive order; ex officio.**

EO DIE on the same day.

EO INSTANTI immediately; instantly.

EO NOMINEE Lat.: by that name.

EPA see **Environmental Protection Agency.**

EQ abbreviation for equity.

EQUAL EMPLOYMENT OPPORTUNITY COMMISSION [EEOC]   see **equal opportunity.**

EQUALITY   possessing the same rights under the same circumstances. Achieving a balance; uniformity. See **equal protection of the laws.**

EQUAL OPPORTUNITY   a term to signify an employer's adoption of employment practices that do not discriminate on the basis of race, color, religion, sex or national origin. Such discrimination was outlawed by Title VII of the Civil Rights Act of 1964.

Title VII also created the EQUAL EMPLOYMENT OPPORTUNITY COMMISSION [EEOC] to implement equal opportunity policy by working with local agencies.

EQUAL PROTECTION OF THE LAWS   constitutional guarantee embodied in the **Fourteenth Amendment** to the U.S. Constitution, which states in relevant part that "No State shall . . . deny to any person within its jurisdiction the equal protection of the laws." The essential purpose of this constitutional doctrine is to ensure that the laws and the government treat all persons alike, unless there is some substantial reason why certain persons or classes of persons should be treated differently.

EXAMPLE: Women and men who perform equal tasks in their jobs for the state receive unequal pay. In a lawsuit seeking equal pay, the fact that a question based on gender is raised forces the state to demonstrate a compelling government interest to justify the distinction.

EQUAL RIGHTS AMENDMENT [ERA]   a proposed amendment hoping to eliminate sex as a basis for any decisions made by a state of the United States. This amendment was never ratified by a sufficient number of states to qualify as a constitutional amendment, but the basic premise underlying the proposal has become an accepted standard in many statutes and court decisions.

EQUAL TIME ACT [RULE]   broadcast requirement that if a candidate for public office is permitted air time, the station must afford equal opportunities to all other candidates for that office. Compare **fairness doctrine.**

EQUIPMENT   see **consumer goods [EQUIPMENT].**

EQUITABLE   according to natural right or natural justice; marked by due consideration for what is fair and impartial, unhampered by technical rules the law may have devised that limit **recovery** or **defense.**

EQUITABLE DISTRIBUTION   see **equitable distribution.**

See **equity.**

EQUITABLE CONSIDERATION see **consideration** [MORAL [EQUITABLE] CONSIDERATION].

EQUITABLE DEFENSE see **defense** [EQUITABLE DEFENSE].

EQUITABLE DISTRIBUTION 1. a just division of property among interested parties; 2. the process by which, as part of a dissolution of marriage proceeding under a no-fault **divorce** statute, the court apportions between husband and wife all **assets** acquired by either or both of them, whether owned jointly or individually, during the marriage See **alimony; community property.**

EQUITABLE EASEMENT see **equitable servitude.**

EQUITABLE ESTATE see **estate** [EQUITABLE ESTATE].

EQUITABLE ESTOPPEL see **estoppel** [ESTOPPEL IN PAIS].

EQUITABLE RECOUPMENT in certain situations in which a **taxpayer** erroneously pays taxes in one **taxable year** when they are properly payable in a later year, this doctrine allows the taxpayer to recoup the additional taxes paid by reducing his or her taxes payable in the later year.

EQUITABLE RELIEF see **relief.**

EQUITABLE SEISIN see **seisin.**

EQUITABLE SERVITUDE a **covenant** that is enforceable only in **equity.** For a covenant to be valid at law, as to remote grantees of the affected property there must exist PRIVITY OF ESTATE (see **privity**) between the covenantor and covenantee, but such a relationship is not necessary to create an enforceable equitable servitude so long as the subsequent grantee has either actual or CONSTRUCTIVE NOTICE (see **notice**) of the covenant.

EQUITABLE TITLE see **title** [EQUITABLE TITLE].

EQUITY generally, justice or fairness Historically, equity refers to a separate body of law developed in England in reaction to the inability of the **common law** courts, in their strict adherence to rigid **writs** and **forms of action,** to consider or provide a **remedy** for every injury. The king therefore established the court of **chancery,** to do justice between **parties** in cases where the common law would give inadequate redress. The principle of this jurisprudence is that equity will find a way to achieve a lawful result when legal procedure is inadequate. Equity and **law** courts are now merged in most jurisdictions, though equity **jurisprudence** and equitable doctrines are still independently viable.

Equity also refers to the value of **property** minus **liens** or other **encumbrances.** For example, one's equity in a home with a **mortgage** is the value of the property beyond the amount of the mortgage debt.

In accounting, equity refers to the ownership interest in a company as determined by subtracting **liabilities** from **assets.** See **balance sheet.** For incorporated business enterprises, equity is owned by the common and preferred **shareholders.** If the corporation is publicly held, the shares will be traded on a **stock exchange** or **over-the-counter market** which together comprise the EQUITY MARKET.

EQUITY CAPITAL   see **securities [STOCK].**

EQUITY OF REDEMPTION   right of mortgagor to redeem his or her property (save it from **foreclosure**) after **default** in the payment of the **mortgage debt,** by subsequent payment of all costs and interest, in addition to the mortgage debt, to the mortgagee.

ERA   see **Equal Rights Amendment [ERA].**

ERGO   *(ĕr'-gō)*   Lat.: therefore; consequently; hence; because.

ERISA [EMPLOYMENT RETIREMENT INCOME SECURITY ACT OF 1974]   a Congressional attempt to attack a multitude of problems that were affecting employee benefit plans, especially the lack of employee information and adequate safeguards concerning their operation. Through various statutes and regulations, the act creates minimum standards to assure the equitable character and financial soundness of these plans.

ERRONEOUS   involving a mistake; signifies a deviation from the requirements of the law, but it does not connote a lack of legal authority, and is thus distinguished from illegal. If, while having the power to act, one commits error in the exercise of that power, he acts erroneously.

ERRONEOUS JUDGMENT   one rendered according to practice of court, but contrary to law, upon a mistaken view of law, or upon erroneous application of legal principles.

ERROR   a mistake; an act involving a departure from truth or accuracy. In a legal proceeding such as a trial, an **ERROR OF LAW** furnishes grounds for the **appellate court** to **reverse** a **judgment.** See **assignment of error; clerical error; harmless error; plain error; reversible error.** See **motion [MOTION IN ERROR]; writ of error.**

ESCALATOR CLAUSE   that part of a **lease** or **contract** that provides for an increase in the rent or contract price upon the occurrence of certain conditions beyond the parties' control, such as an increase in the cost of labor or of a necessary commodity, or the fixing of maximum prices by a government agency. Escalator clauses in leases may permit an increase in rent whenever real estate taxes or interest rates rise. In a divorce decree one's **alimony** payments may increase as the cost of living rises or when the ex-spouse who is paying alimony has a higher income.

ESCAPE CLAUSE a clause in a contract permitting a party to renege on its obligations under certain conditions without incurring a penalty or other liability.

EXAMPLE: Stilton Harvest Corporation agrees to provide a bread company with all the wheat it needs for one year. The agreement includes a provision that, if the annual harvest for a group of states falls below an established level, Stilton is relieved of its obligation.

ESCHEAT assignment of **property** to the state because there is no verifiable legal owner.

ESCROW a written **instrument,** such as a **deed,** temporarily deposited with a neutral third party (the **ESCROW AGENT**), by the agreement of two parties to a valid **contract.** The escrow agent will deliver the document to the benefited party when the conditions of the contract have been met. The depositor has no control over the instrument in escrow. In **common law,** escrow applied to the deposits only of instruments for **conveyance** of land, but it now applies to all instruments so deposited. Money or other property so deposited is also loosely referred to as escrow.

ESOP see **Employee Share Ownership Plan [ESOP].**

ESQUIRE [ESQ.] in English law, a title below knight and above gentleman. Commonly follows the name of an attorney in the United States, as in *Kristen Newlawyer, Esq.*

ESSENCE see **time is of the essence.**

ESTABLISHMENT CLAUSE provision in the **First Amendment** of the U.S. Constitution prohibiting enactment of laws pertaining to "the establishment of religion." It has been said that the establishment clause means that neither a state nor the federal government may set up a church; neither may pass laws that aid one religion, aid all religions or prefer one religion over another. In the words of Jefferson, the clause was intended to erect a "wall of separation between church and state."

ESTATE 1. technically, the nature and extent of a person's **interest** in or ownership of land; 2. broadly, estate applies to all that a person owns, whether **real** or **personal property.**

CONTINGENT ESTATE   see **contingent estate.**

DOMINANT ESTATE   see **dominant estate [tenement].**

EQUITABLE ESTATE   an estate or interest that can be enforced only in **equity;** applies especially to every **trust,** express or implied, that is not converted to a legal estate by the **Statute of Uses.**

ESTATE IN FEE SIMPLE see **fee simple.**

ESTATE IN FEE TAIL see **fee tail.**

FUTURE ESTATE   an estate in land that is not **possessory** but that will or may become so in the future. Future estates are either **vested** or **contingent,** and include **remainders** and **reversions.**

LEGAL ESTATE   originally, an interest in land that was enforced by courts of **common law,** as opposed to an equitable estate, enforced by **courts of equity.**

NET ESTATE see **net estate.**

PRECEDING ESTATE   see **preceding estate.**

RESIDUARY ESTATE see **residuary estate.**

SERVIENT ESTATE   see **servient estate.**

VESTED ESTATE   one either presently in **possession** or owned by a presently existing person to whom (or to whose successors in interest) the property interest will automatically accrue upon the termination of a **PRECEDING ESTATE** Such an estate thus represents a present interest and as such is neither subject to any contingency nor otherwise capable of being defeated.

ESTATE AT SUFFERANCE   see **tenancy** [TENANCY AT SUFFERANCE].

ESTATE AT WILL   see **tenancy** [TENANCY AT WILL].

ESTATE BY THE ENTIRETY   see **tenancy** [TENANCY BY THE ENTIRETY].

ESTATE FOR LIFE   see **life estate.**

ESTATE FOR YEARS   see **tenancy** [TENANCY FOR YEARS].

ESTATE FROM YEAR TO YEAR [PERIOD TO PERIOD]   see **tenancy** [PERIODIC TENANCY].

ESTATE IN COMMON   see **tenancy** [TENANCY IN COMMON].

ESTATE IN COPARCENARY   see **coparcenary.**

ESTATE OF INHERITANCE   a **common law** species of land ownership that could descend to **heirs;** a type of **freehold estate** that the owner can both enjoy during his or her life and **bequeath**

according to an established order of **descent.** Estate of inheritance include estates in **fee simple** absolute, fee simple conditional, fee simple determinable and estates in **fee tail.**

ESTATE PER AUTRE VIE   see **per [pur] autre vie.**

ESTATE TAX   see **tax [ESTATE TAX].**

ESTOPPEL   a restraint; a bar; arises where a person has done some act that the policy of the law will not permit him or her to deny, or where circumstances are such that the law will not permit a certain argument because it would lead to an unjust result. In the context of **contract** law, for example, one is estopped from denying existence of a binding contract where he or she has done something intending that another rely on his or her conduct, and the result of the reliance is detrimental to that other person. Compare **waiver.**

EXAMPLE: Nelson convinces an associate to sign what appears to be a valid contract which gives the associate the right to buy certain items from Nelson. When the contract turns out to harm Nelson more than the associate, Nelson tries to deny the validity of the instrument. A court will find that Nelson is *estopped* (i.e., prevented) from raising that claim since it was Nelson who initiated the offer.

AUTHORITY BY ESTOPPEL   see **authority [AUTHORITY BY ESTOPPEL].**

COLLATERAL ESTOPPEL   see **collateral estoppel.**

DIRECT ESTOPPEL   the prohibition of the relitigation of an issue by two parties who have previously litigated the issue and had it decided by the courts. See **collateral estoppel; res judicata.**

ESTOPPEL BY DEED   a bar that precludes a party from denying the truth and legitimacy of the conveyance represented by a **deed** he or she has given. It may be invoked only in a suit on the deed or concerning a right arising out of it.

ESTOPPEL BY JUDGMENT   see **judgment [ESTOPPEL BY JUDGMENT].**

ESTOPPEL BY LACHES   see **laches [ESTOPPEL BY LACHES].**

ESTOPPEL IN PAIS   [*pá'-ēs*]   Old Fr: the country, the neighborhood. An estoppel that arises out of a person's statement of fact, or out of his or her silence, acts or omissions, rather than from a **deed** or record or written contract; also called an **EQUITABLE ESTOPPEL.**

MUTUALITY OF ESTOPPEL   the doctrine that prohibits one party from raising an issue or a matter which the other party is prohibited from raising.

PROMISSORY ESTOPPEL   see **promissory estoppel.**

ESTOVERS   the right of the **tenant,** during the period of his or her **lease,** to use timber on the leased premises for proper maintenance of the property.

ET AL.   *(ĕt äl)*   Lat.: and others; abbreviation of et alii.

ETHICAL   see **unethical.**

ETHNIC CLEANSING   a policy of removing a particular ethnic population from a geographic area, such as by forced migration. Claims are made that the policy establishes ethnically homogeneous lands but others argue that it serves to remove a population that is a threat to those in power. The practice is often violent and may involve **genocide.** See **crime against humanity.**

ET NON   *(ĕt nŏn)*   Lat.: and not.

ET SEQ.   *(ĕt sĕk)*   Lat.: and the following; abbreviation of et sequentes or et sequentia. Most commonly used in denominating page reference numbers: page 13 et seq.

ET UX.   *(ĕt ŭks)*   Lat.: and wife; abbreviation of et uxor. Used in old legal documents such as **wills** or deeds; for example, "This will made by John Doe *et ux.*"

EURO   unified currency of most nations of the European Union. Replaces units of exchange such as the French franc, the Italian lire, and the German deutsche mark. The euro is intended to simplify pricing, stem inflation, and strengthen the economic policies of the member countries.

EURODOLLAR   a U.S. dollar held as a deposit in a European commercial bank. Eurodollars were created after World War II by United States foreign defense and aid expenditures. Since the dollar was backed by gold, it became a popular reserve currency in Europe and among all the trading partners of the United States.

EUTHANASIA   Greek: easy death. The act or practice of painlessly terminating the life of a person or animal. As applied to animals, it is sometimes referred to as "HUMANE DISPOSAL." As applied to persons, it is accepted in some cultures but in the United States it may be treated as criminal, subjecting those responsible to prosecution under the homicide statutes. Two types of euthanasia exist.

ACTIVE EUTHANASIA refers to the act of putting to death. Also known as "mercy killing," it involves the termination of life as painlessly as possible, such as by an injection of lethal medications. Courts are struggling with this area of law which is also known as "ASSISTED SUICIDE."

PASSIVE EUTHANASIA involves withholding artificial life support, such as breathing or feeding tubes. It is often called the "RIGHT TO DIE."

An exception to prosecution has been developed in some jurisdictions in which the termination of the life of an incurably ill patient is no longer treated as criminal if done by a guardian or immediate family member after consultation with an ethics committee of a hospital, and if accomplished by the negative means of withdrawing life-support systems or extraordinary medical care rather than by some affirmative act. See **brain death.**

EVASION OF TAX   generally applied to any of various fraudulent methods by which a **taxpayer** may pay less than his or her proper tax **liability.**

EXAMPLE: As an independent consultant, Olivia works for many different companies. Her scheme has each company pay her under a different fictitious name. She then sets up bank accounts in each name to facilitate cashing the checks. By that method, she *evades her taxes* because the Internal Revenue Service is unable to locate any of the fictitious individuals.

Evasion is to be distinguished from **avoidance of tax,** which denotes the legal interpretation of relevant tax law to minimize tax liability.

EVASIVE ANSWER   an **answer** that fails to admit or deny the allegations set forth in the **complaint.**

EVEN DATE the same date

EVICTION   the physical expulsion of someone from land by the assertion of **paramount title** or through legal **proceedings.**

ACTUAL EVICTION an actual expulsion of the tenant out of all or some part of the leased premises, and involving a physical ouster or dispossession from the very thing granted. Actual eviction relieves the tenant of any further duty to pay rent.

CONSTRUCTIVE EVICTION   refers to circumstances under the control of the **landlord** that compel the **tenant** to leave the **premises** though he or she is not asked to do so by the landlord. The tenant may be deemed constructively evicted if the premises are rendered unfit for occupancy, or if the use and enjoyment has been substantially impaired. Where the law of the jurisdiction permits the tenant to claim constructive eviction, he or she is not responsible for further rent, but he or she must actually vacate the premises.

PARTIAL ACTUAL EVICTION   an eviction that the law may recognize as having occurred when part of the leased premises has been rendered unusable through the fault of the landlord. If the lease rental is not apportioned by room, nor the premises partitioned in the lease agreement, the tenant may not be responsible for any part of the lease rental while actually evicted from a part of the leased premises, and he or she need not vacate the habitable part of the premises.

RETALIATORY EVICTION eviction of a tenant based on the tenant's good faith complaints against the landlord. Such evictions against residential tenants are illegal in many states. When a landlord seeks to evict a tenant within a specified period of time after the tenant has filed a complaint against the landlord, a presumption may arise that the eviction is in reprisal or retaliation for the tenant's complaints.

EVIDENCE all the means by which any alleged matter of fact, the truth of which is submitted to investigation at judicial **trial,** is established or disproved. Evidence includes the **testimony** of **witnesses,** introduction of records, documents, exhibits or any other relevant matter offered for the purpose of inducing the trier of fact's **(fact finder's)** belief in the party's contention. See **best evidence rule; circumstantial evidence; conclusive evidence; corroborating evidence; demonstrative evidence; direct evidence; documentary evidence; extrinsic evidence; hearsay; illegally obtained evidence; incompetent evidence; indirect evidence; indispensable evidence; insufficient evidence; intrinsic evidence; mere evidence rule; newly discovered evidence; parol evidence rule; preponderance of the evidence; presumptive evidence; real evidence; rebuttal evidence; reputation evidence; suppression of evidence; traditionary evidence; weight of the evidence.**

EVIDENCE ALIUNDE see **aliunde.**

EVIDENCE DE BENE ESSE see **de bene esse.**

EX AEQUO ET BONO *(ex é-quō et bō-nō)* Lat: from equity and conscience.

EXAMINATION see **cross-examination; [DIRECT EXAMINATION].**

EXCEPTION an item that ought to be included in a category but that is eliminated. Exceptions arise in numerous contexts in law: 1. statutory exceptions are intended to restrain the **enacting clause** or to exclude something that would otherwise be within it, or to modify it in some manner. 2. an exception to a court's ruling is an objection to such ruling or the act of calling to the attention of a court an error made by the same or a different court. 3. Exception is also used generally to mean the withholding from conveyance of some **estate** or **interest** in the land conveyed.

EXCESSIVE BAIL an amount of **bail** that is set at a higher figure than is reasonably calculated to fulfill the purpose of assuring that the accused will stand trial and submit to sentence if found guilty. Excessive bail is prohibited by the **Eighth Amendment** to the United States Constitution and by the constitutions of the various states. The prohibition against excessive bails has been held to forbid a person from being capriciously held, by demanding bail in such amount that there is in fact a denial of bail where a right to bail exists. The prohibition against excessive bail has been held not to confer a right to bail on anyone but to provide only that if bail is permitted it may not be set at an excessive amount. See **detention.**

EXCHANGE to give goods or services and to get goods or services of equal value in return. Generally, a transaction is a **sale** where money is received in return for the goods or services and is an exchange when specific **property** susceptible of valuation is received. Exchange is synonymous with **BARTER.**

EXCHANGE, LIKE-KIND see **sale or exchange.**

EXCHEQUER see **court of exchequer.**

EXCISE broadly, any kind of tax not applied to property or the rents or incomes of real estate; a tax upon articles of manufacture or sale and also upon licenses to pursue certain trades or to deal in certain commodities. It is a tax imposed directly and without assessment and is measured by amount of business done, income received, etc.

EXAMPLE: Brycen buys a new set of tires for his car, the price of which includes a federal *excise* tax. The money generated by the tax is used for road maintenance and other transportation expenses and is justified by the rationale that anyone who buys tires must be using them on the roads. The tax is a means of ensuring that users pay for related government services.

EXCITED UTTERANCE a statement relating to a startling event or condition made while the declarant was under the stress of excitement caused by the event or condition. A **hearsay** exception is broader than a **present sense impression** since it (1) need not describe or explain the startling event or condition; it need only relate to it, and (2) need not be made contemporaneously with, or immediately after, the startling event. It is sufficient if the stress of excitement created by the startling event or condition persists as a substantial factor in provoking the utterance. There is no fixed time limit on when a statement is considered to fall under this exception to the hearsay rule. Both a statement made contemporaneously and one made hours later may qualify if the person making the statement is still dominated by the nervous excitement and has not yet entered into a reflective or contemplative state of mind. See **res gestae.**

EXCLUSION   an amount that otherwise would constitute a part of **GROSS INCOME** (see **income**) but that under a specific provision of the **Internal Revenue Code** is excluded from gross income.

EXCLUSIONARY RULE   a constitutional rule of law that provides that otherwise **admissible evidence** may not be used in a criminal trial if it was obtained as a result of illegal police conduct. See **fruit of the poisonous tree doctrine.**

EXAMPLE: The police unlawfully stop a car, order the driver to wait outside, and proceed to search the vehicle. Twenty pounds of marijuana are discovered in the back seat. Since there was never a lawful reason to stop the car in the first place, the subsequent search of the car is unreasonable and in violation of the **Fourth Amendment** of the Constitution. The primary remedy today for the violation is to apply the *exclusionary rule,* which bars the prosecutor from using the confiscated marijuana to convict the driver of possession of the drug. In fact, application of the rule will usually end any prosecution based on items that were discovered but now must be excluded.

EXCLUSIVE USE   see **use [EXCLUSIVE USE].**

EX CONTRACTU   *(ĕks kŏn-trăk'-tū)*   Lat.: arising out of contract.

EXCULPATORY   refers to **evidence** or statements that tend to justify or excuse a **defendant** from alleged fault or **guilt.** Contrast **incriminate; inculpatory.**

EXCULPATORY CLAUSE   a clause in a legal document that excuses a party from liability for its acts other than those caused by willful neglect or gross negligence.

EXCUSABLE NEGLECT   the failure to perform a required act, usually procedural in nature, because of unusual circumstances. The party failing to perform the act is usually given the opportunity by the court to cure his or her neglect.

EX-DATE   see **ex-dividend [EX-DIVIDEND DATE].**

EX DELICTO *(ĕks dĕ-lĭk'-tō)*   Lat.: arising out of wrongs. See **action ex delicto.**

EX-DIVIDEND   without a right to a declared **dividend.** When a stock trades ex-dividend the buyer does not receive the declared dividend because the date on which he or she will officially own the stock will occur after the record date of ownership for purposes of receiving same. A stock will trade ex-dividend during the settlement period, usually five business days, between the execution of an order to buy or sell the security by a broker and the date of settlement when the certificate and funds change hands. The **PAYMENT DATE** refers to the date on which the dividend is actually paid and is usually sometime after the **EX-DIVIDEND DATE** (sometimes called simply **EX-DATE**) and the record date.

EXECUTE 1. to complete, as a legal **instrument;** 2. to perform what is required; 3. to give validity to, as by signing and perhaps **sealing** and **delivering.** For example, a **contract** is executed when all acts necessary to complete it and to give it validity as an instrument are carried out, including signing and delivery.

EXECUTED fully accomplished or performed; leaving nothing unfulfilled; opposite of **executory.**

EXECUTED INTEREST see **interest [EXECUTED INTEREST].**

EXECUTED SALE see **sale [EXECUTED SALE].**

EXECUTION 1. the process of carrying into effect a court's **judgment, decree** or **order.** It gives the successful **party** the fruits of his or her judgment. For instance, when a party has won a judgment on his or her **claim,** the **judgment creditor** can enforce or **execute** the judgment by having the sheriff seize and sell the **judgment debtor's** property and then use the proceeds to pay the judgment. 2. in criminal law, the process by which a sentenced **defendant** serves his or her sentence. For instance, a person sentenced to ten years of imprisonment executes his or her sentence by spending that amount of time in prison, unless released earlier by **parole.** The term also refers specifically to carrying out a death sentence. See **capital punishment.**

EXECUTION OF INSTRUMENT signing of a legal instrument such as a **deed** or **contract** so that it is legally binding and enforceable.

EXECUTION SALE see **sheriff's sale [judicial sale].**

EXECUTIVE AGREEMENT see **treaty.**

EXECUTIVE CLEMENCY the power constitutionally reposed in the President, and by most state constitutions, in the governor, to **pardon** or commute (i.e., reduce) the **sentence** of one convicted by a court within his **jurisdiction.** Compare **reprieve.**

EXECUTIVE ORDER an order issued by the executive head of government, such as the President of the United States or a governor of a state, and that has the force of law.

EXECUTIVE PARDON   see **pardon.**

EXECUTIVE PRIVILEGE   the privilege of the executive branch of government to refuse to disclose confidential communications, the disclosure of which would impair its ability to function. The privilege is based upon the doctrine of **separation of powers,** but it may be overcome in criminal cases, if necessary, in the interest of fundamental fairness.

EXECUTIVE PROCLAMATION   see **proclamation [PRESIDEN-TIAL PROCLAMATION].**

EXECUTOR [EXECUTRESS; EXECUTRIX]   a person who either expressly or by **implication** is appointed by a **testator** [one who dies leaving a **will**] to carry out the testator's directions concerning the dispositions he makes under his will. When the appointee is a woman, she is the executrix or executress. See **personal representative.**

EXAMPLE: Lane's will names Nat *executor* of Lane's estate. As executor, Nat must make sure the provisions in Lane's will are carried out, debts against the estate are paid, and any money owed is collected. If there are ambiguities in the will or the will is contested, Nat is responsible for seeing that a lawsuit is either filed or answered. Nat is compensated for his job, although that may be a small amount, and he is reimbursed by Lane's estate for any expenses.

EXECUTORY   not fully accomplished or completed, but contingent upon the occurrence of some event or the performance of some act in the future; not **vested;** opposite of **executed.** An EXEC-UTORY CONTRACT is one in which some performance remains to be accomplished.

EXECUTORY BEQUEST   see **bequest [EXECUTORY BEQUEST].**

EXECUTORY INTEREST   see **interest [EXECUTORY INTER-EST].**

EXECUTORY SALE   see **sale [EXECUTORY SALE].**

EXECUTORY WAIVER   see **waiver [EXECUTORY WAIVER].**

EXEMPLAR   nontestimonial indentification evidence such as fingerprints, blood samples, handwriting samples, **voice exemplars,** and the like. See **search and seizure.**

EXEMPLARY DAMAGES   see **damages [EXEMPLARY [PUNI-TIVE] DAMAGES].**

EXEMPT   see **tax exempt.**

EXEMPTION   a **deduction** allowed to a **taxpayer** because of his or her status or circumstances rather than because of specific economic costs or expenses during the **taxable year.**

EXAMPLE: Adnan and Emily are married and have three children. Federal income tax laws allow the couple three *exemptions,* one for each child on the couple's joint tax return. The exemption reduces the amount of income upon which the couple is taxed.

EX GRATIA   *(ĕks grä'-shē-à)*   Lat.: out of grace; gratuitously. Describes that which is done as a favor rather than as a required task or as of right.

EXHAUSTION OF REMEDIES   a judicial policy or statutory requirement that certain administrative or non-federal judicial remedies be pursued by a litigant before a state or federal court will consider the controversy.

EXHAUSTION OF ADMINISTRATIVE REMEDIES   the doctrine of all courts, adopted either as judicial policy or by statutory directive, that the courts will not interfere with or review an administrative decision or process until the available administrative channels of review have been attempted. This requirement stems from the usual requirement that courts review only "final" administrative actions. The doctrine avoids piecemeal interruption of administrative processes, conserves scarce judicial resources, and ensures that the expertise of administrative agencies will be fully employed. In some extreme cases, where irreparable harm to public or private interests may be caused by honoring the doctrine, it will be held inapplicable.

EXHAUSTION OF STATE REMEDIES   the practice of federal courts of not intervening in matters where state administrative remedies are available to the litigant seeking federal relief. This is a policy of **comity** and may be excused when it would be unjust or inappropriate to await state administrative consideration. The doctrine applies only to state administrative remedies and not state judicial remedies except in cases involving state prisoners seeking federal habeas corpus relief. In those instances, the federal habeas corpus statute requires that state prisoners first exhaust state judicial remedies, provided they are then currently available. Even in the context of habeaus corpus petitions by state prisoners, the doctrine of exhaustion is not absolute. If the prisoner can demonstrate that resort to state remedies would be "ineffective," he or she need not exhaust; also the prisoner need not present the state with more than one opportunity based on the same issue provided he or she has pursued all available appeals in that previous state application. The Supreme Court has held that exhaustion of state remedies is not required when federal courts are asked to remedy a violation of one's civil rights pursuant to the Civil Rights Act.

EXHIBIT an item of **real evidence** that has been presented to the court.

EXIGENCY an emergency situation that excuses some particular procedure or right from being followed or enforced. Thus, an exigency may justify speeding to the hospital with a critically ill person, breaking into someone's home to secure shelter from life-threatening harm, or dispensing with the **warrant** requirement to effect a **search and seizure** under the **Fourth Amendment.** See **exigent circumstances.**

EXIGENT CIRCUMSTANCES emergency situations or conditions that the law recognizes as excusing compliance with some procedural requirement or recognition of another's property or other interests. Term is most commonly used to refer to the variety of contexts in which a valid **search and seizure** may be conducted without a **warrant.** If the police action must be taken on a "now or never" basis to preserve evidence, it may be reasonable to permit a seizure without obtaining prior judicial approval. Exigent circumstances may be found when substantial risk of harm to others or the police would exist if police were to delay a search until a warrant could be obtained. The mobility of a motor vehicle has been held in itself to create an exigent circumstance. In every instance where a search or arrest warrant has been dispensed with on grounds of **exigency, probable cause** must be present to justify the intrusion.

EXIGIBLE demandable; capable of being required.

EXILE to force out, or cut off from membership or privileges; the punishment, by a political authority, inflicted upon **criminals** by compelling them to leave a city, place or country for a period of time or for life.

EX-OFFENDER see **criminal.**

EX OFFICIO *(ĕks ō-fĭ'-shĕ-ō)* Lat.: from the office; by virtue of his office; officially.

EX OFFICIO MEMBER one who is a member of a board, committee or other body by virtue of his or her title to a certain office, and who does not require further appointment.

EX OFFICIO SERVICES services imposed by law on a public officer by virtue of his office.

EX PARTE *(ĕks pär'-tā)* Lat.: in behalf of or on the application of one party; by or for one party. An ex parte judicial **proceeding** is one brought for the benefit of one party only, without notice to or challenge by an **adverse party.** Therefore, in an ex parte proceeding the adverse party and his or her **evidence** are excluded. For this reason, such proceedings are not favored, and any **relief** obtained ex parte is subject to speedy review.

EXAMPLE: Applications to install wiretaps on telephones are always made *ex parte,* i.e., without notice to the person whose phone is sought to be electronically surveilled. Otherwise, the person will know his or her phone is wiretapped and avoid incriminating conversations. Because the application is ex parte, requirements not usually insisted on must be met to protect privacy, and the person who is recorded may challenge the sufficiency of the application at a later opportunity.

EXPECTANCY **future interest** as to **possession** or enjoyment. In the law of **property, estates** may be either in possession or in expectancy; if an expectancy is created by the parties it is a **remainder;** if created by **operation of law** it is a **reversion.** See **contingent estate.** Compare **vested.**

EXPECTATION DAMAGES see **damages** [**EXPECTATION DAMAGES**].

EXPENSE any business cost incurred in operating and maintaining property. For purposes of information and in reporting to **shareholders** of publicly held **corporations,** expenses are calculated as the cost of goods and services used in the process of profit-directed business activities.

In tax law, expenses are costs that are currently **deductible,** as opposed to CAPITAL EXPENDITURES (see **capital**), which may not be currently deducted but must be **depreciated** or **amortized** over the useful life of the property. **LOBBYING EXPENSE** those incurred in promoting or evaluating legislation.

MEDICAL EXPENSE a limited deduction allowed to a taxpayer for amounts actually expended during the taxable year for diagnoses, cure, mitigation, treatment, or prevention of any disease or affecting any structure or function of the body and associated transportation costs. Expenses for medicine and drugs are allowed as a deduction only if obtained by prescription.

MOVING EXPENSE deduction allowed to a taxpayer for the reasonable expenses of moving his or her residence from one location to another if such move meets certain specified technical requirements regarding distance moved and length of stay.

ORGANIZATION EXPENSE a newly formed corporation or partnership may deduct the costs of organizing the corporation.

PERSONAL EXPENSE in general, a personal living or family expense is not allowable as a deduction from gross **income**. Certain expenses, however, such as mortgage interest, certain taxes, **bad debts**, medical expenses, and **charitable contributions** are deductible if the taxpayer itemizes his or her deductions.

TRADE OR BUSINESS EXPENSE deduction allowed to a taxpayer for all "ordinary and necessary" expenses incurred with respect to the taxpayer's trade or business.

EXPERT TESTIMONY [EVIDENCE] see **expert witness.**

EXPERT WITNESS a **witness** having special knowledge, skill or experience in the subject about which he is to **testify.** Testimony given by such a witness, in his capacity as such, constitutes **EXPERT EVIDENCE** or **EXPERT TESTIMONY.**

EXPLOITATION the act of taking unfair advantage of some person or situation. See **sexual exploitation.**

EXPORT 1. to transport out of one country and into another; 2. the article so transported.

EX POST FACTO *(ĕks pōst făk'-tō)* Lat.: after the fact. Refers especially to a law that makes punishable as a crime an act done before the passing of the law and that was innocent when done. An ex post facto law is also one that makes a crime more serious than when it was committed, inflicts a greater punishment, or alters legal rules of **evidence** to require less or different testimony to convict than the law required when the crime was committed. Such laws violate provisions of the Constitution of the United States, which provide that neither Congress nor any state shall pass an ex post facto law.

EXAMPLE: Knowing that he has no money in the bank, Ji writes a check for $150 and is arrested for the crime. At the time of his arrest, the law made it a crime to write bad checks only for amounts over $200. By the time Ji is brought to trial, the amount that is necessary to make the writing of a bad check criminal had been lowered to $100. Ji must be tried under the law as it was at the time he was arrested and is, therefore, not guilty. To prosecute him under the new, lower limit of $100 would violate the *ex post facto* protection of the United States Constitution.

EXPRESS to set forth an **agreement** in words, written or spoken, that unambiguously signify intent. As distinguished from **implied,** the term refers to something that is not left to inference from conduct or circumstances.

207

EXPRESS AUTHORITY see **authority [EXPRESS AUTHORITY].**

EXPRESSIO UNIUS EST EXCLUSIO ALTERIUS *(ĕks-prĕ'-sē-ō ū'-nē-ūs ĕst eks-klū'-sē-ō äl-tēr'-ē-ūs)* Lat.: the expression of one thing is the exclusion of another. In construing statutes under this maxim, mention of one thing within the statute is said to imply the exclusion of another thing not mentioned. The maxim is an aid to **construction** and is applicable where the contrast between what is expressed and what is omitted enforces the inference that what is omitted must have been intended to have contrary treatment. Thus a statute granting certain rights to "police, fire, and sanitation employees" would be interpreted to exclude other public employees not enumerated in the legislation.

EXPRESS POWERS see **enumerated powers.**

EXPRESS WARRANTY see **warranty [EXPRESS WARRANTIES].**

EXPROPRIATION the taking of private property for public purpose upon the payment of just compensation, which is recognized as an inherent power of the state over its citizens. See **eminent domain.**

EXPULSION see **deportation [EXPULSION].**

EXPUNGEMENT OF RECORDS a procedure whereby a court orders the annulment and destruction of records of an arrest or other court proceedings. Some jurisdictions provide that an individual arrested and not convicted may apply to a court for an order of expungement and that if such an order is granted the individual may regard the arrest and all subsequent proceedings had as having not occurred in contemplation of law. Court-ordered expungements may also be available as a remedy for unlawful arrests. Many states permit an expungement remedy as a means of removing civil disabilities following a period of good behavior after a conviction. Even an expunged record may be used for sentence enhancement and as a basis for denial of a federal firearms permit. Compare **sealing of records.** See **executive clemency, pardon.**

EX REL. *(ĕks rĕl)* Lat.: upon relation or report; abbreviation of ex relatione. Legal **proceedings** that are initiated ex rel. are brought in the name of the state but on the information and at the instigation of a private individual with a private interest in the outcome. The **real party in interest** is called the **RELATOR.** The action will be captioned "State of X [or United States] ex rel. Y versus Z."

EX-RIGHTS refers to stock sold without **rights** to purchase stock subsequently offered by the same **corporation.** Rights normally have value, since the new issue is usually priced at a **discount** from the prevailing market price.

EXTENDED TERM   see **sentence** [EXTENDED TERM].

EXTENDI FACIAS   see **fieri facias** [EXTENDI FACIAS].

EXTENSION   an increase in the date of expiration or due date for a term or obligation. In a **lease,** an extension represents continuation of an existing arrangement on the same terms, whereas a renewal may involve new terms in a different lease instrument. In **procedure,** an extension of time within which a pleading or process must be filed or completed under the rules governing the courts of the particular jurisdiction.

EXTENUATING CIRCUMSTANCES   unusual factors tending to contribute to the consummation of an illegal act, but over which the actor had little or no control. These factors therefore reduce the responsibility of the actor and serve to mitigate punishment or the actor's payment of **damages.** Compare **justification.**

EXTINGUISHMENT   a **discharge** of an obligation or **contract** by **operation of law** or by express agreement.

EXAMPLE: Philippe signs a mortgage with a bank to purchase a new home. After twenty monthly payments, he stops paying the bank. A law in Philippe's state provides that if a bank does not sue on a mortgage where no payment has been made for five years, the obligation is *extinguished.* By operation of that law, if the bank does not sue Philippe within five years from the first payment date that he fails to meet, Philippe is no longer liable on the mortgage.

EXTORTION   1. in common law, the corrupt collection by a public official under **color** of office of an excessive or unauthorized fee; punishable as a **misdemeanor.** 2. under modern statutes the offense includes illegal taking of money by anyone who employs threats, or other illegal use of fear or coercion, to obtain money, and whose conduct falls short of the threat to personal safety required for **robbery.** Extortion is used interchangeably with **blackmail** and is commonly punished as a **felony.**

EXAMPLE: Joel threatens Ming that he will reveal certain aspects of her past that would ruin her career unless she pays him $200 a month. Even if what Joel threatens to say is true, the fact that he has threatened her to obtain money constitutes *extortion.*

Compare **bribery.**

EXTRADITION   the surrender by one state to another of an **accused** or convicted person. A state's chief executive has the right to demand from the **asylum** state the return of a person who was accused of crime based on **probable cause.** Extradition prevents the escape of fugitives who seek sanctuary in another state. It enables the state in which the offense occurred to swiftly bring the offender to trial.

EXTRAJUDICIAL beyond a court's **jurisdiction;** not directly connected with a court or its proceedings; e.g., a **confession** or an identification made outside of court.

EXTRAORDINARY DIVIDENDS see **dividend** [EXTRAORDI-NARY DIVIDENDS].

EXTRAORDINARY REMEDY see **remedy** [EXTRAORDINARY REMEDY].

EXTRAORDINARY RENDITION see **rendition.**

EXTREMIS see **in extremis.**

EXTRINSIC EVIDENCE external evidence. All evidence outside of the writing, including **parol evidence,** may be considered by the court in determining the true intent of the parties if there is any doubt or controversy as to the meaning of the language embodying their bargain.

EXTRINSIC FRAUD see **fraud** [EXTRINSIC [COLLATERAL] FRAUD].

EX TURPI CAUSA NON ORITUR ACTIO *(ĕx tûr'-pē käw'-zà nŏn ôr-ē-tûr äk'-shē-ō)* Lat: no disgraceful [foul, immoral, obscene] matter can be the basis of an **action.**

EYEWITNESS a person who can testify as to what he or she has experienced by his or her presence at an event.

F

FAA see **Federal Aviation Administration [FAA].**

FACE VALUE the value indicated in the wording of the **instrument.** For instance, the face value of a bank check is the amount the check is written for. Compare **market value.**

FACIAL INVALIDITY see **void for vagueness.**

FACILITATION in criminal law, a statutory offense rendering a person guilty when, believing it probable that he or she is aiding someone who intends to commit a **crime,** he or she assists the potential criminal in obtaining the means to commit the crime, and in fact such conduct does aid the person to commit the crime.

EXAMPLE: A very irate man walks into a gun store, screaming loudly that he is going to shoot someone for running a red light and destroying his new car. The man demands to purchase a gun, and the owner allows him to do so once the proper forms are filled out, even though the owner is aware of the man's state of mind. If the man then goes out and shoots the person who ran the light, the store owner may be guilty of criminal *facilitation.*

   In **common law,** facilitation may give rise to **liability** for **aiding and abetting.** Compare **accomplice; conspiracy.**

FACINUS QUOS INQUINAT AEQUAT *(fät'-sĭ-nŭs kwōs ĭn'-kwĭ-nät ī'-kwät)* Lat.: villainy and guilt make all those whom it contaminates equal in character.

FACT an event or circumstance the actual occurrence or existence of which is to be established by the evidence and determined by the **fact finder.** See **conclusion of fact; error [ERROR OF FACT]; mistake [MISTAKE OF FACT].** See **ultimate facts.**

FACTA SUNT PROTENTIORI VERBIS *(fäk'-tà sŭnt pō-tĕn'-tē-ô'-rē vĕr'-bēs)* Lat.: the facts, deeds, or accomplishments are more powerful than words.

FACT FINDER in a judicial or administrative **proceeding,** the person or group responsible for determining the facts relevant to resolving a controversy. It is the role of a **jury** in a jury trial; in a nonjury trial the judge sits both as a fact finder and as a trier of law; in administrative proceedings it may be a hearing officer or a hearing body. The term **TRIER OF FACT** generally denotes the same role.

FACTO *(fäk'-tō)* Lat.: in fact; by a deed. See **de facto.**

FACTOR a person who receives and sells goods for a **commission** (called **FACTORAGE**). He or she is entrusted with **possession** of the goods he or she sells and generally sells them in his or her own name. The term also refers to a **garnishee** in states where factorizing is the name for **garnishment.** Compare **jobber.**

FACTOR'S ACTS the name of certain English statutes, which have also been enacted in a number of states, whose general effect is to make a **factor's [agent's] possession** of property or documents of **title** stand as evidence of ownership to enable him or her to do all things the true owner might do with respect to the property or title documents. The owner thus becomes responsible for the factor's actions. The purpose of such statutes is to protect **bona fide purchasers** where the agent has exceeded his or her authority by giving an appearance that he or she is the true owner.

FACT, QUESTION OF see **question of fact.**

FACTS, PROBATIVE see **probative [PROBATIVE FACTS].**

FACTUAL IMPOSSIBILITY see **impossibility.**

FACTUM *(fäk'-tūm)* Lat.: a deed, or accomplishment. With respect to a change in a person's **domicile,** the factum is the person's physical presence in the new domicile. In civil law the word factum distinguishes a matter of fact from a matter of law.

FACTUM PROBANDUM *(fäk'-tūm prō-bän'-dūm)* Lat.: the fact to be proved. See **evidence.**

FAILURE OF CONSIDERATION see **consideration [FAILURE OF CONSIDERATION].**

FAILURE OF ISSUE termination of one's bloodline. The words are most often used in a **will** or **deed** to refer to a **condition** that operates in the event either no children be born or no children survive the decedent. These words, or the phrase "die without issue," may fix a condition whereby an estate will, in the event of failure of issue, pass automatically to an alternative person or in an alternative manner designated in the will itself. Unless the **instrument** indicated to the contrary, the common law read the condition as operating ad infinitum. This construction is termed **INDEFINITE FAILURE OF ISSUE.** Thus, if children of the first taker themselves fail to leave children, the estate will still go to the alternative. The first taker is regarded as possessing a **fee tail,** and his or her descendants continue to hold the same limited estate. A majority of American jurisdictions by statute have reversed this presumption and construe "die without issue" as a **DEFINITE FAILURE OF ISSUE;** i.e., the condition is satisfied fully if the first taker has issue surviving at the time of his or her death. Alternative expressions include "if he or she dies before he or she has any issue," "for want of issue," "without leaving issue."

FAILURE TO PROSECUTE see **default judgment; dismissal; non prosequitur.**

FAIR COMMENT a **plea** by a **defendant** in a **libel** suit that the statements made, even if untrue, were not intended to create ill will but rather to state the facts as the writer honestly believed them to be. Generally, one will not be held guilty of libel on the basis of honest and unintentional mistakes of fact.

FAIR COMPETITION see **unfair competition.**

FAIR HEARING a statutorily authorized extrajudicial hearing granted primarily where the normal judicial processes would be inadequate to secure **due process,** either because a judicial **remedy** does not exist, or because one would suffer grievous harm or substantial prejudice to his or her rights before a judicial remedy became available. Thus, fair hearings have been authorized as forums for the administrative determination of a citizen's rights in a number of contexts.

FAIR LABOR PRACTICE see **unfair labor practice.**

FAIR MARKET VALUE see **market value.**

FAIRNESS DOCTRINE a requirement that broadcasting stations present contrasting viewpoints on controversial issues of public importance. This doctrine imposes two affirmative responsibilities on the broadcaster: (1) to present adequate coverage of controversial public issues and (2) to ensure that this programming presents differing viewpoints so that the public is fully and fairly informed.

FAIR TRADE LAWS state statutes that permit a manufacturer to establish minimum resale prices that may not be varied by the wholesaler or distributor. Such agreements do not violate the **antitrust laws** when they are entered into under the provisions of state fair trade laws.

FAIR USE in federal **copyright** law, an insubstantial permitted use by another of material protected by copyright.

EXAMPLE: Jenny copyrights an article that she publishes in a medical journal. Although Jenny has the sole right to authorize copies of the article, the fair use doctrine permits a teacher to make as many copies as he or she needs if the teacher uses the copies for classroom discussion.

FALSE ARREST unlawful **arrest;** unlawful restraint of another's personal liberty or freedom of locomotion. It may be a criminal offense or the basis of a **civil action** for **damages.**

FALSE IMPRISONMENT as a **tort,** the intentional, unjustified detention or confinement of a person. Where the restraint is imposed by virtue of one claiming legal authority to do so and an arrest occurs, it will be a **false arrest** as well as a false imprisonment. Compare **kidnapping.**

FALSE OATH see **false swearing.**

FALSE PRETENSE the statutory crime of obtaining money or property by making false representations of fact; also known as **MISREPRESENTATION.**

EXAMPLE: A salesman tells Jackie that the diamond she wants to buy is a perfect cut and therefore very valuable. In reality, the diamond has many flaws and the salesman purposefully made contrary representations. Jackie purchases the diamond based on the salesman's representations since she knows nothing about diamonds. When she learns that the stone is flawed, she can sue the salesman for *false pretense* in the sale.

See **counterfeit; embezzlement; forgery; fraud.**

FALSE [PUBLIC] ALARMS the offense of intentionally making a false statement for the purpose of causing evacuation of a building or a method of public transportation.

FALSE RETURN 1. a **return** to a **writ** made by a ministerial officer (such as a sheriff) in which there is a false statement that is injurious to a party having an interest in the writ. For example, if a sheriff is supposed to serve a **summons** and untruthfully claims on his or her return that he or she did serve it, this would constitute a false return; 2. an incorrect tax return in which there appears either an intent to deceive on the part of the taxpayer, or at least **negligence** that is sufficiently serious to warrant holding the taxpayer liable for his or her error.

FALSE SWEARING the giving of a false oath in connection with some proceeding or matter in which an oath is required by law. It is a **common law misdemeanor** and consists of an act that would amount to **perjury** except that it is not committed in a judicial **proceeding.** See **affidavit.**

FALSE VERDICT a manifestly unjust **verdict;** one inconsistent with the **evidence.** When such a verdict is rendered, the court can enter a judgment **n.o.v.** (notwithstanding the verdict).

FALSI CRIMEN see **crimen falsi.**

FAMILY COURTS see **court [FAMILY COURTS].**

FAMILY THERAPIST PRIVILEGE see **marital communications privilege.**

FAMILY [WIDOW'S] ALLOWANCE an amount awarded to a widow for support during the administration of her deceased husband's estate, regardless of whether the widow has any right in the corpus or income of the estate.

FAMILY, CRIMINAL see **organized crime.**

FAMILY PURPOSE DOCTRINE a doctrine establishing **tort liability** of the owner of a family car when that car is used by another member of the family.

EXAMPLE: A mother explicitly tells her daughter not to use the car at night but leaves a set of keys on the table. The daughter takes the car one night and gets into an accident. The mother is held responsible for any injuries under the *family purpose doctrine,* despite her admonitions to the daughter.

FAMOSUS LIBELLUS *(fä-mō'-sŭs lī-bĕl'-ŭs)* Lat.: a scandalous libel. A **slanderous** or **libelous** letter, handbill, advertisement, petition, written **accusation** or **indictment.**

FANNIE MAE see **mortgage market [FANNIE MAE].**

FARM PRODUCTS see **consumer goods [FARM PRODUCTS].**

FAS see **free alongside.**

FATAL VARIANCE see **variance.**

FAULT generally, **error.** 1. in describing people's conduct, it is the responsibility for or cause of wrongdoing or failure. 2. in describing goods, it is a defect in either the quantity or quality of the goods.

FAVORED BENEFICIARY one who, in a **will,** has been favored over others having equal claim to the **testator's** bounty.

FBI see **Federal Bureau of Investigation [FBI].**

FCI see **jail [FEDERAL CORRECTIONAL INSTITUTION].**

FDA see **Food and Drug Administration [FDA].**

FDIC see **Federal Deposit Insurance Corporation [FDIC].**

FEALTY in feudal times, loyalty sworn by the **tenant** to his lord.

FEATHERBEDDING in labor law, the **unfair labor practice** of creating or spreading employment by unnecessarily maintaining or increasing the number of employees or the time used to complete a particular job. Minimum crew regulations on the railroad is a typical example. Unions attempt to justify such practices on grounds of health and safety although job security is their primary motivation. See **labor organization [union].**

FEDERAL AVIATION ADMINISTRATION [FAA] an agency of the U.S. Department of Transportation, charged with regulating air commerce, promoting aviation safety and overseeing the operation of airports, including air traffic control.

FEDERAL BUREAU OF INVESTIGATION [FBI] an agency of the U.S. Department of Justice, charged by law with investigating violations of all laws of the U.S. government, except those expressly assigned to other agencies.

FEDERAL CLAIMS COURT a court of the United States created in 1855 to hear and determine claims against the United States. The purpose of the tribunal was to relieve Congress of the burden of disposing of such claims through the **enactment** of private bills. At first the court's decisions were merely recommendations for congressional action but in 1866 its decisions were declared by Congress to be final. The TUCKER ACT of 1887 expanded the jurisdiction of the court. The Supreme Court determined that the court was an Article III court and that its judges enjoyed life tenure. In 1982 Congress replaced this court with a new UNITED STATES CLAIMS COURT "established under Article I"; the judges of the new court hold office for 15 year terms and decide CONGRESSIONAL-REFERENCE CASES. These congressional-reference cases are cases in which Congress asks the court to make findings of fact or recommendations that Congress will then use in deciding whether to afford a party legislative relief.

FEDERAL COMMON LAW the body of decisional law developed by the federal courts, not resting on state court decisions. Before the decision in *Erie Railroad* v. *Tompkins,* 304 U.S. 64, it referred primarily to the decisional law that federal courts developed in **diversity of citizenship** cases. After *Erie,* federal courts sitting in diversity cases have been bound to follow the general (substantive) **common law** of the state from which, respectively, each case arose. See **preemption.**

FEDERAL CORRECTIONAL FACILITY see **jail** [FEDERAL CORRECTIONAL INSTITUTION].

FEDERAL COURTS the United States courts (distinguished from the courts of the individual states), including **district courts** (general courts of **original jurisdiction,** which are the federal **trial** courts), courts of appeals (formerly circuit courts of appeals, which are principally **appellate** review **courts),** and the **Supreme Court** (the only court created directly by the constitution, and the court of last resort in the federal system). Other specialized courts in the federal system are **court of claims** (hears suits involving allowable claims against the United States government), COURT OF CUSTOMS AND PATENT APPEALS (reviews customs court decisions), and CUSTOMS COURT (reviews decisions of the customs collectors).

FEDERAL DEPOSIT INSURANCE CORPORATION [FDIC] created by Congress in response to the bank failures of the 1920s and 1930s, it is an independent agency of the federal government that preserves and promotes public confidence in the U.S. financial system by insuring deposits (but not securities, mutual funds, or similar types of investments) in banks and thrift institutions for at least $250,000 per depositor.

FEDERAL EMERGENCY MANAGEMENT AGENCY [FEMA] see **Department of Homeland Security [DHS]** [FEDERAL EMERGENCY MANAGEMENT AGENCY [FEMA]].

FEDERAL EMPLOYERS LIABILITY ACT [FELA] the federal law imposing liability on railroads for injuries sustained by their employees in the course of employment. It is based upon the federal government's power over **interstate commerce.** Compare **Jones Act.**

FEDERAL INSURANCE CONTRIBUTION ACT see **FICA.**

FEDERALISM a system of government wherein power is constitutionally divided between a central government and local governments.

EXAMPLE: The United States Supreme Court decides that the Constitution does not protect a person's privacy from a certain police tactic. Under the doctrine of *federalism,* though, a state court may nonetheless interpret its state constitution as prohibiting the same police conduct. The federal and state judicial systems are sufficiently separate so that a state court can afford greater protection to its citizens than the federal courts by a more liberal interpretation of its own constitution and laws. The state courts must observe any minimum federal rights, however, under the **Supremacy Clause** to the United States Constitution.

FEDERAL MAGISTRATE see **magistrate** [UNITED STATES [FEDERAL] MAGISTRATE].

FEDERAL MAGISTRATE'S ACT OF 1968 see **magistrate** [FEDERAL MAGISTRATE'S ACT OF 1968].

FEDERAL QUESTION JURISDICTION one kind of **original jurisdiction** that allows **federal courts** to hear **cases** wherein the application of something in the Constitution, laws or treaties of the United States is being disputed. See also **diversity of citizenship.**

FEDERAL RESERVE SYSTEM established under the Federal Reserve Act of 1913 to hold cash reserves of member banks and to provide other services, such as furnishing currency for circulation, facilitating clearance and collection of checks, and issuing and redeeming government obligations such as savings bonds. The functions of the agency were expanded in 1933 and 1935 to place greater emphasis on government control of the money supply, the credit structure and the economy in general. Twelve federal reserve banks are located throughout the country. All national banks are member banks; state banks may join at their option.

FEDERAL TORT CLAIMS ACT an act passed in 1946 that confers exclusive **jurisdiction** on United States **district courts** to hear claims against the United States for money **damages,** for injury or loss of property, or personal injury or death, caused by the **negligent** or wrongful act or omission of any employee of the government while acting within the scope of his office or employment, under circumstances where the United States, if a private person, would be liable to the claimant under the laws of the place where the act or omission occurred. The act is a broad waiver of **sovereign immunity,** although there are a number of qualifications on the waiver. Some state governments have enacted similar legislation. See **Tort Claims Act**.

FEDERAL TRADE COMMISSION [FTC] a federal administrative agency established in 1914 to protect consumers against unfair methods of competition and deceptive business practices, including sales frauds and violation of the **anti-trust laws.**

FEDERAL TRADE COMMISSION IMPROVEMENT ACT see **Magnuson-Moss Warranty Act.**

FEE in **real property,** an **estate.** Fee, **fee simple,** and FEE SIMPLE ABSOLUTE are often used as equivalents to signify an estate of absolute ownership that can be sold by the owner or **devised** to the **heirs;** however, the term is used to refer also to ownership that is qualified, as in the case of a **conditional** or **determinable fee,** which are types of estates that might last forever but are subject to termination upon the happening of a certain event.

IN FEE outright ownership of real property; the ownership of all aspects of title, including the ability to transfer the totality of such title.

EXAMPLE: Brianna conveys land to her brother in fee simple absolute. The brother has complete ownership of the land and can do with it as he pleases. If she conveys the land to him restricting its use to religious purposes, that conveyance is called a determinable fee. The moment the land is used for some purpose other than a religious one, it reverts to Brianna or to whomever she designates.

FEE SIMPLE a **freehold estate** of virtually infinite duration and of absolute **inheritance** free of any limitations or restriction to particular heirs; also called **FEE SIMPLE ABSOLUTE.**

FEE SIMPLE CONDITIONAL see **conditional fee [estate].**

FEE SIMPLE DEFEASIBLE see **determinable fee.**

FEE SIMPLE DETERMINABLE see **determinable fee.**

FEE TAIL the estate created by a **conveyance,** by **deed** or **will,** to a person "and the **heirs of his body.**" A fee tail establishes a fixed line of inheritable **succession** and cuts off the regular succession of **heirs** at law. It is a limited estate in that **inheritance** is through lineal descent only, which, if exclusively through males is called **FEE TAIL MALE,** and if exclusively through females is called **FEE TAIL FEMALE.** If the family line runs out **(failure of issue),** the fee **reverts** to the **grantor** or his successors in interest.

FELA see **Federal Employers Liability Act [FELA]; Employers Liability Acts.**

FELLOW SERVANTS co-workers: employees engaged in common pursuits under the same general control, serving the same employer, engaged in the same general business and deriving authority and compensation from a common source; defined for the purpose of the **FELLOW SERVANT RULE,** which absolves an employer of **liability** for **injury** to a worker resulting from the **negligence** of a co-worker. Fellow servants were said to assume the risk of each other's negligence. **Employers' Liability Acts** and **Workers' Compensation statutes** have abrogated the fellow servant doctrine.

FELLOWSHIPS see **scholarships and fellowships.**

FELONY generic term employed to distinguish certain high crimes from minor offenses known as **misdemeanors;** crimes declared to be such by statute or to be "true crimes" by the **common law.** Statutes often define felony as an offense punishable by imprisonment for more than one year or by death or imprisonment generally. The original common law felonies were felonious **homicide, mayhem, arson, rape, robbery, burglary, larceny,** prison breach (escape) and rescue of a felon. See **misprision of felony.**

FELONY, MISPRISION OF see **misprision of felony.**

FELONY MURDER a **homicide** that occurs in the commission or attempted commission of a **felony;** considered first-degree **murder** by operation of this doctrine. In many modern statutes, only homicides that occur in the course of certain specified felonies are felony murders. The **malice** necessary to find someone **guilty** of murder is inferred from the actor's intent to commit a felony.

EXAMPLE: Alan and Kirk hold up a liquor store. The owner attempts to trigger an alarm, and Alan fires at him with a pistol, intending only to frighten him but unfortunately killing him. Even though Alan did not intend to kill the owner, both Alan and Kirk will be guilty of the owner's murder under the doctrine of *felony murder.*

FENCE a structure erected in order to enclose **real property.** A fence may be used to determine a boundary for purposes of **trespass.**

In criminal law, an individual who receives stolen property and resells it for profit. A fence commits the crime of **receiving stolen property.**

FEOFFMENT the name given in common law to the means of conveying title to **freehold** estates, which required **livery of seisin.** At the site of the land and in the presence of neighbors, the **vendor** would point out the boundaries of the purchase and hand over to the vendee the appropriate symbol of **seisin.** The method was used until the use of the written **deed** came to be prescribed by statute.

FERAE NATURAE *(fĕr'-ī nä-tūr'-ī)* Lat.: wild beasts of nature. Animals of natural disposition in that, unlike domestic animals, they are untamed.

FERTILE OCTOGENARIAN refers to a legal fiction that, for purposes of the **Rule Against Perpetuities,** every living person is presumed capable of having children as long as he or she lives, even though it may be biologically impossible. The impact of this fiction under the rule against perpetuities has been modified by statute in many **jurisdictions.**

FEUDALISM a system of government and a means of holding property in England and Western Europe that grew out of the chaos of the Dark Ages. Through a ceremony, called **homage,** in which mutual duties of support and protection were promised, the vassal in effect gave his land to the lord and the lord then had a duty to protect it and the vassal. Though the vassal thenceforth owned no land, he held the land of the lord as a **tenant** and retained a use in that land. The land that the vassal held was called his feud, fief, or feudum. The relationship between the lord and his vassals could become more indirect by the process of **subinfeudation,** so that theoretically there could be placed between the lord and his vassal any number of persons at different levels, each serving as a link in the chain of relations between the lord at the top and the least of the vassals. Eventually, the king became the ultimate lord over all, and all land in England was held of him. Only in England was feudalism the sole method of holding land, although it was the general method elsewhere in Western Europe.

The feudal land holding system influenced all of the early common law concerning real property, and despite the fact that the feudal system never existed in the United States, it has played a vital role in shaping modern land law.

FIAT JUSTITIA *(fē'-ät jūs-tĭ'-shē-à)* Lat.: let justice be done.

FICA [FEDERAL INSURANCE CONTRIBUTION ACT] this Act imposes a tax on employees and employers that is used to fund the **Social Security** system.

FICTION, LEGAL see **legal fiction.**

FIDUCIARY a person having a duty, created by his or her undertaking, to act primarily for the benefit of another in matters connected with the undertaking; one who holds a position of confidence, as, for example, a **trustee.**

FIERI FACIAS *(fēĕ'-rē fā'-shē-ăs)* Lat.: that you cause to be made; a common law writ to enforce the collection of a claim that has gone to judgment and has become final. By this early English writ, a creditor with judgment was, in effect, ordering the sheriff to enforce against the debtor by seizure and sale of the debtor's personal property to the extent necessary to satisfy the judgment. At common law, the real property of the debtor could not be sold at execution. Today, the law of execution is for the most part statutory, and most state laws provide for a single writ for the enforcement of judgments out of the real and personal property of the debtor. Other common law writs made virtually obsolete by modern statutory provisions include:

ELEGIT *(ē-lē'-jĭt)* Lat: that he has chosen; a writ resulting in the appraisal and transfer of a debtor's goods to his or her creditor, and, if necessary to satisfy the judgment, the transfer of an interest in the rents and profits from all (originally only a **moiety**) of his or her real property.

EXTENDI FACIAS *(ĕx-tĕn'-dī fā'-shē-ăs)* Lat.: you cause to be extended; also known as "extent," a writ calling for the setting off of lands of a debtor for purposes of appraisal as to its sufficiency to satisfy the writ of the creditor.

LEVARI FACIAS *(lĕ-vä'-rī fā'-shē-ăs)* Lat.: a writ authorizing enforcement of a judgment out of both the debtor's goods and the profits and rents of his or her land.

FIFO see **first-in, first-out.**

FIFTEENTH AMENDMENT the amendment to the United States Constitution, ratified in 1870, which guarantees each citizen the right to vote, regardless of race, color, or previous condition of servitude.

FIFTH AMENDMENT the amendment to the U.S. Constitution, part of the Bill of Rights, that establishes certain protections for citizens from actions of the government by providing (1) that a person shall not be required to answer for a capital or other **infamous crime** unless an **indictment** or **presentment** is first issued by a grand **jury,** (2) that no person will be placed in **double jeopardy,** (3) that no person may be required to testify against himself or herself, (4) that neither life, liberty nor property may be taken without **due process of law,** and (5) that private property may not be taken for public use, without payment of just compensation.

FIGHTING WORDS those that by their very utterance, in the context in which they are spoken, inflict injury or tend to incite the hearer to an immediate **breach** of the peace.

In **tort** law, one who uses fighting words and thereby creates reasonable apprehension of harm in another person may be guilty of **assault.** See also **defamation.**

FIGURE see **public figure.**

FILE refers to both the physical collection of **documents** (such as **pleadings, motions, briefs,** and other papers) (example: "Where is the *Katherine Nicholas* file?") as well as the act of delivering documents to the proper authority (example: "Please file this **brief** with the court."). See **filing.**

FILIBUSTER see **cloture** [**FILIBUSTER**].

FILING the depositing of **documents** with the **court** or with other **public officials** to become preserved as part of the offical record. Often specific deadlines are imposed by which time the documents must be filed. Failure to meet the deadline may result in the imposition of late fees or may result in the document being excluded from consideration. Court documents must be **served** on the opposing party. See **service.** See also **return [FILING].**

FINAL DECISION [DECREE; JUDGMENT] a decision that settles the rights of **parties** respecting the subject matter of the **suit** until the decision is **reversed** or set aside; ends the **litigation** on the **merits** and leaves nothing for the court to do but execute the **judgment.** Compare **interlocutory.**

FINAL DECREE see **decree [FINAL DECREE].**

FINAL HEARING see **hearing [FINAL HEARING].**

FINAL INJUNCTION see **injunction [PERMANENT [FINAL] INJUNCTION].**

FINAL JUDGMENT see **final decision; judgment [FINAL JUDGMENT].**

FINAL ORDER see **order [FINAL ORDER].**

FINANCE CHARGES any charge for an extension of credit.

FINANCIAL INTERMEDIARY an organization such as a bank that brings together lenders (in the form of depositors) and borrowers. Other examples include savings and loan associations, credit unions, **real estate investment trusts [REITs]** and various kinds of finance companies.

FINANCIAL RESPONSIBILITY LAWS see **assigned risk [FINANCIAL RESPONSIBILITY].**

FINANCIAL STATEMENT see **balance sheet; income statement.**

FINDER OF FACT see **fact finder.**

FINDER'S FEE a fee or commission paid for finding what a customer desires. In **merger** activities, the finder either locates a buyer when the client company wants to sell or locates a seller when the client company is looking for acquisitions. In real estate activities, finder's fees are paid for locating property, for obtaining **mortgage** loans and for referring buyers, sellers and mortgage loans.

FINDING the decision of a court on issues of fact. The decision's purpose is to answer questions raised by the **pleadings** or charges. It is designed to facilitate review by disclosing the grounds on which the **judgment** rests. Findings of fact are made by a **jury** in an **action** at law, or, if there is no jury, they are made by the judge.

FINDING OF FACT factual determinations made by the trier of fact (court or jury), or an administrative body, based upon the evidence which has been presented to it. If the case is presented to a jury, the jury makes the finding of facts, such as "Was the accident the fault of the driver?" Otherwise, the judge or administrative officer will make the findings of fact. When the jury returns a general verdict ("we find for the plaintiff " or "not guilty"), the factual basis of the jury's verdict will not be known and may not easily be ascertained unless there was only one issue of fact in the case. When the jury returns a special verdict, it answers specific factual questions which have been presented to it, such as "Did the accident occur prior to July 5th?" As a general proposition, an appellate court can only set aside a finding of fact made below if it determines that the finding is clearly erroneous, i.e., that reasonable people could not possibly make such a finding.

FINDING OF LAW a determination of the court as to the application of a rule of law to particular facts. Also referred to as a **CONCLUSION OF LAW**.

EXAMPLE: Elon sued his employer for wrongful termination. The court found that Elon did fall under the provisions of the state's whistleblower statute because his firing was a direct result of his complaint regarding the company's failure to provide safety harnesses to its employees.

FINE a sum of money imposed upon a defendant as a penalty for an act of wrongdoing. The fine is payable to the public treasury as opposed to **restitution,** which is payable to the **victim** of the wrongdoing. Modern statutes favor restitution over fines and sometimes provide that courts may not impose a fine if its satisfaction would interfere with the making of restitution. The Court has held that a state has discretion in setting punishment for state crimes and may impose alternative sanctions. However, under the Equal Protection Clause, a state may not subject a certain class of convicted defendants to a period of imprisonment beyond the statutory maximum solely by reason of their indigency. It is a denial of **equal protection** to limit punishment to payment of a fine for those who are able to pay it but to convert the fine to imprisonment for those who are unable to pay it.

FINGERPRINT unique line patterns on each finger that may be left when the finger comes in contact with an object. If a suspect drank from a glass, the glass may be dusted with powder that clings to the oils left by the finger, and an impression may be lifted and later compared against the suspect. No two people (except identical twins) have the same fingerprints. Arrested persons are routinely fingerprinted. The prints are classified and entered into a computer system known as **AFIS** (Automated Fingerprint Identification System). Prints lifted from a gun, for example, can be compared against the hundreds of thousands of prints in the system for a possible match against a suspect. Note: the term "DNA fingerprinting" does not refer to fingerprints but rather to the science of DNA technology and its ability to link an accused person to a particular criminal act. See **DNA testing.**

FIRM OFFER   an offer in writing that states the offer is to be irrevocable for a set time. As long as it is stipulated in a signed writing that the offer is to be held open, it need not be supported by **consideration** to be binding.

   EXAMPLE: A new stationery business undertakes an enthusiastic effort to acquire new customers and develop an excellent reputation. Pursuant to that desire, it makes several *firm offers* to other local businesses, guaranteeing that it will supply all the stationery the others need for ninety days at a fixed price. The others can enforce that offer against the new business at any time during the year, even though they provided no consideration in return for the offer.

FIRST AMENDMENT   the first of ten amendments added to the Federal Constitution in 1791 by the **Bill of Rights,** it guarantees freedoms of speech, assembly, press, petition, and the free exercise of religion. As written, it applies to the federal government but has been applied to states by the **Fourteenth Amendment.** Litigation under this amendment has included the use of prayer in public schools, censorship of the press, and the community's right to regulate obscene materials. See **establishment clause; free exercise clause.**

FIRST DEGREE   see **murder** [FIRST DEGREE MURDER]; **principal** [PRINCIPAL IN THE FIRST DEGREE].

FIRST DEGREE MURDER   see **murder** [FIRST DEGREE MURDER].

FIRST DEVISEE   the first person who is to receive an **estate devised** by **will.**

FIRST IMPRESSION, CASE OF   first discussion or consideration. A case is one of first impression when it presents a **question of law** that has never before been considered by any court, and thus is not influenced by the doctrine of **stare decisis.**

FIRST-IN, FIRST-OUT [FIFO] a method of **inventory** valuation in which cost of goods sold is charged with the cost of raw materials, semi-furnished goods, and finished goods purchased "first" and in which inventory contains the most recently purchased materials. In times of rapid inflation, FIFO inflates profits, since the least expensive inventory is charged against cost of current sales, resulting in "inventory profits." As a consequence, LAST-IN, FIRST-OUT [LIFO] inventory valuation has become a more popular method, since it reduces current taxes by eliminating inventory profits. See **balance sheet.**

FISC the treasury of a political entity.

FISCAL pertaining to the public finance and financial transactions; belonging to the public treasury (called the FISC).

FISCAL POLICY the use of public finance and financial transactions to achieve desired economic goals.

FISCAL YEAR any twelve-month period used by a business as its accounting period.

FIT see **unfit.**

FITNESS see **warranty [WARRANTY OF FITNESS].**

FIXED ASSETS see **asset [FIXED ASSETS]; balance sheet**

FIXED CAPITAL the amount of capital permanently invested in a business.

FIXED INCOME income that does not change; for instance, bonds paying interest at a specified rate that does not change are fixed-income securities.

FIXED INVESTMENT TRUST see **nondiscretionary trust.**

FIXED RATE MORTGAGE see **mortgage [FIXED RATE MORTGAGE].**

FIXED SALARY a salary that is set at a dollar amount and does not increase or decrease as a result of certain events occurring or not occurring, such as a level of business being done by the employer.

FIXING, PRICE see **price fixing.**

FIXTURE something that was once a **chattel** but that is attached to **real property** in such a way that its removal would damage the property, and that is thus considered part of the realty.

EXAMPLE: To install a new chandelier in the house, the occupant had to reinforce the ceiling and attach extra bolts. A few years after the installation, a new room is added that requires construction of a wall near the chandelier. Removal of the chandelier will now require not only a removal of the bolts but destruction of the new wall as well. If the present occupants move, the chandelier must stay behind since it has become a *fixture* of the house.

TRADE FIXTURE see **trade fixture.**

FLAGITIOUS corrupt; shamefully or scandalously disgraceful.

FLIGHT escape; leaving the scene of a crime by one who feels **guilt,** or self-concealment to avoid **arrest** or **prosecution** after arrest. Compare **resisting arrest.** See also **abscond.**

FLOAT checks that are in transit between banks and that have not yet been paid; checks in the process of collection that remain conditional checks in a depositor's checking account until the checks are paid to the bank in currency.

FLOATING DEBT any short-term obligation of a business, such as bank loans due in one year and **commercial paper.** Government floating debt consists of **treasury bills** and short-term **treasury notes.** Long-term debt, such as **treasury bonds,** is referred to as **FUNDED DEBT.**

FOB see **free on board.**

FOIA see **Freedom of Information Act.**

FOOD AND DRUG ADMINISTRATION [FDA] an administrative agency of the Department of Health and Human Services that regulates the safety and quality of foodstuffs, pharmaceuticals, cosmetics, and medical devices.

FORBEAR to refrain from doing an act. See **forbearance.**

FORBEARANCE the act of declining, usually for a period of time, to enforce a legal right. For purposes of the law of **usury,** the term is often used to refer to a contractual obligation of a **creditor** to refrain for a specific period from claiming a debt that has already become payable; such forbearance is in substance a loan for which a creditor may impose a charge. In **contract** law, forbearance of a valid claim, if bargained for, constitutes **consideration.**

EXAMPLE: A grandfather is so distressed by his grandson Brad's smoking habit that he promises Brad $1,000 if Brad discontinues smoking until his 25th birthday. The grandfather dies when Brad is 23, but Brad still refrains from smoking. At age 25, he requests the $1,000, but the executor of the estate claims that Brad never promised anything in return for the money. A court will find that Brad's *forbearance* from smoking constitutes consideration to support the contract and will order the executor to pay.

FORCE physical acts or the threat of physical acts intentionally used to do an act or to commit a crime.

    DEADLY FORCE in criminal law, force that is intended or is likely to cause death or great bodily harm. The doctrine of **self-defense** justifies the use of deadly force only to repel deadly force. See **self-defense.**

    UNLAWFUL FORCE in the law of torts, the use of force without the consent of the person against whom it is directed, for which the user may be liable. See **battery.**

FORCED HEIRS persons who cannot be disinherited, such as a person's spouse or children. In the United States, a spouse may elect to take a share of a decedent's **estate,** usually one-third, instead of taking what the spouse has given the spouse under a last **will** and testament. Civil law countries such as France and Switzerland have forced heirship laws under which members of a person's family, including children, are entitled to **inherit** a certain portion of the estate, regardless of the person's wishes as expressed in a last will and testament.

FORCED LABOR see **involuntary servitude.**

FORCED SALE see **sale [FORCED SALE].**

FORCE MAJEURE superior force. See **act of God [nature].**

FORCIBLE DETAINER see **detainer [UNLAWFUL DETAINER].**

FORCIBLE ENTRY entry on **real property** in the **possession** of another, against his or her will and without authority of law, by actual force, or with such an array of force and apparent intent to employ it that the occupant, in permitting possession to be taken from him or her, must be regarded as acting from a well-founded fear that resistance would be perilous or unavailing. In many states a mere **trespass** without any force will be considered forcible. Compare **detainer [UNLAWFUL DETAINER].**

FORCIBLE ENTRY AND DETAINER a summary statutory **proceeding** for restoring to the **possession** of land one who has been wrongfully deprived of the possession, usually the landlord.

FORECLOSURE generally, the termination of a right to **property;** specifically, an **equitable** action to compel payment of a **mortgage** or other **debt** secured by a **lien.** As to **real property,** foreclosure is precipitated by nonpayment of the debt or other **default** under the loan agreement, and leads to the court's order that the property to which the mortgage or lien is attached be sold to satisfy that debt. As a consequence, the mortgagor's **equity of redemption** is irrevocably destroyed, subject to any statutory **redemption** rights that may survive for a limited time in some jurisdictions. A **security interest** in **personal property** can likewise be foreclosed by a JUDICIAL SALE (see **sale** [FORCED SALE]) of the **collateral.**

FOREIGN belonging to another country or nation. Also, used to describe another jurisdiction or state.

FOREIGN RELATIONS the area of domestic law of the United States that involves decisions and policy concerning international affairs.

FOREMAN [FOREPERSON] OF A JURY the presiding member of the jury and the person who speaks on the jury's behalf when communicating with the court or in rendering the jury's verdict. Normally the individual selected first or seated in the number one position in the jury box is designated the foreperson, but sometimes the jurors themselves elect their foreperson.

FORENSIC belonging to the courts of justice; indicates the application of a particular subject to the law. For example, FORENSIC MEDICINE employs medical technology to assist in solving legal problems.

FORESEEABILITY a concept to limit a party's **liability** for the consequences of his or her acts to effects that are within the scope of a FORESEEABLE RISK, i.e., risks whose consequences a person of ordinary prudence would reasonably expect might occur as a result of his or her actions.

EXAMPLE: During the refueling of a ship, gasoline spills into the harbor. A spark from a nearby welder ignites when it lands on a piece of highly flammable fabric. The fabric falls into the harbor and a fire develops. Consequently, the whole harbor burns down. Even though no fire would have started had the fueling company been more careful, that company is not responsible for the destruction of the harbor. The damage was an *unforeseeable* consequence of spilling a small amount of fuel oil.

In a contract setting, a party's liability for consequential or special **damages** is limited to damages arising from the foreseeable consequences of his **breach.**

In **tort** law, in most cases, a party's actions may be deemed **negligent** only where the injurious consequences of those actions were foreseeable.

FORFEITURE the permanent loss of **property** for failure to comply with the **law;** the **divestiture** of the **title** of property, without compensation, for a **default** or an offense.

FORGERY 1. **fraudulent** making or altering of a writing with intent to prejudice the rights of another; making of a false **instrument** or the passing of an instrument known to be false; 2. fabrication or **counterfeiting** of **evidence.**

FORM model of a document containing the phrases and **words of art** needed to make the document technically correct for **procedural** purposes; used by lawyers in drafting legal documents.

FORMAL CONTRACT see **sealed instrument.**

FORMA PAUPERIS see **in forma pauperis.**

FORMS OF ACTION technical categories of personal **actions** developed in **common law,** containing the entire course of legal proceedings peculiar to those actions. The forms of action are no longer in use, but they continue to affect modern **civil procedure** and **tort** law.

Forms of action consisted of proceedings for recovery of debts, and recovery of money **damages** resulting from **breach** of contract, or injury to one's person, property or relations. The forms can be classified as (*a*) actions in form **ex contract,** including **assumpsit,** covenant, debt and account; and (*b*) actions in form **ex delicto** (i.e., those not based on contracts), including **trespass, trover,** case, **detinue** and **replevin.** The result was a highly formal and artificial system of procedure.

FORNICATION generally, sexual intercourse of two unmarried persons of different sexes, punished as a **misdemeanor** by statute in some states. In some states, it refers to illicit sexual intercourse between a man, whether married or single, and an unmarried woman. In some states, illicit intercourse can be fornication for the party who is not married and **adultery** for the party who is married. It is not a **common law** crime and is not part of modern penal codes, though it remains a criminal offense in many **jurisdictions.**

FORUM a court; a place where disputes are heard and decided according to law and justice; a place of **jurisdiction;** a place where **remedies** afforded by the law are pursued. See also **venue.**

FORUM NON CONVENIENS *(fôr'-ŭm nŏn kŏn-vě'-nē-ĕns)* Lat.: an inconvenient court. Under this doctrine a court, though it has **jurisdiction** of a case, may decline to exercise it where there is no legitimate reason for the case to be brought there, or where presentation in that court will create a hardship on the **defendants** or on relevant **wit-**

nesses because of the court's distance from them. The court will not **dismiss** the case under the doctrine unless the **plaintiff** has another **forum** open to him.

EXAMPLE: A truck lightly hits the rear end of a car, but, because of the vehicle's construction, the car bursts into flames and the driver is seriously injured. The driver, who is from another state, wants to have the case heard in his home state. The car company asks the court to invoke the *forum non conveniens* doctrine and have the case transferred to the state where the accident occurred. That request is granted because the witnesses to the accident, as well as the actual scene, are both in the other state, and it would be more inconvenient to have that information brought to the driver's home state than to have the driver go to the state where the accident occurred.

FOUNDATION in **evidence** law, preliminary evidence necessary to establish the admissibility of other evidence. A lawyer will lay a foundation to establish the relevancy of evidence that does not otherwise appear relevant to the matter at hand.

Also, an organization whose assets are dedicated to charitable purposes. See **charity.**

FOUNDER one who provides the first gift to establish a charitable institution, such as a college.

FOUNDER'S SHARES shares in a **corporation** or **company** issued to the organizers and often carrying special privileges.

401(K) see **retirement plan [401(K)].**

FOUR CORNERS the doctrine that requires that the meaning of a document be derived froms its entire contents as they relate to one another, and not from its individual parts.

FOURTEENTH AMENDMENT one of the so called "Civil War Amendments" to the Constitution in that it was ratified after the Civil War; protects all persons from state laws that attempt to deprive them of "life, liberty, or property, without due process of law," or that attempt to deny them **equal protection of the laws.** The amendment has been used to extend the protection of almost all of the provisions of the **Bill of Rights** to citizens of every state.

FOURTH AMENDMENT constitutional **amendment** guaranteeing the right of persons to be secure in their homes and property from unreasonable **searches and seizures** and consisting of the following elements: (1) the issuance of a **warrant** upon **oath** or affirmation; (2) upon **probable cause,** as determined by a neutral and detached **magistrate;** and (3) particularly describing the place to be searched and the items or persons to be seized.

The Fourth Amendment is most frequently encountered in cases involving the use of illegally seized evidence, or **fruits of the poisonous tree,** and is applied through the **exclusionary rule.** It was initially incorporated in the **Bill of Rights** to counter the abuses from searches conducted without warrants, with general warrants, or with **writs of assistance** and designed to safeguard the public's legitimate or reasonable expectation of privacy. Such expectations of privacy extend to a person's home (in such areas as use of contraceptives, obscene materials, or marijuana in a private residence), and to lesser extents, to a person's place of business, automobile, or even body. Courts have upheld invasions of a person's body in the areas of compulsory vaccinations, blood tests, rectal and vaginal searches, and surgical removal of a bullet. See **search warrant.**

FOUR UNITIES see **unities.**

Fr. abbreviation for French**.**

FRANCHISE 1. a special privilege that is conferred by the government upon individuals that does not of common right belong to citizens. For example, a municipality may grant to a local bus company a franchise that will give it sole authority to operate buses in the municipality for a certain number of years. 2. the right given to a private person or **corporation** to market another's product within a certain area. 3. **ELECTIVE FRANCHISE** (sometimes called simply "the franchise") refers to the right of citizens to vote in public elections.

FRATRICIDE the murder of one's brother.

FRAUD intentional deception resulting in **injury** to another. Fraud usually consists of a misrepresentation, concealment or nondisclosure of a material fact, or at least misleading conduct, devices or contrivance.

BADGES OF FRAUD see **badges of fraud.**

CONSTRUCTIVE [LEGAL] FRAUD comprises all acts, omissions and concealments involving **breach** of **equitable** or **legal duty,** or trust and resulting in damage to another. It is thus fraud that is presumed from the circumstances, without the need for any actual proof of intent to defraud.

EXTRINSIC [COLLATERAL] FRAUD fraud that prevents a party from knowing about his or her rights or **defenses** or from having a fair opportunity to present or litigate them at a trial. It is a ground for **equitable** relief from a **judgment.**

EXAMPLE: Loni obtains a court order requiring a company to give her all relevant information concerning a certain product that she claims injured her. At trial, a judge finds her evidence insufficient and dismisses her claim. Afterwards, Loni finds other documents in the company's possession that she never received but that would have proved her case. The *extrinsic fraud* committed upon her gives rise to both a suit against the company for the fraud and a right for Loni to have a new trial with the new documents.

FRAUD IN FACT [POSITIVE FRAUD] actual fraud; deceit; concealing something or making a false representation with an evil intent **[scienter]** when it causes injury to another. It is used in contrast to **CONSTRUCTIVE FRAUD,** which does not require evil intent.

FRAUD IN LAW fraud that is presumed from circumstances, where the one who commits it need not have any evil intent to commit a fraud; it is a **CONSTRUCTIVE FRAUD** or legal fraud.

FRAUD IN THE FACTUM generally arises from a disparity between the **instrument** executed and the one intended to be **executed,** as for example when a blind or illiterate person executes a deed when it has been read falsely to him or her after he or she asked to have it read.

FRAUD IN THE INDUCEMENT intentional fraud that causes one to execute an instrument, or make an agreement, or render a **judgment.** The misrepresentation does not mislead one as to the paper being signed but rather misleads as to the facts upon which the decision to sign is based.

FRAUD ON THE COURT occurs where it can be demonstrated, clearly and convincingly, that a party has deliberately set in motion some **unconscionable** scheme calculated to interfere with the judicial system's ability to impartially decide a matter by improperly influencing the trier or unfairly hampering the presentation of the opposing party's claim or defense. Unlike **common law** fraud on a party, fraud on the court does not require **reliance.**

INTRINSIC FRAUD fraudulent representation that is considered in rendering a judgment.

LEGAL FRAUD see **CONSTRUCTIVE [LEGAL] FRAUD** (above).

FRAUDULENT CONCEALMENT see **spoilation (of records) [FRAUDULENT CONCEALMENT].**

FRAUDULENT CONVEYANCE any conveyance made, or presumed to have been made, with the intention to delay or defraud **creditors,** where such intention is known to the party to whom the conveyance is made. It is generally characterized by a lack of fair and valuable **consideration** and is usually made by a debtor to place his **property** beyond the reach of creditors.

FREE ALONGSIDE [FAS] a commercial delivery term that signifies that the seller must at his or her own risk and expense deliver the **goods** to the side of the transporting medium in the usual manner and obtain and **tender** a receipt for the goods in exchange for which the carrier must issue a **bill of lading.** Compare **free on board [fob].**

FREE AND CLEAR unencumbered. In property law, a **title** is free and clear if it is not encumbered by any **liens** or restrictions; one conveys land free and clear if he or she transfers a **good title** or **marketable title.**

FREEDOM the state of being free; the absence of restrictions.

FREEDOM OF ASSOCIATION the right to peaceably assembly as guaranteed by the **First Amendment.**

FREEDOM OF EXPRESSION general term referring to the freedom of press, religion, and speech.

FREEDOM OF PRESS the right to publish and circulate one's views, as guaranteed by the First Amendment. Closely related to FREEDOM OF SPEECH (below). See **open court.**

FREEDOM OF RELIGION see **establishment clause.**

FREEDOM OF SPEECH the right to express one's thoughts without governmental restrictions on the contents thereof, as guaranteed by the First Amendment.

FREEDOM OF CONTRACT the liberty or ability to enter into agreements with others, which is a fundamental right reserved to citizens by the United States Constitution.

FREEDOM OF INFORMATION ACT [FOIA] a federal law requiring that, with specified exceptions, documents and materials generated or held by federal agencies be made available to the public and establishing guidelines for their disclosure.

FREE EXERCISE CLAUSE a provision in the First Amendment to the United States Constitution providing that "Congress shall make no laws . . . prohibiting the free exercise" of religion. The "free exercise clause" guarantees against government compulsion in religious matters, while the **establishment clause** insures that the government will maintain neutrality towards religion.

FREEHOLDER originally a responsible person in favor with the King of England who was deemed worthy of land grants in the new Colonies. The term, now unique to New Jersey, refers to persons in elective office comparable to county commissioners or county supervisors.

FREEHOLD [ESTATE] an estate in **fee** or a **life estate; an estate** or **interest** in **real property** for life or of uncertain duration.

FREE ON BOARD [FOB] a commercial term that signifies a contractual agreement between a buyer and a seller to have the subject of a sale delivered to a designated place, usually either the "place of shipment" or the "place of destination," without expense to the buyer. Thus a shipment "fob shipping point" requires the seller to bear the expense and the risk of putting the subject of the sale into the possession of the carrier, but the **duty** to pay the transportation charges from the fob point is on the buyer. Where the shipment is "fob destination point," the seller is required to bear the transportation charges and the risk of transport until the buyer point of destination. Compare **free alongside [fas].**

FREIGHT FORWARDER a shipper who accepts small shipments, consolidates them into larger shipments, and takes responsibility for their safe arrival at their point of destination.

FRESH PURSUIT in criminal law, the **common law** right of a police officer to cross jurisdictional lines in order to arrest a **felon.** The term also refers to the power of a police officer to make an **arrest** without a **warrant** when he or she is in immediate pursuit of a criminal.

FRIENDLY SUIT an action authorized by law brought by agreement between the **parties,** to secure a **judgment** that will have a binding effect in circumstances where a mere agreement or settlement will not; for example, where a claim in favor of an infant or another lacking legal capacity to enter into a binding contract can, for that reason, be settled only through the entry of a judgment. The term also refers to a suit by an administrator or an executor in the name of a creditor, against himself or herself, seeking an order compelling distribution to the creditor of a fixed share of the assets by the estate being administered. Suits that are **collusive,** on the other hand, will be **dismissed.** Compare **declaratory judgment.**

FRIEND, NEXT see **next friend.**

FRIEND OF THE COURT see **amicus curiae.**

FRINGE BENEFIT see **benefit [FRINGE BENEFIT].**

FRISK quick, superficial search; patting outer clothing to detect, by the sense of touch, if a concealed weapon is being carried.

FRIVOLOUS clearly insufficient as a **matter of law;** presenting no debatable question. A **claim** is frivolous if it is insufficient because unsupported by the facts or because the law recognizes no **remedy** for the claim.

FRONT-END LOAD PLAN   a contractual agreement to buy **mutual fund** shares through periodic payments, usually monthly, in which the sales commission and other expenses, called load, are taken out of the initial payments.

FRUCTUS INDUSTRIALES   *(frŭk'-tŭs ĭn-dŭs-trĭ-a'-lēz)*   Lat.: the produce of land resulting from manual labor, such as crops.

FRUCTUS NATURALES   *(frŭk'-tŭs nă-tū-ră'-lēz)*   Lat.: the produce of land that grows naturally, such as timber.

FRUIT OF THE POISONOUS TREE DOCTRINE   a rule under which **evidence** that is the direct result of illegal conduct on the part of an official is inadmissible in a criminal trial against the victim of the conduct. The doctrine draws its name from the idea that once the tree is poisoned (the primary evidence is illegally obtained) then the fruit of the tree (any secondary evidence) is likewise **TAINTED** and may also not be used.

EXAMPLE: The police illegally break into Atsushi's house and obtain a confession from him as to his drug-dealing activities. He also tells the police where they can find more drugs that he intended to sell. The police attempt to use the confession and the drugs to convict Atsushi. Under the *fruit of the poisonous tree doctrine,* neither the confession nor the drugs can be used against him because they are the product of an illegal entry by the police.

FRUITS OF CRIME   the results of a criminal act. See **forfeiture.**

FRUSTRATION (OF PURPOSE)   a doctrine under which the occurrence of unexpected events may justify one of the parties to a contract in **rescinding** the contract. Such frustration (also called **COMMERCIAL FRUSTRATION**) typically occurs when an implied **condition** of an agreement (a circumstance without which the contract would never have been made) does not occur or ceases to exist without fault of either party, so that the absence of the implied condition "frustrates" one party's intentions in making the agreement.

EXAMPLE: Andy signs a contract with a real estate salesman to purchase a house, with the understanding that he will be able to get a zoning change and use part of the house for his office. Contrary to what either party expected, the zoning change is not approved. Andy may seek to renege on his contract to purchase the house because his purpose in purchasing the house has been *frustrated.*

    See **impossibility.**

FTC see **Federal Trade Commission [FTC].**

FUGITIVE FROM JUSTICE   one who commits a crime within a state, and then leaves that state without awaiting the consequences of the crime he or she committed there; also, one who conceals himself or herself within the state in order to avoid its **process.**

FULL FAITH AND CREDIT the federal constitutional requirement that the public acts, records and judicial proceedings of one state be respected by each of the other states. Thus, if a **judgment** is conclusive in the state where it was pronounced, it is equally beyond dispute everywhere in the courts of the United States. The judgment is entitled to full faith and credit when the second court's inquiry discloses that the same questions were properly before the first court and were fully and fairly **litigated** and finally decided there.

EXAMPLE: Following a long trial, a company is found negligent in manufacturing a product that caused Ayad substantial hair loss. The manufacturer's assets in that state are insufficient to cover the full amount of the judgment. Ayad can take that judgment to another state where the manufacturer has assets, sue upon that judgment, and by applying the *full faith and credit* principle, obtain another judgment and collect whatever he is still owed.

FULL DISCLOSURE obligation to reveal details. In a commercial setting, a merchant must disclose to the consumer all details of the consumer transaction, including the cost of financing the purchase. Under federal and state election laws, candidates for public office are required to fully reveal the amount and source of specified campaign contributions.

FUND an amount of money that may be available either for general uses or purposes or that may be dedicated to a specific use or purpose; to pay such an amount.

FUND IN COURT an amount deposited in court because parties are contesting title to it or so that money will be available to pay a liability that is contingent.

GENERAL FUND a fund that is not dedicated to a specific purpose but that may be used to pay any debt or liability.

HEDGE FUND see **hedge fund.**

INDEX FUND see **index fund.**

MUTUAL FUND see **mutual fund.**

SINKING FUND in finance, a bond issue under the terms of which the issuer is obligated to repurchase a portion of the bonds each year until all of the bonds have been repurchased, rather than to redeem all of the bonds at the end of the term of the issue.

TRUST FUND see **trust fund.**

FUNDAMENTAL RIGHT a right that is considered by a court to be expressed, explicitly or implicitly, in the constitution of that state or the United States **Constitution,** and which is implicit in the concept of ordered liberty, such that neither liberty nor justice would exist if they were sacrificed. Examples of fundamental rights include a parent's right to raise his or her own child without governmental intrusion, the right to interstate travel, or the right to become a candidate for election to public office. A court must review laws infringing upon fundamental rights under a standard of **strict scrutiny.** To withstand strict scrutiny, a law must be necessary to promote a compelling governmental interest and must be narrowly tailored to advance that interest. Alternatively, if a court determines the right *not* to be a fundamental right, the **rational basis test** applies. See **privacy, right of.**

FUNDED DEBT see **floating debt.**

FUNGIBLE a term applied to **goods** that are interchangeable or capable of substitution by nature or agreement. Oil, grain and coal are examples of naturally fungible goods. When storing fungible goods, warehousemen are exempt from the legal requirement of keeping stored goods from one depositor separate from the goods of another. **Securities** of the same issue are considered fungible; hence a person obligated to deliver securities may deliver any security of the specified issue.

FUTURE ESTATE see **estate [FUTURE ESTATE [ESTATE IN FUTURO]].**

FUTURE INTEREST an **interest** in presently existing **real property** or **personal property,** or in a **gift** or **trust,** that will commence in **use, possession,** or enjoyment in the future. A **legatee** to receive an annual income upon reaching the age of 21 has a future interest that, when that age is reached, will ripen into a present interest. Future interests may constitute either **vested** or **contingent estates.**

EXAMPLE: A father conveys 200 shares of stock to Shira, his daughter, but if Shira dies before the father, the stock goes to Marcy. Marcy has a *future interest* in the stock that is contingent on Shira's predeceasing the father. If Shira does predecease the father, Marcy's future interest then vests.

FUTURES agreements whereby one person agrees to sell a commodity at a certain time in the future for a certain price. The buyer agrees to pay that price, knowing that the person has nothing to deliver at the time, but with the understanding that when the time arrives for delivery the buyer is to pay him or her the difference between the market value of that commodity and the price agreed upon if the commodity's value declines; and if it advances, the seller is to pay to the buyer the difference between the agreed-upon price and the market price. Thus, if the price of the commodity rises, the buyer makes a profit, and if the price declines, the buyer suffers a loss.

G

GAG ORDER a court-imposed order to restrict information or comment about a case. The ostensible purpose of such an order is to protect the interests of all parties and preserve the right to a fair trial by curbing publicity likely to prejudice a jury. A gag order cannot be directly imposed on members of the press because this constitutes an impermissible prior restraint and violates the First Amendment.

GAIN see **recognition** [NONRECOGNITION OF GAIN; RECOGNITION OF GAIN].

GAINFUL EMPLOYMENT [OCCUPATION] employment suited to the ability of the one employed. For purposes of disability covered by insurance, it may mean the ordinary employment of the insured, or other employment approximating the same livelihood as the insured might be expected to follow in view of his or her circumstances and physical and mental capabilities.

GAIN OR LOSS REALIZED see **realization** [GAIN OR LOSS REALIZED].

GAINS OR LOSSES see **capital** [CAPITAL GAINS OR LOSSES].

GAMBLING a play for value against an uncertain event in the hope of gaining something for value. Includes the payment of a price for a chance to gain a prize. Gambling is illegal in most jurisdictions, although may states permit state-run lotteries or casinos. See **aleatory** [ALEATORY CONTRACT].

GAME LAWS laws whose general aim is to protect from unauthorized pursuit and killing certain birds and animals. These laws may include outright prohibitions, or may restrict the hunting seasons, classes of animals, or type of weapons used.

GAOL the British and early-American spelling of "jail."

GARAGEMAN'S LIEN see **lien** [MECHANIC'S LIEN].

GARNISH to bring a **garnishment** proceeding or to **attach** wages or other property pursuant to such a proceeding.

EXAMPLE: Charles owes money to a department store for several appliances that he purchased on credit. Once Charles stopped paying, the store brought a *garnishment* proceeding against him for the money owed. If the court agrees with the store, it will order that a part of Charles' wages go directly to the store and not to Charles.

GARNISHEE a person who receives notice to retain, until he or she receives further notice from the court, **custody** of **assets** in his or her control that are owed to or belong to another person. The garnishee merely holds the assets until legal **proceedings** determine who is entitled to the property. The term thus signifies one on whom process of **garnishment** is served. In a statutory garnishment proceeding, the garnishee (often an employer) may be directed to pay over to the **creditor** a portion of the **debtor's** property (such as an employee's wages) that is in the garnishee's possession.

GARNISHMENT process in which money or **goods** in the hands of a third person, which are due a **defendant,** are attached by the **plaintiff.** It is a statutory **remedy** that consists of notifying a third party to retain something he or she has that belongs to the defendant (debtor), to make disclosure to the court concerning it, and to dispose of it as the court shall direct.

GATT General Agreement on Tariffs and Trade. See **tariff.**

GAVELKIND at common law, a form of feudal land ownership that required land to descend to all sons equally. By the end of the first quarter of the twentieth century all land ownership, or **tenure,** was reduced to a single form of common **socage** and peculiar customary tenures such as **gavelkind** were abolished.

By distributing land to all sons equally, gavelkind **tenure** differed from the English doctrine of **primogeniture** that allowed only the oldest son to inherit. In the United States, **statutes** of **descent and distribution** in each state govern **intestate succession.** These **statues** generally provide that all children share equally. See **primogeniture** and **descent and distribution.**

GBMI guilty but mentally ill. See **insanity.**

GENERAL APPEARANCE see **appearance** [GENERAL APPEARANCE].

GENERAL ASSUMPSIT see **assumpsit** [GENERAL ASSUMPSIT].

GENERAL CHALLENGE see **challenge** [GENERAL CHALLENGE].

GENERAL CONTRACTOR see **contractor** [GENERAL CONTRACTOR].

GENERAL COURT-MARTIAL see **court-martial; military law** [COURT-MARTIAL].

GENERAL DAMAGES see **damages** [ACTUAL [COMPENSATORY; GENERAL] DAMAGES].

GENERAL DEMURRER see **demurrer** [GENERAL DEMURRER].

GENERAL DENIAL see **denial** [GENERAL DENIAL].

GENERAL FUND see **fund** [GENERAL FUND].

GENERAL INTENT see **intent** [GENERAL INTENT].

GENERAL MENS REA see **mens rea** [GENERAL MENS REA].

GENERAL PARTNER see **partnership** [GENERAL PARTNER].

GENERAL POWER OF APPOINTMENT see **power of appointment** [GENERAL POWER OF APPOINTMENT].

GENERAL WARRANT see **search warrant** [GENERAL WARRANTS].

GENERAL WARRANTY DEED see **warranty deed** [GENERAL WARRANTY DEED].

GENERATION SKIPPING TRANSFER a generation skipping transfer is one more than a single generation removed from the transferor; e.g., a transfer by a grandfather to a grandchild. A GENERATION SKIPPING TRUST is created to make a generation skipping transfer. Certain generation skipping transfers made by a generation skipping trust or its equivalent are subject to a generation skipping transfer tax. If the transfer is not by a **trust** but directly by the donor, such transfer is subject to tax [UNIFIED ESTATE AND GIFT TAX], regardless of whether it skips a generation.

GENERIC general, relating to a group or class of related things; something not specific, not referring to a particular thing. The term "generic" has reference to a class of related things while the term "specific" is limited to a particular, definite, or precise thing.

GENERIC DRUG LAW refers to modern statutes enacted by many states that permit or require pharmacists in certain circumstances to substitute a drug product with the same active ingredients and of the same generic type for the drug prescribed by the physician.

GENEVA CONVENTIONS a set of treaties and protocols that apply during periods of armed conflict and which set forth the expectations under international law for humanitarian treatment of prisoners of war, those wounded in war, war zone civilians, and medical and religious personnel. Compare **enemy combatant.**

GEOGRAPHIC MARKET EXTENSION MERGER see **merger** [GEOGRAPHIC MARKET EXTENSION MERGER].

GERRYMANDER to create a civil division of an unusual shape within a particular locale for improper purpose; to redistrict a state, creating unnatural boundaries and isolating members of a particular political party, in the hope that a maximum number of the elected representatives will be of that political party.

EXAMPLE: A political party finally wins control of a state legislature. At the same time, the legislative districts must be restructured to account for population shifts. The party in power uses the opportunity to insure future control of the legislature by *gerrymandering* the districts. The end result is to create unnatural boundaries that will give the party the least opposition for future elections. The object of gerrymandering is to create districts in which the controlling party maintains a majority among registered voters.

GIFT a voluntary transfer of property made without **consideration,** that is, for which no value is received in return, which is accepted by the recipient. In federal tax law, a gift is excluded from the **gross income** of the recipient, but the transferor may be subject to the unified estate and gift tax. See **tax** [UNIFIED ESTATE AND GIFT TAX].

CLASS GIFT see **class gift.**

GIFT CAUSA MORTIS see **gift causa mortis.**

GIFT IN CONTEMPLATION OF DEATH former provisions of federal tax law provided that transfers made within three years of a donor's death were deemed to have been made in contemplation of death and thus includible in his or her gross estate "unless shown to the contrary." The three-year rule has been continued but without reference to contemplation of death and with certain other exclusions.

GIFT INTER VIVOS see **inter vivos.**

SPLIT GIFT a transfer in which the person receiving the property makes a payment that is less than the value of the property transferred.

GIFT CAUSA MORTIS a gift of personal property made in contemplation of impending death; delivery of the property must be made and death must occur as expected; otherwise, the gift is void.

GIFT IN CONTEMPLATION OF DEATH any gift made by a person within three years of death. Such transfers (except if less than $3,000) are subject to the unified estate and gift tax as if they had occurred at death.

GIFT OVER an estate that is to follow upon the expiration of a **preceding estate.**

GIFT TAX a tax that is imposed on transfers of property by gift during the transferor's lifetime. While the federal government imposes a gift tax most states do not. The federal gift tax is imposed at the same rates as the federal estate tax.

GINNIE MAE see **mortgage market [GINNIE MAE].**

GNP see **Gross National Product [GNP].**

GOING CONCERN VALUE the additional element of value of a trade or business that attaches to property by reason of its existence as an integral part of a going concern. Going concern value includes the value that is attributable to the interruption notwithstanding a change in ownership. Going concern value also includes the value that is attributable to the use or availability of an acquired trade or business (for example, the net earnings that otherwise would not be received during any period were the acquired trade or business not available or operational. **Good will** is the value of a trade or business that is attributable to the expectancy of continued customer patronage, whether due to the name of a trade or business, the reputation of a trade or business, or any other factor. The pre-1993 Act law rule barring amortization for good will and going concern value has produced an enormous amount of litigation. The IRS has generally taken the position that any amount paid for intangibles in the acquisition of a business relates to nonamortizable good will or going concern value, while the taxpayer has attempted to show that amortizable intangibles such as customer lists have a value apart from good will or going concern value and a limited useful life. Currently the code eliminates this IRS-taxpayer conflict by providing that good will and going concern value are amortizable over the same 15-year period applicable to other intangibles. Self-created good will and going concern value generally are not subject to 15-year amortization.

GOLDEN PARACHUTE a financial package with extremely generous terms received by an executive who loses his or her job or resigns due to a corporate merger or takeover.

GOOD CAUSE substantial or legally sufficient reason for doing something. For example, if a statute provides for granting a new **trial** upon a showing of good cause, such good cause might include the existence of **fraud,** lack of **notice** to the **parties** or newly discovered **evidence.**

EXAMPLE: Motions submitted before a judge, which in essence ask the judge to do something, must be supported by a showing of *good cause.* On a motion to exclude or suppress evidence for trial, good cause must be shown by example of illegal police conduct in the seizing of the evidence. For the motion to be granted, the judge must be convinced the conduct occurred and is enough to justify exclusion.

GOOD FAITH total absence of intention to seek unfair advantage or to defraud another party; an honest intention to fulfill one's obligations; observance of reasonable standards of fair dealing.

EXAMPLE: Dion purchases securities for 60 percent of their face value from an associate. The associate had obtained the securities fraudulently, and the real owner then sued Dion for their return. Dion is protected from the owner's claims if he acted in *good faith* and is thus a **bona fide purchaser.** The owner states that Dion could not have acted in good faith since he purchased them at such a low cost in comparison with their face value. But that fact alone does not preclude Dion's good faith defense, since the low price can be justified by the associate's dire need for quick cash.

In property law, a good faith purchaser of land pays value for the land and has no knowledge or notice of any facts that would cause an ordinary, prudent person to make inquiry concerning the validity of the conveyance.

GOODS any species of **property** that is not **real estate,** CHOSE IN ACTION (see **chose**), investment **securities** or the like.

GOOD SAMARITAN one who renders voluntary aid without compensation to a person who is injured or in danger. There is no requirement to intervene; however, if one chooses to be a Good Samaritan, one may face liability if **reasonable care** is not exercised and the rescued party is further injured. Various state statutes may provide limited levels of immunity from lawsuits for the rescuer.

GOOD TENANTABLE REPAIR as used in a lease, describes the obligation of a tenant to maintain the condition of property that has been rented.

GOOD TITLE a **clear title** free from present **litigation,** obvious defects and grave doubts concerning its validity or **mechantability;** a title valid in fact that is **marketable** to a reasonable purchaser or **mortgaged** as security for a loan of money to a person of reasonable prudence. In a **contract** to **convey** good title, the term also signifies that there are no **encumbrances** on the land. See also **recording acts; warranty.**

GOOD UNTIL CANCELLED see **order** [GOOD UNTIL CANCELLED].

GOOD WILL [GOODWILL] an intangible but recognized business asset that is the result of such features of an ongoing enterprise as the production or sale of reputable brand-name products, a good relationship with customers and suppliers, and the standing of the business in its community. Good will can become a **balance sheet** asset when a going business is acquired at a price exceeding the net asset value (**assets** less **liabilities).**

GOVERNMENT the exercise of authority in the administration of the affairs of a state, community, or society; an instrument to preserve an ordered society; the authoritative direction and restraint exercised over the actions of men and women.

In the United States, the federal and state governments operate under a written constitution from which their sovereignty and authority emanate.

GOVERNMENTAL FUNCTIONS activity done or furnished for general public good; legal duties imposed by a state upon its citizens that it may not omit with impunity, but must perform at its peril.

When a jurisdiction engages in a governmental function, such as operating a police department, conducting safety inspections, suing to enforce pubic policy as manifested by city ordinances, or generally is not acting in a proprietary manner, it is immune from tort liability for its actions unless a lawsuit is specifically permitted by statute. See **sovereign immunity.**

GOVERNMENTAL IMMUNITY the **common law** doctrine that the government, be it federal, state, or local, is not amenable to **suit** unless it consents to be sued. See **federal tort claims act; sovereign immunity.**

GOVERNMENT, MILITARY see **military law [MILITARY GOVERNMENT].**

GRACE PERIOD in general, any period specified in a **contract** during which payment is permitted, without penalty, beyond the due date of the debt. In the insurance context, it is a span of time after an insurance policy premium was due to be paid, during which the insurance nevertheless remains in force.

GRADED OFFENSE one where an offender is subject to different penalties for various degrees of the offense, according to terms of a statute. Modern criminal codes rely upon degrees of an offense to vary **sanctions** according to the level of harm to others caused or risked by the actor. See **degree of crime.**

GRAFT fraudulent obtaining of public money by the corruption of public officials; a dishonest advantage that one person by reason of his or her position, influence or trust acquires from another. See **bribery.**

GRANDFATHER CLAUSE a provision permitting persons engaged in an activity before passage of a law affecting that activity to receive a license or prerogative without the necessity of fulfilling all that is legally required of persons subsequently undertaking the same activity.

EXAMPLE: Felix has been selling hot dogs on the street for 15 years. The town council then decides to require licenses for all street vendors. Because the measure includes a *grandfather clause,* Felix can continue selling his food without a license.

GRAND JURY see **jury [GRAND JURY].**

GRAND LARCENY see **larceny [GRAND LARCENY].**

GRANT to give, allow or transfer something to another, with or without compensation; especially, a **gift** of land made by one having authority over it. The one giving the gift or making the transfer is the GRANTOR. The recipient is the GRANTEE. Compare **convey.** Also, generally, to yield or concede, as in to grant a request.

LAND GRANT a governmental grant to another level of government, a corporation, or an individual, without compensation. Many of the first colleges in the United States were established as land-grant colleges, with the land being donated to the schools by federal or state governments.

GRANTEE see **grant [GRANTEE].**

GRANTOR see **assignor; grant [GRANTOR].**

GRANTOR-GRANTEE INDEX see **chain of title.**

GRATIS free; given or performed without reward or **consideration.**

GRATUITOUS BAILMENT see **bailment [GRATUITOUS BAILMENT].**

GRATUITOUS PROMISE one by which a person promises to do, or refrain from doing, something without requiring **consideration** in return.

GRATUITY see **gift.**

GRAVAMEN the essence of a **complaint, charge, cause of action,** etc.

EXAMPLE: A complaint if filed against Bruno alleging that he seriously hurt someone in a barroom brawl and then fled the scene. The *gravamen* of the complaint is that Bruno seriously hurt someone.

GRAVITAS seriousness or weightiness in conduct or speech.

GREAT CARE see **care [GREAT CARE].**

GREAT CHARTER see **Magna Carta [Magna Charta].**

GREAT WRIT see **habeas corpus.**

GREEN AUDIT an evaluation of a business' operations with a focus on finding ways to operate more efficiently and with environmentally responsible methods, including renewable power sources, such as hydroelectric, wind, solar, and geothermal energy.

GREEN CARD a common name for the alien registration card carried by permanent resident aliens in the United States. Permanent resident status is a first step towards becoming a **naturalized citizen.**

GREEN GOODS money which is **counterfeit.**

GRIEVANCE one's allegation that something imposes an illegal burden, or denies some equitable or legal right, or causes injustice. An employee may be entitled by a **collective bargaining** agreement to seek relief through a GRIEVANCE PROCEDURE.

GROSS conduct that is willful and flagrant, out of all measure, beyond allowance, not to be excused, as in **gross negligence.**
   Consideration, profit, or income before charges and deduction as in **gross income.** Compare **net income.** See **easement [EASEMENT IN GROSS].**

GROSS ESTATE see **net estate [GROSS ESTATE].**

GROSS INCOME see **income [GROSS INCOME].**

GROSS NATIONAL PRODUCT [GNP] the total money measure of a nation's annual production of goods and services. GNP is defined both in terms of factor consumption (goods and services purchased by private citizens and government, gross private investment, and the net foreign trade-investment balance), and in terms of factor earnings (wages, taxes, rents, interest and profits, and **depreciation**). GNP is a gross production measure since no allowance is made for capital consumption; i.e., depreciation is part of GNP. Since economists consider GNP to be one of the most important concepts in economic science, the United States and other national governments expend considerable effort in collecting, analyzing, and publishing GNP statistics. Results are reported in both current dollars, including inflation, and constant dollars.

GROSS NEGLIGENCE see **negligence [GROSS NEGLIGENCE].**

GROUND RENT an **estate of inheritance** in the **rent** of lands, i.e., an inheritable **interest** in and right to the rent collected through the **leasing** of certain lands. It is a **freehold** estate, and as such is subject to **encumbrance** by **mortgage** or **judgment** (**lien, attachment,** etc.). The ground rent is an interest distinct from that held by the owner of the property, whose estate is in the land itself. The term most frequently signifies the long-term rent paid on land upon which office buildings, hotels, and other structures are built, where the owner of the land retains title.

GROWTH STOCK the **stock** of a company that has achieved above-average earnings growth in the past and has good prospects for continued increases in the future.

GTC see **order** [GTC].

GUARANTEE 1. to agree or promise to be responsible for the **debt, default** or miscarriage of another; 2. a promise or contract to answer for the debt, default or miscarriage of another; 3. one who receives a guaranty. Compare **save harmless.**

GUARANTEE CLAUSE Article IV, Section 4 of the United States Constitution, which states that "the United States shall **guarantee** to every state in this Union a republican form of government."

GUARANTEED SECURITY a **bond** or **stock** that is **guaranteed** as to principal or interest or both by someone other than the issuer.

GUARANTOR one who makes a **guaranty.**

GUARANTY 1. a promise to be responsible for the **debt, default** or miscarriage of another; 2. a **warranty** or promise to undertake an original obligation; 3. something given as security for the performance of an act or the continued quality of a thing. See **surety.**

GUARDIAN one who legally has care and management of the person or **estate,** or both, of an **incompetent;** an officer or agent of the court who is appointed to protect the interests of minors or incompetent persons and to provide for their welfare, education, and support. See also **committee; next friend; ward.**

   GUARDIAN AD LITEM a person appointed by the court to protect the interests of a ward in a legal proceeding. Compare **next friend.**

GUEST 1. a transient who rents a room at a hotel; 2. someone to whom hospitality is extended without charge.

   An AUTOMOBILE GUEST is one who rides in an automobile for his or her own benefit without giving the driver compensation for the ride; designated by the law as such for purposes of determining **liability** of the owner or driver of the automobile. See **guest statute.**

For purposes of **tort** law, a SOCIAL GUEST is considered a **licensee** with respect to his or her entry upon the host's premises, so that no duty of affirmative care or inspection of the premises for defects is owed to him or her.

EXAMPLE: After a late night of drinking, the host invited Stefan to spend the night at his house. As Stefan was getting into bed, the wooden frame cracked and injured Stefan's foot. Stefan has no cause of action against the host since Stefan was only a **guest** and not a paying customer.

GUEST STATUTE a law that provides that a lesser standard of care is owed by an automobile owner or driver toward his or her nonpaying passenger **[guest].** These statutes differ from state to state, but all require more than ordinary **negligence** on the part of an owner or driver for an automobile guest to recover **damages** in a **civil suit.**

GUILD see **National Lawyers Guild.**

GUILTY the condition of having been found by a **jury** to have committed the crime **charged,** or some **lesser-included offense.** The term may, though rarely does, refer to the commission of a **civil** wrong or **tort.** Compare **conviction.**

GUN CONTROL LAW a law restricting or regulating the sale, purchase or possession of firearms, or establishing a system of licensing, registration or identification of firearms or their owners or users.

H

HABEAS CORPUS *(hā'-bē-ŭs kôr'-pŭs)* Lat.: you have the body. The **writ** of habeas corpus, known as the **GREAT WRIT,** has varied use in criminal and civil contexts. It is a procedure for obtaining a judicial determination of the legality of an individual's custody. Technically, it is used in the criminal law context to bring the petitioner before the court to inquire into the legality of his confinement. The writ of federal habeas corpus is used to test the constitutionality of a state criminal conviction.

EXAMPLE: Luke believes that his conviction in the trial court was obtained unconstitutionally in that he was not provided counsel until three days before his trial. He raised the issue on appeal in the state court system but was denied a new trial. Having exhausted all state remedies, Luke files a writ of *habeas corpus* in the federal district court, alleging that his conviction and present confinement violate his Sixth Amendment right to counsel.

The writ is used in the civil context to challenge the validity of child **custody** and deportations.

HABENDUM that clause of the **deed** that names the **grantee** and defines the **estate** to be granted. It begins with the words "to have and to hold. . . ."

HABITABILITY the condition of residental or other premises being reasonably fit for occupation, and that does not impair the health, safety, or well-being of the occupants. If this condition is not met, due to a failure to provide heat, for example, the occupant may be eligible for a rent **abatement** or may under some circumstances vacate the premises. See **eviction [CONSTRUCTIVE EVICTION]; warranty [WARRANTY OF HABITABILITY].**

HABITUAL OFFENDER see **criminal [HABITUAL OFFENDER]; sentence [EXTENDED TERM]; three strikes [SENTENCE ENHANCEMENT].**

HACK accessing a computer program or network without authorization, often for the purposes of altering the program by way of a **virus.** Some programmers [hackers] seek to find weak points in a security system simply to prove that it can be breached.

HAEC VERBA see **in haec verba.**

HAGUE CONVENTIONS see **neutrality laws.**

HAIRCUT the difference between the market value of a **security** (used as collateral for a loan) and the amount the lender will provide for it.

HALFWAY HOUSE a residence established to assist persons who have left highly structured institutions to adjust to and reenter society and live within its accepted norms. Mental patients and prisoners may be released to facilities of this kind located within the community and usually with no security other than supervised regimen of sign-in, sign-out, and curfew rules. Release to halfway houses is sometimes a first step in a **parole** program. Modern statutes permit courts to sentence defendants directly to such facilities, known as **RESIDENTIAL COMMUNITY TREATMENT CENTERS** as a condition of **probation.**

A **work-release program** may utilize a halfway house instead of a more secure institution for nighttime confinement and weekend supervision. The halfway house provides a supervised and restricted environment in which to ascertain the convict's ability to form a productive life in society while simultaneously fulfilling the functions of a penal institution in its concern for security and rehabilitation.

Although states are not required to utilize such modern correctional concepts as halfway houses, if they choose to do so, the procedures for assigning inmates to such facilities must meet standards of procedural due process and equal protection of the laws.

HALLUCINATION a state of mind whereby a person senses something that in reality does not exist; a perception of an object having no reality. Any of the senses may be involved, although sight or hearing are most commonly affected. The state of hallucination most often results from mental illness or from ingesting drugs designed to create these perceptions. See **controlled substance [HALLUCINOGENS].**

HALLUCINOGENS see **controlled substances [HALLUCINOGENS].**

HANGED, DRAWN, AND QUARTERED a common law punishment for convictions of high treason or other atrocious crimes where the defendant was drawn to the place of execution, disemboweled alive, and then beheaded and quartered. See **cruel and unusual punishment.**

HARASSMENT 1. a **prosecution** brought without reasonable expectation of obtaining a valid conviction; 2. unnecessarily oppressive exercise of authority; 3. conduct motivated by a malicious or discriminatory purpose.

SEXUAL HARASSMENT refers to any policy or practice pursuant to which employees are subject to physical or verbal harassment by their superiors or are denied employment or promotion on the basis of their gender.

HARD CASES cases that produce decisions deviating from the true principles of law in order to meet the exigencies presented by the extreme hardship of one **party.**

It is sometimes said that "hard cases make bad law" because logic is often shortcut in a hard case, and later attempts to justify the new law thus created often compound the original inadequacy of reasoning.

HARD COPY physical document; a printout of a stored document (such as microfilm or computer data). Compare **soft copy** (an electronic file).

HARDSHIP, UNNECESSARY see **unnecessary hardship.**

HARM see **injury; irreparable injury [damage; harm].**

HARMLESS ERROR error that is not sufficiently prejudicial to the losing party in a lawsuit to warrant the **appellate court's** modifying the lower court's decision. A conclusion that an error is harmless reflects the reviewing court's determination that the lower court's decision would have been the same with or without the purported error. Compare **plain error.**

EXAMPLE: The confessions of two codefendants are improperly introduced at Vic's trial. An appellate court may find that the violation was merely *harmless error* and does not require a new trial for Vic if the confessions had little or no effect upon the jury's determination of Vic's guilt.

HATE CRIME see **bias crime.**

HEADNOTE summary, placed at the beginning of a case report, of points discussed and issues decided in a case.

HEAD OF HOUSEHOLD an unmarried **taxpayer** who maintains as his or her home a household that is the principal residence of a designated **dependent.** A qualified head of household is subject to a lower **tax rate** than that applied to a person not a head of household.

HEALTHCARE REFORM see **affordable care act.**

HEALTH INSURANCE PORTABILITY AND ACCOUNTABILITY ACT [HIPAA] see **affordable care act [HEALTH INSURANCE PORTABILITY AND ACCOUNTABILITY ACT [HIPAA]].**

HEARING a **proceeding** where **evidence** is taken to determine an issue of fact and to reach a decision on the basis of that evidence; describes whatever takes place before **magistrates** sitting without **jury.** Thus a hearing, such as an **ADMINISTRATIVE HEARING,** may take place outside the judicial process, before officials who have been granted judicial authority expressly for the purpose of conducting such hearings.

    FINAL HEARING is sometimes used to describe that stage of proceedings relating to the determination of a **suit** upon its **merits,** as distinguished from those of preliminary questions. See also **fair hearing.**

HEARING DE NOVO see **de novo** [DE NOVO HEARING].

HEARSAY RULE a rule that declares not **admissible** as **evidence** any statement other than that by a **witness** while testifying at the **hearing** and offered into evidence to prove the truth of the matter stated. The hearsay statement may be oral or written and includes nonverbal conduct intended as a substitute for words (such as a nodding of the head). If, for example, a witness' statement as to what he or she heard another person say is elicited to prove the truth of what that other person said, it is hearsay. If, however, it is elicited to merely show that the words were spoken, it is not hearsay. The witness' answer will be admissible only to show that the other person spoke certain words and not to show the truth of what the other person said. The reason for the hearsay rule is that the credibility of the witness is the key ingredient in weighing the truth of his or her statement; so when that statement is made out of court, without benefit of cross-examination and without the witness' demeanor being subject to assessment by the trier of fact (judge or jury), there is generally no adequate basis for determining whether the out-of-court statement is true.

    EXAMPLE: Defendant Doug is on trial for robbing Victim Vinnie. Witness Walt wants to testify that Bartender Bart told Walt that Doug had admitted to Bart the commission of the robbery. Walt's testimony would be hearsay if it were offered to prove the truth of the matter (Doug confessed) since Doug did not tell Walt. (Note, however, that if Bart himself were to testify it would not be hearsay since he heard the confession and may be cross-examined about the circumstances). If Walt's testimony were offered for a purpose other than the truth of the confession (such as to establish that Bart was an extremely close friend of Doug and that Doug confided in Bart his closest secrets), some courts would allow the testimony.

    Hearsay is prohibited due to the constitutional guarantee of confrontation (see **confrontation clause**); however, there are many exceptions to the hearsay rule of exclusion based on a combination of trustworthiness and necessity. Thus, official written statements, such as payroll records, where the declarant's statements are based on firsthand knowledge and where the officer is under an official duty to make the report (and hence has no motive to falsify) are admissible under the **BUSINESS RECORDS EXCEPTION.** Another common exception is made for **DYING DECLARATIONS.** Under this rule a statement made by a person with knowledge or hopeless expectation of his or her impending death is admissible through another who overheard that statement where the declarant is unavailable because he or she died. Originally it was strongly believed that a dying person would tell the truth; thus the witness' testimony as to what the dying declarant said became admissible both on the grounds of trustworthiness and necessity. Today, with more skepticism about the effect of religiosity of truth-telling, necessity remains as a major factor in determining admissibility. The question of the witness' credibility is subject to demeanor examination and cross-examination for bias, memory, etc. Some jurisdictions permit any admission by a party to be offered by his or her adversary in a civil proceeding through any competent witness as another broad exception to the hearsay rule. See and compare **admission by a party-opponent; declaration against interest; evidence.**

STATE OF MIND EXCEPTION admits an out-of-court declaration of an existing **motive**, even if the declarant is unable to testify.

HEART-BALM STATUTE legislation that abolishes causes of action for **alienation of affections, breach** of promise to marry, **criminal conversation,** or **seduction.**

HEAT OF PASSION see **manslaughter [HEAT OF PASSION].**

HEDGE FUND an investment partnership or **mutual fund** that uses **selling short** to **hedge** long positions in **stocks.** If stock selection is correct, the stocks sold short decline more in a falling market than the stock owned, and the stocks owned appreciate more in a rising market than the stocks sold short. The goal is to generate trading and investment profits no matter what the direction of the general market. Hedge funds may borrow money to increase their **leverage.**

HEDGING 1. taking measures to counterbalance possible loss. 2. a securities transaction that reduces or limits the risk in investments by taking positions that tend to offset each other. For example, a business can offset the risk of an asset declining by agreeing to sell a specified amount of the asset at a set price at some predetermined point in the future. A potato chip manufacturer can hedge or protect his or her profit margin on a large order of chips to be delivered in the future by buying potatoes in the **futures** market; a potato farmer may sell the futures contract to the process to protect some or all of the investment in raising his or her crop. A speculator in potato contracts might hedge a long position in old crop futures by selling new crop futures in anticipation of a bumper crop and, therefore, lower prices. **Arbitrage** is a type of hedge involving the buying of securities in one market and selling in another market when the price difference between markets offers a profitable trade. Hedged trades are used in the stock **option** market where the various positions are referred to as spreads, straddles, etc. In securities trading and investment, **selling short** is used to hedge stock ownership positions against a decline in the general market. See **hedge fund.**

HEIR APPARENT one who has the rights to **inheritance** provided that he or she lives longer than the donor ancestor. An **antilapse statute** may operate to save a **gift** to the estate of an heir apparent who predeceases the **testator.**

HEIRS strictly, those whom statutory law would appoint to inherit an **estate** should the ancestor die without a **will [intestate];** sometimes referred to as HEIRS AT LAW, RIGHTFUL HEIRS, LEGAL HEIRS. The term is often applied indiscriminately to those who inherit by will or **deed,** as well as by **operation of law.**

AND HIS HEIRS in **common law,** these words had to be included in order to convey a **fee simple absolute.** The formal requirement has been abolished or modified by statute in most of the states, and now one may **convey** or **devise** an absolute interest in **real property** without using these technical words.

COLLATERAL HEIR an heir who is not of the direct line of the deceased, but comes from a collateral line, as a brother, sister, an aunt or uncle, nephew, niece, or a cousin of the deceased.

HEIRS AND ASSIGNS words describing that a **fee simple** estate is being conveyed; words of limitation, not of substitution, or of purchase. When used in a will, the words are descriptive and do not set up an independent class of **legatees.**

LINEAL HEIR one who inherits in a line either ascending or descending from a common source as distinguished from a collateral heir.

HEIRS OF THE BODY issue of the body, offspring engendered by the person named as parent. These words are used in instruments of conveyance, such as **deeds** and **wills,** to create a **conditional fee** or a **fee tail.**

HELOC see **home equity line of credit [HELOC].**

HEREDITAMENTS anything that can be inherited, including **real property** or **personal property. CORPOREAL HEREDITAMENTS** generally are tangible property. **INCORPOREAL HEREDITAMENTS** are less tangible rights connected to land, such as an **easement** or right to **rent.**

HEREDITARY SUCCESSION the passing of **title** according to the laws of descent, acquisition of title to an **estate** by a person by **operation of law** upon the death of an ancestor who has not left a valid **will** affecting the property inherited. See **descent and distribution.**

HIDDEN ASSET a property value that is understated on the **balance sheet** of a company because of accounting convention and/or deliberate action of management.

EXAMPLE: Cubbie Corporation is fearful of being taken over by a large international company and thereby losing its independence. To prevent the takeover, it undervalues the worth of its real estate holdings to make Cubbie look as though the corporation were not worth buying. The real estate holdings constitute *hidden assets.*

HIDDEN DEFECT defect not recognizable upon a reasonable inspection of a good or product, or that is not readily apparent, for which a seller is generally liable and that would give rise to a right to revoke a prior **acceptance.** See **latent defect.** Compare **patent defect.** See **as is.**

HIDDEN INFLATION a price increase implemented by offering a smaller quantity or poorer quality for the old price.

HIDDEN TAX an indirect tax paid unwittingly by the consumer, such as taxes levied on goods at some point in their production or transport prior to retail sale.

HIJACKING the commandeering or seizure of a mode of transportation such as an airplane, truck, or train by force or threat of force for illegal purposes. Such purposes may include theft of the cargo or other contents; redirection of the destination to suit the hijacker's specific purposes; or kidnapping or hostage taking for monetary or political demands. Also known as **piracy,** such acts are governed by international agreements regarding **jurisdiction** over hijackers and **extradition.**

CARJACKING similar in that a motor vehicle such as a car or van is taken from the occupant by force. The driver or other passengers may be forced to remain in the vehicle while it is driven or may be forced out of the vehicle. Carjacking is distinguished from car **theft** by the presence of occupants.

HIPAA see **affordable care act** [HEALTH INSURANCE PORTABILITY AND ACCOUNTABILITY ACT [HIPAA]].

HIT-AND-RUN STATUTES statutes requiring that a motorist involved in an accident stop and identify himself or herself and give certain information about himself or herself to the other motorist and to the police. These laws have been upheld as not violative of the privilege against **self-incrimination** on the ground that they call for neutral acts, not intended to be probative of guilt, and pose only an insignificant hazard of self-incrimination.

HLA DQ ALPHA see **DNA testing** [HLA DQ ALPHA].

HOARDING excess accumulation of commodities or currency in anticipation of scarcity and/or higher prices.

HOBBY LOSS a loss incurred by a **taxpayer** in an activity not pursued for profit. In general, hobby losses are deductible only to the extent of income generated by the hobby.

HOLDER a person in possession of a document of **title** or an **instrument** or an investment **security drawn,** issued or **indorsed** to the holder or to his or her **order** or to **bearer** or in blank.

HOLDER IN DUE COURSE a **good faith holder** who has taken a **negotiable instrument** for value, without **notice** that it was overdue or had been **dishonored** or that there was any **defense** against or **claim** to it. In property law, the innocent buyer or holder in due course is referred to as a **bona fide purchaser.**

EXAMPLE: People's Finance Company regularly buys promissory notes from stores that require the customers to sign these notes in return for merchandise. People's is a *holder in due course* of these notes since it has given value for them. That status protects People's from almost all claims against the notes.

HOLD HARMLESS the assumption by one party to an agreement to relieve the other party of any liability that might attend the situation governed by the agreement. See **save harmless.**

HOLDING 1. in commercial and property law, **property** to which one has legal **title** and of which one is in **possession.** The term may be used to refer specifically to ownership of **stocks** or **shares** of **corporations.** 2. in **procedure,** any ruling of the court, including rulings upon the **admissibility** of **evidence** or other questions presented during trial. Compare **dictum.**

HOLDING CELL see **jail** [HOLDING CELL].

HOLDING COMPANY 1. a **corporation** organized to hold the **stock** of other corporations; 2. any company, incorporated or unincorporated, that is in a position to control or materially influence the management of one or more other companies by virtue, in part at least, of its ownership of **securities** in the other company or companies.

HOLDING PERIOD the period during which property must be held before its disposition will give rise to long-term **capital gain or loss.**

HOLDOVER TENANCY see **tenancy** [TENANCY AT SUFFERANCE].

HOLDUP SUIT a lawsuit that has no legal basis and is instituted solely to prevent or block something from occurring. A party harmed by such a suit may have an action for **malicious prosecution.** See also **strike suit.**

HOLOGRAPHIC WILL a **will** entirely written, dated, and signed by the **testator's** own hand. The word is sometimes written **OLOGRAPHIC.** In some states, such a will need not be witnessed and is valid, under a statute of **descent and distribution,** to pass **property.** In other states, such a will is invalid.

HOMAGE during the **feudal** period, the ceremony wherein the vassal knelt before the lord, acknowledged himself to be his man, and swore **fealty** [an oath of loyalty to the lord]. It was frequently accompanied by a grant of land from the lord to the vassal, the land to be held of the lord by the vassal as **tenant.** As a consequence, any attempt by the vassal [or **tenant**] to convey more than the estate that had been granted him (e.g., an attempt by the vassal to convey a **fee simple** when his grant from the lord consisted only of a **life estate**), was not only **tortious** conduct with regard to the lord, but was also treasonous. See **fealty.**

HOME EQUITY CONVERSION MORTGAGE see **mortgage** [REVERSE MORTGAGE].

HOME EQUITY LINE OF CREDIT [HELOC] line of **credit** secured by the **equity** in the home above the debt outstanding in the mortgage. See **credit** [LINE OF CREDIT]; **loan.** Compare **mortgage.**

HOMELAND SECURITY see **Department of Homeland Security** [DHS].

HOME PORT DOCTRINE in maritime law, refers to the rule that a vessel that is an instrumentality of foreign commerce and engaged therein is subject to property tax only at its "home port" regardless of where it happens to be actually located on tax assessment day. Refers either to the place of a vessel's place of registration or the domicile of the owners. Vessels engaged in interstate commerce may be taxed by jurisdictions other than its home port, but only on an apportioned basis.

The doctrine does not bar the placing of **liens** on vessels in ports other than the vessel's home port for supplies or repairs to the vessel.

HOME RULE a means of apportioning power between state and local governments by granting power to the electorate of a local government unit to frame and adopt a charter of government. The effect of this grant is to enable local government to legislate without first obtaining permission from state legislatures.

EXAMPLE: Since the city was first chartered, it has been run by a mayor with virtually no check on his exercise of power. Exercising their rights under *home rule,* the residents vote to install a city council, which must approve any actions taken by the mayor.

See **preemption.**

HOMESTEAD any house, outbuildings, and surrounding land owned and used as a dwelling by the head of the family. Under modern **HOMESTEAD EXEMPTION LAWS,** enacted in most states, any property designated as a homestead is exempt from **execution** and **sale** by **creditors.** This homestead exemption applies in some states to property taxes as well.

The exemption from claims of creditors may be extended by a **probate** court upon the death of the head of the family to ensure the surviving spouse and minor children uninterrupted **possession** and **enjoyment** of the family home. A home so protected is referred to as a **PROBATE HOMESTEAD.** See **life estate.**

HOMICIDE any killing of a human being by the act, agency, procurement or **culpable** omission of another. An unlawful homicide, or one resulting from an unlawful act, may constitute **murder** or **manslaughter.**

JUSTIFIABLE HOMICIDE the killing of a human being by commandment of the law, in the execution of public justice, in **self-defense,** in defense of habitation, property or person.

HONEST SERVICES anti-corruption statutes based on the concept that it is a crime (fraud) for officials to deprive the public of their intangible rights to honest and impartial government. Prosecutors have convicted politicians and executives based upon nondisclosure of material information even without proof that they received a kickback or bribe, but such statutes have been attacked on vagueness grounds for failing to define a crime.

HONORABLE DISCHARGE a formal final judgment passed by the government upon the entire military record of the soldier. It is an authoritative declaration that he or she has left the service in a status of honor. A person's classification after retirement from the armed services directly affects his or her ability to take advantage of benefits provided to members of the services.

HONORARY generally refers to a position held without profit, fee, or reward, and in consideration of the honor conferred by holding a position of responsibility and trust. A position recognizing honor or commitment. An **HONORARY DEGREE** is one conferred without formal qualification in recognition by an educational institution of an individual's nonacademic accomplishments.

HORIZONTAL MERGER see **merger** [**HORIZONTAL MERGER**].

HORIZONTAL PRIVITY see **privity** [**HORIZONTAL PRIVITY**].

HORNBOOK a book intended to aid one with the fundamentals of the subject being studied; a primer for the student studying in an area of knowledge.

HORNBOOK LAW those principles of law known generally to all in the legal profession and free from doubt and ambiguity. They are therefore such as would probably be enunciated in a **hornbook** (a primer of fundamentals).

HORS *(ôr)* Fr.: outside of, besides, other than. Sometimes DEHORS *(dĕ-ôr')*.

HOSTILE POSSESSION actual occupation or **possession** of real estate, coupled with a claim, express or implied, of ownership, without permission of the holder of **paramount title.** Hostile possession differs from **holding** in subordination to the true owner, as in possession under a **lease.** Hostile does not imply ill will but merely that the occupant claims ownership against all others, including the owner of **record.** The term is usually used as a condition for **adverse possession.** See also **notorious possession.**

EXAMPLE: For 20 years, Ken has lived in a cabin he built in a wooded section of the state. He has cleared an area adjacent to the house where he grows whatever he uses to live, plus some extras to share with neighbors. Ken is not the owner of the land he lives on, but, because no one has come by in 20 years to assert ownership of the land or even to ask him to get off, he claims it as his and is therefore in hostile possession of it.

HOSTILE WITNESS see **witness [ADVERSE [HOSTILE] WITNESS].**

HOSTILE WORKPLACE workplace harassment that is severe or pervasive enough to create a work environment that a reasonable person would consider intimidating, hostile, or abusive. It can involve unwelcome conduct that is based on race, color, religion, sex (including pregnancy), sexual orientation, national origin, age, or disability. Offensive conduct may include offensive jokes, slurs, name calling, physical assaults or threats, intimidation, ridicule or mockery, insults or put-downs, offensive objects or pictures, and interference with work performance. Any person affected by the harassment, not just the person at whom the harassment was directed, may be entitled to relief under state law or federal anti-discrimination laws. See **discrimination; harassment [SEXUAL HARASSMENT].**

HOT BLOOD an emotional state of mind such as rage, anger, resentment, terror, or fear so as to demonstrate an absence of deliberate design to kill, or to cause one to act on impulse without conscious reflection. See **manslaughter [HEAT OF PASSION].**

HOT PURSUIT see **fresh pursuit.**

HOUSE all-inclusive and may include any and every kind of structure, depending upon the context in which it is used and the purpose sought to be effected. Whether a structure is defined as a "house" or "home" may have constitutional implications. For **Fourth Amendment** purposes, "houses" include **curtilage.** See **domicile; dwelling house; residence.** See also **halfway house; prostitution [HOUSE OF PROSTITUTION].**

HOUSE ARREST confinement to one's home as a condition of bail or even as one's sentence. May include the use of electronic devices to monitor compliance. Exceptions may be granted by the judge to allow the person to have a specified curfew, work, or attend religious services or medical appointments.

HUMANE DISPOSAL see **euthanasia.**

HUMAN RIGHTS rights inherent to all human beings on an equal and nondiscriminatory basis. They include but are not limited to the right to life and liberty, freedom of expression, and equality before the law; and economic, social, and cultural rights, including the right to participate in culture, the right to be treated with respect and dignity, and the right to food, work, and education, among other things. All of these rights are without distinction as to race, color, sex, language, religion, political, or other opinion, national or social origin, property, birth, or other status. "Recognition of the inherent dignity and of the equal and inalienable rights of all members of the human family is the foundation of freedom, justice, and peace in the world." United Nations Universal Declaration of Human Rights (1948).

HUMAN RIGHTS VIOLATIONS criminal law violations relating to genocide, torture, war crimes, the use or recruitment of child soldiers as well as sexual abuse, political, racial, or religious persecution, and other inhumane acts which are part of a widespread or systematic practice of atrocities. Victims are persons who individually or collectively suffered harm, including physical or mental injury, emotional suffering, economic loss, or substantial impairment of their fundamental rights, through acts or omissions that constitute violations of human rights laws, or violations of international humanitarian laws.

HUMAN TRAFFICKING see **trafficking [HUMAN TRAFFICKING].**

HUNG JURY one whose members [jurors] cannot reconcile their differences of opinion and that therefore cannot reach a **verdict** by the degree of agreement required (generally unanimity, but sometimes a substantial majority).

HUSBAND-WIFE PRIVILEGE see **marital communications privilege [husband-wife privilege];** compare **spousal disqualification.**

HYPERLINK a word, phrase, or image that links to a new document, or a new section within the current document, when the user clicks on it with a computer cursor. The link interacts with a browser and allows automatic transitioning to the linked page. Hyperlinks are most ofen found in Internet pages but also exist in reference materials and they may be considered a violation of copyright laws if they facilitate illegal copying. In securities law, when an issuer includes a hyperlink in its prospectus, the hyperlinked information becomes part of the prospectus.

HYPNOSIS a state of heightened concentration with diminished awareness of peripheral events, increasing the suggestibility of the subject while hypnotized. In those jurisdictions permitting the use of hypnotically refreshed testimony, the results of hypnosis, as with the results of any scientific test, are admissible only when they have sufficient scientific basis to produce uniform and reasonably reliable results and will contribute materially to the ascertainment of the truth.

HYPOTHECATE to pledge something as security without turning over possession of it. Hypothecation creates a right in the **creditor** to have the pledge sold to satisfy the claim out of the sale proceeds.

EXAMPLE: Nathaniel needs a large amount of cash to put together a business deal. To acquire money from the bank, he *hypothecates* (pledges) his diamond ring as security. The bank allows Nathaniel to retain the ring because he is a good customer and they are not afraid he will disappear with the money and the ring. The loan agreement between Nathaniel and the bank is a hypothecation contract.

A **mortgage** on real property is a form of hypothecation **contract. Intangibles** and **securities** are most often the subject of hypothecation contracts. In the case of buying stock on **margin** the owner signs a hypothecation agreement with the broker who handles the transaction; the broker is then free to pledge the customer's securities as **collateral** for a bank loan or to lend the customer's securities in connection with **selling short.** Compare **replevin.**

HYPOTHETICAL QUESTION a question that assumes facts that the evidence tends to show and calls for an opinion based on the hypothesis. In trials, hypothetical questions can only be posed to an **expert witness** who is qualified to give an opinion on the matter in issue.

I

IB. [IBID.] *(ĭb'-ĭd)* Lat.: in the same place or manner, at the same time; abbreviation of ibidem. Used to mean "in the same book" or "on the same page"; functions in citations to avoid repetition of source data in the reference immediately preceding.

ICC see **Interstate Commerce Commission.**

ICE see **Immigration and Customs Enforcement [ICE].**

ID. *(ĭd)* Lat.: the same; abbreviation of idem. Used in citations to avoid repetition of author's name and title when a reference immediately follows another to the same item.

IDB [INDUSTRIAL DEVELOPMENT BOND] see **guaranteed security.**

IDENTITY THEFT [FRAUD] illegal use of another's personal data (name, driver's license, social security number, medical information, credit cards, or bank accounts) for one's own gain. See also **spam [PHISHING].**

I.E. abbeviation for id est; that is.

IGNORANCE lack of knowledge. Ignorance of the law does not justify an act, since every person is presumed to know the law. However, **mistake** of fact may provide a legal excuse. See **ignorantia legis non excusat.**

IGNORANTIA LEGIS NON EXCUSAT *(ĭg-nō-rän'-shē-à lā'-gĭs nŏn ĕks-kū'-zät)* Lat.: ignorance of the law is no excuse. The fact that a defendant did not think his or her act was against the law does not prevent the law from punishing him or her for the prohibited act.

ILLEGAL against the law. Behavior that can result in either criminal sanctions, such as prison sentences or fines, or civil sanctions, such as liability or injunctions, is illegal.

ILLEGAL ALIEN see **alien; immigration and customs enforcement.** Compare **citizen; legal permanent resident [LPR].**

ILLEGALLY OBTAINED EVIDENCE evidence obtained by the police through circumstances in which the police or a police agent violated a person's right against unreasonable search and seizure as guaranteed by the **Fourth Amendment** or analogous state constitutional provisions. See **exclusionary rule; fruit of the poisonous tree; search and seizure.**

ILLEGITIMATE illegal or improper. Applied to children, it means born out of wedlock, **bastards.**

ILLINOIS LAND TRUST see **land trust [ILLINOIS LAND TRUST].**

ILLUSORY PROMISE a promise too indefinite to be enforced or, because of provisions in the promise itself, one whose fulfillment is optional. Since such a promise is not legally binding, it is not sufficient as **consideration** for a reciprocal promise and thus cannot create a valid **contract.**

EXAMPLE: Tiquan promises his neighbor that, if he remembers, he will water the neighbor's plants twice a week while the neighbor is on vacation. When the neighbor returns, all the plants, including three prize ferns, are dead from lack of water. The neighbor cannot sue Tiquan for the value of the ferns because, legally, Tiquan gave the neighbor only an *illusory promise* that is not enforceable nor is its failure actionable in court.

IMMATERIAL not material; **irrelevant,** nothing to do with the case; not significant.

EXAMPLE: At Zack's trial for robbery, the prosecution wants to introduce evidence that Zack and his wife argue frequently. That evidence is considered *immaterial* and is not allowed at the trial.

IMMEDIATE CAUSE see **cause.**

IMMIGRATION the movement of persons into a foreign country for the purpose of permanently residing in that country. See **alien; citizen; legal permanent resident [LPR]; naturalized citizen.**

IMMIGRATION AND CUSTOMS ENFORCEMENT [ICE] the largest investigative arm of the **Department of Homeland Security,** responsible for identifying and shutting down vulnerabilities in the nation's border, economic, transportation, and infrastructure security. It has four main offices: Detention and Removal (to identify and apprehend illegal aliens, fugitive aliens, and criminal aliens; to manage them while in custody; and to enforce orders of removal from the United States), Investigations, Intelligence, and International Affairs. ICE works closely with a broad range of law enforcement authorities. See *www.ice.gov.* See also **alien; citizen; Citizenship and Immigration Services [USCIS]; deportability; green card; legal permanent resident [LPR]; naturalized citizen.**

IMMIGRATION AND NATURALIZATION SERVICE [INS] former name of an agency whose functions are currently divided into three agencies within the **Department of Homeland Security.** Immigration services (processing citizenship, residency, and asylum requests) fall under the United States **Citizenship and Immigration Services [USCIS].** Investigation services (such as deportability) fall under the United States **Immigration and Customs Enforcement [ICE].** Border and customs services fall under the United States **Customs and Border Protection [CBP].**

IMMORAL CONDUCT behavior opposed to accepted community standards of what is right.

IMMUNITIES, PRIVILEGES AND see **privileges and immunities.**

IMMUNITY right of exemption from a duty or penalty; benefit granted in exception to the general rule. Immunity from prosecution may be granted a **witness** to compel answers he or she might otherwise withhold because of the constitutional privilege to avoid **self-incrimination.**

EXAMPLE: Ben asserts his privilege against self-incrimination when the grand jury asks probing questions about his activities. If the grand jury gives Ben *immunity* from criminal prosecution for anything to which he testifies before the grand jury, Ben can no longer use the privilege. The privilege is only available when Ben is subject to prosecution for what he says, a fear that the immunity eliminates.

OFFICIAL IMMUNITY the immunity of a public official from liability to anyone injured by actions in the exercise of official authority or duty.

See **self-incrimination, privilege against [TRANSACTIONAL** and **USE IMMUNITIES]; sovereign immunity.**

IMO abbreviation for "in the matter of."

IMPACT RULE the requirement of physical contact with an individual person in order for damages for emotional distress to be imposed.

IMPAIRMENT OF COLLATERAL see **collateral [IMPAIRMENT OF COLLATERAL]**

IMPAIR THE OBLIGATION OF A CONTRACT see **obligation of a contract.**

IMPANEL see **panel [IMPANEL].**

IMPANELING 1. selection and swearing in of jurors; 2. listing of those selected for a particular jury.

IMPEACH 1. to charge a public official with wrongdoing while in office; 2. to question the truthfulness of the **testimony** of the **witness** by means of **evidence** that the witness is unworthy of belief.

IMPERTINENT MATTER an inappropriate matter; facts that are irrelevant to the controversy. Under the Federal Rules of Civil Procedure, impertinent matter consists of any allegation that is not responsive nor relevant to issues involved in the action and that could not be put in issue or be given in evidence between the parties.

IMPLEADER the procedure by which a third party is brought into a suit between a **plaintiff** and **defendant,** where that third party may be liable, so as to settle all **claims** in a single **action.** It is a **procedural** device available to any defendant where a third party is or may be liable to him or her for any damages that the defendant owes the plaintiff. The defendant is considered a "third-party plaintiff," vis-à-vis the third party thus joined. The device is also available to a plaintiff against whom a **counterclaim** has been made. Compare **interpleader; joinder.** See also **cross-claim.**

IMPLICATION intention, meaning; though not expressly stated, a deduced state of mind or facts.

NECESSARY IMPLICATION a conclusion resulting from so strong a probability of intention that an opposite intention is incredible.

IMPLIED not explicitly written or stated; determined by deduction from known facts.

IMPLIED AUTHORITY see **authority** [IMPLIED AUTHORITY].

IMPLIED CONSENT consent that is found to exist solely because certain actions or signs would lead a **reasonable person** to believe that consent is present, whether or not that consent is even specifically expressed; in criminal law, generally used as a defense against rape, whereby the defendant claims that he acted under a reasonable and honest belief based on the fact that the woman consented to his advance.

IMPLIED CONTRACT see **contract** [QUASI [IMPLIED] CONTRACT].

IMPLIED EASEMENT see **easement** [IMPLIED EASEMENT].

IMPLIED NOTICE see **notice** [IMPLIED NOTICE].

IMPLIED POWERS those powers not expressly stated but deemed necessary to carry out the stated objectives. Decisions by the **United States Supreme Court** may imply powers in the **Constitution** that are not specifically enumerated. See **Fourteenth**

Amendment; **inherent powers; necessary and proper clause.**
Compare **enumerated powers.**

IMPLIED WARRANTY see **warranty** [IMPLIED WARRANTIES].

IMPORT the transportation of goods into one country and out of
another; also, the article imported. The term under the **customs**
laws requires that the goods be brought voluntarily into this country,
into the proper port of entry, and with an **intent** to unload them.
If customs official determine that an article has been imported into
the United States, it is assessed a **duty** under customs laws unless
clear **evidence** is proved to the contrary. To be imported within the
scope of the tariff laws, the goods must be from a country subject
to our tariff laws and the goods must pass through the custody and
control of the customs officials and into the custody and control of
the importer. See **export.**

IMPORTATION the act of transporting goods into a country from a
foreign country. As used in tariff statutes the term means merchandise
to which the status of an **import** has attached. Compare **exportation.**

IMPOSSIBILITY 1. a **defense** of nonperformance of a **contract**
when **performance** is impossible because of destruction of the
subject matter of the contract (as, for example, by fire) or death of
a person necessary for performance. Performance is then excused
and the contract duty terminated. See also **frustration of purpose.**

EXAMPLE: Grace contracts to purchase a boat at a nearby marina.
Before the boat is ready for use, a storm destroys the marina and
all the boats with it. Grace has an *impossibility* defense against performing the contract because the boat no longer exists.

2. in **civil law,** an excuse for nonperformance of a contract
where the promised performance has become illegal. 3. in **criminal** law, applies to situations in which facts or circumstances render
commission of the crime impossible. Thus, it is impossible to **murder** another if he is already dead.

EXAMPLE: A mugger brings his victim into an alley, robs him and
in a fit of rage shoots him dead. Several hours later, a major drug
deal is transacted in the same alley. One of the dealers sees the person lying there, believes the person is just drunk and shoots him
because he wants no witnesses to the deal. The dealer has an *impossibility* defense to a murder charge because it is impossible to kill a
person who is already dead. The dealer may, however, be subjected
to prosecution for attempted murder.

IMPOST 1. a tax; 2. a charge or levy in the nature of a tax.

IMPOUND to place merchandise, funds or records in the **custody** of an officer of the law.

IMPOUNDING [IMPOUNDMENT] in **common law,** the second step in a **distress** action, in which the distrainer, having seized the **chattels,** must bring the goods to a public pound pending the outcome of the **action.**

IMPRESSION, CASE [MATTER] OF FIRST see **first impression, case of.**

IMPRIMATUR the license granted by the government permitting the publication of a particular book.

IMPRISONMENT the confinement of an individual to a particular place usually as punishment for a crime; any deprivation of liberty or detention of a person contrary to his or her will. The status of imprisonment may affect certain constitutional rights, for example, a right of bail guaranteed to imprisoned persons may not include juveniles held pending delinquency proceedings. Synonymous with **incarceration.** See **false imprisonment.**

IMPROVED LAND raw land with added physical improvements such as roads or utilities.

IMPROVEMENT any permanent, fixed development of land or buildings through expenditure of money or labor that more than merely replaces, repairs or restores to original condition, and supposedly increases the value of the property.

IMPUTE to assign legal responsibility for the act of another, because of the relationship between those made liable and the actor, rather than because of participation in or knowledge of the act. See **vicarious liability.**

IMPUTED INCOME see **income [IMPUTED INCOME].**

IMPUTED LIABILITY see **vicarious liability.**

IN ABSENTIA *(ĭn ab-sĕn'-shē-à)* Lat.: in absence.

EXAMPLE: A defendant who leaves the courtroom without permission after a trial begins may be tried *in absentia.* Such proceedings otherwise require the actual presence of the defendant at all critical stages.

INADMISSIBILITY see **deportation** [inadmissibility]. Also means excludable; not allowable. *Inadmissible* evidence is the opposite of **admissible evidence.** Compare **immaterial.**

INALIENABLE RIGHTS fundamental rights, including the right to practice religion, freedom of speech, due process and equal protection of the laws, that cannot be transferred to another nor surrendered except by the person possessing them. See **Bill of Rights.**

IN ARTICULO MORTIS *(in är-tik'-ū-lō môr'-tis)* Lat.: in the moment of death.

IN BANC see **en banc.**

IN CAMERA *(iň kǎ'-mě-rà)* Lat.: in chambers. A term designating a judicial act while court is not in session in the matter acted upon. Confidential or otherwise sensitive documents are often examined in camera to determine whether information should be revealed to the **jury** and so become public record.

INCAPACITY lack of legal, physical or intellectual power. See **incompetency; minority.** Compare **insanity.**

IN CAPITE *(in kǎ'pēt)* Lat.: in chief; with reference to feudal tenures, as estate in land held by direct grant of the king.

INCARCERATION confinement in prison; **imprisonment.**

INCENDIARY 1. arsonist; one who maliciously sets property on fire; 2. an object capable of starting and sustaining a fire, an incendiary device. See **arson.**

INCEST a criminal offense of sexual intercourse between members of a family, or those between whom marriage would be illegal because of blood relationship.

IN CHAMBERS see **in camera.**

IN CHIEF principal, primary. At trial, the initial presentation of a party's evidence constitutes that party's case in chief, to which rebuttal is allowed.

INCHOATE not yet completed. In inchoate offenses, something remains to be done before the crime can be accomplished as contemplated. See **attempt; conspiracy; solicitation.**

INCHOATE DOWER [INCHOATE RIGHT OF DOWER] the **interest** that a wife has in her husband's lands before his death, and contingent upon his predeceasing her. The right of **dower** is considered inchoate until the husband's death, at which time the widow has a **vested** right to a **life estate.**

INCIDENTAL BENEFICIARY see **beneficiary [INCIDENTAL BENEFICIARY].**

INCIDENTAL DAMAGES see **damages [INCIDENTAL DAMAGES].**

INCIDENT OF OWNERSHIP an aspect of the legal title to property; for federal estate tax purposes, if a decedent possessed any "incidents of ownership" over life insurance at the time of his or her death, the value of these insurance policies would be includable in the decedent's gross estate.

INCLOSURE any land enclosed by something other than an imaginary boundary line, i.e., some wall, hedge, fence, ditch, or other actual obstruction. The word "town" derives from the Anglo-Saxon word "tun," meaning "inclosure." Compare **close.**

INCOME an economic benefit; money or value received.

ACTIVE INCOME earned income. The Internal Revenue Service considers salaries, tips, commissions, and income from businesses in which the taxpayer materially participates to be types of active income. Compare **PASSIVE INCOME** and **PORTFOLIO INCOME** (below).

ADJUSTED GROSS INCOME the gross income of the taxpayer reduced by specified **deductions,** generally business deductions.

CASH EQUIVALENT DOCTRINE the doctrine that property received by a taxpayer is includable in income if it can be converted into cash. The amount of income is the amount of such cash.

CONSTRUCTIVE RECEIPT OF INCOME a doctrine under which a taxpayer is required to include in gross income amounts that, though not actually received, are deemed received during the tax year. Thus there is constructive receipt when income is made available to a taxpayer without substantial restriction or condition on the taxpayer's right to exercise control over the income. Under this theory, interest credited on a savings account must be included in income even though the taxpayer does not withdraw it, since he or she had the right to withdraw it. The doctrine is to be distinguished from the cash equivalent doctrine.

FIXED INCOME see **fixed income.**

GROSS INCOME the total of the taxpayer's income from any source, except items specifically excluded by the Internal Revenue Code and other items not subject to tax, such as **capital** income and **FRINGE BENEFITS** (see **benefit**).

IMPUTED INCOME economic benefit a taxpayer obtains through performance of his or her own services or through the use of his or her own property. In general, imputed income is not subject to **INCOME TAXES** (see **tax**). For example, if a taxpayer is a plumber and repairs his or her own toilet, such repair service is not subject to tax.

INCOME AVERAGE see **income averaging.**

INCOME IN RESPECT OF A DECEDENT income earned by a taxpayer before his or her death but received by, and taxed to, the taxpayer's **heirs** or personal representatives.

INCOME SPLITTING see **income splitting.**

NET INCOME see **net income.**

ORDINARY INCOME income that is fully subject to ordinary income tax rates, as distinguished from income that is subject to the benefit of special deductions for **capital gains and losses.**

PASSIVE INCOME effectively "unearned" income. The Internal Revenue Service considers passive income to be rental activity or trade or business activity in which the taxpayer does not materially participate. Such income is usually taxable and, generally, losses from passive income cannot offset active or portfolio income. Compare **ACTIVE INCOME** (above) and **PORTFOLIO INCOME** (below).

PORTFOLIO INCOME generally defined by the Internal Revenue Service as income from dividends and interest income from securities, royalties, annuities, and capital gains. It does not come from passive income and is not earned from normal business activity. Compare **ACTIVE INCOME** and **PASSIVE INCOME** (above).

TAXABLE INCOME gross income reduced by deductions allowable in obtaining adjusted gross income and further reduced by deductions allowable in calculating itemized deductions.

INCOME AVERAGING a method of calculating tax liability to minimize adverse consequences to a **taxpayer** with substantial fluctuations in income from year to year; permits a taxpayer to compute his or her tax as if the higher amount of income had been earned equally over that year and the previous four years.

INCOME SPLITTING a device that allows married taxpayers to calculate their joint taxes as if one half of their joint taxable income were earned by each spouse. See **return; income tax [JOINT RETURN].** Compare **assignment of income.**

INCOME STATEMENT a financial statement that gives operating results, such as net income and loss, depreciation, for a specific period; also referred to as **EARNINGS REPORT, OPERATING STATEMENT** and **PROFIT-AND-LOSS STATEMENT.** Statements normally cover 12 months of operations with interim statements at quarterly periods in current fiscal or calendar years. Operations divide into two categories of transactions—sales or revenue generation and expenses incurred in the production of sales or revenues.

A typical manufacturing business sells products to its customers which, net of returns and discounts, results in "net sales" income. **Net income** or profit is "net sales" less all expenses. Net income is obtained after taxes are deducted at the prevailing rate. Net income (or "loss" should expenses exceed sales) is available to invest in the business, pay dividends, etc., as decided by owners of the enterprise. The principal expense item is usually COST OF GOODS SOLD, which includes purchase of raw materials, direct labor and factory overhead such as power, rent, etc. Next comes selling, general, and administrative expenses, which include salaries of salespersons, staff personnel, managers and offices, cost of administrative buildings and support services, and advertising expenses. **Depreciation** expense is stated separately since it is not an actual cash outlay and since additional comment on the method used in calculating depreciation is required. See **balance sheet.**

INCOME TAX see **tax [INCOME TAX]; return, income tax.**

INCOMPETENCY inability, disqualification, **incapacity.** 1. lack of legal qualifications or fitness to discharge a required duty; 2. lack of physical, intellectual or moral fitness.

EXAMPLE: Herman is arrested for assault. Prior to his trial, a judge determines that he is *incompetent,* that he cannot aid in his defense nor can he endure the rigors of a criminal trial without suffering a mental breakdown. Herman may at some point be declared competent to stand trial, but at the present time his trial for assault is postponed.

When a person is adjudicated incompetent, a **guardian** is appointed to manage the incompetent's affairs, unless the incompetent recovers competency to the satisfaction of the court. An adjudicated incompetent lacks capacity to **contract** and his contracts are void. Compare **competent.**

INCOMPETENT EVIDENCE **evidence** that is not **admissible.** Compare **competent.**

INCONSISTENT contradictory to one another. In pleading, inconsistent facts or legal theories may be pled in the alternative. See **alternative pleading.**

INCONSISTENT STATEMENT see **prior inconsistent statement.**

INCONTESTABILITY CLAUSE see **noncontestability [incontestability] clause.**

INCONVENIENT FORUM see **forum non conveniens.**

INCORPORATE to organize and be granted status as a **corporation**

by following prescribed legal procedures. See **articles of incorporation.**

INCORPORATION, SELECTIVE see **selective incorporation.**

INCORPOREAL see **corporeal.**

INCORPOREAL HEREDITAMENT see **hereditament.**

INCORPOREAL PROPERTY intangible property, evidencing something of value but having no inherent value independent thereof, such as a **stock certificate.** See **intangible property.**

INCORRIGIBLE uncorrectable; one whose behavior cannot be made to conform to standards dictated by law. See **criminal [HABITUAL OFFENDER]; recidivist.**

INCREMENT an amount of increase in number or value.

INCRIMINATE 1. to hold another, or oneself, responsible for criminal misconduct; 2 to involve someone, or oneself, in an accusation of a crime.

INCROACH to use unlawfully or otherwise impair possession or title to another's property. See **encroach; trespass.**

INCULPATORY tending to **incriminate** or bring about a criminal conviction. Compare **exculpatory.**

INCUMBENT person in present possession of an office or position. See **de facto [DE FACTO INCUMBENT].**

INCUMBRANCE see **encumbrance.**

INDEBITATUS ASSUMPSIT *(ĭn-dĕ-bĭ-tā-tŭs ăs-sŭmp'-sĭt)* Lat.: to be indebted, to have undertaken a debt. At common law, a form of action founded in contract in which the plaintiff alleges that the defendant has undertaken a debt and has failed to satisfy it.

INDEBTEDNESS, INVOLUNTARY see **bankruptcy [INVOLUNTARY PROCEEDING].**

INDECENT vulgar, offensive, obscene.

INDECENT EXPOSURE see **lewdness [INDECENT EXPOSURE].**

INDEFEASIBLE incapable of being defeated or altered. An indefeasible **estate** is absolute and cannot be changed by any **condition.**

EXAMPLE: A sister conveys an *indefeasible* estate to her brother. The brother has perfect title to the land and can do with it as he pleases, since there is no circumstance that can operate to deprive him of title.

INDEFINITE FAILURE OF ISSUE see **failure of issue.**

IN DELICTO *(ĭn dĕ-lĭk'-tō)* Lat.: at fault.

INDEMNIFY 1. to insure; to secure against loss or damage that may occur in the future; 2. to compensate for loss or damage already suffered; 3. to **save harmless.** See **damages; insurance.**

INDEMNITY 1. the obligation to make good any loss or damage another person has incurred or may incur; 2. the right that the person suffering loss or damage is entitled to claim.

EXAMPLE: Beatrice buys a piece of land from Sherman. Unbeknown to Beatrice, the land was encumbered by a lien for several years of back taxes that Sherman had not paid. Beatrice pays the taxes but has a right of *indemnity* against Sherman for the tax liability.

Compare **contribution.**

INDENTURE 1. a **deed** between two parties conveying **real estate** by which both parties assume obligations. Indenture implies a **sealed instrument;** 2. a lengthy written agreement that sets forth terms under which **bonds** or **debentures** may be issued.

INDEPENDENT CONTRACTOR see **contractor [INDEPENDENT CONTRACTOR].**

INDEPENDENT COVENANTS see **covenant [INDEPENDENT [MUTUAL] COVENANTS].**

INDETERMINATE SENTENCE see **sentence [INDETERMINATE SENTENCE].**

INDEX FUND a portfolio of stocks selected to match a stock market index number, usually the Standard & Poor's Industrial Index or the Standard & Poor's Composite Index. The guiding principle is creation of a proxy for the selected index since the index itself contains an unmanageably large number of stocks.

INDIAN CLAIMS COMMISSION see **Indian law [INDIAN CLAIMS COMMISSION].**

INDIAN LAW area of law relating to Native Americans. "Native American" is the preferred term for indigenous Americans; however, many statutes and treaties use the term "Indian" and it is for that reason only that the reference is included herein. Title 25 of the United States Code contains the federal laws regulating Native American affairs. The **BUREAU OF INDIAN AFFAIRS (BIA)** is a bureau of the Interior Department. The BIA and the **ADMINISTRATION FOR NATIVE AMERICANS** are federal agencies concerned with the interaction between the federal government and Native Americans. The **INDIAN CLAIMS COMMISSION** determines claims brought by tribes against the government.

INDIAN RESERVATION lands set aside for the use and occupancy of tribes of Native Americans. The federal government retains title to and exercises supervision and administration over the lands.

INDIAN TITLE also known as **ABORIGINAL TITLE,** inherent right of Native American tribes to occupy certain territory by virtue of their original occupancy of such territory and to the exclusion of other Native American tribes. This **title** cannot be **conveyed** as it consists of possession and not ownership.

INDIAN RESERVATION see **Indian law** [**INDIAN RESERVATION**].

INDIAN TITLE see **Indian law** [**INDIAN TITLE**].

INDICATION OF SOURCE see **appellation of origin** [**INDICATION OF SOURCE**].

INDICIA *(ĭn-dĭ'-shē-à)* Lat.: indications; signs or circumstances that tend to support a belief in a proposition as being probable, but that do not prove to a certainty the truth of the proposition. It is often said to be synonymous with **circumstantial evidence.** Where one exercises dominion and control over **personal property** as if it were his or her own, such behavior is an indicium of ownership. A carbon copy of a bill of sale has also been held to be an indicia of title.

"Indicia" is important in many contexts. Thus, where the owner of property is responsible for giving another indicia of ownership, that other person may effectively transfer the owner's interest to a **bona fide purchaser.** Indicia of reliability are necessary to use information supplied by an informer as a basis to support a **search warrant.**

INDICIUM *(ĭn-dĭ'-shē-ŭm)* Lat.: singular of **indicia.**

INDICTABLE OFFENSES crimes that can be prosecuted by the **GRAND JURY** (see **jury**) indicting the accused. In **common law,** these crimes were known as **felonies** and were defined by the punishment for them—either death, **forfeiture** of all one's property or mutilation. The crimes included **murder, treason, robbery, assault, rape, arson, burglary,** and **larceny.** These crimes could also be prosecuted by individuals bringing lawsuits against the **defendants.** Today felonies, as defined by modern **statutes,** are still prosecuted by **indictment.** Compare **misdemeanor.** See **crime; prosecution; suit.**

INDICTION declaration; proclamation. In Roman times, the determination of land taxes for a 15-year period. Also a method of dating manuscripts.

INDICTMENT a formal written **accusation,** drawn up and submitted under **oath** to a GRAND JURY (see **jury**) by the public prosecuting attorney, charging one or more persons with a **crime.** The grand jury must determine whether the accusation, if proved, would be sufficient for **conviction** of the accused, in which case the indictment is indorsed by the foreman as a TRUE BILL. Once an indictment is filed, the matter passes to the Court. Indictments also serve to inform an accused of the offense with which he is charged and must be clear enough to enable him to prepare his defense adequately. Compare **accusation; charge; complaint; information; presentment.**

INDIGENT 1. generally, a person who is poor, financially destitute; 2. in a legal context, a person found by a court to be unable to hire a lawyer or otherwise meet the expense of defending a criminal matter, at which point defense **counsel** is appointed by the court. See **in forma pauperis; public defender.**

INDIGNITY affront to the personality of another; lack of reverence for the personality of one's spouse. Indignity is a ground for **divorce** in some states; may consist of vulgarity, unmerited reproach, malignant ridicule and any other plain expression of settled hate or estrangement. See **mental cruelty.**

INDIRECT ATTACK see **collateral attack.**

INDIRECT EVIDENCE evidence that supports a factual theory but that does not make it explicit; **circumstantial evidence.**

INDISPENSABLE EVIDENCE **evidence** necessary to prove a submitted fact.

INDISPENSABLE PARTY a **party** who has such an interest in the **litigation** that a final **decree** cannot be issued without either affecting that interest or determining the controversy in a way inconsistent with **equity** and good conscience. Therefore, an **action** may not proceed without an indispensable party, who must be **joined** to the action, because his or her nonjoinder would result in prejudice to his or her rights and the rights of other parties to the action.

INDIVIDUAL RETIREMENT ACCOUNT [IRA] designed for a person to save and invest money for use during retirement. Contributions into the account may range from totally tax deductible to totally non tax deductible, depending upon a person's income tax filing status and adjusted gross income, and whether the person is an active participant in an employer-sponsored qualified **retirement plan.**

INHERITED IRA individual retirement account(s) that are left to one or more **beneficiaries** when the original IRA owner dies. Upon the death of the IRA owner the decedent's beneficiaries inherit the IRA and are allowed to keep the inherited IRA assets tax-deferred—until the **Internal Revenue Service** requires the funds be distributed. A beneficiary of an inherited IRA can either be the original IRA owner's spouse, children, or any non-spouse persons or a corporation but if it is not the spouse, the spouse usually has to sign giving consent to the other beneficiary. See **retirement plan.**

INDORSEE one to whom a negotiable **instrument** is assigned by indorsement. For instance, the payee or holder of a check may write on the back of the check "pay to X" and sign below. X is the indorsee. In the absense of fraud or illegality, an indorsee has all of the right, title, and interest in a negotiable instrument that the indorser had prior to assignment.

INDORSEMENT signature on the back of an **instrument,** with or without other words, the effect of which is to transfer the instrument and to create a new, independent **contract** by which the indorser becomes a party to the instrument and liable, on certain conditions, for its payment.

ACCOMMODATION INDORSEMENT one made without **consideration,** solely to extend **credit** to the holder by the indorser, generally to enable the holder to obtain credit or money from another on the basis of the indorsement.

BLANK INDORSEMENT one that specifies no particular party to whom the indorsed instrument is exclusively payable, and that therefore authorizes negotiation by the **bearer** upon **delivery** alone.

RESTRICTIVE INDORSEMENT one that limits transferability of the instrument.

SPECIAL INDORSEMENT one that specifies to whose **order** the instrument shall be payable. The instrument is then negotiable only by such person unless he or she makes a further indorsement.

INDORSER one who indorses negotiable paper. For instance, the payee or holder of a check may indorse the check by signing it on the back. An indorser is liable to pay the negotiable **instrument** in case it is dishonored.

INDUCEMENT offer enticing or persuading another person to take an action, such as entering into a contract.

INDUSTRIAL DEVELOPMENT BOND [IDB] see **guaranteed security.**

INDUSTRIAL RESERVE BANK [IRB] see **guaranteed security.**

INELIGIBILITY disqualification; legal inability to perform some task or assume some office. See **disqualify.**

IN ESCROW held in an **escrow** account, held by one who is not a party to a transaction for future delivery to a party upon the occurrence or nonoccurrence of a specific event or events.

IN ESSE *(ĭn ĕs'-ē)* Lat.: in existence. Compare **in posse.**

IN EXTREMIS *(ĭn ĕks-trĕ'-mĭs)* Lat.: in extreme circumstances; especially, on the brink of death. Compare **causa [CAUSA MORTIS].**

INFAMOUS CRIME a crime that, in **common law,** rendered the convicted person **incompetent** as a **witness,** because of presumed untrustworthiness. See **crimen falsi; felony; treason.**

INFANCY the legal status preceding **majority; minority.**

IN FEE (SIMPLE) absolute ownership of an **estate** in land. See **fee simple.**

INFERENCE a process of reasoning by which a proposition is derived as a logical consequence from given facts.

INFERENCE, ADVERSE see **adverse inference.**

INFERENCE, NECESSARY see **necessary inference.**

INFERIOR COURT a court whose decision is subject to review by another court, which is referred to as a SUPERIOR COURT.

INFEUDATION the act of granting a **freehold estate;** same as **feoffment** or enfeoffment.

INFIRM sickly; a weak person. In particular circumstances the testimony of an infirm person may be obtained in a manner that differs from regular procedure to prevent its loss through the death of the witness. See **de bene esse.**

INFLUENCE, UNDUE see **undue influence.**

INFORMAL PROCEEDINGS in probate law, the admission of a will to probate without the requirements necessary in an adversarial proceeding, such as notice to interested parties.

INFORMANT see **informer.**

IN FORMA PAUPERIS *(in fôr'-mà paw-pĕr'-ĭs)* Lat.: in the manner of a pauper. In **pleadings,** in forma pauperis grants the right to sue without assuming the burden of **costs** or formalities of pleading. A criminal **defendant** granted permission to proceed *in forma pauperis* may be entitled to court-appointed counsel.

INFORMATION a written accusation of crime signed by the **prosecutor,** charging a person with the commission of a crime; an alternative to **indictment** as a means of starting a criminal prosecution. The purpose of an *information* is to inform the **defendant** of the charges against him or her and to inform the court of the factual basis of the charges.

INFORMATION AND BELIEF verification short of actual knowledge, but based on reasonable, **good faith** efforts to determine truth or falsity. The term is used with reference to documents requiring verification, such as requests for **search warrants,** responses to **interrogatories, complaints, pleadings,** etc.

INFORMATION RETURN see **return [INFORMATION RETURN].**

INFORMED CONSENT consent given only after full disclosure of what is being consented to; constitutionally required in certain areas where one may consent to what otherwise would be an unconstitutional violation of a right.

EXAMPLE: Jan is arrested for burglary. She decides to handle her case by herself, without the assistance of an attorney. Since she has a constitutional right to an attorney and to have one appointed if she cannot afford one, a judge must insure that her decision is based on *informed consent.* Such consent would include an understanding of her right to an attorney and what her decision entails.

The phrase is also used in **tort** law, where a patient must be told the nature and risks of a medical procedure before the physician can validly claim exemption from **liability** for **battery** or from responsibility for medical complications.

Compare **Miranda rule; self-incrimination, privilege against.**

INFORMER one who, on a confidential basis, gives information about some wrongdoing to the police or other governmental authorities. Often the information is given in the hope that some favor or benefit is given to the tipster in return for the useful information provided.

EXAMPLE: Patty called the crime stoppers hotline with the name of a person she recently saw displaying a very large amount of cash. She hoped that the information would lead to a reward for the arrest and conviction of a perpetrator in the case of a recent bank robbery.

INFORMER'S PRIVILEGE the privilege of the government to not reveal the identity of an informer. The identity of an informant need not be disclosed to the defendant at a suppression hearing so long as the person relying upon the informer's information has testified and has been cross-examined as to what the informant told him or her and as to why the information was believed to be trustworthy. The privilege may not survive a demand for disclosure at the trial level, however, if necessary to insure a fair trial. In no event can the informer's true identity be withheld from the accused once the prosecution decides to use the informer as a government witness in a criminal trial.

INFRA *(ĭn'-frà)* Lat.: below; following; beneath. In text the term refers to a discussion or a citation appearing subsequently; the opposite of **supra** ("above").

INFRINGEMENT breach; violation; unauthorized distribution. See **patent infringement.** See **copyright; trademark; plagiarism.**

INFRINGEMENT OF COPYRIGHT see **copyright [INFRINGEMENT]; plagiarism.**

INFRINGEMENT OF PATENT see **patent infringement.**

IN FUTURO *(ĭn fū-tū'-rō)* Lat.: in the future; at a later date.

IN GENERE *(ĭn gĕ'-nĕ-rā)* Lat.: in kind; of the same class or species.

INGRESS AND EGRESS 1. entrance and departure; 2. means of entering and leaving; 3. the right to do so. See **easement.**

IN GROSS at large. See **easement [EASEMENT IN GROSS].**

IN HAEC VERBA *(ĭn hēc vĕr'-bä)* Lat.: in these words.

INHERENT DEFECT a defect that exists in an item regardless of the use made of that item. Although an inherent defect may not be readily detectable, a manufacturer is nonetheless strictly liable for any injury caused by it. Synonymous with **latent defect.**

INHERENT POWERS those powers an authority such as a court or a government must have in order to achieve the purposes for which it was created.

INHERENT CONSTITUTIONAL POWERS the federal government possesses all those inherent and implied powers that, at the time of adopting the Constitution, were generally considered to belong to every government as such, and as being essential to the exercise of its functions. These powers include the ability to conduct foreign affairs, to exclude and deport aliens, to protect persons in federal custody or employment, to protect federal elections, and to protect federally created or federally guaranteed rights.

INHERENT RIGHT a right that exists by reason of an individual's status as an individual and is not derived from any other source.

INHERIT technically, to take as an **heir at law** solely by **descent,** rather than by **devise;** more commonly used to signify taking either by devise (i.e., by **will**) or by descent (i.e., from one's ancestor by **operation of law**).

INHERITANCE **real property** or **personal property** that is received by **heirs** according to the laws of **descent and distribution.** A nontechnical meaning of inheritance includes property passed by **will.**

INHERITED IRA see **individual retirement account [INHERITED IRA].**

IN HOC *(ĭn hŏk)* Lat.: in this; in reference to this.

IN INVITUM *(ĭn ĭn-vē'-tŭm)* Lat.: against the will of the other party.

INITIATIVE a process by which a small percentage of voters may propose legislation and compel officials to submit the proposed legislation to voters. It involves the power of the people to propose bills and laws and to enact or reject them at the polls, independent of legislative assembly. In contrast, **referendum** is the right of the people to have submitted for their approval or rejection an act passed by the legislature. Referendum is a process by which a small percentage of voters may delay effective legislation and compel officials to submit it for voter approval or rejection.

Initiative is a form of direct legislation by the people consisting of two parts: petition and election. An initiative does not become effective until passed by voters and its availability does not remedy the denial of the right to referendum.

IN JEOPARDY see **double jeopardy; jeopardy.**

INJUNCTION a judicial **remedy** awarded to restrain a particular activity; first used by **courts of equity** to prevent conduct contrary to **equity** and good conscience.

The injunction is a preventive measure to guard against future injuries, rather than one that affords a remedy for past injuries.

FINAL INJUNCTIONS see **PERMANENT [FINAL] INJUNCTIONS** (below).

INTERLOCUTORY INJUNCTIONS see **TEMPORARY [INTERLOCUTORY] INJUNCTIONS** (below).

MANDATORY INJUNCTION one requiring positive action, rather than one forbidding a party to act.

EXAMPLE: A landlord refuses to supply his tenants with heat during the winter months. Regardless of the reasons for the landlord's action, a court might issue a *mandatory injunction* forcing the landlord to supply heat.

PERMANENT INJUNCTION one issued upon completion of a trial in which the injunction has been actively sought.

TEMPORARY [INTERLOCUTORY] INJUNCTION one that will expire at a particular time, and that is typically used to maintain the **status quo** or preserve the subject matter of the **litigation** during trial.

INJURIA ABSQUE DAMNO *(ĭn-jū'-rē-à äb'-skwā däm'-nō)* Lat.: wrong without damage; insult without damage. Where a **cause of action** requires that damages be **pleaded,** this maxim expresses the rule that a wrong that causes no legally recognized damage cannot give rise to a cause of action. But see **damages [NOMINAL DAMAGES].**

INJURIA NON EXCUSAT INJURIAM *(ĭn-jū'-rē-à nŏn ĕx-kū'-zät ĭn-jū-rē-äm)* Lat.: one wrong does not justify another.

INJURIOUS FALSEHOOD the **tort** of causing injury to a person's reputation through **libel** or **slander** ("**defamation**") or to a person's business through harmful statements ("**disparagement**").

INJURY wrong or damage done to another, either in his or her person, rights, reputation or property. **LEGAL INJURY** is any damage that results from a violation of a legal right and that the law will recognize as deserving of redress. Compare **damnum absque injuria; depreciation; fault.** See also **damages; relief; remedy.**

EXAMPLE: Federal law prohibits discrimination based on race. May, a black woman, is refused a job because of her race. Even if she gets another job and although no physical injury resulted to her, she has been *injured* in the eyes of the law and can pursue a monetary remedy or an award of the job she was refused.

IN KIND 1. of the same or similar type or quality; 2. in the same or similar manner.

IN LIMINE *(ĭn lĭ'-mĭ-nē)* Lat.: at the beginning or the threshold. See **motion in limine.**

IN LOCO PARENTIS *(ĭn lō'-kō pä-rĕn'-tĭs)* Lat.: in the place of a parent. Refers to a person or agency who has assumed the obligations of a parent. Commonly refers to the role of a residential institution such as a boarding school, in relation to the **minors** in its care.

INMATE one who is committed to an institution, such as a **prisoner** at a prison. See **jail; penal institution.**

INMATE ADVOCATE see **advocate [INMATE ADVOCATE].**

IN MORTMAIN see **mortmain.**

INNOCENT PURCHASER see **bona fide purchaser.**

INNS OF COURT four private societies in England that prepare students for the practice of law and that alone may admit them to the bar; that is, confer the rank of **barrister.** The four inns of court are Inner Temple, Middle Temple, Lincoln's Inn, Gray's Inn.

INNUENDO that part of a **pleading** in an **action** for **libel** that explains, improperly, the spoken or written words that are the basis of the action, thereby attaching to those words more than their plain meaning. The **plaintiff** in a libel action cannot enlarge or change original language by innuendo, since the purpose of innuendo is to explain the application of words used, and words that are not libelous in themselves cannot be made so by innuendo.

IN OMNIBUS *(ĭn ŏm'-nĭ-būs)* Lat.: in all things; in all the world; in all nature; in all respects.

IN PAIS *(ĭn pĕ'-ĭs)* Fr.: in the country, neighborhood. Applies to a transaction handled outside the court or without a legal **proceeding.**

IN PARI DELICTO *(ĭn pä'-rē dē-lĭk'-tō)* Lat.: in equal fault. Refers to an exception to the general rule that illegal transactions or **contracts** are not legally enforceable; thus, where the parties to an illegal agreement are not *in pari delicto,* the agreement may nevertheless be enforceable at **equity** by the innocent or less guilty party. See also **clean hands; duress; fraud.**

IN PARI MATERIA *(ĭn pä'-rē mä-tĕr'-ē-à)* Lat.: on like subject matter. **Statutes** or document provisions that relate to the same person or subject. In the **construction** or interpretation of a statute or instrument, the various provisions of the statute or instrument and all other acts or instruments on the same subject or having the same purpose are to be read together as one law or agreement, giving equal importance to each.

IN PERPETUITY existing forever.

IN PERSONAM *(ĭn pĕr-sō'-näm)* Lat.: into or against the person. In **pleading,** an **action** against a person or persons, founded on personal **liability** and requiring **jurisdiction** by the court over the person sought to be held liable, i.e., the **defendant.**

EXAMPLE: C.J. causes an accident while driving recklessly. He is sued *in personam* in the state where the accident occurred, but he claims that as an out-of-state driver the courts of that state do not have jurisdiction over him and cannot force him to answer the suit. Although that might be true without applicable statutes, every state has laws automatically establishing jurisdiction over persons using their highways. If the victim of the accident wins this suit, based on the merits, he can use the judgment against C.J. in any other state.

In such an action, the **plaintiff** seeks either to subject defendant's general **assets** to **execution** in order to satisfy a money **judgment,** or to obtain a judgment directing defendant to do an act or refrain from doing an act.

Compare **in rem.**

IN POSSE *(ĭn pŏs'-ē)* Lat.: in the future, that which is not yet but that may exist. Compare **in esse.**

IN PRAESENTI *(ĭn prā-zĕn'-tē)* Lat.: in the present. Often signifies a presently effective act or interest, distinguished from one effective **in futuro.**

IN QUANTUM MERUIT see **quantum meruit.**

INQUEST 1. a judicial inquiry; 2. an inquiry made by a **coroner** to determine cause of death of one who has been killed, has died suddenly, or under suspicious circumstances or in prison.

INQUIRY NOTICE see **notice [IMPLIED NOTICE].**

IN RE *(ĭn rā)* Lat.: in the matter of. Usually signifies a legal proceeding with no opponent, but rather judicial **disposition** of a thing, or **res,** such as the **estate** of a decedent.

IN REM *(ĭn rĕm)* Lat.: into or against the thing. Signifies actions against the **res,** or thing, rather than against the person. The goal of a proceeding *in rem* is the **disposition** of property without reference to the **title** of individual **claimants.** Compare **in personam.**

ACTIONS IN REM those that seek not to impose personal **liability** but rather to affect the **interests** of persons in a specific thing (or **res**). A few such actions purport to affect the interests of all persons ("all the world") in the same thing as, for example, in actions to protect the environment; most of them seek to affect the interests of only particular persons in the thing. Typical modern examples are actions for **partition** of, or for **foreclosure** of a **lien** upon, or to **quiet title** to, real estate. The concept of *in rem* actions has been extended to those that seek to affect the condition of a thing as well as the thing itself.

ACTIONS QUASI IN REM actions based on a claim for money damages begun by **attachment** or **garnishment** or other seizure of property where the court has no **jurisdiction** over the person of the defendant but has jurisdiction over a thing belonging to the defendant or over a person who is indebted or under a duty to the defendant.

INSANE DELUSION see **delusion.**

INSANITY mental illness. The term may be used to signify lack of criminal responsibility, need for commitment to a mental institution, inability to transact business, inability to stand trial (i.e., to assist in one's own defense). Compare **incompetency; non compos mentis; non sui juris.** See **Durham rule; M'Naghten rule.**

INSANITY, PLEA OF see **plea [INSANITY PLEA].**

IN SE *(ĭn sā)* Lat.: in and of itself.

INSIDER a person whose opportunity to profit from his or her position of power in a business is limited by law to safeguard the public good. Both federal securities acts and state **blue sky laws** regulate stock transactions of individuals with access to inside information about a corporation, since the prospect of **insider trading** may inhibit investment by the general public due to their concern that the price of securities has been artificially inflated or deflated by such trading.

INSIDER TRADING buying or selling of corporation stock by a corporate officer who profits by his or her access to information not available to the public. Corporate **insiders** who trade on the basis of nonpublic corporate information may be exposed to **liability** under state or federal law, because of a policy that everybody should have equal access to information and that insiders should not profit personally from something that belongs to the corporation.

INSOLVENCY 1. inability to meet financial obligations as they mature in the ordinary course of business; 2. excess of liabilities over assets at any given time. In the absence of definition by statute, the first definition is more widely recognized; however, statutory definition is common today. See **bankruptcy.**

EXAMPLE: Baden Company borrows money from a bank to pay overdue debts in the hope that business will improve. That hope is not realized, and payments to the bank as well as other debts begin to develop again. Baden is finally declared *insolvent.* If any assets remain in the company, Baden's creditors and/or a court will divide them in some fair fashion.

INSOLVENCY PROCEEDINGS see **bankruptcy.**

IN SPECIE *(ĭn spē'-shē)* Lat.: in like form. To repay a loan in specie is to return the same kind of goods as were borrowed.

INSPECTION OF DOCUMENTS right of parties in a **civil action** to view and copy documents in the possession of the court and essential to the **adverse party's cause of action.** This is done as part of the **discovery** process before trial; but apart from the production for pretrial inspection, a party may by the use of a **subpoena duces tecum** require the production of documents at the time of trial for the purpose of introducing them into **evidence.**

INSTALLMENT the partial satisfaction of a debt or other obligation.

INSTALLMENT CONTRACT a contract in which the obligation of one or more of the parties—such as an obligation to pay money, deliver goods or render services—is divided into a series of successive performances.

EXAMPLE: Flavor Bread Company wants to insure supplies of wheat over the next five years. It writes an *installment contract* with a farmer's cooperative to deliver monthly shipments of wheat to its plant over the five-year period, with Flavor's obligation to pay likewise apportioned over the five-year period. Since the contract is long-term, prices are arrived at by a formula that can vary each month.

INSTALLMENT METHOD see **accounting method** [INSTALLMENT METHOD OF ACCOUNTING].

INSTALLMENT SALE a contract by which goods are purchased now but paid for over a period of time by a number of installments. Consumers have extensive protection against abusive installment sales of consumer goods under the Truth-in-Lending Act, which governs advertising, the computation of interest on upaid installments, and other aspects of such sales.

INSTANT MATTER see **sub judice.**

IN STATU QUO *(ĭn stä'-tū kwō)* Lat.: in the existing situation or condition. In the same position a party is in currently or was in at some relevant prior time.

IN STATU QUO ANTE in a contract means being placed in the same position in which a party was at the time of the inception of the contract that is sought to be **rescinded.**

INSTITUTION see **correctional institution; penal institution.**

INSTRUCTION   the judge's directions to the **jury** before their deliberation, informing them of the law applicable to the **case,** to guide them in reaching a verdict according to law and the **evidence.** An instruction to the jury is a **charge** to the jury, more a command than a request.

INSTRUMENT   in commercial law, a written formal document that records an act or agreement and provides the **evidence** of that act or agreement.

INSUFFICIENT EVIDENCE   a term usually referred to in a decision by a judge that a prosecutor or other party charged with proving a crime has failed to provide the minimum of **evidence** necessary to even ask a jury to decide a **question of fact;** results in a **directed verdict** in favor of a defendant. If an **appellate court** decides that the evidence at a defendant's trial is insufficient, it will reverse the conviction and dismiss the charges that the State failed to prove at the trial.

INSURABLE INTEREST   a relationship with a person or thing that supports issuance of an **insurance** policy. A person having an insurable interest can derive financial advantage from preservation of the subject matter insured or suffer loss from its destruction.

An insurable interest in the life of another requires that the continued life of the insured be of real interest to the insuring party. The connection may be financial (as when a **creditor** insures the life of his or her **debtor**) or it may consist of familial or other ties of affection.

EXAMPLE: A basketball team drafts Astor, the best player in college. His contract will pay him over a million dollars a year for ten years. The team has an *insurable interest* in Astor and will undoubtedly take out an insurance policy to protect their investment.

INSURANCE   the benefit from an agreement by one party (insurer) to provide the other (insured), for a **consideration,** money or some other benefit in the event of the loss of, or injury to, a specified person or thing in which the other has an interest.

ENDOWMENT INSURANCE   insurance for a specified amount payable to the insured at the expiration of a certain period or to a designated **beneficiary** immediately upon the death of the insured.

NO FAULT INSURANCE   a system of automobile insurance where a party injured in an automobile accident recovers damages up to a specific amount against his own insurance company regardless of who was at fault in the accident. Damages in excess of the specified amount are recovered by a lawsuit against the party who caused the accident. "No fault insurance" is designed to reduce the amount of _insured_

litigation resulting from minor automobile accidents and to make the system of compensating victims of such accidents more efficient.

TERM INSURANCE insurance for the period for which a premium has been paid. With life insurance it is a **contract** in which the insured pays the actual cost of insurance for each assessment period, without defraying a future deficit from the cost of insuring older persons. Economical premium eliminates cash surrender value and loan value.

TITLE INSURANCE see **title insurance.**

WHOLE LIFE INSURANCE insurance upon the life of the insured for a fixed death benefit at a definite annual premium; synonymous with ordinary life insurance or straight life insurance.

INSURED the person whose interests are protected by an **insurance** policy; the person who **contracts** for a policy of insurance that **indemnifies** him against loss of **property,** life or health.

INSURRECTION a violent uprising of part or all of the people against the government or other authority.

INTANGIBLE ASSET an asset that has no physical being, apart from a writing that evidences its existence. For instance, the debt of another that is evidenced by a **promissory note** is an intangible asset. The intangible assets of a business include **going concern value** and **good will.**

INTANGIBLE PROPERTY possessions that only represent real value, such as **stock certificates, bonds, promissory notes, franchises.**

INTEGRATION 1. the process by which the parties to an agreement adopt a writing or writings as the full and final expression of their agreement; 2. the writing or writings so adopted. 3. the bringing together of different races.

INTELLECTUAL PROPERTY area of law concerning property, such as ideas, creative works, or inventions of human intelligence (including documents, symbols, and images) and the registration thereof (involving copyright, trademark, and patent rights as well as the protection of trade secrets). See also **scène à faire.**

INTENDMENT OF LAW the true meaning of or purpose behind a law.

INTENT a state of mind wherein the person knows and desires the consequences of his or her act. For criminal and certain types of civil **liability,** intent must exist at the time the offense is committed. See **animo; mens rea; scienter.**

DONATIVE INTENT see **gift [DONATIVE INTENT].**

LEGISLATIVE INTENT that which the legislature desired when it enacted legislation. The purpose behind a statute is important in determining the meaning of the words in a statute. See **legislative history.** Compare **plain meaning.**

LETTER OF INTENT see **letter of intent.**

ORIGINAL INTENT view that interpretation of the **Constitution** should be confined to the words themselves and the meaning that those words would have been given by the Founding Fathers themselves, not contemporary interpretations. See **strict construction.**

TESTAMENTARY INTENT see **testamentary intent.**

TRANSFERRED INTENT see **transferred intent.**

INTENTIONAL INFLICTION OF EMOTIONAL DISTRESS see **emotional distress [INTENTIONAL INFLICTION OF EMOTIONAL DISTRESS].**

INTER ALIA *(ĭn'-tèr ä'-lē-à)* Lat.: among other things.

INTERCEPTION see **wiretap.**

INTEREST 1. in commercial law, **consideration** or **compensation** for the use of money loaned or forbearance in demanding it when due; 2. in legal practice, a term connoting bias or concern for the advantage or disadvantage of a party to the **action** or of the subject matter of the action. Interest affects the credibility of **witnesses.** Interest is required for the **intervention** of third parties in a lawsuit and is also a ground for disqualifying a judge or juror; 3. in real property, the broadest term applicable to claims on **real estate,** including any right, **title** or **estate** in or **lien** on real property. Interest thus refers to the legal concern of a person in the property, or in the right to some of the benefits from which the property is inseparable.

COMPOUND INTEREST interest that is paid not only upon the principal sum, but also upon the interest previously paid on that sum. Thus, interest already paid or accrued becomes part of the principal, for purposes of subsequent interest calculations.

EXECUTED INTEREST an interest in property presently enjoyed and possessed by a party.

EXECUTORY INTEREST interest in property that may become actual in the future or upon the occurrence of some event.

INTEREST RATE the amount of interest paid, usually expressed as a percentage of the amount of the underlying debt.

SHIFTING INTEREST a future interest arising in derogation of or out of a preceding interest.

SPRINGING INTEREST a future interest arising from an **estate** in the grantor. Compare **chain of title.**

VESTED INTEREST one in which there is a present fixed right of present or future enjoyment. See also **vested [VESTED INTEREST].**

INTERIM FINANCING debt that is incurred on a short-term basis until permanent financing can be arranged.

INTERIM ORDER a temporary order, made until another or **FINAL ORDER** (see **order**) takes its place or a specific event occurs.

INTERLOCKING DIRECTORATE two or more **boards of directors** of corporations that have one or more common members. Common control of the corporations may result from interlocking directorates, and can be used to restrict competition. Consequently, interlocking directorates are subject to prohibition and regulation under the Clayton Antitrust Act.

INTERLOCUTORY provisional; temporary. An **order** or **judgment** that does not determine the **issues** but directs further **proceeding** preliminary to a final order or **decree.** Until final decree, an interlocutory judgment is subject to change by the court to meet the needs of the case and is often not appealable except by leave of court.

EXAMPLE: Fran wins a suppression motion to exclude certain evidence against her in an upcoming trial. Before the trial begins, the prosecutor seeks leave from the judge to file an *interlocutory* appeal from the suppression order, rather than wait until the trial is concluded before appealing the judge's ruling on Fran's motion. If the prosecutor's request is granted, Fran's trial will not proceed until an appellate court rules on the motion.

INTERLOCUTORY DECREE see **decree [INTERLOCUTORY DECREES].**

INTERLOCUTORY INJUNCTIONS see **injunction [TEMPORARY [INTERLOCUTORY] INJUNCTIONS].**

INTERLOCUTORY ORDER order determining an intermediate issue, made in the course of a pending litigation that does not dispose of the case, but abides further court action resolving the entire controversy. Such orders are not generally appealable until after the entire matter has been disposed of by final order or judgment.

INTERLOCUTORY SENTENCE see **sentence** [INTERLOCU-
TORY SENTENCE].

INTERMEDDLER see **officious intermeddler.**

INTERNAL REVENUE CODE the massive **statute** providing the
foundation for all federal tax law. This statute is located in Title 26,
United States Code. Its various subtitles include **tax** provisions relating to the **INCOME TAX, GIFT TAX** and **ESTATE TAX** (now **UNIFIED
ESTATE AND GIFT TAX**), as well as other less important and less well-
known taxes. As with all federal statutes, it is enacted and amended by
Congress, and is implemented through the **Internal Revenue Service**
by the Commissioner of Internal Revenue, appointed by the President.

INTERNAL REVENUE SERVICE [IRS] the federal agency primarily concerned with the administration of the federal tax laws.

INTERNATIONAL AGREEMENTS agreements between nations
such as **treaties,** conventions, and protocols.

INTERNATIONAL COURT OF JUSTICE the principal tribunal
of the United Nations, consisting of 15 members elected by the
General Assembly and the Security Council for a definite, limited
term. The only **appeal** from a **judgment** of this Court is to the U.N.
Security Council. The seat of the Court is at the Hague, though it
may meet elsewhere at its discretion.

INTERNATIONAL LAW the law governing relations of nations
with one another, which arises principally from international agreements or from customs that nations adopt.

In a broader sense, international law includes both public
law and private law. The public law regulates political relations
between nations. The private law is the **comity** nations grant to
each other's laws in enforcing rights arising under foreign law.

INTER PARES *(ĭn'-tèr pär'-ās)* Lat.: among peers; among those
of equal rank.

INTER PARTES *(ĭn'-ter pär'-tās)* Lat.: between the parties.

INTERPLEADER an equitable **action** in which a **debtor,** not knowing to whom among his or her **creditors** a certain debt is owed, and
having no **claim** on the property in dispute, will petition a court to
require the creditors to litigate the claim among themselves. The person interpleading is called the **stakeholder.** Interpleader is used to
avoid multiple **liability** on the part of the debtor and is used often
by insurance carriers, who deposit the proceeds of a policy in court
where several persons with conflicting rights have made claims.

EXAMPLE: An insurance company immediately realizes that an airline it insures is responsible for a crash that has killed 20 people. The company, by way of *interpleader,* is able to deposit with the court the maximum liability for which the airline is insured for these 20 people and thereby lets the families of each person and the court determine how the money will be allocated.

Compare **cross-claim; joinder.**

INTERROGATION the process by which suspects are rigorously questioned by police. See **Miranda rule.**

INTERROGATORIES in **civil actions,** a pretrial **discovery** tool in which one party's written questions are served on the **adversary,** who must serve written replies under oath. Interrogatories can only be served on **parties** to the **action,** and while not as flexible as **depositions,** which include opportunity of **cross-examination,** they are regarded as a good and inexpensive means of establishing important facts held by the adversary.

IN TERROREM *(ĭn tĕ-rô'-rĕm)* Lat.: in fear. A CONDITION SUBSEQUENT (see **condition**) placed in a **will** or **contract** that, although unenforceable, has the purpose of intimidating the beneficiary and thereby perhaps securing his compliance.

INTER SE [INTER SESE] *(ĭn'-tĕr sā, ĭn'-tĕr sĕ'-sā)* Lat.: among or between themselves; commonly applied to **trust** instruments to signify that only the rights of **shareholders** and **trustees** are involved.

INTERSTATE COMMERCE business activity among inhabitants of different states, including transportation of persons and property and navigation of public waters for that purpose, as well as purchase, sale and exchange of commodities.

INTERSTATE COMMERCE COMMISSION federal **regulatory agency** concerned with **interstate commerce** in the transportation industry (trucks, trains, and bus lines, but not airlines) as well as oil pipelines. The ICC's goal is for the industries to provide reasonable rates and services. See **commerce clause.**

INTERSTATE COMPACT see **compact clause [INTERSTATE COMPACT].**

INTERVAL OWNERSHIP see **time-sharing.**

INTERVENING CAUSE [FORCE] see **cause [INTERVENING [SUPERVENING] CAUSE].**

INTERVENTION a **proceeding** permitting a person to enter a **lawsuit** already in progress; in **civil law,** admission of a person not an original **party** to the suit, to protect a right or **interest** allegedly affected by the proceedings. The **INTERVENOR** may wish to join the **plaintiff** or the **defendant** or demand something adverse to both. A person generally can become an intervenor only by proving he or she has an interest in the subject matter of the original **litigation.** The purpose of intervention is to prevent delay and unnecessary duplication of lawsuits; it may be denied, however, if it interferes excessively with the rights of original parties to conduct the suit on their own terms.

EXAMPLE: The Pope family sues Durable Paperboard Company for using chemicals that contain carcinogens in phone repair products. Two other companies use the same chemicals and fear that a decision adverse to Durable will result in many lawsuits against them based on the same claim. The companies therefore seek to *intervene* in the suit between the family and Durable.

INTER VIVOS *(ĭn'-tèr vē'-vōs)* Lat.: between the living. Transactions inter vivos are made while the parties are living, and not upon death (as in **inheritance**) or upon contemplation of death **(cause mortis).** A **deed,** therefore, is an **instrument** that **conveys** inter vivos a present **interest** in land. **Gifts** are either inter vivos, causa mortis or by **will.**

INTESTATE [INTESTACY] the condition of having died without leaving a valid **will.** An intestate **estate** is property that a **decedent** has failed to dispose of **(devise)** by will.

INTESTATE SUCCESSION the disposition of property to **heirs** according to the laws of **descent and distribution** upon the death of a person who has left no **will,** or who has left a portion of his or her **estate** unaccounted for in the will. See **inheritance.**

IN TOTO *(ĭn tō'-tō)* Lat.: in total.

INTOXICATION state of drunkenness, or a similar condition caused by use of drugs other than alcohol.

INTRINSIC EVIDENCE part of the internal chain composing the process of adjudication. Where allegations of **fraud** in the complaint attacking a judgment in a former action were that false testimony was given, such allegations of fraud concerned "intrinsic fraud" and thus **res judicata** barred the complaint.

INTRINSIC FRAUD see **fraud.**

INTRUST see **entrust.**

INURE to take effect; to serve to the benefit of someone; in property, to **vest.**

IN VACUO *(ĭn vàk'-ū-ō)* Lat.: in space.

INVALID ON ITS FACE see **void for vagueness.**

INVASION OF PRIVACY the wrongful intrusion into a person's private activities by other individuals or by the government. See also **due process of law.** See **privacy, right of [INVASION OF PRIVACY]; wiretapping.**

INVENTION see **patent [PATENT OF INVENTION].**

INVENTORY the category on a **balance sheet** reflecting the cost of **goods** purchased by a business for future sale. Inventories are generally required in every business in which the sale of merchandise is a material **income** producing factor. To determine the gross profit from the business operation involving the sale of merchandise, the **taxpayer** reduces from gross receipts the cost of goods sold. To determine costs of goods sold, the taxpayer adds the inventory on hand at the beginning of the year to the cost of goods purchased during the year and subtracts the inventory on hand at the close of the year. In general, there are two methods available for determining the **basis** of inventory on hand at the end of the year—LIFO and FIFO.

FIRST-IN, FIRST-OUT [FIFO] a method of inventory accounting in which the goods sold during the year are assigned the cost of the goods purchased earliest and the goods on hand at the end of the year are given the value of the goods most recently purchased. The underlying assumption of FIFO is that a business sells its inventory in the order in which it was purchased, i.e., the items purchased first are sold first. During a period of rapid inflation, FIFO will cause large profits to result, since the least expensive goods, i.e., those purchased earliest, are considered sold. To avoid the distortion of income that may result from FIFO, business may change to the **LAST-IN, FIRST-OUT** method of inventory accounting.

LAST-IN, FIRST-OUT [LIFO] a method of inventory accounting under which the goods sold during the year are assigned the cost of the goods most recently purchased, and the goods on hand at the end of the year are given the value of the goods purchased earliest. The underlying assumption of LIFO is that a business sells its most recently purchased goods first. During a period of inflation, LIFO tends to understate profits since the most expensive goods, i.e., those most recently purchased, are considered to be sold.

LOWER COST OR VALUE a method of valuing inventory in which the goods on hand are valued at the lower of the price paid to purchase them or their fair market value at the time of valuation.

IN VENTRE SA MERE *(in vĕn'-trē sä mār)* Leg. Fr: in the mother's womb; an unborn child.

INVERSE ORDER OF ALIENATION see **marshaling [marshalling]** [INVERSE ORDER OF ALIENATION].

INVEST to transfer **capital** to an enterprise in order to secure income or profit for the investor.

INVESTIGATIVE DETENTION see **detention** [INVESTIGATIVE DETENTION].

INVESTIGATORY POWERS the powers given to governmental agencies and other entities to investigate violations of laws and to gather information regarding laws that are proposed to be enacted.

INVESTITURE at **common law,** a ceremony demonstrating the transfer of **possession** of land. An open and notorious **livery of seisin** or corporeal possession in the presence of other vassals was essential to transfer land in the system of feudal **tenure.** During the early English period, when the art of writing was not widely known, this ceremony demonstrated who had title in case title was disputed at a later time. Investitures were probably first used in conquered countries to demonstrate the legitimate possession of lands by the lord. See **seisin.**

INVESTMENT the purchase of property with the expectation of obtaining **income** or **capital gain** in the future.

INVESTMENT BANKER a **broker** of **stocks** who acts as an **underwriter** of **securities.** The investment banker can act as **principal** by buying the entire issue from the selling **corporation** or from selling **shareholders,** or as **agent** by selling the offering on a "best-efforts" basis. In either event the investment banker sells the issue to other dealers who together with the lead banker have formed an underwriting **syndicate.** Members of the syndicate in turn sell the **shares** to the investing public and to institutional investors such as pension funds (see **retirement plan**) or **mutual funds.** Investment banking is not banking as generally defined, and investment banking activities are illegal for commercial banks.

INVESTMENT COMPANY ACT OF 1940 see **Securities Acts** [INVESTMENT COMPANY ACT OF 1940].

INVESTMENT COMPANY [TRUST] a company or trust formed to pool the money resources of many individual investors in a large fund offering potential for investment diversification and professional management. Such a corporation typically invests in real estate or stocks and bonds, distributing the profit therefrom to its shareholders in the form of **dividends.**

INVESTMENT STOCK see **restricted securities** [INVESTMENT STOCK].

INVESTMENT TAX CREDIT see **tax credit** [INVESTMENT TAX CREDIT].

INVESTORS ADVISORS ACT OF 1940 see **Securities Acts** [INVESTORS ADVISORS ACT OF 1940].

INVIDIOUS causing resentment or ill will; discriminatory.

INVITEE one who comes upon private land by the owner's invitation, whether express or implied. In **tort** law, the owner is not an insurer of the safety of invitees, but he or she owes a duty to them to exercise reasonable care for their protection against **latent defects** in the premises that might cause them injury. Compare **licensee; trespass.**

EXAMPLE: Marcos has a vacation home in a wooded area where he lays traps to catch animals. He invites neighbors to take a walk with him in some of the back parts of the property to enjoy the scenic view. One of these invitees steps on a trap that was buried below the ground and injures his foot. Marcos is responsible for the invitee's injuries.

BUSINESS INVITEE [GUEST] one who is invited to enter onto another's land or premises for the purpose of doing business. The person who invites the business invitee onto the property has a high duty of care with regard to the business invitee and must take reasonable care to protect the invitee against injury.

INVOLUNTARY unwilling; forced; opposed; in criminal law, can act as a defense to a charge of committing a crime. See **duress.**

EXAMPLE: Bernice is forced at gunpoint to accompany several men into a bank to aid them in a robbery. Since her actions are *involuntary* and performed under duress, she cannot be charged with criminal responsibility in the crime.

INVOLUNTARY COMMITMENT see **commitment** [INVOLUNTARY].

INVOLUNTARY CONFESSION a confession to a crime obtained in violation of the defendant's right against self-incrimination under the Fifth Amendment. Such confessions can never be used at trial, and their use results in reversal of any subsequent conviction.

INVOLUNTARY CONVERSION the conversion of property into money or similar property as a result of its destruction in whole or in part by theft, seizure, requisition, condemnation or threat thereof. For income tax purposes, gain is not recognized on property that is involuntarily converted, if the taxpayer acquires property similar in service or use within two years of the loss.

INVOLUNTARY DISSOLUTION see **dissolution** [INVOLUNTARY DISSOLUTION].

INVOLUNTARY BAILMENT   see **bailment** [INVOLUNTARY BAILMENT].

INVOLUNTARY MANSLAUGHTER   see **manslaughter** [INVOL-UNTARY MANSLAUGHTER].

INVOLUNTARY NONSUIT   see **nonsuit** [INVOLUNTARY NON-SUIT].

INVOLUNTARY SERVITUDE   forced labor or services, whether or not for pay, that are performed or provided by another person and are obtained or maintained through an actor's threat (either implicit or explicit), scheme, plan, or pattern, or other action intended to cause a person to believe that, if the person did not perform or provide the labor or services, that person or another person would suffer bodily harm or physical restraint; physically restraining or threatening to physically restrain a person; abuse or threatened abuse of the legal process; knowingly destroying, concealing, removing, confiscating, or possessing any actual or purported passport or other immigration document, or any other actual or purported government identification document, of another person; or blackmail. It includes forced prostitution or sexual services, domestic servitude, bonded sweatshop labor, or other debt bondage. See also **trafficking** [HUMAN TRAFFICKING].

INVOLUNTARY TRUST   see **trust** [CONSTRUCTIVE [INVOLUNTARY] TRUST].

IOLTA   acronym for Interest on Lawyers' Trust Accounts. Program in some states where lawyers holding funds belonging to clients, which are too small or short-term for an individual interest-bearing account, deposit such funds into a special bank account containing similar funds from other lawyers. The interest generated from the pooled account helps fund legal programs for the needy.

IPSE DIXIT   *(ĭp'-sā dĭks'-ĭt)* Lat.: he himself said it. Refers to an assertion the sole authority for which is that the speaker has said it.

IPSO FACTO   *(ĭp'-sō făk'-toō)* Lat.: by the fact itself; in and of itself.

IPSO JURE   *(ĭp'-sō jū'-rā)* Lat.: by the law itself; merely by the law.

IRA   see **Individual Retirement Account.**

IRB [INDUSTRIAL RESERVE BOND]   see **guaranteed security.** Also, Individual Retirement Bond.

IRC   see **Internal Revenue Code.**

IRREFRAGABLE   indisputable, not to be refuted or denied.

IRREGULAR RENDITION see **rendition.**

IRRELEVANT   immaterial; not relevant; generally used in the context of a rule of evidence, whereby one party objects to the introduction at trial of evidence that is not connected to the issue being decided.

IRREPARABLE INJURY [DAMAGE; HARM] a type of **injury** for which no **remedy at law (damages)** suffices, and that thus requires a **court of equity** to intervene, often by issuing an **injunction** to prevent the conduct or conditions that are causing or threatening the injury. In fact, showing of imminent irreparable injury is ordinarily prerequisite to a request for an injunction.

IRRESISTIBLE IMPULSE TEST   see **insanity [IRRESISTIBLE IMPULSE TEST].**

IRS see **Internal Revenue Service.**

ISSUE 1. as a verb, to put into circulation, as to a buyer. 2. In **corporation** law, a **STOCK ISSUE** is the process by which a corporation authorizes, executes and delivers shares of stock for sale to the public. The term also describes the shares offered by the corporation at a particular time. 3. in the law of **real property,** the noun issue means descendants.

EXAMPLE: Latonya's will declared that any part of her estate not specifically distributed to someone else be divided among her *issue.* Her children tried to claim the full amount of this residual property, but, as the children were reminded by the court in a lawsuit against them, "issue" refers to all descendants, including children, grandchildren and other more remote descendants.

4. in legal practice, a point of fact or law disputed between **parties** to the **litigation,** generally an assertion by one side and a denial by the other.

ISSUED see **when issued.**

ISSUE PRECLUSION   the rendering of a decision that precludes the issue decided from being relitigated. See **collateral estoppel; res judicata.**

ITEMIZED DEDUCTIONS   see **deductions [ITEMIZED DEDUCTIONS].**

J

J. abbreviation for a **judge** or justice. Other abbreviations include **A.J.**, Associate Judge/Justice; **C.J.**, Chief Judge/Justice; **J.A.G.**, Judge Advocate General; **JJ.**, Judges/Justices; **J.P.**, Justice of the Peace; **L.J.**, Law Judge; **P.J.**, Presiding Judge.

JAG abbreviation for Judge Advocate General; a designation used in **military justice.**

JAIL place used for the detention of persons in the lawful custody of the government, such as a person accused of a crime who is held for **trial,** or a person convicted of a crime who is serving a **sentence.** If the inmate is confined in a local police station, it is generally referred to as a **LOCK-UP;** if temporarily confined in a courthouse during a trial, it is generally called a **HOLDING CELL;** if confined in a county facility for a period of 18 months or less, it is often called a **WORKHOUSE.** Most long-term confinement is now held in a **CORRECTIONAL FACILITY** such as the Federal Correctional Institution at [particular place]. These are referred to as **FCI** at [place]. Older usage called such long-term confinement facilities **PRISONS** or **PENITENTIARIES.** See **penal institution.**

JAILHOUSE LAWYER **inmate** who, through self-study of law, assists fellow inmates in the preparation of their appeals but does not possess formal training and is not licensed to practice law. Reliance upon jailhouse lawyers is often the only means by which indigent prisoners can be assured of access to the courts. Thus, the use of such assistance has been declared to be constitutionally protected.

J.D. Juris Doctor. Degree awarded today upon completion of formal legal studies by most American law schools. The degree was formerly designated **LL.B.**

JENCKS ACT [RULE] a statute entitling a criminal **defendant** in a federal prosecution to **discover** any **witness** statement against him or her that is relevant to the witness's testimony and that is in the possession of the United States government. It was enacted after the U.S. Supreme Court held that defendants were entitled to such material. Since the Act restricts the defendant's access to such material until after the witness has testified in court, pretrial discovery of such material is not permitted. Testimony of a **grand jury** witness is specifically included in the definition of "statement" by virtue of a later-enacted amendment to the Act.

JEOPARDY   the danger of conviction and punishment in which a person is placed when he or she is put on trial for a criminal offense. See **double jeopardy.**

JEOPARDY ASSESSMENT   see **assessment of deficiency [JEOPARDY ASSESSMENT].**

JJ.   abbreviation for judges or justices.

JOBBER   a middleman in the **sale** of **goods;** one who buys from a **wholesaler** and sells to a retailer. A jobber, who actually purchases goods himself or herself and then resells them, is distinguished from a **broker** or **agent,** who sells goods on another's behalf.

JOBS CREDIT   see **tax credit [TARGETED JOBS CREDIT].**

JOHN/JANE DOE   fictional names used to identify persons in a hypothetical situation in order to explain an issue; name used when a person refuses to identify himself or herself or when a person cannot be identified.

JOINDER   uniting of several **causes of action** or **parties** in a single **suit.** In federal practice, a party may join as many claims as he or she has against the opposing party. Compare **class action; impleader; misjoinder.**

COMPULSORY JOINDER   mandatory joining of a person needed in an action for a just adjudication of the **controversy.** All related claims against another must be joined, or the claimant faces the possibility of being barred from **litigating** claims separately on the grounds that such action constitutes **multiplicity of suits.** A defendant must raise related claims as compulsory **counterclaims.**

JOINDER OF ACTIONS OR CLAIMS   the joinder of two or more claims or actions in a single lawsuit. See **PERMISSIVE JOINDER** (below).

JOINDER OF ISSUE   the act by which an issue is formally fashioned and structured for the purpose of its consideration and determination by a court. Under the code system of pleading, an issue is joined when one side asserts a set of facts and the other side denies it. In criminal law joinder of issue occurs when the defendant pleads "not guilty" in response to an indictment filed against him or her.

JOINDER OF PARTIES   the naming of a person or entity as a party to a lawsuit. See **COMPULSORY JOINDER** (above) and **PERMISSIVE JOINDER** (below).

MISJOINDER the improper joinder of a party or a claim. In **civil** cases, the remedy is to remove the improper party or claim from the suit. In **criminal** cases, the remedy is a separate trial of the misjoinder offenses or defendants.. This remedy is also available to criminal defendants if the misjoinder prejudices any of the defendants. See **misjoinder.**

PERMISSIVE JOINDER the joining of persons, so that in a single lawsuit a plaintiff may raise all his or her unrelated claims against another party with the court **severing** claims that ought not be tried together. A defendant may **plead** in his or her **answer** any **PERMISSIVE COUNTERCLAIMS** against the plaintiff.

JOINDER OF ISSUE the act by which an **issue** is formally structured for its determination by a court.

JOINT a common as opposed to individual interest or liability.

JOINT ACCOUNT a bank account belonging to two or more persons, with funds in **JOINT TENANCY** (see **tenancy**).

JOINT AND SEVERAL refers to the sharing of rights and **liabilities** among a group of persons collectively and also individually. Thus, if **defendants** in a **negligence** suit are jointly and severally liable, all may be sued together or any one may be sued for **satisfaction** to the injured party.

EXAMPLE: Emma is injured when a bottle of soda she purchased at a store explodes. She sues both the owner of the store and the manufacturer of the soda. If they are both found liable, their liability will probably be *joint and several.* Emma may choose to collect her entire damage award from one of the parties or may apportion the total owed to her between the two defendants in any manner she chooses.

See **contribution; indemnity.** Compare **severally.**

JOINT CUSTODY see **custody of children.**

JOINT ENTERPRISE undertaking founded on mutual agreement of parties; essential elements are agreement, common purpose, community of interest and equal right of control. Those who engage in a joint enterprise that is unlawful or causes injury may be **liable** as **joint tortfeasors, accessories** or **conspirators.**

JOINT LIABILITY shared **liability** that allows a sued person the right to insist that others be sued jointly with him.

JOINT LIVES a period that lasts until the death of the last to survive of two or more specified persons.

JOINT OWNERSHIP see **joint tenancy [ownership]**.

JOINT RETURN see **return, income tax [JOINT RETURN]**.

JOINT STOCK COMPANY see **company [JOINT STOCK COMPANY]**.

JOINT TENANCY [OWNERSHIP] an interest in property consisting of a single **estate** in land or other property owned by two or more persons, created by the same grantor or grantors under one **instrument** and, at one time, with all such persons having an equal right to share in the use and enjoyment of the property during their respective lives and being entitled to the full ownership of such property upon the death of each other such person. The property can be conveyed by a **deed** joined in by all the co-tenants or by a forced judicial **partition.** See **survivorship; unities.**

JOINT TORTFEASORS two or more persons who owe to another person the same **duty** and whose **negligence** results in injury to such other person, thereby rendering the tortfeasors both **jointly and severally** [individually] **liable** for the injury. To be liable as joint tortfeasors, the parties either must act in concert or must by independent acts cause a single injury.

EXAMPLE: Two friends practice their hunting skills on a reservation that does not permit hunting. A hiker is injured by a stray bullet from one of the friend's guns. Since it cannot be determined which friend shot the bullet that injured the hiker, both friends are liable for the injury as **joint tortfeasors.**

See **contribution**. Compare **conspiracy.**

JOINTURE an **estate** or **property** secured to a prospective wife as a marriage settlement, to be **enjoyed** by her after her husband's decease. The estate existed under the **common law** as a means of protecting the wife's future, upon the death of her husband, in place of **dower.**

JOINT VENTURE a business undertaking by two or more parties in which profits, losses and control are shared. Though the term is often synonymous with **partnership,** a joint venture may indicate an enterprise of more limited scope and duration, though there is the same mutual **liability** of the participants for debts and **torts** of the venture.

EXAMPLE: Several business associates develop a new method of marketing pet food. A *joint venture* is established, limiting business activity to the marketing scheme and obliging each associate to contribute enough money for the new company to last one year. If the company is not successful by that time, any remaining money will be distributed to the associates and the venture will be dissolved.

JONES ACT the federal statute that gives a sailor who suffers a personal injury in the course of employment, or the personal representative of a sailor who dies as the result of a personal injury suffered in the course of employment, the right to sue for **damages** at law. A federal statute provides that all statutes modifying or extending the common law right or remedy in cases of personal injury to railway employees shall apply to sailors. See also **Federal Employers Liability Act.**

JOURNALIST'S [NEWSPERSON'S] PRIVILEGE some states have enacted **shield laws** granting media persons the privilege of declining to reveal confidential sources of information. No constitutional basis for such a privilege has been found in the **First Amendment's** guarantee of freedom of the press. Such a privilege, however, must yield to a defendant's need for discovery and for a fair trial as constitutionally granted under the **Sixth Amendment** and similarly must yield in any circumstance where the interests of justice so require. However, disclosure can only be required if **relevant** to issues at trial.

JOYRIDING the illegal taking of an automobile for the purpose of using if for a short period of time. Joyriding is a specific offense, usually lesser in degree than **larceny,** and is in many states punishable by fines and/or imprisonment. In other states, it is one of many acts that may constitute the more serious crime of **larceny.**

J.P. abbreviation for Justice of the Peace.

JUDGE one who conducts trials or presides over a court of justice. Judges determine controversies between parties based upon evidence and legal argument presented. They are not investigators or advisors.

JUDGE-MADE LAW law made in the **common law** tradition; law arrived at by judicial **precedent** rather than by statute.

JUDGMENT the determination of a court of competent **jurisdiction** upon matters submitted to it; a final determination of the rights of the **parties** to a lawsuit. See **recall a judgment; warrant [WARRANT TO SATISFY JUDGMENT].** Legal circles favor the spelling as judgment instead of judgement.

COGNOVIT JUDGMENT see **confession of judgment.**

CONFESSION OF JUDGMENT see **confession of judgment.**

DEFAULT JUDGMENT a judgment entered on behalf of a plaintiff when the defendant **defaults**, or fails to appear in the proceeding. See **default judgment.**

ERRONEOUS JUDGMENT see **erroneous** [**ERRONEOUS JUDGMENT**].

ESTOPPEL BY JUDGMENT estoppel brought about by the judgment of a court because a similar question or fact in dispute has been determined by a court of competent jurisdiction between the same parties or their **privies.**

FINAL JUDGMENT a conclusive determination of the rights of the parties, disposing of the entire **controversy** before the court, or of some separable portion of the dispute, so that immediately after the judgment, or an appeal therefrom, the enforcement of that judgment can be made. The term also refers to the **sentence** imposed in a criminal case. See **final decision.**

JUDGMENT BY DEFAULT see **default; default judgment.**

JUDGMENT IN PERSONAM see **PERSONAL JUDGMENT** (below).

JUDGMENT IN REM one pronounced upon the status of a particular subject matter, property or thing, as opposed to one pronounced upon persons.

JUDGMENT N.O.V. see **n.o.v.**

JUDGMENT OF CONVICTION the **sentence** in a criminal case formally entered in the clerk's records.

JUDGMENT OF DISMISSAL an order that finally disposes of a matter without a trial of the issues involved on their merits. See **dismissal**.

JUDGMENT ON THE MERITS a binding judgment determined by analysis and adjudication of the factual issues presented, rather than by the existence of a technical or **procedural** defect that requires one party to prevail.

EXAMPLE: Robin files a lawsuit but inadvertently names the wrong parties as defendants. When her case comes to trial, it may be dismissed as against the people she wanted to sue because they were not named. That dismissal would not be a *judgment on the merits,* since the court's action in doing so is necessitated by a procedural error committed by Robin.

JUDGMENT ON THE PLEADINGS see **SUMMARY JUDGMENT** (below).

PERSONAL JUDGMENT a judgment rendered against an individual or an entity such as a corporation for the payment of money damages. To be distinguished from a JUDGMENT IN REM (above). See **in personam; personal judgment.**

SUMMARY JUDGMENT a pre-verdict judgment rendered by the court on the basis of the pleadings because no material issue of fact exists and one party or the other is entitled to judgment as a matter of law. Either party may move for summary judgment at any time after all pleadings have been filed. See **summary judgment.**

JUDGMENT CREDITOR a **creditor** who has obtained against a **debtor** a **judgment** through which the creditor can obtain the sum due him or her. The effect of becoming a judgment creditor is to create against other creditors a certain priority right to have the debt satisfied out of the debtor's assets, and to extend the life of the claim under the **statute of limitations** so that the judgment debt may be sued upon for a longer period than would be possible for a debt without a judgment.

JUDGMENT DEBTOR a person against whom there is a legal **judgment** for repayment of a **debt.** The effect of becoming a judgment debtor is that the debtor's property may be subject to **creditor's** claims. See **creditor's bill; garnishment; lien; sheriff's sale; writ of execution.** Compare **bankruptcy; judgment creditor.**

JUDGMENT PROOF a person who lacks the financial resources necessary to satisfy a judgment for **damages** or whose wages or property is protected from judicial **attachment** by law.

JUDICATURE see **judiciary.**

JUDICIAL ACTIVISM the theory of judicial behavior that advocates basing decisions not on the judicial **precedent** but on achieving what the court perceives to be for the public welfare, or what the court determines to be fair and just on the facts before it. Compare **judicial restraint.**

JUDICIAL ADMISSION see **stipulation.**

JUDICIAL DISCRETION see **discretion.**

JUDICIAL ECONOMY the most efficient use of judicial resources; often used as the rationale underlying doctrines in civil procedure such as **permissive joinder** or **res judicata,** and sometimes offered as the justification for a **judge's** decision in a particular case.

JUDICIAL IMMUNITY the immunity of a judge from civil liability for any acts performed in the judge's official capacity. The immunity is absolute provided only that the judge is acting within his or her jurisdiction. The scope of the judge's jurisdiction must be construed broadly to protect the court's independence; therefore, the judge will not be deprived of immunity because the action taken was in error, was done maliciously, or was in excess of the judge's authority; rather, the judge will be subject to liability only when the action taken was in clear absence of all jurisdiction. Where the relief sought is **injunctive** or **declaratory** and not money damages, immunity is not provided under the **Civil Rights Act of 1964** and state courts may be sued for such relief.

JUDICIAL NOTICE the court's recognition of facts that can be confirmed by consulting sources of unquestioned accuracy, thus removing the burden of producing **evidence** to prove these facts. A court can admit facts that are common knowledge to an average, well-informed citizen.

EXAMPLE: Kristen claims that on the day of the accident the roads were very slick as a result of a torrential downpour. However, the victim of the accident brings in several weather maps and reports showing that for seven days prior to and including the day of the accident, there was not a single raindrop. A court can take *judicial notice* of the maps and reports.

JUDICIAL RESTRAINT the theory of judicial behavior that advocates basing decisions on grounds that have been previously defined by judicial **precedent** rather than on the basis of achieving some public good, which is viewed as the proper role of the **legislature.** Compare **judicial activism.**

JUDICIAL REVIEW the review by a court of law of some act, or failure to act, by a government official or entity, or by some other legally appointed person or organized body; the review of the decision of a **trial** court by an **appellate** court.

In a constitutional law context, judicial review expresses the concept first articulated in *Marbury* v. *Madison,* 5 U.S. (1 Cranch) 137 (1803) that it is "the province and the duty of the judicial department to say what the law is." Under this doctrine the U.S. Supreme Court and the highest courts of every state have assumed the power and responsibility to decide the constitutionality of the acts of the legislative and executive branches of their respective jurisdictions.

JUDICIAL SALE see **sale [FORCED SALE]; sheriff's sale [judicial sale].**

JUDICIARY that department of government established to interpret and administer the law. The courts and all those connected with the practice of law.

JUMP BAIL colloquial expression meaning to leave the **jurisdiction** or to avoid **appearance** as a **defendant** in a **criminal** trial after **bail** has been posted, thus causing a **forfeiture** of bail: to **abscond** after the posting of bail. See **flight.**

JUMP CITATION see **pinpoint citation.**

JURAL of or pertaining to law or justice.

JURAT *(jūr'-ät)* Lat.: has been sworn. The clause at the end of an **affidavit** with the date, location and person before whom the statement was sworn.

JURE UXORIS *(jû'-rē ū-xō-rĭs)* Lat.: right of the wife.

JURIS *(jûr'-ĭs)* Lat.: of law.

JURISDICTION 1. power to hear and determine a case; may be established and described with reference to a particular subject or to parties in a particular category. In addition to power to adjudicate, a valid exercise of jurisdiction requires fair **notice** and opportunity for affected parties to be heard. 2. the geographic or political entity governed by a particular legal system or body of laws. The word "jurisdiction" is also used to refer to particular legal systems, as in "the law varies in different jurisdictions," and in the sense of territory (coupled with authority to reach conduct within the territory), as in "within the jurisdiction of X state."

APPELLATE JURISDICTION the power vested in a superior **tribunal** to correct legal errors of inferior tribunals and to revise their **judgments** accordingly.

CONCURRENT JURISDICTION equal jurisdiction; jurisdiction exercisable by different courts at the same time, over the same subject matter and within the same territory, so that litigants may, in the first instance, resort to either court.

DIVERSITY JURISDICTION jurisdiction that federal courts have when the opposing parties are from different states.

IN PERSONAM JURISDICTION jurisdiction over the person of the **defendant;** necessary where the action is **in personam.**

SUBJECT MATTER JURISDICTION the **competency** of the court to hear and determine a particular category of cases.

See **ancillary jurisdiction; federal question jurisdiction; limited jurisdiction; original jurisdiction; pendent jurisdiction; territorial jurisdiction; title jurisdiction.**

JURISDICTIONAL AMOUNT the minimum value a lawsuit must have for certain courts to have **jurisdiction** to hear the case. The method of determining the jurisdictional amount may vary with the nature of the case; it may be the amount of **damages** claimed, money demanded, the value of **property** in disputed ownership, or the value of a claimed right. In some classes of federal cases, for example, a minimum amount of $10,000 must be in controversy to confer jurisdiction on the federal courts.

JURIS DOCTOR see **J.D.**

JURIS IGNORANTIA EST CUM NOSTRUM IGNORAMUS (*jû'-rĭs ĭg-nō-rän'-shē-ā ĕst kūm nōs'-trŭm ĭg-nō-rä'-mŭs*) Lat.: it is ignorance of the law when we are unfamiliar with our own rights.

JURISPRUDENCE 1. the science of law; the study of the structure of legal systems, such as equity, and of the principles underlying that system; 2. a collective term denoting the course of judicial decision, i.e., case law, as opposed to legislation; 3. sometimes a synonym for law.

JURIST 1. a legal scholar; one versed in law, particularly the **civil law** or the law of nations; 2. a judge.

JUROR 1. person sworn as member of a **jury;** 2. person selected for jury duty, but not yet chosen for a particular case.

JURY a group, composed of the peers of the **parties** or a cross section of the community, summoned and sworn to decide on the facts in issue at a **trial.**

BLUE RIBBON JURY a jury that was chosen from prominent members of the community, such as well-educated persons or persons in positions of high responsibility, thought to be particularly well qualified to serve as jurors. These juries were used for certain highly publicized cases where ordinary juries were thought to be too influenced to judge impartially. Such special juries raised serious constitutional questions of the right to trial by a jury of one's peers and so are no longer used.

EXAMPLE: The murder of a beautiful actress made headlines and television reports across the nation. When someone was finally arrested for the crime, a *blue ribbon jury* was chosen from among bankers, doctors and leaders of the business community. These people were selected for their perceived ability to separate the news stories from the facts they would hear at trial.

DE FACTO JURY see **de facto** [**DE FACTO JURY**].

GRAND JURY a jury to determine whether the facts and accusations presented by the **prosecutor** warrant an **indictment** and eventual trial of the **accused;** called grand because of the relatively large number of jurors **impaneled** (traditionally 23) as compared with a **PETIT JURY**.

JURY OF THE VICINAGE literally, a jury from the neighborhood where a crime was committed; a jury of peers. See **vicinage.**

JURY NULLIFICATION see **nullification.**

PETIT [PETTY] JURY ordinary trial jury, whose function is to determine issues of fact in **civil** and **criminal** cases and to reach a **verdict** in conjunction with those **findings.** While the number of jurors has historically been twelve, many states now permit six-member juries in civil cases, and some states permit six-member juries to hear criminal cases as well.

POLLING THE JURY the practice of a **judge** asking each individual **juror** his or her decision on the **verdict** which has been rendered. The polling of the jury usually takes place at the request of a criminal defendant who has been convicted or a party to a civil suit who has lost, and occurs after the foreman of the jury has announced the verdict of the jury.

See **evidence; hung jury.**

JURY TRIAL the trial of an issue of **fact** before a **jury.** The parties to the action present their evidence to the jury. The judge then instructs the jury as to how the law applies to their **findings of fact.** The jury **deliberates** and renders its **verdict.** The Sixth Amendment to the Federal Constitution guarantees a jury trial to those accused of crime.

JURY VOIR DIRE see **voir dire.**

JUS ACCRESCENDI *(jūs à-krĕ-sĕn'-dī)* Lat.: right of survivorship. See **joint tenancy [OWNERSHIP].**

JUST COMPENSATION full **indemnity** for the loss or damage sustained by the owner of property taken or injured under the power of **eminent domain.** The measure generally used is the fair **market value** of the property at the time of taking.

JUST DESERTS see **desert [JUST DESERTS]**

JUS TERTII *(yūs tĕr'-shē-ī)* Lat.: the right of a third; the legal right of a third. The term often appears in the context of **actions** involving claims of **title** to **real property,** where it is said that because a possessor's title is good against all the world except those with a better title, one seeking to oust a possessor must do so on the strength of his or her own title, and may not rely on a *jus tertii,* or the better title held by a third party.

JUSTICE a **judge.** Often the formal title of a judge of a high court, such as the nine Justices of the United States Supreme Court. In

New York, however, justices are trial judges in the trial courts (which are called the Supreme Court) and judges are in the highest court (the Court of Appeals).

ADMINISTRATION OF JUSTICE judgments by legal processes; the handing out of punishment or reward; the application of law in a manner that is right and equitable.

SYSTEM OF JUSTICE societal method of applying the laws evenly such that all persons are treated fairly and receive the same rights. A standard of conduct holding persons to their legal and moral obligations to others.

JUSTICE OF THE PEACE a judicial officer of inferior rank, who presides in a court of statutorily limited **civil jurisdiction** and who is also a conservator of the peace with limited jurisdiction in criminal **proceedings, prosecutions,** and commitment of offenders, as fixed by **statute.**

JUSTICIABLE 1. capable of being tried in a court of law or **equity;** 2. feasible for a court to carry out and enforce its decision, as opposed to having **jurisdiction**—the authority to hear a case. A court can have jurisdiction, but at the same time have a nonjusticiable **issue** before it.

EXAMPLE: A governor is required by law to extradite a person sought by another state when that state institutes proper legal proceedings. Still, the governor may decide not to extradite if, for example, he or she sees an obvious life-threatening situation should the person be returned to the state seeking him or her. In such instances, a court will usually deem the failure to extradite as a *nonjusticiable* controversy and will take no action to force the governor to extradite.

JUSTICIABLE CONTROVERSY a real **controversy** appropriate for judicial determination, as distinguished from a hypothetical dispute; a dispute that involves legal relations of **parties** who have real adverse **interests,** and upon whom **judgment** may effectively operate through a conclusive **decree.**

JUSTIFIABLE HOMICIDE see **homicide.**

JUSTIFICATION 1. just and lawful cause or excuse; 2. showing in court sufficient reason the **defendant** did what he or she is called upon to **answer** to, so as to excuse liability.

JUVENILE COURTS tribunals designed to treat **youthful offenders** separately from adults. The purpose of this has been to place the state, through the presiding judge, in the position of **parens**

patriae, to replace the adversary nature of normal proceedings with paternal concern for the child's well-being.

JUVENILE DELINQUENT   a **minor** who has committed an offense ordinarily punishable by criminal processes, but who is under the age, set by **statute,** for criminal responsibility. When a juvenile commits an offense it is considered an act of **JUVENILE DELINQUENCY.** See **juvenile courts.**

K

K   abbreviation for **contract.**

KANGAROO COURT   a court that has no legal authority and that disregards all the rights normally afforded to persons; its conclusions are not legally binding. This is a slang term referring to a court that is biased against a party and thus renders an unfair **verdict** or **judgment.**

KEOGH PLAN   see **retirement plans [KEOGH PLANS].**

KEY ENCRYPTION   see **digital certificate.**

KEY NUMBERS   a numbering system used by the West Publishing Company in their publications to break down legal research into manageable topic areas with subcategories. It is a quick and useful method of finding **cases** pertaining to a given subject.

KICKBACK   the practice of a **seller** of **goods** or services paying the purchasing agent of those goods or services a portion of the purchase price in order to induce the agent to enter into the transaction. In the context of public officials, purchasing goods or services for a government entity, kickbacks are plainly illegal, since they cause the official to act in his or her own, not the public's, interest. In most commercial contexts, they are illegal and prohibited by criminal **commercial bribery** statutes. The principal of the purchasing agent may also have a cause of action against the agent to recover the amount of the bribery. For tax purposes, amounts paid as kickbacks or bribes generally are not deductible.

KIDNAPPING   unlawful carrying away of a person against his or her will; **false imprisonment** coupled with removal of the victim to another place. Kidnapping was only a **misdemeanor** in **common law,** but is a serious **felony** in the United States. Compare **abduction.** See **ransom.**

KIN [KINSHIP]   see **consanguinity.**

KIND   see **in kind.**

KIND ARBITRAGE   see **arbitrage [KIND ARBITRAGE].**

KING'S [QUEEN'S] BENCH   Court of King's Bench or Court of Queen's Bench (depending on the reigning monarch); the highest

English **common law** court, both civil and criminal, so called because the king or queen formerly presided; now known as the King's Bench or Queen's Bench Division of the High Court of Justice, embracing the **jurisdiction** of the former Courts of Exchequer and Courts of Common Pleas.

KITING see **check kiting.**

KNOWINGLY see **mens rea.**

KORAN Islamic holy book considered by Muslims to be the source of Islamic law. Often spelled Quran.

L

LABOR-MANAGEMENT RELATIONS ACT see **Taft-Hartley Act.**

LABOR ORGANIZATION [UNION] any association of workers whose main purpose is to bargain on behalf of workers with employers about the terms and conditions of employment including grievances, labor disputes, wages, rates of pay, hours of employment, or conditions of work.

In England, unions were originally indictable as criminal **conspiracies.** When statutes were enacted freeing them from this criminal **liability** they were still condemned by the courts as being organizations in restraint of trade, and therefore not deserving legal enforcement of their rights, an attitude that persisted for some time in the United States. Today, labor unions are recognized in full by the law and are subject to regulation by the federal government under the **National Labor Relations Act.** See also **closed shop; union shop.** Compare **cooperative association.**

LABOR PRACTICE see **unfair labor practice.**

LABOR TRAFFICKING see **trafficking [HUMAN TRAFFICKING].**

LACHES a doctrine providing a party an **EQUITABLE DEFENSE** (see **defense**) where long-neglected rights are sought to be enforced against him or her. Laches signifies an undue lapse of time in enforcing a right of **action,** and **negligence** in failing to act more promptly. It recognizes that on account of the delay the defendant's ability to defend may be unfairly impaired because **witnesses** or **evidence** may have become unavailable or been lost. The doctrine also recognizes that if the delay has led the adverse party to change his or her position as to the **property** or right in question, it is inequitable to allow the negligent delaying party to be preferred in his or her legal right. The consequent barring of the negligent party's action is a kind of equitable **estoppel** known as **ESTOPPEL BY LACHES.**

EXAMPLE: Believing that he had good title to property, Kareem constructs an office building and fully rents it out. George watches Kareem construct the building and waits an additional ten years before asserting an ownership interest in the property. A court might apply the doctrine of *laches* and bar George's claim for two reasons.

George was aware of the construction and took no action until the building was completed, a point at which Kareem had invested a considerable amount of money. Also, George took an inordinate amount of time to raise his claim.

LADING, BILL OF see **bill of lading.**

LAME DUCK an elected official who has not been reelected but who continues to serve until his or her present term of office expires.

LAND 1. **real estate** or **real property,** or any tract that may be **conveyed** by **deed.** 2. an **estate** or **interest** in real property; often refers not only to the earth itself but also to things of a permanent nature found or affixed there. See **grant [LAND GRANT]; run with the land; tide land**.

LANDLORD one who leases **real property.** See **lease.**

LANDLORD'S LIEN see **lien [LANDLORD'S LIEN].**

LANDMARK CASE [DECISION] legal decision of great magnitude. A **precedent**-setting decision. A case such as *Miranda* v. *Arizona,* 384 U.S. 436 (1966) was a landmark case in the area of the rights of criminal suspects and led to the requirement that police give "Miranda rights" to a suspect before taking a statement. See **Miranda rule [warnings].**

LANDRUM-GRIFFIN ACT officially known as the Labor-Management Reporting and Disclosure Act, it created broad reporting and disclosure provisions to eliminate or prevent improper practices on the part of labor organizations, employers, labor relation consultants, their officers and representatives.

LAND TRUST also called an **ILLINOIS LAND TRUST.** This device vests **title** to **real property** in the name of a **trustee** under a recorded deed of trust while a second unrecorded agreement between the trustee and the **beneficiaries** declares the trustee to be vested with full **legal** and **equitable** title subject to certain specified rights of the beneficiaries that are declared to be personal property of the beneficiaries.

LANHAM ACT see **trademark [LANHAM ACT].**

LAPSE to expire. Generally refers to termination of a right or **privilege** that can no longer be exercised because of a particular contingency or the passage of time. See **antilapse statutes.**

EXAMPLE: Ethel signs a 30-day option to purchase a home. That option gives her the exclusive right to purchase the home within 30 days. If 30 days expire and Ethel does not purchase the house, the option *lapses.*

LARCENY the **felonious** taking and carrying away of the **personal property** of another, without his or her consent, by a person not entitled to **possession,** with intent to deprive the owner of the property and to convert it to the use of the taker or another person other than the owner.

Larceny is sometimes classified as either GRAND LARCENY or PETIT [PETTY] LARCENY, according to the value of the property taken or the method employed. Compare **burglary; embezzlement; robbery.**

LAST ANTECEDENT DOCTRINE in statutory **construction,** the doctrine under which relative or modifying phrases are to be applied only to words immediately preceding them, and are not to be construed as extending to more remote phrases unless this is clearly required by the context of the statute or the reading of it as a whole.

LAST CLEAR CHANCE the doctrine that a **defendant** may still be **liable** for the injuries he or she caused, even though the **plaintiff** was guilty of CONTRIBUTORY NEGLIGENCE (see **negligence**), if the defendant could have avoided injury to the plaintiff by exercising ordinary care at the last moment and after the plaintiff's negligence had ceased.

EXAMPLE: A passerby without a hard hat walks on a construction site that is clearly marked "Hard Hats Required." A worker is throwing garbage out of a window so that it will fall into a garbage dump below. One of the pieces of garbage hits the passerby. Although the passerby is at fault for not wearing a hard hat, the worker may be held liable since he had the *last clear chance* to avoid the injury either by being more careful with the garbage or by carrying it to the dump site.

LAST-IN, FIRST-OUT [LIFO] see **first-in, first-out [FIFO]; inventory.**

LAST WILL AND TESTAMENT see **will.**

LAT. abbreviation for Latin.

LATENT AMBIGUITY language of legal effect that can be interpreted to have more than one meaning. **Extrinsic evidence,** when allowable, is often necessary to determine the correct interpretation of a latent ambiguity. In **contract** law, a latent ambiguity that one party interprets differently from the other party can prevent the **meeting of the minds** necessary to the formation of a valid contract.

LATENT DEFECT a defect that is hidden from knowledge as well as from sight and one that would not be discovered even by the exercise of ordinary and reasonable care.

EXAMPLE: A part of a new car engine was prone to wearing down after a few hundred miles, causing the engine to stop immediately. The part was inside the engine and could not be detected by even a very thorough examination unless the engine was dismantled. The faulty part was a *latent defect* of the engine.

Compare **inherent defect; patent defect.** See **products liability; warranty** [WARRANTY OF HABITABILITY].

LATERAL SUPPORT an owner of **real property** has the right to have one's land, in its natural condition, supported and held in place from the sides by one's neighbor's land.

LAW 1. the legislative pronouncement of rules to guide one's actions in society; 2. the total of those rules of conduct put in force by legislative authority or court decisions, or established by local custom. See also **case law; common law; session laws; statute; substantive law; uniform laws; wager of law.**

AT LAW see **at law.**

LAW, CHOICE OF see **conflict of law [choice of law].**

LAW DIV. abbreviation for Law Division.

LAWFUL any act performed within the bounds of law or authorized by law and that does not give rise to any legal liability; activity that is not illegal and is not contrary to public policy.

LAW MERCHANT a body of **commercial law** governing merchants in England, particularly noted for contributions to the law of **negotiable instruments.** The law merchant was the **common law's** recognition of usages and procedures that had developed over a long period among merchants in England and other European countries. As part of the common law of England, it was incorporated into American law and has been largely supplemented by common law evolution and statutory enactment.

LAW OF ADMIRALTY see **maritime law.**

LAW OF CAPTURE see **capture.**

LAW OF THE CASE doctrine whereby courts will refuse to consider matters of law that have been already **adjudicated** by **motion** or **appeal** in the same cause; reflects the courts' unwillingness to reopen **issues** already finally determined in a suit.

EXAMPLE: A judge schedules a pre-trial hearing to decide what evidence will be allowed at trial. Each party is given an opportunity to make arguments, and the judge decides not to allow a statement by one of the plaintiff's witnesses. At trial, the plaintiff attempts to argue for the introduction of the statement. Because of the pre-trial decision, the judge applies the *law of the case* doctrine and refuses to allow the introduction of the statement.

Compare **collateral [COLLATERAL ESTOPPEL]; double jeopardy.**

LAW OF THE LAND 1. phrase first used in **Magna Carta** to refer to the then established law of the kingdom as distinguished from Roman or **civil law;** 2. today, basic principles of justice in agreement with **due process of law;** those rights that the legislature cannot abolish or significantly limit, because they are fundamental to our system of liberty and justice. 3. the law as developed by the courts or in **statutes** in pursuance of those basic principles or rights. The United States Constitution (Article 6, Section 2) establishes itself, and laws made under its authority, and treaties of the United States, as the "supreme law of the land."

LAW, QUESTION OF see **question of law.**

LAW REPORTS see **advance sheets; reports.**

LAWSUIT see **suit.**

LAWYER see **attorney.**

LAY WITNESS any **witness** not **testifying** as an **expert witness** and who is thereby generally precluded from testifying in the form of an **opinion.** However, under federal rules a "lay witness" is able to testify in the form of an opinion or inference if the testimony is (a) rationally based on the perceptions of the witness, and (b) helpful to a clear understanding of his or her testimony or the determination of a fact in issue. The witness may be a **LAY EXPERT WITNESS,** meaning a person whose expertise or special competence derives from experience in a field of endeavor rather than from studies or diplomas.

LEADERSHIP PACS see **political action committee [LEADERSHIP PACS].**

LEADING CASE a case continually cited for a proposition of law that controls in that particular area. For example, *Katz* v. *United States,* 389 U.S. 347 (1967), is a leading case in the area of **search and seizure,** and *Marbury* v. *Madison,* 5 U.S. (1 Cranch) 137 (1803), is a leading case in constitutional law. See also **landmark.**

LEADING QUESTION a question posed by a trial lawyer that is sometimes improper because it suggests to the **witness** the answer he or she is to deliver, or in effect prompts answers in disregard of actual memory.

EXAMPLE: In direct examination during the trial, the witness is asked, "Isn't it true that you saw Ilona standing outside the store waiting for a friend when the robbery occurred?" That question will be objected to as a *leading question* since it suggests to the witness how he or she should explain or recall the event, instead of simply inquiring how the event actually took place. However, leading questions are proper as part of cross-examination since the object of such examination is to test the credibility of the statement made during direct examination.

LEASE   1. an agreement by the **lessor** temporarily to give up **possession** of **property** while retaining legal ownership (**title**); 2. an agreement by the owner **landlord** to turn over, for all purposes not prohibited by terms of the lease, specifically described **premises** to the exclusive possession of the **lessee** for a definite period and for a **consideration** called **rent.** See **release [LEASE AND RELEASE].**

LEASE-PURCHASE see **mortgage [LEASE-PURCHASE].**

NET LEASE while normally a landlord pays costs such as insurance, maintenance, and taxes, under a net lease those costs are borne by the tenant, in addition to rent.

PROPRIETARY LEASE the kind of lease that the resident/stockholder in a cooperative apartment maintains, with the cooperative as owner of the building. See **condominium.**

SUBLEASE [UNDERLEASE] a transition whereby a **tenant** [one who has **leased premises** from the owner, or **landlord**] grants an **interest** in the leased premises less than his own, or reserves to himself a **reversionary** interest in the term. See **assignment,** which connotes the **conveyance** of the whole term of a lease.

LEASEHOLD the **estate** in **real property** of a **lessee,** created by a **lease;** generally an estate of fixed duration, but may also describe **tenancy at will,** a month-to-month tenancy, **PERIODIC** *tenancy,* etc. (see **tenancy**).

LEASE-PURCHASE AGREEMENT [CONTRACT]   see **mortgage [LEASE-PURCHASE AGREEMENT [CONTRACT]].**

LEAVE OF COURT permission obtained from a court to take some action that, without such permission, would not be allowable. This permission in some instances may come before or after the expiration of the period in which the action was to be taken. For instance, a **trustee** may need "leave of court" in order to spend trust **corpus** for the support of the trust **beneficiary;** an attorney will need "leave of court" in order to file papers after the time allowed for filing the papers has elapsed.

LEGACY a disposition by **will** of **personal property;** synonymous with **bequest,** but properly distinguished from **devise,** which is a disposition of **real property.**

ABATEMENT OF A LEGACY see **abatement [ABATEMENT OF A LEGACY].**

ALTERNATE LEGACY disposition whereby testator leaves one of two or more gifts to a person without specifically stating which gift should pass.

CONTINGENT LEGACY a legacy which will only pass upon the happening of some event, such as "if she reaches the age of twenty-five."

DEMONSTRATIVE LEGACY a gift of stated value that identifies a particular asset as the primary source of payment but permits the **executor** to draw on the general assets of the estate once the primary source has been exhausted. Therefore, a "demonstrative legacy" is in nature both a GENERAL LEGACY, because it bequeaths a specified amount, and a SPECIFIC LEGACY in that it designates the fund from which the payment is made.

GENERAL LEGACY one designated primarily by quantity or amount and may be paid out of general assets without regard to any particular fund or thing. For example, a bequest of 270 shares of stock that testator did not describe as specified shares by numbers or otherwise was a general legacy.

LEGATEE recipient of personal property by virtue of a will—i.e., the recipient of a "legacy."

RESIDUARY LEGACY a GENERAL LEGACY (see above) wherein fall all the assets of the estate after all other legacies have been satisfied and all charges, debts, and costs [of the estate and its administration] have been paid. See **residuary legacy**.

SPECIFIC LEGACY a bequest of some definite or specific part of a testator's estate which is capable of being designated, identified and distinguished from other like things composing the testator's estate; that which can be distinguished from other articles of the same general nature in the estate.

LEGAL ADVOCATE an **attorney.**

LEGAL AGE the age, determined by each state, at which a person becomes responsible for his or her actions and is capable of entering into contracts or other business relationships. In many jurisdictions, the legal age is 18, although the legal age for some activities, such as drinking, may be higher, and for others, such as driving a car, may be lower. See **majority, age of.**

LEGAL AID (SOCIETY) state-funded and state-administered offices established throughout the country to deliver legal services to financially needy **litigants,** that is, those unable to afford to retain private **counsel.** See also **Legal Services Corporation; public defender.**

LEGAL ASSISTANT see **paralegal.**

LEGAL CAPACITY TO SUE requirement that a person bringing suit have a sound mind, be of **lawful** age, and be under no restraint or legal disability. The term has no reference to failure of the petition to show a right of action in the plaintiff.

LEGAL CONSIDERATION see **consideration [LEGAL CONSIDERATION].**

LEGAL DETRIMENT giving up something a person was privileged to retain, or doing or refraining from doing something that a person was privileged not to do, or not to refrain from doing. Where a person changes his or her legal position, or assumes duties or liabilities not therefore imposed, that change of position constitutes the **consideration** necessary to form a **contract** and therefore imposes duties on the person benefiting from the detriment.

LEGAL DISCRETION see **discretion [LEGAL DISCRETION].**

LEGAL DUTY that which the law requires be done or forborne. **Breach** of a legal duty owed another is an element of **negligence** and is the essence of most actions in **tort.** Legal duties not otherwise imposed may be created by a **contract** or by one's entering into some other such relationship (**landlord-tenant,** host-**invitee,** etc.).

EXAMPLE: In an apartment house, a landlord usually has the *legal duty* to keep the common areas, such as a hallway, clean and in good repair. If a tenant injures himself or herself because a light bulb in a hallway has gone out and the landlord has been made aware that the bulb is not working, the landlord's breach of the legal duty makes him or her liable.

LEGAL ESTATE see **estate [LEGAL ESTATE].**

LEGAL FICTION a fact presumed in law, regardless of its truth, for the purpose of justice or convenience. For example, the **domicile** of the owner is presumed to be the situs of **personal property** for taxing purposes regardless of where it is actually located. The term legal fiction commonly occurs in cases where adherence to the fiction is perceived as working an injustice. Thus, when the personal property has never been in the state where the owner is domiciled and it would clearly be unfair to tax the property, the court will dispense with the situs presumption as a mere legal fiction.

LEGAL HEIRS see **heirs.**

LEGAL IMPOSSIBILITY see **impossibility** [LEGAL IMPOSSIBIL-
ITY].

LEGAL INJURY see **injury** [LEGAL INJURY].

LEGAL NOTICE see **notice** [LEGAL NOTICE].

LEGAL PERMANENT RESIDENT [LPR] an immigration term
for an **alien** who has entered the United States and has legally established permission to remain. The person receives a document known
as a **green card** and is entitled to live and work (unless the job is
restricted to **citizens**) in the United States on a permanent basis,
provided the person does not commit any actions that would make
him or her removable under immigration law. See **deportability;
inadmissibility.** A permanent resident must follow all laws of the
United States, including paying **income taxes**, but is not entitled to
vote in federal or state elections. Permanent resident status is a first
step toward becoming a naturalized citizen. See **immigration and
customs enforcement [ICE].**

LEGAL SECRETARY secretary having specific familiarity with
legal language and processes, such as the **filing** of court documents.

LEGAL SEPARATION see **divorce** [SEPARATION]; **separation
agreement.**

LEGAL SERVICES CORPORATION a **corporation** established
by Congress in 1974 to provide financial support for legal assistance
in noncriminal proceedings or matters to persons financially unable
to afford legal assistance. The Corporation is empowered to make
grants to qualified programs and to **contract** with outside organizations. See **Legal Aid.**

LEGAL TENDER the kind of money lawfully acceptable for payment of a **debt** where the medium of payment is not specified by
statute or agreement. All legal tender is money, but not all money
is legal tender. Congress has the power to determine what is legal
tender. All coins and paper money of the United States, as well as
Federal Reserve notes and circulating notes of Federal Reserve
banks and national banking associations, are legal tender.

LEGATEE one who takes a **legacy.**

LEGISLATION the act of giving or enacting **laws;** the power to make
laws; the act of legislating; preparation and enactment of laws; the
making of laws by express decree; the exercise of **sovereign** power.

LEGISLATION, SPECIAL see **special legislation.**

LEGISLATIVE HISTORY those recorded events leading up to the passage of a bill including committee reports, hearings, and debates. Published commentary may accompany the legislation itself. **Courts** often look to the legislative history in later determining the meaning of a particular statute. Compare **plain meaning (rule).**

LEGISLATIVE INTENT see **intent [LEGISLATIVE INTENT].**

LEND to part with a thing of value for either a fixed or indefinite period. Such item or something equivalent to it must be returned at the time originally established or when **lawfully** demanded. When used in a will, it means "give" or "devise" unless it is manifest that the testator intended otherwise.

LESSEE one who holds an **estate** by virtue of a **lease;** the **tenant** of a **landlord.**

LESSER-INCLUDED OFFENSE 1. a violation of law that is necessarily established by proof of a greater **offense** and that is properly submitted to the **jury,** should the **prosecution's** proof fail to establish **guilt** of the greater offense charged, without necessity of multiple **indictment;** 2. that necessarily committed lesser offense accompanying the conduct leading to a greater offense.

EXAMPLE: Mei-Li is charged with robbery, which is the taking of property by threat or fear of violence. If Mei-Li cannot be convicted of robbery because there is insufficient proof of a threat or fear, she could still be convicted of larceny, which is simply the taking of another's property. Larceny is a *lesser-included offense* in relation to robbery.

   See **graded offense; plea bargaining.**

LESSOR one who grants a **lease** to another, thereby transferring exclusive temporary right of **possession** of certain **property,** subject only to rights expressly retained by the owner.

LET to **lease;** 1. to grant the use of **realty** for a compensation. 2. The term does not always connote the act of leasing, but the granting of a **license.**

LETTER OF CREDIT in commercial law, a promise by a bank or other issuer that it will honor on behalf of one of its customer's demands for payment upon compliance with specified conditions; intended to facilitate long-distance sales by allowing a buyer to establish a credit line against which a seller can draw. Letters of credit guard against risk **insolvency** and uncertainty in delivery and settlement due to market fluctuations.

LETTER OF INTENT customarily employed to reduce to writing a preliminary understanding of the parties. This letter is not a **contract,** and it does not constitute a binding agreement. Rather, it is an expression of tentative intentions of the parties and creates no liability as between the parties. It is, in essence, "an agreement to agree." If a formal writing is contemplated by the parties, a binding contract may arise between them before the writing is executed as long as there has been a **meeting of the minds** concerning the essential elements of the writing.

LETTER RULING a written statement issued to a taxpayer by the Office of Assistant Commissioner of Tax in which interpretation of the tax laws are made and applied to a specific set of facts.

LETTERS OF ADMINISTRATION document issued by a **probate court** appointing the **administrator** or **administratrix** of the **estate** of a **decedent.** If the decedent left a **will** naming a particular **executor** or **executrix,** the corresponding term for the court document is **LETTERS TESTAMENTARY.** If the decedent left a will but failed to name an executor or the named executor of a will cannot or refuses to serve, the document is termed **LETTERS OF ADMINISTRATION CTA.** CTA stands for the Latin **CUM TESTAMENTO ANNEXO** and means "with the will annexed." If a previous administrator or executor fails to complete the administration of the estate the document is called **LETTERS OF ADMINISTRATION DBN.** DBN stands for the Latin **DE BONIS NON** and means "goods not administered." Modern usage has favored the term **SUCCESSOR ADMINISTRATOR.**

LETTERS ROGATORY see **rogatory letters.**

LETTERS TESTAMENTARY see **letters of administration** [**LETTERS TESTAMENTARY**].

LETTER STOCK a category of stock that derives its name from an inscription on the face of the **stock certificate,** indicating that the shares have not been registered with the **Securities and Exchange Commission** and, therefore, cannot be sold to the general public. See **restricted securities.**

LEVARI FACIAS see **fieri facias** [**LEVARI FACIAS**].

LEVEL PAYMENT MORTGAGE see **mortgage** [**FIXED PAYMENT MORTGAGE**].

LEVERAGE the use of **debt** to finance **capital investment,** for the purpose of increasing the investor's rate of return on his **equity.** As long as the return income and appreciation on the total investment exceed the interest paid on the borrowed money, the investor benefits.

LEVY 1. to raise or collect; 2. to seize; 3. to assess, as to levy a tax; 4. a seizure or levying, as of land or other **property** or rights, through lawful **process** or by force. When one places a levy upon some property, right or a **CHOSE IN ACTION** (see **chose**), it is seized and may be sold to satisfy a **judgment.** See **writ of execution.**

LEWD [LEWDNESS] **criminal** act of sexual indecency committed in public. Exposure of intimate parts for the purpose of arousing or gratifying the sexual desire of the actor (or of any other person) when such exposure is likely to be observed by nonconsenting persons who would be affronted. **INDECENT EXPOSURE** is sometimes synonymous with lewdness but more often is considered to be nudity in public, a lesser offense and punishable generally as a **misdemeanor.** Enforcement may not be practiced in such areas as nude beaches but enforcement may take place if a beachgoer leaves the beach while still nude. Lewd and lascivious behavior means likely to be thought of as sexual conduct.

LEXIS see **search engine.**

LEX LOCI CONTRACTUS *(lĕks lō'-kē kŏn-trăk'-tūs)* Lat.: law of the place of making a contract. See **conflict of laws.**

LEX LOCI DELICTI *(lĕks lō'-kē dĕ-lĭk'-tē)* Lat.: law of the place of the wrong. See **conflict of laws.**

L. FR. abbreviation for Law French.

LIABILITY 1. an **obligation** to do or refrain from doing something; 2. a **duty** that eventually must be performed; 3. an obligation to pay money; 4. money owed, as opposed to an **asset;** 5. responsibility for one's conduct, such as **contractual** liability, **tort** liability, **criminal** liability, etc. See **limited liability; products liability; strict liability; vicarious liability.**

EXAMPLE: Lauren runs a red light and hits another car, injuring both the driver and the passenger. Lauren has incurred *tort liability* for her action.

ABSOLUTE LIABILITY see **strict liability.**

CURRENT LIABILITIES in accounting, **debts** due within one year, including salary payable to employees, purchase costs payable to suppliers, taxes and annual portion due on long-term debt.

JOINT AND SEVERAL LIABILITY when tortious conduct is the cause of a single and indivisible harm, each contributing tortfeasor is liable to the same extent and in the same manner as if they had performed the wrongful act themselves. See **joint and several.**

JOINT LIABILITY created where two or more persons, who may or may not have a legal relationship to each other, owe another a joint duty and by common neglect of that duty the other person is injured. See **joint liability**

LIABILITY WITHOUT FAULT see **strict liability.**.

LONG-TERM LIABILITIES in accounting, debts due after one year, including term bank loans, **mortgages** payable, **bonds** outstanding and liabilities under long-term **lease** and rental agreements.

PRIMARY LIABILITY liability imposed upon the party directly responsible for the loss or injury.

SECONDARY LIABILITY that which arises only when the party directly liable fails to perform or otherwise defaults in performance. Frequently refers to the liability of a **guarantor.**

STRICT LIABILITY see **strict liability.**

VICARIOUS LIABILITY see **vicarious liability.**

LIABILITY WITHOUT FAULT see **strict liability.**

LIABLE responsible for; obligated in law.

LIBEL a **tort** consisting of a false, **malicious,** unprivileged publication aiming to defame a living person or to mar the memory of one dead. Printed or written material, signs or pictures that tend to expose a person to public scorn, hatred, contempt or ridicule may be considered libelous.

EXAMPLE: A candidate for public office reads in the paper of an earlier conviction against him for bribery. After some investigation, the candidate finds out that Victor, who is in contact with his opponent, had planted the story, which is unquestionably false, in order to ruin the candidate's standing in the election. The candidate can sue Victor or the newspaper for *libel*.

See **seditious libel**. Compare **privileged communications; slander.**

LIBERAL CONSTRUCTION see **construction [LIBERAL [EQUITABLE] CONSTRUCTION].**

LIBERTY freedom; the ability to enjoy all the rights granted by the United States and a particular state's constitution, as well as other rights such as the right to earn a living, the right to acquire knowledge, the right to marry, etc.; refers to the fullest scope of freedoms one has but at the same time limits those freedoms so as not to interfere with another person's exercise of them.

LIBERTY, CIVIL see **civil rights.**

LICENSE a grant of permission needed to legalize doing a particular thing, exercising a certain privilege or pursuing a particular business or occupation. Licenses may be granted by private persons or by governmental authority.

In the law of **property,** a license is a personal privilege or permission with respect to some use of **land,** and is revocable at the will of the landowner. The privilege attaches only to the party holding it and not to the land itself, since, unlike an **easement,** a license does not represent an **estate** or **interest** in the land.

EXAMPLE: When Lynn opens a new shop in a small shopping center, a neighboring businessman gives her *license* to use some of his storage space. The businessman can deny Lynn the use of that space at any time, and, most importantly, if Lynn ever sells her store, she could not guarantee that storage space to the purchaser.

Compare **franchise; lease; monopoly.**

LICENSEE one to whom a **license** has been granted; in **property,** one whose presence on the **premises** is not invited, but tolerated. Thus, a licensee is neither a customer, nor a servant, nor a **trespasser,** and does not stand in any contractual relation with the owner of the premises, but is permitted expressly or impliedly to go upon the property of another merely for his own interest, convenience, or gratification. Compare **invitee.**

LICENSE TAX the fee or tax charged by a government to issue the license required for engaging in some regulated activity such as the sale of liquor or the practice of a profession.

LICENSOR one who grants a **license.**

LIE DETECTOR TEST see **polygraph.**

LIEN a charge, hold or claim upon the **property** of another as **security** for some **debt** or charge. The term connotes the right the law gives to have a debt satisfied out of the property to which it attaches, if necessary by the sale of the property.

ARTISAN'S LIEN a statutory lien permitting an artisan to retain possession of a piece of work until payment for the labor performed on it is received.

EQUITABLE LIEN a right in **equity,** but not **at law,** to have specific property applied in satisfaction of a debt. Whenever parties enter into an agreement indicating an intention to post some particular property as security for an obligation, an equitable lien is created on such property. An equitable lien may also be created by implication and is based on the doctrine of **unjust enrichment.**

FACTOR'S LIEN a lien that the **factor** has on goods **consigned** to him or her while in his or her possession for any advances made by him or her and for his or her **commissions.** In **common law,** it was purely a possessory lien and was lost by surrender of **possession,** but today, under the Uniform Commercial Code, a written security agreement is a sufficient substitute for possession.

FEDERAL TAX LIEN a lien of the United States on all property and rights to property of a taxpayer who fails to pay a tax for which he or she is liable to the federal government.

FLOATING LIEN in commercial law, one that covers not only inventory and accounts possessed by the debtor at the time of the original loan, but also his or her **after-acquired property** of inventory or accounts. The floating lien allows a buyer's operations to be completely financed with periodic advances and repayments secured by changing **collateral** of raw materials, work in progress, finished goods, proceeds, etc. This financing may be accomplished in a single security agreement, with only one filing required.

GARAGEMAN'S LIEN see **MECHANIC'S LIEN** (below).

JUDGMENT LIEN a lien on a judgment debtor's property in favor of a judgment creditor. When judgment has been entered in a civil case, and the party liable for the judgment fails to pay it, the judgment creditor may file a lien against the property of the party liable, to give notice that the property is subject to sale in satisfaction of the judgment. The judgment creditor may enforce the lien by having the sheriff seize the property and sell it at a sheriff's sale.

LANDLORD'S LIEN in common law, the **landlord's** right to **levy (distress)** upon the **goods** of a **tenant** in satisfaction of unpaid **rents** or property damage; now generally a statutory lien giving the **lessor** status of a preferred **creditor** with regard to the **lessee's** property.

MECHANIC'S LIEN one created to secure **priority** of payment for value of work performed and materials furnished in erecting or repairing a structure; attaches to the land as well as its buildings and improvements. **Statutes** according priority to the satisfaction of the debt represented by a mechanic's lien are found in most **jurisdictions** and extend to automobiles and other goods as well as to structures. As applied to automobiles, the claim is sometimes called **GARAGEMAN'S LIEN.**

EXAMPLE: Standard Heating and Air Conditioning Company has installed all the ventilation in an office complex. The owner of the complex falls into bankruptcy and cannot pay Standard. By operation of the law of the state in which the work was done, Standard has a *mechanic's lien* equalling the value of the work it performed. That lien attaches to the office complex, so that Standard has a priority of payment for any money that is paid to the complex.

PRIOR LIEN as between two liens, or in a class of liens, the one superior to the others.

STATE TAX LIEN a security interest in the property of a taxpayer established by statute, of which the tax collector may avail himself upon default of payment of taxes. Unlike liens on personal property, which may be made a charge upon other personal property of the owner, such lien on real property does not extend to property other than that being assessed unless expressly authorized by statute. Most jurisdictions give these liens priority over mortgages and other liens existing against the property.

TAX LIEN a statutory lien which exists in favor of a state or municipality and gives the tax collector a security interest in the taxed property. Analogous to a **JUDGMENT LIEN** (above).

WAREHOUSEMAN'S LIEN right of a warehouseman to maintain possession of goods until all storage charges have been paid.

LIEN JURISDICTION **jurisdiction** in which **title** to the **mortgaged premises** remains with the **mortgagor** pending payment of the mortgage price. See **mortgage; title jurisdiction.**

LIEN THEORY OF MORTGAGE see **mortgage [LIEN THEORY].**

LIFE ESTATE an **estate** whose duration is limited by the life of the person holding it or by that of some other person **[per autre vie]**. It is a **freehold** interest in land.

EXAMPLE: A grandfather conveys his summer home to his daughter for life and then to his three grandchildren. Since the daughter's interest in the house exists only so long as she is alive, her interest is considered a *life estate*.

LIFE EXPECTANCY the period of time a person is predicted to live, based on their present age and sex. This figure is most frequently used by **actuaries** to determine **insurance premiums.**

LIFE INTEREST an interest in property measured by the life of either the person using the property or by another's life. See **life estate.**

LIFE TENANT **tenant** whose legal right to remain in possession of certain lands is measured either by his or her life or the life of another. See **life estate.**

LIFO last-in, first-out. See **first-in, first-out; inventory.**

LIKE-KIND EXCHANGE see **sale or exchange.** Compare **boot.**

LIMINE see **in limine.**

LIMITATION a restriction or restraint; the act of limiting. A state constitution constitutes a *limitation* on the power that the state may exercise, not a *grant* of power. "Limitation" also declares the nature and extent of the **estate** granted, and the uses for which the grant is made. For example, in an estate granted "to A and his heirs," the phrase **"and his heirs"** constitutes **words of limitation** and indicates that A has a **fee simple,** and can use the land as he pleases. Also, a limitation determines an estate upon the happening of the event itself without the necessity of doing any act to regain the estate, such as re-entry. See **statute of limitations.**

LIMITATIONS PERIOD see **statute of limitations.**

LIMITATIONS, STATUTE OF see **statute of limitations.**

LIMITATION, WORDS OF see **words of limitation.**

LIMITED JURISDICTION refers to courts that are only authorized to hear and decide certain or special types of cases; also known as SPECIAL JURISDICTION. See **jurisdiction.**

EXAMPLE: The **Court of Claims** has *limited jurisdiction* to only hear claims against the United States based on certain types of violations.

A small claims court is limited to a specified dollar amount that it can litigate.

LIMITED LIABILITY the limitation placed on the amount an investor of a corporation can lose resulting from a lawsuit against the corporation or other loss suffered by the corporation; the **liability** for losses that is limited to the amount an investor or shareholder invests in the corporation. The corporation itself also enjoys limited liability inasmuch as the corporation's obligations are always limited to its **assets** unless, with regard to particular transactions, personal responsibility is assumed by an officer or shareholder of the corporation.

EXAMPLE: Iggy purchases ten shares of a corporation's stock for $5 a share. If the corporation becomes bankrupt with many creditors who are unpaid, Iggy's *liability* is *limited* to the $50 he invested. He can never be charged for a greater amount.

LIMITED PARTNERSHIP see **partnership [LIMITED PARTNERSHIP].**

LIMIT ORDER see **order** [LIMIT ORDER].

LINEAGE race; family; kin; blood. A common ancestor with all ascending and descending persons. See **lineal.**

LINEAL refers to **descent** by a direct line of **succession** in ancestry. See **consanguinity** [LINEAL CONSANGUINITY].

LINEAL HEIRS see **heirs** [LINEAL HEIRS].

LINE OF CREDIT see **credit** [LINE OF CREDIT].

LINEUP the police procedure in which a person suspected of a crime is placed in a line with several other persons and a witness to the crime attempts to identify the suspect as the person who committed the crime. The procedure must not be "unduly suggestive," or the identification will not be admissible in a criminal trial.

LIQUIDATE to settle; to determine the amount due, and to whom due, and then to extinguish the indebtedness. Although the term more properly signifies the adjustment or settlement of **debts,** to liquidate often means to pay.

    LIQUIDATE A BUSINESS to assemble and mobilize the **assets** of the business, settle with **creditors** and **debtors,** and apportion remaining assets, if any, among the **shareholders** or owners.

    LIQUIDATE A CLAIM to determine by agreement or **litigation** the precise amount of the claim, and to settle it on the basis of that determination.

LIQUIDATED AMOUNT [OBLIGATION] amount that may be readily ascertained by a mere computation based on the terms of the obligation or instrument. See **liquidate; sum certain.** Compare **unliquidated.**

LIQUIDATED DAMAGES a stipulated **contractual** amount that the **parties** agree is a reasonable estimation of the **damages** owing to one in the event of a **breach** by the other.

    EXAMPLE: Safety Corporation and Fire Prevention, Inc., enter into a long-term contract whereby Fire Prevention supplies Safety with all the sprinkler systems Safety needs. Instead of leaving a damage figure to a court decision if either party should breach the agreement, the parties include a *liquidated damages* clause in the contract. That clause provides both a dollar figure and a formula for calculating damages, with the higher of the two figures constituting the maximum damages either party could charge.

LIQUIDATED SUM CERTAIN see **sum certain** [LIQUIDATED SUM CERTAIN].

LIQUIDATION DIVIDEND   see **dividend** [LIQUIDATATION DIV-IDEND].

LIS PENDENS *(lēs pĕn'-dĕns)* Lat.: a pending lawsuit. Refers to the maxim that pending the **suit** nothing should be changed; thus, for example, one who acquired an interest in **property** from a party to **litigation** respecting such property takes that interest subject to the **decree** or **judgment** in such litigation and is bound by it.

NOTICE OF LIS PENDENS   in some **jurisdictions,** a publicly recorded notice required to warn persons (such as prospective purchasers) that **title** to the property is in litigation and that they will be bound by a possibly adverse judgment.

LISTED STOCK   a company's stock that is traded on an organized **stock exchange.** To be listed, the company must meet requirements of the selected exchange and file application for listing with both the exchange and the **Securities and Exchange Commission.**

LISTING   in **real estate,** an agency relationship between the seller and broker with the purpose of effecting a juncture between buyers and sellers of **real property** with an ultimate pecuniary reward to the broker for his or her part in "bringing the parties together." See also **listed stock.**

LITE PENDENTE   see **pendente lite.**

LITERAL CONSTRUCTION   see **construction** [STRICT [LITERAL] CONSTRUCTION].

LITERAL DENIAL   see **negative pregnant** [LITERAL DENIAL].

LITIGANTS   the parties actively involved in a lawsuit; **plaintiffs** or **defendants** involved in **litigation.**

LITIGATION   a judicial contest aiming to determine and enforce legal rights. See also **action; case; suit; vexatious litigation.**

LITIGIOUS   most commonly used to refer to one's fondness for or propensity to become engaged in **litigation.** Thus, a citizen who repeatedly sues his or her neighbor over various issues would be called "litigious." Also, the subject of a lawsuit or action. Compare **malicious prosecution.** See also **vexatious litigation.**

LIVERY OF SEISIN   an ancient ceremony signifying an **alienation** of land by **feoffment.** It consisted of a formal delivery of **possession** of the **premises,** symbolized by the manual **delivery** of a clod or piece of turf from the land, all of which was done in the presence of **witnesses.** See **seisin.**

LIVE VIEW TRANSCRIPT see **court reporters [LIVE VIEW].**

LIVING TRUST see **trust [LIVING TRUST].**

L.J. abbreviation for Law **Judge.**

LKA last known address.

LL.B. see **J.D.**

LOAN delivery of a sum of money to another under a **contract** to return at some future time an equivalent amount with or without an additional sum agreed upon for its use; and if such be the intent of the parties the transaction will be deemed a loan regardless of its form. The characterization of a transaction as a loan or some other type of borrowing has significance in ascertaining whether **usury** laws apply to the amount of **interest** being charged. See **mortgage.**

LOANSHARKING the practice of loaning money at **usurious** rates of **interest.** Many states have laws that render unsurious interest and in some instances even the underlying debt uncollectable. The use or the threat to use violence in order to collect the interest or the debt constitutes the crime of **extortion.** See **extortion; usury.**

LOBBYING EXPENSE see **expense [LOBBYING EXPENSE].**

LOBBYIST one engaged in the business of persuading legislators to pass laws that are favorable, and to defeat those that are unfavorable, to the interests of the lobbyist or of his or her clients.

LOCATION see **mining [LOCATION].**

LOCKDOWN a temporary confinement of inmates in a correctional facility to their cells on a 24-hour basis with no outside contact and little if any ordinary privileges or recreation. Such a restriction on normal activity of prisoners is done as a security measure following an escape or riot or during the course of some other prison emergency. Prison officials have been accorded considerable latitude by the courts in the use of such lockdowns both in terms of duration and quality. Any measures taken by prison officials that are "unnecessarily cruel" or completely unjustified may violate an inmate's right to be free from cruel and unusual punishment.

LOCKOUT the employer counterpart of an employee **strike.** The employer locks out the employees preventing them from working in an effort to gain a better bargaining position in labor negotiations. Unemployment benefits may accrue to employees who are locked out as opposed to employees on strike. See **collective bargaining.**

LOCKUP see **jail.**

LOCO PARENTIS see **in loco parentis.**

LOCUS *(lō'-kŭs)* Lat.: the place.

> **LOCUS CONTRACTUS** *(kŏn-trăk'-tūs)* Lat.: the place where the contract was made.

> **LOCUS DELICTI** *(dĕ-lĭk'-tē)* Lat.: the place where the wrong occurred.

> **LOCUS IN QUO** *(ĭn kwō)* Lat.: the place where or in which. Refers to a locale where an offense was committed or a **cause of action** arose.

> **LOCUS POENITENTIAE** *(pō-ĕ-nĭ-tĕn'-shē-ī)* Lat.: a place for repentance. The opportunity for one to change his or her mind.

> **LOCUS SIGILLI** *(sĭ-jĭl'-lē)* Lat.: the place of the **seal;** usually abbreviated L.S. Commonly used within brackets on copies of documents to indicate the position of the seal in the original; also used to call attention of the signer to the place for his or her seal.

LOGROLLING refers to schemes by legislators to force passage of desired bills without convincing their colleagues of the merits of their proposals. One type of logrolling is the inclusion under one bill of secondary bills, each of which probably would not be approved if voted on singly.

> *EXAMPLE:* Conservative legislators are finding it very difficult to get their bills passed on the strength of the bills' own merits. In an attempt to sidestep this problem, the legislators tack their proposals onto a tax bill that has to be passed or government employees cannot be paid. This attempt is called *logrolling.*

> Another practice is for legislators to agree to vote for each other's bills, even if neither has any interest in the other's bill.

LOITER to linger for no evident reason, particularly in a public place, near a school or a transportation facility. There are criminal prohibitions of such behavior as loitering for purposes of begging, gambling, soliciting another to engage in sexual intercourse, or for the purpose of selling or using drugs; being masked or disguised in an unusual manner; or simply not being able to give a satisfactory explanation of one's behavior. Compare **probable cause; void for vagueness.**

LONG-ARM STATUTES laws that allow a local **forum** to obtain **jurisdiction** over nonresident **defendants** when the **cause of action** is generated locally and affects local **plaintiffs.** Such expanded jurisdiction is authorized where the contacts of the nonresident defendant with the forum are regarded as sufficiently substantial.

EXAMPLE: Federated Television Company sells many televisions in a particular state, but the company does not maintain any sales offices, have any corporate headquarters or employ any sales agents in the state. When one of its televisions explodes and burns down Chloe's house, Chloe can use the state's *long-arm statute* to bring Federated into the state court. Without the statute, there may be a procedural difficulty in forcing Federated to come in to Chloe's state and defend against the action or pay for the damages caused.

Long-arm statutes are commonly employed to allow a local court to exercise jurisdiction over nonresident motorists who cause automobile accidents within the state.

LONG POSITION in finance, the ownership of a **stock** or **security,** subjecting the owner to risk of loss in case the security declines in value. Compare **selling short.**

LONG-TERM CAPITAL GAIN see **capital [CAPITAL GAINS OR LOSSES].**

LONG-TERM LIABILITY see **liability [LONG-TERM LIABILITIES].**

LOOKOUT person specifically charged with duty of observing lights, sounds, echoes, or any obstruction to navigation. Such a person must devote his or her undivided attention to the task with that watchfulness that a prudent and reasonable person must maintain for his or her own safety and the safety of others. The doctrine of **PROPER LOOKOUT** requires that one operating a motor vehicle use such care, prudence, and watchfulness as a person of ordinary care and prudence would use under similar circumstances to avoid liability for negligent operation of the vehicle. In popular usage, it refers to a person stationed outside the area where a crime is being committed to watch for police or persons who may alert police or be witnesses to the crime.

LORD at **common law,** one who granted a feudal **estate** in land to a tenant. For instance, the King would be the Lord of the Dukes and other nobles to whom the Crown had granted property; the dukes and other nobles were the lords of the persons to whom they in turn granted property. The lord was responsible for protecting and maintaining order among his tenants, for which purpose he maintained a court. In return, the tenant was responsible for providing services to the lord. Under the English Parliamentary system of government, the House of Lords arose to provide representation for nobles.

Traditionally, membership in the House of Lords was hereditary. In recent times, the Crown has appointed individuals as lords for life only, with the individual's title ceasing at his death.

LORD CAMPBELL ACT the English statute that first provided that the surviving family of a person who suffered a **wrongful death** may sue the **tortfeasor** for **damages.** It is to be distinguished from the **WRONGFUL DEATH STATUTE,** which provides that the personal representative of a person who has suffered a wrongful death may sue for damages, thus contravening the **common law** rule that an action for personal injuries did not survive the plaintiff's death. Most states have enacted some form of a Lord Campbell Act or wrongful death statue.

LOSS the act of losing or the thing lost; synonymous with **"damage";** as used in an insurance policy, a state of fact of being lost or destroyed, ruin or destruction; and where a policy requires notices of a loss, refers to the date that a fraud was discovered. See also **casualty loss; lost property; risk of loss; total loss.**

LOSS OF BARGAIN see **benefit of the bargain (rule) [LOSS OF BARGAIN].**

LOST PROPERTY property involuntarily lost to the owner through neglect, carelessness or oversight. Compare **abandonment; mislaid property.**

LOT, ODD see **odd lot.**

LOTTERY a gambling scheme in which **consideration** is taken in return for the offering of a prize that will be given on the basis of chance and not merit. The use of **interstate commerce,** the U.S. mail, or radio or television to distribute or advertise a lottery constitutes a federal crime. However, these laws do not apply to any lottery conducted by a state, nor to a **SWEEPSTAKES** (for which no consideration is required) conducted by a business entity.

LOWER OF COST OR MARKET a method of valuating **inventory,** using the lower of either the price of the item as of the time it was purchased or the present **market value** of the item.

LPR see **legal permanent resident [LPR].**

L.S. see **locus sigilli.**

LSAT Law School Admissions Test. A standardized examination administered by a private, nonprofit testing organization known as the Educational Testing Service and used by law schools as one factor in accepting applicants.

LUMP-SUM PAYMENT a single amount of money; a sum paid all at once rather than in part or in installments. For instance, under an insurance policy the proceeds may be paid immediately, as a lump-sum payment, or at the option of the payee over time as an annuity or in installment payments.

LUMP-SUM ALIMONY PAYMENT the discharge of one's obligation to pay **alimony** by the payment of a single lump sum. For income tax purposes, the payment of lump-sum alimony may or may not shift the income tax burden on the alimony to the payee, depending on the circumstances.

LUMP-SUM DISTRIBUTION lump-sum payment to an employee from a **pension** or profit-sharing plan upon termination of employment either by retirement or death.

LYING IN WAIT hiding or concealing oneself for the purpose of committing a crime when the opportunity arises. Regarding **murder,** "lying in wait" implies **premeditation** or **malice aforethought** necessary for first-degree murder.

M

MACHINATION that which is devised; a device; a hostile or treacherous scheme; an artful design or plot.

MACRS see **depreciation** [MODIFIED ACCELERATED COST RECOVERY SYSTEM].

MAFIA see **organized crime.**

MAGISTRATE 1. a public **civil** officer, invested with some part of the legislative, executive or judicial power. 2. In a narrower sense, the term includes only inferior judicial officers, such as **justices of the peace.**

UNITED STATES [FEDERAL] MAGISTRATE appointed by U.S. District Court judges, magistrates have powers that include the ability to hear and determine specified pretrial motions pending before a district court, to conduct hearings, including evidentiary hearings, and to submit proposed findings of facts and recommendations for disposition.

MAGNA CARTA [MAGNA CHARTA] the "great charter" to which King John gave his assent in 1215, and that is considered the fundamental guarantee of rights and privileges under English law.

MAGNUSON-MOSS WARRANTY ACT federal statute requiring warranties for consumer products to be written in easily understood language and providing the Federal Trade Commission with better means of protecting consumers.

MAIL BOX RULE a rule that an **acceptance** made in response to an **offer** is valid and forms a binding **contract** at the time of dispatch of the acceptance, as when it is placed in the mailbox, if that method of accepting is a reasonable response to the offer.

MAIM at common law, to deprive a person of such a part of his or her body as to render that person less able to fight or defend himself or herself than that person would otherwise have been. See **mayhem.**

MAIN PURPOSE RULE see **statute of frauds.**

MAINTAIN to continue, to support, to sustain; to hold or keep in any particular state or condition; in terms of "maintaining" a **nuisance,** includes both knowledge of the nuisance and preserving and continuing its existence by some positive act or by acquiescence.

MAINTENANCE see **criminal maintenance.**

MAJORITY, AGE OF the age when a person is considered legally responsible for all his or her activities and becomes entitled to the legal rights held by citizens generally.

MAJORITY OPINION see **opinion.**

MAKER in commercial law, one who **executes** a **note,** or **indorses** it before its delivery to the **payee,** and who thereby assumes an absolute obligation to make payment on the note.

EXAMPLE: Before a supplier ships any goods to Creative Bottle Company, the supplier requires the company to sign a promissory note explaining payment terms and dates and also obliging Creative Bottle to meet those terms. Creative Bottle is the *maker* of the note since it is the one who has to make the payments.

MALA IN SE see **malum in se.**

MALA PROHIBITA see **malum prohibitum.**

MALFEASANCE the doing of an illegal and unlawful act; wrongdoing, especially a violation of the public trust by a public official.

EXAMPLE: Franz hopes to get re-elected and accepts a bribe to fund his campaign from the Widgets Corporation in exchange for the promise of providing them future government contracts. Franz has committed malfeasance.

Compare **misfeasance; nonfeasance.**

MALICE the state of mind that accompanies the intentional doing of a wrongful act without **justification** and in **wanton** or **willful** disregard of the plain likelihood that harm will result.

With respect to **slander** and **libel,** malice is the mental state that accompanies a false statement when the maker knows it to be false or when the maker recklessly disregards the truth or falsity of it. **Tort liability** may also attend the malicious disclosure of true but private facts.

In **malicious prosecution,** there is intent to institute a **prosecution** for a purpose other than bringing an offender to justice.

MALICE AFORETHOUGHT the distinguishing state of mind that may render an unlawful homicide **murder** at common law. It is characterized by a "person-endangering" mental disposition for which there is no justification or excuse and as to which no **mitigating circumstances** exist.

Malice aforethought is the characteristic mark of all murder, as distinguished from the lesser crime of **manslaughter,** which lacks it. It does not mean simply hatred, ill-will, a spite or a grudge. It extends to and embraces generally the state of mind with which one commits a wrongful act. It may be discoverable in a specific deliberate intent to kill, in hardness of heart, cruelty, a wanton and depraved spirit, or in utter disregard of society. It is not synonymous with **premeditation,** however, since a particular person may not be intended to be injured. Murder, therefore, at common law embraces cases where no intent to kill existed, but where the state or frame of mind termed malice, in its legal sense, prevailed. Modern homicide statutes do not employ malice aforethought but instead rely upon an intent to cause death and the absence of extenuating circumstances.

MALICIOUS ARREST the arresting of a person on a criminal **charge** without **probable cause,** with knowledge that the person did not commit the offense charged. See **malicious prosecution.** Compare **false arrest.**

MALICIOUS MISCHIEF see **criminal mischief.**

MALICIOUS PROSECUTION an action for recovery of **damages** that have resulted to person, **property** or reputation from previous unsuccessful **civil** or criminal **proceedings** that were prosecuted without **probable cause** and with **malice.** See also **false arrest.**

EXAMPLE: Avril wants to persuade her estranged husband Eugenio to pay her generous alimony and child support. She contrives a story, which she tells the local prosecutor, connecting Eugenio with child abuse. Her misuse of the criminal process is an example of *malicious prosecution,* for which Eugenio may be able to sue her.

MALPRACTICE a professional's improper or immoral conduct in the performance of his or her duties, done either intentionally or through carelessness or ignorance; commonly applied to physicians, surgeons, dentists, lawyers and public officers to denote negligent or unskillful performance of duties where professional skills are obligatory on account of the **fiduciary** relationship with patients or clients.

MALUM IN SE *(mă'-lŭm ĭn sā)* Lat.: evil in itself. Evil, as adjudged by a civilized community; refers to an act or case involving conduct punishable because of the nature of the conduct, not only because the law has declared it punishable. Compare **malum prohibitum.**

MALUM PROHIBITUM *(mă'-lŭm prō-hĭ'-bĭ-tūm)* Lat.: wrong because it is prohibited. Made unlawful by **statute** for the public welfare, but not inherently evil and not involving **moral turpitude.** Compare **malum in se.**

MANAGEMENT COMPANY see **closed-end management company.**

MANDAMUS Lat.: we command. An extraordinary **writ,** issued from a court to an official, compelling performance of an act that the law recognizes as an absolute duty, as distinct from acts that may be at the official's discretion.

EXAMPLE: A state legislature passes a law that provides that, upon request, a person has the right to see any information the government has on file for that person. Kathy files such a request with the State's Attorney General and is refused access to her information. Unless the refusing party can show some compelling need for secrecy, a court will issue a writ of *mandamus* to the holder of the records, directing the release of the information.

See **ministerial act.**

MANDATE a judicial command; 1. an official mode of communicating the **judgment** of the **appellate court** to the lower court; 2. a **bailment** of something for the performance of some **gratuitous** service with respect to it by the **bailee.**

MANDATORY INJUNCTION see **injunction** [MANDATORY INJUNCTION].

MANDATORY SENTENCING see **sentence** [MANDATORY SENTENCE].

MANDATUM in civil law, a **bailment,** in which the **bailee** performs services without recompense.

MANIFEST WEIGHT see **against the [manifest] [weight of the] evidence.**

MANIPULATION under the Securities Exchange Act of 1934, refers to practices that are intended to mislead investors by artificially affecting market activity. Such practices include WASH SALES or MATCHED ORDERS, i.e., buy and sell orders of substantially the same size at the same time to create a false impression of active trading, or RIGGED ORDERS. See also **wash sale.**

MANN ACT a federal statute prohibiting the transportation of a woman or girl in interstate or foreign commerce for the purpose of **prostitution,** debauchery or any other immoral purpose; also known as the WHITE SLAVE TRAFFIC ACT.

MANSLAUGHTER unlawful killing of another person without **malice aforethought;** distinguished from **murder** with possible attendant death penalty; an explainable, less extreme **homicide.**

Most **jurisdictions** distinguish between voluntary and involuntary manslaughter. VOLUNTARY MANSLAUGHTER is intentional killing committed under circumstances that, although they do not justify the homicide, reduce its evil intent. A charge of manslaughter is appropriate where the **defendant** killed the victim in rage, terror or desperation. INVOLUNTARY MANSLAUGHTER consists of a homicide resulting from criminal negligence or recklessness.

UNLAWFUL ACT MANSLAUGHTER occurs when someone dies as the result of the defendant's doing of an unlawful act, usually a misdemeanor. The unlawful act referred to can be any act prohibited by law. Unlawful acts which are **malum in se**, and which cause a death, constitute involuntary manslaughter. Unlawful acts that are **malum prohibitum** and have death as a foreseeable consequence of committing the act also constitute involuntary manslaughter. Thus, misdemeanor-manslaughter is analogous to **felony-murder**. Many states have been leaning towards the abolition of the unlawful act doctrine.

MARGIN the payment, a percentage of purchase cost, that a buyer of regulated **securities** must make when buying on **credit** from a **stockbroker**.

MARIJUANA [MARIHUANA] see **controlled substance [**CANNABIS**]**.

MARITAL AGREEMENT see **postnuptial agreement; prenuptial agreement; separation agreement**.

MARITAL COMMUNICATIONS PRIVILEGE [HUSBAND-WIFE [SPOUSAL] PRIVILEGE] principle that either spouse is precluded from disclosing a confidential communication (oral, written, or expressive action) made by one to the other. The privilege is only valid during a legal marriage and communications made before the marriage or after the marriage terminates are not protected. However, those communications made during the marriage continue to be protected even after divorce or death. Its purpose is to preserve the marital status and to encourage free and open communication and confidence between spouses. Numerous courts have held that the privilege does not apply to persons living together without being married nor to those in a bigamous marriage. The privilege does not apply if third persons are present whether or not such presence was known to the spouses unless the third party lacks the capacity to be a witness. A presumption does exist that the communication was confidential. Where a spouse or child is the victim of a crime by the other spouse, the privilege does not apply as to that crime. The privilege belongs to the spouse against whom testimony is offered and while it may be waived, many courts feel both spouses, not merely the spouse making the communication, must consent for a valid waiver. The privilege applies in a family therapy or marital counseling setting in a manner similar to the **physician-patient privilege** to protect communications made in a therapeutic environment. This privilege should apply in states that allow **civil unions.** Compare **spousal disqualification.**

MARITAL DEDUCTION an ESTATE TAX (see **tax**) deduction permitting a spouse to take, tax free, up to one half the value of the decedent spouse's total **estate.** The marital deduction thus permits **property** to pass to the surviving spouse without being depleted by the federal estate tax; enacted for all to have tax treatment similar to that enjoyed by surviving spouses in the several **community property** states, where one half of the decedent's gross estate was presumed by law to already belong to the surviving spouse and hence was not subject to an estate tax.

MARITAL ESTATE [PROPERTY] property acquired by spouses during the marriage. Division of the property upon dissolution of the marriage is decided by the **court** unless a **marital agreement** exists. See **community property; equitable distribution.**

MARITIME JURISDICTION see **admiralty and maritime jurisdiction.**

MARITIME LAW the traditional body of rules and practices related to business transacted at sea or to navigation, ships, seamen, harbors and general maritime affairs. It is, and always has been a body of law separate from every other jurisprudence. See **admiralty and maritime jurisdiction; admiralty courts.**

MARKETABLE TITLE one that a reasonably well-informed purchaser would, in the exercise of ordinary business prudence, be willing to accept. A **title,** to be marketable, need not be free from every technical criticism, but it must be demonstrated to be reasonably free of **encumbrances.** See **good title.**

MARKET MAKERS see **over-the-counter market [MARKET MAKERS].**

MARKET ORDER see **order [MARKET ORDER].**

MARKET PRICE price established by public sales or sales in the way of ordinary business; figure fixed by sales in ordinary business transactions, established when other property of the same kind and in the same or comparable location has been bought or sold in so many instances that such value may reasonably be inferred. This price is based on a theoretical transaction between a free seller and buyer dealing at **arm's length.** This term is synonymous with ACTUAL VALUATION, ACTUAL VALUE, MARKET VALUE, and FAIR VALUE. In determining a buyer's damages for nondelivery or repudiation of goods, market price is determined as of the place for tender or, in cases of rejection after arrival or revocation of acceptance, as of the place of arrival.

MARKET VALUE the price that **property** would bring in a market of willing buyers and willing sellers, in the ordinary course of trade. Market value is generally established, if possible, on the basis of sales of similar property in the same locality. Market value is generally regarded as synonymous with ACTUAL VALUE, CASH VALUE, and FAIR MARKET VALUE. See **book value.**

MARRIAGE a voluntary union of two persons for life (or until divorce); the union is solemnized in accordance with local law by a wedding ceremony and the filing of a certificate of marriage. A license is required before a marriage can be performed. Such license can only be obtained after medical testing of the couple and, in the case where either party is a **minor,** by consent of a parent. The Supreme Court has held that the freedom to marry has long been recognized as one of the vital personal rights essential to the orderly pursuit of happiness. The common law recognized a marital status from a period of **cohabitation** between two people but such **common-law marriages** are no longer recognized as valid in most jurisdictions. See **civil union; domestic partnership.** Compare **bigamy.**

MARRIED WOMEN'S ACTS see **tenancy** [TENANCY BY THE ENTIRETY].

MARSHAL 1. an officer of the peace, appointed by authority of a city or borough, to answer calls within the general duties of a constable or sheriff, 2. an officer in each federal district who performs the same duties as sheriffs do for states.

MARSHALING [MARSHALLING] arranging or ranking in order.

MARSHALING ASSETS a rule of ranking assets of a debtor that seeks equitable distribution of those assets among as many claims as possible according to the equities of the parties. Courts of equity sometimes invoke the rule to compel a **creditor,** who has the right to satisfy his or her **debt** out of either of two funds, to resort to the fund that will not interfere with the rights of another creditor who has recourse to only one of these funds.

EXAMPLE: When Triad Corporation goes bankrupt, it owes money to both secured and unsecured creditors. The secured creditors have priority claims over specific property, while the unsecured creditors get paid only after all secured creditors are paid. One of the secured creditors has a claim on Triad's computers. If that creditor now wants to satisfy its debt with something other than the computers and that action will adversely affect the unsecured creditors, a court might apply the rule of *marshaling assets* to force that creditor to take the computers. Under that rule, both types of creditors have a better chance of having their claims satisfied.

MARSHALING LIENS   doctrine whereby one claiming a lien against two or more classes of property, one of which is also subject to a junior lien, a lien inferior to another, will be required to exact satisfaction from the property not subject to the junior lien. Thus, the junior lien is preserved where other assets exist sufficient to satisfy the senior lien.

MARSHALING REMEDIES   where one creditor has security on two funds of his debtor, and another creditor has security for his debt on only one of those funds, the latter has a right in equity to compel the former to resort to the other fund, if such an action is necessary for the satisfaction of both creditors, provided it will not prejudice the rights or interests of the party entitled to the double fund, nor do injustice to the common debtor, nor operate inequitably on the interests of other persons.

Probate courts marshall assets to meet the stated wishes of a **testator** (testatrix) in a **will** when appointed property (property disposed of in the will by **power of appointment**) would, because of technical impediments, pass into an inappropriate **residuary clause** rather than be distributed as intended by the testator. Marshaling of assets in probate courts to achieve this objective is also called **SELECTIVE ALLOCATION.**

MARTIAL LAW   law of military necessity, where the military exercises great control over civilian affairs, generally because of war or civil insurrection. When instituted, martial law represents the unchecked will of the commander, controlled only by consideration of strategy and policy. In America, the President, as Commander-in-Chief of the Armed Forces, would assume unreviewable discretion were martial law declared. Compare **court-martial; military law; separation of powers.**

MARY CARTER AGREEMENT   an agreement by the **plaintiff** to **settle** with some of the **defendants** in a **tort** case for the payment of specified damages even if the case is lost by the plaintiff. If the damages awarded exceed the settled amount, the defendant pays only the agreed upon amount or a specified percentage of the recovery. The case proceeds to the **jury** with all the defendants including the settled defendants who appear to be active **litigants.** Some states allow confidential agreements while others require the information to be disclosed to the jury.

MASSACHUSETTS TRUST a business **trust** that confers limited liability on the holders of trust certificates; also called a common law trust, a voluntary association of investors who transfer contributed cash or other property to trustees with legal authority to manage the business. Ownership **interest** is represented by transferable certificates of beneficial interest, also called trust certificates, and, less properly, **shares.** The business trust is a common form of organization among **real estate investment trusts (REITs).**

MASTER [MASTER IN CHANCERY; SPECIAL MASTER] 1. a judicial officer, often expert in the field with which the litigation is concerned, appointed by **courts of equity** to hear **testimony** and make reports that, when approved by the presiding judge, become the decision of the courts; 2. the employer in an employment relationship. See **master and servant.**

MASTER AND SERVANT the relationship that develops from an **express** or **implied** employment **contract** between a master, or employer, and a servant, or employee. See **agent; respondeat superior; servant.**

MASTER PLAN a long-term, general outline of a project or governmental function. For instance, in **zoning** law, a planning board or zoning commission will adopt a master plan for an area or a development project, which will regulate the height, density, and other characteristics of structures that may be erected.

MATCHED ORDERS see **manipulation [MATCHED ORDERS].**

MATERIAL necessary, meaningful, pertinent to a given matter. In contract law, a material **breach** excuses further performance by the **aggrieved party** and can give rise to an **action** for breach of contract.

EXAMPLE: A contract between Natick, Inc., and a recording company called for 12 separate shipments of blank CDs. The first three shipments were defective and were returned to Natick. The recording company was falling behind in its production schedule when the fourth shipment arrived and that shipment was also defective. The four defective shipments constitute a *material* breach of the contract and permit the recording company to cancel the contract and perhaps to institute a lawsuit against Natick as well.

MATERIAL ALTERATION any alteration of a document that changes its legal effect, i.e., that changes the rights, interests, and obligations of the parties to the instrument.

MATERIAL BREACH see **breach [MATERIAL BREACH].**

MATERIAL ISSUE an issue that is of legal consequence or other importance.

MATERIAL WITNESS see **witness [MATERIAL WITNESS].**

MATERNAL of the mother; belonging to or coming from the mother.

MATRICIDE the crime of killing one's mother.

MATRIMONIAL ACTION a lawsuit for the purpose of establishing or altering the marital status of the parties through an **annulment** or a **divorce.** See **custody; equitable [EQUITABLE DISTRIBUTION].**

MATRIMONIAL COURTS see **court [MATRIMONIAL COURTS].**

MATTER the substantial facts upon which a claim or defense is based; the subject of litigation, upon which issue is brought before the court and joined.

MATTER OF FACT see **question of fact.**

MATTER OF FIRST IMPRESSION see **first impression, case of.**

MATTER OF LAW see **question of law.**

MATURITY the date at which legal rights in something ripen. In the context of **commercial paper [negotiable instruments],** it is the time when the paper becomes **due** and demandable, that is, the date when an **action** can enforce payment.

MAXIMS statements espousing general principles of law; not usually used to justify a court decision based on law, but frequently used to determine the equities of a situation.

EXAMPLE: "Equity treats as done what ought to be done": The court will order the party to do what he or she should in good conscience already have done.

"First in time is first in right": If the claim of two parties is equal, the first in time is the party who will normally prevail.

MAYHEM the common law **felony** of **maliciously** maiming, dismembering or in any other way depriving another of the use of part of his body so as to render the victim less able to fight in the king's army. Many states today treat mayhem as **AGGRAVATED ASSAULT** (see **assault**).

MCNABB-MALLORY RULE a judicial policy, based on federal law, that renders **incriminating** statements not **admissible** in federal court if obtained from a suspect held in violation of the speedy **arraignment** provisions of federal law. i.e., if there is unreasonable delay in arraignment. Compare **miranda rule [warnings].**

MECHANIC'S LIEN see **lien [MECHANIC'S LIEN].**

MED-ARB **mediation** or **arbitration.**

MEDIATE DATA facts from which **ultimate facts** may be inferred for purposes of **collateral estoppel.**

MEDIATELY indirectly; having been deduced from proven facts.

MEDIATION a method of settling disputes outside of a court setting; the imposition of a neutral **THIRD PARTY** (see **party**) to act as a link between the parties; similar to **arbitration** and **conciliation.** See also **alternative dispute resolution.** Compare **negotiation.**

EXAMPLE: Sara and Henry wish to obtain a divorce. Hoping to avoid undue litigation and emotional trauma, they secure the help of a professional divorce mediator, who attempts a *mediation* of their affairs.

MEDIATOR see **mediation [MEDIATOR].**

MEDICAID see **affordable care act [MEDICAID].**

MEDICAL EXAMINER see **coroner.**

MEDICAL EXPENSE see **expense [MEDICAL EXPENSE].**

MEDICAL JURISPRUDENCE see **forensic [FORENSIC MEDICINE].**

MEDICAL MARIJUANA the use of marijuana to treat or alleviate specific conditions or symptoms when prescribed or recommended by a physician. In states where medical marijuana is decriminalized, the approved person who obtains the marijuana from a licensed dispensary (or in some states, grows his or her own) cannot be prosecuted for its possession if all state regulations for its use are followed.

MEDICARE see **affordable care act [MEDICARE].**

MEDIGAP see **affordable care act [MEDIGAP].**

MEETING OF MINDS mutual assent to terms by parties to a **contract.** A traditional rule of contract law is that the agreement, to be legally enforceable, must be accurately expressed within the terms of the contract the parties create for therein lies the required meeting of the minds; a hidden intent of either party will not change the agreement as expressed.

MEGAN'S LAW see **registration of offenders** [MEGAN'S LAW].

MEMBER BANK a member of the **Federal Reserve System.**

MEMBER CORPORATION a **securities brokerage** firm, organized as a **corporation,** with at least one member of the **New York Stock Exchange** who is a director and a holder of voting **stock** in the corporation. See **member firm.**

MEMBER FIRM a **securities brokerage** firm organized as a **partnership** and having at least one general partner who is a member of the **New York Stock Exchange.** See **member corporation.**

MEMORANDUM 1. an informal record; 2. a brief note, in writing, of some transaction; 3. an outline of an intended instrument; 4. an instrument written in concise summary.

MEMORANDUM OF LAW an argument by an **advocate** in support of his or her position; like a **brief** but less formal.

OFFICE MEMORANDUM informal discussion of the merits of a matter pending in a lawyer's office; usually written by a law clerk or junior associate for a senior associate or partner.

MEMORANDUM CHECK see **check** [MEMORANDUM CHECK].

MENACING see **assault.**

MENSA ET THORO see **divorce** [SEPARATION].

MENS REA *(mĕns rā'-à)* Lat.: a guilty state of mind. The mental state accompanying a forbidden act. Criminal offenses are usually defined with reference to one of four recognized criminal states of mind: (1) **intent;** (2) knowledge; (3) recklessness; (4) gross (criminal) **negligence.** In a criminal prosecution, the state must prove beyond a reasonable doubt that the required mental state coexisted with the doing of the proscribed act. Defenses of insanity, intoxication, and mistake may either nullify or mitigate the existence of a specific mens rea. Crimes that are **malum prohibitum** often do not require any specific mens rea. These are usually crimes of **strict liability.** See **assault; larceny.** Compare **insanity.**

MENTAL ANGUISH compensable **injury** embracing all forms of mental pain, distinguished from physical pain, including deep grief, distress, anxiety and fright. See **pain and suffering.**

MENTAL CRUELTY a ground for **divorce,** consisting of behavior by one spouse toward the other that so imperils the mental and physical health of the other that continuation of the marriage is unbearable.

MERCANTILE LAW the branch of law (often called **commercial law**) that deals with rules and institutions of commercial transactions; derived from the **law merchant.**

MERCHANT under the **Uniform Commercial Code,** "a person who deals in goods of the kind or otherwise by his occupation holds himself out as having knowledge or skill peculiar to the practice or goods involved in the transaction or to whom such knowledge or skill may be attributed by his employment of an agent or broker or other intermediary who by his occupation holds himself out as having such knowledge or skill." A one-time **seller** who is not engaged in the business of selling goods in question, or does not hold himself or herself out as a person who deals in such goods, is not a merchant for purposes of implied **warranty.**

Merchants include car dealers, producers of remanufactured engines, manufacturers of mobile homes, and with respect to the leasing of an apartment, landlords.

A warranty of merchantability will only be implied if the seller is a merchant with respect to goods of the kind in the contract of sale.

Under the Uniform Commercial Code, risk of loss passes to the **buyer** upon his or her receipt of goods only if the seller is a merchant; otherwise, the risk passes to the buyer on tender of delivery. See **warranty [WARRANTY OF MERCHANTABILITY].**

MERCHANTABLE 1. salable; 2. reasonably fit for the purpose for which an article is manufactured and sold; 3. having at least average quality, compared to similar products.

MERCHANTABLE TITLE see **marketable title.**

WARRANTY OF MERCHANTABILITY see **warranty [WARRANTY OF MERCHANTABILITY].**

MERCY KILLING see **euthanasia [ACTIVE EUTHANASIA].**

MERE EVIDENCE RULE a former rule of criminal procedure prohibiting the **seizure** of objects of evidential value whether pursuant to a **warrant,** or incident to arrest. The rule is no longer in effect and thus there is no distinction between *mere evidence* and instrumentalities, fruits of crime and contraband, in terms of seizure under the reasonableness standards of the Fourth Amendment. Even private personal papers may be seized as long as the **privilege against self-incrimination** is not violated by compelling a person to make a record or to authenticate the papers by their production.

MERGER 1. in criminal law, the process by which, when a single criminal act constitutes two offenses, the **lesser-included offense**

merges with the more serious offense for purposes of **conviction** and **sentence.**

2. In the law of **corporations,** a merger is effected when one corporation ceases to exist by becoming part of another continuing corporation. The company that continues to exist retains its name and identity and acquires the **assets, liabilities, franchises** and powers of the corporation that ceases to exist. **CONSOLIDATION,** by contrast, occurs when two or more corporations unite to form a new corporation and all the original corporations cease to exist.

3. Procedurally, merger describes the effect of a **judgment** in a **plaintiff's** favor. Such a judgment extinguishes the entire **claim** or **cause of action** that was the subject of a former action, so that it becomes merged in the judgment. Plaintiff is then precluded from making any further claim that was or could have been part of the action that has been ended.

4. In the conveyance of **real property,** once the **deed** is accepted, representations and agreements made before delivery of the executed deed are said to merge with the deed, which is the final expression of the mutual rights and obligations of the parties, replacing the contract of sale and other prior understandings.

5. In **property** law, merger is the absorption of a lesser **estate** into a higher estate when the two estates meet in the same person at the same time, without any intermediate estate separating them. Thus, when a **TENANT FOR YEARS** purchases or **inherits** the **reversion** in **fee simple,** the **tenancy terminates** in ownership.

EXAMPLE: Irwin has the right to possess and use a farm until his death, at which time the land passes to his sister. The sister has no desire to farm or own a country house, so she sells her interest to Irwin. Irwin's right of possession until his death *merges* with the interest he purchases from his sister to give him full ownership of the land forever. The result is that Irwin can now dispose of the property in whatever manner he desires.

Similarly, when the owner of an easement becomes the owner of the land, the easement is terminated by merging into the **possessory interest.**

6. The term also applies to the process by which, since the **Statute of Uses, equitable** ownership becomes legal ownership and conveyance of the former effectively conveys the latter.

CONGLOMERATE MERGER a merger wherein the merged corporations are neither competitors nor potential or actual customers or suppliers of each other where there are no economic relationships between the acquiring and the acquired firm.

GEOGRAPHIC MARKET EXTENSION MERGER a merger between

firms that produce the same or a similar product line but who sell in separate geographic markets and are not direct rivals.

HORIZONTAL MERGER acquisition of one company by another company producing the same or a similar product and selling it in the same geographic market.

MERGER OF PROPERTY INTERESTS merger of a smaller and larger estate whenever successive vested estates are owned by the same person. There cannot be a merger if a vested estate intervenes between the two estates, and, a contingent remainder, which would otherwise be destroyed by a merger of a life estate and the next vested estate, will not be destroyed if those two estates are created simultaneously with the contingent remainder, because that would defeat the intention of the transferor.

PRODUCT EXTENSION MERGER a merger between firms that are not direct rivals but that produce products that are functionally related either in marketing or in production to the other.

PURE CONGLOMERATE MERGER a residual category of mergers in which all mergers are placed that do not fit anywhere else and in which there seems to be no functional or meaningful relationship between the firms involved.

SHORT FORM MERGER a statutory method of merging corporations without the approval of the shareholders of either corporation, usually requiring that the corporation desiring the merger own at least 90 percent of the outstanding shares of each class of the other corporation.

VERTICAL MERGER acquisition of one company which buys the products sold by the acquiring company or which sells the product bought by the acquiring company.

MERGER CLAUSE see **parol evidence [PAROL EVIDENCE RULE].**

MERITS the various elements that qualify **plaintiff's** right to the **relief** sought, or **defendant's** right to prevail in his defense.

MESNE intermediate; between two extremes.

MESNE LORD in English law, a lord who held lands under authority of the King and who then gave others inferior in class to himself the right to use those lands, and thus became a lord to those grantees. See **feoffment; servitudes.**

MESNE PROFITS profits obtained from the land by one without legal right to the land and who thus curtails the rights of the owner.

METES AND BOUNDS the territorial limits of property expressed by measuring distances and angles from designated landmarks and in relation to adjoining properties.

MILITARY JURISDICTION refers to the constitutional setup of three types of military jurisdiction: **military law,** which provides for governing the armed forces in both peace and war; **military government,** which is exercised in times of foreign war outside the United States or in times of rebellion and civil war within states occupied by rebels, supersedes local law, and is exercised by a military commander under the authority of the President; and **martial law,** which can only be declared by Congress, or by the President for a temporary period, to be used in time of invasion or insurrection within the United States where ordinary law no longer adequately secures public safety and private rights. See **court-martial.**

MILITARY LAW a statutory code of rules and articles provided by Congress for the government and discipline of troops. It only applies to those in military service, but is enforced in both peace and war. See **military jurisdiction.** Compare **martial law.**

CODE OF MILITARY JUSTICE see **[UNIFORM] CODE OF MILITARY JUSTICE** (below).

COURT-MARTIAL see **court-martial.**

COURT OF MILITARY APPEAL the final appellate court that may review court-martial convictions of any armed service. It is not an Article III constitutional court but is established by Congress under its power to raise and regulate the land and naval forces of the United States. Its decisions are subject to review by the President of the United States.

COURT OF MILITARY REVIEW an intermediate appellate court established by each branch of the armed forces for purposes of reviewing **court-martial** cases.

MILITARY COMMISSION in time of war, a court appointed by a field commander to try alien enemy combatants for offenses against the laws of war.

MILITARY COURT OF INQUIRY a board of three or more commissioned officers that is convened by any person authorized to convene a general court-martial for the purpose of making an investigation and advising whether futher proceedings shall be had.

MILITARY GOVERNMENT **military jurisdiction** established under the Constitution, superseding local law, and exercised by the military commander under the direction of the President with the express or implied sanction of Congress. It is exercised either outside the boundaries of the United States or in time of rebellion and civil war within states or districts occupied by rebels. When a military government exists, any offense against the "law of war" is tried before a military court. See **martial law.**

[UNIFORM] CODE OF MILITARY JUSTICE the statute that sets forth procedures by which the armed forces may enforce discipline within its ranks. The military justice code establishes a system of courts to try members of the armed forces for service-related crimes. Service-related crimes are those committed on military posts, or while wearing a service uniform, but may extend to "nonmilitary" offenses in appropriate circumstances. The military courts function as a part of the executive branch of government, not the judicial branch, and are specifically exempted from the requirement of a grand jury. The proceedings of the military courts are not generally subject to review by the federal courts; however, the federal courts may hear habeas corpus applications from military prisoners who allege the denial of basic constitutional rights.

MILITARY WILL a relaxation of formal requirements for **wills** for members of the armed services while in actual military service. The will may be oral or written, sometimes without witnesses, and can be made by minors. The will is not contingent on the physical condition of the **testator/testatrix** at the time the will is made.

MINERAL LEASE see **mining [MINING LEASE].**

MINER'S INCH unit of measure involved in water rights of the amount of water passing through a standard opening under a prescribed pressure. Different states have different rates specified by statute (e.g., 1 miner's inch = .02 cu. ft. per sec. in Idaho and .025 cu. ft. per sec. in Arizona).

MINIMUM [MINIMAL] CONTACTS that degree of contact with a **forum** state sufficient to maintain a **suit** there and not offend traditional notions of fair play and substantial justice which are part of the constitutional guarantee of **due process of law.** Such contacts include transacting business within the forum, advertising within the forum, or accepting insurance payments from persons within the forum. The requirement is not met if, for example, a person buys an item outside the forum and is then injured in the normal use of that item within the forum.

MINIMUM WAGE minimum hourly wages established by Congress under the Fair Labor Standards Act to maintain the health, efficiency, and general well-being of workers. That Act has been held inapplicable to state and local governments.

MINING the process of extracting valuable natural resources from the earth including but not limited to gold, silver, diamonds, gas, coal, uranium, oil, and phosphorus.

LOCATION series of acts required by law to acquire a mining claim.

Public notice of the claim and identification of the parameters of the land must be given.

MINING CLAIM portion of land appropriated by an individual according to established rules and allowing for exclusive rights to harvest the natural resources therein.

MINING LEASE an agreement allowing a **lessee** the right to enter upon **real property** to explore for minerals or other natural resources and, if found, to extract them from the earth. The lessee pays the **lessor rent** or a share of the proceeds. A mining lease differs from an ordinary **lease** in that the right exists to take from the soil with only a limited right of possession of the land incidental thereto, as in an oil or gas lease.

MINISTER a person ordained in conformity to the customs of any organized religion. To be exempt from military training and service, but not from registration, under the Universal Military Training and Service Act, a person must be ordained in accordance with the formalities required by their religious denomination and preach and teach its religious tenets as their regular and customary vocation, not merely irregularly or incidentally.

MINISTERIAL ACT an act performed according to explicit directions (often embodied in a **statute**) by a subordinate official, allowing no judgment or **discretion** on the part of that official. See **mandamus.**

MINORITY condition of being under legal age.

MINUTES a transcription or other written record of judicial proceedings. While the minutes kept by the **judge** are neither a memorial of the **judgment** nor a legally required **record,** they are legal **evidence** of the **judgment,** and as such they may serve as the foundation for the correction of **errors.** Compare **transcript.**

MIRANDA RULE [WARNINGS] the requirement to inform a person of his or her privilege against **self-incrimination** (right to remain silent) and his or her right to the presence and advice of a retained or appointed attorney before any custodial **interrogation** by law enforcement authorities. Prior to any questioning, the person must also be warned that any statement he or she does make may be used as **evidence** against him or her.

Statements and evidence obtained in violation of this rule, unless these rights have been knowingly **waived** (and the evidence voluntarily provided), are not **admissible** in the defendant's criminal **trial** and are grounds for federal constitutional challenge to any **conviction** obtained thereby.

MISADVENTURE an accidental and unintentional homicide, distinguished from involuntary **manslaughter** in that the homicide by misadventure must be the result of a lawful act unaccompanied by criminal carelessness or recklessness.

MISAPPLICATION [MISAPPROPRIATION] OF PROPERTY the conscious illegal use of funds or property for a wrongful purpose; particularly applies to the acts of a **fiduciary** [one in a position of trust], public servants as well as private **trustees.** The terms can include misapplication of funds intended for another purpose, e.g., the misapplication of public money, or the **conversion** of another's funds for one's own benefit. Compare **embezzlement; larceny.**

MISAPPROPRIATION see **misapplication [misappropriation] of property.**

MISCARRIAGE OF JUSTICE damage to the rights of one **party** to an **action** that results from errors made by the court during trial and that is sufficiently substantial to require **reversal.** Where the **appellate court** is seriously doubtful that without committed errors the result in the case would have been the same, the errors may require a reversal on the grounds of a miscarriage of justice. See **plain error.**

MISCEGENATION in America and England, a marriage between a Caucasian and a member of any of the other races; the mixture of races in a marriage or cohabitation in a state of **adultery** or **fornication** by a white and a black person.

MISCONDUCT IN OFFICE corrupt misbehavior by an officer in the exercise of the duties of the office or while acting under color of the office; includes any act or omission in breach of a duty of public concern by one who has accepted public office. See **bribery.**

MISDELIVERY includes both **delivery** to the wrong party and delivery of **goods** damaged by the **carrier;** failure to deliver goods within the terms of the **bill of lading;** a total failure to deliver the goods, or leaving them at the wrong place, which is also deemed a **conversion.** In a **bailment** for hire, the bailee is held strictly accountable for a misdelivery and is liable for conversion when such misdelivery occurs. For purposes of commercial **contracts,** a delivery pursuant to a forged delivery order is a misdelivery rather than a **theft.**

MISDEMEANOR a class of criminal offenses less serious than **felonies** and sanctioned by less severe penalties. In a **jurisdiction** where there are no felonies, the more serious misdemeanors are called HIGH MISDEMEANORS. See **degree of crime; felony.**

MISFEASANCE improper and unlawful execution of an act that in itself is lawful. Frequently used when a job is done in a way that is not technically illegal, but is nevertheless mistaken or wrong. Compare **malfeasance; misconduct; nonfeasance.**

EXAMPLE: Tamara is distracted when completing her client's tax return and makes serious errors. Her filing of the document is misfeasance.

MISJOINDER 1. the improper joining together in one trial of distinct unrelated **counts** in a single **indictment** or **complaint;** 2. the improper joining of **parties** or criminal **defendants** in a single action. See **joinder.**

MISLAID PROPERTY **property** that the owner has intentionally placed where he or she can resort to it, but which place is then forgotten. Compare **abandonment; lost property.**

EXAMPLE: Oscar inadvertently leaves his briefcase at the train station. Later that evening, Oscar realizes he no longer has the briefcase and cannot remember where it is. The briefcase is *mislaid property,* and Oscar still has an ownership interest in it. He did not leave the property where he had no intention of recovering it. In that case the property would have been abandoned.

MISNOMER a mistake in a person's name. The MISNOMER RULE, which affords relief from the **statute of limitations,** applies when the **plaintiff** has sued and **served** the party he intends to sue but has mistakenly used the wrong name of the **defendant.**

MISPRISION OF FELONY in common law, the **misdemeanor** of observing the committing of a felony and failing to prevent it, or of knowing about a felony and failing to disclose its occurrence, or of concealing the felony without any previous agreement with or subsequent assistance to the **felon** as would make the concealer an **accessory** before- or after-the-fact. Today, to be guilty of the federal crime of misprision of felony, in addition to knowing about a felony and failing to disclose information about it, one must take an affirmative step to conceal it.

EXAMPLE: Margarita observes a bank robbery taking place at a federally insured bank. As a believer in the axiom of stealing from the rich to give to the poor, Margarita not only does not call the police but picks up a pair of gloves the thieves left behind. Those gloves, which might help solve the crime, are destroyed by Margarita. That destruction makes Margarita guilty of the federal crime of *misprision of felony.*

MISREPRESENTATION See **false pretense.**

MISTAKE an act or omission arising from ignorance or misconception, which may, depending upon its character or the circumstances surrounding it, justify **rescission** of a **contract,** or exoneration of a **defendant** from **tort** or criminal **liability.**

MISTAKE OF FACT mistaken notion as to circumstances, events or facts.

MISTAKE OF LAW ignorance of the legal consequences of one's conduct, though he or she may be cognizant of the facts and substance of that conduct. Compare **ignorantia legis non excusat.**

MUTUAL [BILATERAL] MISTAKE in **commercial law,** an error on the part of both parties regarding the same matter—for example, where both parties understood that the real agreement was what one party alleges it to be, but had unintentionally executed a contract that did not express the true agreement.

EXAMPLE: Otis buys his mother a raincoat for her birthday. The salesperson tells him that one size fits all and believes that to be the case. In fact, the particular coat is tailored for a very large person and is manufactured in several different sizes. The mutual *mistake* will allow the sale to be cancelled by Otis even though it was a final sale with no returns.

UNILATERAL MISTAKE a mistake on the part of only one of the parties.

MISTRIAL a **trial** that has been terminated and declared void prior to the **jury's** returning a **verdict** (or the judge's declaring his or her verdict in a nonjury trial) because of some extraordinary circumstance (such as death or illness of a necessary **juror** or of an attorney), or because of some fundamental error prejudicial to the **defendant** that cannot be cured by appropriate instructions to the jury (such as the inclusion of highly improper remarks in the prosecutor's summation), or most commonly because of the jury's inability to reach a verdict because it is hopelessly deadlocked in its deliberations **(hung jury).** Mistrial does not result in a **judgment** for any party, but merely indicates a failure of **trial.** Compare **double jeopardy.**

MITIGATING CIRCUMSTANCES a set of conditions that, while not exonerating the accused, might reduce the **sentence** or the **damages** arising from the offense. Compare **aggravating circumstances; defense.**

MITIGATION OF DAMAGES 1. a requirement that one injured by another's **breach** of an agreement or **tort** employ reasonable diligence and care to avoid aggravating the injury or increasing the **damages;** 2. a defendant's request to the court for a reduction in damages owed to the plaintiff, a request that the defendant justifies by evidence demonstrating that the plaintiff is not entitled to the full amount that might otherwise be awarded.

DUTY TO MITIGATE DAMAGES the rule that in some circumstances one who is wronged must act reasonably to avoid or limit losses, because he or she cannot recover damages that could have been avoided.

EXAMPLE: Rusty signs a three-year lease with a landlord but has to move out of the apartment after one year. For two years, the landlord lets the apartment stay vacant, even though several people are interested in renting that specific apartment. When the landlord sues Rusty for rent due over the two-year period, Rusty will claim that the landlord's right to collect should be limited because of the landlord's failure to *mitigate his damages.* In this instance, the landlord may have easily rented the apartment to another person so that the landlord's losses, and therefore his damage claims, would have been greatly reduced. The offset for rents that could have been collected will be allowed.

MITOCHONDRIAL DNA see **DNA testing [MITOCHONDRIAL DNA [mtDNA]].**

MIXED NUISANCE see **nuisance [MIXED NUISANCE].**

MIXED QUESTION OF LAW AND FACT see **question of law [MIXED QUESTION OF LAW AND FACT].**

M'NAGHTEN RULE the **common law** test of criminal responsibility under which a person was not responsible for criminal acts and was thus entitled to an **acquittal** by reason of **insanity** if as a result of a mental disease or defect he or she did not understand what he or she did or that it was wrong, or if he or she was under a delusion (but not otherwise insane) that, if true, would have provided a good **defense** (as where the defendant thought he or she was acting in **self-defense** or carrying out the will of God). This is called the **RIGHT AND WRONG TEST** because it is often said that one was not insane under the M'Naghten rule if he or she could distinguish right from wrong. The test has been criticized as too restrictive and has been changed in many **jurisdictions.** See **Durham rule; insanity [M'NAGHTEN RULE].**

M.O. see **modus operandi.**

MOB see **organized crime.**

MODEL ACTS see **uniform laws.**

MODEL RULES OF PROFESSIONAL CONDUCT most recent pronouncement of rules governing professional conduct of lawyers recommended by the American Bar Association in 1983 to replace the **Code of Professional Responsibility.** Generally consists of rules of reason prescribing terms for resolving ethical problems that arise from "conflict between a lawyer's responsibility to clients, to the legal system and to the lawyer's own interest in remaining an upright person while earning a satisfactory living." Preamble to the Rules. The adoption of the Rules recognizes that the legal profession is largely self-governing, a status that can be maintained only as long as the profession can assure that its regulations are conceived in the public interest and not in furtherance of parochial or self-interested concerns of the bar. The Rules, however, simply provide a framework for the ethical practice of law. They do not exhaust the moral and ethical considerations that should guide a lawyer. Moreover, the Rules are not designed to be a basis for civil liability. Each state body that regulates lawyer conduct within its jurisdiction is free to adopt all or part of the Rules, or to reject them.

The Rules address eight separate areas: (1) the client-lawyer relationship, (2) the lawyer as a counselor, (3) the lawyer as an advocate, (4) transactions with persons other than lawyers, (5) law firms and associations, (6) public service, (7) information about legal service, and (8) maintaining the integrity of the profession.

One of the more controversial rules concerns Confidentiality of Information, which essentially requires the lawyer to not reveal any information the client tells to the lawyer, even if that information concerns the commission of a crime or fraud upon others, except if the crime is likely to result in imminent death or substantial bodily harm, or establishes a claim or defense on behalf of the lawyer in a controversy between the lawyer and client.

MODIFIED ACCELERATED COST RECOVERY SYSTEM see **depreciation [MODIFIED ACCELERATED COST RECOVERY SYSTEM].**

MODUS OPERANDI *(mo'-dŭs ŏp-eṙ-än'-dē)* Lat.: the manner of operation. The means of accomplishing an act; especially, the characteristic method employed by **defendant** in repeated criminal acts.

MOIETY a half; a part.

MOLLITER MANUS IMPOSUIT *(mō'-lĭ-tèr mä'-nŭs ĭmpō'-zū-ĭt)* Lat.: the gentle laying upon of hands. In a **tort** action, the term refers to an assertion by one of the **parties** that he or she used only the force necessary to protect himself or herself or his or her property from injury by the other party. Compare **self-defense.**

M-1 [M-2, M-3] see **money supply [M-1, M-2, M-3].**

MONEY coined metal, usually gold or silver, upon which a government has impressed its stamp to designate its value. While money was once limited to "coin of the realm," in common usage the term refers to any currency, tokens, bank notes, or the like accepted as a medium of exchange. Under the **Uniform Commercial Code,** money is defined as "a medium of exchange authorized or adopted by a domestic or foreign government as a part of its currency." Compare **legal tender.**

MONEY DEMAND any demand or **action** arising out of **contract,** tort, or statute, express or implied, where the relief demanded is a recovery of money, and may be enforced by **attachment** when the amount due is fixed or can be ascertained.

MONEY HAD AND RECEIVED in early common law pleading, one of the categories in the action for general **assumpsit.** The plaintiff declared that the defendant "had and received certain money." The other two related declarations in the same category were "for money lent" and "for money paid."

MONEY JUDGMENT a judgment ordering the payment of a sum of money. Such judgments may be executed under a writ of **execution.**

MONEY ORDER a credit instrument, either **negotiable** or non-negotiable, calling for payment of money to a named **payee,** and involving the payee, **drawee,** and remitter.

MONEY SUPPLY [M-1, M-2, M-3] the various measures of money used by the Federal Reserve System. M-1 is currency plus demand deposits or checking account balances; M-2 is M-1 plus net time deposits other than large **certificates of deposit;** M-3 is M-2 plus deposits at nonbank thrift institutions such as savings and loan associations. Various other components and combinations are also used.

MONOGAMY see **polygamy.**

MONOPOLY 1. a market condition where all or so nearly all of an article of commerce within a district is brought within the control of one person or company, that competition or free traffic in that article is excluded. See **antitrust laws.**

2. a privilege or **license** granting a group or company sole authority to deal in certain products, or provide a product or service in a specified area.

EXAMPLE: Public Utilities Gas Company is granted the exclusive right to supply gas to the northern part of a state. The right is granted out of convenience and necessity, since it would be impractical to have several gas company lines running underground. Moreover, it is desirable to have the state control pricing of a necessary item for any household. As a grant by the state, the *monopoly* in favor of Public Utilities is a lawful monopoly.

MONTH-TO-MONTH TENANCY see **tenancy [PERIODIC TEN-ANCY].**

MOOT CASE a case that seeks to determine an abstract question that does not rest upon existing facts or rights, or that seeks a **judgment** in a pretended controversy, or one that seeks a decision about a right before it has actually been asserted or contested, or a judgment upon some matter that, when rendered for any cause, cannot have any practical effect upon the existing controversy. See **advisory opinion.**

EXAMPLE: Tina files a lawsuit against Private University, claiming that the university has denied her admission because of her race. Before the case reaches the trial court. Private admits Tina as a student. Because of the school's actions, the case between Tina and Private is rendered *moot.* Tina can no longer claim that race was a factor in denying her admission, since she has been admitted.

MOOT COURT a fictitious court established to argue a **moot case.** Law schools form moot courts as an instrument of learning.

MORAL CERTAINTY certainty beyond a **reasonable doubt;** a conviction based on persuasive reasons and excluding doubts that a contrary conclusion can exist. A juror is said to be morally certain of a fact when he or she would act in reliance upon its truth in matters of greatest importance to himself or herself.

MORAL CONSIDERATION see **consideration [MORAL [EQUITA-BLE] CONSIDERATION].**

MORAL TURPITUDE vileness or dishonesty of a high degree. A crime of moral turpitude demonstrates depravity in the private and social duties a person owes to others, contrary to what is accepted and customary.

MORATORIUM delay, a period during which certain proceedings or obligations are suspended. During the pendency of **bankruptcy** proceedings, for example, there is a moratorium on the debtor's obligation to pay his debts.

MORTGAGE in **common law,** a conveyance of, or granting of a **lien** upon, **real property** of a **debtor** to his **creditor,** intended as a security for the repayment of a loan, usually the purchase price (or a part thereof) of the **property** so conveyed or **encumbered.** The transfer was rendered **void** upon repayment of the loan; i.e., the property reverted to the debtor upon the discharge of the mortgage by timely payment of the sum loaned.

TITLE THEORY refers to the modern version of the common law mortgage under which the creditor has the legal right to possession (though in fact the debtor remains in possession of his or her property). Under the **HYBRID THEORY** the creditor's right to possession arises only upon **default** by the debtor. Under the **LIEN THEORY,** the mortgagee (creditor) takes a lien on the property, and is not entitled to possession until he or she has pursued remedy in **foreclosure** and the mortgaged **premises** have been sold; i.e., the right to possession arises only when the mortgagor's (debtor's) **equity of redemption** has been foreclosed. In the mortgage relationship, the debtor is called the *mortgagor* and the creditor is called the *mortgagee.*

ADJUSTABLE RATE MORTGAGE   a loan in which the interest rate floats dependent upon periodic adjustments to an index. Such varying rates usually start out lower than fixed rates and may or may not have a cap on the maximum rate. Also called a **VARIABLE RATE MORTGAGE**.

ASSIGNMENT OF MORTGAGE   an agreement transferring mortgage ownership from one party to another.

ASSUMPTION OF MORTGAGE taking upon oneself the obligations of a mortgagor towards a mortgagee, generally as part of the purchase price of a parcel of real estate. By assuming the mortgage rather than taking subject to the mortgage, the purchaser becomes personally **liable** on the debt.

EXAMPLE: Ed wants to buy Kiem's home for $280,000. He can afford a $116,000 down payment and is willing to assume Kiem's $164,000 mortgage. If the bank agrees to the assumption of its mortgage, Ed will be personally responsible for the mortgage payments. If Ed should default, the bank can still hold Kiem liable, since he was the original mortgagor, unless he is released by the bank as part of the assumption.

BALLOON MORTGAGE [NOTE] a promissory note repayable in periodic installments of a specified amount, usually representing interest, with a much larger final payment, usually of the entire principal amount, often called the **BALLOON PAYMENT**.

BLANKET MORTGAGE   a mortgage burdening all of the property present and future.

CHATTEL MORTGAGE conveyance of a present **interest** in **personal property,** generally as security for payment of money, such as the purchase price of property, or for the performance of some other act. Like a mortgage of **real property,** it operates in some states to pass **title** to the mortgagee, but in other states merely to create a **lien;** but in either case the mortgagor retains possession. It is thus distinguished from a **pledge,** which establishes a **bailment** and that therefore establishes the pledgee as bailee and grants him or her possession of the **personalty.**

CLOSED-END MORTGAGE a mortgage that does not permit additional borrowing without the consent of the first mortgagee.

DIRECT REDUCTION MORTGAGE one which requires a fixed payment of principal each period.

EQUITABLE MORTGAGE security transaction that fails to satisfy the legal requirements of a mortgage but that nevertheless is treated in **equity** as a mortgage. It includes cases in which **interest** in the property in the hands of the creditor is full legal ownership, and the aid of equity is necessary to reduce it to a security interest and to establish the rights of the debtor as a mortgagor. Also included are cases where the transaction is technically insufficient to create a mortgage **at law,** but where equity intervenes to protect the mortgagee.

FIXED RATE MORTGAGE one with an interest rate that does not change.

HOME EQUITY CONVERSION MORTGAGE see **REVERSE MORTGAGE** (below).

HOME EQUITY LINE OF CREDIT [HELOC] see **home equity line of credit [HELOC].**

LEASE-PURCHASE AGREEMENT [CONTRACT] a rent-to-own arrangement where the renter's payments go toward the ultimate purchase of the property at a pre-determined price. Often used where there is sufficient income for the monthly payments but no money for a down payment. The lease substitutes for the mortgage.

LEVEL PAYMENT MORTGAGE see **FIXED PAYMENT MORTGAGE** (above).

MORTGAGE COMMITMENT (LETTER) a letter provided by a lender to a borrower legally binding the terms upon which a loan for the purchase or refinance of real property will be granted.

MOTHER HUBBARD CLAUSE see **mother hubbard clause.**

PURCHASE MONEY see **security interest.**

REVERSE MORTGAGE mortgage allowing a homeowner (usually elderly) to convert existing equity into periodic disbursements or a cash advance to be repaid with interest when the home is sold, the borrower dies, or a specified maturity date is reached.

SECOND MORTGAGE a loan with rights secondary to the first loan. A mortgage without intervening liens between it and the first mortgage; one which does not contemplate a mortgage on a buyer's interest in a land contract.

SENIOR MORTGAGE refers to a **FIRST MORTGAGE** and not a

REVERSE MORTGAGE (above). It is not reflective of age.

SHARED APPRECIATION MORTGAGE a loan where the borrower gets a lower than market interest rate in exchange for allowing the lender to share in the future appreciation of the property.

SUBJECT TO MORTGAGE a condition of sale whereby the purchaser takes land encumbered by a preexisting mortgage. The purchaser's obligation to the mortgagee is limited to the value of the property subject to the mortgage, unless the purchaser becomes personally liable on the debt by assuming the mortgage. See **ASSUMPTION OF MORTGAGE** (above)

SUBPRIME MORTGAGE (generally with an adjustable interest rate and often little or no down payment) is one offered to borrowers with low credit ratings. Higher interest rates are charged due to the greater risk of loan default.

SUBPRIME MORTGAGE CRISIS began around 2006, when declining house prices and rising adjustable rates led to the inability of borrowers to refinance and resulted in dramatic numbers of foreclosures. Banking institutions lost huge amounts of their investments and responded by tightening credit, leading to a global economic crisis.

TITLE THEORY see earlier in entry (above).

VARIABLE RATE MORTGAGE see **ADJUSTABLE RATE MORTGAGE** (above).

WRAPAROUND MORTGAGE in real estate law, a second mortgage which allows the borrower to take advantage of a low interest first mortgage without being subject to the usual cash flow demands of carrying both a first and second mortgage. The face amount of the wraparound mortgage is the amount due on the first mortgage plus the amount due on the second mortgage. Annual payments are computed on this combined amount, and are applied to satisfy the payments due on the first mortgage before being applied to the wraparound mortgage. The wraparound mortgage is frequently used in the purchase and sale of realty when the seller's mortgage is at more advantageous terms than financing available to the buyer.

MORTGAGE COMMITMENT (LETTER) see **mortgage [MORTGAGE COMMITMENT (LETTER)]**.

MORTGAGEE the party lending the money to a **mortgagor,** who takes a security interest in property owned by the mortgagor.

MORTGAGE MARKET origination of **mortgage** loans in the primary mortgage market and resale of mortgages in the secondary mortgage market, especially mortgage certificates that are **bond**-like securities backed by blocks of mortgage loans. Primary origination is conducted by mutual savings **banks,** savings and loan associations, mortgage bankers, commercial banks, and insurance companies. The same institutions are active in the secondary market with mortgage certificate issues directed to the general public and traditional investment groups such as pension funds. Mortgage loans represent first **liens** on real estate property that, unlike bonds, require periodic payment (usually monthly) of both principal and interest over the term of the mortgage. The federal government has assumed a major economic role in the mortgage loan market because real estate development is a major sector of the U.S. economy. The Federal Housing Authority and the Veterans Administration promote primary mortgage originations by guaranteeing home mortgages. The Government National Mortgage Association (known as GINNIE MAE) and the Federal National Mortgage Association (known as FANNIE MAE) promote the secondary mortgage market in government-insured loans. The Federal Home Loan Bank Board regulates savings banks, which are the primary originators of home mortgages, and promotes the secondary market in government-insured mortgages, privately insured mortgages and conventional uninsured mortgages.

MORTGAGOR the party borrowing money from a bank or other lending agency, who secures the loan with property the party owns in whole or in part.

MORTIS CAUSA see **cause [CAUSA MORTIS].**

MORTMAIN literally, dead hand; applies to all **property** that, from the nature of the purposes to which it is devoted, or the character of the **ownership** to which it is subjected, is for every practical purpose not freely **alienable.**

MOST FAVORED NATION CLAUSE in international law, a clause in a **treaty** by which each signatory country grants to the other the broadest rights and privileges that it accords to any other nation in treaties it has made or will make.

MOTHER HUBBARD CLAUSE 1. mortgage clause allowing that in the event of a default, the lender may foreclose not only on that mortgage but also any other loans made between the same parties. It is also known as an ANDACONDA CLAUSE or **DRAGNET CLAUSE.** 2. in oil and gas leases, refers to small pieces of land that might be left out of the property description but are included in the lease, such as a ditch or small areas missed by surveyors. As such, it is considered an "all-inclusive" or "catch-all" provision.

MOTION an application to the court requesting an **order** in favor of the applicant. Motions are generally made in reference to a pending **action** and may be addressed to a matter within the discretion of the judge, or may concern a point of law. Motions may be made orally or, more formally, in writing.

MOTION FOR JUDGMENT a motion admitting an agreed-upon statement of facts that leaves the dominant issue in the case as one of a **matter of law**, thereby relegating the issue for a determination by the court rather than by a jury. See **judgment** [JUDGMENT NOTWITHSTANDING THE VERDICT]; **summary judgment.**

MOTION IN ARREST OF JUDGMENT application made by defendant to withhold judgment after verdict. The motion, like a **demurrer**, must point out some fatal defect arising as a matter of law from the record.

MOTION IN ERROR same as **writ of error**, except no notice to opponent is required, because both parties are before the court when a motion in error is made.

MOTION IN LIMINE a motion used to exclude reference to anticipated **evidence** claimed to be objectionable until the **admissibility** of the questionable evidence can be determined either before or during the trial by presenting to the court, out of the presence of the jury, offers and objections to the evidence. The motion seeks to avoid injection into trial of irrelevant, inadmissible, or prejudicial evidence at any point, including the **voir dire** examinations, opening statements, and direct and cross-examinations, and therefore prevents mistrials based on evidentiary irregularities.

MOTION TO SET ASIDE JUDGMENT exactly like **MOTION IN ARREST OF JUDGMENT** (above), except that while a motion to arrest must be made during term of court which renders judgment, a motion to set aside judgment can be made at any time within the applicable **statute of limitations**. Both motions must be based on a legal defect appearing on the face of the **record.**

MOTOR VEHICLE CODE see **code.**

MOVANT the moving party; applicant for an **order** by way of **motion** before a court.

MOVE to make a **motion;** in practice, to make application to a court or other tribunal for a ruling, **order** or particular **relief.**

mtDNA see **DNA testing** [MITOCHONDRIAL DNA [mtDNA]].

MULCT a **fine** or penalty imposed for an offense; a **forfeiture.**

MULIER legitimate child.

MULTIFARIOUS refers to a suit where independent matters are improperly **joined** and thereby confused; also refers to **misjoinder** of **causes of action** and misjoinder of **parties** in a suit.

MULTIPARTITE consisting of two or more parts or **parties,** as where several nations join in a treaty.

MULTIPLICITY OF ACTIONS [SUITS] the existence of several separate **actions at law** brought against the same defendant to **litigate** the same right. In the exercise of its **equity** powers, a court can **enjoin** the proceedings at law and hear all of the claims at a single proceeding. A mere multitude of suits is not sufficient to invoke this remedy. Rather, the court must find that the remedy at law is not sufficient and that the proceedings will be vexatious for the defendant and wasteful for the courts. **Class action** suits are permitted as an attempt to alleviate this problem. See **litigious; malicious prosecution.**

MUNICIPAL BOND a **bond** issued by a state or local government body such as a county, city or town.

MUNICIPAL CORPORATIONS usually **incorporated** cities, towns and villages having subordinate and local powers of legislation. The term is sometimes used in a broader sense to include every **corporation** formed for governmental purposes, so as to embrace counties, townships, school districts and other governmental subdivisions of the state.

MUNICIPAL COURT city court that administers the law within the city. These courts generally have exclusive **jurisdiction** over violations of city **ordinances** and may also have jurisdiction over minor criminal cases arising within the city and over certain **civil** cases.

MUNICIPAL ORDINANCE a law of local application, whose violation is an offense against the city enacting it. See **ordinance.**

MURDER unlawful killing of another human being with premeditated intent or **malice aforethought.**

FIRST DEGREE MURDER unlawful killing that is deliberate and premeditated.

SECOND DEGREE MURDER unlawful killing of another with **malice** aforethought but without deliberation and **premeditation.** Such malice may be in the form of express malice as the actual intention to kill, or of implied malice where there is no intent, but where death is caused by an act that discloses such a reckless state of mind as to be equivalent to an actual intent to kill.

EXAMPLE: Tom becomes very angry at his business partner, Kaz, and throws a brick at him. Since Tom intended to hurt Kaz, if death results the act will be second degree murder. If the provocation was sufficient, the crime might be reduced by the jury to manslaughter. If Tom planned the attack on Kaz and intended to inflict grievous injury, it might be first degree murder.

See also **homicide; manslaughter.**

MUTE see **standing mute.**

MUTINY to rise against lawful or constituted authority, particularly in the naval or military service. At sea, an attempt to usurp command of a vessel from its master. Includes resisting a federal warden or subordinate officers in the free and lawful exercise of their legal authority.

MUTUAL COVENANTS see **covenant [INDEPENDENT [MUTUAL] COVENANTS].**

MUTUAL FUND an investment company that sells its own shares to investors and then invests the proceeds from that sale in other securities, thus affording its investors a diversified **portfolio. OPEN-END MUTUAL FUNDS** do not have a fixed **capitalization** and may issue new shares on a customer-demand basis. **CLOSED-END MUTUAL FUNDS** do have a fixed capitalization and may sell only as many shares as were authorized in the first instance.

MUTUAL FUND SHARE a **security** reflecting an undivided ownership in a **mutual fund** company that is not traded by the shareholders but is redeemable upon its request.

MUTUALITY OF ESTOPPEL see **estoppel [MUTUALITY OF ESTOPPEL].**

MUTUALITY OF OBLIGATION responsibilities imposed on each of the parties to a **contract,** which must be mutual and by which each must be bound. Unless each **party** is bound to perform in some way, the agreement will lack **consideration.**

MUTUALITY OF REMEDY a doctrine that one party should not obtain from **equity** that which the other party could not obtain. Accordingly, whenever a **contract** is incapable of being specifically enforced against one **party** because of the personal nature of the contract, that party cannot specifically enforce it against the other.

MUTUAL MISTAKE see **mistake [MUTUAL [BILATERAL] MISTAKE].**

N

NAKED POWER see **power of appointment [NAKED POWER].**

NALA see **National Association of Legal Assistants [NALA}.**

NALP see **National Association of Legal Professionals [NALP].**

NALS see **National Association of Legal Secretaries [NALS].**

NAMED INSURED the party who contracts for insurance and who is named in the policy. It sometimes happens that one who is a named insured has a claim in tort against another who is an additional insured under the policy. For example, the owner of an insured automobile may lend it to another whose operation of the vehicle injures the owner (the named insured).

NARCOTICS see **controlled substances [NARCOTICS].**

NASD see **National Association of Securities Dealers [NASD].**

NASDAQ the national automated quotation service for **over-the-counter securities.** Operation is supervised by the **National Association of Securities Dealers [NASD]** and input is provided by hundreds of **over-the-counter market** makers. NASDAQ is an acronym for National Association of Securities Dealers Automated Quotations.

NATIONAL ASSOCIATION OF LEGAL ASSISTANTS [NALA] a national organization of **paralegals** and legal assistants providing continuing education, job placement, and professional certification. Use of CLA **(Certified Legal Assistant)** after a name indicates the receipt of certification through NALA.

NATIONAL ASSOCIATION OF LEGAL PROFESSIONALS [NALP] a national organization of **legal secretaries** providing continuing education, professional certification, and job placement.

NATIONAL ASSOCIATION OF LEGAL SECRETARIES [NALS] see **National Association of Legal Professionals [NALP].**

NATIONAL ASSOCIATION OF SECURITIES DEALERS [NASD] a body empowered by the **Securities and Exchange Commission** to regulate **over-the-counter market** brokers and dealers. It is charged to adopt, adminster, and enforce rules of fair practice and rules to prevent fraudulent and manipulative acts and practices, and in general to promote just and equitable principles of trade for the protection of investors. It publishes quotations for national and regional over-the-counter transactions and supervises operation of NASDAQ, the national automated quotation service for over-the-counter stocks.

NATIONAL CRIME INFORMATION CENTER see **NCIC.**

NATIONAL LABOR RELATIONS ACT comprehensive federal law that regulates the relations of employers and establishes the **National Labor Relations Board. See labor organization [union].**

NATIONAL LABOR RELATIONS BOARD [NLRB] an independent agency created by Congress that oversees relationships between unions and employees. The Board has the power to adjudicate claims before it and to enforce its judgments in the federal courts. See **labor organization [union].**

NATIONAL LAWYERS GUILD an association of lawyers, law students, legal workers, and **jailhouse lawyers** dedicated to the need for basic change in the political and economic system of the country. It actively seeks to eliminate racism and to maintain and protect civil rights and civil liberties. It was founded in 1937 as a progressive alternative to the **American Bar Association.**

NATIVE AMERICAN LAW see **Indian law.**

NATIVE FILE original, unaltered computer file.

NATURAL CHILD any child by birth as opposed to an adopted child. Compare **adoption.**

NATURALIZED CITIZEN one who, having been born in another country or otherwise reared as a foreigner, has been granted U.S. citizenship and the rights and privileges of that status. The process by which such a person attains citizenship is called **NATURALIZATION.** See **citizen.** Compare **alien; legal permanent resident.**

NATURAL LAW law that so necessarily agrees with the nature of human beings, that without observing its maxims, the peace and happiness of society cannot be preserved; that law, knowledge of which may be attained merely by the light of reason, and from the facts of its essential connection with human nature. Natural law exists regardless of whether it is enacted as **positive law.** See **positivism.**

NATURAL LAW THEORY in jurisprudence, the view that the

nature and value of any legal order is best understood by studying how the **positive law** of that legal order agrees or contrasts with **natural law.**

NATURAL PERSON a human being, as opposed to an artificial or fictitious person such as a **corporation.**

NATURE, ACT OF see **act of God [nature; providence].**

NAVIGABLE WATERS within meaning of congressional acts, when waters form (in their ordinary condition by themselves or by uniting with other waters) a continued highway over which commerce is or may be carried on with other states or foreign countries in customary modes in which such commerce is conducted by water. See **admiralty and maritime jurisdiction.**

N.B. see **nota bene.**

NCIC National Crime Information Center. Computerized records used by law enforcement agencies to determine **criminal records,** arrest or bench **warrants,** or stolen vehicles and guns.

NECESSARY AND PROPER CLAUSE constitutional provision, U.S. **Constitution,** Art. I, Sec. 8, Cl. 18, empowering **Congress** to make all laws that shall be "necessary and proper" for carrying into execution the enumerated powers of Congress. The phrase is not limited to such measures as are absolutely necessary, but includes all appropriate means that are conducive to the end to be accomplished, and that in the judgment of Congress, will most advantageously effect it. The clause is not a grant of power but a declaration that Congress possesses all the means necessary to carry out its specifically granted powers.

NECESSARY IMPLICATION see **implication [NECESSARY IMPLICATION].**

NECESSARY INFERENCE deduced fact that is unavoidable from the standpoint of reason, so that no other inference may be reasonably drawn from the facts as stated.

EXAMPLE: Cody is in a maximum security prison when a robbery occurs in a local jewelry store. Several witnesses to the robbery are shown pictures of criminals at police headquarters, and one of those witnesses identifies Cody as the robber. Cody cannot be charged because there is a *necessary inference* that he could not have committed the robbery in town while an inmate at a maximum security prison.

Compare **presumption.**

NECESSARY PARTY see **party [NECESSARY PARTY].**

NECESSITY, DEFENSE OF see **justification.**

NE EXEAT *(nē ĕx'-ē-ăt)* Lat.: do not leave. An order (sometimes called a **writ**) forbidding a person from leaving the **court's jurisdiction** unless a suitable **surety,** such as a **bond,** is posted.

NEGATIVE AVERMENT an averment in some of the **pleadings** in which a negative is asserted. Generally a party need not prove a negative averment, but the point in issue is to be proved by the party who asserts the affirmative.

NEGATIVE EASEMENT see **easement** [NEGATIVE EASEMENT].

NEGATIVE PREGNANT in pleading, a **denial** that implies an affirmation of a substantial fact and hence is beneficial to the opponent. Thus, when only a qualification or modification is denied while the fact itself remains undenied, the denial is pregnant with an affirmation of that fact.

LITERAL DENIAL If the complaint alleges that the defendant was at the bar on July 5th and the defendant denies that he was at the bar on July 5th, this would be an admission that he may have been at the bar on July 3rd or July 7th (or any other date).

CONJUNCTIVE DENIAL If the complaint alleges that the defendant injured the plaintiff by kicking and slapping and punching and the defendant denies that he was kicking and slapping and punching, this would constitute an admission that he was guilty but in a combination less than all three. Instead, the defendant should have responded in the disjunctive by denying that he was kicking *or* slapping *or* punching.

NEGLECT the omission of proper attention; avoidance or disregard of duty from heedlessness, indifference, or willfulness; failure to do, use, or heed anything; **negligence,** as neglect of business, of health, or of economy. See **excusable neglect.**

NEGLIGENCE failure to exercise a degree of care that a person of ordinary prudence (a **reasonable man**) would exercise under the same circumstances. The term refers to conduct that falls below the standard established by law for the protection of others against unreasonable risk of harm.

COMPARATIVE NEGLIGENCE the proportionate sharing between **plaintiff** and **defendant** of responsibility for injury to the plaintiff based on the relative negligence of the two. It results in a reduction of the **damages** recoverable by the negligent plaintiff in proportion to his fault.

EXAMPLE: Adib runs across a busy street at a point between two trucks, so that both his vision and the vision of other vehicles is impaired. A car travels down the street over the speed limit, but not excessively fast, and hits Adib. A jury finds Adib 30 percent responsible for the accident and the driver 70 percent. Under a *comparative negligence* theory, if Adib would have normally recovered $10,000 in damages, he now only recovers $7,000.

CONCURRENT NEGLIGENCE the wrongful acts or omissions of two or more persons acting independently but causing the same injury. The independent actions do not have to occur at the same time, but must produce the same result. The actors are all responsible for paying the damages and can usually be sued together in one lawsuit or individually in separate lawsuits.

CONTRIBUTORY NEGLIGENCE conduct on the part of the plaintiff that falls below the standard to which he or she should conform for his or her own protection, and that is a legally contributing cause cooperating with the negligence of the defendant in bringing about the plaintiff's harm. In **common law,** the plaintiff's contributory negligence precludes his or her right to recover from the defendant.

EXAMPLE: On the same facts as in the example under comparative negligence, if the jurisdiction Adib sues in follows a theory of *contributory negligence,* Adib's fault will prevent any recovery against the other driver since Adib's negligence contributed to his injury.

CRIMINAL [CULPABLE] NEGLIGENCE such negligence as is necessary to incur criminal liability. In most jurisdictions, culpable negligence is more than the ordinary negligence necessary to support a **civil action** for damages. Thus, culpable negligence is a reckless disregard of consequences or a heedless indifference to the personal safety of others.

GROSS NEGLIGENCE an intentional or willful failure to perform a clear duty, recklessly disregarding the consequences of injury to person or property that attend such failure.

NEGLIGENCE PER SE negligence as a matter of law; an act or omission recognized as negligent either because it is contrary to the requirements of law or because it is so opposed to the dictates of common prudence that one could say without doubt that no careful person would have committed the act or omission. While negligence ordinarily must be found by the trier of fact (see **fact finder**) from the facts and circumstances disclosed by the **evidence,** negligence per se arises from a violation of a specific requirement of law or ordinance, the only fact for determination by the trier of fact being the omission or commission of the specific act prohibited or required.

RECKLESS NEGLIGENCE see **WANTON NEGLIGENCE** (below).

WANTON NEGLIGENCE an intentional act of an unreasonable character in disregard of a risk known, or so obvious that it must have been known, and so great as to make it highly probable that harm would follow. The act is usually accompanied by a conscious indifference to the consequences amounting almost to willingness that they shall follow. The term "wanton" is used synonymously with willful and reckless. The result is that wanton, willful, or reckless conduct tends to take on the aspect of highly unreasonable conduct, or an extreme departure from ordinary care in a situation where a high degree of danger is apparent.

WILLFUL NEGLIGENCE see **WANTON NEGLIGENCE** (above).

NEGLIGENT INFLICTION OF EMOTIONAL DISTRESS see **emotional distress** [NEGLIGENT INFLICTION OF EMOTIONAL DISTRESS].

NEGOTIABLE INSTRUMENT a writing signed by the **maker** or **drawer,** containing an unconditional promise or order to pay a specific sum, payable on demand or at a definite time, and payable to **order** or to **bearer.** A **draft, check, certificate of deposit** and **note** may or may not be negotiable instruments, depending upon whether the elements of negotiability are satisfied.

EXAMPLE: Mickey takes a loan from a bank and signs a promissory note to repay the bank in twelve months. That note is a *negotiable instrument* and can be transferred by that bank to any other party. Because it is freely transferable, Mickey does not repay the note unless he knows who possesses it, and demands that, upon payment, the note be returned to him so that it is not transferred to another party.

An ordinary check issued by an employer to an employee or by a customer to a store is also a negotiable instrument.

NEGOTIABLE ORDER OF WITHDRAWAL [NOW] see **bank** [NEGOTIABLE ORDER OF WITHDRAWAL [NOW]].

NEGOTIATION a method of dispute resolution where either the parties themselves or the representatives of each party attempt to settle conflicts without resort to the courts; an impartial third party is not involved. Compare **arbitration; mediation.**

NEMO EST SUPRA LEGIS *(nā'-mō ĕst sū'-prà lā-gĭs)* Lat.: nobody is above the law.

NET ASSET VALUE an accounting term similar in meaning to **book value** and net worth; most often used in reference to value of **mutual fund** shares and similar investment companies. Investment companies compute their net asset value at the end of each market day by taking the total market value of securities, cash, etc., owned, less any **liabilities.** See **balance sheet.**

NET ESTATE **estate** that under federal and state statutes is subject to an **estate tax;** generally that estate remaining after all debts of decedent, funeral and administrative expenses, and other deductions prescribed by law have been subtracted from the **GROSS ESTATE** (total valuation of the estate's assets at decedent's death). The term thus refers generally to that estate left to be distributed after all deductions have been made.

NET INCOME the gross [total] income less the deductions and exemptions allowed by law.

NET LEASE see **lease [NET LEASE].**

NET OPERATING LOSS the excess of allowable **deductions** over **GROSS INCOME** (see **income**) with certain specific adjustments set forth in the **Internal Revenue Code,** which are generally designed to limit the net operating loss deductions of individual **taxpayers** to business losses. A net operating loss reduces the **TAXABLE INCOME** (see **income**) of the taxpayer for the **taxable year** by the amount of such net operating loss.

NET WORTH one of several methods used by the **Internal Revenue Service** to reconstruct a **taxpayer's income** when it is determined that either the taxpayer has failed to file a **return** or the tax liability shown is not correct. Under this method the taxpayer's net worth for the start of the period in question is determined, and his or her net worth at the end of the period is also calculated, with the difference, less any nontaxable amounts received, deemed to be the taxpayer's income for the period. This approach is often used in cases involving suspected **evasion** by the taxpayer, but it is also used in normal civil or civil fraud contexts.

NEUTRALITY LAWS laws governing a country's abstention from participating in a conflict or aiding a participant of such conflict, and the duty of participants to refrain from violating the territory, seizing the possession, or hampering the peaceful commerce of the neutral countries. For example, the Neutrality Act of 1939 was passed by Congress for the purpose of preserving the neutrality of the United States and averting the risks that brought the United States into World War I.

NEWLY DISCOVERED EVIDENCE **evidence** in existence at the time of trial of which a party was unaware. Newly discovered evidence may be grounds for a new trial, but an aggrieved party is not entitled to similar relief for evidence that has come into existence after the trial is over since such a procedure could result in perpetual trials. Newly discovered evidence that will entitle a party to a new trial on such grounds must be material, such that it will probably produce a different result on retrial, and it must appear that with reasonable diligence, such evidence could not have been discovered and produced at trial.

NEW MATTER matters raised by **defendant** that go beyond mere denials of **plaintiff's** allegations. New matter consists of new issues, with new facts to be proved, and purports to show that the alleged **cause of action** never did exist and that material allegations are not true.

NEWSPERSON'S PRIVILEGE see **journalist's [newsperson's] privilege.**

NEWSPERSON'S SHIELD see **shield laws.**

NEW TRIAL see **trial [NEW TRIAL].**

NEW YORK CURB EXCHANGE former name of the American Stock Exchange and now known as **NYSE.** NYSE's parent corporation is Intercontinental Exchange.

NEW YORK STOCK EXCHANGE [NYSE] the oldest organized **stock exchange** in the United States, which has been active, since its organization, in establishing listing requirements for companies whose stocks are traded on the Exchange and in encouraging accurate and timely disclosure of listed company **income statement** and **balance sheet** results.

NEXT FRIEND a **competent** person who, although not an appointed **guardian,** acts in behalf of a party who is unable to look after his or her own interests or manage his or her own lawsuit; one who represents an infant, or other party, who by reason of some disability, is not **sui juris.** A next friend is not considered a party to the suit, but is regarded as an **agent** or **officer** of the court to protect the rights of the disabled person.

NEXT-IN, FIRST-OUT [NIFO] a method of inventory valuation. See **inventory [NEXT-IN, FIRST-OUT [NIFO]].**

NEXT OF KIN the term is used generally with two meanings: (1) nearest blood relations according to law of **consanguinity,** and (2) those entitled to take under statutory distribution of **intestates' estates.** In the latter case, the term is not necessarily confined to relatives by blood, but may include a relationship existing by reason of marriage, and may well embrace persons who, in the natural sense of the word, bear no relation of kinship at all.

NEXUS clear, direct connection; core; link.

NGRI not guilty by reason of **insanity.** See **not guilty [NOT GUILTY BY REASON OF INSANITY].**

NIHIL *(nĭ'-hĭl)* Lat.: nothing; not at all, in no respect; **NIL** is an often-used form of the noun. Most commonly used to describe a sheriff's **return** after an unsuccessful attempt to **serve** a **summons** or otherwise gain **jurisdiction** over an individual.

NIL see **nihil.**

NINTH AMENDMENT one of the **Bill of Rights** stating that the rights enumerated in the Constitution shall not be construed to deny or disparage other rights retained by the people. These rights are those so basic and fundamental and so deeply rooted in our society to be truly *essential rights,* and that nevertheless, cannot find direct support elsewhere in the Constitution. The Amendment was included in an abundance of caution and together with the reserved powers amendment (**Tenth Amendment**) was intended to emphasize the limited powers conferred upon the new central government. The Ninth Amendment has been cited by the United States Supreme Court very few times but was relied upon by some members of the Court to identify a right of marital privacy to bar a state from prohibiting the use of contraceptives by married persons.

NISI *(nē'-sē)* Lat.: unless. Used in law after **decree, order,** rule to indicate that the adjudication shall take permanent effect at a specified time unless cause is shown why it should not or unless it is changed by further proceedings. More particularly, a decree *nisi* is a conditional **divorce,** which becomes absolute upon the expiration of a stipulated period unless cause to the contrary is shown within the time period. See **decree [DECREE NISI].**

NISI PRIUS *(nē'-sē prē'-ŭs)* Lat.: unless the first. In American law, sometimes used to describe any court where a case is first heard by a **judge** and **jury,** distinguishing such courts from the **appellate courts.** See **original jurisdiction.**

NLRA National Labor Relations Act. See **labor organization [union].** See **National Labor Relations Board.**

NLRB see **National Labor Relations Board.**

NO BILL see **grand jury [NO BILL]; indictment [NO BILL].**

NO FAULT a system of **insurance** whereby all persons who are injured in an automobile accident may be compensated for any injuries resulting therefrom, without regard to who was at fault.

EXAMPLE: At one o'clock in the morning, two automobile drivers get into an accident. Each claims that the other ran a red light. Under a *no-fault* insurance plan, the argument as to who ran the light is irrelevant. The plan provides each driver with compensation for his injuries from his own insurance company. If the injuries are substantial, fault may be relevant, as suit is generally permitted based on fault, even in no-fault jurisdictions, for injury that exceeds some specified dollar amount. Under a no-fault system, most cases, however, can be settled without litigation.

NO-FAULT DIVORCE see **divorce [NO-FAULT DIVORCE].**

NOLENS VOLENS *(nō-lĕnz vō'-lĕnz)* Lat.: whether willing or unwilling.

NOLLE PROSEQUI *(nōl'-ē prōs'-ē-kwī)* Lat.: unwilling to prosecute; the prosecution's abandonment of a charging document, **count** or part of a count; a discontinued prosecution by the authorized attorney for the state; the formal entry of a declaration that a case will not be further prosecuted. If applicable **statutes of limitation** have not run, the defendant can be re-indicted and prosecuted again. A *nolle prosequi* cannot be pleaded as former jeopardy or **res judicata.** Sometimes abbreviated as **NOL. PROS.** See **dismissal.**

NOLO CONTENDERE *(nō'-lō kŏn-tĕn'-dĕ-rā)* Lat.: I do not wish to contend, fight or maintain (a **defense**). A statement that the **defendant** will not contest a **charge** made by the government. Like a **demurrer** to an **indictment,** it admits all facts stated in the indictment for the purposes of a particular **case,** but it cannot be used as an **admission** elsewhere, or in any other proceeding, such as a **civil** suit arising from the same facts.

EXAMPLE: Zayan is charged with careless driving. He pleads "nolo contendere" and is fined by the court. Since he did not admit guilt, his plea cannot be used against him if he is sued by an injured party.

NOL PROS see **nolle prosequi.**

NOMINAL DAMAGES see **damages [NOMINAL DAMAGES].**

NOMINAL PARTY see **party [NOMINAL PARTY].**

NOMINEE one who has been asked to act for another in a particular context, such as a trustee or an agent; one who has been nominated as a candidate for office; one to whom a party to an agreement may assign his or her rights under a contract.

EXAMPLE: Rohan agrees to buy a property from Blaze. Since Rohan may want to put the title in the name of another person or entity, the agreement will provide for title to be issued "to Rohan or his nominee."

NOMOTHETIC   founded upon or derived from law; lawgiving; legislative.

NONACCESS   see **access.**

NONASSESSABLE STOCK   stock purchased from the issuer at full par value or more per share. Fully paid stock cannot be assessed to pay debts of the issuer in the event of bankruptcy liquidation and is, therefore, non-assessable. Almost all domestic stock issues are non-assessable and instances of assessments against shareholders are extremely rare.

NON ASSUMPSIT   *(nŏn à-sŭmp'-sĭt)* Lat.: he did not promise; he did not undertake. A form of **pleading** in which the defendant claims that he or she did not undertake or promise any obligation in the manner or form that is set forth in the **plaintiff's complaint.** Compare **assumpsit.**

NONBINDING ARBITRATION   see **arbitration [NONBINDING ARBITRATION].**

NONCOMPETITION CLAUSE   see **covenant [COVENANT NOT TO COMPETE].**

NON COMPOS MENTIS   *(nŏn kŏm'-pōs mĕn'-tĭs)* Lat.: not having control over the mind or intellect; not of sound mind; insane. In certain circumstances its effect is lessened to mean only not legally **competent.**

NONCONFORMING USE   a **use** of land that lawfully existed before enactment of a **zoning** ordinance and that may be maintained after the effective date of the ordinance although it no longer complies with use restrictions newly applicable to the area. Continuation of the existing use includes preservation of both the functional use of the land and the physical structures thereon, and neither of these aspects of use may be extended once the zoning restriction has taken effect.

EXAMPLE: Prior to any zoning restrictions, Russ opens a doctor's office adjacent to his home. Subsequently, the town passes an ordinance prohibiting any business in Russ's section of town. Russ is permitted to continue operating his office as a *nonconforming use,* but he cannot expand his office without express permission from the zoning officials.

See **grandfather clause.** Compare **variance.**

NONCONNECTED PACS   see **political action committee [NONCONNECTED PACS].**

NONCONTESTABILITY [INCONTESTABILITY] CLAUSE a provision in an **insurance** policy that precludes the insurer from disputing the validity of the policy on the basis of **fraud** or **mistake** after a specified period. If the insurer wishes to contest the policy on any grounds that would justify **rescission,** it must do so within the prescribed period, either by suing to cancel the policy or by asserting fraud or **misrepresentation** as a **defense** in an action instituted by the policyholder or **beneficiary.** The purpose of the clause is to require the insurer to investigate with reasonable promptness the accuracy of information provided by the policyholder. It prevents the insurer from lulling the policyholder into a sense of security during the time when facts could best be ascertained, only to **litigate** them belatedly.

NONCUSTODIAL SENTENCE see **sentence [NONCUSTODIAL SENTENCE].**

NONDELEGABLE see **delegable duty.**

NONDISCRETIONARY TRUST [FIXED INVESTMENT TRUST] an **investment trust** that may buy only those **securities** on a list set forth when the trust is organized. The percentage of total assets that may be invested in a specific security or type of securities is usually predetermined. See **unit investment trust.**

NONFEASANCE in the law of agency, the total omission or failure of an **agent** to perform a distinct duty that he or she has agreed with his or her **principal** to do; also, the neglect or refusal, without sufficient excuse, to do what is an officer's legal duty to do. Nonfeasance differs from **misfeasance,** which is the improper doing of an act that one might lawfully do, and from **malfeasance,** which is the doing of an act that is wholly wrongful and unlawful. See **misconduct.**

NONMEMBER BANK a bank that is not a member of the **Federal Reserve System** and is regulated only by the banking laws in the state in which it is chartered.

NONNEGOTIABLE INSTRUMENTS see **negotiable instruments.**

NON OBSTANTE VEREDICTO see **n.o.v.**

NONPERFORMANCE the failure to fulfill an obligation. The nonperformance must be material and substantial to justify suspension of another's return performance. See **performance.** See also **consideration [FAILURE OF CONSIDERATION].**

NONPROFIT [NOT-FOR-PROFIT] CORPORATION an incorporated organization chartered for other than profit-making activities and exempt from corporation income tax. Most such organizations are engaged in charitable, educational, or other civic or humanitarian activities, although nonprofit corporations are not restricted to such activities. See **charity.**

NON PROSEQUITUR *(nôn prō-sĕk'-wi-tèr)* Lat.: he has not proceeded. An entry by the defendant that the plaintiff has not continued his or her action. Under modern rules, such failure on the part of the plaintiff would result in either a **dismissal** of the action or in a **default judgment** for the defendant. Abbreviated NON PROS.

NONREBUTTABLE PRESUMPTION see presumption [NONRE-BUTTABLE PRESUMPTION].

NONRECOGNITION OF GAIN see recognition [NONRECOGNI-TION OF GAIN].

NONRECOURSE without personal liability. An obligation that is nonrecourse does not provide a **basis** for federal taxation purposes for individuals or partnerships except in certain limited cases such as when real estate is involved. If a promisor has limited his or her exposure in the event of a **default** to a particular pledged asset such as equity in a building or entity, his or her obligation will be regarded as nonrecourse. Individuals often structure transactions in corporate form to achieve similar limited personal liability.

NONRESIDENT ALIEN see alien [NONRESIDENT ALIEN].

NON SEQUITUR *(nŏn sĕ'-kwĭ-tūr)* Lat.: it does not follow; it does not come after (in time); abbreviated non seq. A non sequitur action or decree is unrelated to the preceding events. A non sequitur has no logical, temporal, or spatial purpose for its place in the progression of events.

NONSTOCK CORPORATION a corporation owned by its members under the membership charter or agreement, rather than through the issue of shares.

NONSUFFICIENT FUNDS CHECK see NSF [NONSUFFICIENT FUNDS] CHECK.

NON SUI JURIS *(nōn swē jū'-rĭs)* Lat.: not by his own authority or legal right. Refers to those who are not legally **competent** to manage their own affairs as regards **contracts** and other causes in which this **incompetency** restricts exercise of sound judgment. Compare **non compos mentis.**

NONSUIT a **judgment** rendered against a **plaintiff** who fails to proceed to trial or is unable to prove his or her case. Since the adjudication is made when the plaintiff has failed to provide **evidence** sufficient to establish a case, it does not decide the **merits** of his or her **cause of action,** and thus does not preclude bringing it again. The term is sometimes broadly applied to various terminations of an action that do not amount to a judgment **on the merits.**

EXAMPLE: Rose sues a local appliance store for selling her a defective washing machine. At the beginning of the trial, she cannot produce any evidence to show that she bought the machine at that particular store. The judge declares a *nonsuit* against Rose and dismisses her claim.

See **dismissal.** Compare **acquit.**

NONSUPPORT the failure to provide **support** that one can provide and that one is legally obliged to provide to a spouse, child, or other dependent. Although nonsupport of wife and child were apparently not crimes at common law, statutes in all states contain provisions making such acts crimes with respect to children and in nearly all states with respect to spouses. Most jurisdictions treat the offense as a **misdemeanor.** See **desertion; support.**

NON VULT *(nŏn vŭlt)* Lat.: abbreviation of non vult contendere ("he will not contest"). Refers to a plea by one charged with a crime that does not expressly admit guilt, but acknowledges that the defendant will not contest the charge and therefore agrees to be treated as though he or she had been found guilty. See **nolo contendere.**

NO-PAR [NONPAR] STOCK stock issued with no value stated on the stock certificate.

NORMAL COURSE OF BUSINESS see **ordinary course of business.**

NOSCITUR A SOCIIS *(nō'-si-tĕr ā sō'-shē-ĭs)* Lat.: it is known by its associates. Under this rule of statutory construction, the meaning of a word in a statute is ascertained in light of the meaning of words with which it is associated. When two or more words in a statute are grouped together, and ordinarily have a similar meaning but are not equally comprehensive, the general word will be limited and qualified by the specific word. Compare **ejusdem generis.**

NO STRIKE CLAUSE a clause in a labor agreement that prohibits employees from striking for any reason during the life of the contract. Such a clause regulates relations between the employer and the employees. It is not an unfair labor practice under the **National Labor Relations Act** for an employer to bargain in good faith for such a clause.

NOTA BENE *(nō'-tà bā-nā)* Lat.: note well. Written on the original note **N.B.** to indicate an important portion of the text to be studied.

NOTARY PUBLIC a public officer authorized to administer oaths, to attest to and certify certain types of documents, to take **depositions,** and to perform certain acts in commercial matters. The seal of a notary public authenticates a document. In some **jurisdictions** an attorney admitted to practice within the jurisdiction can act as a notary public. In many jurisdictions private persons can apply for and receive authority to act as notaries to witness documents.

NOTE a written paper that acknowledges a **debt** and promises payment to a specified party of a specific sum, and that describes a time of **maturity** that is either definite or will become definite. See **commercial paper; treasury note.**

NOT-FOR-PROFIT CORPORATION see **corporation** [NOT-FOR-PROFIT CORPORATION]; **nonprofit [not-for-profit] corporation.**

NOT GUILTY a **plea** by the **accused** in a criminal **action** that denies every essential **element** of the offense charged. A plea of not guilty on **arraignment** obliges the government to prove the defendant's guilt beyond a reasonable doubt and preserves the right of the accused to defend against the charge. A jury **verdict** of not guilty does not mean the jury found the accused innocent, but simply that the state failed to prove its case beyond a reasonable doubt.

NOT GUILTY BY REASON OF INSANITY a special form of verdict or finding that is usually followed by commitment of the defendant to a mental institution. The insanity defense differs from other defenses in that, if successful, it is not an **acquittal** and does not result in the outright release of the accused.

NOTICE information concerning a fact actually communicated to a person by an authorized person, or actually derived by him or her from a proper source. Notice to a **defendant** of a lawsuit that has been instituted against him or her or of an **action** in which he or she may have an interest to defend is accomplished by **service of process** on him or her.

ACTUAL NOTICE direct positive knowledge of fact in question or information sufficient to put a prudent person on inquiry as to such fact. "Actual notice" embraces those things of which one has express information and which reasonably diligent inquiry would have disclosed.

AVERMENT OF NOTICE a statement in the **pleadings** declaring that a **party** to an action has received proper notice thereof.

CONSTRUCTIVE NOTICE notice presumed by law to have been

acquired; often accomplished by posting of notices or by mailing of notification to the defendant if he or she cannot be personally **served** with **process.**

EXAMPLE: Neil sues Quincy for a debt incurred when Neil painted his house. One requirement of filing the suit is that Neil personally notify Quincy of the court action. After several unsuccessful attempts to meet Quincy and physically hand him a copy of the complaint, Neil satisfies the notice requirement by sending a copy to Quincy's business and home addresses and by tacking a copy on Quincy's door. Quincy is considered to have received *constructive notice* of the action whether or not he actually learned of it.

IMPLIED NOTICE notice that may be inferred from facts that a reasonable person had means of knowing but failed to inquire further. A person has no right to avoid information and then say that he or she had no notice. "Implied notice" is distinguished from **CONSTRUCTIVE NOTICE** (above), in that the latter rests upon strictly legal presumptions whereas the former is a form of **ACTUAL NOTICE** (above) arising from inferences of fact.

EXAMPLE: Ronit plans to buy an apartment complex from Maru. Upon touring the property, Ronit observes that all the apartments are occupied. Upon purchasing the property, he is shocked to find out that the tenants have long-term leases. His failure to follow up on the information that the units were occupied will prevent any claim that he had no notice that existing tenants came with the property.

INDIRECT NOTICE see **IMPLIED NOTICE** (above).

INQUIRY NOTICE with respect to one who claims to have been a **bona fide purchaser** without notice of adverse claims to the purchased property, information from whatever source derived that would create in an ordinary mind apprehension about the actual state of ownership of the property and that would prompt a person of average prudence to make inquiry.

JUDICIAL NOTICE see **judicial notice.**

LEGAL NOTICE such notice as the law requires to be given. Legal notice may be notice that the law implies because of knowledge of the actual facts (see **ACTUAL NOTICE**, above), because of specific avoidance of the available knowledge (see **IMPLIED NOTICE**, above), or because of the presumption that knowledge has been acquired (see **CONSTRUCTIVE NOTICE**). Refers also to the act of advertising by **publication** in a legal or general circulation newspaper. Publication includes such notices as the proposal formation or settlement of a **class action** suit, or a person's legal change of name.

NOTICE BY PUBLICATION method of bringing a lawsuit to the attention of parties who may have an interest therein by publishing notification of it in a newspaper of general circulation; permissible only where specifically allowed by **statute** and generally limited to actions involving **land, estates** or status.

PERSONAL NOTICE communication of notice orally or in writing, according to the circumstances, directly to the person affected or to be charged.

RACE NOTICE see **recording acts**.

NOTICE OF APPEAL see **appeal [NOTICE OF APPEAL]**.

NOTICE OF APPEARANCE see **appearance.**

NOTICE OF DISHONOR notice, given in any reasonable manner, that an **instrument** has been dishonored. Notice of dishonor may be given to any person who may be liable on the instrument by or on behalf of the holder or any party who has himself or herself received notice, or any other party who can be compelled to pay the instrument. In addition, an agent or bank in whose hands the instrument is dishonored may give notice to a principal or customer or to another agent or bank from which the instrument was received. Delay without excuse in giving notice of dishonor completely discharges an **indorser.**

NOTICE OF LIS PENDENS see **lis pendens.**

NOTICE OF MOTION see **motion.**

NOTICE TO QUIT formal notification terminating a **tenancy** on a specified date. A notice to quit part of the property is valid only if specifically allowed by the tenancy. The notice may be given by either the landlord or the tenant to the other party.

NOTORIOUS POSSESSION **possession** of **real property** that is open, undisguised, generally known or recognized. The term is one of the elements in defining or determining existence of **adverse possession,** which involves a claim of right to property not by **title** but by possession for a prescribed period. See also **hostile possession.**

N.O.V. [NON OBSTANTE VEREDICTO] *(nŏn ŏb-stăn'-tā vĕr-ĕ-dĭk'-tō)* Lat.: notwithstanding the verdict. A JUDGMENT N.O.V. is one by the trial court that reverses the determination of the **jury,** granted when it is obvious that the jury **verdict** had no reasonable support in fact or was contrary to law. The motion for a judgment n.o.v. provides a second chance for the trial court to render what is, in effect, a **directed verdict** for the **moving** party.

NOVATION substitution of another **party** for one of the original parties to a **contract,** with the consent of the remaining party. The old contract is then extinguished, and a new contract, with the same content but with at least one different party, is created. A novation often involves a transaction whereby the original **debtor** is discharged from liability to his **creditor** by substitution of a second debtor.

NOW ACCOUNT [NEGOTIABLE ORDER OF WITHDRAWAL ACCOUNT] an interest-bearing savings account against which depositors are permitted to write checks. See **bank.**

NSF [NONSUFFICIENT FUNDS] CHECK nonsufficient funds **check.** If the **drawee** (bank) discovers that the **drawer** lacks funds to cover the presented check, the drawee can **dishonor** the check, and the presenter is powerless to make the drawee pay. See **bad check.**

NUDUM PACTUM *(nū'-dŭm päk'-tŭm)* Lat.: a bare **contract.** A **promise** naked of obligation on one side; not enforceable, since contracts must generally be supported by a **consideration** on each side. See **mutuality of obligation.**

NUGATORY **void**; invalid; for example, judicial **proceedings** in courts that lack **jurisdiction.** Compare **voidable.**

NUISANCE 1. anything that disturbs the free use of one's property, or that renders its ordinary use uncomfortable; 2. in **tort** law, a wrong arising from unreasonable or unlawful use of property to the annoyance or damage of another or of the public.

EXAMPLE: Zari rents an apartment in a residential apartment building. In the adjacent apartment, a politically active group meets very frequently at late hours to discuss strategy and to type press releases. The apartment is at no time used for sleep. Even if the group's activities are legal, Zari has a *nuisance* action against the group. Their late hours disturb her, and the apartment is not used for its normal and intended purpose.

ABATABLE NUISANCE a nuisance that can be suppressed, extinguished or rendered harmless, and whose continued existence is not authorized under law.

ABATEMENT OF A NUISANCE the removal or termination of a nuisance by **self-help.**

ATTRACTIVE NUISANCE see **attractive nuisance.**

COMMON NUISANCE see PUBLIC [COMMON] NUISANCE (below).

MIXED NUISANCE a nuisance which is both a public nuisance and a private nuisance at the same time; it interferes with a right of the general public and also interferes with a particular person's use and enjoyment of his or her land.

PRIVATE NUISANCE an **actionable** interference with a person's interest in the private **use** and enjoyment of his or her land.

PUBLIC [COMMON] NUISANCE an unreasonable interference with a right common to the general public; behavior that unreasonably interferes with the health, safety, peace, comfort or convenience of the community.

NUISANCE PER SE an act, occupation, or structure that is a nuisance at all times and under any circumstances, regardless of its location or surroundings; acts that are denounced as illegal by law, when perpetration of them invades rights of others. From an evidentiary point of view once a nuisance per se is established by proof, it becomes a nuisance as a **matter of law.**

NULL AND VOID see **nullity.**

NULLIFICATION cancellation, revocation. See also **annul.** Often refers to the power of a jury to negate a conviction by refusing to follow the judge's instructions (which would have resulted in a guilty finding if literally applied but would have perpetrated an injustice under the particular circumstances). Nullification occurs when, contrary to the evidence, the jury acquits, often in cases involving political causes, civil disobedience, racism, or overzealous or selective prosecution. William Penn benefitted from jury nullification in 1670 when he was acquitted in his unlawful assembly trial for organizing Quaker meetings.

NULLITY in law, a **void** act or an act having no legal force or validity; invalid; null. It is the highest degree of an irregularity, and is such a defect as renders the proceeding in which it occurs of no avail or effect whatever and incapable of being made so. A proceeding that is essentially defective, or that is expressly declared to be a nullity by **statute.**

NUL TIEL RECORD see **trial [TRIAL BY THE RECORD].**

NUNC PRO TUNC (*nŭnk prō tŭnk*) Lat.: now for then.

NUNC PRO TUNC ORDER an **order** used by the courts to correct the **record** usually after a proceeding has been concluded. It supplements a prior **judgment** or order in any matter over which the court originally had **jurisdiction.**

NUNCUPATIVE WILL oral declarations of a person made with dispositive intent during a last illness, where a written **will** would not be possible. Such oral wills are rarely upheld because of the opportunity for fraud and because of the detailed requirements for their validity. Such requirements are that the testator, during sickness, indicate that the disposition is to be a will, that it be reduced to writing by a witness within a short time, that more than one witness prove the will, and that the witnesses are disinterested and competent. The requirements are strictly adhered to, except for persons in actual military service. See **military will.** Nuncupative wills are generally restricted to **personalty** under the **statute of frauds** and thus cannot operate to transfer **real property.**

NYSE see **New York Stock Exchange [NYSE].**

O

OATH a declaration of the truth of a statement. See **affidavit; affirmation.** See also **perjury.**

OATH EX OFFICIO at **common law,** an oath administered by an **ecclesiastical court** whereby a member of the clergy accused of a crime would have to swear to his or her innocence. An accused was also obliged to put forward proof of his or her innocence, after which the ecclesiastical judge, not a jury, decided innocence or guilt.

The phrase has also referred to a process whereby the court, upon an accusation, could order the accused into court to swear an oath. After the courts abused their right by turning their proceedings into inquisitions, the English Parliament abolished the oath.

OBAMACARE see **affordable care act.**

OBITER DICTA (*ō'-bĭ-tėr dĭk'-tà*) Lat.: passing or incidental statements. Statements made or decisions reached in a court opinion that were not necessary to disposition of the case; plural of obiter dictum. See **dictum.**

OBJECT a procedure whereby a party asserts that a particular witness, line of questioning, piece of evidence or other matter is improper and should not be continued, and asks the court to rule on its impropriety or illegality.

EXAMPLE: Elizabeth is on trial for writing a bad check. The prosecution asks a witness whether Elizabeth ever owned a gun without a proper permit. Elizabeth's attorney will *object* and seek to exclude the question and answer on the grounds that the question will introduce improperly "other crimes" (i.e., possession of a gun) into the case.

OBJECTION a procedure whereby a party asserts that a particular witness, line of questioning, piece of **evidence,** or other matter is improper and should not be continued, and asks the court to rule on its impropriety or illegality. A timely objection on the record, stating the grounds thereof, must be made to evidence rulings admitting or excluding evidence if the ruling is to be challenged later on appeal. This is necessary to preserve the point on appeal. As to other rulings or orders entered by a trial court, the failure to object will not prejudice a party's right to challenge on appeal the action taken if he or she had no opportunity to object. See also **challenge; motion [MOTION IN LIMINE].**

OBLIGATION, MUTUALITY OF see **mutuality of obligation.**

OBLIGATION OF A CONTRACT the term refers not to any duty that rises out of the contract itself, but to the legal requirements that bind the contracting parties to the performance of their undertaking.

IMPAIR THE OBLIGATION OF A CONTRACT to weaken the contract in any respect. Any law that changes the intention and legal effect of the original parties, giving to one a greater and to the other a lesser **interest** in the contract, that hastens or postpones the prescribed time of performance, or imposes conditions not included in the contract, or dispenses with the performance of those that are included, impairs the obligation of a contract. Impairment also exists where the right to enforce a contract is eliminated or substantially lessened. State statutes that impair contract obligations are prohibited by Article 1, Section 10 of the United States Constitution.

OBLIGEE one who is entitled to receive a sum of money or to have an act or deed performed as promised or agreed to by the **obligor.**

OBLIGOR one who has promised or is otherwise obligated to perform an act or deed, such as the payment of a sum of money under a promissory **note** or other **contract.** Compare **obligee.**

OBLOQUY blame, censure, reproach; to expose one to obloquy is to subject one to blame or disgrace and may constitute **defamation.**

OBSCENE MATERIAL material that, taken as a whole, appeals to the prurient interest of the average person, depicts sexual conduct in a patently offensive manner, and lacks serious literary, artistic, political or scientific value. Matter so classified is not protected by the free speech guarantee of the **First Amendment.** See **pornography.**

OBSCENITY see **obscene material.**

OBSOLESCENCE the process by which property becomes useless, not because of physical deterioration, but because of scientific or technological advances.

OBSTRUCTION OF JUSTICE the impeding of those who seek justice in a court, or of those who have duties or powers of administering justice therein; includes attempting to influence, intimidate or impede any **juror, witness** or officer in any court regarding the discharge of his duty.

EXAMPLE: Geneva possesses telephone recordings of a contractor offering a bribe to secure a construction grant. When Mack, another contractor, sues to have the grant overturned because of the possibility of a bribe, he requests that Geneva give him the recordings. If Geneva destroys or otherwise loses the recordings after they are requested, she will be charged with *obstruction of justice*.

Statutes addressing this subject may reach beyond interference with the judicial process and also proscribe interference with police officers and other such administrative officials. See **embracery; misprision of felony.**

OBVIOUS RISK a risk that is readily apparent. At common law, a master was not liable to servants for any obvious risks of the employment, rather, the servant was held to have assumed the risk of the employment.

OCCUPANCY the act of occupying or taking possession; to hold or use. See **certificate of occupancy.**

OCCUPANT one who has the actual use or possession of property. See **tenant.** Compare **landlord; title.**

OCCUPATIONAL DISEASE [INJURY] a disease that is the natural result of a particular employment, where that employment involves a risk of contracting the disease greater than the risk in employment and living conditions in general, and that usually develops gradually from the effects of long-continued work at the employment.

OCCUPATIONAL HAZARD a risk distinctively associated with a particular type of employment or workplace.

OCCUPATIONAL SAFETY AND HEALTH ACT [OSHA] a law passed by Congress in 1970 for the purpose of preventing employees from being injured or contracting illnesses in the course of their employment. Under OSHA, the Secretary of Labor is empowered to promulgate national safety and health standards, and to enforce such standards by seeking the imposition of civil and criminal injunctions and penalties. Broad congressional authority granted to OSHA to make warrantless inspections of business premises has been held to be unconstitutional. Thus, an OSHA inspection may be made only in accordance with the administrative inspections permitted in other contexts. See **search and seizure.**

OCCUPYING THE FIELD see **preemption.**

OCCURRENCE TEST see **transactions [occurrence] test.**

ODD LOT in the **securities** trade, **stocks** or **bonds** in a block of fewer than 100 **shares.** In buying or selling an odd lot, a **premium** or **discount** to the round lot price is charged; this charge is referred to as the **ODD LOT DIFFERENTIAL.**

ODIOUS base, vile, scandalous, detestable, disgraceful.

ODIUM hatred, dislike.

OF COUNSEL refers to an attorney who aids in the preparation of a case, but who is not the principal attorney of record for the case. He or she usually assists the attorney who has been hired for the case. See **on the brief**.

OFFENSE any violation of law for which a penalty is prescribed, including both **felonies** and **misdemeanors.** See **degree of crime.**

OFFER 1. a manifestation of willingness to enter into a bargain, so made as to justify another person in understanding that his or her assent to that bargain is invited and will establish a **contract.**

EXAMPLE: A representative of Clay Brick Company sends a letter to a large outlet store informing them of an overstock in several types of bricks the company is hoping to eliminate. The store responds that it will buy the full overstock for the price stated in Clay's letter, and includes a check with their response. The store views Clay's letter as an *offer.* By sending a positive response and a check to Clay, the store believes that a bargain has been struck and a valid contract established.

2. a promise, a commitment to do or refrain from doing some specified thing in the future. 3. In the **securities** trade, an offer indicates price and volume available from open market sellers of **stocks** and **bonds.** 4. an **underwriting** in which a **broker** offers a large quantity of a specific **issue** at a fixed price, called an offering.

OFFER OF PROOF to offer **evidence** for acceptance at **trial.** Such an offer of evidence is governed by the appropriate **jurisdiction's** rules of evidence. For example, if a **party** offers evidence through the **testimony** of a **witness,** certain of the questions asked by counsel may be objected to. Should the court inquire as to the propriety of the questioning, counsel would then ordinarily offer to the court, or **proffer**, the relevance of the question. In such an instance the offer of proof would not ordinarily be made within the hearing of the jury if one is present. If the court sustains the objection, the **appellate court** will assume that the proffer could have been established for the purposes of reviewing the trial court's ruling.

EXAMPLE: In an armed robbery trial Simon testifies for the prosecution that he was in the Nightclub Lounge and saw Charlotte rob the bartender at gunpoint. The defense cross-examines Simon and asks if he has a girlfriend named Dunya. The prosecutor objects that the question is not relevant to the subject at hand, which is a robbery trial and not an inquiry into Simon's dating habits. The defense proffers that Dunya will be called as a witness to state that she was with Simon at the Nightclub Lounge and they were playing pool but they never were close enough to the bar to see any robbery take place.

OFFICER 1. a person invested with the authority of a particular position or office; may be public or private in that the occupied office may or may not be invested with a **public trust.** 2. corporate personnel appointed by the directors and charged with the duty of managing the day-to-day affairs of the **corporation.** See **de facto** [DE FACTO OFFICER].

OFFICIAL IMMUNITY see **immunity.**

OFFICIOUS INTERMEDDLER one who performs an act that confers a **benefit** upon another, although he or she had neither a contractual duty nor a legally recognized interest in performing the act, and who nevertheless seeks **restitution** for the benefit conferred.

OFFSET see **setoff.**

OF RECORD refers to the recordings of **documents** such as **deeds** or **mortgages** with the appropriate entity as well as to the **testimony** recorded as the official **transcript** of a **case.** The ATTORNEY OF RECORD is the official designate of a party upon whom **service** of papers may be made.

OF THE ESSENCE see **time is of the essence.** Compare **on or about.**

OLIGOPOLY 1. an industry in which a few large sellers of substantially identical products, such as automobiles, dominate the market; 2. the condition of a specific products market so dominated. An oligopolistic industry is more concentrated than a competitive one but less concentrated than a **monopoly.**

OLOGRAPHIC see **holographic will.**

OMISSION a failure to do something; something left undone; the neglect to perform what the law requires. Omission will not give rise to **liability** unless there is a **duty** to act.

EXAMPLE: A motorist sees an accident on the highway late at night but fails to call anyone, although he possessed a working cell phone. As a result of that *omission,* one of the victims of the accident dies.

Although common standards may view the motorist as somewhat responsible for the death, the motorist cannot be found liable in a court of law since he has no legal duty to report the accident. If he had been involved in the accident, he would have had a legal duty to summon help and his *omission* in that instance would be the subject of civil and possibly criminal action.

Compare **actus reus.**

OMNIBUS all inclusive; broad. See **in omnibus.**

OMNIBUS CLAUSE a clause in an automobile liability insurance policy that gives categories of persons, in addition to the person named as **assured** (see **insured**), the benefit of the policy, within specified limitations. The clause extends protection to one permitted to use the car, although the assured may not be liable for an accident under the doctrine **respondeat superior.** The object is to cover the liability of the operator of the car as unnamed assured, and to protect any injured person by giving him or her a **cause of action** against the insurer for injuries deemed by law to have been caused by the operation of the car. **Statutes** have been passed in some **jurisdictions** requiring the inclusion of omnibus clauses for the protection of automobile accident victims.

ON ALL FOURS describes a case similar to or identical with the case at hand and therefore possibly useful as **precedent;** derived from the Latin maxim, "Nullum simile est idem nisi quattuor pedibus currit": Nothing similar is identical unless it runs on all four feet.

ON DEMAND when asked for. For example, a note payable on demand is payable when the sum is requested; called a **demand note** if no due date is included.

ONE MAN [PERSON], ONE VOTE see **reapportionment [ONE PERSON, ONE VOTE PRINCIPLE].**

ON ITS FACE see **void for vagueness [FACIAL INVALIDITY].**

ON OR ABOUT language used in legal documents to qualify a time or a place as approximate. Unless the parties expressly provide, any reference to time of performance is presumed to be approximate so that the failure to perform as specified is not a **breach.** Where the parties intend otherwise, they generally provide in the legal document that "**time is of the essence**" or words to that effect.

ON THE BRIEF designation on a **brief** indicating the names of persons who contributed to the written product. Such persons may or may not be listed as the attorneys of record. Many reported cases list the attorneys of record and all persons "on the brief." See **of counsel.**

ON THE MERITS   refers to a **judgment** based upon the essential facts of the case rather than upon a technical rule of practice, such as failure of proper **service** or other **jurisdictional** defect. A decision on the merits is rendered after a full presentation of the **evidence** and determines finally the rights of the parties, barring **appeal** or subsequent relitigation.

EXAMPLE: After several weeks of preparation, the attorneys for both sides presented their arguments to the judge. By carefully considering all the evidence and relevant legal theory, the judge was able to base his decision *on the merits.* Had the judge dismissed the case because one of the attorneys failed to comply on time with a rule of court, the case would have been dismissed because of a procedural flaw and not on the merits.

ON THE PLEADINGS   see **judgment [SUMMARY JUDGMENT].**

OPEN   visible, free from concealment, exposed to public view; unobstructed, such as land without trees or fences. See **notorious possession; plain view.**
   An account or matter that is not final and not closed.
   An attorney *opens* a trial by addressing the trier of fact and briefly summarizing the facts and theory of the case that he or she intends to develop during the trial. This is known as an **OPENING STATEMENT.**

OPEN ACCOUNT   account that has not yet been settled or paid; a series of transactions that give rise to credits and debits, but that results in a single liability.

OPEN AND NOTORIOUS   see **notorious possession.**

OPEN COURT   a court that is formally opened and engaged in the transaction of judicial affairs, to which all persons who conduct themselves in an orderly manner are admitted. Most legal proceedings take place in open court except where confidentiality is a recognized interest (e.g., matrimonial, adoption or juvenile delinquency proceedings).

OPEN END FUNDS   see **investment company [trust].**

OPENING STATEMENT   see **statement [OPENING STATEMENT].**

OPEN POSSESSION   see **notorious possession.**

OPEN PUBLIC MEETINGS LAWS   see **sunshine laws.**

OPEN SHOP   an enterprise that employs workers without regard to whether they are members of a labor union.

OPERATING LOSS see **net operating loss.**

OPERATING STATEMENT see **income statement.**

OPERATION OF LAW the determination of rights and obligations through the automatic effects of the law and not by any private agreement or direct act of the party affected.

EXAMPLE: Chris and Pat own a home as tenants by the entirety. Under that principle of property, when either dies, the survivor has sole ownership of the home. Since this event occurs automatically, it is said to occur by *operation of law.*

OPINION the reason given for a court's **judgment, finding** or conclusion, as opposed to the decision, which is the judgment itself. When the court is composed of more than one judge or justice, and more than one opinion has been written in a given case, the opinion that expresses the view of the majority of the judges presiding, and thus announces the decision of the court, is referred to as the **MAJORITY OPINION.**

CONCURRING OPINION a view basically in accord with the majority opinion, but written to express a somewhat different perception of the issues, to illuminate a particular judge's reasoning or to expound a principle that he or she holds in high esteem. An opinion that concurs "in the result only" is one that rejects the reasoning and conclusions concerning the law or the facts on the basis of which the majority reached its decision, and that expresses a different view that has coincidentally led the judge or justice to recommend the same **disposition** as was agreed upon by the majority.

DISSENTING OPINION a view that disagrees with the disposition made of the case by the court, with the facts or law on the basis of which the court arrived at its decision, or the principles of law announced by the court in deciding the case. Opinions may also be written that express a dissent "in part."

EXPERT OPINION see **expert witness.**

LAY OPINION see **lay witness.**

MAJORITY OPINION one that is joined by a majority of the court. Generally known as "the opinion."

PER CURIAM OPINION an opinion "by the court," which expresses its decision in the case without identifying the author.

PLURALITY OPINION one agreed to by less than a majority of the court but the result of which is agreed to by the majority. A plurality opinion carries less weight under **stare decisis** than does a **MAJORITY OPINION** (above).

Opinion also refers to the conclusions reached by a **witness** that are drawn from his or her observations of the facts. See **expert witness.**

OPT-IN [OPT-OUT]   see **permission-based marketing [OPT-IN] [OPT-OUT].**

OPTION   a **contract** that gives the holder a right or option to buy or sell specified property, such as **stock** or **real estate,** at a fixed price for a limited period. See **option contract; stock option.**

OPTIONAL WRIT   see **peremptory writ.**

OPTION CONTRACT   a binding promise in which the owner of property agrees that another shall have the privilege of buying the property at a fixed price within a stated period of time. It is the offeror's acceptance of **consideration** in exchange for his or her promise to keep the offer open for a designated period of time that renders the offer irrevocable. See **firm offer.**

An option must be supported by consideration, often the payment of a small sum of money that may be, though need not be, applied as a down payment if the option is exercised. It exists only when the option holder alone has the right to determine whether he or she shall require the performance called for by the option. If the agreement states that the option may be exercised only with the consent of the other party, it is not an option even though so-called by the agreement. Some types of option contracts are formed without consideration such as an offer that the offeror should reasonably expect to induce action or forbearance of a substantial character on the part of the offeree before acceptance and that does not induce such action or forbearance. Such action or forbearance is binding as an option contract to the extent necessary to avoid injustice. Under the Uniform Commerical Code a seller can offer a buyer an option contract without consideration by making an irrevocable offer and complying with other statutory requirements. See **stock option.**

ORAL   spoken.

ORAL ARGUMENT   legal arguments given in court proceedings by attorneys in order to persuade the court to decide a legal issue in favor of their client.

ORAL CONFESSION   an acknowledgment by a criminal defendant that he or she did the act of which he or she is accused and is guilty of a crime as a result of it. See **self-incrimination, privilege against.**

ORAL CONTRACT   see **contract [ORAL CONTRACT].**

ORAL DEPOSITION see **deposition** [ORAL DEPOSITION.]

ORAL TRUST a **trust** created by the agreement of the **grantor** and the **settlor,** but for which no document is executed setting forth the terms of the trust. Trusts of land are subject to the **Statute of Frauds.** Most states will recognize an oral trust of **personal property;** however, a few states also subject trusts of personal property to the Statute of Frauds.

ORAL WILL see **nuncupative will.**

ORDER 1. a direction of the court on a matter incident to the main proceeding that adjudicates a preliminary point or directs some step in the proceeding. If an order closes the matter and precludes future **hearing** and investigation, it is a **FINAL ORDER;** but an order that does not completely dispose of the subject matter of the controversy and settle the rights of the **parties** is not final. A final order is an **appealable** order. See **interlocutory.**

2. In the **securities** trade, an instruction to buy or sell a specified security under specified conditions. The most common type of order is a **MARKET ORDER** which is specified as to volume with price determined by the market level at the time of sale. Instructions can include a limit as to price to be paid or received (**LIMIT ORDER**) and a limit as to the time the bid or offer is available. If the order is for the day only, it is a **DAY ORDER**; if it is **GOOD UNTIL CANCELED**, it is a standing order called a **GTC.**

ORDER PAPER see **order paper.**

ORDER BILL OF LADING see **bill of lading** [ORDER BILL OF LADING].

ORDERED LIBERTY a concept in constitutional law that the **due process** requirements applicable to the states through the Fourteenth Amendment to the United States Constitution do not incorporate all the provisions of the first ten amendments (the **Bill of Rights**), but only those measures essential for the preservation of a scheme of ordered liberty.

This restrictive view of due process has been largely replaced by a broader view of incorporating nearly all of the Bill of Rights as representing a national standard of fundamental fairness.

ORDER PAPER in commercial law, a **negotiable instrument** that by its terms is payable to a specified person or his or her **assignee,** rather than, for instance, to cash or to bearer. The **payee** must be named or otherwise indicated with reasonable certainty. Compare **bearer paper; indorsement.**

ORDER TO SHOW CAUSE see **show cause order.**

ORDINANCE a local law that applies to persons and things subject to the local **jurisdiction.** Usually it is an act of a city council or similar body that has the same force as a **statute** when it is duly enacted. See **home rule; preemption.**

ORDINARY COURSE OF BUSINESS the common practices of commercial transactions; refers to a necessary activity that is normal and incidental to the business.

ORDINARY INCOME for tax purposes, income subject to being taxed at the highest rates, as opposed to **capital gains,** which may be taxed at lower rates. Generally, only **capital losses** may be deducted against capital gains, and only ordinary income may be offset by the other **deductions.** See **income [ORDINARY INCOME].**

ORDINARY NEGLIGENCE see **negligence [ORDINARY NEGLIGENCE].**

ORDINARY PRUDENT PERSON see **reasonable man [person].**

ORGANIC LAW the fundamental law of a country, state, or society; the law upon which its legal system is based, whether that law is written, such as a constitution, or unwritten.

ORGANIZATION EXPENSE see **expense [ORGANIZATION EXPENSE].**

ORGANIZED CRIME a syndicate of professional criminals who rely on unlawful activities as a way of life. Often called the FAMILY, the MAFIA, or the MOB. See **racketeering.**

ORGAN TRAFFICKING see **trafficking [HUMAN TRAFFICKING].**

ORIGINAL DOCUMENT RULE see **best evidence rule.**

ORIGINAL INTENT see **intent [ORIGINAL INTENT].**

ORIGINAL ISSUE the initial sale or issue of a **security.**

ORIGINAL JURISDICTION authority to consider and decide cases in the first instance, as distinguished from APPELLATE JURISDICTION (see **jurisdiction**), which is the authority to review a decision or **judgment** of an inferior tribunal.

EXAMPLE: The Constitution of the United States provides that the Supreme Court has *original jurisdiction* in all cases affecting ambassadors. Notwithstanding any issue of diplomatic immunity, if an ambassador from France were sued, the Supreme Court, rather than some lower court, would hear the case.

ORIGINAL PACKAGE DOCTRINE the constitutional prohibition of state and local taxation of **goods** while they are still in their original packages. The U.S. Constitution prohibits states from imposing import or export **duties.** In an early case, the Supreme Court held that an item in its original package retained its character as an import and was thus free of tax by a state while in the original form or package in which it was imported.

OSHA see **Occupational Safety and Health Act [OSHA].**

OSTENSIBLE AUTHORITY see **apparent authority.**

OTC see **over-the-counter market [OTC].**

OUI operating under the influence. See **driving while intoxicated [DWI].**

OUSTER the wrongful **dispossession** or exclusion of a person, usually associated with the acts of a co-owner that exclude other co-owners from their legal right to share **possession.**

OUTLYING POSSESSIONS see **state [OUTLYING POSSESSIONS].**

OUT-OF-COURT SETTLEMENT in civil cases, the resolution of a dispute between parties prior to the rendering of a final judgment by the trial court. Compare **plea bargaining.**

OUT-OF-POCKET EXPENSES those costs for necessary items paid directly (usually by cash) and subject to recovery at a later time. An example would be a tenant's purchase of a tarp to cover a hole in the roof until the landlord is able to make repairs. Said purchase might be deducted from rent or directly reimbursed by the landlord. An attorney often advances expenses for clients and obtains reimbursement from the client or from the final settlement.

OUT-OF-POCKET (RULE) method of measuring **damages** in **breach of contract** or **warranty** cases or cases involving **fraud** or **misrepresentation.** Calculated as the difference between the actual value of what was received and the purchase price. Compare **benefit of the bargain (rule).**

OUTPUT CONTRACT see **contract [OUTPUT CONTRACT].**

OUTSIDE THE RECORD see **record [OUTSIDE THE RECORD].**

OUTSTANDING ISSUE see **authorized issue [OUTSTANDING ISSUE].**

OVERBREADTH the overbroad aspect of a **statute** forbidding or inhibiting conduct that is constitutionally protected. Compare **chill [CHILLING EFFECT]; void for vagueness.**

OVERREACHING in commercial law, the taking of unfair advantage through cunning, cheating, fraud or abuse of superior bargaining power. **Contracts** that are the product of overreaching may be unenforceable under modern concepts of fraud or the **unconscionability** doctrine.

OVERRULE 1. to overturn or make **void** the **holding** (decision) of a prior case; generally accomplished in a different and subsequent case, when a court renders a decision that is substantially opposite the decision made in the prior case. A decision can be overruled only by the same court or a higher court within the same **jurisdiction.** The overruling of a decision generally destroys its value as **precedent.** Compare *reversal.*

2. to deny a **motion,** objection or other point raised to the court.

OVERT ACT open act; especially, an outward act done in furtherance of a crime and as a manifestation of **intent** to accomplish the crime. See also **attempt; conspiracy; treason.**

EXAMPLE: Maneet and Isabelle agree to rob a bank. In preparation, Maneet steals a car and Isabelle buys a ski mask. Both the theft of the car and the purchase of the ski mask as well as any other acts innocent or criminal may be *overt acts* if they are done in furtherance of a criminal conspiracy.

OVER-THE-COUNTER MARKET [OTC] a **securities** dealers market that handles trading in securities that are not **listed stocks** on an organized exchange. OTC trading differs from exchange trading in two significant ways: (1) transactions are carried out through telephone contact and negotiation with a number of dealers, called market makers, as compared to the single specialist, single location auction market mechanism used for listed securities trading, and (2) the market maker acts as principal in the transaction that involves the dealer as buyer and seller from his or her own inventory. The bulk of **bond** trading is carried out in the OTC market.

OWI operating while intoxicated. See **driving while intoxicated [DWI].**

OWNER the person who has legal **title** to property; the person in whom ownership, dominion, or title of property is vested. See also **record owner.**

OWNERSHIP exclusive right of possessing, **enjoying,** and disposing of a thing; often said to include the concept of **possession** and that of **title,** thus to be broader than either.

ALLODIAL OWNERSHIP free ownership, not subject to the restrictions or obligations associated with feudal tenures.

TENURIAL OWNERSHIP the holding of land subject to specific **services** or obligations owed to another. See **fee simple.**

OYER hearing. At **common law,** the reading to a defendant upon his or her demand the writ upon which the action is brought.

OYER AND TERMINER in English law, special tribunals empowered to hear and determine cases within their criminal **jurisdiction,** commissioned by the king when the delay involved in ordinary prosecution could not be tolerated, as in the case of sudden insurrection. The term has been sometimes used in American law to identify high courts of criminal jurisdiction in some states.

OYEZ (often pronounced "O Yes") hear ye. An exclamation used to get attention for an official proclamation or proceeding. In many courtrooms, the **bailiff** normally cries "oyez" to signal the beginning of the court proceeding.

P

P.A. Professional Association. See **professional corporation.**

PAC see **political action committee.**

PACKAGE, ORIGINAL see **original package doctrine.**

PACTUM *(päk'-tŭm)* Lat.: pact, **contract,** agreement. See also **nudum pactum,** a naked or bare agreement.

PAID-IN-SURPLUS in corporate finance, the amount paid for stock in excess of its **par value.**

PAIN AND SUFFERING a species of **damages** that one may recover for physical or mental pain that results from a wrong done. See also **survival statute.**

PAINTING THE TAPE expression for a person or group making transactions without a true change of ownership to give the impression that a stock is trading actively. See **manipulation [RIGGED ORDERS; WASH SALE]; wash sale.**

PAIS *(pā, pās)* Fr.: the countryside.

PALIMONY an award of support like **alimony** but made to a partner in a dissolved nonmarital relationship. Where the partners had an **express contract,** founded on consideration other than sexual services, some courts have held the contract enforceable; where no such formal agreement exists, the court may determine whether the conduct of the parties warrants a finding of **implied** contract or other understanding to support an award.

PALLIATE to mitigate; make less severe or intense.

PANDER to pimp; to cater to the lust of another. A **PANDERER** is a pimp, procurer, male bawd. **PANDERING** is 1. the crime of inducing a female to become a prostitute; 2. the promotion of obscene literature or movies by appeals to prurient interests. See **aid and abet; solicitation.**

PANDERER see **pander; prostitution.**

PANEL the list of persons who have been summoned for **jury** duty and from whom a jury may be chosen. To **IMPANEL** a jury means to summon and select a jury.

Panel also refers to the group of appellate judges who will hear an appeal. Typically, intermediate appellate courts consist of several judges who sit in panels of three.

PAPER see **bearer paper; chattel paper; commercial paper; order paper.**

PAPER PROFIT unrealized gain; profit that exists and is reflected in financial statements but that has not been reduced to cash and realized for tax purposes. See **realization.**

PAR equal to the established value; denotes the face amount or stated value of a **negotiable instrument, stock** or **bond,** and not the actual value it would receive on the open market. Bills of exchange, stocks and the like are AT PAR when they sell for their stated value.

   PAR VALUE is the stated or **face value** of a stock or bond. It has little significance for common stock; current practice is to issue **no-par stock** or stock with an arbitrary low value to avoid taxes. In the case of **preferred stock,** par takes on added importance since it specifies the dollar value upon which dividends are paid, and preferreds are usually offered for sale or exchange at par value. The par value on bonds specifies both the maturity payment and interest base.

PARALEGAL one not a member of the bar who is employed, usually by a law office, to perform a variety of tasks associated with a law practice, any of which may be performed properly and conveniently by one not trained or authorized to practice law.

PARALLELISM see **conscious parallelism.**

PARAMOUNT TITLE a **title** that will prevail over another asserted against it; signifies immediate right of **possession,** and is generally referred to as the basis for **eviction** of a **tenant** by one with a right of possession superior to that of the tenant.

PARAMOUR one's lover; one in the place of a husband or wife, but ordinarily without the legal rights attached to the marital relationship. See **palimony.**

PARCENER in **common law,** one who, jointly with others, as **coparcener,** holds an **estate** by virtue of **descent** (i.e., **inheritance**). The holding of a parcener is generally known as an estate in coparcenary and usually refers to the estate held by each inheritor before the inheritance has been divided (i.e., **partitioned**). The term is no longer widely used, since it is now said to be indistinguishable from a TENANCY IN COMMON (see **tenancy**).

PARDON an exercise of the **sovereign** prerogative to relieve a person from further punishment and from legal disabilities resulting from a crime of which he or she has been **convicted.** Its effect is that of relaxing the punishment and blotting out guilt, so that in the eyes of the law the offender is as innocent as if he or she had never committed the offense. See **amnesty; commutation; executive clemency; parole.**

EXAMPLE: Sofia is convicted of destroying government property in a protest march. As a result of that conviction, Sofia can no longer keep her job as a state employee. A few years later, serious questions are raised as to some of the witnesses' truthfulness, especially in light of the excellent reputation Sofia enjoyed before her conviction. After being presented with the issues, the governor grants Sofia a *pardon.* That pardon enables Sofia to work once more for the state.

CONDITIONAL PARDON any pardon imposing some condition, precedent or subsequent, that is not illegal, immoral, or impossible of performance.

UNCONDITIONAL PARDON goes no further than to restore the accused to his civil rights and remit the penalty imposed for the particular offense of which he was convicted in so far it remains unpaid.

PARENS PATRIAE *(pă'-reňz pă'-trē-ī)* Lat.: parent of his country. The role of the state as sovereign and guardian of persons under legal disability. By exercising this authority the state emphasizes that a child is not the absolute property of a parent but is a **trust** reposed in a parent by the state as parens patriae.

PARENTAL LIABILITY responsibility of parents for tortious acts committed by their minor children. While at common law, parents did not have such liabilities, the fact that juvenile misbehavior resulted in uncompensated victims led many states to enact statutes imposing liability on parents for the tort of their minor child. These statutes vary widely, but usually limit the parents' liability to a small dollar amount.

PARENT CORPORATION see **subsidiary.**

PARI DELICTO see **in pari delicto.**

PARI MATERIA see **in pari materia.**

PARITY equality.

PARLIAMENT a legislative body. The term was first used to describe the legislative body of England, Scotland, and Ireland and still is used to describe that of the United Kingdom. Many countries and localities that are former British colonies call their legislative bodies "Parliament."

PARLIAMENTARY LAW   general body of rules governing the orderly procedure of any legislative or other deliberative body. The most commonly followed rules are "Robert's Rules of Order."

PAROLE   in criminal law, a conditional release from imprisonment that entitles the person receiving it to serve the remainder of his or her term outside prison if he or she complies with all the conditions connected with his or her release. Compare **pardon; probation.**

PAROL EVIDENCE   oral rather than written **evidence.** See **parol evidence rule [merger clause].**

PAROL EVIDENCE RULE [MERGER CLAUSE]   a rule that declares that when terms of a **contract** have been embodied in a writing (called the **integration** of the agreement) to which both parties have assented, *parol* (oral) evidence of contemporaneous or prior oral agreements is not **admissible** for the purpose of varying or contradicting the written contract.

EXAMPLE: Mateo signs a contract with a home improvement builder to construct a pool at certain specifications. When the project is completed, Mateo claims that the builder orally agreed to change the specifications at Mateo's request. Because the specifications were never changed, Mateo refuses to pay, and the builder sues him. Unless the circumstances allow Mateo to introduce as *parol* [oral] *evidence* the builder's statement agreeing to the changes, the builder will probably prevail on the basis of his written contract with Mateo.

PARTIAL ACTUAL EVICTION   see **eviction [PARTIAL ACTUAL EVICTION].**

PARTIAL BREACH   a **breach** that gives rise to a claim for **damages** but that is so slight that it does not substantially impair the value of the **contract** to the injured party and thus does not give the injured party cause to abandon the whole contract. See **breach [PARTIAL BREACH].**

PARTIALLY DISCLOSED PRINCIPAL   see **principal.**

PARTICULARS, BILL OF   see **bill of particulars.**

PARTITION   a judicial separation of the respective interests in land of joint owners or TENANTS IN COMMON (see **tenancy**), so that each may take **possession** of, **enjoy** and control his or her separate **estate.** Partition is thus the dissolution of the **unity** of possession existing between common owners, with the result that the parties hold their estates in **severalty.** Partition is available whenever desired by any co-tenant in a tenancy in common.

A **JOINT TENANCY** (see **tenancy**) can be destroyed by either the **sale** or the **mortgaging** of a joint owner's interest in the estate, and the resultant tenancy in common is then subject to partition, thus defeating the **survivorship** rights of other joint tenants in the sold or mortgaged property.

EXAMPLE: Marwan and his friend own a large piece of undeveloped land as tenants in common. Marwan uses his ownership interest to obtain a loan from the bank. When he defaults on the loan, the bank can seek a *partition* of the land. With a partition, the bank owns one-half of the land and Marwan's friend owns one-half. Subsequent to a partition, the parties own particular portions of the land. If the land cannot be divided equitably, the land would be sold and the proceeds divided.

PARTNERSHIP 1. a **contract** of two or more persons to place their money, effects, labor and skill, or some or all of them, in lawful business, and to divide the profit and bear the loss in certain proportions; 2. an association of two or more persons to carry on as co-owners a business for profit. Partners are individually liable for the **debts** of the partnership, and assets individually owned will be subject to **execution** to satisfy any such debt when partnership assets are insufficient. A partnership is not subject to tax; rather the income is divided and taxed as personal income to the individual partners, unlike profits in corporations. The decision whether to form a partnership or to incorporate is generally controlled by the tax consequences.

ARTICLES OF PARTNERSHIP the written agreement, setting forth each partner's rights in and obligations to the partnership.

LIMITED PARTNERSHIP an entity in which one or more persons, with unlimited liability (called **GENERAL PARTNERS**), manage the partnership, while one or more other persons contribute only **capital.** This latter group of partners (called **LIMITED PARTNERS**) have no right to participate in the management and operation of the business and assume no liability beyond the capital contributed. Compare **corporation; joint venture.** See **distribution [PARTNER-SHIP DISTRIBUTION].**

PART PERFORMANCE see **statute of frauds.**

PARTY 1. in a judicial **proceeding,** a **litigant** (**plaintiff** or **defendant**); a person directly interested in the subject matter of a case; one who would assert a **claim,** make a **defense,** control proceedings, examine **witnesses** or **appeal** from the **judgment.** 2. a person or entity that enters into a **contract, lease, deed,** etc.

AGGRIEVED PARTY see **aggrieved party.**

INDISPENSABLE PARTY one whose involvement in the subject matter of a **controversy** is such that his or her **interests** will be affected, or one whose **joinder** in the **action** is required to enable a complete **adjudication** of the issues as well as the fashioning of an effective **remedy.** A **suit** cannot in **equity** and good conscience proceed without one who is regarded as an **indispensable party**.

EXAMPLE: Ball Corporation is the largest maker of a chemically based ceiling tile, although other smaller companies also produce the product. The tiles were installed in school buildings, and the chemical in them has had an adverse effect on the children. It could not be determined which company's tiles had been used, but only the smaller companies are named in a suit by the children. Ball is never mentioned. The other companies want Ball named as an *indispensable party* because, by numbers alone, it is most likely that Ball's tiles were used in schools. Ball also wants to be named because it fears that a judgment against the other companies will be used against it, even though it did not have an opportunity to participate in the litigation, and because otherwise a favorable outcome for the other companies would not prevent Ball from being sued later for the same thing.

NECESSARY PARTY one whose interests will be affected by the suit or without whom complete relief cannot be granted, but who will not be joined if doing so would deprive the court of **jurisdiction** in the case.

NOMINAL PARTY party appearing on the **record** not because he or she has any real interest in the case, but because technical rules of **pleading** require his or her presence in the record.

PARTY WALL see **party wall**.

POLITICAL PARTY a group of people united in pursuit of common political goals, specifically including the election of their members to public office.

PREVAILING PARTY see **prevailing party**.

PROPER PARTY one who has an interest in the subject matter of the **litigation,** but without whom a substantial **decree** may nevertheless issue, though such decree will not settle all questions in the controversy with respect to such party.

REAL PARTY IN INTEREST see **real party in interest.**

SECONDARY PARTY see **secondary party.**

THIRD PARTY someone other than the parties directly involved in the action or transaction; an outsider with no legal interest in the matter.

PARTY TO BE CHARGED see **statute of frauds.**

PARTY WALL a dividing wall between adjoining landowners that exists for the common benefit of both properties that it separates, and of which any use may be made by either party, so long as such use is not detrimental to the other. The two landowners own the wall as **TENANTS IN COMMON,** (see **tenancy**), where the wall stands upon ground that is itself held in common, or where it stands partly upon each of the two adjoining properties. A *party wall* may be constructed wholly upon property belonging to one of the parties, or it may be owned entirely by only one of them; in either case the wall is subject to an **easement** to have it maintained. A party wall is often one that provides support for one or more separately owned structures.

PAR VALUE see **par [PAR VALUE].**

PASSIVE inactive, usually used to describe permissive behavior, such as toleration of or failure to correct a dangerous condition on one's property as opposed to an affirmative act threatening the safety of another. In tax law, **PASSIVE INCOME**, such as dividends, is a separate category from active income. See **income.**

PASSIVE EUTHANASIA see **euthanasia [PASSIVE EUTHANASIA].**

PASSIVE INCOME see **income [PASSIVE INCOME].**

PASSIVE USE see **use [PASSIVE USE].**

PATENT evident; obvious.

PATENT OF INVENTION (often called simply a patent) a grant of right to exclude others from the making or selling of an invention during a specified time. It gives to its owner a legitimate **monopoly.** See **patent infringement.**

PATENT OF LAND an instrument by which the government conveys a **fee simple** interest in land to another.

PATENT PENDING (often abbreviated **PAT. PEND.**) a notice that the product on which it is inscribed has been the subject of an application for patent protection and that if a patent does issue, those with notice will be subject to the applicant's prior rights.

PATENT APPEALS see **federal courts [COURT OF CUSTOMS AND PATENT APPEALS].**

PATENT DEFECT a defect that could be recognized upon reasonably careful inspection or through ordinary diligence.

EXAMPLE: Alex examines a warehouse space prior to renting it for himself. Normal examination would reveal that water leaked into the warehouse in several spots. Some of Alex's property in the warehouse is subsequently damaged by water. Since the leakage is a *patent defect,* which he should have discovered, Alex cannot sue for the damage.

Compare **latent defect.**

PATENT INFRINGEMENT the act of trespassing upon the rights secured by a **patent.** The test of infringement is whether the device in question does substantially the same work in substantially the same way and accomplishes the same result as the device that has been patented.

Copyrights and **trademarks** can also be the subject of an infringement action.

PATERNITY SUIT [BASTARDY PROCEEDINGS] a suit initiated to determine the paternity of a child born out of wedlock and to provide for the support of that child once paternity is proved. See **DNA testing.**

PATIENT PROTECTION AND AFFORDABLE CARE ACT [PPACA] see **affordable care act.**

PAT. PEND. see **patent [PATENT PENDING].**

PATRICIDE the killing of one's own father.

PATRIOT ACT Act of Congress to combat terrorism signed into law after the events of 9-11 involving the World Trade Center and the Pentagon. The act is called the "Uniting and Strengthening America by Providing Appropriate Tools Required to Intercept and Obstruct Terrorism Act of 2001" or USA Patriot Act. A four-year "Sunsets Extension Act" was signed in 2011, extending the provisions of the act involving roving wiretaps, searches of business records, and surveillance of individuals suspected of terrorist-related activities. The act focused upon combatting chemical-weapons offenses, the use of weapons of mass destruction, the killing of Americans abroad, and terrorism financing. To fight the threats, the act provided for many things, including strengthening border security and establishing an electronic crime task force and funding for it. It expanded search powers for law enforcement, including interception of telephone, e-mail, and bank records, often without the need for judicially sanctioned wiretap warrants. It allows notification of search warrants to be delayed, meaning that the individual would not be notified of the search until after it was carried out. It also provides for indefinite detention of persons suspected of terrorism. The act also added crimes considered to be acts of terrorism to include mass transit system attacks, use of a biological weapon, supporting terrorism, and computer hacking. The penalties for terrorist crimes also increased. The balance between national security and personal civil liberty concerns has led to numerous challenges to the act's provisions, with some provisions being found to be unconstitutional and other provisions expiring without renewal by Congress.

PATRONAGE giving either protection or support. **POLITICAL PATRONAGE** is the use of political office to protect one's friends and supporters through the influence of the office, and to support them by hiring them for government jobs. The **CIVIL SERVICE COMMISSIONS** were established to create professional bodies of government employees who would be free of political patronage.

PAUPER indigent; one who is unable to provide his or her own support and is otherwise without financial resources. Under the **Equal Protection Clause** to the United States Constitution, indigents and paupers may be excused from paying certain court costs and other legal fees so that they may have equal access to the courts. See **in forma pauperis; indigent.**

PAWN to deposit personal property with another as security for the payment of a **debt.**

PAYABLES see **account [ACCOUNT PAYABLE]; balance sheet; liabilities.**

PAYABLE TO BEARER see **bearer paper.**

PAYABLE TO ORDER see **order paper.**

PAYEE any **person** to whom a **debt** should be paid; one to whose order a **bill of exchange, note** or check is made payable.

PAYER [PAYOR] one who pays a **debt** or is obligated to pay a debt under a promissory **note** or other **instrument.**

PAYMENT satisfaction of a claim or **debt.** Delivery of money in fulfillment of an obligation.

PAYMENT DATE see **ex dividend [PAYMENT DATE].**

PAYMENT IN DUE COURSE payment of a **negotiable instrument** at or after its date of maturity, made to its **holder** in good faith and without notice of any defect in his or her **title.**

EXAMPLE: Uri fraudulently obtains a negotiable promissory note made out by Raoul and payable to a third party. When the note becomes due, Uri presents it to Raoul and Raoul *pays it in due course.* The third party cannot force Raoul also to pay him, because Raoul had no knowledge of the earlier fraud and, therefore, had no reason to suspect that the third party did not legitimately negotiate the note to Uri.

PAYMENT INTO COURT the payment by a party of a sum of money or other subject matter of a lawsuit into court for the duration of the lawsuit. The court disposes of the money or other property as the parties agree in their settlement of the lawsuit, or in accordance with the court's judgment.

PAYOR see **payer [payor].**

PAY TO PLAY term used to describe the practice of government (whether federal, state, or local) contractors making campaign contributions or giving things of value to those responsible for issuing the contracts. Many states are enacting legislation to ban such practices by limiting the amount and timing of certain gifts or campaign contributions.

P.C. see **probable cause; professional corporation; protective custody.** Also an abbreviation for personal computer; politically correct.

PCR see **DNA testing [PCR].**

PCR ACTIONS see **postconviction relief proceedings [PCR actions].**

P.D. **public defender**. Also, police department.

PEACEABLE POSSESSION possession that is not interrupted by adverse **suits** or other hostile action intended to **oust** the possessor from the land. The existence of adverse claims is not precluded, so long as no actual attempt to **dispossess** is made. See **quiet title.**

PEACEFUL ENJOYMENT see **quiet enjoyment.**

PECULATION the fraudulent **misappropriation** to one's own use of money or goods entrusted to one's care. See **embezzlement; larceny.**

PECUNIARY consisting of money or that which can be valued in money. A **PECUNIARY LOSS** is a loss of money or one that can be translated into economic loss.

PENAL ACTION a civil suit brought for the recovery of a statutory penalty imposed as a punishment for an offense againse the public.

PENAL INSTITUTION any place of confinement for **convicted** criminals. Penal institutions include local and county jails and workhouses, reformatories, penitentiaries, prison camps and farms, as well as the modern **CORRECTIONAL INSTITUTION** (new nomenclature used to describe many penal institutions previously called "prisons"). See **jail**.

PENAL LAW [CODE] a law to preserve public order that defines an offense against the public and inflicts a penalty for its violation. **Statutes** that grant a private **(civil) action** against a wrongdoer are not considered penal, but **remedial,** in nature.

PENALTIES see **civil penalties.**

PENALTY sanction, usually an amount of money, imposed as punishment for civil or criminal wrongdoing. The term also refers to a sum fixed by contract to be payable by one party to the other for the failure of either to perform his or her obligations under the contract. See **civil penalties; liquidated damages.**

PENALTY CLAUSE a **contract** clause that provides for the payment of an amount as forfeiture in the event a party defaults. Penalty clauses are generally not enforced by the courts when the amount of the penalty is unrelated to the damages incurred. However, the courts will sometimes enforce a penalty on the grounds that the parties were free to agree to it. Courts will enforce a **liquidated damage clause** when the amount of actual damages is difficult to ascertain and the liquidated damages are a reasonable attempt to approximate the actual damages.

PENDENTE LITE [LITE PENDENTE] *(pĕn'-dĕn'-tā lē'-tā)* Lat.: suspended by the lawsuit; pending the lawsuit. Contingent upon the determination of a pending lawsuit. See **lis pendens**.

EXAMPLE: Tenants in an apartment building sue their landlord for not providing heat. The tenants do not want to pay full rent since they are not getting heat, but state law requires full rent each month or else the landlord can evict. To protect themselves, the tenants commence a lawsuit and set up a bank account *pendente lite* where they deposit their rent each month while the suit is in court. At the end of the suit, the money in the account is applied to past-due rents less whatever amount the court says the tenants are entitled to for lack of heat.

A spouse will seek alimony and child support payments *pendente lite* in most cases after he or she sues for divorce.

See **lis pendens.**

PENDENT JURISDICTION federal court doctrine whereby a plaintiff, notwithstanding the limitations of **federal question jurisdiction,** may rely upon both federal and nonfederal grounds for the **relief** sought in a **complaint.** Thus, where the plaintiff joins a federal claim with a state law claim based on closely related or identical conduct of the defendant, the federal courts have jurisdiction to hear and determine the state law claims as well as those arising under federal law. See **abstention; jurisdiction [PENDENT JURISDICTION].** Compare **ancillary jurisdiction.**

PENITENTIARY see **jail** [PENITENTIARIES]; **penal institution.**

PEN REGISTER see **WIRETAP** [PEN REGISTER].

PENSION FUND see **retirement plan** [PENSION FUND (PLAN)].

PENSION PLAN see **retirement plan** [PENSION FUND (PLAN)].

PENSION PROTECTION ACT pension legislation passed in 2006 providing a number of significant tax incentives to enhance and protect retirement savings and strengthen workers' retirement security. Its provisions include **inherited IRAs; DB(k)s;** and increased contribution amounts to retirement accounts. See **retirement plan.**

PEONAGE see **Thirteenth Amendment** [PEONAGE].

PER ANNUM *(pĕr ăn'-nŭm)* Lat.: by the year; annually.

PER [PUR] AUTRE VIE *(pĕr [pūr] ô'-tr vē)* Fr.: for or during the life of another. A **life estate** measured by the life of a third person rather than the life of the **grantee.**

PER CAPITA *(pēr kăp'-ĭ-tà)* Lat.: by the heads. Anything figured per capita is calculated by the number of individuals, (heads) involved and is divided equally among all.

PER CURIAM *(pĕr kū'-rē-äm)* Lat.: by the court. See **opinion** [PER CURIAM OPINION].

PER DIEM *(pĕr dē'-ĕm)* Lat.: by the day. l. pay for a day's services. 2. Government and private business travel allowances are often allocated on a per diem basis.

PEREMPTORY absolute, final, not admitting of question or appeal. A peremptory trial date may be established by the court on its own **motion** or at the request of a **party** to insure timely disposition of the case. In selection of a **jury** each side has a right to a fixed number of PEREMPTORY CHALLENGES to the seating of potential **jurors,** which means that **counsel** may reject a certain number of potential jurors for any reason, or for no reason. See **challenge** [PEREMPTORY CHALLENGE]; **peremptory writ.**

PEREMPTORY CHALLENGE see **challenge** [PEREMPTORY CHALLENGE].

PEREMPTORY PLEA see **plea** [PEREMPTORY PLEA].

PEREMPTORY WRIT a peremptory **writ** is a form of **mandamus** that requires the act commanded be done absolutely. In comparison, a usual writ of mandamus permits the public official the choice of either doing the act commanded or showing legal cause why it need not be done. Before a peremptory writ can issue, the official must be given notice of the legal action and an opportunity to defend.

In **common law,** peremptory writs were a species of original writs by which lawsuits were begun. The peremptory original writ commanded the sheriff to cause the **defendant** to appear in court and to defend the suit. It was used when general damages to be assessed by the jury were requested. A suit was otherwise begun by the use of an optional writ, which commanded the defendant to do the acts requested or to show cause why they should not be done. This writ was used when the plaintiff requested a specific remedy, such as the return of a parcel of land or the payment of a specific sum. **Compare prerogative writ.**

PERFECTED completed, executed, enforceable, merchantable; refers especially to the status ascribed to **security interests** after certain events have occurred or certain prescribed steps have been taken, such as filing evidence of the interest, taking possession of the collateral, etc. A perfected security interest has **priority** over an unperfected interest. The date of perfection is also the time from which courts judge priority contests among other holding perfected interest.

In practice, after the accomplishment of all steps necessary to entitle a litigant to proceed in an **appellate court,** the appeal is said to be *perfected.*

PERFORMANCE the fulfillment of an obligation or a promise; especially, completion of one's duty under a **contract.** See **specific performance; substantial perfomance.** See also **nonperformance.** Compare **obligation of a contract.**

PERFORMANCE BOND a bond that guarantees against **breach of contract;** generally used in building contracts to guarantee that a contractor will perform the contract. In the event the contractor defaults or otherwise breaches the contract, the owner of the building project may use the proceeds of the bond to complete the project. Depending upon its terms, the proceeds of a performance bond may also be used to pay subcontractors who furnish labor and materials See **bond [PERFORMANCE BOND].**

PERIL risk, such as the risk that is insured in an insurance policy.

PER INFORTUNIUM *(pèr ĭn-fôr-tū'-nē-ŭm)* Lat.: by accident.

PERIODIC TENANCY see **tenancy [PERIODIC TENANCY].**

PERJURY criminal offense of making false statements under **oath.** In **common law,** only a willful and corrupt sworn statement made without sincere belief in its truth, and made in a judicial **proceeding** regarding a material matter, was perjury. Today, **statutes** have broadened the offense so that in some jurisdictions any **false swearing** in a legal instrument or legal setting is perjury. See also **subornation of perjury**.

EXAMPLE: Sheila is charged with robbery. At her trial, Tomas, Sheila's boyfriend, admits to the crime, which results in a "not guilty" verdict for Sheila. Because of a procedural technicality, Tomas cannot be tried for the robbery. But if the prosecution can prove that Tomas lied about committing the crime, he could then be prosecuted for *perjury.*

PERMANENT FIXTURE see **fixture.**

PERMANENT INJUNCTION see **injunction [PERMANENT [FINAL] INJUNCTION].**

PERMANENT RESIDENT see **legal permanent resident [LPR].**

PERMISSION-BASED MARKETING e-mail messages, mail, or newsletters sent to a person who has given the sender permission. Compare junk mail and **spam.**

OPT-IN granting permission for receipt of such communications by registering or affirmatively responding to a request.

OPT-OUT request by a recipient to cease delivery or to unsubscribe from such communications.

PERMISSION OF COURT see **leave of court.**

PERMISSIVE COUNTERCLAIM see **counterclaim [PERMISSIVE COUNTERCLAIM]; joinder [PERMISSIVE JOINDER].**

PERMISSIVE JOINDER see **joinder [PERMISSIVE JOINDER].**

PERMISSIVE USE see **use [PERMISSIVE USE].**

PERMISSIVE WASTE see **waste [PERMISSIVE WASTE].**

PER MY ET PER TOUT *(pĕr mē ā pĕr tū)* Law Fr.: by half and by whole. In joint **tenancy,** each tenant's share is the whole, for purposes of **tenure** and **survivorship** [tout], and each share is an **aliquot** portion for purposes of **alienation** [my]. Compare **per tout et non per my.**

PERPETUITIES, RULE AGAINST see **rule against perpetuities.**

PERPETUITY see **in perpetuity.**

PER QUOD *(pĕr kwŏd)* Lat.: through which; by which; whereby. Requiring extrinsic circumstances (context); acquiring meaning only by reference to external facts.

PER SE *(pĕr sā)* Lat.: through itself, by means of itself. Not requiring extraneous evidence or support to establish its existence. In defamation, statements that damage a person's reputation, without reference to the circumstances that give the language their injurious meaning, are **libelous** or **slanderous** *per se*. Language imputing any of the following characteristics to a person is slanderous per se: having a loathsome disease; having committed a crime; unchastity in a woman; and incompetence in one's profession.

ACTIONABLE PER SE act which on its face constitutes a **cause of action.** No proof of damages is required. Applies in defamation cases, although free speech constitutional considerations may prevail.

In antitrust law, some types of business conduct are considered per se restraints of trade. Because proof of such conduct proves a violation of the **Sherman Antitrust Act**, there is no need to prove any injury to competition, which is otherwise a necessary element in an antitrust claim. One example of a per se violation is **price fixing**.

PERSON in law, an individual or **incorporated** group having certain legal rights and responsibilities. See **natural person**.

PERSON AGGRIEVED see **aggrieved party**.

PERSONAL ATTACK RULE see **fairness doctrine [PERSONAL ATTACK RULE]**.

PERSONAL CHATTEL see **chattel [PERSONAL CHATTEL]**.

PERSONAL EFFECTS a vague phrase used to describe tangible property having an intimate relation to the decedent, such as clothing and jewelry.

PERSONAL EXPENSE see **expense [PERSONAL EXPENSE]**.

PERSONAL EXPENSES DEDUCTIONS see **deductions [PERSONAL EXPENSES DEDUCTIONS]**.

PERSONAL HOLDING COMPANY a **corporation** having a limited number of **shareholders** and a high percentage of passive **income,** such as **interest, dividends, rents, royalties,** and **capital gains.** A special income tax was imposed on personal holding companies in 1937 in order to prevent taxpayers from avoiding taxes by placing their **assets** in corporations. Previously, taxpayers would avoid income taxes by placing their assets in one or more corporations, thereby splitting their income among several taxpayers and taking advantage of the lower marginal tax brackets. The **PERSONAL HOLDING COMPANY TAX** is imposed on the undistributed income of such corporations at a flat rate. The purpose of the tax is to force the shareholders to distribute the corporation's income to themselves as dividends so they may be taxed on it at their regular rate of income tax.

PERSONAL JUDGMENT **judgment** imposed on defendant requiring sums to be advanced from whatever assets he or she has within the jurisdiction of the issuing court, as opposed to a judgment directed against particular property (called an **in rem** judgment) or a judgment against a **corporate** entity. See **jurisdiction [IN PERSONAM JURISDICTION].**

PERSONAL JURISDICTION see **judgment [PERSONAL JUDGMENT]; jurisdiction [IN PERSONAM JURISDICTION].**

PERSONAL NOTICE see **notice [PERSONAL NOTICE].**

PERSONAL PROPERTY [PERSONALTY] things movable, as distinguished from **real property** or things attached to the **realty.** See **chattel; fixture.**

EXAMPLE: An agreement between a buyer and seller of a house provides that the sale covers only the land and home and not the seller's *personal property.* This agreement means that the seller can remove items such as furniture and rugs, but not the heating system.

PERSONAL RECOGNIZANCE see **release on own recognizance [ROR].**

PERSONAL REPRESENTATIVE a person who manages the affairs of another, either under a **power of attorney** or due to the incapacity of the principal either through death, incompetency, or infancy; for example, the **executor** appointed under the will of a decedent or the **committee** of an incompetent.

PERSONAL SERVICE see **service [PERSONAL SERVICE].**

PERSONALTY see **personal property [PERSONALTY].**

PERSONAM see **in personam.**

PER STIRPES *(pĕr stûr'-pāz)* Lat.: through or by roots; by family stock representation. The essential characteristic of a distribution of an **intestate's estate** per stirpes is that each beneficiary receives a share in the property, representing the accurate fraction of the fraction to which the person through whom he or she claims from the ancestor would have been entitled. It is distinguished from a distribution **per capita.**

EXAMPLE: Keith dies without a will. His wife has predeceased him, and he is survived by two children. A third child has also predeceased him but has left two children. Under a *per stirpes* distribution, Keith's two children each receive one-third of his estate. The remaining one-third is distributed to the children of the third child who had predeceased Keith.

PERSUASION BURDEN see **burden of proof.**

PER TOUT ET NON PER MY *(pĕr tū ā nōn pĕr mē)* Law Fr.: by the whole and not by the half. Describes the type of **seisin** that exists in a **JOINT TENANCY** or **TENANCY BY THE ENTIRETY** (see **tenancy**). Thus, the joint tenants or man and wife who own property by the entirety own an **undivided interest** in the whole of the property but not an individual interest in only a part of the property. See **partition; tenancy [TENANCY IN COMMON].** Compare **per my et per tout.**

PERVIOUS open to arguments; receptive to new ideas; approachable; open-minded.

PETITION in **equity** procedure, the functional equivalent of a **complaint at law.** It is a written application addressed to a court or judge, stating facts and circumstances relied upon as a cause for judicial action, and containing a **prayer** (formal request) for relief.

PETITIONER one who presents a petition to a court or other body either to institute an **equity** proceeding or to take an **appeal** from a **judgment.** The adverse party is called the **respondent.**

PETITION IN BANKRUPTCY the petition by which an insolvent debtor declares bankruptcy and invokes the protection of the bankruptcy court from creditors. Under the United States Constitution, Congress is given power to establish uniform laws of bankruptcy. It has used this power to preempt all state laws and state court actions by granting an automatic stay of any proceedings against the bankrupt debtor upon the filing of a bankruptcy petition. Creditors must seek their remedies against the debtor in the bankruptcy court.

PETIT [PETTY] JURY see **jury [PETIT [PETTY] JURY].**

PETIT [PETTY] LARCENY see **larceny [PETIT [PETTY] LARCENY].**

PETTY JURY see **jury [PETIT [PETTY] JURY].**

PETTY LARCENY see **larceny [PETIT [PETTY] LARCENY].**

PHISHING see **spam [PHISHING].**

PHYSICAL WASTE see **waste.**

PHYSICIAN-PATIENT PRIVILEGE see **privileged communication.**

P.I. personal injury; private investigator.

PICKETING the practice, used in labor disputes, of patrolling, usually with placards, to publicize a dispute or to secure support for a cause; a constitutionally protected exercise of free expression when done peaceably.

PIERCING THE CORPORATE VEIL the process of imposing liability for corporate activity, in disregard of the corporate entity, on a person or entity other than the offending **corporation** itself.

Generally, the corporate form isolates both individuals and **PARENT CORPORATIONS** (see **subsidiary [SUBSIDIARY CORPORATION]**) from liability for corporate misdeeds. However, there are times (such as when incorporation itself was accomplished to perpetrate a **fraud**) when the court will ignore the corporate entity and strip the organizers and managers of the corporation of the limited liability that they usually enjoy. In doing so, the court is said to pierce the corporate veil.

PILOT [PILT] abbreviations for "payment in lieu of taxes." Federal payments to local governments that help offset losses in property taxes due to nontaxable federal lands within their boundaries. States also apply the concept to universities and hospitals due to the public benefits derived from them.

PIMP see **pander; prostitution.**

PINK SHEETS see **listed stock [PINK SHEETS].**

PINPOINT CITATION particular location of a quotation within an opinion. In legal brief writing, the reader may then go directly to the relevant area to find the quoted material. For example, "lawyers in criminal courts are necessities, not luxuries" is cited as *Gideon v. Wainwright*, 372 U.S. 335, 344 (1963). Page 335 directs the reader to the first page of the *Gideon* opinion and page 344 directs the reader to the specific page within the opinion where the quotation (or concept) is found.

PIRACY at **common law,** the commission of acts of robbery and depredation on the high seas that, if committed on land, would constitute felonies. See **hijacking.** Piracy is also used to refer to the commercial reproduction and distribution of property protected by copyright, patent, trademark, or trade secret law. Pirated works, such as videotapes or records, constitute copyright infringement. See also **plagiarism.**

P.J. presiding **judge.**

PL. [P.L.] plaintiff; public law.

PLAGIARISM appropriation of the literary composition of another and passing off as one's own the product of the mind and language of another. The offense of plagiarism, known in the law as **INFRINGEMENT OF COPYRIGHT,** comes into being only when the work allegedly copied is protected by **copyright.**

PLAIN ERROR (RULE)   rule applicable to **appellate courts** that requires the **reversal** of a conviction and the award of a new trial where an obvious error in the trial **proceedings** affecting the fundamental right of the accused to a fair trial was not objected to at the time it occurred and went uncorrected by the trial court.

EXAMPLE: The prosecutor introduces very prejudicial evidence at Roy's trial. The judge fails to instruct the jury to limit their consideration of that evidence, despite the obvious need for such an instruction. Roy is convicted and the case is appealed. Even though Roy's attorney did not object to the introduction at the time it occurred—a procedure that would normally be required before a new trial could be granted—the appellate court may apply the *plain error* rule and grant Roy a new trial.

Compare **harmless error; miscarriage of justice.**

PLAIN LANGUAGE STATUTE[S]   increasing tendency of state and federal legislatures and courts to require clear, understandable language in statutes, contracts, and opinions such that a person not familiar with legal terms can readily understand the context.

EXAMPLE: Zoe provides a lease to her tenant Li Ming that clearly states the rental terms, including what is covered by the security deposit, when the rent is due, and when late penalties apply. Due to the simple but clear language, Li Ming also understands that while he may have pets, he can only have a maximum of two dogs and that each dog cannot weigh more than 50 pounds. He also understands what would be considered pet damage rather than normal wear and tear.

PLAIN MEANING (RULE)   minority view that the words themselves determine the meaning of a **statute.** See **strict construction.** The majority view looks to the **legislative history** (committee hearings, commentary) or other **extrinsic evidence** in determining the **intent.** See **four corners.**

PLAINTIFF   the one who initially brings the **suit;** one who, in a personal **action,** seeks a **remedy** in a court of justice for an injury to, or a withholding of, his or her rights.

PLAINTIFF IN ERROR   one who appeals from a judgment against him or her in a lower court, whether he or she was plaintiff or defendant in that court.

THIRD PARTY PLAINTIFF refers to a **defendant** who files a **complaint** against a third party not named as a defendant by the plaintiff, and so not otherwise a party to the **proceeding.**

PLAIN VIEW a doctrine that may legitimize a **search** or **seizure** without a **search warrant,** which otherwise is generally required.

EXAMPLE: While walking on the sidewalk, a policeman sees a marijuana plant growing in someone's house. Under the *plain view* doctrine, the policeman can enter the house without a search warrant, even though a house represents a highly protected privacy area that in almost every other instance requires a search warrant prior to a policeman's entrance.

PLAN see **master plan.**

PLAT in property law, a map that shows the location of real estate in a town or county in relation to adjoining lots and landmarks such as roads.

PLEA 1. in **equity,** a special answer relying upon one or more things as a reason for the **suit** to be dismissed, delayed, or barred; 2. **at law,** broadly, any one of the common law **pleadings;** 3. technically, the **defendant's** or **respondent's** answer refuting the factual basis for the **plaintiff's** petition or **complaint,** as distinguished from a **demurrer,** which is an answer asserting no cause of action exists as a matter of law. 4. In criminal procedure, the defendant will enter a plea at his or her **arraignment,** of not guilty, guilty or, in some jurisdictions, **nolo contendere** or **non vult** (meaning no contest). Pleas are either dilatory or peremptory. The past tense is pleaded or pled.

AFFIRMATIVE PLEA one that sets up a single fact not appearing in the bill, or sets up a number of circumstances all tending to establish a single fact, which, if existing, destroys the complainant's case.

ALFORD PLEA a guilty plea entered without a factual admission of guilt by the defendant. There must be evidence indicating actual guilt. It is done to accept the favorable aspects of a **plea bargain** rather than risk a harsher sentence if convicted at trial. Not all jurisdictions permit Alford pleas. See **nolo contendere**.

DILATORY PLEA one that tends to defeat the actions to which it refers by contesting grounds other than the **merits** of plaintiff's case. Hence, the plea raises issues such as improper **jurisdiction,** wrong defendant, or other procedural defects. See **dilatory plea.**

DOUBLE PLEA one which consists of several distinct and independent matters alleged to the same point and requiring different answers.

INSANITY PLEA one by which the defendant claims innocence because of a mental disorder or inability to reason that prevented him or her from having a culpable mental state, i.e., from having the sense of purposefulness (intent, willfulness, recklessness) that is a necessary element of the crime charged. See **insanity.**

PEREMPTORY PLEA a type of **PLEA IN BAR** (below), which answers the merits of the plaintiff's complaint, as compared to a **DILATORY PLEA** (above), which defends on grounds other than the merits.

PLEA IN ABATEMENT a **DILATORY PLEA** (see above) objecting to the place, mode, or time of asserting the plaintiff's claim, but not addressing any of the underlying merits. These errors can be corrected, as opposed to claims made in a **PLEA IN BAR**, at which time the claim can be renewed. Compare **PEREMPTORY PLEA** (above).

PLEA IN BAR a plea that sets forth matters which per se destroy the plaintiff's right of action and bar its prosecution absolutely, such as a bar due to a statute of limitations or a constitutional guarantee against self-incrimination. This plea denies a plaintiff's right to maintain the action and which, if established, will destroy the action.

PURE PLEA see **AFFIRMATIVE PLEA** (above).

PLEA BARGAINING the process whereby the accused and the prosecutor negotiate a mutually satisfactory disposition of the case. The defendant may plead guilty to a lesser offense or to only one or some of the counts in a multicount **indictment.** In return, the defendant seeks concessions on the type and length of his or her **sentence** or a reduction of counts against him or her.

EXAMPLE: Fred is charged with robbery while armed with a deadly weapon. All witnesses say that Fred was seen with a gun. However, the only gun found at the scene of the crime is on Fred's partner. In Fred's state, robbery with a deadly weapon carries a much greater sentence than robbery. Fred *plea bargains* with the prosecutor, offering to plead guilty to robbery if the prosecutor will dismiss the charge relating to the weapon and thus insure a shorter sentence. The State is spared the expense and uncertainty attendant to a trial, and defendant minimizes his overall exposure.

PLEAD 1. to make any **pleading;** 2. to answer **plaintiff's common law declaration;** 3. in criminal law, to answer to the **charge,** either admitting or denying guilt.

PLEADED the past tense of **plea.** Synonymous with pled.

EXAMPLE: After Weber pleaded guilty to fraud, the judge revoked bail, ordered the preparation of a presentence report, and set a sentencing date.

PLEADING BURDEN see **burden of proof.**

PLEADINGS statements, in logical and legal form, of the facts that constitute plaintiff's **cause of action** and defendant's ground of **defense.** Pleadings are either **allegations** by the parties affirming or denying certain matters of fact, or other statements in support or derogation of certain principles of law, which are intended to describe to the court or jury the real matter in dispute.

AFFIRMATIVE PLEADINGS any defensive pleadings that affirmatively allege the existence of facts, rather than merely deny the existence of the facts alleged by the plaintiff. For instance, if a plaintiff alleges the nonpayment of a promissory note, the defendant may deny that the note exists, or he may affirmatively plead that the note has been paid.

AMENDED PLEADINGS pleadings submitted to the court later in time than the original pleadings and which correct the original pleadings or arguments therein, such as by the addition of a cause of action or a defense.

CODE PLEADINGS see **code pleading**.

DEFECTIVE PLEADING see **defective pleading.**

PLEADINGS IN THE ALTERNATIVE see **alternative pleading.**

RESPONSIVE PLEADINGS answers that either admit or deny the allegations contained in the complaint, and thus respond to them, rather than raise grounds upon which the complaint should be dismissed, such as the expiration of the **Statute of Limitations**.

SUPPLEMENTAL PLEADINGS pleadings that assert a claim or a defense based upon events occurring after the filing of the original pleading which they supplement.

PLEADING THE FIFTH (AMENDMENT) see **Fifth Amendment; self-incrimination, privilege against.**

PLEA IN ABATEMENT see **dilatory plea.**

PLEASURE one who serves "at pleasure" can be fired without warning or cause.

PLED see **pleaded.**

PLEDGE a deposit of **personal property** as security for a **debt;** delivery of goods by a **debtor** to a **creditor** until the debt is repaid; generally defined as a **lien** or a **contract** that calls for the transfer of personal property only as **security.** See **bailment; collateral.**

PLEDGEE   person who takes property to hold as security for a debt in accordance with a contract.

PLEDGOR   person who delivers the property.

PLENARY   full or unqualified. In judicial proceedings, denotes a complete, formally **pleaded** suit wherein a **petition** or **complaint** is filed by one or more persons against one or more other persons who file an **answer** or a response. A **PLENARY ACTION** is one in which a full trial or **PLENARY HEARING** is had on the merits of a complaint following full **discovery,** as distinguished from a **summary proceeding.** See de novo.

PLURALITY OPINION   see **opinion [PLURALITY OPINION].**

PLUS TICK   see **up [plus] tick.**

POCKET VETO   a means by which the President of the United States may effectively veto an act of Congress without exercising the presidential veto right. Under the U.S. Constitution the President must veto legislation within ten days after it has been passed by both the Senate and the House of Representatives, or else the legislation will become law. However, if Congress adjourns before the end of the ten-day period the legislation will only become law if the President has signed it. Accordingly, the President may effectively veto legislation that was passed within the last ten days of the congressional session merely by not signing it into law.

P.O.D.   pay on death; pay on delivery.

POINT RESERVED   at **trial,** the holding of a legal issue in abeyance for argument, so that the testimony or other matters at hand may proceed.

POISONOUS TREE   see **fruit of the poisonous tree.**

POLICE COURT   an inferior **municipal court** with limited **jurisdiction** in criminal cases. Minor cases can be disposed of by such courts, but otherwise they generally have power only to **arraign** the **accused** and set **bail.**

POLICE POWER   inherent power of state governments, often delegated in part to local governments, to impose upon private rights those restrictions that are reasonably related to promotion and maintenance of the health, safety, morals and general welfare of the public. Restrictions upon the use of one's property, such as **zoning** laws, or upon the conduct of one's business, such as environmental regulations, are imposed by state and local governments pursuant to the police power.

EXAMPLE: A federal law sets out certain requirements for processing milk. One state has conclusively found that, because of conditions peculiar to the state, the requirements are insufficient to protect its citizens' health. Under the state's *police power,* the state legislature may enact greater precautions that all milk must meet to be sold in that state.

POLITICAL ACTION COMMITTEES special-interest groups formed to provide money for a candidate's election campaign or a legislative initiative, or to counter against the same. The money is generally spent on commercials and other advertising. The names of donors are publicly reported but in some instances the filing of donor names is not required to occur (if, for example, quarterly) until after an election has taken place. The amount of money **CONNECTED, NON-CONNECTED** or **LEADERSHIP** PACs may spend is regulated by federal or state election laws. **SUPER-PACS** do not have a limit on donations.

CONNECTED PACS businesses, organized labor, or health organizations raising money from a "restricted class," generally consisting of managers, shareholders, or members.

LEADERSHIP PACS groups formed by politicians to help fellow candidates.

NON-CONNECTED PACS also known as **IDEOLOGICAL** PACs. They are committees focusing on a single issue. These organizations may accept funds from any individual, group, or connected PAC.

SUPER-PACS INDEPENDENT-EXPENDITURE ONLY COMMITTEES that may raise funds from individuals, businesses, organized labor, and other groups without any legal limit on donation size and can spend the funds independent of any specific candidate campaign. They must not directly coordinate with a candidate or party.

POLITICAL ASYLUM see **asylum [POLITICAL ASYLUM].**

POLITICAL CONTRIBUTION see **charitable contribution [POLITICAL CONTRIBUTION].**

POLITICAL CORPORATION see **corporation [PUBLIC CORPORATIONS].**

POLITICAL PARTY see **party [POLITICAL PARTY].**

POLITICAL PATRONAGE see **patronage [POLITICAL PATRONAGE].**

POLITICAL QUESTION a question that a court determines not to be properly subject to judicial determination (not to be **justiciable**), because resolution is committed exclusively to the jurisdiction of another branch of government (legislative or executive), or because adequate standards for judicial review are lacking, or because there is no way to insure enforcement of the court's judgment.

EXAMPLE: The Constitution provides that the Senate shall have advise and consent power for all treaties entered into by the President with other nations. After the Senate consents to a certain treaty, a suit is brought challenging the extent to which the Senate deliberated over the treaty. A court will rule that the issue is a *political question* that cannot be decided by the judiciary.

POLLING THE JURY see **jury [POLLING THE JURY].**

POLL TAX a direct tax of a fixed amount upon all persons, or upon all persons of a certain class, resident within a specified territory, without regard to their property or their occupation.

POLYGAMY in criminal law, the offense of having more than one husband or wife at one time.

POLYGRAPH a lie detector; an electromechanical instrument that measures and records certain physiologic changes that it is believed are involuntarily caused by the subject's conscious attempts to deceive the questioner. Once the machine has recorded the subject's responses to the questions propounded by the operator, the operator interprets the record and determines whether the subject is lying.

PONZI SCHEME deceptive investment operation that offers extraordinarily high rates of return that other investments cannot match, with low risk to the investor. Such an operation pays returns to investors from incoming deposits by new investors rather than from the profits accrued by the investments.

POOL 1. a group or combination of individuals or entities organized for the purpose of eliminating competition between the members and combining their resources in order to acccomplish a benefit for each member. A pool sufficiently large or powerful so as to restrict competition throughout a particular trade or industry is illegal under the **Sherman Antitrust Act** of 1890. 2. **jury [POOL].** 3. Monies combined for betting purposes. Such a process is often illegal under **antitrust** laws. See **gambling.**

POPULAR NAME TABLE database of statutes listed by common or popular name.

EXAMPLE: Bryan looked up the "Americans with Disabilities Act" in a Popular Name Table and found that he could locate the text in the Code at 42 U.S.C. § 12101.

PORDITION see **treason.**

PORNOGRAPHY books, magazines, films, pictures, and other such material depicting sexual acts that appeal to one's **prurient interest.** See **obscene material.**

PORTFOLIO a group of **securities** held by an individual or institutional investor, which may contain a variety of common and preferred **stocks,** corporate and municipal **bonds, certificates of deposit** and **treasury bills**—that is, appropriate selections from the **equity, capital** and money markets. See **income [PORTFOLIO INCOME].**

POSITIVE FRAUD see **fraud [FRAUD IN FACT].**

POSITIVE LAW standards of conduct dictated by validly enacted laws, rather than by principles of **natural law.**

POSITIVISM in **jurisprudence,** the view that any legal system is best studied by concentrating on the **positive law** of that system. Compare **natural law.**

POSSE see **in posse.**

POSSE COMITATUS *(pŏ'-sā kŏm-ĭ-tä'-tus)* Lat.: able to be an attendant. Refers to those called to attend the sheriff to assist him in making an **arrest** for a **felony.** A person so summoned is neither an officer nor a mere private person, but occupies the legal position of a posse comitatus, and, while acting under the sheriff's orders, is as much clothed with the protection of the law as the sheriff himself. See **immunity.**

POSSESSION the having, holding or detention of **property** in one's control. When distinguished from mere **custody,** possession involves custody plus the assertion of a right to exercise dominion.

ACTUAL POSSESSION immediate and direct physical control over property. In **real property,** it involves actual occupation of the property or direct appropriation of the benefits it yields.

EXAMPLE: Yuna is in actual possession of betting slips in her pocket because she knows what they are; has knowledge of their character (as illegal items) and has them on her person.

ADVERSE POSSESSION see **adverse possession.**

CHOSE IN POSSESSION see **chose [CHOSE IN POSSESSION].**

CONSTRUCTIVE POSSESSION the condition of having the conscious power and intention to exercise control over property, but without direct control or actual presence upon it.

EXAMPLE: Kent is arrested for unlawful possession of handguns found in the trunk of his car. Kent argues that he did not have *actual possession* of the guns, since the trunk was locked and he was driving the car. Although that fact may be true, he is still liable for prosecution if he had *constructive possession,* which in this case is shown by the fact that he is the only person with keys to the trunk.

CRIMINAL POSSESSION possession for which criminal sanctions are provided, because the thing (or property) either may not lawfully be possessed, may not be possessed by a particular category of persons or may not be possessed under certain circumstances.

HOSTILE POSSESSION see **hostile possession.**

NOTORIOUS POSSESSION see **notorious possession.**

PEACEABLE POSSESSION see **peaceable possession.**

POSSESSORY ACTION a lawsuit brought for the purpose of obtaining or maintaining possession of real property. See **tenancy** [**TENANCY AT SUFFERANCE**].

POSSESSORY INTEREST a right to exert exclusive control over certain land, coupled with intent to exercise that right. Compare **remainderman.**

POSSIBILITY OF A REVERTER the possibility of the return of an **estate** to the **grantor,** should a specified event occur or a particular act be performed in the future. It is thus a **reversionary** interest subject to a **CONDITION PRECEDENT** (see **condition**). The possibility does not itself constitute an estate, present or future. It describes the interest remaining in the grantor who conveys a **conditional** or **determinable fee.**

EXAMPLE: A father conveys a piece of real estate to his daughter as long as she remains unmarried. The possibility of the land returning to the father or his estate if the daughter marries creates a *possibility of a reverter* in the father.

Compare **reentry.**

POSSLQ see **CUPOS** [**POSSLQ**].

POSTCONVICTION RELIEF PROCEEDINGS [**PCR ACTIONS**] a statutory or court rule procedure whereby a criminal **defendant** may challenge collaterally a **judgment** of **conviction** that has otherwise become final in the normal **appellate** review process. See **collateral** [**COLLATERAL ATTACK**]. Compare **habeas corpus.**

A **writ of coram nobis** is available in some states as a form of PCR. In other states an out-of-time motion for a new trial to correct a miscarriage of justice can afford this relief.

POST FACTO see **ex post facto.**

POST HOC ERGO PROPTER HOC *(pōst hōk ĕr'-gō prôp'-tèr*

hōk) Lat.: after this, therefore because of this; a maxim setting forth the false logic that because one event occurs after another event, it was caused by the prior event.

POSTING to affix physically in order to display. 1. In civil procedure, posting of certain required information is a substitute form of **service of process;** 2. In commercial law, posting is the procedure that a bank follows in deciding to finally pay a **negotiable instrument** and in recording its payment. It includes verifying any signature, ascertaining that sufficient funds are available, marking the item paid, charging the customer's account and correcting or reversing an entry or erroneous action with regard to the item; 3. Posting also refers to the exhibition of notices on real property, warning potential trespassers that trespass for fishing or hunting is not permitted by the property owner.

POST MORTEM *(pōst môr'-tĕm)* Lat.: after death. Examination of the body of a deceased to determine cause of death; may comprehend only examination by a **coroner** and may consequently not produce a true medical determination of cause of death, which involves **autopsy** and dissection. See **inquest.**

POSTNUPTIAL AGREEMENT an agreement entered into by a married couple to determine the rights of each in the other's property in the event of death or divorce. Generally, each spouse must disclose his or her assets to the other and must have independent counsel for a postnuptial agreement to be valid. Even then, most jurisdictions will not permit a postnuptial agreement unless it is made to accommodate the rights of the parties in an already failing marriage. See **separation agreement.** Compare **prenuptial agreement.**

POT slang for marijuana. See **controlled substance [CANNABIS].**

POUROVER 1. a provision in a will, or a whole will, that distributes money or other valuables to a previously established **trust;** 2. in rare instances, a provision in a trust placing the trust assets in a will.

POVERTY AFFIDAVIT document detailing financial circumstances which is required to qualify a person as **indigent.**

POWER, COMMERCE see **power, constitutional [COMMERCE POWER].**

POWER, CONSTITUTIONAL in a constitutional form of government, **enumerated** and **implied** power vested in a particular branch or designated authority, for example, the **spending power** and the **taxing power** under the United States Constitution. In addition, the

COMMERCE POWER describes the whole range of authority granted the Congress to regulate **interstate commerce.** See **inherent powers** [INHERENT CONSTITUTIONAL POWERS]; **necessary and proper clause; privileges and immunities.**

POWER, CORPORATE a corporation's capacity or right to do certain acts or engage in certain activities, such as to sue or be sued, to enter into contracts, to borrow money, and to do such other things as are necessary to obtain its purposes.

POWER COUPLED WITH AN INTEREST a power over property that is accompanied by or connected with an interest in the property subject to the power. Under the law of agency, when an agent has a power over property and also has a beneficial interest in that property, the principal may not revoke the agent's power until the interest has expired or unless the principal and agent have agreed otherwise.

POWER, DELEGATED see **delegate** [DELEGATED POWER].

POWER, ENUMERATED see **enumerated powers.**

POWER, IMPLIED see **implied powers.**

POWER, INHERENT see **inherent powers.**

POWER OF ACCEPTANCE the ability of an offeree to create a binding **contract** by consenting to the terms of an **offer.** An offer can be accepted only by the individual invited by the offeror to furnish the **consideration.**

The power of acceptance is always terminated by rejection or counteroffer by the offeree, **revocation** by the offeror, lapse of time specified in the offer, or death or incapacity of the offeror or offeree.

POWER OF APPOINTMENT authority given to a person to dispose of **property** of another, or of an **interest** therein. The authority must be to do an act that the grantor of the authority might lawfully do. **Title** to the property or interest passes directly from the **donor** of the power; the party having the power of appointment acts merely as a conduit through which title passes.

A power of appointment does not itself constitute an **estate** or interest, but the **donee** of the power may also be granted, in the same **instrument,** a present or **future interest** in the subject or property over which the power is to be exercised. The donee is then said to have a **POWER COUPLED WITH AN INTEREST.**

Powers of appointment are exercisable **inter vivos** (by **deed** or similar instrument) or by **testamentary disposition (will.)** A **GENERAL POWER** may be exercised by the donee in favor of any person(s) he or she chooses, including himself or herself or his or her estate. The donee of a **SPECIAL POWER** is limited in the choice of **beneficiaries** by the donor of the power, and so must appoint in favor of member(s) of the class specified in the instrument creating the power.

EXAMPLE: A trust instrument created by a grandmother gives her son a special *power of appointment* to distribute the income generated by the trust principal to all of the grandmother's living grandchildren. The son has no power to touch the principal, but he has discretion to determine which grandchildren get how much of the interest.

POWER OF ATTORNEY an **instrument** in writing by which one person, as **principal,** appoints another as his or her **agent** and confers upon him or her the authority to perform certain specified acts or kinds of acts on behalf of the principal. The primary purpose of a power of attorney is to evidence the authority of the agent to third parties with whom the agent deals.

POWER OF DISPOSITION see **power of appointment.**

POWER OF POLICE see **police power.**

PP. pages.

PPACA see **affordable care act.**

PRACTICE refers to the rules governing all aspects of a court proceeding.

PRAECIPE *(prē'-si-pė)* Lat.: order; command. A writ commanding the defendant to do the thing required or to show reason why it has not been done. The clerk of the court is ordered by a *praecipe* to issue an **execution** for a **judgment creditor.**

PRAESENTI see **in praesenti.**

PRAYER (FOR RELIEF) request contained in a **complaint** or **petition** that asks for relief to which plaintiff thinks himself entitled.

PREAMBLE an introductory clause in a **constitution, statute** or other legal instrument that states the intent or underlying reason for the instrument.

PRECATORY advisory or in the form of a recommendation or request rather than a command; applied to language, usually in a **trust** or a **will,** by which the **settlor** or **testator** expresses a wish to benefit another but does not impose an enforceable **obligation** upon any party to carry out this wish. Depending upon how equivocal the language is, the trust or disposition may or may not be enforceable by the person whose benefit the testator seeks. See **trusts [PRECA-TORY TRUSTS]**.

EXAMPLE: Valentina's will leaves her home to her son. Other language in the will provides that if her home is ever sold by the son, she hopes that it will be sold to some other member of the family. That *precatory* language creates a doubt as to whether the son has an obligation to sell the house to another family member and as to what will happen should the son sell to someone else.

PRECEDENT previously decided case recognized as authority for the disposition of future cases. In **common law,** precedents were regarded as the major source of law. A precedent may involve a novel question of common law or it may involve an interpretation of a **statute.** To the extent that future cases rely upon the precedent or distinguish it from themselves without disapproving of it, the case will serve as a precedent for future cases under the doctrine of **stare decisis.**

PRECEDENT CONDITION see **condition [CONDITION PRECEDENT].**

PRECEDING ESTATE a prior estate upon which a **future interest** is limited. Thus, a **remainder** is said to **vest** upon the termination of a preceding estate, such as a **life estate.**

PRECLUSION OF ISSUE see **estoppel; issue preclusion.**

PREEMPTION a doctrine based on the **supremacy clause** of the federal constitution, under which a state may be deprived of **jurisdiction** over matters embraced by an Act of Congress, regardless of whether the state law coincides with, is complementary to or opposes the federal legislation. When Congress legislates in an area of federal concern, it may specifically preempt all state legislation (thus **OCCUPYING THE FIELD**) or may bar only inconsistent legislation; where Congress does not directly indicate its intention in this regard, the court will determine that intention based on the nature and legislative history of the enactment.

EXAMPLE: A state owns a railroad that operates in interstate commerce and uses guidelines to insure safety. Congress then passes legislation establishing greater safety requirements for railroads nationwide. Since Congress has the power to regulate interstate commerce, its guidelines *preempt* the state guidelines and the state must follow the national requirements.

State legislatures may preempt local governments in the same manner.

In international law, the term expresses the right of a nation to detain goods of a stranger in transit so as to afford its citizens a chance to purchase those goods.

PREEMPTIVE RIGHTS the right specified in the **charter** of a **corporation,** granting to existing **shareholders** the first opportunity to buy a new issue of **stock.** Corporations implement such a charter provision by distributing, in advance of a new issue, subscription rights or **warrants** to existing shareholders in proportion to their current holdings. Shareholders have the choice of exercising the rights by purchasing shares of the new issue or of selling the rights in the open market. Rights usually have market value due to pricing of the new issue slightly below the prevailing market.

PREFERENCE the paying or securing by an **insolvent debtor,** to one or more of his or her **creditors,** the whole or a part of their claims, to the exclusion or detriment of other creditors. Under the Bankruptcy Act, a **bankrupt** is deemed to have given a preference if within four months preceding the filing of his or her petition for bankruptcy, he or she procures or suffers a judgment against himself or herself, or makes a transfer of any of his or her assets; the effect of this is to give a creditor a greater percentage of his or her debt than any other creditor of the same class.

VOIDABLE PREFERENCE a transfer of property by a bankrupt person to a creditor within a specified time period of filing the petition in bankruptcy. Because such transfers deprive the bankrupt's other creditors from sharing in the property, the transfer is set aside and the property is brought back into the bankrupt's estate.

PREFERENCE ITEMS see **tax preference items.**

PREFERRED DIVIDEND see **dividend [PREFERRED DIVIDEND].**

PREFERRED RIGHTS see **First Amendment [PREFERRED RIGHTS].**

PREFERRED STOCK part of the CAPITAL STOCK (see **capital**) of a **corporation** that enjoys **priority** over the remaining stock, or **common stock,** in the distribution of profits and, in the event of dissolution of the corporation, in the distribution of assets as well. See **security [PREFERRED STOCK].**

PREGNANT, NEGATIVE see **negative pregnant.**

PREJUDICE bias; a leaning toward one party in a lawsuit; a prejudging of a case. See **dismissal [DISMISSAL WITH PREJUDICE; DISMISSAL WITHOUT PREJUDICE].**

PREJUDICIAL ERROR see **reversible error.**

PRELIMINARY HEARING in criminal law, 1. a **hearing,** before **indictment,** to determine whether **probable cause** for the arrest of a person existed; 2. a hearing to determine whether there is sufficient **evidence** to warrant the **defendant's** continued detention and whether submission of such evidence to the **GRAND JURY** (see **jury**) is warranted. Compare **arraignment.** See **fair hearing.**

PRELIMINARY INJUNCTION see **injunction; restraining order [TEMPORARY RESTRAINING ORDER].**

PREMEDITATION forethought. As one of the **elements** of first-degree murder, the term is often equated with **intent** and deliberateness.

PREMISE in logic, the propositions upon which a conclusion is based.

PREMISES land and its **appurtenances;** land or a portion thereof and the structures thereon. For purposes of insurance on a building, or in defining the crime of **burglary,** or with respect to the scope of a **search warrant,** the range of the term may vary.

EXAMPLE: A search warrant lists 118 South Street as the *premises* to be searched. If there is a garage at 118 South Street that is not attached to the house, the warrant would not extend to the garage. It is not considered part of the premises, because a search warrant must list with particularity the places to be searched. To cover the garage, the warrant would have to list 118 South Street and the adjacent garage.

With respect to **Workers' Compensation Acts,** premises may include any place where the employee may go in the course of his employment.

PREMIUM 1. the sum paid to the insurer as **consideration** for a policy of **insurance;** 2. money paid by a buyer for an **option** to buy or sell corporate **stock;** 3. a reward for an act done.

PRENUPTIAL AGREEMENT an agreement entered into by two people who intend to marry each other, which sets forth the rights of each person in the property of the other in the event of divorce or death. Generally, the entering into marriage constitutes sufficient consideration to make a prenuptial agreement enforceable. Such an agreement is also termed an **ANTENUPTIAL AGREEMENT.**

PREPONDERANCE OF THE EVIDENCE general standard of **proof** in civil cases. The phrase refers to the degree of proof that will lead the **TRIER OF FACT** (see **fact finder**) to find that the existence of the fact in issue is more probable than not. See **clear and convincing.**

PREROGATIVE WRIT a written order issued by a court in further-ance of its **discretionary** powers. The prerogative writs are the writs of **procedendo, mandamus, prohibition, quo warranto, habeas corpus** and **certiorari.**

EXAMPLE: A corporation files a suit in federal district court chal-lenging a part of a federal securities statute. It loses in the district court and also in the Court of Appeals. It asks the Supreme Court to issue a writ of certiorari to the Court of Appeals so that the Supreme Court can rule on the question. The Supreme Court has the discre-tion to issue the writ, making the writ a *prerogative writ.*

PRESCRIPTION a means of acquiring an **easement** on the land of another by continued regular use over a specified period of time. Compare **adverse possession.**

PRESCRIPTIVE EASEMENT see **easement [PRESCRIPTIVE EASEMENT [EASEMENT BY PRESCRIPTION]].**

PRESENT DANGER see **clear and present danger.**

PRESENTENCE REPORT material prepared by a probation depart-ment to assist the trial court in **sentencing** a criminal defendant after he or she has been convicted. Pre-sentence reports usually include prior convictions, prior arrests, employment history, education his-tory, and family and social background.

PRESENTMENT 1. a written accusation of crime by the **GRAND JURY** (see **jury**) upon its own initiative, without consent or participa-tion of a prosecutor, in the exercise of the jury's lawful inquisitorial powers; 2. the presenting of a **bill of exchange** or **promissory note** to the party on whom it is **drawn,** for his or her acceptance, or to the person bound to pay, for payment.

PRESENT SENSE IMPRESSION a statement describing or explain-ing an event or condition made while the declarant was perceiving the event or condition, or immediately thereafter.

For this exception to apply, the declarant need not be excited or otherwise emotionally affected by the event or condition perceived. The trustworthiness of the statement arises from its timing. The requirement of contemporaneousness, or near contemporaneous-ness, reduces the chance of premeditated prevarication or loss of memory. Compare **excited utterance.** See also **res gestae.**

PRESIDENTIAL PROCLAMATION see **proclamation [PRESI-DENTIAL PROCLAMATION].**

PRESUMPTION an assumption of fact resulting from a rule of law that requires such fact to be assumed from another fact or set of facts. The term indicates that the law accords to a given evidentiary fact heavy enough weight to require the production of contrary **evidence** to overcome the assumption thereby established. This rule of evidence thus has the effect of shifting either the **burden of proof** or the burden of producing evidence.

EXAMPLE: Burton writes a check to a car repair establishment that the bank refuses to cash. The law in Burton's state establishes a *presumption* that he knowingly intended to write a bad check if (1) there is no account in Burton's name at the bank named on the check or (2) the shop was refused payment for lack of funds within thirty days of the date on the check and Burton did not pay the amount owed within ten days of being informed of the bank's refusal to honor the check.

Compare **inference.**

CONCLUSIVE [NONREBUTTABLE] PRESUMPTION one that no evidence, however strong, no argument, or consideration will be permitted to overcome. Since a presumption always properly refers to a rebuttable assumption of fact, when the term presumption is used in this conclusive sense, it is not a true presumption but is a statement by the court of a rule of law.

REBUTTABLE PRESUMPTION an ordinary presumption that, as a matter of law, must be made once certain facts have been proved, thus establishing a certain conclusion **prima facie;** but it may be rebutted. If it is not overcome through contrary evidence, it becomes conclusive. The prevailing doctrine is that competing facts are weighed on their own merits, without further reference to the presumption.

PRESUMPTION OF INNOCENCE prevailing assumption that the **accused** is innocent until proven **guilty.** Because of this **presumption,** the government bears the **burden of proof** that the **defendant** is guilty beyond a **reasonable doubt.**

PRESUMPTIVE EVIDENCE evidence that is indirect or **circumstantial; prima facie** evidence or evidence that is not conclusive and admits of explanation or contradiction; evidence that must be treated as sufficient unless rebutted by other evidence, such as evidence that a **statute** deems to be presumptive of another fact unless rebutted.

PRETERMITTED HEIR an **heir** who was born after a **decedent executed** his or her **will,** but before he or she died. Because the heir was not alive when the testator executed the will, the pretermitted heir is not mentioned in and may not take under the will. However, most states have statutes that allow a child of the decedent who was born after the will was executed but before the time of death to take a share of the decedent's estate equal to the share the child would have received if the decedent had died **intestate.** A child who may so take a share of the decedent's estate is called a pretermitted heir.

PRETRIAL CONFERENCE in civil procedure, a conference held after the pleadings have been filed and before the trial begins, for the purpose of bringing the parties together to outline **discovery** proceedings and define the issues to be tried. Courts often use the pretrial conference as an opportunity to encourage settlement.

In criminal procedure, a *pretrial conference* is also used to review evidentiary issues prior to trial, but because of the privilege against **self-incrimination** and the **presumption of innocence,** it is not as comprehensive or useful to the parties as in civil cases.

PRETRIAL DETAINEE see **detention [PRETRIAL DETAINEE].**

PRETRIAL DETENTION see **detention [PRETRIAL DETENTION].**

PRETRIAL DISCOVERY see **discovery.**

PRETRIAL INTERVENTION [PTI] a remedial program by which first-time or petty criminal offenders are not subjected to the regular judicial process, but rather are immediately placed under probationary supervision for a period usually no longer than one year. The program allows persons accused of crime to avoid the stigma of conviction and a permanent criminal record by correcting their criminal behavior during the period of probation. Pre-conviction probationary programs divert persons from the ordinary criminal process without an admission of guilt or a conviction, and, for this reason, are called **DIVERSIONARY PROGRAMS.**

PREVAILING PARTY the party in a lawsuit who has successfully obtained a judgment in his or her own favor. Federal law allows for the awarding of attorney's fees to the prevailing party, other than the United States, in proceedings in vindication of civil rights. Courts have broadened the interpretation of "prevailing party" in such a context to include preliminary relief or relief obtained as the result of a consent decree, or settlement, and the party need only prevail on the merits of some of the claims. The plaintiff's lawsuit must be found to be causally linked to the achievement of relief obtained, and the defendant must not have acted gratuitously in response to a frivolous or legally insignificant claim.

PREVARICATION deceitful, dishonest, or unfaithful conduct.

PREVENTIVE DETENTION pretrial confinement imposed upon a criminal defendant under the terms of a statute authorizing the denial of **bail** to certain defendants charged with particular offenses. A hearing is required at which the court must determine that the defendant is likely to be found guilty of an enumerated serious offense and that he or she poses an immediate danger to the public if released on bail. The constitutionality of preventive detention has been upheld by one court but has yet to receive review by the United States Supreme Court. Only a small number of jurisdictions have such statutes. In many instances, however, the same result is accomplished **de facto** by a magistrate setting bail beyond a defendant's reach. See **detention.**

PRICE DISCRIMINATION the practice of charging different persons different prices for the same goods or services. When price discrimination is engaged in for the purpose of lessening competition, for instance, through tying the lower prices to the purchase of other goods or services, it constitutues a violation of the **Sherman Antitrust Act.** Unlawful price discrimination is also specifically covered by the **Clayton Act,** and the **Robinson-Patman Act.**

PRICE FIXING under federal **antitrust laws,** a combination or **conspiracy** for the purpose and with the effect of raising, lowering or stabilizing the price of a commodity in interstate commerce.

HORIZONTAL PRICE FIXING price fixing engaged in by competitors at the same commercial level.

VERTICAL PRICE FIXING price fixing engaged in by members of different levels of production, such as manufacturer and retailer.

PRIEST-PENITENT PRIVILEGE communications made by a person to a priest, rabbi, or minister in the course of confession, or similar course of discipline by other religious bodies, that are privileged from disclosure. The communications to clergy members must be made while clergy members are acting in the professional capacity of a spiritual adviser and with the purpose of dispensing religious counsel, advice, solace, or absolution. Some states have broadened their privilege to include all forms of individual or group counseling for marital and other personal problems. The definition of "clergy" is the subject of controversy, but has not been found to include nuns.

PRIMAE IMPRESSIONIS *(prī'-mē im-prĕ-shĕ-ō-nis)* Lat.: first impression.

PRIMA FACIE *(prī'-mà fā'-shà)* Lat.: at first view, on its face. Not requiring further support to establish existence, validity, credibility.

EXAMPLE: Sylvain is caught with untaxed cigarettes. In the state where he is caught, untaxed cigarettes are designated *prima facie* contraband and are immediately subject to forfeiture to the state.

PRIMA FACIE CASE 1. a case sufficient on its face, supported by at least the requisite minimum of **evidence,** and free from obvious defects; 2. state of facts that entitles a party to have his case go to the **jury;** sufficient to avoid a **directed verdict** or a **motion to dismiss;** 3. a case that will usually prevail in the absence of contradictory evidence; 4. a case in which the evidence is sufficient to support, but not to compel, a certain conclusion and does no more than furnish evidence to be weighed, but not necessarily to be accepted, by the TRIER OF FACT (see **fact finder**).

PRIMARY DISTRIBUTION see **underwriting.**

PRIMARY LIABILITY see **liability [PRIMARY LIABILITY].**

PRIMARY OFFERING see **underwriting.**

PRIMOGENITURE *(prē-mō-jĕn'-ĭ-tūr)* ancient **common law** doctrine governing **descent,** under which the eldest son takes all property of decedent father. The opposite of primogeniture, **BOROUGH ENGLISH,** existed under local custom in at least one **jurisdiction** even while primogeniture prevailed elsewhere in England; the youngest son inherited on the death of the father. Under the local custom of **gavelkind** all sons took equally. In the event all **issue** of the decedent were daughters, they took equal shares in **coparceny.**

PRINCIPAL most important. 1. in criminal law, one who commits an offense, or an **accomplice** actually or constructively present during commission of the offense. 2. in commercial law, the amount received in loan, or the amount upon which interest is charged; 3. in the law of **agency,** one who has permitted or engaged another to act for his or her benefit, in accordance with his or her direction and subject to his or her control. 4. chief, superintendent. Compare **principle.**

DISCLOSED PRINCIPAL one whose identity is known to the party dealing with the agent.

PARTIALLY DISCLOSED PRINCIPAL one whose identity is not known, but whose existence is known, to the party with whom the agent deals.

UNDISCLOSED PRINCIPAL one of whose existence the party dealing with the agent is not aware—i.e., the third party does not know he or she is dealing with an agent.

EXAMPLE: Tara buys property for Sphinx Mall Company. Sphinx desires to be an *undisclosed principal* because it believes that land prices would skyrocket if sellers knew the identity of the real purchaser.

PRINCIPLE fundamental doctrine; a settled rule. Compare **principal.**

PRIOR INCONSISTENT STATEMENT in evidence, a **witness's** out-of-court statement that contradicts his or her testimony in court; a prior inconsistent statement may constitute **hearsay,** since the evidence of the prior inconsistent statement may be based only on the witness's out-of-court statement rather than the evidence about which he or she testified. Regardless of its character as hearsay, a prior inconsistent statement is nonetheless admissible in evidence for purposes of **impeaching** the witness. **Extrinsic** evidence of a prior inconsistent statement is not admissible unless the witness is first given the opportunity to explain or deny the same, and the opposite party is given an opportunity for interrogation thereon, or the interests of justice otherwise require. Compare **admission by a party-opponent; declaration against interest.**

PRIORITY preference; the condition of coming before, or of coming first, in a **bankruptcy** proceeding; the right to be paid before other **creditors** out of the assets of the bankrupt party. The term may also be used to signify such a right in connection with a **prior lien,** prior **mortgage,** etc.

PRIOR LIEN a first or superior **lien,** entitled to satisfaction before others.

PRIOR RESTRAINT any prohibition on the publication or communication of information prior to such publication, or communication under the First Amendment's guarantees of the right to free speech and free press. Prior restraints are subject to strict scrutiny and bear a heavy presumption against constitutional validity.

PRISON see **jail, penal institution.**

PRISONER generally, anyone who is held against his or her will. Specifically, one who has been committed to a prison, **jail,** or **penal institution** for the purpose of detention until he or she may be tried for a crime of which he or she is accused, or for the purpose of punishment after conviction of such crime. See **detention; sentence.** Compare **inmate.**

PRIVACY see **privacy, right of.**

PRIVACY, INVASION OF see **invasion of privacy.**

PRIVACY, RIGHT OF a general right to be left alone, including protections from governmental interference in personal relationships or activities. It allows the individual freedom to make fundamental choices involving oneself, one's family and one's relationship with others but it is not absolute and does not apply to private conduct which is harmful to individual participants or to society.

The federal **constitution** does not specifically provide for this right but zones of privacy have been implied from the general thrust of the **Bill of Rights,** specifically the **First, Third, Fourth, Fifth,** and **Ninth** Amendments through the **Fourteenth Amendment.** Such privacy rights include the right to have an abortion (subject to certain state regulations), or to keep certain types of information private.

An **INVASION OF PRIVACY** constitutes a **tort** for which remedies are available. Examples of different types of torts are: (1) **appropriation** (the use of a person's name, picture, or likeness as a symbol of his or her identity without compensation); (2) an intrusion upon a person's physical solitude or seclusion; (3) the public disclosure of private facts; and (4) placing a person in a false light in the public eye by associating this person with beliefs or activities with which this person has no connection.

PRIVATE CORPORATION   see **corporation [PRIVATE CORPORATION].**

PRIVATE DWELLING   see **dwelling house [PRIVATE DWELLING].**

PRIVATE FOUNDATIONS see **charity [PRIVATE FOUNDATIONS].**

PRIVATE NECESSITY see **justification [PRIVATE NECESSITY].**

PRIVATE NUISANCE see **nuisance [PRIVATE NUISANCE].**

PRIVATE OFFERING [PLACEMENT]   generally, any sale of securities in a corporation not subject to registration requirements under the Securities Act of 1933. Transactions by an issuer not involving any public offering are exempt. These include placements with large institutional investors such as insurance companies and pension funds, securities issued to key employees of a company, and securities issued to acquire the stock of a closely held corporation. The **Securities and Exchange Commission** has general authority to issue regulations concerning exempt transactions and is specifically authorized to issue regulations exempting offerings if the aggregate amount of the securities to be sold does not exceed $5,000,000. The SEC issued **REGULATION D** in 1982, under which offerings of various amounts of securities are exempt from registration if they meet specific requirements, the most important of which is that the purchasers of the securities by **ACCREDITED INVESTORS,** that is, an institutional investor such as a bank, an insurance company, a pension fund, or a charitable foundation with assets of at least $5 million; a director or officer of the issuer; an individual with a minimum net worth of $1 million or a minimum annual income of $200,000; or an individual who purchases at least $150,000 of the securities offered, provided that the purchase does not exceed 20 percent of his or her net worth. If the securities issued total less than $5 million, then up to 35 percent of the purchasers do not have to be accredited investors.

PRIVATE PLACEMENT see **private offering [placement].**

PRIVATE RULING see **revenue ruling [PRIVATE RULING].**

PRIVILEGE 1. a particular benefit enjoyed by a person, company or class beyond the advantages of other citizens; 2. an exceptional exemption, or an immunity held beyond the course of the law; 3. an exemption from some burden or attendance, with which certain persons are indulged, from a supposition of the law that the public offices or duties require so much time and care that, without this indulgence, their duties could not be performed to the advantage that the public good demands. See **executive privilege; informer's privilege; privileged communication.**

EXAMPLE: All citizens of a county are required to be available for jury duty. Doctors are *privileged* to avoid this requirement, because of their constant need to attend to their patients.

PRIVILEGE AGAINST SELF-INCRIMINATION see **self-incrimination, privilege against.**

PRIVILEGED COMMUNICATION communication that occurs in a setting of legal or other recognized professional confidentiality. Designating a communication as privileged allows the speakers to resist legal process to disclose its contents. When communications are termed privileged, a **breach** by one party of the concurrent confidentiality can result in a **civil suit** in **tort** by the other party to the communication. Communications that are privileged may include: (1) communications in the sanctity of the marital relationship; (2) communications between physicians and their patients; (3) communications of psychological counselors and their clients; (4) priest-and-penitent communications; (5) communications between attorney and client; and (6) in some **jurisdictions,** communications between journalists and their sources. See **attorney-client privilege; journalist's privilege; marital communications privileges; physician–patient privilege** (including PSYCHOTHERAPIST–PATIENT PRIVILEGE); **priest–penitent privilege; rape crisis counselor privilege.** See also **informer's privilege; self-incrimination, privilege against.**

ATTORNEY-CLIENT PRIVILEGE an evidentiary **privilege** protecting the confidential communications between a client and his or her attorney from disclosure to any other party; can be waived by the client but not by the attorney.

EXAMPLE: Joaquin discusses with his attorney a past wrong he is alleged to have committed. If the attorney is asked to discuss this without Joaquin's permission, she will not be permitted to do so since the communication was privileged.

PRIVILEGE FROM ARREST the right of certain persons, granted by either a constitution, statute, or public policy, against being arrested while engaging in certain activities. For instance, the U.S. Constitution grants senators and representatives the privilege from arrest during their attendence at the session of their respective houses, and in going to or returning from the same.

PRIVILEGES AND IMMUNITIES the phrase used in the **Fourteenth Amendment** to the Constitution to describe the rights that citizens of the United States have by virtue of their citizenship. These rights derive from the establishment and existence of the federal government and thus were assumed to exist prior to the enactment of the Fourteenth Amendment. That provision makes it clear that the federal government may protect such rights from the state as well as individual denials. Privileges and immunities include the right to travel; the right to vote in federal elections; the right to assemble to petition federal officers and to discuss national legislation; and any other personal right arising out of federal statutes. Such rights are to be distinguished from those that exist regardless of the federal government, such as the right to assembly or of jury trial.

PRIVITY a relationship between parties out of which arises mutuality of interest.

HORIZONTAL PRIVITY privity of estate between the covenantor and covenantee. Horizontal privity is satisfied any time an estate is **conveyed** from one party to another, provided that the **covenant** is made at the time of the transfer.

EXAMPLE: Janan sells some of her land to a neighbor, who by the sale acquires ownership of a lake. Three months later the neighbor conveys to Janan the right to use the lake. Janan then sells her portion of the land to another party. That party does not have the right to use the lake. The requirements of *horizontal privity* are not met because the covenant is made after the transfer of the land between Janan and the neighbor.

PRIVITY OF CONTRACT the relationship between two or more contracting parties. To maintain an **action** on any contract, there must be a privity between the plaintiff and defendant in respect to the matter sued on.

PRIVITY OF ESTATE mutual or successive relation to the same right in the same property. A privy in **estate** derives from another person's **title** to property, by contract (**grant, will** or other voluntary transfer of possession) or law (**descent, judgment,** etc.).

VERTICAL PRIVITY the privity of estate between the covenantor and his or her successor in interest who acquires the property subject to the *covenant.*

See **easement [RECIPROCAL NEGATIVE EASEMENTS]; run with the land.**

PRIVY a person connected with another or having mutual interest with him or her in the same **action** or thing, by **contract** or otherwise.

PROBABLE CAUSE a requisite element of a valid **arrest** or **search and seizure;** consists of knowledge of facts and circumstances sufficient in themselves to warrant belief that a crime has been committed (in the context of an arrest) or that property subject to seizure is at a designated location (in the context of a search and seizure). Compare **stop and frisk.**

EXAMPLE: A policeman, patrolling a high crime area where narcotics offenses are particularly troublesome, observes two men exchange money on a street and then go to a nearby car to retrieve a package from the trunk. One of the men sticks his finger in the bag, puts his finger in his mouth to taste something, stuffs the bag in his pocket and walks away. This routine occurs several times. The owner of the vehicle is known to the officer as a drug dealer. The policeman has *probable cause* to obtain a warrant to search the vehicle and any person who receives a package from the trunk.

PROBATE 1. act of proving that an **instrument** purporting to be a **will** was signed and otherwise executed in accordance with the legal requirements for a will, and of determining its validity; 2. combined result of all procedures necessary to establish the validity of a will. In some **jurisdictions** a **PROBATE COURT** is a special court having jurisdiction of proceedings incident to the settlement of a decedent's **estate.** In such situations the court may appoint a **committee, conservator,** or **guardian.** See **surrogate.** See also **homestead [PROBATE HOMESTEAD].**

PROBATION procedure whereby a **defendant** found guilty of a crime, upon a **verdict** or **plea** of guilty, is released by the court without imprisonment, subject to conditions imposed by the court, under the supervision of a **PROBATION OFFICER.** Compare **parole.**

PROBATIVE tending to prove a particular proposition or to persuade one of the truth of an allegation.

PROBATIVE FACTS 1. matters of **evidence** required to prove **ultimate facts;** 2. facts from which the ultimate and decisive facts may be properly inferred.

PROBATIVE VALUE the relative weight properly accorded particular evidence.

EXAMPLE: The prosecutor wants to introduce an accused's past criminal record as evidence of the accused's guilt of the offense with which he is presently charged. In the past the accused has committed similar offenses. The accused replies that if his record is introduced, the jury might convict him exclusively because of his prior record as opposed to the evidence before it. The judge refuses to allow the introduction of the evidence, finding that the *probative value* of the prior record is far outweighed by the prejudicial effect it will have on the jury's consideration of the evidence. Although the prior record is relevant, that relevance is not sufficient to overcome the right of the accused to be judged on the basis of the evidence of the present offense and not upon demonstration of a criminal disposition. If the defendant decides to testify, the record may be used to impugn his credibility. In that event, the court will instruct the jury that it may only consider the prior record for that limited purpose.

PRO BONO PUBLICO *(prō bō'-nō pūb'-ly-kō)* Lat.: for the public good or welfare. When an attorney takes a case without compensation to advance a social cause, or to fill a perceived social need to offer legal representation to the poor, the attorney represents the party *pro bono publico.* The phrase *pro bono* is sometimes used.

PROCEDENDO *(prō-sā-děn'-dō)* Lat.: duty to have proceeded. Refers to a **writ** issued by a superior court when a cause has been improperly removed to it, as by **certiorari,** commanding the inferior court from which it was removed to assume **jurisdiction** and proceed to judgment on the cause. It is more frequently called a **remand.**

PROCEDURAL DUE PROCESS see **due process of law.**

PROCEDURE legal method; the machinery for carrying on the **suit,** including **pleading, process, evidence** and **practice.** The term thus refers to the mechanics of the legal process—the body of rules and practice by which justice is meted out by the legal system—rather than the substance and content of the law itself. See **adjective law.** Compare **substantive law.**

CIVIL PROCEDURE The Federal Rules of Civil Procedure guide the federal courts in conducting all aspects of cases before them, from the filing of a suit to the trial itself. The rules also instruct attorneys how they must proceed with these cases. Although these rules

449

govern only *procedure,* not the actual merits of the case, a failure to abide by the rules could easily result in a valid claim being dismissed by the court. Each state court also has rules of procedure.

CRIMINAL PROCEDURE the process by which the government imposes sanctions for crimes, from the investigation of the crime, through the arrest and trial of the person accused of committing the crime, to the punishment of the convicted criminal. The primary sources of criminal procedure are: statutes governing police activities, court procedures and sentencing matters; and court rules, such as the Federal Rules of Criminal Procedure. Constitutional limitations on criminal procedure to protect the rights of defendants are found in state and federal guarantees, such as the ban on unreasonable searches and seizures, and the privilege against self-incrimination.

PROCEEDING 1. the succession of events in the process of judicial action; 2. the form in which actions are to be brought and defended, the manner of intervening in suits, of conducting them; the mode of deciding them, of opposing and of executing **judgments.**

COLLATERAL PROCEEDING any proceeding not instituted for the express purpose of annulling, correcting, or modifying a **judgment.** Instead, a collateral proceeding will attempt to change or affect the result of the judgment while allowing the judgment to remain intact. See **collateral estoppel.**

INFORMAL PROCEEDING see **informal proceeding.**

SUMMARY PROCEEDING see **summary proceeding.**

PROCESS 1. a formal writing **(writ)** issued by authority of law; 2. any means used by the court to acquire or to exercise its **jurisdiction** over a person or over specified property; 3. usually refers to the method used to compel attendance of a **defendant** in court in a **civil** suit. See **abuse of process; compulsory process; due process of law; service of process.**

PROCLAMATION a public announcement giving notice of an act done by the government or to be done by the people. A **PRESIDENTIAL PROCLAMATION** is the President's official, public announcement of an **executive order** or act.

PROCTOR 1. one who manages another's affairs, acting as that person's **agent;** 2. an attorney who is admitted to practice in a **probate, admiralty** or **ecclesiastical** court. Compare **administrator.**

PRODUCT see **work product.**

PRODUCT EXTENSION MERGER   see **merger** [PRODUCT EXTENSION MERGER].

PRODUCTION BURDEN see **burden of proof.**

PRODUCTS LIABILITY a concept in the law of **torts** holding a manufacturer **strictly liable** in tort when an article the manufacturer places on the market, knowing it is to be used without inspection for defects, proves to have a defect that causes injury to a human being. One who sells any defective product unreasonably dangerous to the consumer or to his or her property may be liable for physical harm thereby caused to the consumer or to his or her property, even though there is no contractual or other relationship between seller and user, and even though the seller has not been **negligent.** See **warranty.**

EXAMPLE: A manufacturer sells a food processor to a department store, which in turn sells it to Ann. The rotary mechanism in the machine has a tendency to engage when the top of the processor is off. Ann's finger is cut when this problem occurs. She can sue the manufacturer under a *products liability* theory.

PROFESSIONAL ASSOCIATION see **professional corporation** [association].

PROFESSIONAL CONDUCT see **code of professional responsibility; model rules of professional conduct.**

PROFESSIONAL CORPORATION [ASSOCIATION] a corporation formed for the purpose of engaging in one of the learned professions, such as law, medicine, or architecture. Traditionally, corporations were prohibited from engaging in such professions because they lacked the human, personal qualifications necessary to pursue them. However, within recent years most states have enacted a professional corporation or association act that allows professional persons to practice in the corporate form provided that all shareholders are members of the profession. A professional corporation has at least two advantages. First, it allows a professional to join together with one or more other professionals without assuming personal liability for the acts or omissions of the others. Second, it allows the professional to enjoy certain tax advantages not available to him or her as an individual taxpayer.

PROFESSIONAL CRIMINAL see **criminal** [HABITUAL OFFENDER]; **sentence** [EXTENDED TERM].

PROFESSIONAL RESPONSIBILITY see **code of professional responsibility; model rules of professional conduct.**

PROFFER to offer **evidence** at **trial.** The **admissibility** of evidence so offered is governed by the appropriate **jurisdiction's** rules of evidence. See **offer of proof.**

PROFILING 1. collecting and analyzing information that individuals have provided about themselves (see **registration**) or information about their web site purchases or visits for marketing purposes; 2. behavioral analysis of serial murder suspects providing information on the causality, motivations, and characteristics of serial killers to assist in their apprehension; 3. police targeting of suspects by utilizing a set of characteristics to decide whether an individual (who possesses those characteristics) might be guilty of some crime. One method known as **RACIAL PROFILING** is particularly violative of individuals' rights because it involves the police's use of race as the sole factor in decisions to stop, interrogate, or search people. However, reliance on such criteria in combination with other identifying factors when seeking a specific suspect whose race, ethnicity, national origin, gender, or religious dress is part of the description of the suspect is not racial profiling.

PROFIT gain; the excess of an amount received over the amount paid for goods and services. See **capital gains or losses; earnings and profits; paper profit; realization.** See also **profit à prendre.**

PROFIT-AND-LOSS STATEMENT see **income statement.**

PROFIT À PRENDRE *(prō-fĕ ah prŏn-drè)* Fr.: the right to take. In **real property** law, the right to take soil, gravel, minerals, and the like from another's land.

PRO FORMA *(prō fôr'-mà)* Lat.: for the sake of form; as a matter of form. 1. In practice, the term usually means that an **appealable decree** or **judgment** was entered by the court, not because of an intellectual conviction that the decision rendered was right, but merely to facilitate further proceedings; 2. In accounting, the term is used in reference to the presentation of financial statements that represent proposed events in the form in which they would appear if or when the event actually occurred. Examples include presentation of consolidated statements in connection with a proposed corporate **merger** and presentation of **balance sheet** data showing the effect of a proposed financing.

PROGRESSIVE TAX see **tax [PROGRESSIVE TAX].**

PRO HAC VICE *(prō häk vē'-chā)* Lat.: for this turn; for this one particular occasion. The allowance of that which under ordinary circumstances is not permitted. Usually the term is used to describe the permission granted an out-of-state lawyer to appear in a particular case with the same standing as a local attorney admitted to practice in the **jurisdiction.**

PROHIBITION see **writ of prohibition.**

PROLIXITY any unnecessary language or facts in **pleadings** or in **evidence.**

PROMISE a declaration of one's intention to do or to refrain from doing something.

> BREACH OF PROMISE see **breach (of contract)** [BREACH OF PROMISE].
>
> COLLATERAL PROMISE see **collateral** [COLLATERAL PROMISE].
>
> GRATUITOUS PROMISE see **gratuitous promise.**
>
> ILLUSORY PROMISE see **illusory promise.**

PROMISE, BREACH OF see **breach (of contract)** [BREACH OF PROMISE].

PROMISSORY ESTOPPEL an **equitable** doctrine that declares that if injustice can be avoided only by enforcement of a promise, the pledge is binding, though there is no **consideration** for the promise and it cannot therefore be enforced as a contract. The promisor, having induced in the promisee **reliance** on the promise for certain action or forbearance, is said to be **estopped** to deny the existence of a contract, though in fact one has not been made. See also **estoppel; waiver** [EXECUTORY WAIVER]. Compare **assumpsit.**

PROMISSORY NOTE a kind of **negotiable instrument** wherein the **maker** agrees to pay a specific sum at a definite time.

PROMOTER in corporate law, generally anyone who undertakes to form a corporation and to procure for it the rights, instrumentalities, and capital by which it is to carry out the purpose set forth in its charter. The **Securities and Exchange Commission** defines a promoter as any person who, acting alone or in conjunction with one or more persons, directly or indirectly takes initiative in founding or organizing the business or enterprise of an issuer of securities or any person who receives 10 percent or more of any class of securities of an issuer on the proceeds therefrom in consideration for services or property.

PROOF [PROOFS] the quantity or quality of **evidence** that tends to establish the existence of a fact in issue. See **burden of proof; degree of proof; inference; judgment proof; moral certainty; offer of proof; preponderance of the evidence; presumption; reasonable doubt.**

PROOF BEYOND A REASONABLE DOUBT see **reasonable doubt.**

PROOF TO A MORAL CERTAINTY see **moral certainty.**

PRO PER Lat.: in propria persona ("for oneself") and written *in pro per*. See **pro se.**

PROPER see **necessary and proper clause.**

PROPER LOOKOUT see **lookout [PROPER LOOKOUT].**

PROPER PARTY see **party [PROPER PARTY].**

PROPERTY every species of valuable right or **interest** that is subject to **ownership,** has an exchangeable value or adds to one's wealth or **estate.** Property describes one's exclusive right to possess, use and dispose of a thing, as well as the object, benefit or prerogative that constitutes the subject matter of that right.

COMMON PROPERTY 1. that which belongs to the citizenry as a whole; 2. property owned by TENANTS IN COMMON (see **tenancy**), or in some **jurisdictions** where designated by **statute,** that are owned by husband and wife. Compare **community property.**

INCORPOREAL PROPERTY see **incorporeal [INCORPOREAL PROPERTY].**

INTANGIBLE PROPERTY see **intangible property.**

PERSONAL PROPERTY see **personal property.**

PUBLIC PROPERTY see **public property.**

REAL PROPERTY see **real property.**

TANGIBLE PROPERTY see **tangible property.**

PROPERTY SETTLEMENT in martrimonial law, the division of property owned or acquired by spouses during their marriage. Since a property settlement merely allocates the property between the parties and does not satisfy the obligation of either spouse to support the other, it is not subject to judicial modification if the circumstances of either spouse later change. See **postnuptial agreement; prenuptial agreement; separation agreement.**

PROPERTY TAX see **tax [PROPERTY TAX].**

PROPORTIONAL REPRESENTATION a system of election designed to insure that different groups will have their interests represented, something that may not necessarily occur in a majority rule scheme.

EXAMPLE: A university faculty is comprised of 65 percent full-time and 35 percent part-time members. Under a *proportional representation* system for election of an appointments committee, each class will be able to have a voice on the committee.

PROPRIETARY owned by a particular person. In **trade secrets** law, proprietary property is information or knowledge in which the person developing it has ownership rights. Such rights are usually protected by contract and have not been the subject of a **patent** application. In the law of municipal corporations, a proprietary function is one that a government may undertake for the benefit of its citizens. Government activities fall into two general categories: those fundamental to its nature as a government, such as passing of legislation or providing police services, and those proprietary or done for the benefit of particular citizens, such as providing a swimming pool. Generally speaking, a government may not be held liable for the former, but it may be liable for negligence with regard to the latter. See **governmental function; sovereign immunity; Tort Claims Act.**

PROPRIETARY INTEREST any right in relation to a **chattel** that enables a person to retain its **possession** indefinitely or for a period of time.

PROPRIETARY LEASE see **lease [PROPRIETARY LEASE].**

PROPRIETOR owner; the person who holds **title** to property. See **proprietary.** See also **sole proprietorship.**

PRO RATA *(prō rā'-tà)* Lat.: according to the rate, i.e., in proportion. According to a measure that fixes proportions. Thus, a lease terminated by agreement before the expiration of the full term may call for the payment of rent on a *pro rata* basis for the expired term of the lease.

PRO SE *(prō sā)* Lat.: for himself; in one's own behalf. One appears *pro se* in a legal **action** when one represents oneself without aid of counsel. See **pro per.**

PROSECUTION 1. the act of pursuing a lawsuit or criminal **trial;** 2. the party initiating a criminal **suit,** i.e., the state. Where the civil **litigant,** or the state in a criminal trial, fails to move the case towards final resolution or trial as required by the court schedule, the matter may be dismissed for **WANT OF PROSECUTION** or for **FAILURE TO PROSECUTE.** See **malicious prosecution.**

PROSECUTOR public official who prepares and conducts the **prosecution** of persons accused of **crime.** In certain cases, the legislature may appoint a **SPECIAL PROSECUTOR** to conduct a limited investigation and prosecution. The state prosecutors are usually called district attorneys or county prosecutors. The federal prosecutor is known as the United States Attorney for a certain federal district. The prosecutor is charged with the duty to see that the laws of his or her **jurisdiction** are faithfully executed and enforced.

PROSECUTRIX term used to refer to the complaining witness in a rape case; less frequently, it refers to a female prosecutor.

PROSECUTORIAL DISCRETION see **discretion** [**PROSECUTORIAL DISCRETION**].

PROSECUTORIAL MISCONDUCT see **summation [summing up]** [**PROSECUTORIAL MISCONDUCT**].

PROSPECTIVE future, in the future. A law or decision that is to be applied "prospectively" is to be applied only after the date it was enacted or decided. Constitutional decisions in the area of criminal procedure are often applied prospectively only to minimize the disruptive effect on law enforcement and the administration of justice. If the new decision does not affect the integrity of the fact-finding process and represents a clear break from prior **precedent,** it will be applied prospectively only. Compare **retroactive.**

EXAMPLE: Richard's conviction for selling drugs in a school zone was overturned. In its opinion the court declared that in the future prosecutors must prove that the school was in session at the time of the offense. Loni was convicted before Richard under similar facts yet her conviction will not be overturned since the court specifically applied their ruling to only Richard's case and those that follow.

PROSPECTUS a document that discloses financial information about a corporation to potential investors and explains the company's plans and objectives. Under federal **securities acts,** a corporation making a public offering of its securities must file a copy of its prospectus with the **Securities and Exchange Commission** and must provide a copy of it to each purchaser of securities.

PROSTITUTION the giving or receiving of the body for sexual intercourse for hire. A person who sells his or her body for sexual intercourse is a **PROSTITUTE.** See **pander; solicitation.**

PRO TANTO (*prō tän'-tō*) Lat.: for so much; to the extent, but only to the extent.

PROTECT [PROTECTION] to preserve in safety; to keep intact; to take care of and to keep safe. "Protection" is any measure that attempts to preserve that which already exists. For instance, trade protection attempts to preserve domestic industry through the imposition of tariffs and custom duties on imported goods. See **tariff [PROTECTIVE TARIFF];** see also **consumer protection.**

PROTECTIVE CUSTODY the confinement of an individual by the state in order to protect the individual from being harmed either by himself or herself or some other person. For instance, a prisoner who is the subject of attack by other prisoners will be segregated from those prisoners and placed in protective custody.

PROTECTIVE ORDER any order issued for the purpose of protecting a party from some abuse of the legal system. Under federal rules of civil procedure the court may make any order that justice requires to protect a party or person from annoyance, embarrassment, oppression or undue burden or expense. The rule specifically mentions various discovery matters, including the time, place, and subject matter of discovery, and the protection of trade secrets. Under federal rules of criminal procedure the court is specifically authorized to limit discovery in criminal cases as may be appropriate.

PRO TEMPORE [PRO TEM] *(prō tĕm'-pō-rā)* Lat.: for the time being.

PROTEST 1. a demand for payment of a **note,** its nonpayment, and consequent **dishonor;** 2. a formal certification by a consul, **notary** or the like that an **instrument** has been dishonored. A protest must identify the instrument and certify that due **presentment** has been made, or show why it has been excused, and that the instrument has been dishonored by non-acceptance or nonpayment.

EXAMPLE: Fernando deposits one of his customer's checks in the bank, but the check is returned for lack of sufficient funds in the customer's account. Fernando files a *protest* with the customer and demands that the debt now be paid in cash.

PROTHONOTARY in some jurisdictions, a chief clerk of the court.

PROVISIONAL REMEDY see **remedy [PROVISIONAL REMEDY].**

PROVISO a condition or stipulation. Its general function is to except something from the basic provision, to qualify or restrain its general scope, or to prevent misinterpretation.

PROXIMATE CAUSE see **cause [PROXIMATE CAUSE].**

PROXY 1. recipient of a grant of authority to act or speak for another; 2. one permitted to vote in place of a **stockholder** of a **corporation,** who is thereby presumably voicing the will of his or her **principal.** 3. the instrument used to grant this authority.

PRUDENT MAN [PERSON] RULE a flexible legal investment standard that allows a **fiduciary** to purchase **securities** that a person of discretion and intelligence would choose to earn a reasonable income and to preserve the **principal.** See also **trustee.**

EXAMPLE: A father sets up a trust for his two sons, naming a bank as trustee. The trust instrument provides no definition of how the trust principal should be invested. The trustee is bound by the *prudent-person rule* and must purchase securities that may not offer the highest return possible but are very safe investments.

PRURIENT INTEREST shameful and morbid interest in nudity, sex, or excretion. It is one criterion in determining whether or not something is obscene. See **obscenity.**

P.S. public statute.

PSYCHOTHERAPIST-PATIENT PRIVILEGE see **physician-patient privilege [PSYCHOTHERAPIST-PATIENT PRIVILEGE].**

PTI see **pretrial intervention.**

PUB. L. public law.

PUBLICATION the act of making something known to the public. Also the document itself, such as a newspaper or book. Publication can be accomplished by a physical posting (such as placing a paper on a bulletin board), an electronic Internet posting, or by a printed method, such as a magazine or newsletter. Publication of **slander** can constitute **defamation.** It can also be a means of **service (of process)** of a legal document (such as notice of a class action suit, a legal name change or a sheriff's sale) if statutory requirements are followed. See **notice.**

PUBLICATION, SERVICE BY see **service [SERVICE BY PUBLICATION].**

PUBLIC CHARITY see **charity [PUBLIC CHARITY].**

PUBLIC CORPORATION see **corporation [PUBLIC CORPORATION].**

PUBLIC DEFENDER an attorney hired by the government to defend persons accused of crimes and unable to afford an attorney. Under the **Sixth** and **Fourteenth Amendments,** a defendant in a criminal proceeding who faces possible incarceration if convicted, is entitled to the assistance of counsel in conducting his or her defense, and an attorney must be provided at government expense if the defendant is indigent.

PUBLIC DOCUMENT see **public record.**

PUBLIC DOMAIN 1. all lands and waters in the possession of the United States, and all lands owned by the several states, as distinguished from lands possessed by private individuals or corporations; 2. information, the source of which is available to anyone and is not subject to **copyright.**

PUBLIC EASEMENT any **easement** enjoyed by the public in general, such as the right of passage over the surface of streets and highways. Also called a **DEDICATION,** meaning that use of the land has been devoted for such purposes by the owner of the **fee.**

EXAMPLE: A developer wants to construct a tall office building but needs part of the sidewalk adjacent to the area. The city is willing to allow this infringement of a *public easement* if the builder will provide other access to the public, such as an open passageway through the building or an alternate facility for public usage.

PUBLIC FIGURE in **libel** law, a person of general fame or notoriety in the community, and extensive involvement in the affairs of society. Under the **First Amendment,** a public figure is required to show actual **malice** before recovering damages for libel.

PUBLIC INTEREST that which is best for society as a whole; a subjective determination by an individual such as a judge or governor, or a group such as a township committee or state legislature or what is for the general good of all people. Providing an adequate education and maintaining libraries, hospitals, and playgrounds are examples of concerns that are in the public interest.

AFFECTED WITH A PUBLIC INTEREST connotes the need for regulation. An example of a business affected with a public interest would be a public utility. **PUBLIC POLICY** is virtually synonymous with public interest but tends to have more specific connotations. For example, police act in the public interest but public policy dictates that citizens shall not be subjected to undue detention or arrest. **AGAINST PUBLIC POLICY** is a determination that a specified act or course of conduct does not further society's best interests. Usage of drugs within a private residence is nonetheless illegal as against the public policy of a drug-free society.

PUBLIC NECESSITY see **justification [PUBLIC NECESSITY].**

PUBLIC NUISANCE see **nuisance [PUBLIC [COMMON] NUISANCE].**

PUBLIC OFFERING see **offer [OFFERING].**

PUBLIC OFFICIAL any elected or appointed person holding a public office and having duties relating to the **sovereign** powers of government. The term does not apply to public employees having purely **ministerial** duties.

PUBLIC POLICY see **public interest [PUBLIC POLICY].**

PUBLIC PROPERTY that which is dedicated to the use of the public, or that over which the state has dominion; describes the use to which the property is put, or the character of its ownership. Compare **public domain; public easement.**

PUBLIC PURPOSE generally, the goal of society to benefit its citizens. Specifically, the doctrine examining governmental action and measuring the ultimate benefit to the public, as with the taking of private property to build a private correctional facility. See **eminent domain; public use.**

PUBLIC RECORD any record a governmental body is required by law to keep, and that must be filed and be accessible to the public.

PUBLIC SALE see **sale [PUBLIC SALE].**

PUBLIC SECURITIES see **securities [PUBLIC SECURITIES].**

PUBLIC TRIAL see **open court.**

PUBLIC TRUST 1. **CHARITABLE TRUST** (see **trust**); 2. the public's confidence reposed in their elected officials and expectation that these elected officials will faithfully perform the duties of public office.

PUBLIC TRUST DOCTRINE A doctrine under which the state is said to own lands lying under navigable waters and to hold such lands in trust for the benefit of the people of the state. According to this doctrine, these submerged lands may not be sold or otherwise alienated by the state except in a manner that promotes the public interest.

PUBLIC USE the public's right to use or to benefit from the use of **property** condemned by the government through the exercise of its power of **eminent domain.** One of the limitations upon the use of this power is that property so taken must be for a public use.

PUBLIC UTILITY a company that, because of the nature of its business, has characteristics of a natural **monopoly.** For instance, an electric company will have a natural monopoly over the sale of electricity to that area, since having a single supplier of electricity for any given area is the most efficient method of producing and distributing electricity. Because no free market or competition exists for the services or goods sold by public utilities, they are subject to government regulation of the price they may charge and the means in which they may distribute their goods.

PUBLIC UTILITY HOLDING COMPANY ACT OF 1935 see **Securities Act [PUBLIC UTILITY HOLDING COMPANY ACT OF 1935].**

PUBLISH to make known to the general public. In the law of torts, a statement does not constitute defamation unless it is **published,** that is, made known to some third party other than the party making the statement or the party defamed. In the law of wills, a will is not valid unless the testator **publishes** it, by informing the witness that he or she is signing the document as his or her will. In civil practice, service of process may be effected by publication, usually in a local newspaper, when notice of a lawsuit cannot be given by any other means.

PUFFING a statement of belief not meant as fact; a seller's extravagant statements, made to enhance his or her wares and induce others to enter into a bargain. Salesmanship talk, characterized as puffing, cannot be the basis of a charge of **fraud** or **express warranty,** since the buyer is said to have no right to rely on sales talk.

EXAMPLE: Jean Claude *puffs* his cooking utensils by stating that they are the best quality utensils money can buy or the easiest to clean or the least expensive compared to other brands. A purchaser of these utensils then finds a nearly identical set that costs a few dollars less. Jean Claude's comments cannot be taken as facts and do not give rise to a cause of action against Jean Claude by the customer for misleading advertising or the like.

PUNISHMENT sanctions imposed on a person because that person has been found to have committed some act. Historically, punishment for various acts has included fines, prison sentences, loss of rights or privileges, banishment or deportation, physical dismemberment, and execution. Some forms of punishment, such as banishment and dismemberment, have fallen into disuse. The Constitution specifically forbids **cruel and unusual punishment.** This prohibition has been held to apply to torture or other treatment beyond the limits of civilized standards. However, courts have generally had difficulty in defining the exactness of the constitutional limitation. See **capital punishment; corporal punishment.**

PUNITIVE DAMAGES see **damages** [EXEMPLARY DAMAGES].

PUR AUTRE VIE see **per autre vie.**

PURCHASE the acquisition of property by furnishing valuable **consideration.** Compare **descent and distribution; succession.**

PURCHASE-MONEY SECURITY INTEREST see **security interest.**

PURCHASER one who acquires property by giving valuable consideration for it. See **bona fide purchaser.**

PURCHASER IN DUE COURSE see **holder in due course.**

PURCHASE, WORDS OF see **words of purchase.**

PURE CONGLOMERATE MERGER see **merger** [PURE CONGLOMERATE MERGER].

PURE PLEA see **plea [PURE PLEA].**

PURE RACE ACTS [STATUTES] see **recording acts [PURE RACE].**

PURLOIN to steal; to commit **larceny.**

PURPOSELY deliberately or intentionally. As used in criminal statutes to define murder, *purposely* means intentionally, and as an act of the will, not accidentally. In the Model Penal Code it is one of the four defined mental states, along with knowingly, recklessly, and negligently. A person acts purposely with respect to a material element of an offense when it is his or her conscious object to engage in conduct or cause a result. See **mens rea.**

PURSUIT OF HAPPINESS one of the "unalienable rights" of people enumerated in the Declaration of Independence, along with "life" and "liberty." The right of persons to pursue any lawful business or vocation, in any manner not inconsistent with the equal rights of others, which may increase their prosperity or develop their faculties, so as to give them their highest enjoyment. Because the right is not set forth in the Constitution, it is not enforceable by the courts. However, the right to the pursuit of happiness is often raised in arguments against government regulations, because its mention in the Declaration of Independence gives it a degree of forcefulness.

PURVIEW the enacting part of a statute distinguished from other parts, such as the **preamble.** Conduct is WITHIN THE PURVIEW of a statute when such conduct properly comes within the statute's purpose, operation or effect.

  EXAMPLE: The legislature passes a statute prohibiting the possession of burglar's tools. Workmen such as locksmiths or window repairmen commonly have these tools as part of their trade. Their possession of the tools would not come *within the purview* of the statute.

PUTATIVE alleged; supposed. Thus, a putative marriage is one that is actually void, but that has been contracted in good faith by the two parties, or by one of the parties. The putative father in a **paternity suit** is the person alleged to have fathered the child whose parentage is at issue in the suit.

PUT OPTION see **stock option [PUT OPTION].**

PYRAMIDING the use of paper profits from an investment to finance purchases of additional investments. Compare **margin.**

Q

Q AND A   question and answer.

QDRO   see **Qualified Domestic Relations Order.**

QSBS   qualified small business stock. See **capital [CAPITAL GAINS OR LOSSES].**

QUAERE   *(kwē'-rē)* Lat.: a **query.**

QUALIFIED DISCLAIMER   see **disclaimer [QUALIFIED DISCLAIMER].**

QUALIFIED DOMESTIC RELATIONS ORDER [QDRO]   any **judgment, decree,** or **order** that grants to a person the right to participate in another's **pension.** The person who is granted a specific participation in the other person's pension must be a spouse, a former spouse, or a dependent child. This person is called an **ALTERNATE PAYEE** and the original sole owner of the pension being divided is called a **PARTICIPANT.** The pension itself is referred to as a **PLAN.** A QDRO is an exception to the antialienation provision of the federal law governing pensions, known as **ERISA.**

QUALIFIED PENSION OR PROFIT-SHARING PLAN   see **retirement plans [QUALIFIED PENSION OR PROFIT-SHARING PLAN].**

QUALIFIED SMALL BUSINESS STOCK   see **capital [CAPITAL GAINS OR LOSSES].**

QUANTUM MERUIT   *(kwän'-tūm mě'-rū-ĭt)* Lat.: as much as he deserved. l. Historically, it was a common **count** in the action of **assumpsit,** allowing recovery for services performed for another on the basis of a **contract** implied in law or an implied promise to pay the performer for what the services were reasonably worth.

2. It refers today to a theory under which a **plaintiff** may recover for reasonable value of services or materials furnished to another who has enjoyed those materials or services under circumstances that reasonably notified him or her that the plaintiff expected to be paid. The doctrine imposes **liability** for a contract implied by law, which arises not from the consent of the parties but from the law

of natural justice and **equity,** and which is based on the doctrine of **unjust enrichment.** See quasi [QUASI CONTRACT] Compare **officious intermeddler.**

EXAMPLE: A physician renders emergency services to an unconscious accident victim. Consent to those services by the injured party is implied in law, so that the physician may bring an action in *quantum meruit* to recover the reasonable value of the services.

QUANTUM VALEBANT *(kwän'-tūm văl-ē'-bănt)* Lat.: as much as they were worth. A common law action of **assumpsit** for goods sold and delivered, founded on an implied assumpsit or promise by the defendant to pay the plaintiff as much as the goods are reasonably worth.

QUARE CLAUSUM FREGIT *(kwä'-rā klaù'-zūm frā'-gĭt)* Lat.: wherefore he broke the close. An early form of **trespass** designed to obtain **damages** for an unlawful entry upon another's **land.** The **form of action** was called trespass quare clausum fregit, or trespass qu. cl. fr. **BREAKING A CLOSE** was the technical **common law** expression for unlawful entry upon land. Even without an actual fence the complainant would **plead** that the "defendant with force and arms broke and entered the close of the **plaintiff,**" since in the eyes of the common law every unauthorized entry upon the soil of another was a trespass.

QUASH to annul, overthrow or vacate by judicial decision.

QUASI *(kwā'-zi; kwä'-zē)* Lat.: as it were, so to speak; about, almost, like.

QUASI CONTRACT one that, unlike a true **contract,** is not based on the apparent intention of the **parties** to undertake the **performances** in question, but is an obligation created by law for reasons of justice and fairness. The doctrine of quasi contract is based upon the principle that a party must pay for a benefit he or she desired and received under circumstances that render it inequitable for him or her to retain it without making compensation. See **quantum meruit; unjust enrichment.**

EXAMPLE: A car owner brings his car in for brake repairs. The mechanic fixes the brakes and in doing so he also fixes a separate part of the axle that has a direct relationship to the car's ability to brake correctly. Although the axle repair was not specifically contracted for, a *quasi contract* is implied for which the owner must pay the mechanic.

QUASI CORPORATION see **corporation** [QUASI CORPORATION].

QUASI CRIMINAL describes a **proceeding** that, though not actually a criminal **prosecution,** is sufficiently similar in terms of the substantial **sanction** (civil fine, loss of employment, loss of license, suspension from school, etc.) or the stigma attached to warrant some of the special **procedural** safeguards of a criminal proceeding. See also **due process.**

QUASI IN REM describes proceedings that are not purely **in rem** but that are brought against the defendant personally, although the real object is to deal with particular property; refers to **actions** for money **damages** begun by **attachment, garnishment** or other seizure of property, where the court has no **jurisdiction** over the defendant but has jurisdiction over a thing belonging to the defendant or over a person who is indebted or under a duty to the defendant.

QUEEN'S BENCH see **King's [Queen's] Bench.**

QUERY question; indicates that the proposition or rule it introduces is unsettled or open to some question.

QUESTION, LEADING see **leading question.**

QUESTION OF FACT disputed factual contention that is traditionally left for the jury to decide, unless the judge is serving as **TRIER OF FACT** (see **fact finder**) in the case.

EXAMPLE: The jury is asked to decide if Butch developed a product while he was employed by his company or after he was fired. That issue is a *question of fact,* and the legal significance of the answer (who is entitled to what) is for the judge to determine.

Compare **question of law.**

QUESTION OF LAW disputed legal contentions that are traditionally left for the judge to decide. The occurrence or nonoccurrence of an event is a **question of fact;** its legal significance is a question of law.

EXAMPLE: Two parties stipulate [agree] on the facts of the situation in which they are involved. The judge is then asked to only rule on the *question of law* that those facts present.

QUESTION, POLITICAL see **political question.**

QUIA EMPTORES, STATUTE OF *(quī'-ă ĕmp-tō'-rēz)* Lat.: an act passed by Parliament in 1290 that abolished the restraint upon alienation or transfer of land that had been imposed under the feudal system. The process of **subinfeudation** [creation of new manors by the subject of a lord] was terminated, and after that date only the king was able to infeudate. The statute's practical effect on land transactions and ownership was that after the land was sold, the seller had no further connection with it. Thus, subinfeudation was replaced by strict **alienation.**

QUIA TIMET *(quī'-ă tī'-mĕt)* Lat.: because he fears. A type of

injunction sought in a court of **equity** to restrain an anticipated (feared) damage. Such a remedy would be granted only upon a showing of imminent and **irreparable harm.**

QUICK alive, living.

QUICKENING the point at which a fetus first moves within the womb. The term **VITALIZED** [alive] applies to the fetus both before and after quickening.

QUID PRO QUO *(kwĭd prō kwō)* Lat.: something for something. In some legal contexts, synonymous with **consideration;** sometimes referred to as the quid and always indicating that which a party receives or is promised in return for something he or she promises, gives or does.

QUIET ENJOYMENT the right to unimpaired use and enjoyment of **property.** For **leased** premises, a guarantee of quiet enjoyment is usually expressed by a **COVENANT OF QUIET ENJOYMENT** in a written lease, but such a **covenant** may be implied today from the landlord-tenant relationship, even where it is not so expressed. This covenant is violated if the tenant's enjoyment of the premises is substantially disturbed either by wrongful acts or omissions of the landlord or by persons claiming a superior **title** against the landlord.

EXAMPLE: A company agrees to lease a warehouse owned by a landlord. When the company's lease is to begin, the tenants who were in the warehouse are still there. Their presence violates the company's right to *quiet enjoyment.* A few states may place the burden of removing the tenants on the company, but most states place the burden on the landlord. In that majority of states, if those tenants do not leave after a certain amount of time, the company can rescind the lease without penalty.

The covenant may be and often is included in a **deed** conveying title to property. If it is present in a deed, the **grantor** is obligated to protect the estate of his **grantee** against lawful claims of ownership by others. See **constructive eviction; covenant.**

QUIET TITLE a **suit** in **equity** brought to obtain a final determination as to the **title** of a specific piece of property. A quiet title action is distinguished from an action to **REMOVE CLOUD ON TITLE,** which is brought to determine and resolve problems of **instruments** conveying a particular piece of land, rather than to resolve the actual claims to that land.

EXAMPLE: Rahul believes he is the rightful owner of a parcel of land, but there is a question concerning the transfer of the land 25 years ago. In order to satisfy any doubts so that he may sell the property,

Rahul brings a *quiet title* action to confirm his ownership by judicial decree.

QUIETUS final discharge from debt or obligation. Rest or death.

QUI TAM *(quī täm)* Lat.: who as well. A *qui tam* action is a lawsuit under a statute, which gives to the plaintiff bringing the action a part of the penalty recovered and the balance to the state. The plaintiff describes himself as suing for the state as well as for himself.

QUITCLAIM DEED a **deed** that conveys only that right, **title** or **interest** that the **grantor** has, or may have, and that does not warrant that the grantor actually has any particular title or interest in the property. The grantor under a quitclaim deed represents merely that whatever interest he may have he conveys to the grantee.

QUORUM the number of members of any body who must necessarily be present in order to transact the business of that body.

QUOTATION 1. in commercial usage, a statement of the price of an item; 2. the price stated in response to an inquiry.

QUOTIENT VERDICT see **verdict** [QUOTIENT VERDICT].

QUO WARRANTO *(kwō wär'-rän-tō)* Lat.: by what right or authority. An ancient **common law writ** that was issued out of **chancery** on behalf of the king against one who claimed or usurped any office, **franchise** or liberty, to inquire by what authority he asserted such a right, in order that the legitimacy of the assertion might be determined. Formerly a criminal method of **prosecution,** it has long since lost its criminal character and is now a **civil** proceeding, expressly recognized by **statute,** and usually employed for **trying the title** to a corporate franchise or to a corporation or public office.

Quo warranto proceedings may be brought against **corporations** where the company has abused or failed for a long time to exercise its franchise. In the case of an official, it may be brought to cause him or her to forfeit an office for misconduct. If in these cases a quo warranto proceeding determines that a company no longer properly holds a franchise or that an officer no longer properly holds his or her office, it will oust the wrongdoer from enjoying the franchise or office. The purpose of the writ is not to prevent an improper exercise of power lawfully possessed; its purpose is to prevent an official, corporation or persons acting as such from usurping a power that they do not have.

QURAN see **Koran.**

R

R. registered. See **trademark.**

RACE a term commonly used in antidiscrimination statutes that refers to ancestry, as opposed to national origin. For use in a property law context, see **recording acts.**

RACE-NOTICE see **recording acts [RACE-NOTICE].**

RACIAL PROFILING see **profiling [RACIAL PROFILING].**

RACKETEER INFLUENCED AND CORRUPT ORGANIZATIONS ACT [RICO] see **racketeering.**

RACKETEERING originally, an organized **conspiracy** to commit extortion. Today, punishable offenses created by Congress aimed at eradicating organized crime by providing for enhanced sanctions and new remedies to be used in dealing with the illegal activities of persons involved in organized crime.

RADAR an electrical device used for determining the speed, direction, or range of an object. The term stands for Radio Detection and Ranging. Radar was developed during World War II and since the late 1940s has been used by police to monitor the speed of motor vehicles. Radar is generally admissible in court as probative **evidence** that a person was driving in excess of the speed limit. However, the accuracy of a particular radar reading may be attacked on the grounds of the inadequacy of the training of the police officer operating the unit, whether the unit has been recently tested for accuracy or is properly calibrated, and whether it was operated properly on a given occasion. Furthermore, the type of radar device used may affect whether the evidence produced by it is admissible.

RAISED CHECK a **check** whose face amount has been increased from the amount for which the check was originally issued. That change constitutes a **material alteration** under the **Uniform Commercial Code** and discharges any party whose contract is thereby changed unless that party assents or is precluded from asserting the defense. A **holder in due course** of the raised check may enforce it for its original amount.

RAKE-OFF skim profits; bribe.

RANSOM 1. money or other consideration paid for the release of a kidnapped or otherwise captured person or thing; 2. to redeem from captivity by payment.

RAPE   intercourse by force or threat, or under circumstances where the victim is unable to resist due to intoxication or lack of consciousness. State statutes general refer to "SEXUAL ASSAULT" or "SEXUAL ABUSE" instead of the term "rape." Where "rape" is used in common parlance, it refers to sexual penetration. Both sexual assault and sexual abuse refer to engaging in sexual acts, or forcing or encouraging another person to engage in sexual acts alone or with another person of any age, whether of the same sex or of the opposite sex. Sexual assault or sexual abuse statutes criminalize offenses involving penetration as well as other sexual offenses, including SEXUAL CONTACT (the touching of another's intimate body parts without their consent) and non-touching offenses such as **lewdness** or indecent exposure of one's genitals, as well as exposing a child to sexually explicit magazines or videos. State statutes vary greatly with regard to the criminal punishments available for various sexual offenses.

Types of behavior that include verbal comments of a sexual nature, that are unwelcome or reasonably could be expected to be unwelcome, generally fall under the heading of "sexual harassment." Examples of sexual harassment include sexually suggestive or obscene comments, gestures, or jokes; requests for sexual favors; unwelcome inquiries or comments about a person's sex life; or unwelcome sexual flirtations or advances. State statutes generally provide only civil remedies for the victims of sexual harassment. See **harassment** [SEXUAL HARASSMENT].

DATE RAPE   a situation where initially the victim willingly accompanied the attacker on a social outing but then a sexual assault occurred.

STATUTORY RAPE   sexual intercourse with a person under the **age of consent**. See **carnal knowledge.**

RAPE CRISIS COUNSELOR PRIVILEGE   privilege against disclosure of records and notes afforded by some states to professionals who give victims of sexual assault counseling and emotional support. The privilege is usually available in both civil and criminal proceedings. The privilege is relatively novel and is presently recognized in only a small number of jurisdictions. Where it has been adopted, its availability represents a judgment that the confidentiality of a rape victim and a rape crisis counselor is sufficiently important to justify limiting the right of the criminal defendant to confront the witnesses against him or her under the Sixth Amendment.

RAPE SHIELD LAWS see **shield laws.**

RAPINE forcible taking of property.

RAP SHEET see **criminal record.**

RASURE erasure or alteration to a document.

RATABLE proportional, capable of estimation; taxable. Thus, a ratable **estate** is a taxable estate. In **bankruptcy,** a ratable distribution is a **pro rata** share of the bankrupt's **assets.** Ratable does not mean equal, but rather pro rata according to some measure fixing proportions.

RATE a stated or fixed price for some commodity or service measured by a specific unit or standard or that may be stated as a percentage of a fixed figure, such as a percentage of profits; an amount of charge or payment with reference to some basis of calculation.

RATE OF RETURN a return on investment, frequently used to describe the rate that a **utility,** such as an electric company or telephone company, is entitled to earn on its investment, and is determined by combining the capital structure of the utility with the proper cost of capital. It is expressed as a percentage of the utility's rate base.

RATE OF TAX see **tax rate.**

RATIFICATION to sanction or affirm confirmation of the act of another regardless of whether the act was originally authorized. The process by which society approves a fundamental change in the law. Congress may, by a two-thirds vote, propose a constitutional amendment or call for a convention to propose amendments to the Constitution. Any proposed amendment must then be ratified either by the legislature or by conventions in three-fourths of the states before they become effective.

RATIOCINATION the process of reasoned, rational, exact thought.

RATIO DECEDENDI *(rä'-shē-ō dā-sā-děn'-dē)* Lat.: the reason for the decision; the principle that the case establishes.

RATIO LEGIS *(rä'-shē-ō lā'-gĭs)* Lat.: legal reasoning or grounds; the underlying principle; theory, doctrine or science of the law.

EXAMPLE: A loitering statute permits law enforcement officers to disperse crowds of people rather than arrest each person and go through a series of formalities not actually necessary in the circumstances. The *ratio legis* of the statute is to allow the officers more latitude in attempting to prevent crime rather than to rely solely on apprehension and sentencing as a deterrent.

RATIONAL BASIS TEST a method of constitutional analysis under the **equal protection clause** used to determine whether a challenged law bears a reasonable relationship to the attainment of some legitimate governmental objective. See **fundamental right.**

RAVISH generally, synonymous with **rape.** Literally, to ravish is to seize or snatch by force. Traditionally, a valid **indictment** for rape required the use of the term ravished, which implied force or violence; it would thus constitute an essential word in all indictments for rape, importing not only violence on the part of one party but resistance on the part of the other.

RAVISHMENT see **sexual assault.**

RE see **in re.**

READY WILLING AND ABLE to be prepared to act, and capable of acting, in a given situation, such as the buyer or seller in a real estate transaction.

REAL CHATTEL see **chattel [REAL CHATTEL].**

REAL ESTATE every possible **interest** in land, except for a mere **chattel** interest.

REAL ESTATE INVESTMENT TRUST [REIT] a specialized investment organization that functions as a financial intermediary in the real estate debt market and that qualifies under Internal Revenue Code requirements to act as a conduit with respect to income distributions. The **Massachusetts Trust** is a popular legal form for REITs. **Trusts** fall into two basic categories: **equity** trusts, which invest in income properties under terms that provide equity ownership and/or participation in income, and **mortgage** trusts that lend funds on a short-term basis for development and construction and on a long-term basis for first and second mortgages.

REAL EVIDENCE an object relevant to facts in issue at a trial and produced for inspection at trial rather than described by a witness. Real evidence may include any object produced for inspection at a trial, from the murder weapon to a tape recording of a telephone conversation or a photograph of where an event occurred to the exhibition of a physical injury. Real evidence is one type of **demonstrative evidence.**

REALIZATION 1. the conversion of an asset into money; 2. in tax law, the occurrence of a transaction deemed to be a sufficiently substantial economic change for the **taxpayer** to warrant imposition of **INCOME TAX** (see **tax**). If the tax is imposed, the event gives rise to **recognition.**

GAIN OR LOSS REALIZED the difference between the amount realized on a **sale or exchange** of an asset and the taxpayer's **basis** in such asset.

EXAMPLE: A taxpayer buys stock for $5 a share. Ten years later, he sells the stock for $15. The taxpayer has a *realization* of $10 on each share and must pay tax on the total gain. If the stock is sold at $1, he has a loss of $4 a share, and his income is reduced by that amount before his tax liability is calculated.

REAL PARTY IN INTEREST the person who will be entitled to the benefits of the legal **action** if it is successful; one who is actually and substantially interested in the subject matter, as opposed to one who has only a nominal, formal or technical interest in it. For example, if an insurance company pays its insured for damage done to his automobile under a collision insurance provision of his policy and if the insurance company attempts to collect its loss from the responsible party, the suit may be brought in the name of the insured, but the real party in interest will be the insurance company.

REAL PROPERTY 1. land and whatever is erected or growing on it, or affixed to it; 2. rights issuing out of, annexed to, and exercisable within or about, the land. See **fixture.** Compare **chattel.**

REAL TIME TRANSCRIPT see **court reporters [REAL TIME].**

REALTOR real estate broker. Compare **relator.**

REALTY an interest in land; another word for **real property.**

REAPPORTIONMENT changing of a legislative district or of the number of seats a state is entitled to in the Congress to more clearly reflect the population of that district or state; an attempt to meet the right of every person to vote on a one-person, one-vote basis. Compare **gerrymander.**

EXAMPLE: Each legislative district elects one person to represent them in Congress, but one district has only 10,000 people whereas another district covers 20,000 people. *Reapportionment* will attempt to make each district equal in size.

REARGUMENT the oral presentation of additional arguments to a court after it has already heard argument, for the purpose of demonstrating that there is some decision or principle of law that would have a controlling effect and that has been overlooked, or that there has been a misapprehension of facts. Reargument usually occurs prior to the court rendering a decision in a matter and may be distinguished from a **rehearing** that also presents some new or overlooked principle of law or fact but that usually occurs after the court has rendered its decision.

REASONABLE a subjective standard for what is fair, just, or appropriate; that which is ordinary or usual under the circumstances. Rational and logical. Compare **unreasonable.**

REASONABLE BELIEF 1. in criminal law, similar to the **probable cause** standard in that it is a subjective standard used to validate a **warrantless search and seizure** or **arrest** and that considers whether an officer acted on personal knowledge of facts and circumstances that are reasonably trustworthy, and that would justify a person of average caution to believe that a crime has been or is being committed; 2. in insurance law, a subjective standard used to determine the extent to which an automobile insurance policy covers a driver, based on the reasonableness of the driver's belief that the owner's permission had been granted to use the vehicle, whether or not such permission was directly granted.

REASONABLE CARE that degree of **care** that under the circumstances would ordinarily or usually be exercised by or might be reasonably expected from an ordinary prudent person. The exercise or absence of reasonable care, which is a jury question, is often dispositive of tort cases or of cases involving injury to others. See **care [REASONABLE CARE]; reasonable man [person].**

REASONABLE DILIGENCE see **diligence.**

REASONABLE DOUBT refers to the degree of certainty required of a **juror** before he or she can make a legally valid determination of the guilt of a criminal **defendant.** These words are used in **instructions** to the **jury** in a criminal trial to indicate that innocence is to be presumed unless the jury can see no reasonable doubt of the guilt of the person charged. The term does not require that proof be so clear that no possibility of error exists; it means that the evidence must be so conclusive that all reasonable doubts are removed from the mind of the ordinary person. See also **moral certainty; preponderance of the evidence.**

EXAMPLE: Jay is charged with first degree murder, which requires that he intentionally planned the death. At his trial, he attempts to show that the killing occurred on the spur of the moment in a fit of rage. He is trying to create in the jurors a *reasonable doubt* that he planned the murder. If he is successful in that effort, he may lower the degree of his guilt to **manslaughter.**

REASONABLE MAN [PERSON] a phrase used to denote a hypothetical person who exercises qualities of attention, knowledge, intelligence and judgment that society requires of its members for the protection of their own interest and the interests of others. Thus, the test of **negligence** is based on either a failure to do something that a reasonable person, guided by considerations that ordinarily regulate conduct, would do, or on the doing of something that a reasonable and prudent person would not do.

REASONABLE TIME a subjective standard based on the facts and circumstances within a particular case, with applicability in a variety of contexts. Within commercial law, the term applies to the amount of time in which to accept an **offer,** to inspect goods prior to payment or acceptance, to await performance by a party who repudiates a contract, or the time in which a seller may substitute conforming goods for goods rejected by a buyer as nonconforming. If not governed by statute, the term may also refer to the time allowed to set aside a **default judgment,** to inform an insurance company of an accident, to file certain claims, and to make various motions. Compare **time is of the essence.**

REBUTTABLE PRESUMPTION see **presumption.**

REBUTTAL generally, the time either party is given to refute or oppose a claim or claims made by the opposing party that would not otherwise belong in that party's case in chief. Also refers to the time given to the party who presented the first closing argument to rebut any claims made by the opposing party in the closing argument, which followed. This rebuttal can only attack those claims made in the opposing party's argument and cannot raise any new issues.

REBUTTAL EVIDENCE any **evidence** that refutes, counteracts or explains away evidence given by a **witness** or an adverse party. Rebuttal evidence is offered to contradict other evidence or to rebut a **presumption** of fact.

REBUTTER a form of common law **pleading** that was a defendant's answer of fact to the plaintiff's response to the defendant's **rejoinder.**

RECALL a method of removing a public official from office by submitting to popular vote the issue of whether the official should continue in office. In insurance law, the invalidation of an insurance policy before it becomes effective. Under the federal Consumer Safety Act, a recall is the process by which a manufacturer is required to replace or repair potentially defective products in order to bring them into conformity with consumer product safety rules.

RECALL A JUDGMENT **reverse** or **vacate** a decision based on a **matter of fact,** as opposed to a **matter of law.**

RECAPITALIZATION a recasting of the **capital** structure of a **corporation.** A typical **capitalization** will contain **bonds** (called funded debt), **preferred stock** and **common stock.** Voluntary recapitalization could involve exchanging an existing bond issue or exchanging a preferred stock issue for bonds.

EXAMPLE: A corporation finds that the amount of its outstanding loans to banks is greater than the corporation wants. The directors *recapitalize* the corporation by exchanging shares of the corporation's stock for money to repay the loans. The corporation thus receives additional equity investors in return for reduction of its debt.

Recapitalizations are common when public companies emerge from **bankruptcy.** See **refinancing.**

RECAPTURE a term generally applied when an event or transaction requires a **taxpayer** to repay earlier tax savings by payment of additional tax in the present **taxable year.** Thus, upon a **sale** or **exchange** of property that constitutes a CAPITAL ASSET (see **capital**), the gain realized on such sale or exchange constitutes **capital gain.** However, under certain circumstances, if the taxpayer has taken excess **depreciation** (ACCELERATION DEPRECIATION over STRAIGHT LINE DEPRECIATION) with respect to real property or any depreciation with respect to personal property, to the extent of such depreciation the gain realized on the sale or exchange of that property is taxed as ORDINARY INCOME (see **income**) and not as capital gains. This taxation of the proceeds of the sale or exchange or the capital asset as ordinary income is recapture.

RECEIVABLES see **account** [ACCOUNT RECEIVABLE]; **balance sheet.**

RECEIVER 1. a neutral person appointed by the court to receive and preserve the property that is the subject of **litigation** during the period of litigation, or to manage and dispose of the property as the court or officer may direct. The court takes possession of the property in controversy through its **agent,** the receiver, during the litigation or after the **decree** or **judgment,** for the benefit of the people entitled to the property, when the court does not deem it proper that either party have control of it during that time. Although the assets involved in the litigation are in **custody** of the receiver, **title** to the assets remains in the owners who are parties to the litigation, and the receiver manages the property for the benefit of the parties.

A receiver is frequently appointed in **insolvency** proceedings to manage the property of the insolvent for the benefit of his **creditor.**

2. In criminal law, one who obtains possession of property that he or she knows or believes to have been stolen is a receiver of stolen property and commits an offense thereby.

RECEIVERSHIP 1. an **equitable** remedy whereby property is by order of the court placed under the control of a **receiver** so that it may be preserved for the benefit of affected parties. A failing company may be placed in receivership in an **action** brought by its **creditors.** The business is often continued but is subject to the receiver's control. A receivership is ancillary to or in aid of the main **relief** sought in an action; it is sometimes used to carry out an **order** or **decree** but is generally used for the purpose of preserving property during **litigation** involving rights in the property; 2. the status of property affected by this remedy; property is said to be in receivership.

EXAMPLE: The Antique Furniture Company is heavily indebted to several creditors and is only showing average sales. In a court-approved agreement between the owners of the company and the creditors, Antique is placed in *receivership*. The court appoints a receiver to oversee Antique's expenditures and orders. At the same time, the creditors settle for a partial payment of the debt and dismiss the rest of the debts against Antique.

Compare **bankruptcy.**

RECEIVING STOLEN PROPERTY a crime at common law, and under most modern statutes, requiring as its elements, that property be stolen by someone other than the person charged with receiving it; that the person receiving it has actually received the property or aided in concealing it; that the person has knowledge that the property has been stolen; and, in some jurisdictions, that the person received it with wrongful intent. The receiver is popularly known as a **fence,** and his or her blameworthiness is sometimes considered greater than the thief's since the fence has induced the thief to commit the crime. The crime may be a **felony** or **misdemeanor,** or its degree may vary, depending on the value of the property received. See **fence.**

RECESS 1. temporary adjournment of a trial or hearing after commencement of the trial or hearing. The recess may be short, for lunch, overnight or for a few days. If it amounts to a substantial delay in the proceedings, it is called a **continuance;** 2. the intermission between sittings of the same legislative body at its regular or adjourned session, but not the interval between the final adjournment of one body and the convening of another at the next regular session. Compare **sine die.**

RECIDIVIST a second offender or habitual criminal, who is often subject to extended terms of imprisonment under **habitual offender** statutes. See **criminal; sentence [EXTENDED TERM].**

RECIPROCAL NEGATIVE EASEMENT see **easement [RECIPROCAL NEGATIVE EASEMENT].**

RECIPROCITY generally, a relationship between persons, corporations, states, or countries whereby privileges granted by one are returned by the other. Compare **comity.**

RECISSION see **rescission.**

RECKLESS careless, inattentive to duty; foolishly heedless of danger; rashly adventurous; indifferent to consequences; mindless; very negligent.

In criminal law, the term connotes conscious disregard of a substantial and unjustifiable risk, a gross deviation from the standard of care that a **reasonable person** would observe in the actor's situation, a wanton indifference to the consequences of one's acts. Compare **negligence.**

RECKLESS DISREGARD refers to conduct without concern for consequences or danger. Compare **negligence.**

EXAMPLE: Fully aware that his conduct creates a risk of harm, Louis lights a pack of firecrackers and throws them into a crowd. Regardless of whether anyone is hurt, Louis has acted with *reckless disregard.*

RECKLESS NEGLIGENCE see **negligence** [WANTON NEGLI-GENCE].

RECOGNITION imposition of tax under the federal income tax system. Income or loss that the **taxpayer** has **realized** is recognized when it is subject to **tax.**

NONRECOGNITION OF GAIN gain or loss from the sale or exchange of an asset is not recognized when such gain or loss is not subject to tax. For example, if a taxpayer sells his or her principal residence, and within a period ending two years after the date of the sale of such principal residence, the taxpayer reinvests the proceeds from the sale, the gain realized (the excess of the selling price over the basis of the property) is not recognized.

RECOGNITION OF GAIN gain or loss realized from the sale or exchange of property is recognized when such gain or loss is subject to tax. In general, whenever an asset is disposed of, the gain realized is taxed unless specifically exempted from recognition.

RECOGNIZANCE an obligation of record, entered into before a court or other officer duly authorized for that purpose, with a condition to do some act required by law, upon failure of which the recognizor is obligated to pay a specific sum to the court or a party. For instance, in criminal law, a recognizance is an undertaking entered into before a court of record by the defendant and his or her sureties by which they bind themselves to pay a sum of money to the court unless the defendant appears for trial. See **bond; release on own recognizance [R.O.R.].**

RECOGNIZANCE, ONE'S OWN   see **release on recognizance [R.O.R.].**

RECORD 1. to preserve in writing, printing, on film, tape, etc.; 2. a precise history of a **suit** from beginning to end, including the conclusions of law thereon, drawn by the proper officer to perpetuate the exact facts.

EXAMPLE: A court rule provides that a judge must inform a person convicted of a crime of his or her right to an attorney to pursue an appeal if he or she so desires. Since all comments by the judge are transcribed, a *record* is produced that will eliminate any question whether the person was informed of his or her rights.

The **RECORD ON APPEAL** consists of those items introduced in **evidence** in the lower court, as well as a compilation of **pleadings, motions, briefs** and other papers filed in the proceeding in the inferior court. 3. in real property law, to enter in writing in a repository maintained as a public record any mortgage, sale of land or other interest affecting real property located within the jurisdiction of the government entity maintaining the public record. See **criminal record; of record; recording acts.**

RECOMBINANT DNA TECHNOLOGY   see **DNA testing [RECOMBINANT DNA TECHNOLOGY].**

RECORD DATE   the date on which a **shareholder** must be registered on the books of a **corporation** in order to receive **dividends** and other distributions or to vote on company business. See **ex-dividend.**

RECORDING ACTS   in real property law, statutes that afford a means of giving **CONSTRUCTIVE NOTICE** (see **notice**) to others of ownership respecting **estates** or **interests** in land, by providing for recording the existence of that estate or interest. These statutes generally provide for recording **deeds, mortgages, EXECUTORY CONTRACTS** (see **executory**) of sale and **leases** of specified duration. When one's interest or ownership in land is recorded, the recording prevents a subsequent purchaser or **mortgagee** of the land from qualifying as a **bona fide purchaser** for value without notice, because the instrument recorded would provide at least constructive notice of another's prior ownership or interest in the land.

Under a **RACE** type of recording act, the first person who records takes in preference to other persons who receive an interest from the same source, even if the first recorder had notice of a prior unrecorded conveyance. A **RACE-NOTICE** type of act operates like the race statute, but only if the first recorder had no notice of the prior unrecorded conveyance. **NOTICE** type recording acts provide that a bona fide purchaser is favored even though a prior purchaser is the first to record, so long as the second purchaser had no knowledge of the prior conveyance at the time he made his purchase.

Where there is a **GRACE PERIOD** provided by a recording act, a prior conveyee is protected against a subsequent conveyee even if he or she doesn't record first, as long as he or she records within the period of grace defined by the recording act. See **chain of title.**

RECORD OWNER the owner of **real estate** or other property, such as **stocks, bonds,** etc., at the time in question as revealed by public records. The term is frequently found in tax statutes, and therefore has importance in terms of which party is liable for a certain tax. It also may permit a party to have notice of certain events, such as land **foreclosure.**

RECOUPMENT 1. the right of **defendant** to have **plaintiff's** award of **damages** against defendant reduced; 2. a right of deduction from the amount of the plaintiff's claim by reason of either a payment thereon or some loss sustained by the defendant because of the plaintiff's wrongful or defective **performance** of the **contract** out of which his or her claim arose; 3. a withholding, for an equitable reason, of something that is due. The word is nearly synonymous with discount, deduction or reduction. Compare **counterclaim; cross-claim.**

RECOURSE the act of satisfying a claim, i.e., "recourse in the courts." If persons fail to obtain a desired result in court, they might claim that they will seek "recourse in the legislature." In financing, the ability to pursue a judgment for a default on a **note** not only against the property underlying the note, but against the party or parties signing the note. In **nonrecourse financing,** only the property used as **collateral** for the underlying loan may be reached to satisfy a **default judgment.** See **without recourse.**

RECOVERY 1. the establishment of a right by the **judgment** of a court, though recovery does not necessarily imply a return to whole or normal; 2. the amount of the judgment; 3. the amount actually collected pursuant to the judgment.

RECOVERY OF BASIS see **basis [RECOVERY OF BASIS].**

RECUSAL disqualification of a judge, jury or administrative officer for prejudice or interest in the subject matter. A judge may be recused as a result of objection by either party, or may voluntarily disqualify himself or herself if he or she fears that he or she may not act impartially, or that some circumstance will lead to a suspicion of bias.

EXAMPLE: Zhang Wei has been before a judge several times on criminal charges and has been acquitted each time. After each trial, the judge makes certain disparaging comments indicating to the press that he believes Zhang Wei is guilty. When Zhang Wei comes before the judge again, Zhang Wei seeks a *recusal* based on the earlier comments. Zhang Wei contends that the comments indicate prejudice on the judge's part and will prevent his getting a fair trial.

In most states, a judge may also be disqualified because he is related within certain degrees to a party litigant.

RECUSATION the process of disqualification of a judge, jury, or administrative hearing officer by reason of prejudice, bias, or interest in the subject matter. Judges may be recused by the objections of either party or they may voluntarily disqualify themselves if they fear they may not act in an impartial manner. Under most state statutes, judges may also be disqualified because they are closely related to a party litigant. The appearance of impropriety must be avoided at all costs.

REDEEMABLE BOND a bond that is callable for payment by the issuer.

REDEMPTION a regaining of possession by payment of a stipulated price; especially, the process of annulling a **defeasible title,** such as is created by a **mortgage** or tax sale, by paying the **debt** or fulfilling other obligations.

For tax purposes, a redemption is any purchase by a **corporation** of its own stock.

RIGHT OF REDEMPTION statutory right in some jurisdictions to redeem property that has been **forfeited** because the **mortgagor** had **defaulted** on the mortgage payments. It can be exercised only after the **foreclosure** and sale of the property, by paying the amount due on the mortgage, plus interest. It is a personal privilege and not an interest or **estate** in land, and it can be exercised only by the persons and on the condition named in the statute that grants the right. This right arises only after the **equity of redemption** period ends. It frequently applies to foreclosure under tax foreclosure statutes.

RED HERRING an issue, whether legal or factual, raised in a case or law school exam that may be important generally but that has no relevant importance to the question at hand. Also, a preliminary **prospectus,** concerning a future stock issue, distributed during the **WAITING PERIOD**—the period from the filing date to the effective date of a registration statement.

RE-DIRECT EXAMINATION see **cross-examination [RE-DI-RECT EXAMINATION].**

REDLINING an unlawful credit discrimination based on the characteristics of the neighborhood surrounding a would-be borrower's dwelling.

REDRESS relief or **remedy.** It may be damages or equitable relief. See **recovery; restitution.**

REDUCTIO AD ABSURDUM *(rā-dŭk'-tē-ō äd äb-sûr'-dŭm)* Lat.: to reduce to the absurd. To disprove a legal argument by showing that it ultimately leads to an absurd position.

REENTRY the resumption of **possession** pursuant to a right reserved when the former possession was surrendered. It was a remedy given by the feudal law for nonpayment of rent, and also refers to a right reserved in the conveyance of a **fee** that is subject to a **CONDITION SUBSEQUENT** (see **condition**). See **conditional fee.** Compare **ejectment; quiet title.**

REFEREE a quasi-judicial officer appointed by a court for a specific purpose, to whom the court refers power and duty to take **testimony,** determine issues of fact and report the findings for the court to use as a basis for judgment.

REFERENDUM referring of legislative acts to the voters for final approval or rejection.

REFINANCING **refunding** existing elements of the **capital** structure; usually implies selling a new **bond** issue to provide funds for **redemption** of a maturing issue. See **recapitalization.**

REFORM to correct, modify, or rectify; synonymous with **amend.**

REFORMATION an **equitable** remedy consisting of a revision of a **contract** by the court, in cases where the written terms of the contract do not express what was actually agreed upon. Thus, reformation is generally only decreed upon a **clear and convincing** showing of **MUTUAL MISTAKE** (see **mistake**); if only one party was mistaken, reformation is not appropriate unless the mistake of one party resulted from the other party's **fraud.**

EXAMPLE: Two parties negotiate a contract that inadvertently calls for a delivery date that predates the signing of the contract. Neither party realizes this mistake at the time, but, subsequently, one of the parties tries to use this fault as a reason for cancelling the contract. Since a delivery date can never come before a contract is completed, the court *reforms* the contract and does not permit the one party to cancel.

REFUND see **claim for refund; tax [TAX REFUND].**

REFUNDING the process of selling a new **issue** of **securities** to obtain funds needed to retire existing securities. Debt refunding is done to extend maturity and/or to reduce debt service cost. See **refinancing.**

REFUSAL the rejection of something to which a person is entitled, such as the rejection of **goods** under a **contract;** the denial of an obligation to perform a legal duty such as the refusal to complete a contract.

A refusal may be an affirmative act, or it may be the mere failure or neglect to perform an act that one is obligated to do without a demand therefore, such as the payment of money.

REG. abbreviation for registered; regulation.

REGIONAL STOCK EXCHANGE a domestic exchange located outside New York City. See **stock exchange.**

REGISTER to record formally and exactly; to enroll; to enter precisely in a list or the like. For **corporations,** to record the names of **stock** and **bond** holders on the books of the company. The **REGISTRAR** may be an **agent,** such as a bank, or it may be the corporation. The registrar is responsible for preventing unauthorized issuance of stock by a company. See **draft**.

REGISTERED BOND see **bond [REGISTERED BOND].**

REGISTERED [COUPON] BOND see **bond.**

REGISTERED REPRESENTATIVE a commission sales person who is qualified to take orders for **securities** from the general public. A securities sales trainee must be trained in the securities trade for at least six months and must pass tests prepared by the **National Association of Securities Dealers** [NASD] and the **New York Stock Exchange;** when training and testing are successfully completed, the trainee is registered with the **Securities and Exchange Commission,** the NASD, New York Stock Exchange and regional exchanges, and is registered in the various states in which the sales person intends to do business.

REGISTRAR a record keeper, such as the official at a university who is responsible for maintaining academic records. In corporate law, an agent appointed by a corporation to record the names of stock- and bondholders. See **register.**

REGISTRATION the act of making a list, catalogue, schedule, or register which has the purpose and effect of giving notice and preventing fraud and deception; within the meaning of election laws, a method of proof for ascertaining and identifying electors who are eligible to vote. In **securities** law, registration is the process by which a company submits financial data to the **Securities and Exchange Commission** so that it may have its securities bought and sold on public markets.

REGISTRATION OF OFFENDERS **statute** requiring lifetime registration of convicted **sex offenders** (including those found **not guilty by reason of insanity**) with law enforcement, and allowing law enforcement to notify the community of the sex offender's known address and vehicle. Failure to register is punishable as a criminal action. Federally, and in many states, such a statute is called MEGAN'S LAW. The provision of COMMUNITY NOTIFICATION is intended to prevent tragedies such as the sexual assault and murder of a seven-year-old girl (Megan) at the hands of her next-door neighbor, a twice-convicted sex offender whose past status was not known by the community.

REGISTRATION STATEMENT a document that must be approved by the **Securities and Exchange Commission [SEC]** before a company makes a public offering of new securities through the mails or in interstate commerce. The registration statement must describe the securities and must disclose in detailed information on the nature of the business, including accounting statements, the identity of the management and key stockholders, the purpose of the offering, and the use to be made of the proceeds.

REGISTRY (OF DEEDS) an officially maintained book that provides a place and mechanism for registering evidences of **conveyances** of interests in **real property,** so that notice may be available to all third parties that there has been a change in the ownership of property effected by a conveyance of that property.

REGULAR COURSE OF BUSINESS see **ordinary course of business.**

REGULATION A the "small-issues" exemptions governing the sale of **securities** that are exempt from registration filing requirements.

REGULATION D see **private offering [placement] [REGULATION D].**

REGULATIONS rules or other directives issued by administrative agencies to implement laws. These agencies must have specific authorization to issue directives and must usually adhere to prescribed procedures and conditions. See **Administrative Procedure Act [APA].**

REGULATION T a regulation of the **Securities and Exchange Commission** that governs the maximum amount of credit that **securities** brokers and dealers may extend to customers for the initial purchase of regulated securities.

REGULATION U a rule of the **Securities and Exchange Commission** that governs the maximum amount of credit that banks may extend for the purchase of regulated **securities.**

REGULATION Z the body of regulations promulgated by the Federal Reserve Board pursuant to the federal **Truth in Lending Act** that entrusts that administrative agency with supervision of compliance by all banks in the Federal Reserve System with the cost of credit disclosure requirements established under the Act.

REGULATORY AGENCY a government body responsible for control and supervision of a particular activity or area of public interest. For example, the Federal Communications Commission (FCC), in addition to its other duties, administers the laws regulating access to communication facilities such as television and radio airwaves. Regulatory agencies are also called **ADMINISTRATIVE AGENCIES.**

EXAMPLE: The Environmental Protection Agency was created by Congress to protect the quality of the nation's air, water and land. Pursuant to that goal, the agency monitors air pollution in cities, sewage treatment plants, chemical landfills, etc. The Federal Trade Commission regulates commercial practices and takes action against deceptive advertising and monopolistic activity. There are many federal and state *regulatory agencies* that enforce federal and state policies in particular areas of governmental regulation.

REGULATORY OFFENSE a deed that is not inherently evil but is a crime only because prohibited by legislation, i.e., **malum prohibitum.** Regulatory offenses are also called **STATUTORY OFFENSES** and may impose **strict liability** upon defendants for their violation.

REHABILITATION restoration of good repute; reformation. The term has many specific connotations. In the context of a **witness** it means restoring a witness' credibility after **cross-examination** has successfully **impeached** it. In **bankruptcy** it means the **reorganization** of a business or an arrangement with **creditors** that will restore **solvency** to the corporation. In **matrimonial actions,** the term **REHABILITATIVE ALIMONY** refers to temporary spousal support necessary to train a divorced person in useful skills so he or she will become employed and self-supporting and not be dependent upon society for financial survival. In criminal contexts, the term refers to efforts to become drug- or alcohol-free, to perform community service, to obtain educational or vocational training, or to otherwise demonstrate that the circumstances that were underlying the criminal behavior are not likely to recur and the person having bettered his or her situation can now be a productive member of society. **Judges** and **parole** boards look at rehabilitative efforts in sentencing and paroling criminals. See **mitigating circumstances.**

REHEARING a **retrial,** a new hearing and a new consideration of the case by the court (or other body) in which the suit was originally heard, and upon the **pleadings** and **depositions** already in the case.

REHEARING EN BANC see **en banc.**

REINSTATE restore to a former state, authority, station, or status from which one has been removed; as applied to insurance, to restore all benefits accruing under a policy. As applied to employment practices, if the former position no longer exists or is occupied by another with senior service, an obligation to reinstate may be satisfied by placing the person on a preferential employment list rather than by restoring the person to active employment.

REIT see **real estate investment trust [REIT].**

REJOINDER in **pleadings,** in **common law,** an answer to **plaintiff's** replication by some matter of fact, in an **action at law.**

RELATION BACK the principle that an act done at a later time is deemed by law to have occurred at a prior time, often for purposes of the **statute of limitations** or rules of procedure permitting amendment of **pleadings.**

RELATIVE refers to relationships by blood **(consanguinity),** marriage **(affinity),** or **adoption.**

RELATOR the **real party in interest** in whose behalf certain suits are brought by the state or the Attorney General when the right to sue resides solely in that official; the real party in interest in an **ex rel.** suit; also a person in whose behalf certain **writs** are issued, such as **informations** in the nature of **quo warranto.** Thus, a **habeas corpus** action is styled "United States ex rel. [defendant] vs. [warden]."

RELEASE a written document or the act of writing by which some **claim,** right or interest is given up to the person against whom the claim, right or interest could have been enforced.

In the law of property, the holder of a **fee simple** may **convey** to another a term of years and then subsequently release his or her **reversionary** interest **[LEASE AND RELEASE]** to the possessor of the term of years.

RELEASE ON RECOGNIZANCE [R.O.R.] a method by which an individual is released in lieu of providing **bail,** upon his or her promise to appear and answer a criminal charge. The R.O.R. procedure permits release on nonmonetary conditions, generally involving only the promise to appear, but sometimes involving special conditions (e.g., remaining in the **custody** of another, abiding by travel restrictions).

RELEVANCY [RELEVANT] a test concerning the admissibility of evidence. Evidence is relevant if it has a logical tendency, however slight, to prove a fact in issue.

RELEVANT MARKET a term used by the courts in determining whether a violation of an **antitrust** statute has occurred. Identification of the relevant market of a product takes into account not only the product but also its geographic area of distribution. Compare **monopoly.**

RELIANCE dependence, confidence, repose of mind upon what is deemed sufficient authority.

DETRIMENTAL RELIANCE reliance by one party on the acts, representations, or promises of another, which causes the first party to allow or to effect a worsening change in his position.

RELICTION gradual and imperceptible withdrawal of water from land that it covers, by lowering of the water's level from any cause. If the retreat of the waters is permanent, not merely seasonal, the owner of the contiguous property acquires ownership of the dry land thus created. Compare **avulsion; dereliction.**

RELIEF the redress or assistance awarded to a **complainant,** by the court, especially a **court of equity,** including such **remedies** as **specific performance, injunction, rescission** of a contract, etc.

EXAMPLE: Carlos ordered 200 items at a set price from a company that happens to be the only manufacturer of the item. Although his order has been produced, the company refuses to deliver unless Carlos pays a price increase. Carlos seeks *relief* from a court, which in this instance should be to order delivery since the item cannot be purchased elsewhere.

The term generally does not comprehend an award of money **damages.** Thus the term **AFFIRMATIVE RELIEF** is often used to indicate that the gist of relief is protection from future harm rather than compensation for past injury.

RELIEF TO LITIGANTS see **contempt of court.**

RELIGIOUS FREEDOM RESTORATION ACT federal law (held

unconstitutional as applied to states) preventing laws that substantially burden the personal free exercise of religion. The purpose is to prevent the federal government from substantially burdening religious exercise without compelling justification. Often applied to Native American religious claims as well as claims arising from religious exception to contraceptive requirements under the **Affordable Care Act.**

RELINQUISHMENT see **abandonment; abstention (doctrine).**

REM see **in rem.**

REMAINDER that part of an **estate** in land that is left upon the termination of the immediately preceding estate (often a life estate or estate for a term of years) and that does not amount to a **reversion** to the original grantor or his or her heirs. The remainder must be created by the same **conveyance** and at the same time, as the preceding estate; the remainder must **vest** in right during the continuance of the preceding estate; and no remainder can be created in connection with a **fee simple.**

CONTINGENT [EXECUTORY] REMAINDER any remainder subject to a CONDITION PRECEDENT (see **condition**), created in favor of an unborn person, or in favor of an existing but unascertained person. Such an interest was not, according to the older **common law** definition, an estate, but the possibility of an estate. A contingent remainder becomes a **vested** remainder only if any condition precedent is fulfilled and the **remainderman** is identified prior to the termination of the preceding estate.

EXECUTED REMAINDER a remainder interest that is vested as of the present time, though the enjoyment of it may be withheld until a future date.

VESTED REMAINDER a remainder created in favor of an existing and ascertained person who has the right to immediate possession at the termination of the preceding estate, or estates, subject only to another person's prior right to possession.

EXAMPLE: A grandfather conveys a house to his son for life, then to his oldest grandson. The grandson has a *vested remainder* in the house since he is entitled to it at the son's death. If the grandson predeceases the son, the house is distributed according to the provisions of the grandson's will.

REMAINDERMAN one who has an interest in the **estate** that becomes possessory **in futuro,** after the termination, by whatever reason, of a present possessory interest. Remainderman usually refers to one who holds an interest in a **remainder** whether **vested** or **contingent.**

REMAND to send back, as for further deliberation; to send back to the tribunal (or body) from which the matter was appealed or moved. When a judgment is **reversed,** the **appellate court** usually remands the matter for a new trial to be carried out consistent with the principles announced by the appellate court in its opinion ordering the remand.

REMEDY the means employed to enforce or redress an injury. The most common remedy **at law** consists of money **damages.**

EXTRAJUDICIAL REMEDY see **extrajudicial** [EXTRAJUDICIAL REMEDY].

EXTRAORDINARY REMEDY a **remedy** not usually available in an action at law or in **equity,** and ordinarily not employed unless the **evidence** clearly indicates that such a remedy is necessary to preserve the rights of the party. Examples include the appointment of a **receiver,** a decree of **specific performance,** the issuing of a **writ of mandamus** or **writ of prohibition** or of an **injunction.**

PROVISIONAL REMEDY one provided pursuant to a proceeding incidental to and in connection with a regular **action,** invoked while the primary action is pending, to assure that the claimant's rights will be preserved or that he or she will not suffer irreparable injury. Its connection to the primary action is termed **collateral.** Examples include **attachment,** temporary **restraining orders,** preliminary **injunctions,** appointment of **receivers.**

REMEDY, MUTUALITY OF see **mutuality of remedy.**

REMITTER the act by which a person, who has a good **title** to land, and enters upon the land with less than his or her original title, is restored to his or her original good title; the doctrine whereby the law will relate back from a defective title to an earlier valid title.

REMITTITUR *(rē-mǐ'-tǐ-tūr)* Lat.: reduction. The procedural process by which the **verdict** of a **jury** is diminished; describes any reduction made by the court, without the consent of the jury, to decrease an excessive verdict.

EXAMPLE: A jury awards several million dollars to a small electronics corporation as compensation for anticompetitive practices by a multinational company. The judge is unsure whether the evidence supports a finding against the large company but is not willing to overturn the jury's decision on that issue. Still, he feels that the award is much too great and by *remittitur* reduces the award to one million dollars. If the reduction is not accepted by the plaintiff, the judge will set the entire verdict aside and order a new trial.

REMOTE CAUSE see **cause** [REMOTE CAUSE].

REMOVAL 1. a change in place or position, as the removal of a **proceeding** to another court, especially from state to federal court; 2. the process by which a public official is stripped of office for cause.

REMOVE CLOUD ON TITLE see **quiet title** [REMOVE CLOUD ON TITLE].

RENDER to officially announce a decision, either orally in open court or by memorandum filed with the clerk.

RENDITION the covert transportation for interrogation of a foreigner suspected of crimes, such as terrorism, to another country known to have harsher and less stringently regulated methods of interrogation.

RENEWAL continuation in force and effect of a previously existing arrangement for a new period, as a **lease** or a **note,** on the same or different terms. Insurance policies are renewed from term to term.

RENOUNCE an affirmative declaration of abandonment; giving up of a title or claim. See **renunciation.**

RENT a profit in money, goods, or labor issuing periodically out of land and **tenements,** constituting a return for the privilege of use.

RENUNCIATION in criminal law, the voluntary and complete abandonment of criminal purpose prior to the commission of a crime, or an act otherwise preventing its commission. In some jurisdictions it is an **affirmative defense** (see **defense**) to inchoate, or incipient, offenses such as **attempts, conspiracy, solicitation** or offenses dependent upon the conduct of another (i.e., **accessorial** crimes).

EXAMPLE: Vladimir devises an intricate plan to rob a bank, but, on the evening on which he plans to carry it out, he finds that workmen are redecorating the bank's interior. He postpones the robbery until he can formulate a new plan. He has not *renunciated* the crime since he plans to rob the bank at another opportunity, even if that opportunity never arises or the new plan is not carried out. If he has a genuine change of heart and voluntarily destroys the blueprint of the bank, this might satisfy the requirements of *renunciation.*

Compare **withdrawal.**

RENVOI *(rähn'-vwä)* Fr.: rule in some jurisdictions that in a **suit** by a nonresident upon a cause arising locally, his or her capacity to sue will be determined by looking to the law of his or her **domicile** rather than to the local law. The problem of *renvoi* is nothing more than the question whether the whole law including its **conflict of laws** of a foreign state is looked to for solution when a reference is made to the law of another state. If the reference is to the whole law, as is often the case, an application of the *renvoi* concept is involved. Take, for example, the case of a citizen of the United States permanently residing in France who dies leaving movables in New York. Assuming the New York conflict of laws rule to be that the law of the **decedent's domicile** will govern this matter, the New York **forum** would look to the "law" of France. If the forum should look to the law applicable to a French person dying in France leaving movables there, the court would be rejecting the use of *renvoi*. If, however, the forum looks to the whole law, i.e., including the French conflicts rule, this is using the *renvoi*.

REORGANIZATION the transaction by which the **stock** of property of one **corporation** is exchanged for the stock or property of another corporation. The **shareholders** of the old corporation generally hold the same proportion of stock in the new corporation. The term is most often used to mean reorganization under Chapter X of the Federal Bankruptcy Act. See **bankruptcy.**

In corporate income tax law, a group of transactions including mergers, consolidations, recapitalizations, acquisitions of the stock or assets of another corporation, and changes in form or place of organization. The common element in each of these transactions is that if various technical requirements are met, the corporations or shareholders involved may not recognize any gain for income tax purposes, and the transation will occur tax free.

REPAIR see **tenantable repair.**

REPEAL abrogation or annulling of a previous law by the enactment of a subsequent statute, which either expressly declares that the former law shall be revoked, or contains provisions so irreconcilable with those of the earlier law as to abrogate the earlier law by necessary **implication.** Compare **amend.**

REPEAT OFFENDER see **criminal [HABITUAL OFFENDER]; three strikes.**

REPLEVIN a legal form of **action** ordinarily employed only to recover **possession** of specific **personal property** unlawfully withheld from the plaintiff, plus **damages** for its detention. In this primarily possessory action, the issues ordinarily are limited to the plaintiff's **title** to the goods.

EXAMPLE: Arthi leaves a shipment of goods in a warehouse and prepays storage costs for three months. At the end of that time, she goes to pick up the goods, but the warehouse refuses to release them until she pays for the storage. Arthi sues for *replevin* to obtain the goods.

REPLEVY to secure, especially by an **action** in **replevin,** redelivery of goods that have been kept from the rightful owner.

REPLICATION the plaintiff's answer or reply to the defendant's **plea** or **answer.** See **pleadings.**

REPLY a defensive **pleading** by one who has made a complaint; the sole purpose of reply is to interpose a **defense** to **new matter** pleaded in the **answer.** In modern practice a reply is an extraordinary pleading and is not permitted except to respond to a **counterclaim** or by leave of court to an answer or third-party answer.

EXAMPLE: A store owner sues Annika for failure to pay a debt. Annika files a counterclaim against the store owner claiming that the washer and dryer Annika purchased, which gave rise to the debt, have never worked properly. The store owner can *reply* to the counterclaim that he is not responsible for the problem or that Annika has not operated the machines correctly.

REPORTERS see **court reporters; reports.**

REPORTS official published court or administrative agency decisions that are collectively grouped by date and court of issuance into bound volumes thus comprising the **case law** for that jurisdiction. The reports (also known as reporters) have **headnotes** written by the publisher. Some examples of reports are found in the Table of Abbreviations. The United States Supreme Court has three reporters: United States Reports, Supreme Court Reporter, and Lawyer's Edition Supreme Court Reports.

REPOSE in civil actions, the maximum time period within which an **action** may be brought, regardless of injury. While a **statute of limitations** limits the remedy of going to court, a **STATUTE OF REPOSE** limits the underlying cause of action. See also **res judicata.**

REPOSSESSION seizure or foreclosure. Either by judicial action or **self-help,** the secured **creditor,** to satisfy the **debtor's** obligation, takes **possession** of the **property** after the debtor **defaults** on his payments.

REPRESENT [REPRESENTATION] to stand in another's place; to speak with authority on behalf of another; to appear on one's behalf. As an element of actionable fraud, representation includes deeds or acts calculated to mislead another, as well as words or positive assertions. In insurance law, a representation is an oral or written statement preceding the insurance policy and, though not part of it, is used to enable the **underwriter** to form a judgment as to whether he or she will accept the risk. Only a false misrepresentation that materially affects the risk will permit the insurer to rescind the policy. In commercial law, a representation is anything short of a **warranty** and is sufficient to create a distinct impression of fact conducive to action.

In constitutional law, the **Sixth Amendment's** right of assistance of counsel in a criminal case includes the right to adequate and effective representation. This standard includes the right to an attorney who knows the relevant law, does not have any conflicts in the case at hand, adheres to all legal procedural requirements so as not to forfeit any rights, and vigorously pursues a client's cast at trial through direct and cross-examinations, the filing of motions, and the raising of objections. Representation so lacking in competence creates a duty on a trial judge to correct such to prevent a mockery of justice.

In property law, "representation" permits children or more remote lineal descendants of a predeceased relative of the **intestate** to stand in their predeceased ancestor's shoes for purposes of inheritance. Representation is equivalent to **per stirpes** (meaning by the stock or roots). Compare **per capita.** See **proportional representation; virtual representation.**

REPRESENTATIVE agent; one who acts for another in a special capacity. One's status as a representative entitles the person to a number of rights including the right to discovery of trial preparation materials, and the right to bargain collectively on behalf of employees. See **personal representative; registered representative.**

REPRIEVE in criminal law, the postponement of a **sentence** for an interval in which the execution is suspended. Compare **commutation; pardon.** See also **executive clemency.**

REPUBLICATION an affirmative act of **reviving** a **will** after it has been destroyed or otherwise replaced by a subsequent will, and is frequently accomplished by use of a **codicil.** In those jurisdictions permitting republication, the mere revocation of the subsequent will shall not revive the earlier will without some type of affirmative act.

REPUDIATION refusal by one party to perform a contractual obligation to another party. See **anticipatory breach.**

REPUTATION EVIDENCE see **witness [CHARACTER WITNESS].**

REQUIREMENTS CONTRACT see **contract [REQUIREMENTS CONTRACT].**

RES *(rās)* Lat.: a thing. The subject matter of **actions** that are primarily **in rem,** i.e., actions that establish rights in relation to an object, as opposed to a person (**in personam**). For example, in an action that resolves a conflict over **title** to **real property,** the land in question is the *res*. Tangible **personal property** can also be a *res,* as in the **corpus** of a **trust.**

EXAMPLE: A mother creates a trust for her children, providing that the rentals from an office building be distributed to each child every month. The office building is the trust *res* since it generates the income that is distributed to the children.

In a QUASI IN REM (see **quasi**) **proceeding,** land or **chattels** that are seized and **attached** at the beginning of the action, in order that they may later be used to satisfy a personal **claim,** are the *res* of such suits. The term refers as well to the status of individuals. Thus, in a divorce suit, the marital status is the *res*. The purpose of a *res* is to establish a court's **jurisdiction:** if the property lies within the state where the action is brought, or an individual in a divorce action is a **domiciliary** of the state, then jurisdiction is established.

RES AJUDICATA see **res judicata.**

RESCIND to abrogate a **contract,** release the parties from further obligations to each other and restore the parties to the STATUS QUO ante, (see **status quo**) or the positions they would have occupied if the contract had never been made. Compare **rescission.**

RESCISSION cancellation of a **contract** and the return of the parties to the positions they would have occupied if the contract had not been made (see **status quo [STATUS QUO ANTE]**). Grounds for rescission may include original invalidity of the agreement, **fraud,** failure of **consideration,** or **material breach** or **default.** Rescission may be brought about by the mutual consent of the parties, by the conduct of the parties or by a decree by a **court of equity.** See **repudiation; revocation.** Compare **rescind.**

RESCRIPT a statement of the decision of the highest appellate tribunal; a direction from that tribunal to a lower court to enter a **decree** in accordance with that direction, in effect remanding the case to the lower court for the entry of a decree.

RESCUE the act of aiding a person in imminent and serious peril, which, as a matter of law, cannot give rise to a charge of contributory negligence against the rescuer in risking his or her own life or serious injury in attempting to effect the rescue, provided the attempt is not made recklessly or rashly.

RESCUE DOCTRINE tort rule that holds a **tortfeasor** liable to his or her victim's rescuer, should the latter injure himself or herself during a reasonable rescue attempt. The premise is that the wrong is not only to the imperiled victim, but also to the rescuer. See **Good Samaritan.**

RESERVATION 1. a clause in any **instrument** of **conveyance,** such as a **deed,** that creates a lesser **estate,** or some right, interest or profit in the estate granted, to be retained by the **grantor;** 2. a tract of land, usually substantial, set aside for specific purposes such as military grounds, parks, Indian lands. Compare **reversion; under protest.**

RESERVE funds kept available to meet future contingencies. Examples include funds banks must keep on hand to meet depositors' withdrawals, insurance company liabilities, and pension payments. The funds that must be presently retained are usually a percentage of the institution's full liability for the particular need. See **accumulation depreciation; depreciation reserve.**

RESERVE CLAUSE clause generally found in sports contracts, giving a team that first signs a player a continuing and exclusive right to that player's services, even beyond the length of the contract, and to the point of obligating other teams to respect and enforce those rights. Such clauses have less effect than they once did, and players in most sports are free to move to other teams after their contract expires.

RESERVE DECISION see **reservation [RESERVE DECISION].**

RESERVED POINT see **point reserved.**

RESERVED POWERS see **Tenth Amendment.**

RES GESTAE *(rās gĕś -tí)* Lat.: the thing done. Spontaneous exclamations or statements so closely connected to an occurrence they are considered part of that occurrence. Declarations that are subject to the **hearsay rule** may be admissible if they qualify as *res gestae;* i.e., if they constitute a part of the thing done under a recognized exception to the hearsay rule.

RESIDENCE broadly, any place of abode that is more than temporary. See **retreat, duty to; search and seizure; self-defense.** Compare **domicile.**

RESIDENT ALIEN see **alien.**

RESIDENTIAL COMMUNITY TREATMENT CENTERS see **halfway houses.**

RESIDUARY BEQUEST see **bequest [RESIDUARY BEQUEST]; residuary legacy.**

RESIDUARY CLAUSE clause in a **will** that conveys to the beneficiary of a **residuary legacy** (residuary **legatee**) everything in a **testator's estate** not **devised** to a specific legatee; a testamentary clause that includes in its gift any property or interest in the will that, for any reason, eventually falls into the general residue, because specific legacies were **void,** the disposition was illegal, or because for any other reason it was impossible that the legacy should take effect; and it includes such legacies as may lapse by events subsequent to the making of the will. It operates to transfer to the residuary legatee such portion of his or her property as the testator has not perfectly disposed of.

EXAMPLE: In his will Manny leaves his antique car to a cousin who predeceases him. He also provides a *residuary clause* that leaves any of his property not already disposed of in the will to his oldest son. In addition to receiving all of Manny's property not left to others, the son, as the residuary legatee, also receives the antique car.

RESIDUARY ESTATE that part of a **testator's estate** that remains undisposed of after all of the estate has been discharged through the satisfaction of all claims and specific legacies with the exception of the dispositions authorized by the **residuary clause.**

RESIDUARY LEGACY a general **legacy** into which all the assets of the estate fall after satisfaction of other legacies, payment of all debts of the estate and all costs of administration.

RESIDUUM the substance or part remaining after some other part has been taken away.

RESIDUUM RULE in administrative law, the principle that a decision rendered by an administrative agency and based in part on incompetent **evidence** will be upheld on judicial review if it is supported by a residuum of competent evidence. The federal courts have rejected the residuum rule.

RES IPSA LOQUITUR *(rās ĭp'-sà lō'-kwĭ-tûr)* Lat.: the thing speaks for itself. Refers to a rule of **evidence** whereby **negligence** of the alleged wrongdoer may be inferred from the mere fact that the accident happened, provided (1) that in the absence of negligence the accident would not have occurred and (2) the thing that caused the injury is shown to have been under the exclusive control of the alleged wrongdoer. The procedural effect of successful invocation of the doctrine is to shift the **burden** of going forward with the evidence, normally borne by the plaintiff, to the defendant, who is thereby charged with introducing evidence to refute the **presumption** of negligence that has been created.

EXAMPLE: An accident occurs when the brakes of a new car fail

495

on its first trip from the dealer. The victim claims negligence on the part of the car manufacturer and points to the failed brakes as evidence. Under the doctrine of *res ipsa loquitur,* the manufacturer must now provide evidence to show that some cause other than its negligence is responsible for the accident.

RESISTANCE see **utmost resistance.**

RESISTING ARREST common-law offense involving physical efforts to oppose a lawful arrest.

RES JUDICATA *(rās jŭ-dĭ-kä'-tà)* Lat.: a thing decided; a matter adjudged. The phrase reflects a rule by which a final **judgment** by a court of competent **jurisdiction** is conclusive upon the **parties** in any subsequent **litigation** involving the same **cause of action.** See **bar; merger.**

EXAMPLE. Two parties litigate an issue in one federal district court, and the defendant loses. Under the principle of *res judicata,* the defendant could not then go to another federal district court and litigate the same issue a second time.

Compare **collateral [COLLATERAL ESTOPPEL].**

RESPITE 1. a delay, postponement or **forbearance** of a **sentence,** not comprehending a permanent suspension of **execution** of the **judgment;** 2. a delay in repayment, granted to a debtor by his creditor. See **grace period; reprieve.**

RESPONDEAT SUPERIOR *(rā-spôn'-dā-ät sū-pĕr'-ē-ôr)* Lat.: let the superior reply. This doctrine is invoked when there is a master-**servant** relationship between two parties. The premise is that when an employer (master) is acting through the facility of an employee or **agent** (servant), and tort **liability** is incurred during the course of this **agency** because of some fault of the agent, then the employer or master must accept the responsibility. Implicit is the **common law** notion that everyone must conduct his or her affairs without injuring another, whether or not he or she employs agents or servants. See **scope of employment.** Compare **vicarious liability.**

EXAMPLE: A truck driver employed by a manufacturing company causes an accident while delivering a shipment to a buyer. The doctrine of *respondeat superior* allows the victims to sue the company for any injuries caused by the driver. Under normal principles of tort responsibility, the driver can also be sued. Since it is unlikely that he has the money to pay a damage award, the doctrine acts to assure that the victims will be paid the full amount of the award because the company by law will be required to carry adequate insurance or have sufficient assets for such contingencies. Absent this doctrine, companies would be able to hire judgment-proof drivers and in that fashion avoid all liability for injuries caused by such drivers.

RESPONDENT 1. in **equity,** the party who answers a **pleading.** 2. the party against whom an **appeal** is prosecuted.

RESPONSIBILITY the obligation to answer for an act and to repair any injury caused by that; the state of being answerable for an obligation. As used in statutes such as those governing awards of local public contracts to **RESPONSIBLE BIDDERS,** the term refers to the characteristic the absence of which would cause fair-minded and reasonable persons to believe it was not in the best interest of the municipality to award the contract to the lowest bidder, and may involve experience, financial ability and adequate facilities.

RESPONSIBILITY, DIMINISHED see **diminished capacity.**

RESPONSIVE PLEADING see **pleadings [RESPONSIVE PLEAD-INGS].**

RESTATEMENT an attempt by the American Law Institute [A.L.I.] to present an orderly statement of the general **common law** of the United States, including not only the law developed by judicial decision, but also the law that has evolved from the application of statutes by the courts. Restatements are compiled according to subject matter: **contracts, torts, property, trusts, agency, conflict of laws, judgments, restitution, security** and **foreign relations**.

RESTITUTION act of making good or of giving the equivalent for loss, damage or injury. As a remedy, restitution is available to prevent **unjust enrichment,** to correct an erroneous payment and to permit an **aggrieved party** to recover deposits advanced on a contract. As a contract remedy, restitution is limited to the value of a performance rendered by the injured party, and ordinarily requires that both parties to a transaction be returned to the STATUS QUO (see **status quo**).

In criminal law, restitution is sometimes ordered as a condition of a **probationary sentence.** Compare **indemnity.**

RESTRAINING ORDER an **order** granted without notice or hearing, demanding the preservation of the **status quo** until a hearing can be held to determine the propriety of **injunctive** relief, temporary or permanent. A restraining order is always temporary, since it is granted pending a hearing; thus it is often called a **T.R.O.,** a **temporary restraining order.**

EXAMPLE: A federal agency grants a lumber company permission to cut wood on federal lands. An environmental group immediately goes to court and seeks a *restraining order* prohibiting the cutting of any trees until the validity of the grant is determined. The order probably will be issued since irreparable damage will be caused by cutting the trees, provided the group can produce a minimum of evidence that their position as to the illegality of the grant is correct.

RESTRAINT, JUDICIAL see **judicial restraint.**

RESTRAINT OF TRADE in **common law** and as used in the antitrust laws, illegal restraints interfering with free competition in commercial transactions, which tend to restrict production, affect prices or otherwise control the market to the detriment of consumers of goods and services.

RESTRAINT ON ALIENATION restriction on the ability to **convey** real property interests, any attempt at which is in **derogation** of the **common law** policy in favor of free alienability. Such restrictions often are void or voidable as unlawful restraints on **alienation.**

RESTRAINT, PRIOR see **prior restraint.**

RESTRICTED SECURITIES **securities** acquired from an issuer in a nonpublic transfer, that is, on terms and at a price not offered to the general public through an **underwriter.** Since the securities were not part of a public offering and thus not subject to the safeguards of the Securities Act of 1933, such as the registration of the securities and the issuing of a prospectus, their sale to the public is restricted. Under S.E.C. rules, restricted stock must be held at least two years prior to its sale on an established securities market, and may only be sold in small amounts. Restricted stock is often referred to as LETTERED STOCK since the certificate must bear a legend reciting the restrictions to which it is subject. It is also known as INVESTMENT STOCK.

RESTRICTIVE COVENANT a promise as part of an agreement, restricting the use of **real property** or the kind of buildings that may be erected. The promise is usually expressed by the creation of a **covenant, reservation** or exception in a **deed.** In order for a grantor to enforce the covenant against remote grantees [subsequent owners who take **title** from the first grantee], the covenant must **run with the land.**

EXAMPLE: When Marshall sells a plot of land next to his house, he includes a *restrictive covenant* with the deed that no structure over two and one-half stories will be constructed on the land. Since the covenant is included with the deed, it is valid against any and all other purchasers of the land.

RESTRICTIVE INDORSEMENT see **indorsement [RESTRICTIVE INDORSEMENT].**

RESULTING TRUST see **trust [RESULTING TRUST].**

RESULTING USE see **use [RESULTING USE].**

RETAIL INSTALLMENT CONTRACT generally, a **contract** consisting of a promissory **note** and a **chattel mortgage;** a contract whereby the seller retains **title** to, or a security or property interest in, **goods** purchased by a buyer who is obligated to make periodic payments for the goods. In some states, the term also includes certain types of **leases. See installment contract.**

RETAINER compensation paid in advance to an attorney for services to be performed in a specific case. A retainer may be the whole sum to be charged (plus expenses) but more often is a deposit, with the attorney furnishing a periodic or final statement of how much the client owes for services rendered.

RETALIATORY EVICTION see **eviction [RETALIATORY EVICTION].**

RETIRE 1. in reference to **bills of exchange,** to recover or redeem by payment of a sum of money; to withdraw from circulation or from the market.

2. A **jury** is retired when the judge has submitted the case for its consideration and **verdict.**

RETIREMENT PLAN a plan provided by an employer or a self-employed individual for an employee's or self-employed individual's retirement. Because of the tax advantages, most retirement plans are designed to insure a present **deduction** to the employer while the employee is permitted to avoid **recognizing** the **income** until he or she has actually or **constructively** received it.

DB(K) see **db(k).**

DEFERRED COMPENSATION a plan under whose terms an employee defers payment of a portion of his or her salary in return for the employer's promise to pay the employee the salary at some time in the future. Generally, if such plan is not financed by irrevocably setting the fund aside for the employee or guaranteed by insurance, the employee will not recognize income from such plan until he or she is actually paid, and the employer does not obtain a deduction under such plan until the employee recognizes the income.

401(K) named after a section in the U.S. Internal Revenue Code. A 401(k) is a type of employer-sponsored defined contribution retirement plan. Employees select the portion of their wages to be directed to their account. Some employers will match a portion of their employees' contributions.

INDIVIDUAL RETIREMENT ACCOUNT [IRA] an account to which the employee pays a specified tax-exempt sum, whose earned income is also tax-exempt when specified limitations upon withdrawal are adhered to.

INHERITED IRA individual retirement account(s) that are left to one or more beneficiaries when the original IRA owner dies.

KEOGH PLAN a pension or profit-sharing plan set up by a self-employed individual.

NON QUALIFIED PENSION OR PROFIT-SHARING PLAN a plan created by an employer for an employee that does not qualify for a present deduction to the employer and deferral of income recognition to the employee. In such cases the employer is generally not permitted to take a deduction for the amount set aside until the employee recognizes such amount as income.

PENSION FUND [PLAN] any plan, fund, or program that provides retirement income to employees or results in a deferral of income by employees for periods extending to the termination of covered employment or beyond. This definition is intended to reach a wide variety of retirement benefit structures, including profit-sharing plans that meet these requirements, with the only limitation being the express language of the plan providing for retirement benefits or deferral of income.

QUALIFIED PENSION OR PROFIT-SHARING PLAN a plan set up by an employer for an employee or a group of employees that allows the employer to pay into a **trust** a certain sum or percentage of compensation for the employees. The employer obtains a present deduction for the contributions but the employee does not recognize the income until it is actually paid to him.

ROLLOVER a method whereby an employee converts from one qualified plan to another without the recognition as income of the sum rolled over.

ROTH 401 (K) a type of retirement plan that combines the features of a **Roth IRA** and a traditional **401(k).** Starting in 2006, businesses were able to offer their employees the Roth IRA type of tax treatment for their 401(k) contributions.

ROTH IRA this is a special variant of the traditional IRA which does not provide a tax deduction for contributions but which under strict rules, does allow the gains to be distributed, tax free and at ages beyond age 59 ½.

RETIREMENT SECURITY ACT see **ERISA.**

RETRACTION the withdrawing of a **plea,** declaration, **accusation,** promise, etc.

RETRAXIT a voluntary renunciation by a **plaintiff** in open court of his or her suit and cause of action and that bars a second action between the same parties on the same grounds; it is **dismissal with prejudice,** equivalent to a **verdict** and **judgment on the merits** of the case.

RETREAT, DUTY TO a duty found in some jurisdictions obligating a person to retreat from a dangerous situation rather than employ **self-defense** and injure another. However, one is not usually required to retreat when attacked in one's own home. In tort law, the failure to exercise one's duty to retreat may create liability in the party who could have retreated. In criminal law, the failure to retreat except from one's home or from a robber will foreclose the defense of self-defense in a minority of states.

RETRIAL a new trial in which an issue or issues already litigated, and as to which a verdict or decision by the court has been rendered, are reexamined by the same court for some sufficient reason, such as a recognition that the initial trial was improper or unfair as a result of procedural errors. Compare **mistrial.**

RETROACTIVE refers to a rule of law, whether legislative or judicial, that relates to things decided in the past. "Retroactive" includes both retrospective and **ex post facto,** the former technically applying only to **civil** laws, the latter to criminal or penal laws. A **RETRO-SPECTIVE LAW** is one that relates back to a previous transaction and gives it some different legal effect from that which it had under the law when it occurred. A retrospective law is constitutionally objectionable if it impairs **vested** rights acquired under existing laws, or creates a new obligation or attaches a new disability with respect to past transactions. Similarly, an ex post facto law retroactively imposes criminal liability on behavior that took place prior to enactment of the criminal statute. State constitutions may prohibit their legislatures from enacting retrospective laws; ex post facto laws are prohibited by the Constitution of the United States.

Judicially created law (common law) is often retroactive in its effect, since the court's decision is made on the basis of old facts as to which the litigants could not possibly have predicted at the time of their actions the court's eventual interpretation of the law; nevertheless they are bound by it.

In constitutional law, decisions announcing new or different rights favoring criminal defendants are often given full retroactive effect so as to permit a **COLLATERAL ATTACK** (see *collateral)* on previously finalized judgments.

EXAMPLE: The state supreme court rules that any person affected by the use of a particular police procedure can exclude evidence so obtained. The court also rules that this right is only available after the date of this decision. The latter ruling means that the law is prospective only and has no *retroactive* effect and that any person already tried cannot take advantage of the new rule. If the decision had retroactive effect, every person who has been convicted or whose trial is in progress and who has not been permitted to challenge the legality of the evidence used against him could now raise the issue.

Compare **statute of limitations.**

RETROSPECTIVE see **retroactive.**

RETURN 1. a report from an official, such as a sheriff, stating what he or she has done in respect to a command from the court, or why he or she has failed to do what was requested. See **false return.**

2. a report from an individual or **corporation** as to its earnings, etc., for tax or other governmental purposes.

RETURN, INCOME TAX a document by which a **taxpayer** or his representative provides information to the **Internal Revenue Service** relevant to the determination of the taxpayer's tax liability for a specified period.

AMENDED RETURN a return by which a taxpayer or his or her representative corrects information contained in an earlier return. An amended return may require an additional payment of tax (possibly with interest and/or penalties) or be accompanied by a **claim for refund.**

DECLARATION OF ESTIMATED TAX a return required of those taxpayers who do not regularly withhold income, as in the case of self-employed taxpayers, who expect that the total amount of their withholdings will not cover their tax liability for the tax year, and whose filing is accompanied by payments of estimated tax.

FALSE RETURN see **false return.**

FILING the process by which the taxpayer transmits the return to the Service. The **Internal Revenue Code** sets forth the due dates for the filing of the various returns and rules exist for determining whether or not the returns are timely filed.

INFORMATION RETURN any of a number of returns that only communicate information to the Service relevant to tax liability but that do not compute the actual liability of any taxpayer or accompany the actual payment of tax.

JOINT RETURN a return filed by a husband and wife, setting forth tax information concerning each of them, and computing a joint tax liability.

REVALUATION SURPLUS see **unearned surplus [REVALUA-TION SURPLUS].**

REV. abbreviation for revenue, review, revised.

REV'D abbreviation for "reversed."

REVENUE **income** from whatever source derived; that which returns or comes back from an investment.

REVENUE BILLS bills that levy taxes. Federal revenue bills are required to originate in the House of Representatives. Many states have similar constitutional provisions requiring that such bills originate in a particular house of a legislature, or that the bills shall not be passed in the last five days of the legislative session.

REVENUE PROCEDURE see **revenue ruling [REVENUE PROCE-DURE].**

REVENUE RULING a published decision by the **Internal Revenue Service** in the Internal Revenue Bulletin applying the federal tax laws to a particular set of facts. Revenue Rulings (as opposed to **PRIVATE RULINGS**) may be relied upon by **taxpayers** in determining the **tax** impact upon them of a similar set of facts.

PRIVATE RULING a determination by the Internal Revenue Service issued to a taxpayer who has asked for a determination as to the tax impact upon such taxpayer of a particular transaction. The determination is binding with respect to that taxpayer only and may not be relied upon by other taxpayers. These private rulings are published with the identifying characteristics of the taxpayer and the transaction deleted.

REVENUE PROCEDURE a published determination by the Internal Revenue Service concerning the administrative practices in the Internal Revenue Service. For example, the method and requirements for obtaining a private ruling are often published in revenue procedure.

REVERSAL as used in **opinions, judgments** and **mandates,** the **vacating** or changing to the contrary the decision of a lower court or other body. Compare **affirm; overrule; remand.**

REVERSE DISCRIMINATION a term referring to the practice of excluding a classification or race of people who have not been historically discriminated against, usually whites, from positions that are made available exclusively to persons or groups that have traditionally been the subject of discrimination, or who otherwise benefit from **affirmative action** programs. The term has been applied to the practice of reserving positions for minorities in school admissions programs, corporate promotions, and rehiring of blacks with less job seniority than whites. The contention that affirmative action violates the **equal protection clause** of the **Fourteenth Amendment** and Title VI of the **Civil Rights Act,** has been the cause of differing opinions by members of the Supreme Court.

REVERSE MORTGAGE see **mortgage [REVERSE MORTGAGE].**

REVERSIBLE ERROR error substantially affecting **appellant's** legal rights and obligations that, if uncorrected, would result in a miscarriage of justice and that justifies **reversing** a **judgment** in the inferior court; synonymous with **PREJUDICIAL ERROR.** See **error; plain error; harmless error.**

EXAMPLE: In his summation to the jury, a prosecutor makes disparaging remarks concerning the defendant Jules' failure to take the stand, thus violating the defendant's constitutional right to remain silent. The defendant objects and the judge tells the jury to disregard the remarks. The jury finds Jules guilty. On appeal, the appellate court finds the prosecutor's remarks so blatant that no amount of instructions by the judge could eliminate the prejudice that was caused. The remarks constitute *reversible error,* and Jules is granted a new trial.

REVERSION an **interest** created by operation of law by a **conveyance** of less than an absolute interest in property, thus leaving in the **grantor** some present or future right or interest in the property; a **FUTURE ESTATE** (see **estate**) created by operation of law to take effect in possession in favor of a **lessor** or a grantor or his or her **heirs,** or the heirs of a **testator,** after the natural termination of a prior particular estate **leased,** granted or **devised.** Compare **remainder; reservation.**

REVERTER see **reversion.** See also **possibility of a reverter.**

REVEST returning to the possession of the **donor** or the former **proprietor.**

REV'G abbreviation for "reversing."

REVIEW judicial reexamination of the proceedings of a court or other body; a reconsideration by the same court or body of its former decision; also, an **appellate court's** examination of the **record** of a lower court or agency's determination that is on **appeal** to the appellate court. See **bill of review; judicial review.**

REVISED STATUTES statutes that have been altered, reorganized or reenacted. Their enactment is generally regarded as repealing and replacing the former laws.

REVIVAL in the law of **wills,** the act reinstituting a former will (which had been **revoked** by a latter will) once the latter will is canceled or destroyed. A few jurisdictions recognize the former will automatically upon the latter will's cancellation; most require some affirmative act, such as **republication,** before the former will is effective.

REVOCABLE able to be terminated at the **maker's** discretion. See **revocation.**

REVOCATION 1. recall of authority conferred; 2. cancellation of an **instrument** previously made; 3. cancellation of an **offer** by the offeror, which, if effective, terminates the offeree's power of **acceptance.**

EXAMPLE: Steel Pipe Company offers to buy used pipe from a supplier at 15 cents a foot. Before the supplier responds, Steel realizes it has offered to buy the wrong type of pipe and *revokes* its offer. Since the supplier has not acted, the revocation is effective.

REVOCATION OF PAROLE [PROBATION] see **probation [REVOCATION OF PAROLE; REVOCATION OF PROBATION].**

REVOCATION OF WILL an affirmative act, such as writing "annulled" or "void" across the face of the **will,** or other marks on the words of the instrument and not just on the margin; or by tearing off the signatures at the end of the will, all of which operate to render the instrument invalid for purposes of **probate.** Some courts require that the markings must affect the entire will or there is not revocation, while others allow particular names to be eliminated, although attempts to write in a new name will not be effective unless independently signed and witnessed.

REVOKE 1. to recall a power previously conferred; 2. to **vacate** an **instrument** previously made; 3. to annul, **repeal, rescind** or cancel privileges, e.g., **parole, probation,** driver's license.

EXAMPLE: Eric is involved in numerous accidents and moving violations and accumulates enough points on his driving record for Massachusetts to revoke his driving privileges.

REVOLVING CREDIT renewable **credit** line over a set period of time. The term refers generally to credit extended by a banker or merchant for a certain amount that can be paid off periodically.

REV. STAT. see **revised statutes.**

RFLP see **DNA testing [RFLP].**

RFRA see **religious freedom restoration act.**

RICO see **Racketeer Influenced and Corrupt Organizations Act [RICO].**

RIDER 1. an amendment or addition attached to a document usually found as an attachment to an insurance policy identifying changes or increases in coverage; 2. in the legislative process, a provision in a bill that is not germane to the main purpose of the law.

EXAMPLE: The president wants to increase the federal excise tax on gasoline five cents to raise revenues needed to repair the nation's roads and bridges. Knowing that the president is anxious to approve the bill, a senator attaches to it a *rider* providing for an unrelated measure he was having difficulty getting support for by itself.

RIGGED ORDERS see **manipulation [RIGGED ORDERS].**

RIGHT see **civil rights; claim of rights; constitutional right; inalienable rights; inherent right; preemptive rights; rights; subscription rights; vested [VESTED RIGHTS]; visitation rights; voting right; Voting Rights Act.**

RIGHTFUL HEIRS see **heirs.**

RIGHT OF ACTION see **cause of action.**

RIGHT OF ELECTION in probate law, the statutory right of a surviving spouse to elect to take either what the deceased spouse gave under the **will,** or a share of the deceased spouse's estate as set forth by statute. Compare **dower.**

RIGHT OF FIRST PUBLICATION see **copyright [RIGHT OF FIRST PUBLICATION].**

RIGHT OF FIRST REFUSAL right of a purchaser to be given the opportunity to purchase before any other buyer. If the purchaser declines the offer, the seller may then offer the transaction to others. Similar to a call option, see **stock option [CALL OPTION],** but ROFR applies in various contexts, including real estate and real property ventures.

RIGHT OF FIRST OFFER by contrast, a ROFO only means an agreement to negotiate in good faith before negotiating with other potential purchasers.

RIGHT OF PRIVACY see **privacy, right of.**

RIGHT OF REDEMPTION see **redemption [RIGHT OF REDEMPTION].**

RIGHT OF REENTRY see **reentry, right of.**

RIGHT OF WAY 1. in property law, an **easement** to use another's land for passage; 2. in the context of vehicular traffic, the right of a vehicle or pedestrian to proceed on the road, while others yield.

RIGHT OR WRONG TEST see **insanity [M'NAGHTEN RULE].**

RIGHTS 1. individual liberties in a constitutional sense; 2. **proprietary,** contractual or legal rights. 3. in the context of securities trading, a negotiable privilege to buy a new **issue** of stock at a subscription price lower than the market price of outstanding stock. Compare **stock option; warrant.** See **civil rights; claim of rights; constitutional right; inalienable rights; inherent right; preemptive rights; rights; subscription rights; vested [VESTED RIGHTS]; visitation rights; voting right; Voting Rights Act.**

RIGHT TO CONVEY see **covenant [COVENANT OF SEISIN AND RIGHT TO CONVEY].**

RIGHT TO COUNSEL **Sixth Amendment** guarantee that an accused person shall have effective legal counsel for his or her defense to a criminal charge. **Indigent** persons are entitled to have an attorney appointed to represent them. See **public defender.**

RIGHT TO DIE see **euthanasia [PASSIVE EUTHANASIA].**

RIGHT TO REMAIN SILENT see **Miranda rule.**

RIGHT TO WORK LAWS see **open shop.**

RIGHT, WRIT OF see **writ of right.**

RIGOR MORTIS *(rĭ-gôr môr'-tĭs)* Lat.: stiffness of death. Medical terminology depicting the rigidity of the muscles after death.

RIPARIAN RIGHTS rights that accrue to owners of land on the banks of bodies of water, such as the use of such water, and ownership of soil under the water. The lands to which these natural rights are attached are called in law **RIPARIAN LANDS.**

RIPE FOR JUDGMENT the point in a case when everything seems to have been done that ought to be done before entry of a final adjudication upon the rights of the parties. See **ripeness.**

RIPENESS doctrine in constitutional law under which courts will not decide cases in advance of the necessity of deciding them, i.e., in advance of their being ripe for decision. Compare **justiciable; moot case.**

RISK hazard, danger, peril, exposure to loss, injury, disadvantage or destruction. In **tort** law, the risk that should be reasonably perceived and avoided defines the common law duty concerning the probability or foreseeability of injury to another. See **assigned risk; obvious risk.**

RISK ASSUMPTION see **assumption of the risk.**

RISK, AT see **tax shelter [AT-RISK RULES].**

RISK CAPITAL money invested in a business venture for which **stock** is issued; in **security** law, a security transaction whereby an investor subjects money to the risks of an enterprise over which he or she exercises no managerial control. If a transaction is so characterized, it is subject to the various securities laws.

RISK, FORESEEABLE see **foreseeability [FORESEEABLE RISK].**

RISK OF LOSS 1. a phrase used to signify who bears the financial risk of damage or destruction when property is being transferred from a buyer to a seller.

EXAMPLE: In a contract between Dynamic Boat Company and a buyer, the buyer agrees to assume *risk of loss* only when the boat is in his or her possession. Therefore, if anything should happen to the boat after its completion but while it is being transported to the buyer, from the buyer's point of view Dynamic must take responsibility for the damage.

2. In insurance law, the term refers to the contingencies or unknown events that are contemplated by the insured and that are covered by the insurance.

RISK OF NONPERSUASION see **burden of proof.**

ROBBERY forcible stealing; the **felonious** taking of property from the person of another by violence or by putting him in fear.

ARMED ROBBERY robbery aggravated by the fact that it is committed by a defendant armed with a dangerous weapon, whether or not the weapon is used in the course of committing the crime. Compare **burglary.**

ROBERT'S RULES OF ORDER see **parliamentary law.**

ROBINSON-PATMAN ACT section 2(a) of the **Clayton Act,** the Robinson-Patman Act, also known as the **ROBINSON-PATMAN ANTI-DISCRIMINATION ACT,** prohibits price discrimination between purchasers of commodities of like grade and quality, where the effect of the discrimination may be to substantially lessen competition or tend to create a **monopoly** in any line of commerce. The illegal discrimination may include payment or acceptance of commisisons, brokerage fees, or other compensation, payment for services or facilities for processing or sale, furnishing services or facilities for processing or handling, knowingly inducing or receiving discriminatory price, or the discriminatory use of rebates, discounts, advertising service charges, or underselling in particular localities. See **antitrust laws.**

ROGATORY LETTERS a formal communication from a court in which an **action** is pending, to a foreign court, requesting that the **testimony** of a **witness** residing in such foreign **jurisdiction** be taken under the direction of the court, addressed and transmitted to the court making the request.

ROLLOVER see **retirement plan.**

ROR see **release on own recognizance [ROR].**

ROTH 401(K) see **retirement plan [ROTH 401(K)].**

ROTH IRA see **retirement plan [ROTH IRA].**

ROUND LOT SHAREHOLDERS **shareholders** holding blocks of 100 shares per block. The term also refers to bondholders holding **bonds** with a $1,000 **par value.**

ROYALTY a share of the product or of the proceeds therefrom, reserved by an owner for permitting another to exploit and use his or her **property;** the rental paid to the original owner of property, based on a percentage of profit or production. The term is employed with respect to mining **leases, conveyances,** literary works, inventions and other intellectual productions. Compare **commission.**

R.S. see **revised statutes.**

RUBRIC the title of a statute; a statute regarded as authoritative.

RULE prescribed guide for action or conduct, regulation or principle; includes commands to lower courts or court officials to do **ministerial acts.** If a standard or directive by a governmental agency is characterized as a rule, it must be promulgated in accordance with the procedures set down in the **Administrative Procedure Act.** A rule of a **court,** such as a federal rule of civil or criminal procedure, is adopted by the court itself and is subject to legislative action.

RULE AGAINST PERPETUITIES the rule that no contingent **interest** is good unless it must **vest,** if at all, not later than 21 years after some life in being at the creation of the interest. The rule against perpetuities is directed against the remoteness of vesting of **estates** or interests in property, and against unreasonable restraints of the power of **alienation.**

RULE IN SHELLEY'S CASE when in the same **conveyance,**

an **estate** for life is given to the ancestor with **remainder** to the ancestor's **heirs,** then the ancestor takes the **fee simple** (or fee tail) remainder estate and the heirs take nothing. If, for example, A, fee owner, conveys *"to B for life, then to the heirs of B,"* then B takes both the life estate and the remainder in fee simple. The rule, created in 1324, has been abolished in England and in a majority of American jurisdictions.

RULE IN WILD'S CASE a rule of **construction** by which a **devise** to "B and his children," where B has no children at the time the gift **vests** in B, was read to mean a gift to B in **fee tail,** the words "and his children" thus being construed as **words of limitation** and not **words of purchase.** The popularity of the fee tail has declined, and most American jurisdictions have repudiated the Rule in Wild's Case, so that such conveyances are construed to be a gift of a **life estate** to B, with a **remainder** to his children.

RULE NISI procedure by which one party by an **ex parte** application or an order to **show cause** calls upon another to show cause why the rule set forth in his or her proposed order should not be made final by the court. If no cause is shown, the court orders the rule absolute (final), thereby requiring whatever was sought to be accomplished.

RULE OF AVOIDABLE CONSEQUENCES see **mitigation of damages.**

RULE OF CAPTURE see **capture.**

RULE OF LAW see **question of law.**

RULE OF REASON in **antitrust law,** the principle first enunciated by the Supreme Court in 1911 that the law is to be applied only to "unreasonable" restraints of trade. Since then, the rule of reason has evolved into a complex set of factors that may be considered in resolving an antitrust case. The rule of reason has been rejected for certain types of business conduct such as **price fixing** agreements, which have been found to be illegal **per se,** that is, likely to harm competition and so lacking in potential benefit that they are illegal in and of themselves. See **Sherman Antitrust Act.**

RULES OF PROFESSIONAL CONDUCT see **Code of Professional Responsibility; Model Rules of Professional Conduct.**

RUN WITH THE LAND a phrase used with respect to **covenants** in the law of real property to mean that the burdens and/or the benefits of the covenant pass to the persons who succeed to the interests of the original contracting parties. Covenants so characterized bind the owners of the property to which they attach (with which they "run"), no matter who those owners are; such covenants therefore represent an essentially permanent limitation upon the **estate** held by the owner of the "burdened" property, and an enhancement of the estate held by the owner of the "benefitted" property.

EXAMPLE: Luigi divides a large building so that he can sell one-half to another businessman. There is only one alley through which deliveries can be made, but the alley is on Luigi's side of the property. In the deed of sale, Luigi includes a covenant that allows the other businessman to use the alley. That covenant *runs with the land* so that anyone who buys the store from the other businessman can enforce the covenant against any owner of the other half of the building.

Compare **chain of title.**

S

SAILOR'S WILL see **military will.**

SALABLE **merchantable;** an item fit for sale in usual course of trade, at usual selling prices. The item salable shall be of ordinary marketable quality, bring the average price, be lawful merchandise, be good and sufficient of its kind, and be free from any remarkable defects.

SALARY, FIXED see **fixed salary.**

SALE a **contract** by which property, real or personal, is transferred from the seller **(vendor)** to the buyer **(vendee)** for a fixed price in money, paid or agreed to be paid by the buyer. This is in contrast to **BARTER,** which is an exchange of goods or services for another's goods or services. See **arm's length.**

   ABSOLUTE SALE a sale whereby the property passes to the buyer upon completion of the agreement between the parties.

   AUCTION SALE a public sale of goods or **real property** to the highest bidder, by public outcry and competitive bidding.

   BARGAIN AND SALE see **bargain and sale.**

   BILL OF SALE see **bill [BILL OF SALE].**

   CASH SALE see **cash sale.**

   CONDITIONAL SALE 1. a sale in which the vendee receives **possession** and right of use of the **goods** sold, but transfer of title to the vendee is dependent upon **performance** of some condition, usually full payment of purchase price. The conditional sale becomes absolute on fulfillment of the condition. 2. a purchase accompanied by an agreement to resell upon particular terms. See also **SALE ON APPROVAL.**

   EXECUTED SALE in contrast to an **EXECUTORY SALE,** one wherein nothing remains to be done by either party to effect **delivery** and complete transfer of title.

   EXECUTION SALE see **FORCED SALE** (below); **sheriff's sale.**

   EXECUTORY SALE in contrast to an **EXECUTED SALE,** an agreement to sell wherein something remains to be done by either party before delivery and passing of title.

FORCED SALE a sale that the seller must make immediately, without opportunity to find a buyer who will pay a sum approaching the reasonable worth of the item (often land). The phrase is synonymous with **JUDICIAL SALE** (see **sheriff's sale**), whereby the court forces the sale of property as a result of a prior **adjudication.**

EXAMPLE: Marquise owes money to several creditors as a result of work they performed on a building he owns. He avoids the creditors, and they obtain a judicial order demanding payment. His continued refusal to pay results in a *forced sale* of the building. The excess of the sale price over the money owed is returned to Marquise.

INSTALLMENT SALE see **installment sale.**

JUDICIAL SALE see **FORCED SALE** (above); see also **sheriff's sale.**

PUBLIC SALE a sale upon notice to the public and in which members of the public may bid.

SALE BY SAMPLE a sale of **goods** in existence in bulk, but not pres-ent for examination, where it is mutually understood that the goods not exhibited will conform to the sample. Such a sale carries with it an **implied** warranty that the goods purchased conform to the sample.

SALE IN GROSS sale of land by the tract or as a whole, without **warranty** of quantity (acres); sometimes referred to as a **CONTRACT OF HAZARD.**

SALE ON APPROVAL a transaction in which goods delivered primarily for use may be returned if the buyer is unsatisfied with them, even though they may conform to the contract. If the goods are delivered primarily for resale, rather than for use, the transaction is termed a **SALE OR RETURN,** or the arrangement is termed a **CONSIGNMENT.**

SALE ON INSTALLMENT see **installment sale.**

SALE OR EXCHANGE see **sale or exchange.**

SALE WITH RIGHT OF REDEMPTION sale where seller reserves the right to take back **title** to property he has sold upon repayment of the purchase price.

SHERIFF'S SALE see **FORCED SALE** (above); **sheriff's sale.**

TAX SALE a sale of land for the nonpayment of taxes. See **foreclosure.**

SALE AND LEASEBACK a procedure whereby an owner of property sells it to another party who immediately leases the property back to the original owner. This method is frequently employed for tax purposes or for situations where the original owner needs cash rather than property.

SALE BY SAMPLE see **sale** [SALE BY SAMPLE].

SALE IN GROSS see **sale** [SALE IN GROSS].

SALE IN INSTALLMENTS see **installment sale.**

SALE ON APPROVAL see **sale** [SALE ON APPROVAL].

SALE OR EXCHANGE disposition of property in a value-for-value exchange, as opposed to a disposition by **gift,** contribution or the like. For **income tax** purposes, the **realization** of **gain or loss** on the disposition of property is based on the sale or exchange of that property.

SALES TAX see **tax** [SALES TAX].

SALE WITH RIGHT OF REDEMPTION see **sale** [SALE WITH RIGHT OF REDEMPTION].

SALVAGE generally, the value of property following its destruction or loss. In maritime law, a service rendered to a vessel that removes it from some distress; to be entitled to a salvage award, the distressed vessel must be in impending peril of the sea from which it is rescued by the voluntary efforts of others. In insurance law, the value of the property following a loss, which can be deducted from the amount recovered by the insured. In tax law, the amount, determined at the time of the acquisition, which is estimated will be realizable upon sale or other disposition of an asset when it is no longer useful in the taxpayer's business and is to be retired from service. That amount is then calculated into a taxpayer's permissible **depreciation** of the asset.

The **accelerated cost recovery system** does not provide for salvage value. EQUITABLE SALVAGE is an equitable right of the last person to preserve a property's value to have priority over others in either that property or its value upon realization, since without that person's actions the property would be worthless.

SALVAGE VALUE see **depreciation** [SALVAGE VALUE].

SAME-SEX MARRIAGE see **civil union; marriage.**

SAMPLE that which is taken out of a large quantity as a fair representation of the whole; a part shown as evidence of the quality of the whole. Under the Uniform Commercial Code, any sample or model that is made part of the basis of the bargain creates an express warranty that the whole of the goods shall conform to the sample or model.

SANCTION 1. to approve; 2. to reward or punish; 3. a consequence of punishment for violation of accepted norms of social conduct, which may be of two kinds: those that redress **civil** injuries (civil sanctions) and those that punish crimes (penal sanctions).

SANE [SANITY] the state of sound mental condition; all persons are presumed sane until the opposite is demonstrated. All jurisdictions require the defendant in a criminal case to produce some evidence to challenge this presumption. In some jurisdictions, the burden of persuasion is borne by the state; in others, the defendant carries the ultimate burden of proof. The allocation of this burden is apparently within the individual state's rules of procedure and placing the burden on the defendant does not violate the presumption of innocence. Compare **insanity.**

SANITY HEARING a proceeding authorized by statute for investigating the sanity of a person accused of a felony. Such a hearing is not a **trial** placing the accused in jeopardy, but is a "collateral inquiry" in the nature of an inquest to determine the competency of a person to stand trial.

SANS without.

SATISFACTION (OF A DEBT) a release and discharge of the obligation in reference to which performance is executed. See **accord and satisfaction; ademption.**

SAVE HARMLESS protect from loss or liability; **indemnity;** guarantee.

In **contract** law, signifies a commitment by one party to **repay** another party to an agreement in the event of a specified loss.

EXAMPLE: A lease provides that the tenant shall *save harmless* the landlord against claims for injuries to persons on the premises. As a result of this clause, the tenant is required to reimburse the landlord in the event such a claim is successfully prosecuted and damages are recovered against the landlord.

SAVING CLAUSE a clause in a **statute** restricting the scope of the **repeal** of prior statutes; language inserted in a statute to maintain existing rights provided in the repealed law. See also **grandfather clause.**

SAVINGS AND LOAN ASSOCIATION see **bank** [SAVINGS AND LOAN ASSOCIATION].

SAVINGS BANK see **bank** [SAVINGS BANK].

SAVING TO SUITORS CLAUSE see **admiralty courts** [SAVING TO SUITORS CLAUSE].

SCÈNE À FAIRE Fr.: for scenes to be made. **Intellectual property**

term involving **copyright** protection for nonliteral elements of dramatic works. Software or program code is generally considered a literary work for the purposes of copyright law. As such, nonliteral elements are copyright-protected, but only the expression of an idea and not the idea itself. That which is standard in the treatment of a given topic is not copyrightable.

SCHOLARSHIPS AND FELLOWSHIPS tuition or subsistence aid given to an individual for participation in an educational program. In general, a fellowship or scholarship grant at an educational institution is not subject to income taxes. However, it must not constitute compensation for services primarily for the benefit of the grantor of the fellowship or scholarship unless the employment is required in order for the taxpayer to obtain a degree. If the individual receiving the grant is not a candidate for a degree, the grantor must be a tax-exempt educational organization or a governmental unit. The amount **excludable** in any one year is $300 multiplied by the number of months for which the recipient received amounts under the scholarship or fellowship grant during the **taxable year.**

SCIENTER *(sī'-ĕn-tûr)* Lat.: knowledge. Previous knowledge of operative facts; frequently signifies guilty knowledge. As used in **pleadings,** the term signifies that the alleged **crime** or **tort** was done designedly or with guilty knowledge. The term is usually employed in relation to **fraud,** and means a person's knowledge that he was making false representations, with **intent** to deceive.

EXAMPLE: A corporation files a registration statement, containing false representations, with the Securities and Exchange Commission so that the corporation may sell stock to the public. Applicable law holds a party liable if with *scienter* he or she signs a statement that contains false representations. The requirement of scienter means that the party must know of the false representations and know that the statement will be used to deceive others into purchasing stock.

See **culpable; mens rea.**

SCINTILLA (OF EVIDENCE) **evidence** that is speculative and conjectural and is something less than substantial evidence. If at least a scintilla of evidence is presented, some courts have held that the party against whom the evidence is offered should not be granted a **summary judgment.**

SCOPE OF AUTHORITY in the law of agency, those acts proper for the accomplishment of the goal of the agency, including not only the actual authorization conferred upon the agent by his or her principal, but also that which has apparently or impliedly been delegated to the agent. As applied to doctrine of **respondeat superior,**

masters are liable civilly for damages occasioned by the torts of their servants and agents committed while acting within the scope of their authority. The proper inquiry is whether the act was done in the course of the agency and by virtue of the authority as agent. See also **apparent authority.**

SCOPE OF EMPLOYMENT those acts done while performing one's job duties. The phrase was adopted by the courts for the purpose of determining employer's **liability** for the acts of his or her employees. The master (usually, the employer) is said to be **vicariously liable** only for those torts of the servant (employee) that are committed within the range of his or her job activities. See **respondeat superior; employee's liability acts; Workers' Compensation acts.**

EXAMPLE: A professional driver employed by Escort Service, Inc., decides to stop home and see his wife while he is driving from one job to another. As he drives to his home, he hits a child playing in the street. Escort will not be responsible for the injury to the child if the driver was not in the *scope of his employment.*

S CORPORATION see **corporation [S CORPORATION].**

SCRIP DIVIDEND see **dividend.**

SCRIVENER 1. an old English term referring to a writer or scribe, particularly one who draws legal documents; 2. one who acts as **agent** for another, investing and managing that other's property for a fee.

SCRUTINY see **strict scrutiny.**

SCUTAGE in feudal law, a tax imposed on landholders to help pay for the king's army.

SEAL in **common law,** an impression on wax or other substance capable of being impressed. The purpose of a seal is to attest to the execution of an **instrument.** The word seal or the letters **L.S.** (**LOCUS SIGILLI,** place of the seal) have the same significance and are commonly used for the same purpose today.

A seal of a corporation is sometimes called a **COMMON SEAL.**

SEALED INSTRUMENT one that is signed and has the seal of the signer attached. To render a **contract** a sealed instrument, it must be so recited in the body of the instrument and a seal must be placed after the signature. In **common law,** a sealed contract was a **FORMAL CONTRACT** (as opposed to a contract without a seal, called a **SIMPLE CONTRACT**) and is often called a **CONTRACT UNDER SEAL;** such a contract or a **deed** under seal did not require **consideration.** Today any symbol, even the printed word seal or the letters L.S. will, if so intended, constitute the necessary seal. In most states, **statutes** have eliminated most of the special effects of sealed instruments in common law.

SEALING OF RECORDS the sealing of criminal records, permitted in some states with respect to **youthful offenders,** so that such records may be examined only by court order.

SEARCH AND SEIZURE a police practice whereby a person or place is searched and **evidence** useful in the investigation and **prosecution** of crime is seized. The search and seizure is constitutionally limited by the **Fourth Amendment** and **Fourteenth Amendment** to the United States Constitution and by provisions in the several state constitutions, statutes and rules of court. See also **probable cause; search warrant.** Compare **unreasonable search and seizure.**

SEARCH, CONSENT FOR see **consent search.**

SEARCH ENGINE a computerized system that enables the user to type in various search terms and receive information that fits the designated query. For legal research, there are two main fee-based search engines known as "LexisNexis" and "Westlaw." See **Boolean search.**

SEARCH OF TITLE see **title search.**

SEARCH WARRANT an order issued by a judge or **magistrate** authorizing certain law enforcement officers to conduct a search of specified premises for specified things or persons. In those cases where **warrants** are required, only a judge or magistrate who has not previously considered the facts giving rise to the application can issue a search warrant, and only upon a showing of **probable cause** that the described item is located in the designated place and that it was involved in the planning or commission of a crime.

SEASONABLE timely; in due season or time; the time in which action is appropriate and can be effective. The word *seasonably* has been used synonymously with *reasonably* to mean in a timely manner. See **time is of the essence.**

SEASONAL relating to a specific time of the year. Seasonal employment is the kind of occupation that can be performed only during certain periods of the year, and does not include such occupations that may be carried on throughout the entire year. Compare **seasonable.**

S.E.C. see **Securities and Exchange Commission [S.E.C.].**

SECOND AMENDMENT the provision in the U.S. Constitution that gives each state the right to maintain a "well regulated Militia" and "the people to keep and bear Arms." The debates that led to the adoption of the Second Amendment indicate that its purpose was to prevent federal interference with state militia and the creation of a national army that would destroy local autonomy. The Second Amendment thus does not apply to private conduct, to **state action,** or to federal gun control laws that do not interfere with state militia.

SECONDARY AFFINITY see **affinity [SECONDARY AFFINITY].**

SECONDARY BOYCOTT see **boycott [SECONDARY BOYCOTT].**

SECONDARY DISTRIBUTION an organized **offering** of **stock** that is already issued and outstanding, usually distributed by a **syndicate.** Typical sources of large blocks of stock for redistribution are **founders, insiders** and major investors.

SECONDARY LIABILITY see **liability [SECONDARY LIABILITY].**

SECONDARY PARTY a person obligated to pay a debt if the person incurring the debt fails to pay the **creditor.** The parties to whom the creditor may then go for repayment are secondarily **liable.**

EXAMPLE: Abe receives a check for a debt owed to him. He signs the check and turns it over to a friend to whom he owes money. Abe is *secondarily liable* on the check, so that if the check is dishonored, the friend can look to Abe for payment.

SECOND-DEGREE see **murder [SECOND-DEGREE MURDER]; principal [PRINCIPAL IN THE SECOND-DEGREE].**

SECOND MORTGAGE see **mortgage [SECOND MORTGAGE].**

SECRET SERVICE see **Department of Homeland Security [DHS] [UNITED STATES SECRET SERVICE].**

SECRETS OF TRADE see **trade secrets.**

SECTION 1231 PROPERTY see **capital [§1231 PROPERTY].**

SECUNDUM *(sĕ-kūn'-dŭm)* Lat.: immediately after; next to.

SECURED CREDITOR a **creditor** who holds **security** that will cover the amount the **debtor** owes him or her. Among these securities may be mortgages, deeds, bills of sale, liens upon goods, etc. The definition in the Bankruptcy Act is narrower in that it applies only to those creditors who hold security for the debt on property belonging to the bankrupt. See **credit; security interest.**

SECURED TRANSACTIONS see **security interest.**

SECURITIES **stock certificates, bonds,** or other **evidence** of a secured indebtedness or of a right created in the holder to participate in profits or **assets** distribution of a profit-making enterprise; more generally, written assurances for the return or payment of money; **instruments** giving to their legal holders the right to money or other property. As such, securities have value and are used in regular channels of commerce. The basic purpose of the sale of securities is to raise capital for businesses and government. Historically, securities have been an area of major investment and speculation by **banks** and individuals. Unbridled trading by unscrupulous speculators that led to inflated securites markets and contributed to the great financial crash of the late 1920s resulted in the passage of the **Securities Act of 1933,** and the **Securities Exchange Act of 1934** (see **Securities Acts**), both of which strictly regulate the buying and selling of securities. Securities are also regulated by state laws known as **Blue Sky laws.**

The most common types of securities are:

BLUE CHIP STOCK see **blue chip stock.**

BOND essentially, a loan agreement respresenting a debt. In return for the **capital** given to a corporation or a government entity, the bondholder gets a promise of repayment of **principal** and **interest** over time, instead of ownership rights. Since the holder of a bond is a **creditor** instead of an owner, his or her claims against the assets of a corporation are satisfied first in case of a failure of the business venture. Most bonds are secured by some kind of **collateral,** so that in case of **default,** the debt might still be satisfied. Consequently, bonds are generally a lower risk investment. Unsecured bonds are called **debentures.** Bonds raise money commonly known as **DEBT CAPITAL.** See **bond.**

BONUS STOCK see **bonus stock.**

CAPITAL STOCK see **capital [CAPITAL STOCK].**

CLASSIFIED STOCK see **classified stock.**

COMMON STOCK see **STOCK** (below).

CONVERTIBLE SECURITY see **convertible securities.**

DEBT CAPITAL see **BOND** (above).

DIVIDEND see **dividend.**

EQUITY CAPITAL see **STOCK** (below).

GROWTH STOCK see **growth stock.**

GUARANTEED SECURITY see **guaranteed security.**

INVESTMENT STOCK see **restricted securities.**

JOINT STOCK COMPANY see **company [JOINT STOCK COMPANY].**

LETTER STOCK see **restricted securities.**

LISTED STOCK see **listed stock.**

NONASSESSABLE STOCK see **nonassessable stock.**

NONSTOCK CORPORATION see **nonstock corporation.**

NO-PAR [NONPAR] STOCK see **no-par [nonpar] stock.**

PREFERRED STOCK see **STOCK** (below).

PUBLIC SECURITIES those certificates and other **negotiable instruments** evidencing the debt of a governmental body.

RESTRICTED SECURITIES see **restricted securities.**

STOCK an equity or ownership interest in a **corporation,** usually created by a contribution to the **capital** of the corporation. Its unit of measurement is the **share,** and the owner of one or more shares of stock in a company is entitled to participate in the company's management and profits, and in distribution of assets upon **dissolution** of the company. Ownership of stock may be evidenced by a written **instrument** known as a **stock certificate.** Distribution of profits to stockholders occurs through the payment of **dividends.** However, for tax purposes, not all corporations pay dividends to their stockholders, but rather reinvest profits in the business, thereby increasing the value of the stock to the investor.

There are two general types of stock. **COMMON STOCK** is the ordinary stock of the corporation that entitles the owner to pro rata dividends without any priority or preference over any other shareholders or class of shareholders but equally with all other shareholders except preferred stockholders. **PREFERRED STOCK** is a class of stock entailing certain rights beyond those attached to common stock; corporate stock having preference rights over other kinds of stock in the payment of **dividends.** It represents a contribution to the capital of the corporation and is in no sense a loan of money. The dividends come out of earnings [income] and not out of **capital.** Unless there are net earnings there is no right to dividends. Other rights that may be attendant to preferred stock are limitless; however, whatever rights are given must be clearly noted. It is part of the capital **stock** of a **corporation** that enjoys **priority** over the remaining stock, or **common stock,** in the distribution of profits and, in the event of dissolution of the corporation, in the distribution of assets as well. The issuance of stock raises money commonly known as **EQUITY CAPITAL.**

STOCK ISSUE see **issue [STOCK ISSUE].**

TREASURY STOCK see **treasury stock.**

UNLISTED STOCK see **unlisted security.**

WATERED STOCK see **watered stock.**

WHEN ISSUED SECURITIES see **when issued securities.**

SECURITIES ACT OF 1933 see **Securities Acts [SECURITIES ACT OF 1933].**

SECURITIES ACTS popular name of the two primary federal statutes regulating the issuing of and market trading in corporate **securities.** The **Securities Act of 1933** deals primarily with initial distribution of securities by the issuer: its objective is to provide full disclosure of **material** facts about securities for sale so that investors may be able to make informed investment decisions. The **Securities Exchange Act of 1934** is designed to regulate postdistribution trading in securities and provides for the registration and regulation of securities exchanges, as well as for the prohibition of fraud and manipulation in sale or purchase of securities.

INVESTMENT COMPANY ACT OF 1940 regulates publicly owned companies engaged primarily in the business of investing and trading in securities.

INVESTORS ADVISERS ACT OF 1940 act that establishes a scheme of registration and regulation of investment advisers comparable to that contained in the SECURITIES EXCHANGE ACT OF 1934 (above) with respect to broker–dealers but not as comprehensive. A limited private cause of action for **rescission** but not **damages** has been found to be implied in the act.

PUBLIC UTILITY HOLDING COMPANY ACT OF 1935 act that regulates the financing and operation of electric and gas public utility holding company systems.

SECURITIES INVESTOR PROTECTION ACT OF 1970 act that established the **Securities Investor Protection Corporation [S.I.P.C.]** and gave it the power to supervise the liquidation of financially troubled securities firms and the payment of the claims of their customers.

TRUST INDENTURE ACT OF 1939 act that regulates public issuers of large debt securities—i.e., over $5,000,000.

SECURITIES AND EXCHANGE COMMISSION [SEC] the federal agency empowered to regulate and supervise the selling of **securities,** to prevent unfair practices on security exchanges and **over-the-counter markets,** and to maintain a fair and orderly market for the investor. The **Commodity Futures Trading Commission** fulfills a similar role in the regulation of commodity futures and option markets. See also **Administrative Procedure Act; proxy.**

SECURITIES EXCHANGE ACT OF 1934 see **Securities Acts** [SECURITIES EXCHANGE ACT OF 1934].

SECURITIES INVESTOR PROTECTION ACT OF 1970 see **Securities Acts** [SECURITIES INVESTOR PROTECTION ACT OF 1970].

SECURITIES INVESTOR PROTECTION CORPORATION [SIPC] a nonprofit corporation supported by its membership of **securities brokers** and dealers, developed to protect their customers and to promote confidence in the securities markets. In principle, SIPC provides certain amounts of insurance on cash and securities left on deposit in a brokerage account.

SECURITY protection, safety; the instrument of protection or safety; a person who becomes the **surety** for another. Generally, instruments for the payment of money, or evidencing title or equity, with or without some collateral obligation, and which are commonly dealt in for the purpose of financing and investment. Also, an investment in some private or public business enterprise. Components of a security are: (1) an investment of money, (2) in a common enterprise, (3) with an expectation of profits solely from the efforts of others. See **bankruptcy; Securities Exchange Act of 1934.** See generally **securities; securities acts.**

SECURITY DEPOSIT money that a **tenant** deposits with the **landlord** to assure that the tenant will abide by the **lease** agreements; a fund from which the landlord may obtain payment for **damages** caused by the tenant during his or her occupancy.

SECURITY INTEREST an **interest** in **real property** or **personal property** that secures the payment of an obligation. In common law, security interests are either consensual (by agreement) or arise by **operation of law,** as in the case of judgment **liens** and statutory liens.

EXAMPLE: In order to obtain a loan from a bank, Omar uses a very valuable painting as collateral. The bank has a *security interest* in the painting and can acquire ownership of it if the loan is not repaid.

PURCHASE-MONEY SECURITY INTEREST one taken or retained by the seller of the collateral to secure all or part of its price.

SEDITION illegal action that tends to cause the disruption and overthrow of the government.

EXAMPLE: Cathy sabotages a Federal Bureau of Investigation computer that lists the names of all of the most wanted criminals, thus committing a *seditious* act. Liability for such an act extends beyond a mere charge of destroying government property.

See **treason.** Compare **clear and present danger.**

SEDITIOUS LIBEL in English law a misdemeanor involving the publishing of any words or document, with an intention to promote feelings of ill will or contempt between the classes or towards the government. The law of seditious libel is not severely circumscribed in the United States by the **First Amendment** to the Constitution. See **freedom [FREEDOM OF PRESS]; [FREEDOM OF SPEECH].**

SEDUCTION inducing a chaste, unmarried woman, by means of temptation, deception, acts, flattery or a promise of marriage, to engage in sexual intercourse. Compare **rape.**

SEGREGATION setting apart; the separation of some persons or things from others. For instance, a contract may require a party to keep certain funds segregated so that they will be available for payment.

In constitutional law, segregation is the maintenance of separate facilities and institutions for people of different races. The racial segregation that prevailed in this country until the 1950s was based on the theory that **separate but equal** facilities met the constitutional requirements of the equal protection clause. In the **landmark** case of *Brown* v. *Board of Education,* 347 U.S. 483 (1954), segregation resulting from **state action** was held to be violative of the **equal protection clause.** After a period of 15 years, the **deliberate speed** with which all vestiges of public school segregation was to end was rejected in favor of a standard of immediate implementation. See **de facto [DE FACTO SEGREGATION].**

SEIGNEUR [SEIGNIOR] *(sē'-nyôr)* generally, Fr.: master, lord; more specifically, the lord of a **fee** or of a manor.

SEISED the condition of legally **owning realty.** The phrase imports legal **title** as opposed to **beneficial ownership.**

EXAMPLE: A father owning apartment houses that are fully rented conveys the houses to his son. The son is thus *seised* of the buildings. He has legal title to them, but, because the tenants have leases that allow them to remain in their apartments, he cannot do with the buildings as he pleases until all the leases expire.

SEISIN in early English property law, the term to describe the **interest** in land of one who held a **freehold estate.** The term **ownership**

was not used, since the **sovereign** (king) was technically owner of all lands in England; a landholder was instead said to be **seised** of his estate. A voluntary transfer of the holder's interest was accomplished by **livery of seisin.** Today, seisin is generally considered synonymous with ownership.

SEISIN, COVENANT OF see **covenant** [COVENANT OF SEISIN AND RIGHT TO CONVEY].

SEIZURE 1. the act of forcibly dispossessing an owner of property, under actual or apparent authority of law; 2. the taking of property into the **custody** of the court in **satisfaction** of a **judgment,** or in consequence of a violation of law. See **attachment; garnishment; in rem; levy.** See **search and seizure.**

SELECTIVE ALLOCATION see **marshaling [marshaling]** [SELECTIVE ALLOCATION].

SELECTIVE INCORPORATION the process by which certain of the guarantees expressed in the **Bill of Rights** become applicable to the states through the **Fourteenth Amendment.** Under the TOTAL INCORPORATION APPROACH, an approach never adopted by a majority of the Supreme Court, all the Bill of Rights and the attendant case law interpreting them, are applied to the states. Under the selective incorporation approach, select guarantees in the Bill of Rights and their related case law are applied to the states.

SELECTIVE SERVICE SYSTEM the system established under the Selective Service Act by which persons are selected to serve in the armed forces in order to ensure the security of this country. Every male citizen or resident of the United States who is between the ages of 18 and 26 years is required to register for potential selection to serve in the armed forces. The requirement that only men and not women register does not violate the **Fifth Amendment.** Since women are not eligible for combat duty and the purpose of the registration system is to ensure the availability of combat troops, the statute has been found to bear a reasonable relationship to a legitimate legislative purpose. While males are required to register, none has been drafted into the armed forces since the end of the Vietnam War. See **military law.**

SELF-DEALING type of securities trading in which a party acts upon secret information obtained by his or another's special position in the corporation. It may involve sale or purchase of stock by the director, officers and majority **shareholders** of a **corporation.** See **fiduciary; insider.**

SELF-DEFENSE the self-protection of one's person, or preservation of members of one's family, and, to a lesser extent, one's property, from harm by an aggressor, in a way and under circumstances that the law recognizes as justifying the protective measures. It is a valid **defense** to a criminal **charge** or to **tort** liability. See **justification.**

EXAMPLE: Ty is assaulted and in an act of *self-defense* hits the mugger. Even if that blow was strong enough to knock the mugger unconscious, Ty still has a valid defense for his assault against the mugger. If the mugger is unconscious and Ty then hits him with a brick and kills him, Ty would not be able to assert he was acting in self-defense since the mugger was no longer in a position to harm him. Ty would be liable in that circumstance to prosecution for murder.

SELF-HELP the right or fact of redressing or preventing wrongs by one's own action, without resort to legal proceedings, but without **BREACH OF THE PEACE** (see **breach**).

EXAMPLE: Tim's car is stolen. Two weeks later he sees the car in a downtown auto repair shop. Tim can employ *self-help* and drive the car away without calling the police to aid him if he so desires. Likewise, if Tim had been behind in his car payments, the creditor could come and take the car to satisfy the debt without legal process so long as there is no breach of the peace.

SELF-INCRIMINATION, PRIVILEGE AGAINST the constitutional right of a person to refuse to answer questions or otherwise give **testimony** against himself or herself that will create substantial likelihood of criminal incrimination.

The privilege can be displaced by a grant of **USE IMMUNITY,** which guarantees that neither the compelled testimony nor any fruits will be used against the witness. Given such immunity, the witness is no longer exposed to the hazard of self-incrimination and thus must respond to questions or provide evidence. Some states still give such witnesses a broader form of immunity known as **TRANSACTIONAL IMMUNITY,** which protects the witness not merely from use of his or her testimony but from any prosecution relating to transactions about which relevant testimony was elicited. It should be emphasized that the privilege against self-incrimination, like all constitutional rights, may be **waived. Miranda** warnings are generally necessary before such a waiver will be found to qualify a **confession** as admissible evidence in a criminal trial.

See **Fifth Amendment.** Compare **contempt of court; immunity.**

SELLER in commercial law, a person who sells or contracts to sell goods; in securities law, entities who conduct is a substantial factor in causing a purchaser to buy a **security.** Compare **merchant.**

SELLING SHORT the selling of **securities, commodities** or foreign currency that are not actually owned by the seller. In making the short sell, the seller hopes to cover—that is, buy back—sold items at a higher price and thus earn a profit.

COMMODITY SHORT SALES short sales accomplished in the **futures** market. A speculator wishing to take advantage of an expected decline in a commodity can sell a large quantity of the commodity for future delivery. Compare **margin.**

SEMINAL leading; contributing the seed of later development; original, creative, and influential.

SENILE DEMENTIA insanity that occurs as the result of old age, progressive in character, and resulting in collapse of mental faculties that, in its final state, deprives one of **testamentary** capacity because of loss of power to reason or act sanely.

EXAMPLE: Warren had a valid will, but as he neared death, he changed certain provisions. When the will was read subsequent to Warren's death, there was a challenge as to Warren's capacity to change it. After hearing evidence that Warren claimed he spoke to dead people and was king of a nonexistent country, the court found that he had suffered from *senile dementia,* and therefore disallowed the changes.

See **competent; incompetency.**

SENIOR MORTGAGE see **mortgage [SENIOR MORTGAGE].**

SENTENCE punishment ordered by a court for a person convicted of a crime, usually either a **NONCUSTODIAL SENTENCE** such as **probation** or a fine, or a **CUSTODIAL SENTENCE** such as a term of imprisonment.

CONCURRENT SENTENCE a sentence that overlaps with another as opposed to a consecutive [cumulative] sentence, which runs by itself, beginning after or ending before the running of another sentence.

CONDITIONAL DISCHARGE SENTENCE see **SUSPENDED SENTENCE** (below).

CONSECUTIVE [CUMULATIVE] SENTENCE a sentence that runs separately from one or more other sentences to be served by the same individual. The sentence is cumulative to the extent that it begins after an existing sentence has terminated either by expiration of the maximum term of the existing sentence, or by release from the present sentence through **parole.** If the consecutive sentence is a custodial one, the parole will be "to the cell" (called **CELL PAROLE**), so that the consecutive sentence may be served during the period of the parole.

527

DEFERRED SENTENCE   a sentence not imposed unless the defendant violates the conditions of probation.

DETERMINATE SENTENCE   a sentence imposed for a definite rather than indefinite term. It may be a mandatory sentence or a sentence imposed within a permissible range by the exercise of judicial discretion.

ENHANCED SENTENCE   see **three strikes [SENTENCE ENHANCEMENT].**

EXTENDED TERM   heavier punishment imposed on a criminal **defendant** by virtue of his or her criminal record and the perception that as a persistent or multiple offender an increased sentence is warranted.

INDETERMINATE SENTENCE   a sentence for the maximum period prescribed by law for the particular offense committed, subject to the provision of the statute that the custodial portion may be terminated sooner by the board of parole any time after the expiration of the minimum period required for parole eligibility.

EXAMPLE: Carter, a youth, is given an *indeterminate sentence* for burglary. Since the maximum sentence for any youth in Carter's state is three years, his punishment will not exceed that length. But, as an indeterminate sentence, the time he actually serves will be determined by the prison authorities based on his adjustment at the prison. He is thereby encouraged to make a positive adjustment.

INTERLOCUTORY SENTENCE   1. a temporary or provisional sentence, pending the imposition of a final sentence; 2. a sentence on a supplementary question derived from the main cause of action.

MANDATORY SENTENCE   a custodial sentence that the legislature has required to be imposed upon persons convicted of certain offenses. If the criminal statute requires a certain minimum period of incarceration, no discretion to suspend the sentence exists in the trial court. The legislative command must be unequivocal, because courts hesitate to find their judicial discretion curtailed; the legislature normally provides explicitly for the mandatory sentence by stating that a certain minimum sentence shall be imposed and that it may not be suspended nor may the defendant be released on probation or parole until that minimum term has been served. Only executive clemency by way of commutation of the minimum term can relieve the defendant of a mandatory sentence.

PRESENTENCE REPORT   see **presentence report**.

SENTENCE ENHANCEMENT   see **three strikes [SENTENCE ENHANCEMENT].**

SPLIT SENTENCE a sentence part of which is served in jail and the remainder of which is served on probation.

SUSPENDED SENTENCE one whose imposition or execution has been withheld by the court on certain terms and conditions. An **implied** condition is always that the defendant not commit further violation of the law during a fixed period. Where no such period is fixed by the court, the practical effect of the suspended sentence is similar to an **UNCONDITIONAL DISCHARGE** sentence, i.e., the matter is terminated without conditions. A **CONDITIONAL DISCHARGE** is a suspended sentence on particular conditions for a period that is expressly fixed by the court or by statute. See also **pretrial intervention.**

SENTENCE ENHANCEMENT see **three strikes [SENTENCE ENHANCEMENT].**

SENTIENT aware; perceptive; responsive to or conscious of sensory impressions.

SEPARABLE CONTROVERSY within **removal** statute, a claim or cause of action that is part of the entire controversy yet by its nature can be severed from the whole. For a case to present a separable controversy within the statute providing for removal of causes to the federal court, federal statute provides that whenever a separate and independent claim or cause of action, which would be removable if sued upon alone, is joined with one or more otherwise nonremovable claims or causes of action, the entire case may be removed and the district court may determine all issues therein, or in its discretion, may remand all matters not otherwise within its original jurisdiction.

SEPARATE BUT EQUAL a doctrine under which equality of treatment is accorded when the races are provided substantially equal facilities, even though these facilities are separate. Although the doctrine has not been **per se** eliminated from American jurisprudence, its application to most aspects of society has been found to violate the **equal protection clause** of the **Fourteenth Amendment.** The violation is not so much directed toward the physical aspects of separate facilities, but rather the intangible harm that results from the segregation that is a by-product of the doctrine. For example, the Supreme Court has found that the mere segregation of minority and white students in public education creates a sense of inferiority that significantly impedes the educational and mental development of minority children.

SEPARATION see **divorce [SEPARATION [DIVORCE A MENSA ET THORO]].**

SEPARATION AGREEMENT a written agreement by a husband

and wife who are separated or about to separate or divorce; provides for the distribution of marital property and, when applicable, support by one spouse for the other. See **divorce [SEPARATION]; postnuptial agreement; prenuptial agreement.**

SEPARATION OF POWER the doctrine prohibiting one branch of government, at any level, federal, state or local, from infringing or encroaching upon or exercising the powers belonging to another branch.

SEQUESTER to separate from; to hold aside.

SEQUESTRATION 1. in **equity,** the act of **seizing** property belonging to another and holding it until profits have paid the demand for which the property was taken.

2. In **common law, juries** (at least in capital cases) were always sequestered, i.e., kept together throughout the trial and jury deliberations, and guarded from improper contact until they were discharged. This common law right to demand jury sequestration has been replaced in most **jurisdictions** with **discretion** in the trial court to grant sequestration in the interests of justice.

3. Sequestration of **witnesses** is frequently ordered by the court at the request of one of the parties to insure that in-court testimony of each witness not be colored by what another witness said.

EXAMPLE: The prosecutor believed that defense witnesses might alter their versions of the facts if they were permitted to hear the State's witnesses testify. To avoid that problem, he asked for the *sequestration* of all witnesses. The judge agreed and excluded all potential witnesses from the courtroom until they were called to testify.

SERIAL BOND see **bond [SERIAL BOND].**

SERIATIM *(sĕr'-ē-ä'-tĭm)* Lat.: in due order; in succession; one by one.

SERIES BOND see **bond [SERIES BOND].**

SERVANT one who works for, and is subject to, the control of his **master;** a person employed to perform services for another and who in the performance of the services is subject to the other's control or right to control.

In determining whether one acting for another is a servant or an independent contractor, the following matters of fact, among others, are considered: (1) the extent of control which, by the agreement, the master may exercise over the details of the work; (2) whether or not the one employed is engaged in a distinct occupation or business; (3) the kind of occupation, with reference to whether, in the locality, the work is usually done under the direction of the employer or by a specialist without supervision; (4) the skill required in the particular occupation; (5) whether the employer or the workman supplies the instrumentalities, tools and the place of work for the person doing the work; (6) the length of time for which the person is employed; (7) the method of payment, whether by the time or by the job; (8) whether or not the work is a part of the regular business of the employer; (9) whether or not the parties believe they are creating the relation of master and servant; and (10) whether the principal is or is not in business. A master is in many instances liable, under the theory of **respondeat superior,** for the torts of his servant, but not for those of an independent contractor. See **fellow servant rule; master and servant.** Compare **agent; contractor [INDEPENDENT CONTRACTOR].**

SERVE see **service.**

SERVICE (OF PROCESS) delivery of a **pleading,** notice or other paper in a suit, to the opposite party, to charge that party with receipt of it and subject him or her to its legal effect; communication of the substance of the **process** to the defendant, either by actual delivery or by other methods, whereby defendant is furnished with reasonable notice of the proceedings against him or her, to afford defendant the opportunity to appear and be heard.

EXAMPLE: Tamara files a lawsuit against a company, but the company never responds. Before entering a default judgment against the company, the judge demands proof that the company was *served* with notice of the suit. Without such proof, the judge cannot be sure that the company knows there is a suit against it.

PERSONAL SERVICE actual delivery to the party to be served.

SERVICE BY MAIL may be permitted either by court rule or, under unusual circumstances, as the court may authorize.

SERVICE BY PUBLICATION CONSTRUCTIVE SERVICE accomplished by publishing the **notice** in a newspaper designated by the court, and in some **jurisdictions,** by mailing that newspaper to the last-known address of the party.

SUBSTITUTED SERVICE constructive service accomplished by service to a recognized representative or **agent** of the party to be served.

SERVICES at common law, the acts done by an English **feudal tenant** for the benefit of his lord, which formed the **consideration** for the property granted to him by his lord. Services were of several types, including knight's service, military service, and the more varied kind of certain and determinate service called socage. See also **tenure.**

SERVIENT ESTATE in relation to an **easement,** an **estate** that is burdened by the **SERVITUDE,** i.e., an estate that is subject to some use by the owner of the **dominant estate;** also called **SERVIENT TENEMENT.**

SERVITUDE, EQUITABLE see **equitable servitude.**

SERVITUDES in constitutional law, a condition of enforced compulsory service of one to another that is prohibited by the U.S Constitution, **Thirteenth Amendment,** except as punishment fo a convicted criminal; charges or incumbrances that follow the land, and are distinguishable from **easements** in that easement usually refers to a right enjoyed whereas servitudes refer to a burden imposed.

SESSION LAWS laws bound in volumes in the order of their enactment by a state legislature, before possible codification. See **code.**

SET ASIDE to **annul** or make **void.** See **reversal.**

SETBACK legal minimum distance between new construction and an existing structure or the street. Setbacks are regulated by **ordinances** and building codes.

SETOFF 1. a **counterclaim** by **defendant** against **plaintiff** that grows from an independent **cause of action** and diminishes the plaintiff's potential **recovery;** a counterdemand arising out of a transaction different from that on which the plaintiff's cause of action is based It does not deny the justice of the plaintiff's claim but seeks to bala ce it in whole or in part by a counterobligation alleged to be due by he plaintiff to the defendant in another transaction.

2. In tax law, setoff allows the amount of refund that a **taxpayer** could claim to be offset against the amount of deficiency that co ld be properly assessed; conversely, the amount of deficiency the g ernment could assess can be offset by the amount the taxpayer co d properly claim as a refund for the same **taxable year.**

SETTLEMENT conclusive resolving of a matter; especially, a compromise achieved by **adverse parties** in a **civil suit** befc final **judgment,** whereby they agree between themselves upon their respective rights and obligations, thus eliminating the necessity of judicial resolution of the controversy.

EXAMPLE: A company is accused of discriminatory hiring practice by the Equal Employment Opportunity Commission (EEOC). The Commission will usually file with the company a notice of its ac ns sations and will attempt to reach a *settlement* before looking to courts. That method generally gives each party more flexibility. In certain instances, a judge may have to approve the settlement.

Compare **plea bargaining.**

SETTLOR [DONOR; TRUSTOR] one who creates a **trust** by giving **real** or **personal property** in trust to another (the **trustee**) for the benefit of a third person (the **beneficiary**). One who gives such property is said to settle it on, or bring **title** to rest with, the trustee.

SEVENTH AMENDMENT the amendment to the U.S. Constitution that guarantees the right to a **jury trial** in any **civil** case before a federal court if the amount in controversy exceeds $20. Each civil litigant in a federal court is entitled to a jury of 6 to 12 persons before a judge capable of instructing them on the law, and a unanimous verdict. However, trial by jury is not automatic; rather a party must specifically request it. A litigant is not entitled to have a jury decide **equitable** claims. However, when a case includes both legal and equitable causes of action, each litigant is entitled to have the legal issues decided by the jury prior to the resolution of the equitable issues.

SEVER see **severance.**

SEVERABLE CONTRACT one that, in the event of a **breach** by one of the parties, may be justly considered as several independent agreements expressed in a single **instrument.** Where a **contract** is deemed severable, a breach thereof may constitute a **default** of only part of the contract, saving the defaulting party from the necessity of responding in **damages** for breach of the entire agreement.

A severable contract may in fact be a series of **DIVISIBLE CONTRACTS** so that each part may be supported by a separate **consideration** and involve separate suits for breach of contract.

SEVERABLE STATUTE one the remainder of which is still valid when a portion has been declared invalid, because the parts of the **statute** are not wholly interdependent. If the remaining part of the statute is capable of separate enforcement, the statute is said to be severable. The legislature may express its intent in a **SEVERABILITY CLAUSE** at the end of the act. See **saving clause.**

EXAMPLE: Congress passes a comprehensive piece of legislation attacking racial discrimination in all areas. If the Supreme Court finds a part of the legislation unconstitutional, the Court will eliminate it. Since the legislation is *severable,* the rest of the provisions remain in force.

SEVERAL [SEVERALLY] separate. 1. In a **note,** each who severally promises to pay is responsible separately for the entire amount. 2. In a **judgment** against more than one defendant, arising out of one **action,** each may be **liable** for the entire amount of the judgment, thereby permitting the successful plaintiff to recover the entire amount of the judgment from any defendant against whom he chooses to institute a suit. See **contribution; joint and several; joint tortfeasors.**

SEVERALTY   refers to the sole holding of property. A tenant in severalty holds land exclusively for the duration of his or her **estate** without any other person holding **joint** rights.

SEVERANCE   act of separating; state of being disjoined. l. a process for selecting a particular **charge** against the **defendant,** so that only one charge or only properly joined charges are before the **jury** in one trial. 2. the disjoinder, for separate trials, of two or more **defendants** named in the same **indictment** or **information;** a useful device where prejudice might arise to one or more of the defendants if they were tried together.

EXAMPLE: Liu Wei is on trial with two other well-known criminals. He feels that the association between him and the others will sway a jury to convict him regardless of the evidence. Liu Wei asks the trial judge for a *severance* so that he will have a better opportunity for a fair trial.

3. Severance of **claims** is also available in **civil** trials to prevent prejudice or for the convenience of the parties. A court may sever the issue of **liability** from the issue of **damages** and direct that the question of liability be determined first. Once liability is established the parties may agree upon the damages, avoiding a lengthy trial on that issue.

SEVERE   of an extreme degree, beyond endurance. For example, in determining whether a plaintiff has succeeded in showing severe emotional distress, both the intensity and duration of the emotional distress suffered must be considered in determining whether the distress is of such substantial quantity or enduring quality that no reasonable person in a civilized society should be expected to endure it.

SEX OFFENDER   person convicted of a sexual offense such as **rape (sexual assault), sexual contact,** or **lewdness.** In some states sexual activity between consenting adults of the same sex is classified as criminal. Some states house sex offenders together and offer specialized counseling programs in an effort to successfully treat such offenders and thus prevent **recidivism.** Many states require lifetime **registration of offenders** with law enforcement.

SEXTING   act of an individual sending photographs or text messages by cellphone to others or for posting on the Internet that contain sexually suggestive messages or images, including nude or seminude photographs of the sender. Often the sender is a young person and the courts must balance prosecution for dissemination of child pornography with normal adolescent development in the age of digital technology.

SEXUAL ABUSE see **rape [SEXUAL ABUSE].**

SEXUAL ASSAULT see **rape [SEXUAL ASSAULT].**

SEXUAL CONTACT see **rape [SEXUAL CONTACT].**

SEXUAL EXPLOITATION the participation by a person in prostitution, sexual servitude, or the production of pornographic or **obscene materials** as a result of being subjected to a threat, deception, coercion, abduction, force, abuse of authority, debt bondage, or fraud. Even in the absence of any of these factors, where the person participating in prostitution, sexual servitude, or the production of pornographic materials is under the age of 18, sexual exploitation shall be deemed to exist. **CHILD PORNOGRAPHY** means any visual depiction, including any photograph, film, video, picture, or computer-generated image or picture of a minor (person under 18) engaging in sexually explicit conduct. Possession and distribution of child pornography is strictly regulated. The **PROTECT ACT** ("Protect" is an acronym for Prosecutorial Remedies and Other Tools to end the Exploitation of Children Today) is a federal statute making it a crime to offer or solicit sexually explicit images of children, regardless of whether the material turns out to consist solely of computer-generated images or digitally altered photographs of adults, or even if the offer is fraudulent and the material does not exist at all. Among its many provisions, the Act also bars pretrial release of persons charged with specified offenses against or involving children; provides for mandatory life imprisonment of sex offenses against a minor if the offender has a similar prior record; authorizes wiretapping in cases related to child abuse or kidnapping; and eliminates statutes of limitations for child abduction or abuse and establishes a program to obtain criminal history background checks for volunteer organizations. The **First Amendment** has been held not to apply to offers to provide or requests to obtain child pornography.

SEXUAL HARASSMENT see **harassment [SEXUAL HARASSMENT].**

SEXUAL SERVITUDE see **involuntary servitude; trafficking [HUMAN TRAFFICKING].**

SHALL often used to denote an obligation or direction to do some act; however, it is sometimes considered to be permissive where it is necessary to give effect to the intent of the word, and to mean the same as the word "may."

SHAM PLEADING one so clearly false that it presents no **issue** of fact to be determined by a **trial.** A **complaint** or **answer** will be stricken as sham only when it is undisputed that the alleged claim or **defense** is wholly unsupported by facts.

SHAM TRANSACTION see **transaction [SHAM TRANSACTION].**

SHARE a portion of something; an **interest** in a **corporation.** See **stock; stock certificate.**

SHARE AND SHARE ALIKE in equal shares. The phrase is normally used to describe the division of property among a class of persons on a **per capita** basis; however, other language in the controlling legal document, such as a **will** or a **trust,** may require the property to be divided **per stirpes.**

SHARED APPRECIATION MORTGAGE see **mortgage [SHARED APPRECIATION MORTGAGE].**

SHARE, ELECTIVE see **widow's election.**

SHAREHOLDER proprietor of one or more shares of the **stock** of a **corporation.** A **stockholder** possesses the evidence, usually **stock certificates,** of real ownership of a portion of the property in actual or potential existence held by the company in its name for the common benefit of all the owners of the entire **capital** stock of the company. See also **round-lot shareholders**.

EXAMPLE: Grace feels that a small company named Venta has a great future profit potential. She has some money that she can afford to risk so she becomes a *shareholder* in Venta. By purchasing shares, she becomes a part owner of the company and is entitled to share in dividends and to vote on certain company affairs.

SHAREHOLDERS' DERIVATIVE ACTION see **stockholders' derivative action.**

SHAREHOLDER'S EQUITY see **equity.**

SHELL CORPORATION see **corporation [SHELL CORPORATION.]**

SHELLEY'S CASE, RULE IN see **Rule in Shelley's Case.**

SHELTER see **tax shelter.**

SHEPARDIZING see **spading [SHEPARDIZING].**

SHERIFF'S SALE [JUDICIAL SALE] a **sale** of **property** by the sheriff under authority of a court's **judgment** and **writ of execution** in order to satisfy an unpaid judgment, **mortgage, lien** or other **debt** of the owner **(judgment debtor).** See **sale.**

SHERMAN ANTITRUST ACT see **antitrust laws.**

SHIELD LAWS in the case of news persons, laws designed to protect a journalist's confidential sources of information and to protect other information, notes and materials from disclosure. In the case of rape victims, laws that limit the questions a defendant may ask about the lifestyle of the victim unless those questions can be shown to be essential for a fair trial. See **journalist's privilege; privileged communication.**

SHIFTING INTEREST see **interest [SHIFTING INTEREST].**

SHIFTING THE BURDEN OF PROOF transferring to the other party in a litigation the burden that one party has in producing evidence to support his or her claim; requires that the person who originally had the burden make out a **prima facie** case or defense by some minimum of evidence. See **burden of proof.**

SHIFTING USE see **use [SHIFTING USE].** See also **interest [EXECUTORY INTEREST].**

SHIPMENT CONTRACT see **tender [TENDER OF DELIVERY].**

SHOP see **closed shop; open shop; union shop.**

SHORT AGAINST THE BOX see **selling short [SHORT AGAINST THE BOX].**

SHORT FORM MERGER see **merger [SHORT FORM MERGER].**

SHORT RATE in insurance law, a term applied to a mutual **rescission** of **insurance** by both parties, who then contract for a new policy that is identical with the original except for a shortened term and lower earned premium.

SHORT SELLING see **selling short.**

SHORT SWING PROFITS see **insider [SHORT SWING PROFITS].**

SHORT TANDEM REPEATS [STR] see **DNA testing [SHORT TANDEM REPEATS [STR]].**

SHORT-TERM CAPITAL GAIN see **capital [CAPITAL GAINS OR LOSSES].**

SHOW CAUSE ORDER an **order,** made upon the **motion** of one party, requiring a party to appear and show cause (demonstrate) why a certain thing should be permitted or not permitted. It requires that party to meet the **prima facie case** made by the applicant's verified **complaint** or **affidavit.** An order to show cause is an accelerated method of beginning a **litigation** by compelling the adverse party to respond in a much shorter period of time than he or she would normally have to respond to a complaint.

EXAMPLE: A group of prisoners petitions a court to allow them greater visitation rights than their present one-visit-a-month allotment. The judge is inclined to agree with them and orders prison officials to *show cause* why greater visitation privileges should not be granted immediately. The officials must then provide at least some rationale for the limit, or the court will order a change, pending a trial on the petition.

Compare **restraining order; summons.**

SHOW UP a one-to-one confrontation between a suspect and a witness to a crime. Although the term is frequently used interchangeably with **lineup,** the two are distinguishable in that lineup refers to a group of persons being shown to a witness.

SHRINKWRAP LICENSE see **clickwrap license [SHRINKWRAP LICENSE].**

SIC Lat.: thus. Used to make clear that the quoted material contains a grammatical mistake or spelling error in the original writing.

SICK PAY refers to compensation an employee receives while away from a job due to illness or injury. In general, when an employee receives payments as reimbursement for medical care or for permanent injury, such payments constitute an **exclusion** from **gross income.** If an employee receives wages or payments in lieu of wages under a disability plan provided by the employer, of which payments are made to the employee on account of permanent and total disability, a portion of such payment is not subject to income taxes.

SIDE-BAR the area of the courtroom that is within the hearing of the judge but out of the hearing of the jury and the witness. When court is in session and the attorneys must discuss with the judge issues that are not appropriate for the jury to hear, the attorneys and the judge will hold a conference at side-bar. Such side-bar conferences are preserved by the stenographer and appear in the transcript for purposes of appeal.

SIGHT DRAFT a **bill of exchange** for the immediate payment of money. See **demand note; draft [SIGHT DRAFT].**

SIGNATURE a writing or other mark that is placed upon an instrument for the purpose of authenticating it or giving it legal effect. Statutes define *signature* differently in different contexts, such as in corporate documents, wills, books, etc. For instance, under the **Uniform Commercial Code,** a signature is made by use of any name, including any trade or assumed name, upon an instrument, or by any word or mark used in lieu of a written signature.

SILENT PARTNER an investor in a business enterprise who either does not take an active role in the management of the business, or whose identity is not revealed to third parties; a principal whose identity is not disclosed by his or her agent. While the identity of a silent partner may or may not be disclosed, the silent partner, nonetheless, participates in the profits or loses of the enterprise. See **principal** [UNDISCLOSED PRINCIPAL].

SILVER PLATTER DOCTRINE the doctrine, now discredited, that allowed evidence seized by state officers in an illegal search and seizure to be used against the defendant in a federal criminal trail. It was subsequently declared unconstitutional.

SIMONY see **barratry** [SIMONY].

SIMPLE CONTRACT see **sealed instrument.**

SIMPLE NEGLIGENCE the failure to exercise ordinary care; to be distinguished from **gross negligence.** See **negligence.**

SIMPLE TRUST see **trust** [SIMPLE TRUST].

SIMPLICITER simply, directly, summarily.

SIMULTANEOUS DEATH ACT a uniform state law passed in most states providing for the distribution of property when distribution depends upon the time of death of more than one person and it cannot be determined that the persons died other than simultaneously. In cases governed by the Act, the law presumes each person died before the other, with the effect that one half of the property of each passes to the estate of the other.

SINE DIE *(sē'-nā dē'-ā)* Lat.: without day, without time. A legislative body adjourns *sine die* when it does not set the next date of assembly.

SINE QUA NON *(sē'-nā kwä nŏn)* Lat.: without which not. That without which the thing cannot be, i.e., the essence of something. Compare **cause.**

EXAMPLE: Jayla purchases a new refrigerator. She puts the old one on the street to be carted away but does not remove the door or lock it shut. A child is severely injured when he is trapped inside the refrigerator. The *sine qua non* is Jayla's failure to do something about the door, which made the refrigerator an **attractive nuisance.**

SINKING FUND an accumulation, by a corporation or government body, of money invested to repay a **debt.**

EXAMPLE: A university borrows money from a bank to build a library. In its appeal to alumni, the school stresses that it wants to develop a *sinking fund* to pay off the loan. It is hoped that the fund will generate enough interest income so that the principal is never touched.

In government bodies, a sinking fund, whose sources are taxes, **imposts** or duties, is appropriated toward payment of interest on a public loan and for eventual payment of the **principal.**

S.I.P.C. see **Securities Investor Protection Corporation [S.I.P.C.].**

SISTERN (awkward) term for a female member of the **United States Supreme Court.** Prior to the appointment of female Justices, the reference **brethren** (brothers) was used.

SITUS the location or place of a thing. The situs of **real property** and of **tangible personal property** is determined by its physical location. The situs of **intangible property,** such as a debt or note, is more theoretical and may depend upon the location of the debtor, creditor or other variables. This determination frequently becomes one of **jurisdiction,** that is, whether a particular **court** has the power to **issue** an **order** affecting the **rights** or **interests** of the parties in such property, and whether such an order can be enforced.

SIXTH AMENDMENT the amendment to the U.S. Constitution that entitles the accused in a criminal trial the right to a **speedy trial** by an impartial jury, to be informed of the charges against him or her, to be confronted with witnesses against him or her, to have **compulsory process** for obtaining witnesses in his or her favor, and to have effective assistance of counsel.

Through the process of **selective incorporation,** each of these rights has been applied to the states under the **due process clause** of the **Fourteenth Amendment.** While these rights form the foundation of the accused's right to a fair trial, the accused has been accorded additional rights, such as the right to conduct his or her own defense as necessary to a fair trial under the due process clause.

SKIPTRACING the location of missing persons such as heirs, debtors, spouses, or witnesses, frequently done by a specialized agency or private investigator, often so **service of process** can be made.

SKYJACKING see **hijacking.**

SKY LAWS see **blue sky laws; sunshine laws.**

S.L. session or statute laws.

SLAMMING   the deceptive practice of switching a person's long-distance telephone provider (or other public utility) without that person's knowledge or permission. The FCC will take action against slammers.

SLANDER   to engage in **defamation** orally; spoken words that tend to damage another's reputation. If defamatory meaning is apparent on the face of the statement, it is said to be **SLANDEROUS PER SE.** If the defamatory meaning is not self-evident, but arises only from extrinsic facts, the statement is **SLANDEROUS PER QUOD.** Compare **libel.**

SLANDER OF GOODS [TITLE]   see **bait and switch.**

SLAPP SUIT   Strategic Lawsuit Against Public Participation. Refers to suits filed without merit against an activist or group to chill their actions and draw effort away from their cause by forcing them to defend themselves against the suit. The suits are filed to retaliate against critics (claiming libel or slander or restraint of business for example) or to intimidate the person(s) into silence. SLAPP-BACKS are lawsuits filed by a defendant against the person(s) who filed the original SLAPP suit. Many states have passed ANTI-SLAPP STATUTES providing for speedy hearings and the possibility of recovering legal fees and punitive damages.

SLIGHT CARE   see **care [SLIGHT CARE].**

SLIGHT NEGLIGENCE   see **negligence [SLIGHT NEGLIGENCE].**

SLIP OPINION   see **advance sheets.**

SMALL CLAIMS COURT   a **court** of **limited jurisdiction,** usually able to adjudicate claims of $500 or less, depending on statute. Proceedings are less formal than in other types of courts and parties usually represent themselves.

SOCAGE   in feudal England, a type of tenure founded upon certain and designated services performed by the vassal for his lord, other than military or knight's service. Where the services were considered honorable it was called **FREE SOCAGE** and where the services were of a baser nature it was called **VILLEIN SOCAGE.** By statute, most all tenures by knight-servants were converted into **FREE AND COMMON SOCAGE.** See also **homage.**

SOCIAL GUEST   see **guest [SOCIAL GUEST].**

SOCIAL SECURITY   federal legislation known as the Social Security Act, which provides a national program of contributory social insurance and is administered by the Social Security Administration. Employees, employers, and the self-employed pay involuntary contributions during their years of employment in the form of a **tax** on payroll earnings, known as **F.I.C.A.** Upon death, disability, or retirement the worker or the worker's family is provided monthly cash benefits. The Act also provides assistance in the form of **AID TO FAMILIES WITH DEPENDENT CHILDREN [A.F.D.C.]**, which provides poor parents with funds for food and shelter for their children and **SUPPLEMENTARY SECURITY INCOME [S.S.I.]**, which provides minimum monthly income to persons who are at a certain retirement age, blind, or disabled and have income below a specified level.

SOCRATIC METHOD type of instruction often used in law schools and patterned after the Greek philosopher Socrates' dialectical method of hypothesis elimination. The process of layering questions and answers is designed to stimulate critical thinking and analysis of the material.

SODOMY **crime against nature,** including **bestiality,** buggery (copulation per anus) and, in many **jurisdictions,** other acts of unnatural sexual intercourse as defined and proscribed by statute. Sodomy was a common law **felony** in the United States.

SOFT COPY electronic copy or video display of a computer file or e-mail. Compare **hard copy** (a physical document).

SOLDIER'S WILL see **military will.**

SOLEMNITY OF CONTRACT the concept that two persons are free and entitled to make whatever **contract** or agreement they wish, and that if the requisite formalities are observed and no defenses exist, their contract should be respected and enforced.

SOLE PROPRIETORSHIP a business or financial venture that is carried on by a single person and that is not a **trust** or **corporation.**

SOLICITATION an **offense** developed by later common law courts to reach conduct whereby one incited another to commit a **felony** or certain **misdemeanors** injurious to public welfare. If the actor agrees to join the other in an offense, **conspiracy** can be established. Compare **aid and abet; pander.**

SOLICITOR see **barrister.**

SOLICITOR GENERAL person appointed by the President to assist the Attorney General in performing his or her duties. The Solicitor General may attend to the interests of the United States in any court, and except when otherwise authorized, only the Solicitor General or the Attorney General shall conduct and argue suits and appeals in the Supreme Court and suits, in which the United States is interested, in the court of claims.

SOLIDARITY STRIKE see **boycott [SECONDARY BOYCOTT].**

SOLVENCY 1. ability to pay all **debts** and just claims as they come due; 2. term to signify that **property** is adequate to satisfy one's obligations when sold under **execution.** 3. In certain contexts, solvency is an excess of **assets** over **liabilities.**

SOUND good physical condition; free from defects. See **sane.**

> **SOUND AND DISPOSING MIND AND MEMORY** language often used in a **will** as a declaration by the **testator** that he or she had **testamentary capacity** when he or she executed the will.

> **SOUND BODY** free from disease or infirmity.

> **SOUND MIND** able to know and understand the nature of one's acts; synonymous with **testamentary capacity.**

SOUNDS IN has a connection with. Thus, though a party to a lawsuit has **pleaded damages** in **tort,** it may be said that the **action** nevertheless *sounds in* **contract** if the elements of the offense charged appear to constitute a contract, rather than a tort, action.

SOVEREIGN that which is preeminent among all others; the King; the State.

EXAMPLE: A state wants to build a highway that requires the use of private property. Negotiations with the property owners fail to persuade them to sell to the state. The state can then use its *sovereign* power of eminent domain over all property within the state to take private property and put it to public use upon payment of just compensation.

SOVEREIGN IMMUNITY **immunity** precluding **suit** against the **sovereign** (government) without the sovereign's consent when the sovereign is engaged in a government function. Compare **Federal Tort Claims Act.**

SPACE ARBITRAGE see **arbitrage [SPACE ARBITRAGE].**

SPADING cite checking; the use of an electronic or printed citator to check the history or current status of a case or piece of legislation. One may also look up parallel citations by this method. *Shepard's Citations* is such a well known citator that it has led to the term "SHEPARDIZING" to commonly describe the process of tracing the history of decisions which follow, distinguish, or overrule the case or legislation being checked.

SPAM unsolicited bulk e-mail [UBE] messages providing commercial advertising or attempting scams at low cost to the sender. **PHISHING** e-mail directing the recipient to other sites (via a **hyper-**

link) or to a phone number, and requesting personal information in order to commit identity theft. Such an e-mail may appear to come from a regularly visited site or legitimate company. **SPEAR PHISHING** e-mail appearing to come from the recipient's employer, human resources, or information technology office. The **Federal Trade Commission** handles charges against those who produce and distribute such mass disruptions, particularly where they contain fraudulent business schemes or offensive messages.

SPECIAL APPEARANCE see appearance [SPECIAL APPEARANCE].

SPECIAL ASSUMPSIT see assumpsit [SPECIAL ASSUMPSIT].

SPECIAL CONTRACT see sealed instrument; specialty.

SPECIAL COURT-MARTIAL see court-martial; military law [COURT-MARTIAL].

SPECIAL DAMAGES see damages [CONSEQUENTIAL DAMAGES].

SPECIAL DEMURRER see demurrer [SPECIAL DEMURRER].

SPECIAL INDORSEMENT see indorsement [SPECIAL INDORSEMENT].

SPECIAL JURISDICTION see jurisdiction [LIMITED [SPECIAL] JURISDICTION]; limited jurisdiction.

SPECIAL LEGISLATION acts of the legislature for the benefit of a certain individual or group, as opposed to general legislation enacted for the general population. Special laws may be constitutional if there is a rational basis for limiting application of the statute to the special group, such as small municipalities.

EXAMPLE: A state legislature passes a law requiring all municipalities to provide sewage systems. Because of the peculiarities of the soil in one municipality, *special legislation* is passed postponing the requirements until appropriate technology can be developed.

SPECIAL MASTER see master [master in chancery; special master].

SPECIAL POWER OF APPOINTMENT see power of appointment [SPECIAL POWER].

SPECIAL PROSECUTOR see prosecutor [SPECIAL PROSECUTOR].

SPECIAL TRAVERSE see traverse [SPECIAL TRAVERSE].

SPECIALTY common law category of formal **contracts** that were valid without **consideration.** It is synonymous with **SPECIAL**

CONTRACT. The usual form of the formal contract that was called a *specialty* was an instrument under seal. Other examples include **recognizances, negotiable instruments** and documents, and **letters of credit.** See **sealed instrument.**

SPECIE money with intrinsic value, e.g., gold and silver coins.

SPECIFIC BEQUEST see **bequest [SPECIFIC BEQUEST].**

SPECIFIC DENIAL see **denial [SPECIFIC DENIAL].**

SPECIFIC INTENT see **intent [SPECIFIC INTENT].**

SPECIFIC LEGACY see **legacy [SPECIFIC LEGACY].**

SPECIFIC MENS REA see **mens rea [SPECIFIC MENS REA].**

SPECIFIC PERFORMANCE an **equitable remedy** available to an aggrieved party when remedy **at law** is inadequate. A decree of specific performance requires the party guilty of **BREACH OF CONTRACT** (see **breach**) to complete performance of his or her obligations under the contract on pain of punishment for contempt. Money **damages,** in contrast, are enforceable only by a **judgment** against property. Specific performance is available only where the **subject matter** of the contract is unique such as a particular parcel of real property or a rare painting, or in other unusual circumstances.

SPECIFIC RELIEF see **specific performance.**

SPECIFIC WARRANTY DEED see **warranty deed [SPECIFIC WARRANTY DEED].**

SPECULATION purchase of property with the expectation of obtaining a quick profit as a result of price change.

SPEECH, FREEDOM OF see **freedom [FREEDOM OF SPEECH].**

SPEECH OR DEBATE CLAUSE constitutional provision that protects members of Congress from prosecution "for any speech or debate in either House." The clause was designed to assure Congress wide freedom of speech, debate, and deliberation without intimidation or threats from any other branch of government, and to protect members of Congress against prosecutions that directly impinge upon or threaten the legislative process.

SPEED see **controlled substances.**

SPEED, DELIBERATE see **deliberate speed.**

SPEEDY TRIAL constitutional guarantee that anyone accused of a crime is entitled to a trial conducted according to prevailing rules, regulations and proceedings of law, free from arbitrary, vexatious or oppressive delays.

SPENDING POWER   in the U.S. Constitution the power of Congress to spend money in order to provide for the general welfare of the United States. At least since 1936, this power has been recognized not only to apply to purposes other than those specifically enumerated in Article I of the Constitution, but to include purposes such as Social Security, desegregation, and environmental control.

SPENDTHRIFT TRUST   a **trust** to provide a fund for maintenance of a **beneficiary** that is so restricted that it is secure against the beneficiary's improvidence, and beyond the reach of his **creditors.**

EXAMPLE: Ross is well-known for his ability to spend large sums of money quickly and foolishly. Fearful that his habits may one day leave him without enough to live on, his mother creates a *spendthrift trust* with Ross as beneficiary. The trust is restricted so that he receives only income and cannot invade the principal except with special permission.

SPLIT GIFT   see **gift [SPLIT GIFT].**

SPLIT SENTENCE   see **probation [SPLIT SENTENCE].**

SPLITTING A CAUSE OF ACTION   impermissible practice of bringing an **action** for only part of the **cause of action** in one **suit,** and initiating another suit for another part. Under the policy against splitting of causes of action, the law **mandates** that all **damages** accruing to one as a result of a single wrongful act be claimed in one action or not at all.

EXAMPLE: Matt develops a new product and obtains a patent for it. Two months later, one of Matt's assistants goes to work for a company that introduces the exact same product. Matt sues the company but *splits his cause of action* by filing one suit for copyright infringement and another for profits derived from the sale of his product. The court does not permit this and forces Matt to combine both suits at the same time in one action.

Compare **multiplicity of suits; joinder; misjoinder.**

SPOLIATION (OF RECORDS)   the hiding or destruction of litigation **evidence.** Remedies include the "spoliation inference" which tells the fact finder that an **adverse inference** may be drawn that the evidence concealed would have been harmful to the case of the person who concealed it; discovery sanctions; or a separate tort action. Some jurisdictions feel the tort of FRAUDULENT CONCEALMENT is sufficient to deal with issues of spoliation. Fraudulent concealment has the following elements (1) the defendant had a legal obligation to disclose evidence in connection with existing or pending litigation; (2) the evidence was **material** to the litigation; (3) the plaintiff could not have reasonably obtained access by other means; (4) the defendant intentionally withheld, altered, or destroyed the evidence with the purpose of disrupting the litigation; and (5) the plaintiff was damaged in the underlying litigation by having to rely on an evidential record that did not contain the evidence the defendant concealed. See also **concealment.** Spoilation also refers to the violent seizure of real or personal property.

SPOOFING see **spam [PHISHING].**

SPOT ZONING see **zoning [SPOT ZONING].**

SPOUSAL DISQUALIFICATION common law rule that disqualified the husband or wife from testifying either for or against the spouse in any civil or criminal case. Today, statutes generally consider a husband or wife fully competent to testify either for or against a spouse, subject to the limitations of the **marital communications privilege.** The witness-spouse alone has a privilege to refuse to testify adversely. The witness may be neither compelled to testify nor foreclosed from testifying.

SPRINGING INTEREST see **interest [SPRINGING INTEREST].**

SPRINGING USE see **use.** See also **interest [EXECUTORY INTEREST].**

SQUEEZE-OUT in corporate law, any transaction engaged in by the parties in control of a corporation for the purpose of eliminating minority **shareholders.** The use of corporate control vested in the statutory majority of shareholders or the **board of directors** to eliminate minority shareholders from the enterprise or to reduce to relative insignificance their voting power or claims on corporate assets. Furthermore, it implies a purpose to force upon the minority shareholder a change that is not incident to any other business goal of the corporation. Although the form of such freeze-out transaction may vary and is not confined to merger or consolidation, the policy considerations are generally the same.

SSI see **Social Security [SUPPLEMENTARY SECURITY INCOME].**

SSN Social Security number. See **Social Security.**

STAKEHOLDER a third party chosen by two or more persons to keep in deposit **property** whose **title** is in dispute, and to deliver the property to the one who establishes his right to it.

STALKING persistent, distressing, or threatening behavior consisting of at least two elements: the actor must repeatedly follow the victim and must engage in conduct that annoys or alarms the victim and serves no legitimate purpose. Constitutionally protected activities such as **picketing** are not intended to be covered by such statutes. Compare the charge of **harassment,** which is generally considered less serious than stalking.

STANDARD DEDUCTIONS see **deductions** [STANDARD DEDUCTIONS].

STANDARD OF CARE the uniform standard of behavior upon which the theory of **negligence** is based. The standard of care requires the actor to do what the "reasonable person of ordinary prudence" would do in the actor's place. If the actor's conduct falls below the standard that a reasonable person would conform to under like circumstances, the actor may be liable for injuries or damages resulting from his or her conduct.

STANDING the legal right to challenge in a judicial forum the conduct of another. In the federal system, **litigants** must satisfy constitutional standing requirements in order to create a legitimate **case or controversy** within the meaning of Article III of the Constitution. In construing this language, courts have held that the gist of the question of standing is whether the party seeking **relief** has alleged a personal stake in the outcome of the controversy so as to insure that real, rather than remote or possible, adverseness exists to sharpen the presentation of issues.

EXAMPLE: Payne, a resident of one state, files a suit claiming that another state prevents its own citizens from voting. Since Payne is not affected by the fact that citizens of another state may not be getting the opportunity to vote, he has no *standing* to bring this challenge. There are procedures whereby a court has the discretionary power to allow Payne to participate in a suit if someone files it who does have standing. Payne might also have standing in the suit first referred to if the challenged state action adversely impacts on a national election that affects Payne.

STANDING MUTE in a criminal trial, refusing to **plead;** today equivalent to a **plea** of **not guilty.** Compare **self-incrimination, privilege against.**

STANDING ORDER see **order** [STANDING ORDER].

STAR CHAMBER an ancient court of England that received its name because the ceiling was covered with stars. It sat with no jury and could administer any penalty but death. The Star Chamber was abolished when its jurisdiction was expanded to such an extent that it became too onerous for the people of England. The abuses of the Star Chamber were a principal reason for the incorporation in the federal consitution of the privilege against **self-incrimination.**

STARE DECISIS *(stä'-rā dĕ-sī'-sĭs)* Lat.: to stand by that which was decided. Rule by which **common law** courts are reluctant to interfere with principles announced in former decisions and therefore rely upon judicial **precedent** as a compelling guide to decision of cases raising issues similar to those in previous cases.

EXAMPLE: A state supreme court rules that a person's privacy interests demand court protection of telephone toll records from police investigations. Several years later, the issue is brought back to the court. The prosecutor claims that other states allow the records to be used without interference in privacy and that other privacy protections can be employed if necessary. Even if some new members of the court agree with the prosecutor, the court most likely will apply *stare decisis* and abide by the previous decision.

STAT. abbreviation for **statute;** also, informal for immediately.

STATE 1. an institution. An organized community of persons living within territorial limits. Pertaining to government, a nation, or sovereignty generally. Also, one of the parts of a nation, such as a state of the United States. The term *state in the United States of America* includes the 48 continental states and Alaska and Hawaii. Puerto Rico, Guam, and the Virgin Islands of the United States are examples of U.S. Territories, while the term **OUTLYING POSSESSIONS** of the United States means only American Samoa and Swains Island. 2. character; 3. condition, status, or situation; 4. circumstance; 5. display, say, or declare.

STATE ACTION generally, term used to describe claims arising under the due process clause of the **Fourteenth Amendment** and the Civil Rights Act for which a private party is seeking damages or other proper remedy because the state has violated that party's civil rights. See **color of law.**

STATEMENT a declaration of fact; an allegation by a witness. See also **prior inconsistent statement; registration statement.**

CLOSING STATEMENT in litigation, a **summation** made by the attorney, at the end of the case, which sets forth that client's case. In real estate law, a document prepared in the closing of a sale of real estate that summarizes the transaction and sets forth its financial terms.

OPENING STATEMENT in litigation, a statement made by the attorney for each party after the jury has been selected and before any evidence has been presented. A defendant may reserve an opening statement until after the conclusion of the plaintiff's case. An opening statement outlines for the jury the evidence that each party intends to present and informs the jury of the party's theory of the case.

STATE OF MIND one's mental processes. See **hearsay rule** [state of mind exception]; **mens rea.**

STATE OR MUNICIPAL BONDS state or municipal bonds are debt instruments issued by state or local governments. The interest paid or accrued on such bonds is generally an **exclusion** from **gross income,** and thus not subject to **income tax.**

STATE REMEDIES see **exhaustion of remedies** [EXHAUSTION OF STATE REMEDIES].

STATE'S ATTORNEY see **prosecutor.**

STATE SECRETS information which the federal government withholds in court proceedings for national security reasons. It is a common law rule of evidence not codified in any statute. Congress is considering procedures and standards for resolving claims of state secret privilege.

STATE [STATE-SPONSORED] TERRORISM see **terrorism** [STATE [STATE-SPONSORED] TERRORISM].

STATU QUO see **in statu quo.**

STATUS CRIME an offense where there is no wrongful deed that would render the actor criminally liable if combined with **mens rea.** The imposition of any punishment for such an offense violates the **cruel and unusual punishment** prohibition of the **Eighth Amendment.** For example, although one may be convicted for the use of drugs one may not be convicted for the mere status of addiction to drugs. See also **vagrancy.**

STATUS QUO *(stă'-tŭs kwō)* Lat.: the positions or conditions that exist.

    STATUS QUO ANTE the situation that existed at the inception of a **contract.**

    See **injunction; rescission; restraining order.**

STATUTE an act of the legislature, adopted under its constitutional authority, by prescribed means and in certain form, so that it becomes the law governing conduct within its scope. Statutes are enacted to prescribe conduct, define crimes, create inferior government bodies, appropriate public monies, and in general to promote the public welfare. Compare **common law; judge-made law; ordinance; police power.** See **declaratory statutes; severable statute.**

STATUTE OF DESCENT AND DISTRIBUTION   see **descent and distribution** [STATUTE OF DESCENT AND DISTRIBUTION].

STATUTE OF FRAUDS   statutory requirement that certain kinds of **contracts** be in writing to be enforceable. Contracts to answer to a **creditor** for the **debt** of another, contracts made in **consideration** of marriage, contracts for the sale of land or affecting any **interest** in land and contracts not to be performed within one year from their making normally must be evidenced by a written memorandum and be signed by the **party** sought to be bound by the contract.

STATUTE OF LIMITATIONS   any law that fixes the time within which parties must take judicial action to enforce rights or else be thereafter barred from enforcing them. Equity proceedings are governed by an independent doctrine called **laches.**

The enactment of such laws and invocation of the doctrine of laches to bar suits in equity derives from the belief that there is a point beyond which a prospective defendant should no longer worry about a future possibility of an action against him or her, that the law disfavors "stale evidence," and that no one should be able to "sit on his (her) rights" for an unreasonable time without forfeiting claims.

STATUTE OF QUIA EMPTORES   see **Quia Emportes, Statute of.**

STATUTE OF REPOSE   see **repose** [STATUTE OF REPOSE].

STATUTE OF USES   an English statute, enacted in 1536, to prevent separation of legal and EQUITABLE ESTATES (see **estate**) in land, a separation that arose whenever a **use** was created at **common law.** The purpose was to unite all legal and equitable estates in the **beneficiary** (the holder of the equitable estate) and to strip the **trustee** (the holder of the legal **title**) of all interest.

STATUTE OF WILLS   an early English statute prescribing conditions necessary for valid disposition through a **will.** Today the term is used broadly to refer to the statutory provisions of a particular **jurisdiction** relating to requirements for valid testamentary dispositions.

STATUTE, TITLE OF A   see **title** [TITLE (OF A STATUTE)].

STATUTORY ARSON   see **arson** [STATUTORY ARSON].

STATUTORY CONSTRUCTION   the process by which one determines the meaning of statutes by drawing conclusions with respect to matters that lie beyond the direct expression of the text from elements known and given in the text. The meaning of a law may be ascertained from examining extraneous connected circumstances, laws, writings or legislative history bearing on the same or connected matter, and seeking therefrom the probable aim and purpose of the statute. The courts have developed principles of statutory construction, such as **ejusdem generis** and **expressio unius est exclusio alterius.** See **liberal construction; severable statute [SEVERABILITY CLAUSE]; strict construction**.

STATUTORY EXCEPTIONS see **exceptions [STATUTORY EXCEPTIONS]**.

STATUTORY LAW the law created by legislatively enacted **statutes.** Compare **common law.**

STATUTORY OFFENSE those crimes created by **statutes** and not by **common law**; offenses **malum prohibitum**. See **regulatory offense.**

STATUTORY RAPE see **carnal knowledge; rape [STATUTORY RAPE]**.

STAY a halt in a judicial **proceeding** where, by its **order,** the court will not take further action until the occurrence of some event.

STAY OF EXECUTION process whereby a **judgment** is precluded from being executed for a specific period.

EXAMPLE: An apartment dweller is found in default under his lease. He seeks a *stay of execution* of the eviction order until he can make new living arrangements. A stay may be granted, but not for an excessively long time.

STEP TRANSACTION see **transaction [STEP TRANSACTION]**.

STEP-UP BASIS see **basis [STEP-UP BASIS]**.

STIMULANTS see **controlled substances [STIMULANTS]**.

STIPULATION an agreement or concession made by parties in a judicial proceeding or by their attorneys, relating to a matter before the court.

EXAMPLE: Two parties in a contractual dispute agree as to most of the facts except those occurring immediately prior to the breach of contract. To avoid unnecessary delays in proving facts that the parties agree on, they enter a *stipulation* with the court as to those facts. If one of those facts is actually a legal conclusion based on the facts, the court will not accept that part of the stipulation.

STIRPES see **per stirpes.**

STOCK 1. a merchant's inventory; 2. the **capital** of a corporation, consisting of proceeds from the sale of shares and evidenced by the total number of shares issued; 3. the number of shares owned by an individual shareholder and the proportionate **equity** interest in the corporation represented thereby. See **securities.**

BONUS STOCK see **bonus stock.**

COMMON STOCK see **common stock.**

NO-PAR STOCK see **no-par [nonpar] stock.**

PREFERRED STOCK see **preferred stock.**

STOCKBROKER see **broker** or **registered representative.**

STOCK CERTIFICATE written **instrument** evidencing a **share** in the ownership of a **corporation.**

STOCK CLEARING a so-called "back office" function in the securities trade that involves physical delivery of securities and money payments between buyers and sellers.

STOCK CORPORATION see **nonstock corporation.**

STOCK DIVIDEND see **dividend [STOCK DIVIDEND].**

STOCK EXCHANGE a place where the business of buying and selling **securities** is transacted. See **New York Stock Exchange; regional stock exchange.**

STOCKHOLDER see **dummy [DUMMY SHAREHOLDER]; security; shareholder.**

STOCKHOLDERS' DERIVATIVE ACTION see **derivative action.**

EXAMPLE: The shareholders of a corporation believe that the corporation is not pressing a debt owed to it by another company. The shareholders bring a *stockholders' derivative action* to force the officers to take steps against the other company to secure payment of the debt.

STOCK, INVESTMENT see **restricted securities [INVESTMENT STOCK].**

STOCK ISSUE see **issue [STOCK ISSUE].**

STOCK, LETTER see **restricted securities [LETTER STOCK].**

STOCK MARKET an organized market, such as a **stock exchange** or an **over-the-counter market,** where **stocks** and **bonds** are actively traded. See also **brokers; dealers; securities.**

STOCK OPTION the granting to an individual of the right to purchase a corporate stock at some future date at a price specified at the time the option is given rather than at the time the stock is obtained. The option may be purchased or sold, as in a **CALL OPTION,** or may be granted to an individual by the company as is an **EMPLOYEE STOCK OPTION.** The option will always involve a specified number of shares, state a time period within which it may be exercised and state a price to be paid upon exercise. A **PUT OPTION** is the reverse of a call option in that the holder has a right to compel the seller of the option to purchase his shares at a fixed price during a set time period for a predetermined price per share.

EXAMPLE: Santiago acquires the right to buy *x* number of shares of corporate stock in two months at $20 a share. The price of the *stock option* depends on the price of the stock at the time the option is purchased. Santiago hopes that the stock will be worth over $20 in two months. If it is worth $25 at that time, he may decide to exercise his option to purchase at $20 and then choose to sell the stock immediately at a profit for its market value of $25. If it is worth less than $20 in two months, however, Santiago will probably not exercise his option and will only lose whatever he paid for the option. At any time before expiration, Santiago can sell the option for its then market value.

STOCK RIGHTS see **subscription rights.**

STOCK SPLIT a dividing up of the outstanding shares of the corporation into a greater number of units without disturbing the stockholder's original proportional participating interest in the corporation. Stock split involves no change in the capital account, while a **stock dividend** involves a transfer of accumulated earnings to the capital account. In the event of a corporate *stock split,* no change is made in any corporate accounts, and although more shares are issued to present holders by reducing **par** (or stated) **value,** there is no distribution in any sense.

STOLEN PROPERTY see **receiving stolen property.**

STOP AND FRISK in reference to police conduct on the street, a limited search for weapons confined to outer clothing.

EXAMPLE: A policeman observes two men walk in front of a jewelry store several times and discuss what they see after each trip. The policeman is permitted to *stop* the men and question them until the purpose of their activity is sufficiently explained. He can *frisk* them if he sees a bulge that appears to be a weapon or if he otherwise has a reasonable belief that one of them possesses a weapon. To do anything beyond this "stop and frisk" requires a more concrete belief that the pair will commit or have committed a crime.

Compare **search and seizure.**

STOWAWAY for immigration purposes, any alien who obtains transportation without the consent of the owner, charterer, master, or person in command of any vessel or aircraft through concealment aboard such vessel or aircraft.

STRADDLE in the securities trade, refers to an **option** position in which a holder has both a **put** (contract to sell) and a **call** (contract to buy) on the same **stock** or **commodity** at the same or nearly the same exercise price. Profit is gained if the optioned stock has a large price movement in either direction. If the price remains stable, a loss results. Thus, straddles are of interest when the underlying stock or commodity is very volatile, but the direction of the next move is uncertain. See **hedging.**

STRAIGHT BILL OF LADING see **bill of lading [STRAIGHT BILL OF LADING].**

STRAIGHT-LINE METHOD see **depreciation [STRAIGHT-LINE DEPRECIATION].**

STRAW MAN [PERSON] 1. a colloquial expression designating arguments in **briefs** or **opinions** created solely for the purpose of refuting them. Such arguments are like straw men because they are, by nature, insubstantial.

2. In commercial and property contexts, the term may be used when a transfer is made to a third party, the straw man, simply to retransfer to the transferror or to transfer to another in order to accomplish some purpose not otherwise permitted.

STREET NAME refers to **securities** held in the name of a **broker** or the broker's nominee instead of the name of the owner. This is required when securities are purchased on **margin.** Many cash buyers leave their securities with their broker, who normally holds them in street name, although arrangements can be made to hold the securities as custodian in the customer's name.

STRICT CONSTRUCTION 1. adherence to the literal meaning of the words in **statutes** or **contracts;** 2. an interpretation that confines a statute or **instrument** to subjects or applications obviously within its terms or purposes.

STRICT LIABILITY in **tort** and criminal law, liability without a showing of fault, or the need to show fault. See **ultrahazardous activity.**

EXAMPLE: Adrienne harbors wild animals on her estate. A child accidentally enters the estate and is harmed by one of these animals. Adrienne will usually be held *strictly liable* for the injury regardless of the fact that the child did not belong there or that the child scared the animal. Society imposes that cost on Adrienne merely for keeping the animals.

STRICT SCRUTINY a test to determine the constitutional validity of a statute that creates a category of persons, including classifications based upon nationality or race. Under this test, if a grouping scheme affects fundamental rights—such as the right to vote—it requires a showing that the classification is necessary to, and the least intrusive means of achieving, a compelling state interest.

STRIKE a concerted action or combination effort by a group designed to exert pressure on an individual or entity to accede to certain demands. For instance, the mass refusal to work overtime by a group of employees constitutes a strike. The right to strike by employees is generally governed by the **National Labor Relations Act.** However, the use of the term *strike* is not limited to the labor context. For instance, the refusal of a group of tenants to pay rent until the landlord makes improvements in the rented property is commonly referred to as a **RENT STRIKE.** See **no strike clause.**

STRIKES, THREE see **three strikes.**

STRIKE SUIT a suit brought primarily for its nuisance value by a small **shareholder** whose interest in the corporation is insignificant. Knowing that the cost of defending such a suit is high, the shareholder sues hoping for a private settlement. These suits are also called **BLACKMAIL SUITS** and **HOLDUP SUITS.** Compare **stockholders' derivative action.**

SUA SPONTE *(sū'-à spŏn'-tā)* Lat.: of itself or of one's self. Without being prompted; refers especially to a court's acting of its own volition (on its own motion), without a **motion** being made by either of the **adverse parties.**

EXAMPLE: A party files a lawsuit and the opponent replies, so that both parties are prepared to litigate the issue. If the judge realizes for some reason that he has no jurisdiction over the case, he will on his own initiative dismiss the case. His action is taken *sua sponte.*

SUBCHAPTER S CORPORATION see **corporation [SUBCHAPTER S].**

SUBCONTRACTOR one to whom a principal (general) contractor or other subcontractor sublets part or all of a contract.

SUBDIVISION any reduction in size of a parcel or tract of land by division into two or more smaller parcels. See **zoning.**

SUBINFEUDATION the process that developed under **feudal** law whereby the **grantee** of an **estate** in land from his lord granted a smaller estate in the same land to another. In 1066, William the Conqueror claimed all the land of England for the crown. Subsequently, he granted land to barons for their use in exchange for **services,** but retained ultimate **ownership,** this grant process being called **infeudation.** Such barons held land **in capite.** Subinfeudation was the process by which barons further divided the land by making grants to knights in return for knight services, and the term also includes all subsequent grants and subdivisions by knights and their grantees. Owners under subinfeudation held land "in service" to their grantor and owed nothing directly to the king.

Subinfeudation was made illegal by the statute of **Quia Emptores** and was replaced by the modern concept of **alienation.** See **servitudes.**

SUBJACENT SUPPORT the support of the surface by the underlying strata of the earth. Compare **lateral support.**

SUBJECT MATTER the thing in dispute; the nature of the **cause of action;** the real **issue** of fact or law presented for **trial;** also, the object of a **contract.**

SUBJECT MATTER JURISDICTION see **jurisdiction [SUBJECT MATTER JURISDICTION].**

SUBJECT TO MORTGAGE see **mortgage [SUBJECT TO MORTGAGE].**

SUBJECT TO OPEN describes the **future interests** of a class of persons in **real property** or a **trust** when the number of persons who could comprise the class may increase or decrease. For example, A, fee owner, conveys to B for life, remainder to B's children. At the time of the grant, B has a child C. C has a vested remainder subject to open to let in later born children. Thereafter, children D and E are born to B and upon their births the remainder opens and vests in C, D, and E as co-tenants. The term is also known as **SUBJECT TO PARTIAL DEFEASANCE.**

SUB JUDICE *(sŭb jū'-dĭ-sā)* Lat.: under a court. Before a court or judge for consideration.

EXAMPLE: Two attorneys are arguing their respective positions before a judge. One attempts to prove his point by using related examples. The other, seeking to weaken his opponent's tactic, reminds the judge that the facts of the case *sub judice* are sufficiently different from the examples to warrant a different outcome.

SUBLEASE a transaction whereby a **tenant** (one who has **leased** premises from the owner, or **landlord**) grants to another an **interest** less than his or her own in the leased premises. Compare **assignment [ASSIGNMENT OF A LEASE]**.

EXAMPLE: Priya has two years remaining on her rental agreement when she marries her boyfriend and moves into his apartment. Except in rare circumstances, Priya will be able to *sublease* her apartment to someone else. But unless the landlord makes a different arrangement, Priya is still responsible for seeing that rent is paid each month.

SUBLET to make a **sublease**.

SUBMIT to yield to the will of another. In mediation procedures, committing to discretion of another or presenting for determination.

SUB MODO *(sŭb mō'-dō)* Lat.: under a qualification. Subject to a **condition**.

SUB NOMINE *(sŭb nō'-mē-nā)* Lat.: under the name; often abbreviated *sub nom.* Indicates that the title of a case has been altered after the beginning of the proceedings.

SUBORDINATION establishment of priority of one **claim** or **debt** over another. A **SUBORDINATION AGREEMENT** is one in which a **creditor** agrees in a **contract** that claims of other creditors must be fully paid before there is any payment to the subordinated creditor.

EXAMPLE: A company wants to borrow money from a lender, but it runs into difficulty because of two outstanding debts, both of which are owed to company directors. In order to obtain the money, the directors sign a *subordination agreement,* which provides that the lender will be fully repaid before the directors receive any money toward their loans.

In real estate law, subordination refers to the establishment of priority between different existing interests, claims, **liens** and **encumbrances** on the same parcel of land.

SUBORNATION OF PERJURY a crime consisting of encouraging and persuading another to make a false oath. See **false swearing**.

SUBPOENA *(sŭ-pē'-nà)* Lat.: under penalty. A **writ** issued under authority of a court to compel the **appearance** of a **witness** at a judicial proceeding; disobedience may be punishable as **contempt of court**.

SUBPOENA AD TESTIFICANDUM *(äd tĕs-tĭ-fĭ-kän'-dūm)* subpoena to testify. Technical name for the ordinary subpoena.

SUBPOENA DUCES TECUM *(dū'-chĕs tā'-kūm)* under penalty you shall bring it with you. Type of subpoena issued by a court at the request of one of the parties to a **suit.** A witness having under his or her control documents relevant to the controversy is **enjoined** to bring such items to court during the trial or at the **deposition.**

EXAMPLE: Several years ago, Wynn was a marketing consultant to a large firm. The firm is being sued by a company that claims the firm gave it false information. Wynn is not personally being sued, but he is issued a *subpoena duces tecum* to testify at the trial and bring with him any papers relevant to the firm's relationship with the company.

SUBPRIME MORTGAGE see **mortgage [SUBPRIME MORT-GAGE].**

SUBPRIME MORTGAGE CRISIS see **mortgage [SUBPRIME MORTGAGE CRISIS].**

SUBROGATION the substitution of another person, the **subrogee,** in the place of the **creditor,** to whose rights to the debt the other person succeeds.

Subrogation typically arises when an insurance company pays its insured under the provisions of an insurance policy; in that event the company is subrogated to the cause of action of its insured against the one responsible for the damage for which the insurance company has paid.

EXAMPLE: While making a delivery, a home fuel oil company negligently performs its task and a home burns down as a result. If the home is protected by fire insurance, the insurance company will pay for the damages. The homeowner's claim against the oil company is then *subrogated* to the insurance company.

SUBROGEE one who, by **subrogation,** succeeds to the legal rights or claims of another.

SUBROGOR one whose legal rights or claims are acquired by another through **subrogation.**

SUB ROSA literally "under the rose"; secretly, covertly, privately.

SUBSCRIBER a person who has agreed to take and pay for the original unissued **shares** of a corporation.

SUBSCRIPTION 1. affixing a **signature** to a document. 2. purchase made for a specified period of time, such as a monthly delivery or a purchase for a series of events. 3. in a **securities** context, see **subscription rights.**

SUBSCRIPTION RIGHTS the **contractual** right of an existing **shareholder** to purchase additional **shares** of **stock** of the same kind as that already held when and if new shares are issued by a corporation. Also called **STOCK RIGHTS.** Compare **stock option; warrant [STOCK WARRANT].**

SUBSEQUENT CONDITION see **condition subsequent.**

SUBSIDIARY an inferior portion or capacity; usually describes a relationship between **corporations.**

SUBSIDIARY CORPORATION one in which another corporation owns a majority of shares and thus has control. It has all normal elements of a corporation **(charter, bylaws, directors),** but its **stock** is controlled by another corporation known as the **PARENT CORPORATION.**

SUB SILENTIO (*sŭb sĭ-lěn'-shē-ō*) Lat.: under silence; silently. When a later opinion reaches a result contrary to what would appear to be controlling authority, the later case, by necessary **implication,** overrules *sub silentio* the prior holdings.

EXAMPLE: An early case holds that a homeowner has no obligation to remove the snow in front of his or her house. A later case ruled upon by a higher court then decides that the homeowner does have that obligation. The later case does not make specific reference to the earlier case. By necessary implication, the later case overrules *sub silentio* the prior case.

SUBSTANTIAL CAPACITY TEST see **insanity [SUBSTANTIAL CAPACITY TEST].**

SUBSTANTIAL COMPLIANCE see **substantial performance [compliance].**

SUBSTANTIAL PERFORMANCE [COMPLIANCE] **perfor-mance** of a contract that, while not full performance, is so nearly equivalent to what was bargained for that it would be unreasonable to deny the one who has promised to perform the full contract price, subject to the right of the one who agreed to pay for that performance to recover whatever **damages** may have been occasioned him or her by the promisor's failure to render full performance.

EXAMPLE: A student contracts to paint a neighbor's house during the summer. He has almost completed the task when he is overwhelmed by the desire to spend the rest of the summer at the shore. The only part of the house unpainted is the window moldings, which are the same color as the house but lack a fresh coat. The student is entitled to payment since there is **substantial performance** of the contract, but there will be a slight reduction in the price because of the unfinished moldings.

Compare **breach [BREACH OF CONTRACT].**

SUBSTANTIAL PRESENCE TEST see **alien** [**SUBSTANTIAL PRESENCE TEST**].

SUBSTANTIVE DUE PROCESS see **due process of law.**

SUBSTANTIVE LAW the **positive law** that creates, defines and regulates the rights and duties of the **parties** and that may give rise to a **cause of action,** as distinguished from **adjective law** that pertains to and prescribes the practice and **procedure** or the legal machinery by which the substantive law is determined or made effective.

SUBSTITUTED BASIS see **basis** [**SUBSTITUTED BASIS**].

SUBSTITUTED SERVICE see **service** [**SUBSTITUTED SERVICE**].

SUBSTITUTION putting in place of another thing, serving in lieu of another. In respect to **wills,** the putting of one person in the place of another so that he or she may, on failure of the original **devisee** or **legatee** or after such person, have the benefit of the **legacy,** particularly, the act of the **testator** in naming a second legatee who is to take the legacy on failure of the original legatee or after such person.

SUBTENANT one who **leases** all or part of rented **premises** from the original **lessee** for a term less than that held by the original lessee; the original lessee becomes the sublessor. Most leases either prohibit subletting or require the lessor's permission in advance. The original lessee remains responsible for the subtenant's obligations to the lessor.

EXAMPLE: A supplier rents space in a warehouse but finds that he does not need the full amount that he rented. He then leases part of the space to a large retail discount store that needs some extra storage space. The discount store, which is the *subtenant,* may pay rent to the supplier or to the warehouse owner. The supplier, though, is still liable for the full rent unless some other agreement with the warehouse owner is reached.

Compare **assignment** [**ASSIGNMENT OF A LEASE**].

SUCCESSION refers to the process by which the property of a decedent is inherited through **descent** or by **will.** See **hereditary succession; inheritance; intestate succession.**

SUCCESSIVE TERMS a series of terms where one term follows the term immediately preceding it.

SUCCESSOR one who succeeds to the role, rights, duties or place of another.

SUCCESSOR ADMINISTRATOR see **letters of administration** [SUCCESSOR ADMINISTRATOR].

SUE OUT to apply for and obtain a **writ** or court **order,** as to sue out a writ in **chancery.**

SUFFERANCE see **tenancy** [TENANCY AT SUFFERANCE [HOLD-OVER TENANCY]].

SUFFICIENT CONSIDERATION see **consideration** [SUFFI-CIENT CONSIDERATION].

SUICIDE the voluntary and intentional killing of oneself.

EXAMPLE: Suzanne is very upset over the loss of a boyfriend, so she goes out and drinks heavily. When she comes home, she decides to take some aspirin in the hope that there will be no hangover in the morning. Unfortunately, she never wakes up. Suzanne is not a victim of *suicide* because she had no intention of killing herself.

SUICIDE, ASSISTED see **euthanasia.**

SUI GENERIS *(sū' ē jĕn'-ĕr-ĭs)* Lat.: of its own kind; unique; in a class by itself. See also **ejusdem generis.**

SUI JURIS *(sū'-ĕ jūr'-ĭs)* Lat.: of his own right. Describes one who is no longer dependent, e.g., one who has reached **majority,** or has been removed from the care of a **guardian.** Compare **emancipation; incompetency.**

SUIT any **proceeding** in a court of justice by which an individual pursues a **remedy** that the law affords.

CLASS SUIT see **class action.**

[STOCKHOLDERS'] DERIVATIVE SUIT see **stockholders' derivative action.**

SUITOR a claimant; a litigant. A party to an action in a court of law.

SUM CERTAIN any amount that is fixed, settled, stated or exact. It may refer to the value of a **negotiable instrument,** to a price stated in a **contract,** or to a measure of **damages.** The sum must be ascertainable at the time the instrument is made and computable solely from examination of it.

EXAMPLE: A long-term contract includes a very technical formula for determining the cost of wheat. The formula allows for fluctuations in the market place, weather, demand and other factors. Although the price can therefore vary each time a price is paid, the fact that there is a formula means that the contract includes a *sum certain.*

SUMMARY COURT-MARTIAL see **court-martial; military law** [COURT-MARTIAL].

SUMMARY JUDGMENT preverdict **judgment** of the court in response to a **motion** by plaintiff or defendant, rendered when the court perceives that only questions of law are in dispute, or that the court's decision must be the same regardless of which party's version of the facts is accepted. It is a device designed to effect a prompt disposition of controversies on their **merits** without resort to a lengthy trial.

EXAMPLE: Dale erects a structure on his property that almost completely blocks the sun from the pool area that his neighbor just built, and the neighbor sues Dale to remove the structure. Dale and the neighbor agree on that set of facts. The only question is whether Dale may do as he wants, which in this instance is a question of law. Both parties, therefore, seek a *summary judgment* supporting their respective positions.

Compare **directed verdict.**

SUMMARY PROCEEDING a method by which the **parties** to a legal controversy may achieve a more prompt disposition of their case by use of simplified **procedural** rules, usually involving more limited **discovery** or fact finding than is normally permitted in the particular type of proceeding. Summary proceedings have been commonly used in **arbitration, bankruptcy, landlord-tenant** and unlawful entry and **detainer** cases.

SUMMATION [SUMMING UP] the final step in a **trial,** wherein each party's counsel reviews the **evidence** that has been presented and attempts to show why its position should prevail; also known as **CLOSING ARGUMENTS.** In a jury trial, this step immediately precedes a judge's **instructions** to a jury. The party with the **burden of proof** always closes or sums up last. Therefore, in a civil case, the defendant closes first and then the plaintiff follows. In criminal cases, the procedure varies among jurisdictions. Federal rules of criminal procedure provide that the prosecution closes first the defendant following. In most cases, the prosecution is also afforded an opportunity to rebut the defendant's closing as well.

A prosecutor has the special burden to prove the state's allegations beyond a **reasonable doubt.** During summation a prosecutor must not: comment on a defendant's failure to testify, refer to evidence not in the record, interject personal opinions concerning the veracity of witnesses, appeal to a jury based on passion or prejudice rather than facts, or imply that the prosecutor believes that the defendant is guilty of the crime charged. In addition, a prosecutor cannot be argumentative in his or her closing. It is as much the prosecutor's duty to refrain from improper methods calculated to produce a wrongful conviction as it is to use every legitimate means to bring about a just one. Failure of the prosecutor to comply with the above is referred to as **PROSECUTORIAL MISCONDUCT** and may result in a **mistrial.** Still, the prosecutor is entitled to a certain degree of latitude in summation, and his or her closing must be viewed in the context of the entire trial rather than in the abstract.

SUMMONS a mandate requiring the **appearance** of the defendant under penalty of having **judgment** entered against him or her for failure to appear. The object of the summons is to notify the defendant that he has been sued.

EXAMPLE: Nico sues a landscaper for installing a defective sprinkler system. His attorney prepares a *summons* notifying the landscaper of the court action. The clerk of the court stamps the summons, and it is then issued.

See **process; service.** Compare **subpoena.**

SUNDAY CLOSING LAWS any state or local laws that restrict activities on Sunday, as for instance forbidding the sale of goods on Sunday.

BLUE LAWS any state or local laws that, for moral or religious purposes, restrict activities on Sunday or that restrict certain activities all the time, such as an ordinance prohibiting the operation of a movie theater in a municipality. The name "blue laws" comes from the blue paper the laws were written on.

SUNSHINE LAWS laws requiring that government agencies and departments permit the public to attend their meetings. Often called **OPEN PUBLIC MEETING LAWS.**

SUO NOMINE *(sū'-ō nō'-mē-nā)* Lat.: in his own name.

SUPERIOR COURT see **inferior court [SUPERIOR COURT].**

SUPER-PACS see **political action committee [SUPER-PACS].**

SUPERSEDEAS *(sū-pėr-sē'-dē-às)* Lat.: you shall forbear. A **writ** commanding a "stay of proceedings." The purpose of such a writ is to maintain the status quo that existed before the entry of a **judgment** or **decree** of the court below.

SUPERSEDING CAUSE see **cause [SUPERSEDING CAUSE].**

SUPERVENING CAUSE see **cause [INTERVENING [SUPERVENING] CAUSE].**

SUPPLEMENTAL something added to cure a deficiency or otherwise complete a document or act. Compare **amendment.**

SUPPLEMENTAL ACT that which supplies a deficiency, adds to or completes, or extends that which is already in existence without changing or nullifying the original; an act designed to improve an existing statute by adding something thereto without changing the original text.

SUPPLEMENTAL AFFIDAVIT a subsequent affidavit in addition to the original one. Generally used to explain or correct the original affidavit, but may also be used to set up a new and different defense.

SUPPLEMENTAL ANSWER an answer in addition to the original answer that corrects, enhances, or explains the original one.

SUPPLEMENTAL BILL in equity, a bill in addition to the original bill, that brings into controversy some matter that occurred after the original bill was filed, or that corrects a defect in the original bill.

SUPPLEMENTAL CLAIM a filed claim seeking additional relief after the filing of the original claim.

SUPPLEMENTAL PLEADING [COMPLAINT] see **pleading [SUPPLEMENTAL PLEADING]**.

SUPPLEMENTAL PROCEEDING a proceeding in an action against a **judgment debtor** to discover property of the debtor subject to **execution** and apply such property to the satisfaction of the judgment. Such a proceeding is separate from the original action and is generally governed by the rules of the court.

SUPPLEMENTARY SECURITY INCOME see **Social Security [SUPPLEMENTARY SECURITY INCOME]**.

SUPPORT see **alimony**. See **lateral support; subjacent support**.

SUPPRESS to effectively prevent; to restrain; to end by force. See **suppression of evidence**.

SUPPRESSION OF EVIDENCE the refusal to produce evidence or to allow evidence to be produced for use in litigation. Suppression of evidence refers most commonly to the sanction in a criminal case for an **unreasonable search or seizure** that violates a defendant's constitutional rights. In 1914, the U.S. Supreme Court held that illegally seized evidence must be excluded from use in federal criminal trials. In 1961, the Court expanded the **exclusionary rule** to include state criminal trials.

Suppression of evidence also refers either to a party's refusal to produce evidence or to interference by a party with the production of evidence when another party seeks the evidence pursuant to the law. In civil cases, the failure to produce evidence may constitute an admission that the evidence is unfavorable to the party refusing to produce it.

SUPRA *(sū'-prà)* Lat.: above; before. In a written work, refers to a part preceding that which is presently being read.

SUPREMACY CLAUSE popularized title for Article VI, Section 2 of the United States Constitution, which is the main foundation of the federal government's power over the states, providing that the acts of the federal government are operative as supreme law throughout the union.

EXAMPLE: The United States Supreme Court rules that no person can be arrested in his or her home without an arrest warrant issued by a judge. Regardless of the procedures the various states used before the Supreme Court decision, the *Supremacy Clause* mandates that the Supreme Court's decision govern future police practice.

SUPREME COURT the highest **appellate court** in most **jurisdictions** and in the **federal court** system. It is usually the appellate state court of last resort, and in the absence of a **federal question,** its decisions cannot be reviewed by other courts and must be respected. In some states this court is an inferior court and not the court of last resort.

In the federal court system, the United States Supreme Court is expressly provided for in the **Constitution,** which vests judicial power in "one Supreme Court" and such inferior courts as Congress shall establish. It consists of a Chief Justice and eight Associate Justices appointed by the President with the advice and consent of the U.S. Senate.

SUPREME COURT OF APPEALS West Virginia's highest state court.

SUPREME COURT OF ERRORS Connecticut's highest state court.

SUPREME JUDICIAL COURT Massachusetts' and Maine's highest state courts.

SURCHARGE 1. an additional charge that has been omitted from an account stated; 2. a penalty for failure to exercise common prudence and common skill in the performance of a **fiduciary's** duties.

3. SURTAX is a tax added to the normal tax, imposed on certain kinds of income.

SURETY one who undertakes to pay money or perform other acts in the event that his or her **principal** fails therein. See also **indorsement.**

EXAMPLE: A corporation wants to issue bonds so that it has sufficient money to develop a new product. If the reputation of the corporation is such that people are unwilling to buy the bonds without some guarantee, the corporation will seek a *surety* who in fact guarantees payment of the corporate bonds.

SURETY BOND see **bond [SURETY BOND].**

SURPLUS the remainder of a fund appropriated for a particular purpose. In corporations, surplus denotes **assets** left after liabilities and debts, including capital **stock,** have been deducted.

EARNED SURPLUS the portion of surplus derived from the net earnings, gains or profits retained by a corporation rather than paid to **shareholders** as **dividends.**

PAID-IN SURPLUS the portion of surplus derived from the sale, exchange or issuance of capital stock at a price above the **PAR VALUE** (see **par**) of the stock. Thus, the difference between par value and the actual price received is the paid-in surplus. In the case of **no-par stock,** it is the amount received that has been allocated to paid-in surplus. The term is sometimes used interchangeably with capital surplus, although the latter term is often used to denote the entire surplus of a corporation other than its earned surplus. See also **unearned surplus.**

SURREBUTTER in **common law pleading,** a **plaintiff's** answer to the **defendant's rebuttal (rebutter).**

SURREJOINDER in **common law pleading,** a **plaintiff's** answer to the **defendant's rejoinder.**

SURRENDER the yielding or delivery of **possession** in response to a demand. In property law denotes the yielding of the **leasehold estate** by the lessee to the landlord, so that the **TENANCY FOR YEARS** (see **tenancy**) merges in the **reversion** and no longer exists.

SURROGATE a judicial officer of limited **jurisdiction,** who administers matters of **probate** and **intestate succession** and, in some cases, **adoptions.**

EXAMPLE: After Malik's death, his will is submitted to a *surrogate,* who oversees the distribution of the estate. A question arises concerning a fraudulent transfer of money outside the estate, giving rise to possible criminal and civil liability. Since the surrogate is limited in what he can rule upon, the question must be raised in a court that has broader jurisdiction.

SURROGATE MOTHER one who bears a child for a person or a couple unable to have children, usually for monetary compensation. The surrogate mother often uses her own egg and is impregnated with the semen of the future father, but she may have a fertilized egg from the future parents implanted in her uterus. Upon the child's birth, the surrogate mother relinquishes all rights, duties, and responsibilities to the child. Various states have adopted statutes specifically regulating this relationship. Surrogate parenting contracts were previously held to be illegal under laws prohibiting baby selling.

SURROGATE PARENT one who is not a child's parent, but who stands in the place of the parent and is charged with a parent's rights, duties, and responsibilities, either by virtue of voluntary assumption or court appointment. See **guardian; in loco parentis.**

SURROGATE'S COURT see **court [SURROGATE'S COURT].**

SURTAX see **surcharge [SURTAX].**

SURVEILLANCE oversight or supervision. In criminal law, an investigative process by which police gather evidence about crimes or suspected crime through continued observation of persons or places. Wiretapping, electronic observation, tailing or shadowing are examples of this type of law enforcement procedure.

SURVIVAL STATUTE a statute that preserves for his or her **estate** a decedent's **cause of action** for infliction of **pain and suffering** and related **damages** suffered up to the moment of death. Compare **wrongful death statute.**

SURVIVORSHIP a right whereby a person becomes entitled to property by reason of having survived another person who had an **interest** in it. It is one of the elements of a **JOINT TENANCY** (see **tenancy).**

EXAMPLE: Morgan and Brandon own a house as tenants by the entirety. When Morgan dies, Brandon acquires full ownership of the house by his right of *survivorship.*

SUSPECT as a verb, it is to have a slight or even vague idea concerning, but not necessarily involving knowledge or belief or likelihood; ordinarily used in place of the word "believe." As a noun, a person reputed to be involved in crime; a broad term for anyone being investigated by law enforcement authorities. If the individual is formally charged with an offense, the reference is generally to a **defendant,** rather than a suspect.

SUSPECT CLASSIFICATION see **equal protection of the laws.**

SUSPENDED SENTENCE see **sentence [SUSPENDED SENTENCE].**

SUSPENSION temporary interruption or cessation; abeyance.

SUSTAIN to support; to approve; to adequately maintain.

SWEARING, FALSE see **false swearing.**

SWEAT EQUITY the process of volunteering hours of labor in lieu of financial contributions. A start-up company may provide ownership shares of the company in exchange for the labor of employees at lower-than-market salaries.

EXAMPLE: Saba and Colin worked countless hours painting numerous homes for Habitat for Humanity. Their sweat equity allowed them to receive a home built with the labor provided by others working for the organization. They then make interest-free mortgage payments into a fund providing capital for building additional homes.

SWEEPSTAKES see **lottery [SWEEPSTAKES].**

SWITCH see **bait and switch.**

SYLLABUS a **headnote** preceding a reported case and summarizing the principles of law established in that case. Under the practice of the United States Supreme Court, the headnotes are prepared for the convenience of readers by the Reporter of Decisions; as such, the syllabus constitutes no part of the opinion of the Court.

SYMBOLIC DELIVERY see **delivery [SYMBOLIC DELIVERY].**

SYMBOLIC SPEECH conduct or activity expressing an idea or emotion without the use of words. Some forms of speech, such as flag burning or the wearing of black armbands to protest war have been held to be protected under the **First Amendment;** however, other forms, such as the burning of draft cards have not been held to be protected due to the government's substantial interest in the regulation of the draft.

SYMPATHY STRIKE see **boycott [SECONDARY BOYCOTT].**

SYNALLAGMATIC CONTRACT see **contract [BILATERAL].**

SYNDICATE a group of individuals or companies who have formed a joint venture to undertake a project that the individuals would be unable or unwilling to pursue alone.

EXAMPLE: A large corporation frequently offers stock for sale. An underwriting *syndicate* made up of investment bankers and stockbrokers will first buy the stock, a step made possible by the fact that the syndicate can pool the resources of its individual members. The syndicate will then use the combined strength of its members to market the stock and sell it to the public.

SYSTEM OF JUSTICE see **justice [SYSTEM OF JUSTICE].**

T

T abbreviation for **treasury** (as in T- bill, T-bond, and T-note). Also, an abbreviation for **term, testamentum (will),** and **title.** A letter branded on the thumb of a person who claimed **benefit of clergy** to prevent a future claim.

T/A abbreviation for "temporarily assigned." Often used to designate a retired **judge** who has been recalled to limited duty.

TACIT implied or indicated, but not actually expressed; arising without express contract or agreement. Compare **latent.**

TACKING adding together; l. in property law, the uniting of the periods of possession of successive holders to complete the period necessary to establish title by **adverse possession,** which is possible provided that there is **privity** of estate between the successive adverse possessors. Thus, the original adverse possessor must transfer the property either by a voluntary **conveyance** or by **inheritance** for tacking to be permitted; 2. As a legislative phrase, tacking designates the practice of adding a measure that is of doubtful strength on its own merits onto a general appropriations bill in order to compel the legislature to vote for it; 3. As applied to mortgages, tacking is joining of a third purchaser's **encumbrance** with his original **mortgage** debt so as to close out the second mortgagee.

TAFT-HARTLEY ACT the popular name for the Labor-Management Relations Act of 1947, whose stated purpose is to protect employers' rights by broadening their rights to free speech on unionization; by permitting them to disregard unions formed by supervisory personnel; by outlawing the closed shop; by permitting employees to refrain from union activity; by limiting employee elections on whether to unionize to one per year; by prohibiting unions from forcing employees to join, from forcing an employer to discriminate against nonunion employees, from refusing to bargain collectively with the employer, from engaging in wildcat strikes, from charging discriminatory membership fees, and from extracting favors or kickbacks from employers.

EXAMPLE: A construction company is not allowed to send any trucks onto a construction site unless the driver is a union member. The company therefore cannot hire any drivers unless they belong to a union. The company has the right to bring a suit for a violation of the *Taft-Hartley Act.*

TAIL see **fee tail.**

TAIL, ESTATE IN see **fee tail.**

TAINTED EVIDENCE [TAINT] see **fruit of the poisonous tree doctrine.**

TAKE [TAKING] 1. acquire property by **will** or intestate succession. 2. obtain by possession, whether acquiring legally as in a purchase, or illegally as in a **theft.** 3. seize. 4. pay or discharge as in a debt.

TAKING THE FIFTH the popular term given to a person's assertion of his **Fifth Amendment** right not to give evidence that will incriminate himself. See **self-incrimination, privilege against; Fifth Amendment.**

TALMUD ancient scriptures containing the oral laws and Rabbinic writings that provide the foundation for the religious laws of Judaism.

TANGIBLE PROPERTY **property,** either **real** or **personal,** capable of being **possessed.** Tangible property is capable of being perceived by the senses, as distinguished from intangible property or incorporated rights in property, such as **franchises, copyrights, easements.** For taxation purposes, tangible property generally refers to (**personal property**) personalty, and is that movable property that has a value of its own, rather than merely the evidence or representation of value.

TARGET CORPORATION see **corporation [TARGET CORPORATION].**

TARGETED JOBS CREDIT see **tax credit [TARGETED JOBS CREDIT].**

TARIFF tax; used most frequently in reference to taxes on imported and exported goods; a **customs duty.** Also, a public document setting forth the services offered of a public utility or carrier, rates and charges with respect to the services, and governing rules, regulations, and practices relating to those services.

GATT [GENERAL AGREEMENT ON TARIFFS AND TRADE] an international agreement signed by most of the nations of the free world, including all of the major industrial nations, which establishes rules for the conduct of international trade. The purpose of GATT was to promote the expansion of world trade by the removal of trade barriers such as tariffs and customs duties. Under GATT, each signatory country was granted **most favored nation** status vis-à-vis each other signatory country. Now replaced by the **World Trade Organization.**

TARP abbreviation for Troubled Asset Relief Program. A program created by an Act of Congress to address the **subprime mortgage** crisis. The EMERGENCY ECONOMIC STABILIZATION ACT OF 2008 established a treasury fund to purchase troubled assets, such as commercial and residential mortgages, to aid in stabilizing financial institutions against further losses. With increased liquidity and lessened fear of future losses, banks would be encouraged to increase their lending instead of holding onto their cash, thus bringing order, stability, and improved confidence to the financial marketplace.

TAX a rate or sum of money assessed on a citizen's person, property or activity for the support of government, levied upon assets or real property (property tax), upon income derived from wages, etc. (income tax), or upon sale or purchase of goods (sales tax).

ABATEMENT OF TAXES see **abatement** [ABATEMENT OF TAXES].

AD VALOREM TAX see VALUE ADDED TAX (below).

ALTERNATIVE MINIMUM TAX see **alternative minimum tax [AMT].**

AVOIDANCE OF TAX see **avoidance of tax.**

CAPITAL GAINS TAX see **capital** [CAPITAL ASSETS]; **capital gains or losses.**

CLAIM OF RIGHT see **claim of right.**

DEDUCTIONS see **deductions; tax deduction.**

ESTATE TAX state death taxes imposed upon the net value of a decedent's **estate.** The same tax result is accomplished in some jurisdictions through imposition of a TRANSFER TAX, which is a tax upon the transfer of the property from the estate to the **beneficiary.** See **inheritance.**

ESTIMATED TAX income taxes that are paid periodically by a taxpayer on income that is not subject to **withholding** taxes, in an amount that represents a projection of ultimate tax liability for the taxable period.

EXCISE TAX a federal tax imposed upon the purchase of certain items, such as gasoline. See **excise.**

FEDERAL INSURANCE CONTRIBUTION ACT see **FICA.**

FICA see **FICA.**

FRANCHISE TAX a tax generally imposed by the states upon **corporations,** often divided into two components: (1) a tax upon the net income of the corporation attributable to activities within the state, and (2) the tax on the net worth of the corporation located in the state.

EXAMPLE: A state imposes a tax on "the privilege of doing business" in the state. As long as the tax is only imposed on the income that the corporation earns in the state or on the value of the corporation's assets in the state, the tax is a valid *franchise tax* on the corporation.

GIFT TAX see **gift tax.**

HIDDEN TAX see **hidden tax.**

INCOME TAX a tax imposed upon value received by the taxpayer, reduced by the allowable **deductions** and **credits.** See **return.**

INHERITANCE TAX see **ESTATE TAX** (above)**; inheritance.**

LICENSE TAX see **license tax.**

PERSONAL HOLDING COMPANY TAX see **personal holding company.**

POLL TAX see **poll tax.**

PROGRESSIVE TAX a tax whose rate increases as the amount subject to tax increases.

PROPERTY TAX a tax imposed by municipalities upon owners of property within their **jurisdiction,** based upon the **assessed** value of such property.

PROPORTIONAL TAX a tax imposed at a fixed and uniform rate in proportion to the property subject to the tax.

REFUND see **tax refund**.

REGRESSIVE TAX a tax whose rate of tax remains the same regardless of the amounts involved, or decreases as the amount to which the tax is applied increases.

RETURN see **return.**

SALES TAX a tax imposed on the retail sale of certain items.

SURTAX see **surcharge [SURTAX].**

TAX LIEN see **lien [TAX LIEN].**

TAX REFUND money paid as regards application of limitation statute governing actions to recover refunds; "refund" is to pay back, return, restore, make restitution. A "tax exemption" implies that no tax is payable, while "refund" implies that tax paid is subject to reimbursement.

TAX SALE see **sale [TAX SALE].**

TRANSFER TAX see **ESTATE TAX** (above).

UNIFIED ESTATE AND GIFT TAX a federal tax imposed upon the net value of an **estate** and on **gifts** of certain amounts. Usually, the transferror is liable for gift taxes, but if the transferror fails to pay, the transferee may be held liable for payment.

USE TAX a tax imposed upon property when it is brought into the taxing jurisdiction, usually because the taxing jurisdiction has no jurisdiction over the sale and therefore cannot impose a sales tax.

EXAMPLE: A state requires a bus company to obtain certificates of title to operate their buses in that state. The certificates will not be issued until a tax is paid, based on the fair market value of the buses. The tax is permitted as a *use tax* to offset the cost of maintaining the state highways.

VALUE ADDED TAX [AD VALOREM TAX] a tax imposed upon the difference between the cost of an asset to the taxpayer and the present fair **market value** of such asset.

WITHHOLDING TAX the amount of income taxes that an employer is required to withhold from an employee's salary when the salary is paid. The amount withheld is a credit against the amount of income taxes the employee must pay on his or her income earned for the taxable year.

TAXABLE ESTATE the amount to which the rate of **estate** tax is applied in order to determine the amount of estate tax payable. For federal estate tax purposes, it is the **decedent's** gross estate, i.e., all property in which the decedent had an interest at the time of death as well as specified other property, less the estate tax deductions, such as **marital** and **charitable deductions.** See **tax [ESTATE TAX].**

TAXABLE GIFT the amount to which the rate of **gift tax** is applied in order to determine the amount of gift tax payable. For federal gift tax purposes, it is the total amount of gifts made, less the gift tax deductions allowed, such as the **marital** and the **charitable deductions.** The aggregate of all lifetime gifts that are taxable is added to the **decedent's estate** to determine the applicable estate tax under the unified estate and gift tax.

TAXABLE INCOME the amount applied to the rate of income tax in order to determine the income tax payable. For federal income tax purposes, it is defined differently for corporations and individuals. The taxable income of a corporation is its gross income less its income tax deductions. The taxable income of an individual is **gross income,** less the deductions allowed in computing the adjusted gross income, less the excess of itemized deductions over the zero bracket amount. See **deductions [ZERO BRACKET AMOUNT].**

TAXABLE YEAR the period during which the tax liability of an individual or entity is calculated, or, in the case of certain non-taxable entities, the period for which tax information is provided. Compare **fiscal year.**

TAX BENEFIT DOCTRINE a theory that provides for the inclusion in **GROSS INCOME** (see **income**) of amounts deducted in earlier **taxable years** and recovered in later years, but only to the extent that the earlier **deductions** resulted in a reduction in income tax liability for the earlier years.

TAX COURT an independent 16-judge federal administrative agency that functions as a court to hear appeals by **taxpayers** from adverse administrative decisions by the **Internal Revenue Service.** Although such suits may be considered in federal district courts or in the Court of Claims, the Tax Court does not require the tax-payer to pay the alleged deficiency prior to suit. Headquartered in Washington, D.C., the Tax Court holds hearings in several principal cities as well. Tax court trials are **de novo** and an adverse decision may be appealed as of right to the Court of Appeals and in rare cases to the United States Supreme Court.

TAX CREDIT a dollar-for-dollar reduction in the amount of tax that a taxpayer owes. Unlike **deductions** or **exemptions,** which reduce the amount of income subject to tax, a credit reduces the actual amount of tax owed.

    INVESTMENT TAX CREDIT tax credit allowed for investments in **personal property** devoted to business or income-producing activity, when certain specific requirements are met.

    TARGETED JOBS CREDIT a credit allowed to businesses for increasing the number of employees they hire.

TAX DEDUCTION an item that may be deducted from a gross amount subject to tax, in order to yield the net amount. By reducing the amount subject to tax, a tax deduction will usually reduce the amount of tax imposed. See **deductions.**

TAX EVASION the fraudulent and willful underpayment of or nonpayment of taxes. The term is usually applied to activities that constitute criminal tax fraud. Evasion is to be distinguished from tax avoidance, whereby proper interpretation or relevant tax law is made to minimize tax liability legally.

TAX EXEMPT not subject to tax. Most commonly used to describe tax exempt **interest,** which is interest paid by the states or their subdivisions and is exempt from federal income taxes. Interest paid by the states was initially exempted from federal income taxation in 1913 under the belief that taxing such interest would unconstitutionally interfere with the state's ability to raise funds. The exemption is now retained by Congress as a form of revenue sharing with the states.

TAX EXPENDITURE   revenue losses that are suffered by the federal government as a result of provisions of the **Internal Revenue Code** that grant special tax benefits to certain kinds of **taxpayers** or certain activities engaged in by taxpayers.

TAX EXPENDITURE BUDGET a compilation of various tax expenditures inherent in the tax system for the year in question.

TAXING POWER   under the U.S. Constitution, the power of Congress to lay and collect taxes, duties, imports, and excises provided that all duties, imports, and excises shall be uniform throughout the United States, and to lay and collect taxes on incomes, from whatever source derived, without apportionment among the several states, and without regard to any census or enumerations. The taxing power is used primarily to raise revenue. However, some taxes, such as the estate, gift, and generation-skipping taxes attempt to affect social policy, while other taxes, such as the excise tax on gambling and marijuana are used to regulate or deter certain activities.

TAXPAYER   the person who is determined to bear the tax liability for a given **transaction,** activity or status.

TAX PREFERENCE ITEMS   those items of **income, deduction** or **tax credit** deemed to reflect a preference in the tax law for the **taxpayer** benefited by the preference item. Since it is thought that these items result in preferential treatment that may result in minimal tax liability for certain taxpayers, notwithstanding substantial **GROSS INCOME** (see **income**), a minimum tax is imposed on the aggregate of the tax preference items in an attempt to insure a minimum tax liability for each taxpayer.

TAX RATE   the percentage rate of **tax** imposed. Tax liability is computed by applying the applicable tax rate to the tax base.

EFFECTIVE TAX RATE   the rate at which the taxpayer would be taxed if his or her tax liability were taxed at a constant rate rather than progressively. This rate is computed by determining what percentage the taxpayer's tax liability is of the taxpayer's total taxable income. See **tax [PROGRESSIVE TAX].**

MARGINAL TAX RATE   the highest percentage at which any part of the taxpayer's income is taxed.

TAX RETURN see **return, income tax.**

TAX SALE see **sale [TAX SALE].**

TAX SHELTER any device by which taxpayers can reduce their tax liability by engaging in activities that provide them with **deductions** or **credits** that they can apply against their tax liability. In such cases, the activities engaged in are said to shelter taxpayers' other **income** from tax liability.

EXAMPLE: An individual in a high tax bracket may choose to make an investment in real estate or oil and gas in order to take advantage of tax losses that these investments create. The investor, in effect, uses money he or she would have paid in taxes to offset part of his or her investment. And if the investment is a good one, he or she may also make a profit when he or she sells the interest. These types of investments are referred to as *tax shelters.*

AT-RISK RULES provisions of the Internal Revenue Code that limit the amount of loss from business and investment activities that a taxpayer may deduct to the total amount that he or she has "at risk" in the activity. A taxpayer is "at risk" in an activity only to the extent of the cash or other property he or she has invested in the activity and to the extent he or she is personally liable for the debts of the activity secured by his or her property.

TEMPORARY that which is to last for a limited time; ephemeral; transitory. Temporary has no fixed meaning in the sense that it designates a fixed period of time, but is used in contradistinction to permanent. See **injunction; interim financing; interim order; restraining order.**

TEMPORARY INJUNCTION see **injunction; restraining order.**

TEMPORARY RESTRAINING ORDER see **restraining order.**

TEMPORE *(tĕm'-pō-rā)* Lat.: for the time of; thus, the "President pro tempore" of the United States Senate is the Senate President for the present time (when the Vice President is not presiding over the Senate).

TENANCY a **tenant's** right to possess an **estate,** whether by **lease** or by **title;** 1. refers generally to any right to hold property; 2. refers to holding in subordination to another's title, as in the landlord-tenant relationship.

COTENANCY see **cotenancy.**

HOLDOVER TENANCY see **TENANCY AT SUFFERANCE** (below).

JOINT TENANCY a single **estate** in **property,** real or personal, owned by two or more persons, under one **instrument** or act of the parties, with an equal right in all to share in the enjoyment during their lives; and on the death of a joint tenant, the property descends to the survivor or survivors and at length to the last survivor. Joint tenancy originally was a technical feudal estate in land, but now also applies, through **statutes,** to **personal property** (**stocks, bonds,** bank accounts, with right of **survivorship**). See **joint tenancy [ownership].**

PERIODIC TENANCY in landlord-tenant law, a tenancy for a particular period (a week, month, year or number of years), plus the expectancy or possibility that the period will be repeated. In contrast to a **TENANCY FOR YEARS,** a periodic tenancy must be terminated by due notice by either the landlord or the tenant, unless one party has failed to perform some part of his obligation. A periodic tenancy is considered a form of **TENANCY AT WILL** and is created either by express agreement of by implication from the manner in which rent is paid. A periodic tenancy is alienable.

TENANCY AT SUFFERANCE [HOLDOVER TENANCY] a tenancy that comes into existence when one at first lawfully possesses land, as under a lease, and subsequently holds over beyond the end of one term of the lease or occupies it without such lawful authority. A tenancy at sufferance therefore cannot arise from an agreement, distinguishing it from a **TENANCY AT WILL.** A tenant at sufferance differs from a **trespasser** only in that he originally entered with the landlord's permission. The landlord has a right to establish a landlord-tenant relationship (i.e., extend the lease) of a tenant at sufferance.

EXAMPLE: Lance has completed the one-year lease on his apartment. He continues to reside there although the landlord does nothing to acknowledge that he is there, including not accepting rent checks. Lance is a *tenant at sufferance.* He may have certain rights, though, depending on the state he is in, possibly including a right to one week's or thirty days' notice before eviction.

TENANCY AT WILL a leased estate that confers upon the tenant the right to possession that both parties agree is for an unpredetermined period and that either party may terminate upon proper notice. A tenancy at will may arise out of an express contract or by implication. Because a tenancy at will is determinable at any time, the tenant cannot **assign** or **grant** his estate to another.

TENANCY BY THE ENTIRETY ownership of property, real or personal, **tangible** and **intangible,** by a husband and wife together. Neither husband nor wife is allowed to **alienate** any part of the property so held without consent of the other. The survivor of the marriage is entitled to the whole property. A divorce severs the tenancies by the entirety and usually creates a **tenancy in common.** Under the **MARRIED WOMAN'S ACTS** each tenant by the entirety is a tenant in common of the **use,** and is therefore entitled to one half of the rents and profits while both are alive.

TENANCY FOR YEARS an estate in land created by a lease that is limited to a specified and definite term, whether in weeks, months or years. If the tenant stays beyond expiration of the term, the tenancy may be converted into a **TENANCY AT SUFFERANCE, TENANCY AT WILL,** or a **PERIODIC TENANCY.** A tenancy for years is alienable, subject to lease restrictions against assignment or **sublease.**

TENANCY FROM MONTH TO MONTH   see **PERIODIC TENANCY** (above).

TENANCY FROM YEAR TO YEAR   see **PERIODIC TENANCY** (above).

TENANCY IN CAPITE   tenancy-in-chief. In feudal law, the holding of land direct from the crown.

TENANCY IN COMMON   an interest held by two or more persons, each having a possessory right, usually deriving from a title (though perhaps also from a lease) in the same piece of land. Tenancy in common also applies to personalty. Though co-tenants may have unequal shares in the property, they are each entitled to equal use and possession. Thus, each is said to have an undivided interest in the property. An estate held as a tenancy in common may be **partitioned,** sold or **encumbered.**

TENANT 1. one who holds land by any kind of **title** or right, whether permanently or temporarily; 2. one who purchases an **estate** and is entitled to **possession,** whether exclusive or to be shared with others; 3. one who **leases** premises from the owner **(landlord)** or from a tenant as his **subtenant.** See also **tenancy.**

TENANTABLE REPAIR   see **good tentable repair.**

TENANT FOR LIFE   see **life tenant.**

TENANT IN FEE (SIMPLE)   a tenant in fee simple who has lands, tenements, or hereditaments to hold to him or her and the heirs forever. The word *fee* alone, without any qualifying words, serves to designate a **fee simple estate,** and is not frequently used in that sense.

A tenant in fee simple or fee simple absolute holds the greatest estate known to law. The word *simple* is used to indicate that there are no restrictions with respect to the inheritance characteristics of the estate. The word *absolute* emphasizes that the estate is not **defeasible** upon the happening of any event.

TENANTS IN TAIL see **failure of issue [TENANTS IN TAIL].**

TENDER an unconditional offer to pay or **perform** in full an obligation owed to another, together with either actual presentation of the thing or sum owed, or some clear manifestation of present ability to pay or perform.

LEGAL TENDER any kind of currency or other such medium of commerce designated by law as one that must be accepted in satisfaction of monetary debt.

TENDER OFFER a publicly announced effort to purchase the stock of a company, not through open market transactions but through direct dealings with present shareholders, for the purpose of acquiring controlling ownership of that company.

TENDER OF DELIVERY the seller's placement at the buyer's disposal of goods sold to him or her. A seller's failure to tender delivery at the proper place, according to **contract,** may constitute a **breach** unless he or she has a lawful excuse; a buyer's refusal to take delivery at the proper place may constitute a breach on his or her part.

EXAMPLE: Scholarly Book Publishers contracts with a book wholesaler to distribute its books nationwide. Scholarly arranges to have the books shipped to the wholesaler's main warehouse on a specific date, and the wholesaler agrees to pick them up there. Scholarly fulfills its obligation, but the wholesaler does not take the books on the date agreed upon. Two days later, the books are destroyed by fire. Since Scholarly completed its *tender of delivery,* the wholesaler must pay for the damage. See **CIF [COST, INSURANCE AND FREIGHT]; free alongside [FAS]; free on board [FOB].** See also **bill of lading.**

TENDER OFFER a public offer made to **shareholders** of a particular **corporation** to purchase from them a specific number of shares of **stock** at a specific price. The price quoted in such an offer is payable only if the offeror is able to obtain the total amount of stock specified in the offer. The number is usually sufficient to give the offeror control of the corporation.

TENEMENT permanent and fixed property including both **corporeal** and **incorporeal real property.** In modern usage, tenement applies to any structure attached to land, and also to any kind of dwelling inhabited by a **tenant.** Tenement is frequently used to indicate dilapidated apartment dwellings.

10-K an audited, annual, comprehensive overview of the business and financial condition of a corporation registered to sell securities that is filed with the **Securities and Exchange Commission.** Compare **10-Q.**

10-Q a comprehensive quarterly report filed with the **Securities and Exchange Commission** by all corporations registered to sell securities. A 10-Q provides information similar to that reported on the **10-K.**

TENTH AMENDMENT the amendment to the U.S. Constitution, referred to as the **RESERVED POWERS AMENDMENT,** that reserves to the states or the people any powers not delegated to the United States nor prohibited to the states by the Constitution. It expresses the original framers' intent that the central government be a government of limited powers and was included in the **Bill of Rights** to prevent the federal government from attempting to exercise powers it was not specifically given. Traditionally, the Tenth Amendment has been viewed as a mere truism that restates the relationship between the states and the federal government. However, the Supreme Court has held that the amendment bars Congress from exercising power that impinges directly upon state functions essential to the states' separate and independent existence.

TENURE right to hold; 1. in real property, an ancient hierarchical system of holding lands; 2. a statutory right of certain civil servants, teachers in the public schools and other employees to retain their positions permanently, subject only to removal for adequate cause or economic necessity.

TENURIAL OWNERSHIP see **ownership [TENURIAL OWNERSHIP].**

TERMINABLE INTEREST an **interest** in **property** that will fail or terminate on the lapse of time, on the occurrence of an event or a contingency, or on the failure of an event or a contingency to occur. The term is used to describe a class of property that generally does not qualify for the marital deduction for federal estate and gift **tax** purposes.

TERMINER see **oyer and terminer.**

TERM INSURANCE see **insurance [TERM INSURANCE].**

TERM OF ART see **words of art.**

TERM OF COURT a definite time period prescribed by law for a court to administer its duties. Term and session are often used interchangeably, but, technically, term is the statutory time prescribed for judicial business and session is the time a court actually sits to hear cases. In general, terms of court no longer have any special significance, fixed periods of days having replaced the stated terms of court.

TERMS OF SERVICE [USE] rules which must be agreed to in

order to use a service; a disclaimer. See **clickwrap [clickthrough] license.**

TERM, SUCCESSIVE see **successive terms.**

TERRITORIAL COURT a **court** established by Congress under the Constitution, which gives Congress the power to make all needful rules and regulations respecting the territory or other property belonging to the United States.

TERRITORIAL JURISDICTION the territory over which a government or a subdivision thereof has **jurisdiction;** relates to a tribunal's power with regard to the territory within which it is to be exercised, and connotes power over property and persons within such territory.

TERRITORIAL WATERS all inland waters, waters between the line of mean high tide and mean low tide, and all waters seaward to a line three geographical miles from the coastline generally constitute the territorial waters of a country.

TERROREM see **in terrorem.**

TERRORISM the use or threatened use of fear or violence as a means of coercion. Often used for political, ideological, or religious advantage. If sponsored or sanctioned by a government, it is known as STATE [STATE-SPONSORED] TERRORISM. Compare **false [public] alarm.**

TERRORISTIC THREAT [THREATENING] see **threat [TERRORISTIC THREAT].**

TESTACY the condition of leaving a valid **will** at one's death. Compare **intestacy.**

TESTAMENT strictly, a testimonial or just statement of a person's wishes concerning the disposition of his personal property after death, in contrast to a **will,** which is strictly a **devise** of **real estate.** Commonly, however, will and testament are considered synonymous.

TESTAMENTARY CAPACITY the mental capacity that a person must have at the time of the execution of his or her will in order for the will to be valid. Testamentary capacity usually requires that the person comprehend the nature and extent of his or her property, the persons who are the natural objects of his or her bounty, and the dispositive effect of the act of executing the will. It is synonymous with sound mind.

TESTAMENTARY DISPOSITION a gift of property that **vests** (takes effect) at the time of the death of the person making the disposition. It can be effected by **deed,** by an **inter vivos** transaction or by **will.** All instruments used to make testamentary dispositions must comply with the requirements of the **statute of wills.** See **causa mortis.**

EXAMPLE: A father owns 100 shares of stock. He makes a gift to his son as follows: "To myself for life, then to my son." The gift to the son is a *testamentary disposition* since it does not take effect until the father's death.

TESTAMENTARY INTENT a determination that must be made by a **probate** court that the document was intended by the writer to be a **will** and as such reflects his or her true wishes. If **fraud** or **undue influence** is found, then the will is not admitted to probate. See **testator [testatrix].**

TESTAMENTARY TRUST see **trust [TESTAMENTARY TRUST].**

TESTATOR [TESTATRIX] one who makes and executes a **testament** or **will,** testator applying to a man, testatrix to a woman. See **intestate; testacy; testament; testamentary disposition.** Compare **administrator; executor.**

TEST CASE [ACTION] a lawsuit that tests the validity of a law or a legal principle. Usually, the case is one of many similar cases pending, and is chosen for decision prior to the others because its facts are most representative of the issue. Often the case is brought about intentionally by a group interested in determining the validity of the law.

Such cases are limited by the case or controversy doctrine that prohibits parties from bringing collusive suits before the court. See **controversy [CASE OR CONTROVERSY].**

TESTIFY the making of a statement under **oath** or **affirmation** in a judicial proceeding; to make a solemn declaration under oath or affirmation for the purpose of establishing proof of some fact to the court. See **examination; false swearing; perjury; testimony; witness.**

TESTIMONIAL IMMUNITY see **self-incrimination, privilege against [TESTIMONIAL [USE] IMMUNITY].**

TESTIMONY statement made by a **witness,** under oath, usually related to a legal **proceeding** or legislative hearing; **evidence** given by a competent witness under oath or **affirmation,** as distinguished from evidence derived from writing and other sources.

TESTIS Lat.: witness.

THEFT see **larceny.**

THING IN ACTION see **chose** [CHOSE IN ACTION].

THIRD DEGREE imposing mental (by intense questioning or threats) or physical (food or sleep deprivation) coercion upon a suspect in order to obtain a confession. Compare **torture.** Also, a level of crime (such as third-degree theft) having a lower sentencing exposure than a more serious second- or first-degree crime.

THIRD PARTY see **party** [THIRD PARTY].

THIRD PARTY BENEFICIARY a person having enforceable rights created by a **contract** to which he or she is not a **party** and for which he or she gives no **consideration.** The third person is a **DONEE BENEFICIARY** if the promisee expressed an intention to confer a benefit upon the third person as a **gift** in the form of the promised performance. He or she is a **CREDITOR BENEFICIARY** if the promisee, or some other person, is under an obligation under the contract, or the making of the **executory** contract itself, will satisfy and discharge that obligation. To be enforceable by the third party beneficiary, the contract must be primarily for his or her benefit.

THIRD PARTY PLAINTIFF see **plaintiff** [THIRD PARTY PLAINTIFF].

THIRTEENTH AMENDMENT the amendment to the United States Constitution that prohibits slavery and **involuntary servitude** and empowers Congress to enforce the amendment by appropriate legislation. The Thirteenth Amendment was passed in 1863 during the Civil War. It not only prohibits slavery but also forbids **PEONAGE,** which is a condition of involuntary servitude based on indebtedness. The Thirteenth Amendment is self-enacting as regards slavery, and permits Congress to pass legislation forbidding badges of slavery such as all forms of racial discrimination, private and public, in the sale and rental of property. Further, a state may not enact laws designed to force employees to stay on their jobs by, for example, making it a crime to terminate private employment. However, a state may punish a crime through forced labor, and may compel labor on behalf of the government, such as highway labor.

THREAT a declaration of an intention or determination to inflict punishment, loss, or pain on another, or to injure another by some wrongful act. A threat may be made by means of innuendo or suggestion as well as by express language. Threats may be the basis of criminal or civil liability. Mere words, however violent, have been held not to amount to an **assault.** See **coercion; extortion; fighting words; mental cruelty.**

THREE STRIKES laws imposing longer prison sentences for certain repeat offenders. Most significantly, they require that a person who is convicted of a felony and who has been previously convicted of two or more violent or serious felonies receive a sentence enhancement. A **SENTENCE ENHANCEMENT** is additional time added to a criminal defendant's sentence for specified reasons relating to the nature of the crime or the offender's criminal history. Examples include the addition of five years for possession of a firearm during the commission of a felony or an additional 10 years for an offender who commits a violent felony and who has served a prior prison term for a violent felony. The Three Strikes law is an example of a sentence enhancement because third strikers receive additional time in prison for their current offense because of their prior convictions for serious or violent crimes. See **criminal [HABITUAL OFFENDER]; sentence [EXTENDED TERM].**

EXAMPLE: Maxwell has two prior aggravated assault convictions. When he is arrested for carjacking, the state moves to prosecute him under the three strikes' provisions. Maxwell's prison exposure for carjacking is thereby raised from 20 years to life without parole.

THRIFT INSTITUTIONS generic name for savings banks and savings and loan associations. See **bank.**

TIDE LAND land covered and uncovered by ordinary tides. See also **avulsion; reliction.**

TIERED SERVICE offerings on the Internet at various price levels. One level (of limited information) may be free, and other levels may require a **subscription** or provide a specific period of time within which usage is allowed.

TIME see **reasonable time.**

TIME ARBITRAGE see **arbitrage [TIME ARBITRAGE].**

TIME DRAFT see **draft [TIME DRAFT].**

TIME IS OF THE ESSENCE a term used in contracts that fixes time of **performance** as a vital term of the **contract,** the **breach** of which may operate as a discharge of the entire contract. The phrase emphasizes that performance by one party at the time specified in the contract is essential in order to enable him to require performance from the other party.

TIME SHARING an arrangement by which either (1) multiple owners (or long-term **lessees**) of a **condominium** unit agree contractually to reserve to one another exclusively the use of the unit (and of the common elements associated with unit ownership) for a portion of the year, at the same time each year, or (2) individual owners purchase an interest in the unit (and associated common elements) that is limited in duration to a specified portion of each year and thereby divide the ownership of the unit into intervals, also referred to as **INTERVAL OWNERSHIP.**

EXAMPLE: A group of friends purchase a condominium at a ski resort. They develop a *time-sharing* arrangement to fit each person's desire, with Pedro reserving two weeks in the spring. Unless the agreement states otherwise, as an owner Pedro can do whatever he wants with those weeks, including renting to others.

TIME, UNITY OF see **unities** [UNITY OF TIME].

TITHE in old English law, a right of the clergy to exact for the use of the Church one-tenth of the produce of the lands and personal industry of the people.

TITLE ownership; a term used in property law to denote the composite of facts that will permit one to recover or to retain possession of a thing.

EXAMPLE: Marty's car is stolen, and the thief sells it to another person who pays a fair value for the car and has no knowledge or suspicion that it is stolen. Marty still has superior *title* to the car over the other person even though the person paid money for the vehicle. As a basic principle of law, ordinarily one cannot take title from a thief.

ADVERSE TITLE a title asserted in opposition to another; one claimed to have been acquired by **adverse possession.**

AFTER-ACQUIRED TITLE see **after-acquired title.**

BAD TITLE see **bad title.**

CERTIFICATE OF TITLE see **certificate of title.**

CHAIN OF TITLE see **chain of title.**

CLEAR TITLE see **clear title.**

CLEAR TITLE OF RECORD a title that the **record** shows to be an **indefeasible** unencumbered **estate.**

CLOUD ON TITLE see **cloud on title.**

COLOR OF TITLE see **color of title.**

DEFECTIVE TITLE see **defective title.**

DOCUMENT OF TITLE see **document of title.**

EQUITABLE TITLE ownership that is recognized by a **court of equity** or founded upon **equitable** principles, as opposed to formal legal title. The purchaser of real property can require **specific performance** of his contract for purchase and as a result, prior to the actual **convey-**

ance, he has an enforceable equitable title that can be terminated only by a **bona fide purchaser.**

GOOD TITLE see **good title.**

MARKETABLE TITLE see **marketable title.**

PARAMOUNT TITLE see **paramount title.**

QUIET TITLE see **quiet title.**

TITLE (OF A STATUTE) the heading of a **statute** or legislative bill, which introduces it by giving a brief description or summary of the matters it embraces.

UNITY OF TITLE see **unities** [UNITY OF TITLE].

TITLE INSURANCE insurance policy guaranteeing **clear title** to the purchaser of **real property.** Should any defects or encumbrances, such as liens or competing claims, exist in the title, the insurer will correct the problem or pay damages to the **mortgagee** or owner.

TITLE JURISDICTION a jurisdiction in which **title** to **mortgaged premises** passes to the **mortgagee,** and only passes back to **mortgagor** when full payment is made. See **lien jurisdiction.**

TITLE SEARCH an investigation of documents in the public record office to determine the state of a **title,** including all **liens, encumbrances, mortgages, future interests,** etc., affecting the property; the means by which a **chain of title** is ascertained.

TITLE THEORY see **mortgage; title jurisdiction.**

TOLL 1. to bar, defeat. To toll the **statute of limitations** means to suspend the limitation.

EXAMPLE: State law provides that a person has 45 days to file an appeal from a conviction and that a judge must inform the person of that limit. At the end of Randolph's trial, the judge fails to inform him of the limit. When he is informed five months later, it is technically too late to file. A court may *toll* the 45-day limit until Randolph is informed of its existence, which in this case would be five months after the conviction. If an appeal is then not filed within 45 days, the opportunity will not be granted again.

2. charge for the use of another's property. 3. **consideration** for the use of roads, bridges, ferries or other public facilities.

TOMBSTONE AD a common expression for a newspaper advertisement announcing the sale or purchase of **securities** in a **corporation.** The term derives from the fact that such advertisements usually consist of all copy and no illustrations, and thus look like a tombstone. A tombstone ad is merely a public announcement concerning such transactions and does not constitute either an offer to sell or to buy the securities. Such offers constitute and may only be made by a **prospectus.**

TONNAGE in commercial usage, the weight (in number of tons) a ship or vessel will carry, as estimated by the official measurement and computation prescribed by public authority.

TONNAGE DUTY a tax imposed on ships that enter the United States; it is called tonnage duty since it is based upon the ship's tonnage.

TORT a wrong; a private or **civil** wrong or injury resulting from a **breach** of a **legal duty** that exists by virtue of society's expectations regarding interpersonal conduct, rather than by **contract** or other private relationship. The essential elements of a tort are existence of a legal duty owed by **defendant** to **plaintiff,** breach of that duty and a causal relation between defendant's conduct and the resulting damage to plaintiff. See also **derivative tort.**

EXAMPLE: Chandler places a large object on a railroad track to see what happens when it is hit by an oncoming train. The train derails in a set of circumstances that would not have occurred if there had been no object on the track. Chandler has committed an intentional *tort* against the railroad and its passengers. He committed a crime as well.

TORT CLAIMS ACT statute passed by Congress and most states that waives **sovereign immunity** from liability in tort and allows a suit to be brought against a governmental entity under certain circumstances. See **Federal Tort Claims Act.**

TORTFEASOR one who commits a **tort.**

JOINT TORTFEASORS those who act together or independently to commit a **tortious** act, causing a single injury. See **contribution; joint tortfeasors.**

TORTIOUS describes conduct that subjects the actor(s) to **tort** liability; unlawful.

TORTURE any act by which severe pain or suffering, whether physical or mental, is intentionally inflicted on a person for such purposes as obtaining from him or her or a third person information or a confession, punishing him or her for an act he or she or a third person has committed or is suspected of having committed, or intimidating or coercing him or her or a third person, or for any reason based on discrimination of any kind, when such pain or suffering is inflicted by or at the instigation of or with the consent or acquiescence of a public official or other person acting in an official capacity. It does not include pain or suffering arising only from, inherent in, or incidental to lawful sanctions.

TORTURE VICTIM PROTECTION ACT see **alien tort claims act [TORTURE VICTIM PROTECTION ACT]**.

TOS terms of service. See **clickwrap [clickthrough] license.**

TOTAL DISABILITY as used in insurance contracts, a person's inability to perform the material duties of some occupation for which he or she is qualified by experience or training. Absolute physical disability or helplessness is not necessary for "total disability" to exist. See **workers' compensation acts.**

TOTAL INCORPORATION see **selective incorporation [TOTAL INCORPORATION APPROACH]**.

TOTALITY OF THE CIRCUMSTANCES TEST a test used to determine whether certain constitutional rights of a defendant have been violated. The test looks to all the circumstances attending the alleged violation, rather than to any particular factors. While some factors may recur more frequently than others, the relative importance of any one factor depends upon the particular facts of a case. The test was originally used to determine whether a confession was coerced from a defendant in violation of his or her privilege against **self-incrimination,** until the **Miranda** case required that a defendant have his or her rights read to him or her. The test is currently used to determine whether a defendant consented to a **warrantless** search, and whether **probable cause** exists for the issuance of a **search warrant.**

TOTAL LOSS in insurance contracts, the destruction of property such that it is no longer useful for its intended purpose, or that renders it of little or no value to the owner.

TOTO see **in toto.**

TOU terms of use. See **clickwrap [clickthrough] license.**

TOUCH AND CONCERN in real property law, a requirement for a covenant that "**runs with the land**" is that it touch and concern the land involved. A covenant runs with the land when the rights or liabilities of the covenant pass to the succeeding owners with the title to the land. A covenant touches and concerns the land when it enhances the enjoyment of one parcel of real property by burdening the enjoyment of another. For instance, a covenant in a building development that each property owner paint his or her house a specific color would run with the land.

TO WIT namely; that is to say.

TRACT INDEX see **chain of title.**

TRADE EXPENSE see **expense [TRADE OR BUSINESS EXPENSE].**

TRADE, FAIR see **fair trade laws.**

TRADE FIXTURE property placed on or annexed to rented **real estate** by a **tenant** for the purpose of aiding the tenant in the conduct of a trade or business. The law makes provision for, and leases often expressly permit (or require), the tenant to remove such **fixtures** at the end of his or her tenancy, though the tenant is responsible to the landlord for any damage to the premises resulting from such removal. Other fixtures, which are considered **improvements,** the tenant must leave intact. Compare **waste.**

TRADEMARK any mark, word, letter, number, design, picture or combination thereof in any form, which is adopted and used by a person to denominate goods that he or she makes, is affixed to the goods, and is neither a common or generic name for the goods nor a picture of them, nor is merely descriptive of the goods.

Protection from infringement upon a trademark is afforded by the common law action for **unfair competition.**

TRADE NAME name under which a person identifies his or her business or vocation. A trade name or *commercial name* applied to the business and its **good will.** Compare **trademarks,** which apply only to vendable commodities and have different legal protections.

TRADE, RESTRAINT OF see **restraint of trade.**

TRADE SECRETS any formula, pattern, machine or process of manufacturing used in one's business that may give the user opportunity to obtain advantage over competitors; a plan or process, tool, mechanism or compound, known only to its owner and those of the owner's employees to whom it is necessary to disclose it. A trade secret is distinguished from a **patent** in that the owner holds no exclusive rights to it as against the public, though the owner may seek an **injunction** or **damages** for trade secrets unlawfully obtained from him or her.

EXAMPLE: Janeen works for a whiskey distilling company. There is no patent on the formula for making the liquor, although the formula has been used for over one hundred years. Janeen leaves the company to work for someone else. The company can legally prevent Janeen from using the formula since it is a *trade secret* that no one has ever been able to duplicate.

TRADE USAGE a practice widely accepted and relied upon in numerous transactions in a particular trade or industry. A meaning given to language due to its general acceptance in a trade or industry and the reasonable reliance of the parties on such meaning. The **Uniform Commercial Code** uses the synonymous term USAGE OF TRADE, which is defined as any practice or method of dealing having such regularity of observance in a place, vocation, or trade as to justify an expectation that it will be observed with respect to the transaction in question. The existence and scope of such a usage are to be proved as facts. If it is established that such a usage is embodied in a written trade code or similar writing, the interpretation of the writing is for the court.

A COURSE OF DEALING is to be distinguished from a trade usage in that the course of dealing is based upon a sequence of previous conduct between the parties to a particular transaction that is fairly to be regarded as establishing a common basis of understanding for interpreting their expressions and other conduct. The express terms of an agreement and an applicable course of dealing or trade usage should be construed wherever reasonable as consistent with each other, but when such construction is unreasonable, express terms control both course of dealing and trade usage while course of dealing controls trade usage.

TRADITIONARY EVIDENCE statements of fact based upon tradition, long-standing reputation, and statements made by deceased persons that are admissible to prove pedigree and ancient boundaries when no living witnesses are available to testify about such matters.

TRAFFICKING illegally transporting or trading goods or people. HUMAN TRAFFICKING is (1) the recruitment, transportation, transfer, harboring, enticement, provision, obtaining, or receipt of a person by any means, for the purpose of: (i) debt bondage or forced labor or services, (ii) slavery or practices similar to slavery, or (iii) the removal of organs through the use of coercion or intimidation; or (2) receiving profit or anything of value, knowing or having reason to know it is derived from one of the acts described. It includes forced prostitution or sexual services, domestic servitude, bonded sweatshop labor, or other debt bondage. See also **involuntary servitude.**

TRAK FLYER Technology to Recover Abducted Children: a computer-generated system to create and disseminate (among law enforcement agencies and the media) images of a missing child or a wanted criminal, similar to a wanted poster.

TRANSACTION an event or series of events that have **tax** consequences.

CLOSED TRANSACTION a deal in which all events have occurred to allow the transaction to be subject to tax.

OPEN TRANSACTION a deal in which events have not occurred to allow the transaction to be subject to tax.

SHAM TRANSACTION one that will be ignored because it is deemed to have no substance.

STEP TRANSACTION one that consists of a number of interdependent steps and will, generally, be subject to tax based upon all the various steps rather than upon each intermediate step.

TRANSACTIONAL IMMUNITY see **self-incrimination, privilege against.**

TRANSACTIONS OR OCCURRENCE TEST in civil practice, the requirement that a party must make a **counterclaim** for all **causes of action** arising from the same transaction or occurrence that is the subject matter of the opposing party's claim. The failure to bring the counterclaim may result in the party being barred from ever litigating his or her claim. See counterclaim [**COMPULSORY COUNTERCLAIM**]. The purpose of the rule is to avoid the expense that would result from a multiplicity of lawsuits. *Transaction* is liberally construed to encompass any series of occurrences that are logically connected.

TRANSCRIPT an official and certified copy of proceedings in court or at an out-of-court deposition. The transcript is usually prepared by a court reporter from shorthand notes made during the proceeding.

TRANSFER to **convey** or remove from one person or place to another; to sell or give; specifically, to take over **possession** or control as in the transfer of **title** to land.

TRANSFER AGENT individual or firm that keeps a record of the **shareholders** of a **corporation** by name, address, and number of shares owned. When stock is sold, the new owner through his or her agent presents the shares purchased to the transfer agent, who cancels the old certificates and issues new certificates registered in the name of the owner. Not every stock transaction results in a transfer, since a significant portion of most **issues** is held in **street name** to support **margin** or for the convenience of the owner.

TRANSFEREE LIABILITY a tax liability of a **taxpayer** that is imposed upon another person who is the transferee of property from the taxpayer under specified circumstances, in which the taxpayer is unable, because of the transfer, to pay tax liability. In general, the transferee can be liable only to the extent of the value of the property transferred, although the liability is personal and can be recovered from any assets of the transferee. TRANSFEREE, for purposes of imposition of this liability, includes **heirs**, donees of **gifts** and **shareholders** of dissolved **corporations,** but does not include people who act as mere **agents** for others.

TRANSFER IN CONTEMPLATION OF DEATH see **cause** [CAUSA MORTIS]; **gift** [GIFT IN CONTEMPLATION OF DEATH].

TRANSFERRED INTENT a doctrine in **tort** law and **criminal** law that provides that if a defendant intends harm to A but harms B instead, the *intent* is said to be *transferred* to the harm befalling the actual victim as far as defendant's liability to B is concerned. This is only a *fiction,* or a legal conclusion, created in order to accomplish the desired result in terms of liability. The doctrine is applicable in criminal law and finds most frequent application in a **homicide** context (T.J. shoots at Wang Jun but misses and kills an innocent bystander).

TRANSPORTATION see **deportation** [TRANSPORTATION].

TRANSPORTATION SECURITY ADMINISTRATION [TSA] see **Department of Homeland Security** [DHS] [TRANSPORTATION SECURITY ADMINISTRATION [TSA]].

TRAVERSE a common law **pleading** that denies the opposing party's **allegations** of fact.

GENERAL TRAVERSE a blanket denial, stated in general terms, intended to cover all the allegations.

SPECIAL TRAVERSE a denial that is not absolute, but that seeks to establish a denial through the presentation of supplementary facts (or **new matter**) that, if accurate, would render the allegations untenable.

TREASON a crime defined by the Constitution: "treason against the United States shall consist only in levying war against them, or in adhering to their enemies, giving them aid and comfort."

EXAMPLE: The United States is engaged in war with another country. A U.S. arms manufacturer sells munitions to a private party but with the express knowledge that the munitions will be transferred to the other country at war. The manufacturer may be guilty of *treason.*

Compare **sedition.**

TREASURE TROVE money, coin, gold, silver, plate, bullion, or any other item of value found hidden in the earth or in a private place, such as a house, whose owner is unknown. Treasure trove is distinguished from **lost property** in that it must have been hidden by the owner for safekeeping and not parted with voluntarily. In the absence of **statute,** the finder of treasure trove has a legal claim to it against all the world except the true owner. See **abandonment.**

TREASURY the subdivision of a government, corporation, or other entity that is responsible for its financial affairs. The United States Department of the Treasury includes the Bureau of Alcohol, Tobacco and Firearms, the Office of the Comptroller of the Currency, the United States Customs Service, the Bureau of Engraving and Printing, the Federal Law Enforcement Training Center, the Bureau of Government Financial Operations, the Internal Revenue Service, the Bureau of the Mint, the Bureau of the Public Debt, the United States Savings Bond Division, and the United States Secret Service. The basic functions of the Department of the Treasury are to develop and propose national and international economic and tax policies; to serve as the government's financial agent, to collect taxes, to disburse funds, and to manage the public debt; to produce currency and coins; and to enforce specific groups of laws.

TREASURY BILL a U.S. government **promissory note** issued by the U.S. Treasury, having maturity periods up to one year. Notes having longer maturities are called **Treasury notes** and very long maturities are called **Treasury bonds.** Treasury bills are sold at a discount to face value, which is paid at maturity. Denominations are $10,000 or multiples thereof, although smaller denominations are offered when money is in short supply. Money market trading is very active with large dollar amounts of Treasury bills, which are **bearer** instruments, changing hands daily. Also known as **T-BILLS.**

TREASURY BOND 1. a long-term debt **instrument** issued by the U.S. Government. Issues of the U.S. Government have the highest rating among so-called fixed income or debt **securities** and, therefore, offer the lowest taxable yield of any **bonds.** Also known as **T-BONDS.**

2. a bond that has been bought back by the issuing corporation. See **treasury stock.** Such Treasury bonds are usually retired as part of **sinking fund** requirements or held in the corporate treasury, which reduces interest expense.

TREASURY NOTE an intermediate term (one to five years) obligation of the U.S. Government that bears interest paid by **coupon.** Like all direct U.S. Government obligations, Treasury notes carry the highest domestic credit standing and thus have the lowest taxable yield available at equivalent maturity. Also known as **T-NOTES.**

TREASURY SHARES [STOCK] common or preferred **stock** that had been issued by a company and later reacquired. The stock may be used for a variety of corporate purposes, such as a stock bonus plan for management and employees or to acquire another company, or it may be held indefinitely, resold or retired. While held in the company treasury, the stock earns no dividends and has no vote in company affairs.

TREATY a compact made between two or more independent nations with a view to the public welfare: Under the Constitution, the President has the sole power to initiate and make treaties, which must be approved by the Senate before they become binding on citizens of the United States as law. An **EXECUTIVE AGREEMENT** is often substituted for a treaty and does not require the advice and consent of the Senate, though it may be entered into pursuant to formal authority delegated by the Congress in particular legislation. Executive agreements, however, are restricted to narrower topics. Trade agreements, for example, are often executive agreements rather than treaties.

TREATY CLAUSE portion of the United States Constitution providing that the President shall have power, by and with the advice and consent of the Senate to make treaties, provided two-thirds of the Senators present concur.

TREBLE DAMAGES the amount of **damages** awarded to an injured party, whereby the judge triples the amount that the jury awards; it acts to punish the wrongdoer in addition to compensating the injured party. This is a statutory remedy most often awarded in antitrust violations. See **damages [DOUBLE [TREBLE] DAMAGES]**.

TRESPASS 1. in common law, a **form of action** instituted to recover **damages** for any unlawful injury to the plaintiff's person, property or rights, involving immediate force or violence; 2. the violent act that causes such injury; 3. most often connotes a wrongful interference with the **possession** of property and is applied to **personal property (personalty)** as well as to **realty.**

EXAMPLE: Jun erects a fence that inadvertently crosses adjoining property. He *trespasses* on that property and is responsible for all damage that results from his action.

CONTINUING TRESPASS one that is not intermittent or transient, as where one dumps garbage upon the land of another. In such a case, there is a continuing wrong so long as the offending object remains.

TRESPASS DE BONIS ASPORTATIS *(dā bō'-nĭs äs-pôr-tä'-tĭs)* Lat.: trespass for goods carried off. A common law action brought to recover damages from a person who has taken **goods** or property from the rightful owner.

TRESPASS ON THE CASE one of the two early English actions at common law dealing with what are now known as **torts** (the other being simply trespass). Trespass on the case afforded remedy against injury to person or property indirectly resulting from the conduct of the defendant. The action of trespass covered only directly resulting injury.

TRESPASS QUARE CLAUSUM FREGIT see **quare clausum fregit.**

TRESPASS VI ET ARMIS *(vē ĕt är'mĭs)* Lat.: force and arms. 1. trespass with force and arms, or by unlawful means; 2. a remedy for injuries accompanied with force, or where the act done is itself an immediate injury to another's person or property.

TRESPASSER one who enters or remains upon land of another without the owner's permission. The owner of the land has no duty to guard against injury of a trespasser and is not liable if a trespasser injures himself or herself unless an unjustified risk of injury to such persons is created, such as by the use of spring guns or human traps. See **trespass.** Compare **invitee; licensee.**

TRESPASS ON THE CASE see **trespass [TRESPASS ON THE CASE].**

TRIAL an examination, usually involving the offering of **testimony,** before a competent **tribunal** according to established procedures, of facts or law put in **issue** in a **cause** for the purpose of determining such issue.

BENCH TRIAL the trial of a matter where the court sits without a jury; trial by a judge. Both parties must waive any constitutional or statutory right to trial by jury. Compare **jury trial**.

NEW TRIAL a re-examination in the same court of an issue of fact or law after the **verdict** by a jury, a decision by the court or a report of a **referee**. The trial court can grant a new trial on its own motion or an **appellate court** can remand the matter for the **trial court** to rehear. Usual grounds for a new trial are: errors of the court in rulings during the trial or in charging the jury; misconduct of any party, juror, or witness; newly discovered evidence which the party seeking the new trial could not have discovered with due diligence; surprise which prevented a party from adequately presenting their case; ineffective assistance of counsel or any other irregularity which renders it probable that an impartial trial had not been held.

TRIAL BY JURY see **jury trial**.

TRIAL BY RECORD a trial in which a party pleads that a record exists supporting his or her claim, and the adversary denies the record's existence, or pleads **NUL TIEL RECORD** (no such record). If the record can be produced, it is considered by the court in reaching a verdict. If it is not produced, judgment is given to the adversary.

TRIAL DE NOVO historically described an appeal from a decision of a court of **chancery.** It signifies a proceeding in which both issues of law and issues of fact are reconsidered as if the original trial had never taken place. Appeals from **probate** court or from minor courts, such as local municipal courts, are often by trial de novo. New testimony may be adduced or the matter may be determined **de novo** on the basis of the evidentiary **record** already produced. When the trial de novo is "on the record," no new evidence is taken by the reviewing court, but a fresh consideration of the law and facts is nevertheless undertaken without deference to the decision reached in the initial trial.

TRIAL COURT court of **original jurisdiction,** where matters are to be litigated first and where all evidence relative to a cause is received and considered. All states differentiate between trial courts and **appellate courts.** The distinction is that it is the function of the trial court first to determine the facts and the law in a case, with the appellate court acting predominantly as a court of review of law, but not fact.

TRIAL LIST see **court calendar.**

TRIBUNAL an officer or body having authority to **adjudicate** matters. See **administrative agency; court; forum; trial court.**

TRIER OF FACT see **fact finder.**

TRIGGER LAWS laws which are presently unenforceable but may achieve enforceability in the future. They contain both substantive provisions, which would be held unconstitutional if presently challenged, and a *trigger* provision, which would allow them to be upheld by the courts if the change occurs. Examples would be making all abortions illegal, requiring presidential elections to be decided by popular vote, or prohibiting human cloning.

TRIPARTITE having three parts.

TRO temporary **restraining order.**

TROUBLED ASSET RELIEF PROGRAM see **TARP.**

TROVER an early common law **tort** action to recover **damages** for a wrongful **conversion** of **personal property** or to recover actual **possession** of such property. Originally, the action was limited to cases in which **lost property** had been found and converted by the finder to his or her own use. Later the action was expanded to include property not actually lost and found, but only wrongly converted. Compare **detine; replevin; tenancy** [TENANCY AT SUFFERANCE]; **trespass; unlawful detainer.**

TRUE BILL see **indictment.**

TRUST 1. an entity that holds assets (the **res** or corpus) for the benefit of certain other persons or entities. The person holding legal title or interest, who has responsibility for the assets and distribution of the assets or distribution of the income generated by such assets, is the **trustee.** The CESTUI QUE TRUST, or **beneficiary,** for whose benefit the trust is created, holds the EQUITABLE TITLE (see **title**) or interest. 2. any relationship in which one acts as **guardian** or **fiduciary** in relation to another's property. Thus, a deposit of money in a bank is a trust, or the receipt of money to be applied to a particular purpose or to be paid to another is a trust.

ACTIVE TRUST a trust in which the trustee has affirmative duties to perform, requiring the exercise of sound personal discretion. Compare PASSIVE TRUST (below).

BANK TRUST see TOTTEN TRUST (below).

BREACH OF TRUST see **breach (of contract)** [BREACH OF TRUST].

CESTUI QUE TRUST $(s\breve{e}s\text{-}tw\bar{e}\ k\bar{a})$— Old Fr.: beneficiary; one for whose benefit the trust is created. The property given in trust is called the subject matter, or trust **res** (or **corpus**).

CHARITABLE TRUST a trust created to advance some public purpose, such as education, religion or science; also called a PUBLIC TRUST.

COMPANY see **trust company.**

COMPLEX TRUST a trust that under the **instrument** of its creation or under state law may either distribute or retain income.

CONSTRUCTIVE TRUST [INVOLUNTARY TRUST] one that is found to exist by operation of law or by **construction** of the court, regardless of lack of express intent on the part of the parties. When one party has been wrongfully deprived, either by mistake, fraud or some other breach of faith, of some right, benefit or title to property, a court may impose upon the present holder of legal title to that property a constructive trust for the benefit of the wronged party. Thus, to prevent **unjust enrichment** of the legal holder, such person is deemed to hold the property as a trustee for the **beneficial use** of the party wrongfully deprived of rights.

DECLARATION OF TRUST an instrument by which the owner of property declares that he or she is holding that property in trust, thus making himself or herself a **trustee** of the property. A declaration of trust creates a valid trust of the property subject to it, even though the settlor receives no consideration for declaring the trust, and even though the property is not formally transferred. The settlor must only satisfy the **Statute of Frauds** to create the trust, unless it is in substance a **testamentary** disposition, in which case the **Statute of Wills** must be satisfied.

DEED OF TRUST see **deed of trust; trust deed.**

DIRECT TRUST see EXPRESS [DIRECT] TRUST (below).

DISCRETIONARY TRUST a trust that gives the trustee the discretion to pay to or apply for the benefit of the beneficiary so much or all of the trust income or principal as the trustee deems appropriate. Compare **spendthrift trust.**

DISTRIBUTION OF A TRUST see **distribution** [TRUST DISTRIBUTION].

EXPRESS TRUST [DIRECT TRUST] a trust created from the free and deliberate act of the parties, including affirmative intention of the **settlor** [the one granting the property] to set up the trust, usually evidenced by some writing, **deed** or **will.**

FIXED INVESTMENT TRUST see **nondiscretionary trust.**

FUND see **trust fund.**

GENERATION-SKIPPING TRUST see **generation-skipping transfer** [GENERATION-SKIPPING TRUST].

GRANTOR TRUST a trust that has beneficiaries other than the grantor but, because of retention of certain interests or certain powers over the trust, all income of the trust is taxed to the grantor.

IMPLIED TRUST one that is inferred from the parties' transactions by **operation of law,** in contrast to an **EXPRESS TRUST** that is created by the parties' deliberate acts or expression of intent. Implied trusts can be either CONSTRUCTIVE or RESULTING.

INDENTURE see **indenture; trust indenture.**

INTER VIVOS TRUST a trust created during the grantor's lifetime.

INVESTMENT TRUST see **investment company.**

INVOLUNTARY TRUST see CONSTRUCTIVE [INVOLUNTARY] TRUST (above).

LAND TRUST see **land trust.**

LIVING TRUST an **inter vivos** trust; a trust established and in operation during the settlor's life. Compare TESTAMENTARY TRUST.

MASSACHUSETTS TRUST see **Massachusetts trust.**

NONDISCRETIONARY TRUST see **nondiscretionary trust**.

ORAL TRUST see **oral [ORAL TRUST].**

PASSIVE TRUST a trust imposing no active duties on the trustee, but rather the trustee merely holds legal title to the property. Under the **Statute of Uses,** the legal estate in a passive trust rests in the beneficiary.

POUROVER TRUST a trust that either distributes assets to another trust, or that receives assets from another trust or some other source.

PRECATORY TRUST one frequently created by a **will,** arising from words of expectation, request or recommendation that are expressed therein. Though they do not amount to actual directives, such words are effective to create a trust so long as they are not so modified by the context as to amount to no more than mere suggestions, to be acted upon or not, according to the caprice of the supposed trustee.

PUBLIC TRUST see **CHARITABLE TRUST** (above).

REAL ESTATE INVESTMENT TRUST   see **real estate investment trust [REIT].**

RESULTING TRUST a trust arising by implication of law when it appears from the nature of the **transaction** that it was the intention of the parties to create a trust. Thus, a resulting trust involves the element of intent, which though implied, makes it more like an **EXPRESS TRUST.** A constructive trust, in contrast, is sometimes found contrary to the parties' intent, in order to work equity or frustrate **fraud.**

EXAMPLE: Kelly purchases a piece of land, but the purchase agreement names a close friend as the purchaser. Since the friend is not considered a natural object of Kelly's affection, which is usually a family member or relative, a presumption arises that Kelly did not make a gift to his friend. Unless other evidence is shown to invalidate that presumption, a court finds that the friend holds title to the property as a *resulting trust* for Kelly.

SAVINGS ACCOUNT [BANK] TRUST see **TOTTEN TRUST** (below).

SIMPLE TRUST   a trust required, by the terms of its creation or under state law, to distribute all of its income currently.

SPENDTHRIFT TRUST see **spendthrift trust.**

TESTAMENTARY TRUST a trust that is established during the settlor's life but is contained in the settlor's will and does not take effect until the settlor's death; created with the formalities necessary for a will.

TOTTEN TRUST a bank account established by a depositor who describes himself or herself as trustee for another, other than a trustee under a will, trust agreement, or court order. During the depositor's lifetime, a Totten trust is fully revocable; upon the depositor's death, the account is payable to the named beneficiary, subject to the claims of the depositor's creditors. The purpose of a Totten trust is to create a testamentary substitute, i.e., a means of passing one's money upon one's death other than by will. Totten trusts are statutorily recognized in some states and are given various effect in others. Totten trusts are also known as **SAVINGS ACCOUNT [BANK] TRUSTS.**

TRUSTEE see **trustee.**

TRUST INDENTURE ACT OF 1939 see **securities acts [TRUST INDENTURE ACT OF 1939].**

TRUSTOR see **trustor.**

UNIT INVESTMENT TRUST see **unit investment trust.**

VOTING TRUST see **voting trust.**

TRUST CERTIFICATE an **instrument** issued to finance the purchase of railroad equipment, under which the **trustees** hold **title** to the equipment as **security** for the load.

TRUST COMPANY a financial organization that provides **trust** services such as acting in the capacity of **trustee, fiduciary** or **agent** for both individuals and companies; **transfer agents** are typically provided by trust companies. Duties include administering **trust funds,** acting as custodian for property held in trust, providing investment management for trust funds, executing wills. Trust companies often engage in banking activities as well, and are regulated by state law.

TRUST DEED see **deed of trust.**

TRUSTEE 1. one who holds legal **title** to property in **trust** for the benefit of another person, and who is required to carry out specific duties with regard to the property, or who has been given power affecting the disposition of property for another's benefit.

EXAMPLE: A father creates a trust for his children. He wants to control the disposition of the money generated by the trust, so he names himself as *trustee.* In that position, he can be sure that his desires in relation to the trust are carried out.

2. also used loosely as anyone who acts as a **guardian** or **fiduciary** in relationship to another, such as a public officer towards his or her constituents, a state toward its citizens, or a partner to his or her copartner.

TRUSTEE IN BANKRUPTCY an officer, elected and approved by the **referee** or judge of a **bankruptcy** proceeding, who takes legal title to the property or money of the bankrupt and holds it in trust for equitable distribution among the bankrupt's **creditors.**

TRUST FUND **real property** or **personal property** held in **trust** for the benefit of another person; the **corpus [res]** of a trust.

TRUST INDENTURE an instrument that states the terms and conditions of a **trust,** particularly a trust created as **security** for a **bond issue.**

TRUST INDENTURE ACT OF 1939 see **Securities Acts [TRUST INDENTURE ACT OF 1939].**

TRUSTOR one who creates a **trust;** more often called the **settlor.**

TRUTH IN LENDING ACT a federal law, the provisions of which assure individuals applying for commercial credit information relating to the cost of credit, enabling them to decide which credit source offers them the most favorable credit terms. Under this law, the commercial lender must inform the borrower of the dollar amount of the interest charges and the interest rate, computed on an annual basis according to the specified formula, and must afford borrowers who pledge **real property** as **security** for the loan a three-day period in which to **rescind** the transaction.

EXAMPLE: A merchant allows his customers to buy goods on credit. He does not force them to sign any papers evidencing the debt, but, in return, he charges a fluctuating interest rate. This practice may violate the *Truth in Lending Act,* and the merchant may be liable for penalties.

TRY TITLE to submit to judicial scrutiny the legitimacy of **title** to property.

TSA see **Department of Homeland Security [DHS] [TRANSPORTATION SECURITY ADMINISTRATION [TSA]].**

TUCKER ACT see **Federal Claims Court [TUCKER ACT].**

TURNTABLE DOCTRINE see **attractive nuisance.**

TURPITUDE see **moral turpitude.**

1231 ASSET see **capital [§1231 ASSET].**

TWO FUNDS DOCTRINE see **marshaling [marshalling] [TWO FUNDS DOCTRINE].**

TWO PARTY CONSENT see **wiretap [TWO PARTY CONSENT].**

TYING ARRANGEMENT the sale of one product on the condition that the purchaser also buy another product, or agree to not buy the other product from anyone else. A tying agreement is a *per se* violation of the **Sherman Antitrust Act,** in that it allows the seller to exploit his or her control over the tying product to force the buyer into the purchase of a tied product that the buyer either did not want at all or might have preferred to purchase elsewhere on different terms. But, if a seller does not possess sufficient market power to cause an actual adverse effect on competition, a court will not find a tying arrangement and therefore the **per se** rule will not apply. See **antitrust laws.**

U

UBI *(ū'-bē)* Lat.: where.

UBI SUPRA *(ū-bē sū'prä)* Lat.: where stated above.

UCC see **Uniform Commercial Code [UCC].**

UCCC see **Uniform Consumer Credit Code [UCCC].**

ULTIMATE FACTS the essential and determining facts on which the final conclusion of law is predicated. They are facts deduced by **inference** from evidentiary facts, which can be directly established by **testimony** or **evidence.** Compare **mediate data.**

ULTRAHAZARDOUS ACTIVITY an uncommon activity, giving rise to **strict liability,** that necessarily involves risk of serious harm to the person, land or **chattels** of others.

EXAMPLE: As part of the demolition of a building, a construction company uses various methods of blasting. These methods are permitted even though they may cause damages elsewhere because of the need to use explosive devices. But since blasting is an *ultrahazardous activity,* the company must pay any damage that results, whether or not the damage was forseeable.

ULTRA VIRES *(ŭl'-trä vĭ'-rēz)* Lat.: beyond, in excess of powers. That which is beyond the power authorized by law. 1. an action of a **corporation** that is beyond the powers conferred upon it by its **charter,** or by the **statute** under which it was created. 2. acts of public officials beyond their authority. See **quo warranto.**

UNAVOIDABLE ACCIDENT see **accident [UNAVOIDABLE ACCIDENT].**

UNCLEAN HANDS one of the **equitable** maxims embodying the principle that a party seeking redress in a court of equity (equitable relief) must not have done any unethical act in the transaction upon which that party maintains the action in **equity,** since a court of conscience will not grant relief to one guilty of **unconscionable** conduct, i.e., to one with unclean hands.

UNCONDITIONAL DISCHARGE see **sentence [SUSPENDED SENTENCE].**

UNCONDITIONAL PARDON see **pardon** [UNCONDITIONAL PARDON].

UNCONSCIONABLE so unreasonably detrimental to the interest of one party to a contract as to render the **contract** unenforceable. The term refers to a bargain so one-sided as to amount to an absence of meaningful choice on the part of one of the parties (typically as a result of greatly unequal bargaining power), together with contract terms unreasonably favorable to the other party.

EXAMPLE: Renata needs money quickly to meet her monthly car payments. She contracts with a company to work at extremely low wages in return for their making her car payments. The contract may be declared *unconscionable* because Renata entered into it in a distressed state and the company took great advantage of her position.

UNCONSTITUTIONAL conflicting with some provision of the **Constitution.** A **statute** found to be unconstitutional is considered void or as if it had never been, and consequently all **rights, contracts** or duties that depend on it are void. Similarly, no one can be punished for having refused obedience to the law once it is found to be unconstitutional.

UNCONTROLLABLE IMPULSE TEST see **insanity** [UNCONTROLLABLE IMPULSE TEST].

UNDERAGE shortage; deficiency; an amount of money or goods actually on hand falling short of the listed amount in the records. Also, being below the legal age for voting, drinking, or consensual sexual activities.

UNDER COLOR OF LAW see **color of law.**

UNDER COLOR OF TITLE see **color of title.**

UNDERLEASE see **sublease.**

UNDER PROTEST the making of a payment or the doing of an act under an obligation while reserving the right to object to the obli-gation at a later date. Typically, a party will make the payment or perform the act, but will at the same time inform the other party in writing that the performance is under protest. The statement *under protest, without prejudice, with reservation of right,* or the like will prevent an **accord and satisfaction** and will prevent prejudice to the rights reserved.

UNDER SEAL see **seal; specialty.**

UNDER THE INFLUENCE see **driving while intoxicated** [DWI].

UNDER THE WILL, ELECTION see **election under the will.**

UNDERWRITE to insure the satisfaction of an obligation, such as by an **insurance** contract or sale of **bonds.** To underwrite an insurance contract is to act as the insurer, or assume the risk for the life or property of another.

EXAMPLE: Nocturn Company transports highly flammable liquids across the country. It locates an insurance company to *underwrite* an insurance policy, thereby shifting the risk and consequences of an accident onto another company. Nocturn will have to pay a high price for the underwriting, and the insurance company may require frequent supervision of Nocturn's safety practices.

To underwrite a **stock** or bond issue is to insure the sale of stocks or bonds by agreeing to buy the entire issue if they are not sold to the public before a certain date.

UNDISCLOSED PRINCIPAL see **principal [UNDISCLOSED PRINCIPAL].**

UNDIVIDED INTEREST [RIGHT] that interest or right in **property** owned by **TENANTS IN COMMON, JOINT TENANTS** or **TENANTS BY THE ENTIRETY** (see **tenancy**), whereby each tenant has an equal right to make use of and enjoy the entire property. An undivided interest may be of only a fractional share, e.g., "an undivided one-quarter interest," in which case the holder is entitled to one quarter of all profits and sale proceeds from the property but has a right to possession of the whole. See **partition; severalty.**

UNDUE INFLUENCE influence of another that destroys the requisite free will of a **testator** or **donor** and creates a ground for nullifying a **will** or invalidating an improvident **gift.** The exercise of undue influence is suggested by excessive insistence, superiority of will or mind, the relationship of the parties or pressure on the donor or testator by any other means to do what he or she is unable, practically, to refuse.

EXAMPLE: A mother has her son draft her will, which provides the son with most of her estate. The son is also her attorney. If the two other sons, both of whom had relationships with the mother equal to the attorney's, are virtually excluded from the mother's will, most courts will find *undue influence* on the part of the attorney and invalidate the gift to him.

Compare **duress.** See **unconscionable.**

UNEARNED SURPLUS in finance, surplus not part of earned surplus. It may include **paid-in-surplus, REVALUATION SURPLUS,** which arises upon the revaluation of assets above their cost, or **DONATED SURPLUS,** which arises from capital contributions other than for shares of **stock.**

UNETHICAL   not ethical; not in accordance with the standards followed in a business or a profession. See **conflict of interest.** See also **Code of Professional Responsibility** and **Model Rules of Professional Conduct.**

UNEXECUTED USE   see **use [UNEXECUTED USE].**

UNFAIR COMPETITION   1. unfair, untrue or misleading advertising likely to lead the public to believe that certain goods are associated with another manufacturer; 2. imitating a competitor's product, package or **trademark** in circumstances where the consumer might be misled; 3. representations or conduct that deceive the public into believing that the business name, reputation or good will of one person is that of another.

Unfair competition is a **tort** and a **fraud** for which the courts afford a **remedy.** Fraudulent or deceptive practices that are disparaging or injurious to the trade of a competitor may be **enjoined.**

UNFAIR LABOR PRACTICE   any activities by either a **labor organization** (union) or an employer that are unlawful under the **National Labor Relations Act.** Unions are specifically forbidden to engage in the following activities: restraint or coercion of employees or employers; coercion of employers to discriminate against employees; refusal to bargain; coercion or inducement of **strikes** or **boycotts** for a prohibited purpose; excessive or discriminatory initiation fees; **featherbedding;** picketing for organizational purposes under certain circumstances; in the health care industry, picketing or striking on less than ten days' notice.

Employers are specifically forbidden to engage in the following activities: interference with employees in exercise of their rights; domination of a labor organization; encouragement or discouragement of membership in labor unions through discriminatory terms and conditions of employment; discrimination against employees for filing labor grievances or testifying in regard to them; refusal to bargain collectively with the representative of a majority of the employees; entering into contracts that discriminate against other employers. See **collective bargaining.**

UNFIT   unsuitable, incompetent, or not adapted for a particular use or service. Compare **warranty [WARRANTY OF FITNESS].** In the context of a parent child relationshop the term *unfit* usually, although not necessarily, imports something of moral delinquency.

UNIFIED ESTATE AND GIFT TAX   see **tax [UNIFIED ESTATE AND GIFT TAX].**

UNIFORM ARBITRATION ACT   see **arbitrator [UNIFORM ARBITRATION ACT].**

UNIFORM CODE OF MILITARY JUSTICE   see **military law** [(UNIFORM) CODE OF MILITARY JUSTICE].

UNIFORM COMMERCIAL CODE [UCC]   a code of laws governing various commercial transactions, including the sale of **goods,** banking transactions, secured transactions in **personal property,** and other matters, that was designed to bring uniformity in these areas to the laws of the various states, and that has been adopted, with some modifications, in all states (except Louisiana) as well as in the District of Columbia and in the Virgin Islands.

UNIFORM CONSUMER CREDIT CODE [UCCC]   one of several **uniform laws** that states may or may not adopt, the UCCC was passed to simplify and further consumer understanding of all aspects of credit and credit transactions and to encourage the development of sound consumer credit practices. Sometimes called U3C.

UNIFORM GIFTS TO MINORS ACT [UGMA]   a **uniform law** adopted by every state that creates a statutory method for making a **gift** in **trust** to minors.

   The law usually applies only to certain types of personal property, such as securities, annuity, life insurance and endowment policies, partnership interests, or tangibles. The gift is made and the **trust** is created by the donor either by registering the property in the name of the custodian, followed by the language "as custodian for . . ." or by delivering the property to the custodian together with a statement that the property is to be held as custodian under the Uniform Gifts to Minors Act. The statutes set forth the terms of the trust, under which the custodian may apply the trust fund for the benefit of the minor and is obliged to pay over the funds upon the minor attaining age 18, unless the donor indicates at the time of the gift that it is to be held until age 21.

UNIFORM LAWS   laws that have been approved by the Commissioners on Uniform State Laws and are proposed to all state legislatures for their consideration and adoption. Some uniform laws are passed by only a few states; others are passed by all the states with minor differences in language.

   EXAMPLE: The **Uniform Commercial Code,** a *uniform law,* has been adopted by almost all states, with some variations by several states. The UCC governs banking and secured transactions, and sale of goods.

UNIFORM SYSTEM OF CITATION   a legal **citation** guide of accepted and standard rules of citation and style. Published by The Harvard Law Review Association in updated editions. It is a guide to citations related to cases, statutes, periodicals, debates, hearings, and other specific forms of authority; known as the **BLUE BOOK** for its blue cover. Properly cited **briefs** are said to be in blue book form.

UNIFORM TRADE SECRETS ACT see **trade secrets** [UNIFORM TRADE SECRETS ACT].

UNILATERAL CONTRACT see **contract** [UNILATERAL CONTRACT].

UNILATERAL MISTAKE see **mistake** [UNILATERAL MISTAKE].

UNION see **labor organization** [union].

UNION SHOP a workplace where all the employees are members of a union. Nonunion members may work in such shops provided they agree to join the union.

UNIT see **commercial unit.**

UNITED STATES ATTORNEY see **district attorney; prosecutor.**

UNITED STATES CLAIMS COURT see **Court of Claims.**

UNITED STATES CODE the official codification of the federal statutes in a multivolume bound set that is issued every six years and supplemented during the intervening years. It is updated by the supplement, United States Code Congressional and Administrative News. The **UNITED STATES CODE ANNOTATED (U.S.C.A.)** includes case notes, historical references, and cross-references.

UNITED STATES COURTS see **federal courts.**

UNITED STATES MAGISTRATE see **magistrate** [UNITED STATES [FEDERAL] MAGISTRATE].

UNITED STATES TRUSTEE see **bankruptcy** [UNITED STATES TRUSTEE].

UNITIES the **common law** requirements necessary to create a **JOINT TENANCY** or a **TENANCY BY THE ENTIRETY** (see **tenancy**). A joint tenancy requires the four unities of interest, possession, time and title, and a tenancy by the entirety requires, in addition to the four unities, unity of person. Tenants in common, as a result of the kind of estate they hold, have a unity of possession, but no unity is required to create such an estate.

UNITY OF INTEREST the requirement that **interests** of the co-tenants in a joint tenancy or tenancy by the entirety be equal. An individual joint tenant cannot encumber his or her share by **mortgage** without destroying this unity; to preserve the joint tenancy the mortgage must be agreed to by all. Tenants in common are not subject to this unity of interest rule and may have unequal shares in the same property. See **tenancy [TENANCY IN COMMON]**.

UNITY OF PERSON the common-law requirement for the creation of a tenancy by the entirety that the co-tenants be husband and wife, based on the conception that marriage created a unity of person.

UNITY OF POSSESSION the equal right of each co-owner of property to the **use** and **possession** of the whole property.

UNITY OF TIME the requirement that the interests of the co-tenants in a joint tenancy or tenancy by the entirety must commence (or **vest**) at the same moment in time.

UNITY OF TITLE the requirement that all tenants of a joint tenancy or both tenants of a tenancy by the entirety acquire their interests under the same **title.** Thus, such co-tenants cannot hold by different **deeds;** their interests are created by the same instrument or event.

UNIT INVESTMENT TRUST an unmanaged **portfolio** of **bonds** that is sold to investors in units of $1,000 each. A bank or **trust company** serves as custodian and **trustee** for the portfolio of bonds, and collects and periodically disburses interest payments and principal when bonds mature. Since the portfolio is fixed, the trust is self-liquidating because of both unit holder redemptions and bond maturities. Compare **nondiscretionary trust.**

UNIVERSAL AGENT an **agent** authorized to transact all the business of his or her **principal.**

UNIVERSAL DECLARATION OF HUMAN RIGHTS an international bill of rights adopted by the United Nations General Assembly in 1948 calling for specified rights and freedoms for all persons. See **human rights.**

UNJUST ENRICHMENT gain or benefit that is the result of another's efforts or acts but for which that other has received no recompense, and for which the one receiving the benefit has not paid. A person who is deemed by law to have been unjustly enriched at the expense of another is required to make **restitution** to the other. Restitution and unjust enrichment are modern designations for the older doctrine of quasi contracts, which are not true contracts, but are obligations created by the law when money, property or services have been obtained by one person at the expense of another under such circumstances that in **equity** and good conscience he or she ought not retain it. The law then may impose a duty to pay compensation in order to prevent unjust enrichment.

EXAMPLE: Louie plants shrubbery under a contract with Kimani.

Kimani dies before Louie is paid, and Mia then buys Kimani's house. Mia must pay Louie for the shrubbery, for if she does not, she will be *unjustly enriched* and Louie will be out the value of the plantings.

Compare **quantum meruit.**

UNLAWFUL ACT MANSLAUGHTER see **manslaughter** [UNLAWFUL ACT MANSLAUGHTER].

UNLAWFUL ASSEMBLY 1. a **misdemeanor** in common law consisting of a meeting of several persons with a common plan that, if carried out, would result in a riot; 2. a meeting of persons who intend to commit a crime by open force; 3. a meeting to execute a common design, lawful or unlawful, in an unauthorized manner that is likely to cause fear of a **BREACH OF THE PEACE** (see **breach**). Compare **association; conspiracy.**

UNLAWFUL DETAINER the act of holding **possession** without right, as in the case of a **tenant** whose **lease** has expired. UNLAWFUL DETAINER STATUTES often create a right to oust, by summary **process,** a holdover tenant and to determine speedily the landlord's right to possession of real property. The **summary proceeding** determines only the question of possession; no ultimate determination of **title** or **estate** can be made in such a proceeding. See **tenancy** [TENANCY AT SUFFERANCE]. See **detainer; forcible entry.**

UNLAWFUL [ENEMY] COMBATANT see **enemy combatant.**

UNLAWFUL ENTRY the statutory crime of entering onto someone else's property without their consent by fraud or force. Unlawful entry is broader than and should be distinguished from the common law crime of **burglary** that requires the breaking and entry of the dwelling of another at night and with felonious intent. Statutes prohibiting unlawful entry were passed to protect society from acts not prohibited by burglary. See **trespass.**

UNLAWFUL FORCE see **force** [UNLAWFUL FORCE].

UNLIQUIDATED see **sum certain** [UNLIQUIDATED].

UNLISTED SECURITY a **stock** or **bond** that is not listed on a **stock exchange** and is therefore traded only in the **over-the-counter market.**

UNNATURAL ACT [OFFENSE] see **crime against nature.**

UNNECESSARY HARDSHIP in **zoning** law, a permissible ground for a **variance.** Unnecessary hardship exists when the physical characteristics of the real estate are such that it cannot be used for a permitted purpose, or that it can only be used for a permitted purpose at a prohibitive expense.

UNREALIZED APPRECIATION see **appreciation [UNREALIZED APPRECIATION].**

UNREASONABLE arbitrary, capricious, absurd, immoderate, or exorbitant; not conformable to reason, irrational, beyond bounds of reason or moderation.

UNREASONABLE PUNISHMENT see **cruel and unusual punishment.**

UNREASONABLE RESTRAINT OF TRADE see **restraint of trade.**

UNREASONABLE SEARCH AND SEIZURE a search and/or seizure of a person, a house, papers or effects that are protected against it by the **Fourth** and **Fourteenth Amendments** and state constitutions, where the basis for the search and/or seizure does not meet constitutional requirements.

EXAMPLE: An officer receives an anonymous tip that Samir is growing marijuana in his house. The officer waits until Samir leaves his house, and then the officer enters through an open window. Since the entry was conducted without a **warrant** and without **probable cause,** the *search and seizure* would be found *unreasonable* and evidence obtained thereby would be **suppressed** and would not be used to prove that Samir had marijuana in his house.

UNUSUAL PUNISHMENT see **cruel and unusual punishment.**

UP [PLUS] TICK indicates that the latest trade in a **stock** is at a higher price than the previous trade. A **ZERO-PLUS TICK** is a trade at the last price with the preceding different price registered as an up tick.

UPZONING see **zoning [UPZONING].**

URBAN ENTERPRISE ZONE designated zones in a state which allow the charging of a significantly lower sales tax to buyers. Such zones are designed to revitalize otherwise blighted communities by encouraging sales and thereby the creation of jobs. A UEZ may also allow tax free purchases of equipment for the business, energy sales tax exemptions and tax credits as well as other state financial assistance to the business.

URL see **domain [URL].**

USAGE OF TRADE see **trade usage.**

USCIS see **Citizenship And Immigration Services [USCIS].**

USE the right to enjoy the benefits flowing from **real property** or **personal property; equitable** ownership as distinct from legal **title.** Historically in the law of property the term referred to every form of beneficial ownership enforceable in the courts of **chancery.** Historically, uses have been created by provision in a **deed,** by implication to the conveyer when property is transferred without **consideration** [called a RESULTING USE]; by **bargain and sale** deed or by a covenant to stand **seised.** Under the **Statute of Uses,** the party in whom a use was created was deemed to be the owner of legal title to a like **estate** as he had in the use; hence "A to B for the use of C for life" was operative under the statute to convey to C a life estate.

An important effect of the Statute of Uses was the validation **at law** of executory **interests** (a species of **future interests**) that had previously been recognized only in equity. A SHIFTING USE is a use that arises in derogation of another, i.e., shifts from one beneficiary to another, depending on some future contingency. A SPRINGING USE is a use that arises upon the occurrence of a future event and that does not take effect in derogation of any interest other than one that results to the grantor, or remains in him or her in the meantime. Thus, a shifting use is one that cuts short a prior use estate in a person other than the conveyor; a springing use is one that cuts short a use estate in the conveyor.

In patent law, use refers to the rights of the licensee of the patent.

BENEFICIAL USE see **beneficial use.**

CESTUI QUE USE see **cestui que** [CESTUI QUE USE].

CONFORMING USE see **conforming use.**

EXCLUSIVE USE in real property law, one of the elements of a **prescriptive easement**. Exclusive use in this regard means that the rights of the party claiming the easement do not depend upon similar rights in others. Exclusive use does not mean that no other persons have physically used the property in question. In **trademark** law, *exclusive use* refers to the exclusive use of both a specific mark or symbol and of any confusingly similar mark or term.

FAIR USE see **fair use.**

PERMISSIVE USE use with the knowledge or consent of the owner; a license terminable at the will of the owner or when the acts contemplated in the permission are completed.

PUBLIC USE see **public use.**

USE IMMUNITY see **self-incrimination, privilege against** [TESTIMONIAL [USE] IMMUNITY].

USES, STATUTE OF   see **Statute of Uses.**

USE TAX   see **tax [USE TAX].**

USEFUL LIFE   see **depreciation [USEFUL LIFE].**

USE IMMUNITY   see **self-incrimination, privilege against.**

USE, PUBLIC   see **public use.**

USICE   see **Immigration And Customs Enforcement [ICE].**

USUFRUCT   in **civil law,** the right to use and enjoy **property** vested in another, and to draw from it all the profit and utility it may produce, provided it be without altering the substance of the thing. See **beneficial use.**

USURIOUS CONTRACT   a contract that imposes **interest** on a debt at a rate in excess of that permitted by law. See **loansharking; usury.**

USURY   an unconscionable or exorbitant rate of **interest;** an excessive and illegal requirement of compensation for **forbearance** on a **debt;** a bargain under which a greater profit than is permitted by law is paid, or is agreed to be paid, to a **creditor** by or on behalf of the **debtor** for a loan of money, or for extending the maturity of a pecuniary debt. The state legislatures today determine the maximum allowable rates of interest that may be demanded in any financial transaction.

EXAMPLE: Darrell needs money but cannot obtain a loan from a bank. A close friend agrees to lend him what he needs but at an interest rate over the maximum allowed by law. Darrell agrees to the arrangement and in fact does not think it unfair. Still, the friend is guilty of *usury* and can be prosecuted for usury if the rate reaches a criminal level, which varies in each state. The friend may also be made to return any interest he has received. More importantly, the usurious rate of interest, and in some jurisdictions the debt as well, is not enforceable against Darrell in the event he has failed to make payments.

UTILITY   see **public utility.**

UTMOST CARE   the highest degree of care. In tort law, such a degree of care as would be exercised by a very careful, prudent, and competent person under the same or similar circumstances. See **negligence.**

UTMOST RESISTANCE   the degree of resistance that a woman traditionally has been required to offer her attacker in order to charge that she has been raped; the maximum resistance of which a woman is capable in resisting rape.

UTTER   to put forth, to execute; especially, to offer, whether accepted or not, a forged **instrument** with representations by words or acts, directly or indirectly, that the instrument is valid.

UTTERANCE, EXCITED see **excited utterance.**

UXOR see **et ux.**

V

V. abbreviation for 1. versus, the Latin for "against." Also abbreviated as "vs." however "v." is preferred. Used in case captioning such as "Roe v. Wade" to indicate the parties involved in a lawsuit. 2. volume. 3. verb.

VACATE 1. to render **void;** to **set aside;** 2. to move out; to render vacant.

VAGRANCY general term for a class of minor offenses such as idleness without visible means of support, **loitering,** wandering around from place to place without any lawful purpose.

VAGUENESS see **void for vagueness.**

VALUABLE CONSIDERATION see **consideration [VALUABLE CONSIDERATION].**

VALUATION determination of the worth of real or personal property. See **appraise; book value; face value; market value.**

VALUE the monetary worth of a thing; marketable price; estimated or assessed worth. The method of determining an object's value will vary depending upon the purpose for which it is being determined. For instance, for estate and gift **tax** purposes, value is the price a willing buyer would pay a willing seller if neither is compelled to buy or sell and both have reasonable knowledge of the relevant facts. However, for insurance purposes, value may refer to **REPLACEMENT VALUE,** that is, the cost of replacing an object, rather than its fair **market value.** See **book value; capitalized value; cash surrender value; diminution in value; face value; going concern value; net asset value; par value; probative [PRO-BATIVE VALUE].**

VALUE ADDED TAX see **tax [AD VALOREM TAX].**

VANDALISM see **bias crime; criminal mischief.**

VARIABLE NUMBER OF TANDEM REPEATS [VNTR] see **DNA testing [SHORT TANDEM REPEATS [STR]].**

VARIABLE RATE MORTGAGE see **mortgage [ADJUSTABLE RATE MORTGAGE].**

VARIANCE 1. in procedure, a discrepancy between what is **charged** or **alleged** and what is proved or offered as proof. A **FATAL VARIANCE** is, in both civil and criminal cases, a material and substantial variance: in criminal cases, it must also tend to mislead the defendant in making his or her defense, or tend to expose the defendant to the injury of **double jeopardy.**

EXAMPLE: Neerja files a lawsuit against a package delivery service for damaging a package they delivered to her. At the trial, she offers proof to show that she never received the package. The difference between her original claim and the claim that she offers to prove constitutes a *fatal variance,* and Neerja's case will probably be dismissed.

2. in zoning law, an exemption from the application of a zoning ordinance or regulation permitting a use that varies from that otherwise permitted. The exception is granted by the appropriate authority in special circumstances to protect against undue hardship wrought by strict enforcement. See **nonconforming use.**

VASSAL at common law, a person who was granted **real property** in return for a promise to perform services for his or her **grantor** or lord. For instance, the king of England was the lord of the country and granted land to his nobles; the nobles were then obligated to perform various feudal services for the king, and were vassals to him. Upon a vassal's failure to perform the required services, the property reverted to the lord. While the nobles were vassals of the king, they also could grant land in return for feudal services, and thus be lords to other vassals. See **subinfeudation.** The abuses of the feudal system led the term to acquire a meaning similar to slave.

VEIL, PIERCING see **piercing the corporate veil.**

VEL NON *(vĕl nŏn)* Lat.: or not.

VENAL dishonest; readily bribed or corrupted.

VEND the habit of selling and exposing to sale; to transfer to another for a pecuniary equivalent.

VENDEE buyer, especially in a **contract** for the **sale** of **realty.**

VENDOR seller, especially person who sells **real property.**

VENDOR'S LIEN the right to enforce payment of the purchase price by suit against the **vendee's** equitable estate.

VENIRE *(vĕ-nē'-rā)* Lat.: to come. Refers to the **common law** process by which **jurors** are summoned to try a case.

VENIRE DE NOVO *(dā nō'-vō)* Lat.: to come anew. Refers to summoning of a second **jury** for the purpose of proceeding to a second trial. Such a second trial is awarded where a **verdict** (by the jury) or finding (by the court) is so defective or ambiguous upon its face that no **judgment** can be rendered upon it. The term is sometimes used simply to denote a new trial.

VENUE a neighborhood, a neighboring place; synonym for place of trial; refers to the possible or proper place for trial of a **suit,** among several places where **jurisdiction** could be established. Venue essentially involves the right of the party sued to have the action heard in a particular judicial district, for reasons of convenience. In a criminal trial where publicity surrounding the crime would virtually preclude fair trial, the court will direct a CHANGE OF VENUE, or **removal** of the proceedings to a different district or county. See **forum non conveniens.**

VERACITY honesty, truthfulness. See **witness** [CHARACTER WITNESS]. Compare **credibility.**

VERBOTEN forbidden, prohibited, banned.

VERDICT the opinion rendered by a **jury,** or a **judge** where there is no jury, on a question of fact. A verdict differs from a **judgment** in that a verdict is not a judicial determination, but rather a finding of fact that the trial court may accept or reject and utilize in formulating its judgment.

COMPROMISE VERDICT a verdict resulting from improper surrender of one juror's opinion to another on a material issue.

DIRECTED VERDICT see **directed verdict.**

FALSE VERDICT a manifestly unjust **verdict**; one not true to the **evidence**, arrived at by any process (such as a coin flip or a **quotient verdict**) that departs from the legitimate methods by which jurors may reach a decision. When such a verdict is rendered, the court can enter a **judgment n.o.v.** ("notwithstanding the verdict").

GENERAL VERDICT ordinary verdict declaring simply which party prevails, without any special findings of fact.

PARTIAL VERDICT in criminal law, a finding that the defendant is guilty of certain charges but innocent of others.

QUOTIENT VERDICT improper and unacceptable kind of compromise verdict resulting from an agreement by the jurors that their verdict will be an award of **damages** in an amount to be determined by the addition of all jurors' computations of damages and its division by the number of jurors.

SPECIAL VERDICT one rendered on certain specific factual issues posed by the court. The special verdict requires the jury to make a specific finding on each ultimate fact put in issue by the **pleadings** rather than a general finding for one party or the other. The court will then apply the law to those found facts.

VERIFICATION confirmation of correctness or authenticity of **pleading** or other paper **affidavit,** oath or **deposition;** an affidavit attached to a statement insuring the truth of that statement.

VERSUS against. The preferred abbreviation is "v." (especially in the captioning of a case, such as *Gideon v. Wainwright*), but "vs." is also used.

VERTICAL MERGER see **merger [VERTICAL MERGER].**

VERTICAL PRICE FIXING see **price fixing [VERTICAL PRICE FIXING].**

VERTICAL PRIVITY see **privity [VERTICAL PRIVITY].**

VESTED fixed, accrued or absolute; not **contingent;** generally used to describe any right or **title** to something that is not dependent upon the occurrence or failure to occur of some specified future event (**CONDITION PRECEDENT**—see **condition).**

VESTED ESTATE a property **interest** that either is presently in possession or will necessarily come into **possession** in the future merely upon the determination, or end, of the preceding **estate.**

EXAMPLE: A mother conveys a house to her son, who will keep it until he has his first child, at which time the house is to pass to her daughter. Not until the son's child is born can it be determined whether the daughter will get the house. But immediately upon the birth, the daughter's interest in the house vests, giving rise to a *vested estate.*

VESTED INTEREST a present right or title to a thing that carries with it an existing right of **alienation,** even though the right to possession or enjoyment may be postponed to some uncertain time in the future.

VESTED REMAINDER a **remainder** that is limited to an ascertained person whose right to the estate is fixed, certain and not dependent upon the happening of any future event, but whose enjoyment of the estate is postponed to some future time.

VESTED RIGHTS in relation to constitutional guarantees, a broad shield of protection that consists of a vested interest that the government should in **equity** recognize and protect, and of which the individual could not be deprived arbitrarily without injustice. The term is frequently used to designate rights that have become so fixed that the owner cannot be deprived of them without his consent.

VETO see **pocket veto.**

VEXATIOUS LITIGATION **civil action** shown to have been instituted maliciously and without **probable cause,** and that may be protected against by **injunction.** See **litigious; malicious prosecution.**

VIATICAL SETTLEMENT assignment, transfer, or sale of a life insurance policy's death benefit to another for substantially less than the full death benefit value where the policy owner has a terminal illness and is thereby able to recover some monetary value to provide for his or her immediate needs.

VICARIOUS LIABILITY **liability** imputed to one person for the actions of another, where the law contemplates that the other should be held responsible for a wrong in fact committed by someone else. Sometimes this doctrine is called IMPUTED LIABILITY.

EXAMPLE: Mekhi drives a truck for Speedy Delivery Service. While pulling out of a driveway, he hits a pedestrian. Speedy will be *vicariously liable* for the pedestrian's injuries under the doctrine of **respondeat superior.**

EXAMPLE: Taye agrees to drive the getaway car in a robbery. Donna, who enters the bank, kills a teller during the robbery. In most states, Taye is *vicariously liable* for the killing.

Compare **strict liability.**

VICE CRIMES activities such as gambling, prostitution, and pornography that are illegal because they offend the moral standards of the community.

VICINAGE neighborhood; vicinity. Contemporary meaning denotes a particular area where a crime was committed, where a **trial** is being held, or from which **jurors** are called.

VICTUALS prepared food; food ready to eat.

VICTUALER [VICTUALLER] one who sells food or drink prepared for consumption on the premises.

VIDELICET see **viz.**

VIDUITATE [VIDUITY] widowhood.

VI ET ARMIS see **trespass [TRESPASS VI ET ARMIS].**

VIEW see **plain view.** See also **lineup; show up.**

VILLEIN SOCAGE see **socage.**

VILLENAGE a menial form of feudal **tenure** in which the **tenant** [the **villein**] was required to perform all **services** demanded by the lord of the manor.

VIOLATION OF PROBATION see **probation** [VIOLATION OF PROBATION].

VIOLENCE [VIOLENT] moving, acting, or characterized by physical force, especially by extreme and sudden or unjust or improper force. The degree of force implied by the word *violence* depends upon the context in which it is used. For instance, its use in an insurance policy may imply a lesser degree or a different type of force than its use in a criminal statute.

VIR *(vĭr)* Lat.: man.

VIRTUAL REPRESENTATION representation in a **lawsuit** without being named as a **party.** A type of **class action** where nonparty members have a close relationship to the named parties and have similar interests such that a **judgment** is binding upon the nonparties. A preferable alternative is the appointment of a **guardian ad litem** to ensure that the nonparty interests will be adequately protected.

VISA a recognition of the validity of a passport; issued by proper officials of the country that the bearer wishes to enter; more broadly, a symbol made on a document certifying that it has been examined and approved.

VISITATION, CONJUGAL see **conjugal rights** [CONJUGAL VISITATION].

VISITATION RIGHTS in family law, the right granted by a court to a parent or other relative who is deprived custody of a child to visit the child on a regular basis.

VIS MAJOR *(vĭz mä-yôr')* Lat.: a greater force. In civil law denotes an **act of God,** an irresistible natural cause that cannot be guarded against by ordinary exertions of skill and prudence. Once treated as equivalent to act of God, *vis major* now includes any insuperable interference.

VITALIZED see **quickening.**

VITIATE to **void;** to render a nullity; to impair.

VIZ *(vĭz)* Lat.: namely; that is to say; abbreviation of the Latin videlicet. Used in **pleadings** to specify or explain what goes before it.

VOICE EXEMPLAR a recording of a person's voice made for the purpose of identification, usually in a criminal investigation. The Supreme Court has held that requiring a person to make a voice **exemplar** does not violate the privilege against **self-incrimination,**

since it is used for identification purposes only, and that it does not constitute an unreasonable **search or seizure.**

VOID empty, having no legal force, incapable of being ratified.

VOIDABLE capable of being later **annulled;** refers to a valid act that, though it may be rendered void, may accomplish the thing sought unless or until the defect in the transaction has been effectively asserted or judicially ascertained and declared.

VOIDABLE PREFERENCE see **preference** [VOIDABLE PREFERENCE].

VOID FOR VAGUENESS a doctrine that renders a criminal statute unconstitutional and unenforceable when it is so vague that persons of common intelligence must guess at its meaning and differ about its application. A statute is **void** when it is vague about either what persons are within the scope of the statute, what conduct is forbidden or what punishment may be imposed. The principle derives from the requirement of the **due process** clause of the **Fifth Amendment** that criminal statutes give reasonably certain notice that an act has been made criminal before the act is committed and a person is charged with a crime for having so acted.

VOID, NULL AND see **nullity.**

VOID ON ITS FACE see **void for vagueness.**

VOIR DIRE *(vwŏr dēr)* Fr.: to speak the truth. 1. A **VOIR DIRE EXAMINATION** by the court or by the attorneys of prospective jurors is to determine their qualification for **jury** service, to determine if there is cause to challenge (i.e., to excuse) particular jurors, and to provide information about the jurors so that the parties can exercise their statutory **peremptory** challenges (objections to particular jurors without need to state cause).

EXAMPLE: A doctor is on trial for performing an abortion. In a *voir dire* examination of potential jurors by counsel or the court, it is revealed that a prospective juror has strong religious beliefs concerning abortions that would bias any possibility of a fair and independent judgment. That juror will most likely not be used at the doctor's trial.

2. A voir dire examination during the trial refers to a **hearing** by the court out of the presence of the jury upon some **issue** of fact or law that requires an initial determination by the court or upon which the court must rule as a matter of law alone.

VOLENTI NON FIT INJURIA *(vō-lĕn'-tē nŏn fĕt ĭn jū'-rē-à)* Lat.: the volunteer suffers no wrong. No legal wrong is done to one who consents. In **tort** law, the principle that usually **damages** cannot be claimed by one who has consented to the activity that caused the damages.

VOLUNTARY APPEARANCE   see **appearance** [VOLUNTARY APPEARANCE].

VOLUNTARY COMMITMENT   see **commitment** [VOLUNTARY].

VOLUNTARY DISABLEMENT   see **anticipatory breach.**

VOLUNTARY DISSOLUTION   see **dissolution** [VOLUNTARY DISSOLUTION].

VOLUNTARY MANSLAUGHTER   see **manslaughter** [VOLUNTARY MANSLAUGHTER].

VOLUNTARY NONSUIT   see **nonsuit** [VOLUNTARY NONSUIT].

VOLUNTARY WASTE   see **waste** [VOLUNTARY WASTE].

VOTER OWNED ELECTIONS   see **clean elections.**

VOTING   see **cumulative voting.**

VOTING RIGHT   the right of a common **shareholder** to vote in person or by **proxy** on the affairs of a company.

VOTING RIGHTS ACT   the federal law passed in 1965 to effectuate the right of each citizen to vote under the **Fifteenth Amendment** to the U.S. Constitution. The law prohibits imposition of any qualification, prerequisite to voting or practice or procedure by any state or political subdivision to deny or abridge the right of any U.S. citizen to vote because of race or color. The law forbids restrictions, such as literacy, on the right to vote.

VOTING TRUST   The accumulation in a single hand, or in a few hands, of shares of corporate **stock** belonging to many owners, for the purpose of exercising control over the business of the company. A device whereby two or more **shareholders** divorce the voting rights of their stock from its ownership, retaining their ownership but transferring their voting rights to **trustees** in whom the voting rights of all the depositors in the trust are pooled.

VOUCHER   a document or receipt showing a payment. Also, an authorization for a disbursement.

VS.   see **v.**

W

WAGE EARNER'S PLAN see **bankruptcy [WAGE EARNER'S PLAN].**

WAGE, MINIMUM see **minimum wage.**

WAGER OF LAW under early English law, the giving of a pledge or **surety** by a **defendant** to appear in court with the required number of **compurgators** [character **witnesses**] who would testify that they believed the defendant to be telling the truth. The number of compurgators was usually 11 but could vary. The form of the oath they had to recite was very strict. If one of them used the wrong word, the oath "burst" and the plaintiff won. In England, this procedure had largely died out by the thirteenth century but was still used occasionally as late as the eighteenth century in cases of **debt** and **detinue.**

Compurgation originally became the accepted mode of **trial** adapted to members of the church when the duel and ordeal lost favor. The defendant would then be expected to bring a required number of priests and/or kinsmen as compurgators because they should best know the defendant's character. Later, for practical reasons, neighbors became acceptable compurgators. The compurgators were not witnesses but merely expressed their confidence in the veracity of the defendant; therefore, a comparative value was attached to their **oaths.** For example, the oath of one competent witness may have outweighed the oaths of six compurgators. The defense of wager of law was much abused. Since it was only available in actions of debt, the courts permitted the creditor to sue in **assumpsit,** an action in which that defense was not available.

WAGNER ACT see **labor organization [union]; National Labor Relations Act; Taft-Hartley Act.**

WAIT see **lying in wait.**

WAITING PERIOD generally, any period of time that must expire before a party may attempt to pursue legal rights. For instance, most states require a waiting period after a blood test or the issuance of a marriage license before a marriage may occur. A waiting period may be unconstitutional if it interferes with a citizen's right to travel freely. For instance, a law requiring that a person be a resident of the state for one year before he or she may be eligible for welfare benefits was held unconstitutional on that ground. See also **red herring** [WAITING PERIOD].

WAIVER an intentional and voluntary surrender of some known **right,** which generally may either result from an express agreement or be inferred from circumstances. See **informed consent.**

EXAMPLE: Spencer enters into a plea bargain with the prosecutor in the hope that he will receive a lighter sentence. Since the plea represents an admission of guilt and a *waiver* of the right to a jury trial, the judge must be sure that Spencer realizes the consequences of his actions. Therefore, the judge will inform Spencer that he has a right to have a trial and that there is no guarantee that a plea will necessarily result in any different sentence than from a trial. Without these precautions, the judge cannot be sure that Spencer's waiver is knowing and intelligent.

EXECUTORY WAIVER one that affects a still unperformed duty of the other party to a **contract.**

IMPLIED WAIVER the waiver of substantial rights based upon the conduct of the waiving party. For an implied waiver to occur, the party alleging the waiver must have acted in detrimental **reliance** on the conduct constituting the waiver, and the conduct relied upon must demonstrate a clear, decisive, and unequivocal purpose to waive the legal rights involved. Compare **estoppel.**

WANT OF CONSIDERATION see **consideration** [WANT OF CONSIDERATION].

WANT OF PROSECUTION see **prosecution** [WANT OF PROSECUTION].

WANTON grossly **negligent** or careless; with a reckless disregard of consequences.

WARD 1. a person whom the law regards as incapable of managing his or her own affairs, and over whom or over whose property a **guardian** is appointed. 2. one of the sections into which a town is divided for educational or election purposes.

WARDSHIP the office of **guardian.** At common law, a form of guardianship. The guardian was entitled to the wardship of a male **heir** who was under age 21, or a female under age 14. The guardian had custody of both the body and the lands of the heir, and was not required to account to the heir for the profits derived from the land.

WAREHOUSEMAN'S LIEN see **lien** [WAREHOUSEMAN'S LIEN].

WAREHOUSE RECEIPT a receipt issued by a person **(bailee)** engaged in the business of storing goods for hire. A warehouse receipt constitutes a **document of title** under the Uniform Commercial Code, which evidences that the person in possession of the document is entitled to receive, hold, and dispose of the document and the goods it covers. A warehouse receipt may be a **negotiable instrument,** depending upon its terms.

WARRANT a written **order** from a competent authority directing the doing of a certain act, especially one directing the **arrest** of a person or persons, issued by a court, body or official. See also **bench warrant; search warrant.**

The word warrant is also used in commercial and property law to refer to a particular kind of guarantee or assurance about the quality and validity of what is being **conveyed** or sold.

ARREST WARRANT an order of a court directing the sheriff or other officer to seize a particular person to answer a **complaint** or otherwise appear before the court. If a defendant fails to appear as required in court, the judge will issue a **bench warrant** for arrest. For less serious offenses, it is common to issue a **summons** in lieu of an arrest warrant. An arrest warrant is constitutionally required to enter a person's home to effect an arrest except in **exigent circumstances** such as hot **(fresh) pursuit.** See **arrest; search and seizure.** Compare **warrantless arrest.**

BENCH WARRANT see **bench warrant.**

GENERAL WARRANT see **search warrant [GENERAL WARRANTS].**

SEARCH WARRANT an order that certain premises or property be searched for particularized items which if found are to be seized and used as **evidence** in a criminal **trial** or destroyed as contraband. See **search and seizure; search warrant.**

STOCK WARRANT a certificate that gives the holder the right to purchase shares of **stock** for a specified price and within a specified time. Unlike **subscription rights,** stock warrants offer the holder the right to purchase shares of a different kind from those already held. Thus a holder of common stock may purchase **preferred stock.** Stock warrants usually originate as a bonus with new **issues** of **bonds, notes** or preferred stock where they serve as an inducement to the buyer. Warrants so offered come attached to the new security and usually cannot be separated for a short period; once separated, the warrants can be traded like any other security.

WARRANT TO SATISFY JUDGMENT an authorization issued by the judgment **creditor's** attorney to the clerk of the court directing the clerk to enter a **satisfaction** of the **judgment** in the official court records.

WARRANTLESS ARREST an **arrest** made without a warrant. At common law, an officer was justified in making an arrest without a warrant if the officer reasonably believed that the defendant had committed a **misdemeanor** in his or her presence or had committed any **felony.** There is a constitutional preference for arrest upon a warrant, however, and the Supreme Court has held that a warrantless arrest will be judged by a somewhat higher standard of **probable cause** than if the same arrest had occurred under the direction of a neutral and detached magistrate. While warrantless arrests in public places have been upheld, an arrest in a private residence requires an arrest warrant unless there are exigent circumstances. See **search and seizure; warrant [ARREST WARRANT].**

WARRANTY an assurance by one **party** to a **contract** of the existence of a fact upon which the other party may rely, intended precisely to relieve the promisee of any duty to ascertain the fact for himself or herself; amounts to a promise to **indemnify** the promisee for any loss if the fact warranted proves untrue. Such warranties are made either overtly (**EXPRESS WARRANTIES**) or by implication (**IMPLIED WARRANTIES**).

A **COVENANT OF WARRANTY** in **real property** is a covenant **running with the land,** insuring the continuing validity of **title.**

BREACH OF WARRANTY see **breach [BREACH OF WARRANTY]**

WARRANTY OF FITNESS a warranty that the goods are suitable for the special purpose of the buyer, which will not be satisfied by mere fitness for general purposes.

EXAMPLE: Constant Trucking Company orders a specially enforced truck for a new type of service it is starting. Constant places the order with a dealership with whom it has often worked in the past, and explains the need and purpose for the vehicle. The vehicle is delivered to Constant, which finds after one shipment that the truck is not built as specified. A warranty *of fitness,* which either is written in the contract between Constant and the dealer or is implied, has been breached. Constant can return the truck and demand its money back.

WARRANTY OF HABITABILITY a promise by the landlord that at the inception of a residential **lease** there are no **latent defects** in facilities vital to the use of the premises for residential purposes, and that these facilities will remain in usable condition for the duration of the lease.

WARRANTY OF MERCHANTABILITY a warranty that the goods are reasonably fit for the general purposes for which they are sold.

WARRANTY ACT see **Magnuson-Moss Warranty Act.**

WARRANTY DEED a **deed** that warrants that the grantor has the **title** he or she claims to have. It purports to **convey** property free and clear of all **encumbrances.** As a guarantee of title, the warranty deed creates liability in the grantor if the title transferred is defective. Compare **quitclaim deed.**

WASH SALE a sale or other disposition of **stock** or **securities** as to which no loss is recognized for tax purposes, because within 30 days before or after the date of sale or disposition the taxpayer purchased substantially identical stock or securities.

WASTE generally, an act, by one in rightful **possession** of land who has less than a **fee simple** interest in the land, which decreases the value of the land or the owner's **interest** or the interest of another who has a future interest in the land (such as a **remainderman, lessor, mortgagee, reversioner**).

AMELIORATING WASTE a change in the physical structure of the occupied premises by an unauthorized act of the tenant that, though technically waste, in fact increases the value of the land.

ECONOMIC WASTE in the law of oil and gas, a production practice that, in light of alternatives, reduces net value of hydrocarbons that may be produced from a reservoir.

EQUITABLE WASTE such acts as at law would not be deemed to be waste under the circumstances of the case but that in the view of a court of **equity** are so viewed because of their manifest injury to the property, although they are not inconsistent with the legal rights of the party committing them.

PERMISSIVE WASTE injury to the inheritance caused by the tenant's failure to make the expected reasonable repairs to the premises.

PHYSICAL WASTE in the law of oil and gas, a production practice that, in light of alternatives, reduces the quantity of hydrocarbons that may be produced from a reservoir.

VOLUNTARY WASTE injury to the inheritance caused by an affirmative act of the tenant.

WASTING ASSET an asset that will be consumed through its use; property exhausted over a period of years through the progressive loss of value or consumption of the property. For instance, a coal mine is a wasting asset, since it contains a limited amount of coal that will be exhausted by regular mining activity.

WATERED STOCK a stock **issue** that is offered to public investors by founders and promoters of a company at a greatly inflated price compared to **book value** or cost; stock that a company issues for property that is worth less than the stock. Stock may be identified as watered stock by comparison of market or offering value to net asset value of a share.

WATERS see **territorial waters.**

WATER TABLE   the distance between the surface of the land and the depth where natural water is located. Used in determining the possibility of and cost of drilling a well.

WAY, RIGHT OF see **right of way.**

WEAPON   see **dangerous weapon [instrumentality]; deadly weapon; force; gun control law.**

WEIGHT OF THE EVIDENCE   a phrase that indicates the relative value of the totality of **evidence** presented on one side of a judicial dispute, compared to the evidence presented on the other side; refers to the persuasiveness of the testimony of the **witnesses.**

WESTLAW see **search engine.**

WHEN ISSUED   short for "when, as and if issued," which is a conditional trading basis for a new **stock** or **bond** issue that has been authorized for issuance but does not actually exist. WHEN ISSUED SECURITIES can be bought or sold like ordinary securities, except that transactions do not settle until the actual security is formally issued and the **stock exchange** involved or the National Association of Securities Dealers decides on a specific settlement date. The most common occasion for *when issued* trading is in connection with stock splits. After the split is announced but before the new shares issue, the split stock may be traded on a when issued basis. Such trading has speculative appeal since a down payment of only 25 percent is required and since no **margin** or loan debt is required for the balance until settlement date, which might be weeks in the future.

WHIPLASH INJURY   neck injury commonly associated with rear-end automobile collisions. Caused by a sudden, unexpected forced forward movement of the body while the unsupported head of an automobile occupant attempts to remain stationary consistent with the laws of physics, subjecting the neck to a severe strain while in a relaxed position.

WHITE-COLLAR CRIME   a catch-all phrase connoting a variety of **frauds,** schemes and commercial offenses by business persons, confidence men and public officials; includes a broad range of non-violent offenses that have cheating as the central element.

EXAMPLE: Directors of a bank arrange for friends of theirs to obtain large loans from the bank. The friends use fake names and businesses so that they cannot be traced when the loans are not repaid. The directors always approve the loans, and the money is split between the directors and friends. The scheme represents *white-collar crime* and each participant is liable for criminal prosecution.

Consumer fraud, **bribery** and stock manipulation are other examples of white-collar crime. See **organized crime; racketeering**.

WHITE SLAVE TRAFFIC ACT see **Mann Act.**

WHOLE LIFE INSURANCE see **insurance [WHOLE LIFE INSURANCE].**

WHOLESALER middleman; person who buys large quantities of goods and resells to other distributors rather than to ultimate consumers. Compare **jobber.**

WHOLLY completely, utterly, entirely.

WIDOW'S ALLOWANCE see **family allowance.**

WIDOW'S [WIDOWER'S] ELECTION see **right of election.**

WILDCAT STRIKE unauthorized strike; strike for which the representing labor union disclaims responsibility.

EXAMPLE: Working conditions have always been poor at a certain train yard, but the workers' representatives have never been able to get improvements. Tired of waiting for the representatives to negotiate something, the workers engage in a *wildcat strike* and take matters into their own hands. The success of the strike depends on how long it lasts and how many people participate, although such strikes are generally illegal. Even if the strike does not change conditions immediately, it indicates the workers' discontent and may prod both their representatives and their employer to change the conditions.

WILD'S CASE, RULE IN see **Rule in Wild's Case.**

WILL a person's declaration of how he or she desires his or her property to be disposed of after death. A will may also contain other declarations of the **testator's** desires as to what is to be done after he or she dies so long as it disposes of some property. See **causa mortis; codicil; holographic will; nuncupative will; revocation of will.** Compare **gift; inter vivos; testamentary disposition.**

JOINT AND MUTUAL WILL a single will executed by two or more persons, the provisions of which are reciprocal and which show on its face that the devises and bequests are made one in consideration of the other.

JOINT WILL   a single instrument which is made the will of two or more persons and is jointly signed by them. It is not necessarily either mutual or reciprocal.

LAST WILL AND TESTAMENT   an expression commonly used to refer to the most recent document directing the disposition of the real and personal property of the party.

MUTUAL WILLS   separate wills of two persons which are reciprocal in their provisions.

RECIPROCAL WILLS   wills in which two or more testators make testamentary dispositions in favor of each other. This may be done by separate wills [**MUTUAL WILLS**] or by one will [**JOINT AND MUTUAL WILL**].   Such wills may be revocable by the surviving testator, although some states have created a presumption in favor of irrevocability.   A joint will may be both a will contractual in character, and a contract testamentary in nature, giving rise to appropriate remedies in contract for any breach thereof.

WILLFUL [WILFUL]   intentional, as distinguished from accidental. In a criminal statute, the term signifies an act done with a bad purpose and without justifiable excuse.

WILLFUL NEGLIGENCE   see **negligence [WANTON NEGLIGENCE]**.

WILLIAMS ACT   see **tender offer.**

WILLS, STATUTE OF   see **Statute of Wills.**

WINDING UP   the process of **liquidating** a corporation. It consists of collecting the **assets,** paying the expenses, satisfying creditors' claims and distributing the net assets, usually in cash but possibly in kind, to **shareholders,** according to their liquidation preferences and rights. Compare **dissolution.**

WIRETAP   the acquisition of the contents of communication through the use of any electronic, mechanical or other device. Use of wiretaps by government authorities is subject to the constitutional prohibition against unreasonable **search and seizure,** and they can be used only after a finding of **probable cause.** Use of wiretaps by private citizens against other private citizens may constitute a **tort** based on **invasion of privacy** and thereby give rise to a claim for **damages.**

WITHDRAWAL   1. removal of money or the like from the place where it is kept, such as a bank; 2. separation of oneself from a criminal activity to avoid liability for **conspiracy,** by conduct evincing disapproval of or opposition to the criminal activities. Compare **renunciation.**

WITHHOLDING   that portion of wages earned that an employer retains, usually for income **tax** purposes, from each salary payment made to an employee. The amount so deducted is forwarded to the government to be credited against the total tax owed by the employee at the end of the **taxable year.** See **tax [WITHHOLDING TAX].**

WITHHOLDING TAX   see **tax [WITHHOLDING TAX].**

WITHOUT FAULT [LIABILITY]   see **strict liability.**

WITHOUT PREJUDICE   see **dismissal [DISMISSAL WITHOUT PREJUDICE]; prejudice.**

WITHOUT RECOURSE   generally, without further rights in regard to some matter. In finance, without recourse, or *nonrecourse,* refers to the fact that the borrower is not personally liable on a loan, and that the lender must look to other **security** for repayment. See **nonrecourse.**

WITHOUT RESERVE   see **sale [AUCTION SALE].**

WITH PREJUDICE   see **dismissal [DISMISSAL WITH PREJUDICE]; prejudice.**

WITH RESERVATION   see **under protest.**

WITNESS   1. one who gives **evidence** in a cause before a court and who **attests** or swears to facts or gives **testimony** under oath; 2. to observe the **execution** of, as that of an **instrument,** or to sign one's name to it to authenticate it (attest it).

ADVERSE [HOSTILE] WITNESS   one whose relationship to the opposing party is such that his or her testimony may be prejudiced against that party.

CHARACTER WITNESS   a witness who testifies at another person's trial, vouching for that person's high moral character and standing in the community, but who does not have knowledge of the validity of the charges against that person.

EXAMPLE: The preacher testified as a *character witness* at Brian's trial, giving many examples of Brian's service to the elderly and poor. Looking only at the charitable work Brian had done, the preacher could not believe Brian would burglarize a house.

EXPERT WITNESS   see **expert witness.**

HOSTILE WITNESS   see **ADVERSE [HOSTILE] WITNESS** (above).

LAY WITNESS   see **lay witness.**

MATERIAL WITNESS   one who can give testimony that might have a bearing upon the outcome of a cause and that no one else is able to give. In criminal law, the term refers particularly to a witness about whom there is reasonable expectation that he or she can give testimony bearing upon the defendant's guilt or innocence.

WITNESS AGAINST ONESELF see **self-incrimination, privilege against.**

WORDS OF ART words that have a particular meaning in a particular area of study and that have either no meaning or different meanings outside that field.

WORDS OF FIGHTING see **fighting words.**

WORDS OF LIMITATION words used in an **instrument** conveying an interest in **property** that seem to indicate the party to whom a **conveyance** is made, but that actually indicate the type of **estate** taken by the **grantee.** Compare **words of purchase.**

WORDS OF PURCHASE words in a property transfer that indicate who takes the **estate.** The term designates the **grantee** of the estate, while **words of limitation** define the property rights given to the grantee.

WORKERS' COMPENSATION ACTS **statutes** that in general establish **liability** of an employer for injuries or sicknesses that arise out of and in the course of employment. The liability is created without regard to the fault or **negligence** of the employer. Benefits generally include hospital and other medical payments and compensation for loss of income; if the injury is covered by the statute, compensation thereunder will be the employee's only **remedy** against the employer. See **scope of employment; strict liability.** See also **employers liability acts.**

WORKHOUSE see **jail [WORKHOUSE].**

WORK PRODUCT work done by an attorney in the process of representing his or her client that is ordinarily not subject to **discovery.** It encompasses writings, statements or testimony that would substantially reflect or invade an attorney's legal impressions or legal theories about a pending anticipated **litigation,** including the attorney's strategy and opinions.

EXAMPLE: Ivan is charged with tax evasion. He hires an attorney to prepare the case, and the attorney hires an accountant to compute Ivan's income. Because the attorney hires the accountant, the accountant is working for the attorney, not for Ivan. The accountant's report is the *work product* of the attorney and therefore cannot be obtained by the Internal Revenue Service. If Ivan hires the accountant and then presents the accountant's report to the attorney, the report would not be considered a privileged work product and would be discoverable by the IRS.

WORK RELEASE PROGRAM   program that allows a prisoner to work at paid employment or participate in a training program in the community on a voluntary basis while continuing as a prisoner of the institution or facility to which he or she is committed. A lawfully confined prisoner does not have a **Fourteenth Amendment** liberty interest in his or her continued participation in a work release program. State prisoners in a temporary release program may not be removed from the program unless a due process hearing is held concerning the inmate's eligibility in light of the threat that the inmate presents to the security of the community. Compare **halfway house.**

WORLD INTELLECTUAL PROPERTY ORGANIZATION [WIPO]   see **Digital Millennium Copyright Act.**

WORLD TRADE ORGANIZATION [WTO]   the WTO is the only global international organization dealing with the rules of trade between nations. Its predecessor was GATT (see **tariff**). The WTO members account for over 97 percent of world trade. The goal is to help producers of **goods** and **services,** exporters and importers conduct their business.

WORTH   see **net worth.**

WORTHIER TITLE, DOCTRINE OF   early **common law** rule whereby a **gift** by **devise (will)** to one's **heir** that amounted to exactly what the heir would have taken under the statutes of **descent and distribution** had the ancestor died **intestate,** was disregarded and the heir took instead by descent, which was considered as conferring a worthier (better) **title.**

    The rule also has an application to transfer of property **inter vivos;** thus, a grantor may not grant a limited estate to another, with a remainder to the grantor's own heirs. This has been recognized in many American jurisdictions as a rule of **construction** in fulfilling the intent of the grantor. Thus, a **reversion** in the grantor is preferred to a **remainder** in his heirs.

WRAPAROUND MORTGAGE   see **mortgage [WRAPAROUND MORTGAGE].**

WRIT   a legal order issued by the authority and in the name of the state to compel a person to do something therein mentioned. It is issued by a court or other competent **tribunal,** and is directed to the sheriff or other officer authorized to execute it. In every case the writ itself contains directions for doing what is required. See **peremptory writ; prerogative writ.**

WRIT OF ASSISTANCE at common law, a general **warrant** under which an officer of the crown, such as a customs official, had blanket authority to search where he or she pleased for goods imported in violation of the British tax laws. Writs of assistance were greatly abused and hated in this country prior to the American Revolution, and ultimately resulted in the adoption of the constitutional ban against unreasonable **searches and seizure** and especially the requirement of particularization.

In modern practice, a writ of assistance is an equitable remedy used to transfer property where the title has been previously adjudicated. The issuance of a writ of assistance is a **summary proceeding,** not a new lawsuit, which is incidental or auxiliary to a prior judgment or decree and is issued to enforce such judgment or decree.

WRIT OF CAPIAS see **capias.**

WRIT OF CERTIORARI see **certiorari.**

WRIT OF CORAM NOBIS [WRIT OF ERROR CORAM NOBIS; CORAM NOBIS] *(kôr'-äm nō'-bĭs)* Lat.: before us; in our presence, i.e., in our court. The writ aims to bring the attention of the court to, and obtain relief from, errors of fact not appearing on the **record.** Knowing these facts in time would have prevented the **judgment** questioned. Thus, the writ does not correct errors of law. It is addressed to the court that rendered the judgment in which injustice was allegedly done, in contrast to **appeals** or review, which are directed to another court.

WRIT OF ERROR an early common law **writ** issued by the **appellate court,** directing the trial judge to send up the **record** in the case. The appellate court reviews only alleged errors of law. It is similar to a writ of **certiorari,** except that a writ of error is a writ of right and lies only where **jurisdiction** is exercised according to the course of the **common law.**

WRIT OF EXECUTION a routine court order by which the court attempts to enforce the **judgment** granted a **plaintiff,** by authorizing a sheriff to levy on the property belonging to the **judgment debtor,** which is located within the county, to satisfy the judgment obtained by the judgment creditor.

WRIT OF HABEAS CORPUS see **habeas corpus.**

WRIT OF MANDAMUS see **mandamus.**

WRIT OF NE EXEAT see **ne exeat.**

WRIT OF POSSESSION see **writ of assistance.**

WRIT OF PROHIBITION a prerogative **writ** issued by a superior court that prevents an inferior court or **tribunal** from exceeding its **jurisdiction** or usurping jurisdiction it has not been given by law. It is an extraordinary writ because it issues only when the party seeking it is without other means of redress for the wrong about to be inflicted by the act of the inferior tribunal. Sometimes it is referred to simply as **PROHIBITION.**

WRIT OF QUO WARRANTO see **quo warranto.**

WRIT OF RIGHT 1. a **writ** generally issued as a matter of course or granted as a matter of right, in contrast to **prerogative writs** that are issued only at the discretion of the issuing authority; 2. the name of an ancient writ for the recovery of real property.

WRIT OF SUPERSEDEAS see **supersedeas.**

WRIT, PEREMPTORY see **peremptory writ.**

WRIT, PREROGATIVE see **prerogative writ.**

WRITTEN INSTRUMENT anything reduced to writing; the **agreement** or **contract** the writing contains; a document or writing that gives formal expression to some act. Many acts are required to be set forth in a written instrument in order to have legal effect. See **Statute of Frauds.**

WRONG generally, the violation of the legal rights of another; the breach of a legal duty. See **crime; tort.**

WRONGFUL ACT any act that in the ordinary course will infringe upon the rights of another to his or her **damage,** unless the act is done in the exercise of an equal or superior right. Thus, the scope of the term is not limited to acts that are illegal, but includes acts that are deemed immoral, antisocial or tortious.

WRONGFUL DEATH STATUTE a statute that provides relief from the **common law** rule that the death of an individual cannot be the basis of a **cause of action** in a **civil** suit. Every U.S. state has a wrongful death statute, providing that action for damages can be maintained by the **executor, administrator** or **beneficiaries** of the decedent for the wrongful act, neglect or default that caused his death.

WRONGFUL LIFE a **tort** action concerning childbirth, such as the birth of a child after the negligent performance of an operation to sterilize the parent, or the birth of a child with serious defects due to the doctor's failure to advise the parents properly. Compare **wrongful death statutes.**

WTO see **World Trade Organization.**

X

X a mark that may be used as **signature** by one who is unable to write his or her name. The mark may be placed wherever the signature could be placed and does not have to be attested unless so required by statute. A name may accompany a mark, and the mark will be sufficient even if the name is invalid due to an incorrect spelling or other error.

Y

Y CHROMOSOME ANALYSIS see **DNA testing** [Y CHROMOSOME ANALYSIS].

YEAR AND A DAY RULE in criminal law, the common law rule that a death must occur within one year and one day of the act alleged to cause the death, for the death to constitute **murder.** The rule was not incorporated into the Model Penal Code and has been abandoned by most states.

YEARLY see **per annum.**

YELLOW DOG CONTRACT an employment **contract** expressly prohibiting the named employee from joining **labor unions** under pain of dismissal. Most state constitutions guarantee the right to union affiliation and to **collective bargaining.** Federal and state **statutes** now generally declare that such contracts will not form the basis for legal or **equitable** remedies.

YIELD the current return as a percentage of the price of a **stock** or **bond.**

YIELD-TO-MATURITY a calculation of **yield** on a **bond** that takes into account the **capital gain** on a discount bond or capital loss on a premium bond. In the case of a discount bond, the yield-to-maturity, YTM, is higher than the current yield or the coupon yield. The reverse is true for a premium bond with YTM lower than both current yield and coupon yield.

YOUTHFUL OFFENDERS youths accused of crime who are processed in the **juvenile court** system, and so are treated as delinquents rather than as adult criminals. The age beyond which an offender is considered an adult for prosecution and punishment purposes has not been uniformly established and so varies from state to state. See **juvenile delinquency.**

Z

ZERO-PLUS TICK see **up [plus] tick [ZERO-PLUS TICK].**

ZONE OF EMPLOYMENT that physical area within which injuries to an employee are compensable by **workers' compensation** laws; it denotes the place of employment and surrounding areas (including the means of entrance and exit) that are under control of the employer.

ZONING legislative action, usually on the municipal level, that divides municipalities into districts for the purpose of regulating the use of private property and the construction of buildings within the zones established. Zoning is said to be part of the state **police power,** and therefore must be for the furthering of the health, morals, safety or general welfare of the community.

CLUSTER ZONING departure from zoning regulations regarding lot sizes and permitting multiple houses on smaller lots in exchange for open space for public parks, ball fields, or the like.

DOWNZONING reduction in the density of a parcel such as rezoning from commercial use to low-density residential use. Compare UPZONING below.

NONCONFORMING USE see **nonconforming use.**

SPOT ZONING specific zoning classification for one parcel of land (or several parcels in the same area) that differs from surrounding parcels. Such a specialized grant is generally the result of favored treatment and not the general welfare of the community and may therefore be unlawful.

UPZONING rezoning to increase the density of a parcel. Compare **DOWNZONING** above.

USE VARIANCE a **variance** that would allow a use other than what is currently permitted. For example, allowing the owner of a premises to operate a veterinarian clinic in a zone otherwise limited to general office use.

ZONING VARIANCE see **variance.**

DEC _ _ 2015